Closing the Gate

Race,

Politics,

and the

Chinese

Exclusion

Act

ANDREW GYORY

Closing the Gate

The

University

of North

Carolina

Press

Chapel Hill

& London

© 1998 The University of North Carolina Press

All rights reserved

Designed by April Leidig-Higgins

Set in Minion by Keystone Typesetting, Inc.

Manufactured in the United States of America

The paper in this book meets the guidelines
for permanence and durability of the Committee on Production Guidelines for Book Longevity of the Council on Library Resources.

Library of Congress Cataloging-in-Publication
Data. Gyory, Andrew. Closing the gate : race,
politics, and the Chinese Exclusion Act / by
Andrew Gyory. p. cm. Includes bibliographical
references (p.   ) and index.

ISBN 0-8078-2432-1 (alk. paper)

ISBN 0-8078-4739-9 (pbk. : alk. paper)

1. Chinese Americans—History—19th century.
2. Chinese Americans—California—History—
19th century. 3. Chinese Americans—Legal
status, laws, etc.—History—19th century.
4. United States—Emigration and immigration—History—19th century. 5. California—
Emigration and immigration—History—19th
century. 6. Labor policy—United States—
History—19th century. 7. Labor policy—
California—History—19th century. 8. United
States—Race relations. 9. California—Race
relations. I. Title.

E184.C5G9   1998   97-47746

325.73′089′951—dc21   CIP

02 01 00 99 98   5 4 3 2 1

To Cathy

Contents

Acknowledgments xi

Introduction 1

ONE The Very Recklessness of Statesmanship
Explanations for Chinese Exclusion, 1870s–1990s 3

TWO To Fetch Men Wholesale
Framing the Chinese Issue Nationally in the
1860s and the First Chinese Scare in 1869 17

THREE Yan-ki vs. Yan-kee
Americans React to Chinese Laborers in 1870 39

FOUR All Sorts of Tricks
Defining Importation, 1871–1875 60

FIVE To Overcome the Apathy of National Legislators
The Presidential Campaign of 1876 76

SIX The Reign of Terror to Come
Uprising and Red Scare, 1877–1878 92

SEVEN An Unduly Inflated Sack of Very Bad Gas
Denis Kearney Comes East, 1878 109

EIGHT Rolling in the Dirt
The Fifteen Passenger Bill of 1879 136

NINE An Earthquake of Excitement
California and the Exodus East, 1879–1880 169

TEN   No Material Difference

The Presidential Campaign of 1880 185

ELEVEN   The Gate Must Be Closed

The Angell Treaty and the Race to Exclude, 1881–1882 212

TWELVE   A Mere Question of Expediency

The Chinese Exclusion Act of 1882 242

APPENDIX   Text of the Chinese Exclusion Act 261

Notes 265

Bibliography 317

Index 339

Figures

2.1 Uncle Sam's Thanksgiving Dinner 27

2.2 The Youngest Introducing the Oldest 28

3.1 Yan-ḳi vs. Yan-kee 49

3.2 William M. Stewart 55

3.3 The New Pandora's Box 57

5.1 Philip A. Roach 81

5.2 Aaron A. Sargent 83

7.1 The Progress of One of Kearney's Speeches 114

7.2 Up Hill Work for the California Drayman 117

7.3 Adolph Strasser 133

8.1 James G. Blaine 139

8.2 Will History Repeat Itself? 144

8.3 A Matter of Taste 149

8.4 Hannibal Hamlin 152

8.5 The Chinese Question Would Be Settled If the Chinee, Chinee, Would Votee! Votee!! Votee!!! 154

8.6 The Demagogues' Triumph 157

9.1 California's New Constitution 171

9.2 Yung Wing 178

9.3 The Chinese Plague 180

9.4 Strikes and Their Results 181

10.1 The "*Magnetic*" Blaine 188

10.2 Where Both Platforms Agree 191

10.3 William M. Evarts 199

10.4   The Morey Letter 207

11.1   James B. Angell 214

11.2   George Frisbie Hoar 226

11.3   George F. Edmunds 231

11.4   Senator Edmunds's Greatest Effort 234

12.1   Joseph R. Hawley 253

12.2   (Dis-) "Honors Are Easy" 255

Acknowledgments

The original spark for this book came from my professor Herbert Gutman. One day long ago, he remarked, "This event in North Adams needs to be looked at in a fresh light. Who wants to tackle it?" Little did I realize that his suggestion would evolve into the present work. Herb's guidance and wisdom, along with his passionate love for people and history, inspired me to become a historian. Before his untimely death in 1985, he read only a very rough draft of what later became Chapter 3. We never had a chance to discuss the chapter, but I like to think he sensed where it was headed. Herb's spirit and vision infuses every page of this book, and I thank him for his scholarship, his commitment to his students, and his deep humanity.

I owe an equally great debt to my professor and mentor Bruce Laurie, who encouraged me through every step of this manuscript. From his tough but respectful criticisms I learned to think historically: to study with an open mind the process and complexity of history. Bruce also made sure I kept my eye on the larger picture of Gilded Age politics and its connection to today. As both a historian and a friend, Bruce constantly criticized my work and challenged my thinking—and always with humor, kindness, and warmth. He made this book possible. Thanks, Bruce, for your personal generosity, solid integrity, and high professional standards.

I also thank Paula Baker for forcing me to adhere to the most rigorous standards and for asking me the hardest questions. I thank the many teachers who inspired me early on with a love for history and a love for writing, including Lorraine Spencer, Toni Abramson, Dan Smith, and Eileen Simnica. I thank the many professors who taught me history, sharpened my thinking, and freely offered their time and advice: Ed Pessen, Jesse Lemisch, Ron Story, Gerald Friedman, Frances Fox Piven, David Rosner, Hans Trefousse, Barbara Welter, Evelyn Ackerman, Eric Foner, and David Montgomery. I am grateful to the Rutgers Graduate Student Conference and the Lowell Conference on Industrial History for giving me the opportunity to present my ideas in public. I also thank the outstanding librarians at both the New York Public Library in New York City and the Tamiment Institute Library at New York University, where I performed the bulk of my research. Thanks as well to Lew Bateman, Ron Maner, and my copyeditor, Nancy Malone, at the University of North Carolina Press, who believed in this book and made it the best it could be.

Some of the finest criticism and best encouragement I received came from colleagues and fellow students. For their wise and invaluable contributions, as well as for their enduring friendship, I thank Jeff Kroessler, Mike Musuraca, Tim Coogan, and Jim Cemint. In a similar vein, I gratefully thank Clarence Taylor, Elizabeth Baker, Elissa Krauss, Ivan Greenberg, Karen Hoppes, Ron Mendel, Jon Birnbaum, Jeff Schneider, Linda Nieman, Peter Bunten, Robert Weir, and in a very special way, Catherine Low. Many friends outside of the profession also played a vital role, including Chris and Dana Morgan, Judy Gutman, Sam Friedman, Eric Oatman, Terry Eastland, Ruthanne Lum Mc-Cunn, and Andy Wells.

I happily thank everyone in my incredibly supportive extended family for standing behind me and encouraging me each step of the way, particularly my loving parents, Esther and Richard Gyory; my sister, Anne Gyory; my mother-in-law, Tamara Casriel; and my uncle Cliff. I reserve a special thanks to Madeleine, Willy, and Lila, the three most wonderful children a father could ever be blessed with. Their inspiring love, patience, and excitement for life contributed greatly to this book, and with its publication they can at last explain to their friends what their daddy does.

And finally, and most of all, I thank Cathy, to whom I owe my greatest and most unrepayable debt. Cathy nurtured my ideas and refined my writing. With astonishing goodness and care, she read every page of every version of this book—no mean feat—and improved every sentence of every paragraph. In what often seemed an interminable project, Cathy supported me and believed in me in every way possible. She taught me to be a much better thinker and, more important, a much better husband and father. Without her critical eye and loving heart, this book could never have been completed. The depth of her love still dazzles me. To Cathy I owe everything, and to her this book is lovingly dedicated.

Closing the Gate

Introduction

This book answers a simple question: Why did the United States pass the Chinese Exclusion Act in 1882? This Gilded Age statute, which barred practically all Chinese from American shores for ten years, was the first federal law ever passed banning a group of immigrants solely on the basis of race or nationality. Congress renewed the law in 1892, 1902, and 1904, each time with increasingly less opposition. Historians have identified three forces behind the Chinese Exclusion Act: pressure from workers, politicians, and others in California, where most Chinese had settled; a racist atmosphere that pervaded the nation in the nineteenth century; and persistent support and lobbying by the national labor movement. As the evidence will show, the first two forces were important but not decisive. The third was nonexistent; contrary to the claims of numerous scholars, most workers evinced little interest in Chinese exclusion. Organized labor nationwide played virtually no role in securing the legislation. The motive force behind the Chinese Exclusion Act was national politicians who seized and manipulated the issue in an effort to gain votes, while arguing that workers had long demanded Chinese exclusion and would benefit from it. As one midwestern congressman declared, "To protect our laboring classes . . . the gate . . . must be closed."

In slamming the gate on an entire race of people, the Chinese Exclusion Act reversed not only an American policy but also American tradition, changing forever the nation's image of itself as a beacon of hope, a refuge for the poor and the oppressed the world over. Much like the Fugitive Slave Act of the antebellum era, the Chinese Exclusion Act proved to be the most tragic, most regrettable, and most racist legislation of its era. But unlike the Fugitive Slave Act, which provoked outrage in parts of the country and ignited a fury that led to civil war, the Chinese Exclusion Act rapidly forged a consensus that led to more far reaching exclusion of immigrants—Japanese, Koreans, and other Asians in the early 1900s, and Europeans in the 1920s. The Chinese Exclusion Act set the precedent for these broader exclusion laws and fostered an atmosphere of hostility toward foreigners that would endure for generations. It also fostered a bleaker atmosphere of racism, a racism that swiftly led to Jim Crow legislation in the 1880s, *Plessy v. Ferguson* in the 1890s, and decades of state-sponsored segregation in the 1900s. In legitimizing racism as national policy, the Chinese Exclusion Act set the stage for these developments. "It is the first break in the levee," one congressman observed in 1882. "I would deem the new country we will have after this bill becomes law as changed from the old country we have to-day as our country would have been changed if the rebellion of 1861 had succeeded." By separating the old America from the new, exclusion became the American tradition, and the arguments first invoked by Gilded Age politicians in favor of restriction have reverberated in every debate on immigration down to the present day. At the dawn of a new century, the Chinese Exclusion Act still casts a long, dark shadow over American immigration policy.

> I feel and know that I am pleading the cause of the free American laborer and of his children and of his children's children.
> —James G. Blaine, February 24, 1879

CHAPTER ONE

The Very Recklessness of Statesmanship

Explanations for Chinese Exclusion, 1870s–1990s

"Ought we to exclude them?" asked Senator James G. Blaine on February 14, 1879. "The question lies in my mind thus: either the Anglo-Saxon race will possess the Pacific slope or the Mongolians will possess it." Championing the Fifteen Passenger Bill, a measure aimed at limiting Chinese immigration, Blaine declared on the Senate floor: "We have this day to choose . . . whether our legislation shall be in the interest of the American free laborer or for the servile laborer from China. . . . You cannot work a man who must have beef and bread, and would prefer beer, alongside of a man who can live on rice. It cannot be done."[1]

With this speech, James Blaine became the nation's foremost politician to vigorously advocate Chinese exclusion. In a widely reprinted letter to the *New York Tribune* a week later, he elaborated his position, calling Chinese immigration "vicious," "odious," "abominable," "dangerous," and "revolting. . . . If as a nation we have the right to keep out infectious diseases, if we have the right to exclude the criminal classes from coming to us, we surely have the right to exclude that immigration which reeks with impurity and which cannot come to us without plenteously sowing the seeds of moral and physical disease, destitution, and death." Leaving no doubt as to where he stood, the Maine Republican concluded, "I am opposed to the Chinese coming here; I am opposed to making them citizens; I am opposed to making them voters."[2]

As the most prominent statesman of the Gilded Age, Blaine single-handedly made racist attacks on Chinese immigrants an honorable act. His racist words in 1879 elevated the issue nationally from the streets of San Francisco to the Senate of the United States and made the cries of demagogues respectable. Blaine's polemic broadened the issue from one affecting only the West, where 97 percent of the nation's 105,000 Chinese immigrants lived, to one that supposedly affected the entire country, from one that generated political support from all classes on the Pacific Coast to one that might attract a single class nationwide—the working class. "There is not a laboring man from the Penobscot [River in Maine] to the Sacramento [River in California] who would not feel aggrieved, outraged, burdened, crushed, at being forced into competition with the labor and the wages of the Chinese cooly. For one, I would never consent, by my vote or my voice, to drive the intelligent workingmen of America to that competition and that degradation." But Chinese immigration, Blaine said, involved more than the issue of class. It also affected racial harmony: "I supposed if there was any people in the world that had a race trouble on hand it was ourselves. I supposed if the admonitions of our own history were anything to us we should regard the race trouble as the one thing to be dreaded and the one thing to be avoided. . . . To deliberately sit down and . . . permit another and far more serious trouble seems to be the very recklessness of statesmanship." As Blaine concluded, "It is a good deal cheaper . . . to avoid the trouble by preventing the immigration." Chinese exclusion could thus minimize further racial conflict and preclude another civil war. It could also reduce class tensions. Citing the divisive national railroad strike of 1877 when "unemployed thousands . . . manifested a spirit of violence," Blaine envisioned Chinese exclusion as a palliative measure giving working people what they wanted. "I feel and know that I am pleading the cause of the free American laborer and of his children and of his children's children."[3]

As the front-runner for his party's nomination for president in 1880, Blaine aimed his message at two constituencies—the West Coast and workers nationwide. During three days of debate, he was the only Republican senator east of the Rocky Mountains to speak out against Chinese immigration. But he was hardly alone in his party. When the Senate passed the Fifteen Passenger Bill, which would have limited to fifteen the number of Chinese passengers on any ship coming to the United States, 11 Republicans east of the Rockies supported the measure, and in the House of Representatives, 51 Republicans joined 104 Democrats to pass the bill by a comfortable margin. By 1879, congressional support for Chinese immigration restriction was becoming broad and bipartisan. But for a presidential veto it would have become law.[4]

Three years later, in 1882, Congress debated the Chinese Exclusion Act, a measure far more extreme than the Fifteen Passenger Bill of 1879. Although Blaine had lost the Republican nomination to James A. Garfield in 1880, his racial and class arguments against Chinese immigration carried the day. Republican after Republican denounced the Chinese with a firmness and venom once the preserve of westerners. "Alien in manners, servile in labor, pagan in religion, they are fundamentally un-American," thundered Representative Addison McClure (R-Ohio). "There is no common ground of assimilation," Senator George F. Edmunds (R-Vt.) asserted, to which Senator John Sherman (R-Ohio) added, the Chinese "are not a desirable population. . . . They are not good citizens." Invoking visceral racist images, eastern and midwestern Republicans echoed former senator Blaine. Representative George Hazelton (R-Wisc.) called the Chinese immigrant a "loathsome . . . revolting . . . monstrosity . . . [who] lives in herds and sleeps like packs of dogs in kennels." Other congressmen likened the Chinese to rats and swarming insects whose "withering and blighting effect," in the words of Representative Benjamin Butterworth (R-Ohio), "leave in their trail a moral desert." They "spread mildew and rot throughout the entire community," concluded Representative William Calkins (R-Ind.). Permit them to enter and "you plant a cancer in your own country that will eat out its life and destroy it."[5]

Although condemning the Chinese on racial, cultural, and religious grounds, congressmen across the country emphasized that they favored Chinese exclusion because they favored the working person. "My chief reason for supporting such a measure," said Representative Edwin Willits (R-Mich.), "is, that I believe it is in the interest of American labor." Likewise, Representative Stanton Peelle (R-Ind.) backed the law "upon the ground of protection to American labor as distinguished from protection to American society." As Edward K. Valentine (R-Nebr.) argued, "It is our opportunity to do justice to the American laborer, and injustice to no one." Senator Henry M. Teller (R-Colo.) was blunter: "I see no other way to protect American labor in this country." Lest anyone doubt that workers demanded the law, Representative John Sherwin (R-Ill.) declared that Chinese exclusion "is a question which comes home after all to the men and women who labor with their hands, more than to anyone else. And I think we can trust them in determining it better than we can trust anyone else."[6]

Senator Blaine's endorsement of the Fifteen Passenger Bill in 1879 had given anti-Chinese racism legitimacy, and within three years a strong bipartisan consensus emerged to outlaw Chinese immigration. Scurrying to take credit for the Chinese Exclusion Act, politicians echoed Blaine in claiming to have passed the measure in response to workers' needs and long-stated demands. Although congressional opposition to Chinese immigration had actually begun forming in the mid-1870s, its swiftness amazed many observers. "If such a bill had been proposed in either House of Congress twenty years ago," Senator Sherman noted in 1882, "it would have been the death warrant of the man who offered it."[7] Indeed, when Congress first debated Chinese citizenship in 1870, virtually no one suggested tampering with the nation's century-old policy of open immigration. During the next twelve years, however, Chinese exclusion would become an article of faith in both parties that would dictate political platforms and shape presidential campaigns.

The creation of Chinese immigration as a national issue and the passage of the Chinese Exclusion Act on May 6, 1882, mark a turning point in American history. It was the first immigration law ever passed by the United States barring one specific group of people because of their race or nationality. By changing America's traditional policy of open immigration, this landmark legislation set a precedent for future restrictions against Asian immigrants in the late nineteenth and early twentieth centuries and against European immigrants in the 1920s. Despite the broad significance of the Chinese Exclusion Act, it has received remarkably little attention from historians. And much of what has been written is wrong.

Historians have ascribed two theories to explain the origins of the Chinese Exclusion Act: the California thesis and the national racist consensus thesis. The California thesis, advanced by Mary Roberts Coolidge in 1909, posits California and its working people as the key agents of Chinese exclusion. The Chinese first emigrated to America in large numbers in 1849, when, like thousands of people the world over, they joined the gold rush and raced to California. By 1852, about twenty-five thousand Chinese had arrived in Gam Saan, or Gold Mountain, as they called California, some staking claims in the mines, others working as cooks, launderers, and laborers. During the first three years, Coolidge argued, white Californians welcomed the Chinese. Called "one of the most worthy [classes] of our newly adopted citizens" by the state's second governor, the Chinese took part in services commemorating President Zachary Taylor's death in 1850 and marched in the parade celebrating California's admission to the union later that year. "The China Boys will yet vote at the same polls, study at the same schools, and bow at the same altar as our own countrymen," the *San Francisco Alta California* predicted in 1852. Yet long before this newspaper rolled off the press, racial hostilities had erupted in the mining camps when whites tried to drive all "foreigners"—Mexican, South American, and Chinese—from the region. Some Chinese immigrants had signed contracts in their native land to work for a set period of time at substandard wages. Miners and other Californians targeted them for abuse, and politicians exploited the situation for their own benefit. Several officials, such as Governor John Bigler and State Senator Philip Roach, denounced the Chinese and urged restrictions on their entry as early as 1852. Which came first—the anti-Chinese sentiment in the mining camps or the anti-Chinese rhetoric in the state capital—Coolidge did not say, but each fed on the other, and with miners a key voting bloc in the new state, politicians eagerly courted their support. In the course of the decade, the California legislature passed numerous discriminatory laws against the Chinese, culminating with an 1858 exclusion act. Most of these laws and others passed subsequently were declared unconstitutional by state or federal courts.[8]

Despite bigotry and violence directed at them by whites, Chinese immigrants kept coming to Gam Saan, their numbers augmented when the Central Pacific Railroad Company imported thousands of workers directly from China in the 1860s to build the western portion of the transcontinental railroad. "They are very trusty, they are very intelligent, and they live up to their contracts," railroad president Charles Crocker observed, praising their "reliability and steadiness, and their aptitude and capacity for hard work." By 1870, the census counted 49,310 Chinese in California, making up 8.5 percent of the state's population. In San Francisco, the state's largest city, they composed one-fourth of the population; because most Chinese immigrants were single men, they were a third of the workforce. With the decline of mining, the Chinese entered a variety of occupations, including agriculture, manufacturing, and construction, often accepting wages below those of white workers. Combined with racism—the Chinese looked different, practiced a different religion, and seemed reluctant to "assimilate" into American society—this economic competition, Coolidge argued, led white workers to oppose the Chinese, and abetted by politicians, a revived labor movement in San Francisco after the Civil War mobilized against them. Because the courts had ruled that only Congress possessed the power to restrict immigration, western politicians turned to Washington, where as early as 1867 they began introducing bills aimed at limiting Chinese immigration.[9]

In 1876, Democrats and Republicans locked horns in the most competitive presidential election since the Civil War and believed that the electoral votes of the West Coast could make the difference. Both parties embraced the Chinese issue and pushed for immigration restriction. Labor militancy in San Francisco kept the issue in the forefront in the late 1870s, Coolidge maintained, and the same dynamic recurred nationally in the election of 1880. By advocating anti-Chinese legislation to attract votes, national politicians pursued the identical strategy local politicians had used in California in the 1850s and 1860s. "The struggle on the part of both parties . . . to carry California became fiercer and fiercer," Coolidge wrote, "and gave her demands for legislation a prominence in the national legislature out of all proportion to their normal value." Coolidge blamed workers, and particularly Irish immigrants, for fanning the flames of racial hatred. "The clamor of an alien class in a single State—taken up by politicians for their own ends—was sufficient to change the policy of a nation and to commit the United States to a race discrimination at variance with our professed theories of government."[10]

Although marred by class prejudice, numerous inaccuracies, and a polemical tone, Coolidge's presentation of the California thesis has remained the dominant explanation for Chinese exclusion. Succeeding generations of historians have refined but not overturned her argument. In *The Anti-Chinese Movement in California* (1939), Elmer Clarence Sandmeyer offered a more scholarly and balanced account, stressing that anti-Chinese sentiment on the West Coast was not confined to workers but crossed all classes. By 1876, middle-class and conservative Californians vied with workers in opposing Chinese immigration, Sandmeyer contended, while Chinese exclusion "found strong support in the growing labor organizations of the country." Despite these important additions, Sandmeyer essentially reaffirmed Coolidge's thesis.[11]

Three decades later, Alexander Saxton provided the most sophisticated study of anti-Chinese politics. In *The Indispensable Enemy: Labor and the Anti-Chinese Movement in California* (1971), Saxton traces the roots of anti-Chinese sentiment to working-class ideology of the Jacksonian era. As the franchise spread to propertyless white men in the early 1800s, northern Democrats embraced an egalitarian philosophy that appealed to workers wary of class hierarchy and special privilege. In the South, Democrats (like virtually all white southerners) possessed a proslavery outlook that necessarily implied black inferiority. To win presidential elections, the Democratic Party needed both sections of the country, and northern Democrats of all classes readily accepted southern positions on slavery and race. "Workingmen alone of the northern white population came into direct competition with free Negroes," Saxton argues, and spurred on by this economic imperative, they incorporated racial supremacy into their ideology. Republicans, on the other hand, descended from a Federalist-Whig tradition that accepted divisions in society based on class and property and, by implication, race. This acceptance of social and class distinctions contributed to a distrust of the poor and a fear of immigrants. Although seemingly patrician in origin, nativism appealed to workers who believed that foreigners threatened their jobs. As the nation expanded westward during the 1840s and 1850s, Whigs and many Democrats wanted to keep the territories free of slavery and free of blacks. Defending his proviso to ban slavery from the vast region soon to be acquired from Mexico, Representative David Wilmot (D-Pa.) stated in 1847: "I plead the cause and the rights of white freemen. I would preserve to free white labor a fair country . . . where the sons of toil, of my own race and own color, can live without the disgrace which association with negro slavery brings upon free labor." This free-soil impulse, Saxton contends, was as much antiblack as antislavery. When these three forces—"whiggishness," nativism, and free soil—converged in the early 1850s to create the Republican Party, the goal of abolishing slavery played a small role. Only during the Civil War, when emancipation became necessary to win the war and preserve the union, did abolitionism become central to Republicans. But these changes during the Civil War and Reconstruction, Saxton claims, had little impact on white workers' racism: "Meanwhile, thousands of Americans, including workingmen and immigrants, passed through the free-soil and unionist phases of anti-slavery without modifying their previously held attitudes toward the Negro. Not much of abolition rubbed off on them." Saxton argues that despite their political differences, Democratic and Republican workers—the pioneers who headed west to California during and after the gold rush—carried with them a nearly identical ideological baggage steeped in racism. In California, however, they encountered not blacks but Chinese, and the transfer of their hostile attitudes from the former to the latter was a logical step, especially when they believed the Chinese posed an economic threat. In the anti-Chinese movement, Saxton concludes, racist white workers found a common foe—an indispensable enemy—that would unite them for generations.[12]

Like Coolidge and Sandmeyer, Saxton pinpoints 1867 as the inauguration of labor's campaign in California against Chinese immigration. By 1870, workers and politicians statewide had made the cause their own, with Democrats and Republicans united on the issue. Saxton elaborates Sandmeyer's claim that 1876 saw a major diffusion of anti-Chinese sentiment across class lines, as most of California's labor organizations had collapsed during the depression in the mid-1870s. "Trade unionism in San Francisco . . . almost ceased to exist during the depression years," Saxton writes, leaving workers "leaderless, embittered, and disorganized." A bipartisan establishment of "respectable" citizens—employers, manufacturers, and business leaders—took the reins of the anti-Chinese movement in the centennial year. Saxton agrees with Sandmeyer that by 1870, organized labor nationally had adopted the issue of Chinese exclusion. Although Saxton's account is by far the most complete, the most textured, and the most persuasive explanation of the origins of the anti-Chinese movement in California, he scarcely connects it to the national debate over Chinese immigration. Like Coolidge and Sandmeyer of generations past, Saxton offers virtually no explanation of how Congress and the rest of the nation came to support Chinese exclusion.[13]

The only serious challenge to the California thesis came in 1969 from Stuart Creighton Miller in *The Unwelcome Immigrant: The American Image of the Chinese, 1785–1882*. Examining thousands of books, magazines, and news-papers from the nineteenth century, Miller finds relentlessly negative stereo-types of the Chinese, a negative image that long preceded their arrival in North America. Merchants, diplomats, and missionaries—the only Americans in the first half of the century to interact with the Celestial Empire, as China was often called—sent back images of "Chinese deceit, cunning, idolatry, despo-tism, xenophobia, cruelty, infanticide, and intellectual and sexual perversity." This racist image, Miller writes, coincided with the emerging scientific contro-versy over racial origins and differences and whether human beings con-stituted one or multiple species. Because scientists on both sides accepted the inferiority of the "Mongolian" and "Ethiopian" races, the debate provided a solid basis for "Caucasian" superiority and "heightened American conscious-ness of racial differences." Racist iconography of the Chinese gained broad currency during the Opium War (1839–42), the first major event involving the Celestial Empire covered by American newspapers, and this negative imagery spread more widely in following decades with the rise of the penny press. "The important point to keep in mind," Miller argues, "is that the unfavorable image of the Chinese is discernible among American opinion makers long before the first Celestial gold seeker set foot upon California soil." It is this unfavorable image, Miller maintains, that served as the key agent of Chinese exclusion: "The accepted interpretation of the Chinese exclusion laws, referred to . . . as the 'California thesis,' does not stand up under close scrutiny and should be substantially modified, if not completely altered. To view the policy of exclusion simply as a victory for the obsessive prejudice of Californians is neither accurate nor fair. Although that state unquestionably catalyzed and spearheaded the movement for exclusion, there were much more potent na-tional and historical forces at work than the mere accident of evenly balanced political parties."[14]

Although Miller effectively illustrates the prevalence of anti-Chinese imag-ery in nineteenth-century America, his explanation for Chinese exclusion pos-sesses a fundamental flaw: it is entirely intellectual. Racist thought does not necessarily produce racist action, and by leaving the politics out, Miller fails to make the connection of how racist imagery—or racism itself—gained expression in national legislation. Anti-Chinese imagery provided a climate conducive to exclusion but did not in itself cause it. In tracing causation, Miller repeats and magnifies earlier assumptions on working-class agency: "It would not be difficult to indict organized labor as the backbone of the anti-Chinese movement on a national level. Labor leaders in every section of the country attacked the coolie issue with the monomania of men whose backs are to the wall. . . . Virtually every labor newspaper and organization opposed Chinese immigration after 1870."[15]

In emphasizing the role of the national labor movement, Miller joined the ranks of nearly every labor historian who has treated the subject. In 1918, John R. Commons, founder of the Wisconsin school of labor history and dean of labor historians, wrote that as early as 1870, the "national labour movement consistently" supported the exclusion of Chinese immigrants. His student Selig Perlman later called the Chinese Exclusion Act "the most important single factor in the history of American labor." These two set the tone for future labor historiography on the subject. Historians Philip Taft, Joseph G. Rayback, and Gerald N. Grob stressed the national labor movement's opposition to Chinese immigration in the 1870s, a point echoed by Herbert Hill, who has argued that nationally, "organized labor took up the anti-Chinese litany after 1870" and formed "the vanguard of the anti-Asian campaign" during the decade and that "the great effort generated in the ranks of labor" contributed to the Chinese Exclusion Act in 1882. Labor and immigration historians Robert D. Parmet and A. T. Lane, as well as Roger Daniels and Ronald Takaki, leading scholars of the Asian American experience, have also accepted this interpretation. As David R. Roediger writes, "Rare is the modern labor historian who does not recoil from regarding Chinese exclusion as *the* historic victory of the American working class."[16]

The historian who most forcefully connects the national labor movement with the Chinese Exclusion Act is Gwendolyn Mink. In her 1986 study, *Old Labor and New Immigrants in American Political Development: Union, Party, and State, 1875–1920*, Mink argues that after the Civil War, "immigration, rather than immigrants, played the decisive role in formulating an American version of labor politics." Squeezed from below by newcomers from abroad, "the trade-union response to this pressure was to mobilize, and then to lobby, for immigration restriction." The overriding force galvanizing the labor movement and driving it toward this xenophobic goal was anti-Chinese hostility. "From the mid-1870s a profound racial and nativist strain would be at the political core of trade unionism," Mink writes. "Although the 'Chinese menace' was geographically contained, the anti-Chinese movement must be viewed in a national context. It invigorated national union solidarity." In providing "a peculiar bridge between unionism and national politics," she adds, Chinese exclusion became the dominant issue uniting the labor movement after the Civil War.[17]

By placing anti-Chinese politics at the heart of the national labor movement and the national labor movement at the heart of the anti-Chinese campaign, Mink profoundly distorts the evolution of working-class ideology and organized labor after the Civil War. Like countless historians before and after, she misunderstands the positions of workers and working-class leaders nationwide toward Chinese immigration in the late 1860s and 1870s. One reason for Mink's faulty interpretation stems from her heavy reliance on secondary sources—many of which she misreads. She claims, for example, that as a result of working-class militancy in San Francisco in 1877–78, Republicans included an anti-Chinese plank in their national platform in 1880—ignoring completely that Republicans had included an anti-Chinese plank in 1876, well before this labor militancy erupted. Her assertion that in 1882 Chinese exclusion was "a Democratic issue" overlooks the many prominent Republicans such as Blaine who strongly supported the Chinese Exclusion Act, vigorously campaigned on it, and took credit for it. Mink also errs by stating that in 1885, "Congress passed the Foran Act, repealing Republican Civil War legislation that had authorized the recruitment of European contract labor." Congress had actually repealed this legislation seventeen years earlier, in 1868. This fact debunks her conclusion that organized labor's successful campaign against Chinese immigration "prodded" the labor movement to oppose contract labor. The labor movement needed no such prodding. As the historical record makes clear, the fight to outlaw contract labor long preceded any effort by the national labor movement to restrict Chinese immigration. Perhaps Mink's most egregious error lies in repeatedly stressing, with virtually no original evidence, that workers in the eastern United States backed the cries of their brethren in California and that their support for Chinese exclusion thereby "nationalized labor politics." By misrepresenting workers' attitudes toward Chinese immigration, Mink seriously skews the development of the labor movement after the Civil War and presents a thesis on the origin of the Chinese Exclusion Act that is patently invalid.[18]

In placing race at the core of white working-class formation, Mink echoes the work of Saxton and Hill and anticipates that of Roediger. No one has analyzed this theme more brilliantly than Saxton himself. In *The Rise and Fall of the White Republic: Class Politics and Mass Culture in Nineteenth-Century*

America (1990), he dissects images and themes in popular culture to show how white racism evolved in the 1800s from a vague construct to a vital ideological force that helped justify slavery, American Indian extermination, and Chinese exclusion. Saxton's genius rests in portraying multiple racisms—Republicans could be "soft" on blacks but "hard" on Native Americans (and a little of both on the Chinese)—and in identifying politics as the conduit for crystallizing and propagating racial discourse. Whether dealing with slavery, westward expansion, or industrialization, politics served as the crucible for racism to be defined, refined, and perpetuated. Stressing the importance of American Indian removal to the ideological formation of both political parties, Saxton argues that for Democrats, strong proponents of slavery and manifest destiny, extermination of American Indians reinforced white superiority, whereas for Republicans, driven more by industrialization than by antislavery or territorial growth, extermination helped harden racial attitudes and legitimize racist policies. As class boundaries solidified after the Civil War, racial identification became more central to working-class ideology, and white workers effortlessly transferred antiblack and anti-Indian hostility to the Chinese. Although Saxton convincingly traces the evolution of Democratic racial thought, he is less persuasive and less comprehensive in his analysis of Republican racial attitudes. He claims that Free-Soilers, while virulently anti-Indian, remained silent on blacks, a silence he doesn't explain. As a result, a key strand of Republican ideology—abolitionism and racial equality—remains unexplored and unconnected to the party's Reconstruction policies. To Saxton, Reconstruction was a momentary blip in the nation's history with little lasting impact on party policy or working-class ideology. This failure to analyze the antislavery, free-labor heritage with the same rigor he applies to other forces leads Saxton to discount the significance of this heritage and obscures the manner in which workers adapted it to their ideology after the Civil War.[19]

One of Saxton's major contributions is his emphasis on the complexity of racism, his assertion that neither economic competition nor psychological needs can explain the prevalence and pervasiveness of racism in American history. Racism, he argues, is ultimately an ideological construct that has served different functions for different groups and classes in different eras. As he contends, "neither trade unionists nor anyone else in nineteenth-century America arrived at conclusions involving matters of race simply through processes of economic reasoning." There is a corollary, however, that Saxton does not explore: white workers, like other white Americans, could be deeply racist and possess a deeply racist ideology, but that does not mean they necessarily acted on this racist ideology or pursued or supported racist policies. Thought is not action; ideology is not policy. Workers could be racist and still oppose exclusion.[20]

Saxton's failure to integrate the abolitionist legacy undercuts his analysis of working-class attitudes toward Chinese immigration. By endorsing the view that eastern workers united with western workers in support of Chinese exclusion after the Civil War, Saxton and all his predecessors miss a key development and a key moment in working-class history. Racist as white workers may have been in this era, they were neither much more nor much less racist than other segments of American society. And although they were the only group with a distinct economic motive to favor Chinese exclusion, eastern workers— who made up the vast bulk of the working classes and the national labor movement—were largely indifferent to Chinese exclusion and played practically no role in the passage of the Chinese Exclusion Act.

One other historian bears noting. In *The Wages of Whiteness: Race and the Making of the American Working Class* (1991), David Roediger stresses the concept of whiteness as the signal force unifying workers before the Civil War. Whiteness provided psychological distance from blacks and elevated white workers, especially Irish immigrants, to a common equality as American citizens. Although Roediger offers numerous examples of working-class racism, his survey is ultimately impressionistic, giving little sense of working-class policies or working-class demands. He acknowledges but minimizes workers' roles as Free-Soilers and abolitionists and yet contends, unlike Saxton, that the war transformed workers' attitudes. Quoting Karl Marx, Roediger writes: "There was . . . a stunning 'moral impetus' . . . injected into the working-class movement by the Civil War and emancipation. Anti-slavery luminaries were not just welcomed onto labor platforms but courted by workers' organizations." Attempts at interracial unity "set it [the postwar labor movement] dramatically apart from the antebellum labor movement." But such unity had its limits, Roediger argues, citing as evidence the "tremendous working-class response in areas such as Chicago and Massachusetts . . . [to] the anti-Chinese movement." Much like Mink, Roediger relies heavily on secondary sources. Consequently, despite his careful attention to the meanings of working-class terminology (such as "wage slavery" and "white slavery"), he misses some of the nuances of that terminology and thus misconstrues working-class attitudes toward Chinese immigration. "Race is constructed differently across time by people in the same social class," Roediger argues, "and differently at the same time by people whose class positions differ." But to go one step further, race is also constructed differently at the same time by people in the *same* social class. Workers' myriad attitudes toward Chinese immigration demonstrate this point and reveal the dangers of generalizing too broadly about the extent and uniformity of racism in any single group.[21]

Both the California thesis of Coolidge and Sandmeyer and the national racist consensus thesis of Miller provide valid insights into the origins of the Chinese Exclusion Act, but neither thesis explains the process by which Chinese exclusion came to be enacted. Nor does either thesis explain how national politicians appropriated and packaged the issue. The California thesis, in which West Coast activists agitated for Chinese exclusion and national politicians then picked up the issue for their own personal gain, remains accurate, but the emphasis on agency should be reversed. The single most important force behind the Chinese Exclusion Act was national politicians of both parties who seized, transformed, and manipulated the issue of Chinese immigration in the quest for votes. In an era of almost perfectly balanced party strength, presidential elections pivoted on a few thousand ballots, and candidates flailed desperately to capture them. Chinese immigrants, powerless and voteless, became pawns in a political system characterized by legislative stalemate and presidential elections decided by razor-thin margins. Politicians also used Chinese immigration as a smoke screen. In a period of rising class conflict, they aimed both to propitiate working-class voters and to deflect attention from genuine national problems—economic depression, mass poverty, and growing unemployment—by magnifying and distorting a side issue of paltry significance into one of seemingly overriding national importance. Chinese immigrants became the indispensable enemy not to workers but to politicians, who, in a period of converging political consensus, needed a safe, nonideological cause to trumpet. Politicians—not California, not workers, and not national racist imagery—ultimately supplied the agency for Chinese exclusion.

The Chinese Exclusion Act provides a classic example of top-down politics and opens a unique window for viewing the political system of the Gilded Age. The act also illustrates the transformation of the Republican Party from an antislavery force to a mere electoral apparatus. This transformation was neither swift nor sudden. Nor was it complete. As late as 1882, many principled Republicans fought exclusion adamantly. The difference, however, was that in 1870 this idealistic wing of the party, the wing that had fought for emancipation and civil rights for freed slaves, was still influential and respected even by its enemies. But by 1882, this once prominent force had been relegated to the party's fringe. Formerly revered as the conscience of the nation, these altruistic leaders were now considered a nuisance and portrayed as doddering sentimentalists, "humanitarian half thinkers." The passage of the Chinese Exclusion Act reflects the passing of an era, revealing this fundamental change in both the Republican Party and the nation at large.

The Chinese Exclusion Act marks the coda of Reconstruction, with North, South, and West uniting to usher in a new era of state-sponsored segregation. After a brief period of federal efforts to protect civil rights and promote integration, politicians found restrictive, racist legislation a simpler and easier way to handle the nation's race problems. With antiblack bigotry temporarily in eclipse (at least among many) in the late 1860s and 1870s, anti-Chinese racism filled the vacuum and provided a convenient alternative in the hunt for scapegoats amid a sputtering economy. Anti-Chinese racism served as a bridge from the antebellum era to the rise of Jim Crow in the 1880s when racism again became fashionable. The Chinese Exclusion Act, by which Congress and the United States government legitimized racism as national policy, remains a key legacy of the nineteenth century, and its lingering impact of anti-Asian bigotry remains to this day.

The origins of Chinese exclusion are neither simple nor direct. They involve numerous twists and turns through a decade and a half of industrial upheaval and mounting class tensions. While Chinese immigrants flocked to Gam Saan in the nineteenth century, Californians, workers, and the national labor movement put the Chinese question on the map, but Gilded Age politicians redrew the map's boundaries and recast the issue. Abetted by the press, politicians such as James Blaine and countless others convinced the nation that American workers demanded Chinese exclusion and would be better off without Chinese immigrants. Nationally, however, workers remained generally uninterested in Chinese exclusion. This, then, is the double tragedy of the Chinese Exclusion Act: not only did politicians close the gate on an entire race of people, but they also blamed this act on a group that did not seek it. Historians should no longer be misled by their arguments.

Two facts are patent—China has the labor that we need, and it can be procured to an unlimited extent.
—Report of the Memphis Chinese Labor Convention, July 1869

CHAPTER TWO

To Fetch Men Wholesale

Framing the Chinese Issue Nationally in the 1860s and the First Chinese Scare in 1869

China is a "disgustful . . . booby nation," its civilization "a besotted perversity," its people distinguished by "their cheerless . . . stupidity." So wrote Ralph Waldo Emerson in 1824. A generation later, Horace Greeley, editor of the influential *New York Tribune*, called Chinese immigrants "uncivilized, unclean and filthy beyond all conception, without any of the higher domestic or social relations. . . . Pagan in religion, they know not the virtues of honesty, integrity or good faith." In voicing these sentiments, Emerson and Greeley were largely in the mainstream of American intellectual opinion in the nineteenth century. As the globe-trotting journalist Bayard Taylor wrote in 1855, in one of the most frequently quoted passages of the era: "The Chinese are, morally, the most debased people on the face of the earth . . . [with a] depravity so shocking and horrible, that their character cannot even be hinted. . . . Their touch is pollution." On the eve of the Civil War, Samuel Goodrich, the nation's most popular author of juvenile literature, taught children that "men [from China] are

17

servile, deceitful and utterly regardless of the truth. From the emperor to the beggar through every rank of society . . . there is a system of cheating, and hypocrisy, practiced without remorse. . . . No faith whatever, can in general, be reposed in the Chinese." Caleb Cushing, first U.S. commissioner to China and negotiator of the first treaty between the two nations, stated in 1859, "I do not admit as my equal . . . the yellow man of Asia."[1]

To many Americans in the nineteenth century, perceived physical differences reinforced cultural differences. Newspapers called Chinese immigrants "almond-eyed, spindle-legged," "yellow-skinned," "pig-tailed," and "bald-pated." Political affiliation mattered little. The Democratic *New York Star* described the Chinese immigrant as "filthy, unnatural, and abominable," while the Republican *Cincinnati Gazette* labeled him a "dependent, ignorant . . . animal machine." Nicknamed "John Chinaman" or simply "John," these common epithets, like "Sambo" for black men and "Bridget" for Irish women, stereotyped male Chinese immigrants as an anonymous, undifferentiated mass. Editors and journalists portrayed them as childlike, feminine, and submissive, and metaphors frequently linked them to insects and vermin, which the Chinese allegedly consumed. Hinton Rowan Helper called them "counterfeit human beings." Religious differences compounded the racism. The *New York Times* noted their "heathenish souls and heathenish propensities," while the *New York Herald*, the most widely read newspaper in the country, claimed that the "Chinese people remain as barbarous as ever. Their pagan savageness appears to be impregnable to the mild influences of Christian civilization."[2]

Speaking before the American Social Science Association in 1869, Charles Francis Adams Jr. described the Chinese as "semi-civilized, ignorant," and unable to "change or assimilate." Better to "organize an emigration from Sodom" than from China, said this descendant of two presidents, fearing that "contact with such a race will brutalize the inhabitants of the Pacific States more than contact with the harmless African ever brutalized the South." Even Wendell Phillips, the former abolitionist who would defend unrestricted Chinese immigration to his dying day, called the Chinese "barbarous," of an "alien blood," and capable of "dragging down the American home to the level of the houseless street herds of China." And liberal-thinking John Stuart Mill worried that Chinese immigration could result in "a permanent harm" to the "more civilized and improved portion of mankind."[3]

Stuart Creighton Miller has amply documented many of these anti-Chinese statements and images; such racist iconography reached every class and every region of the country in the nineteenth century. But the fundamental questions are, How did Americans react to these racist portrayals, and how did this racism get translated into public policy? To answer these questions and trace the development of the Chinese issue nationally, it is necessary to examine the labor movement and political situation in the United States after the Civil War. The eight-year period from the surrender of the Confederacy in 1865 to the onset of the depression in 1873 was a vibrant era in American working-class history. David Montgomery contends that several hundred thousand wage earners joined unions, marking the highest proportion of organized industrial workers in any period of the century. The chief issue uniting the labor movement during Reconstruction was the eight-hour workday. Several states passed laws mandating an eight-hour day for government workers, and in 1868 Congress enacted the eight-hour workday for federal employees. This legislation was seldom enforced, however, and the eight-hour day would remain the lightning rod for working-class protest for the next two generations. A cadre of other issues galvanized workers in the early Reconstruction era: arbitration to settle strikes, an end to convict labor, and government inspection of factories and mines. Another major working-class grievance was the importation of contract labor—workers hired in a foreign country and brought to work in the United States.[4]

Imported contract labor in the form of indentured servitude was older than the nation itself, dating to the earliest white settlements in British North America. Prior to the Revolution, more than half the nation's immigrants south of New England came as indentured servants, signing contracts to work for several years in exchange for passage to the colonies. The institution practically died out by the early 1800s but revived in modified form when manufacturers began importing skilled workers from Britain to operate the nation's new factories. Despite the range of workers brought over, importation remained limited and uncontroversial. Meanwhile, millions of voluntary immigrants poured in from Ireland and Germany after 1845, amply supplying hands for the nation's burgeoning industrial economy.[5]

Labor relations changed during the Civil War when massive enlistment in the Union army decimated the male workforce. To ease this labor shortage, influential economist Henry C. Carey, long a proponent of increased immigration, lobbied for the importation of workers from abroad. Endorsing the idea, bankers, lawyers, railroad presidents, and politicians incorporated the American Emigrant Company (AEC) in Hartford, Connecticut, in 1863 to procure "miners, mechanics (including workers in iron and steel of every class), weavers, and agricultural, rail-road and other laborers . . . in any numbers, and at a reasonable cost." With the same goal, Boston manufacturers established the Foreign Emigrant Aid Society a few months later. Across the Northeast and Midwest, manufacturers and merchants (as well as steamship companies) supported these groups, and the AEC soon had operating capital of half a million dollars. Secretary of State William H. Seward, Treasury Secretary Salmon P. Chase, and Senator Charles Sumner (R-Mass.) backed these ventures, and in his annual message to Congress in 1863, President Abraham Lincoln gave his blessing to federal support for immigration. On July 4, 1864, the U.S. government approved "An Act to Encourage Immigration," authorizing the federal government to enforce contracts made on foreign soil in which emigrants pledged up to one year's worth of labor in exchange for transport to America. This law officially sanctioned imported contract labor.[6]

Setting up offices in England, Scotland, Wales, Prussia, Scandinavia, Belgium, and France, AEC agents scoured western Europe for immigrants and advertised in local newspapers. The U.S. government assisted labor importers by instructing consular officials abroad to serve as recruiting agents and distribute pamphlets, maps, and information to potential contract immigrants. With this joint private-public effort, the president of the AEC looked forward to importing twenty thousand workers a year. Other companies jumped into the act. Within days of the law's passage, agents of mine owners from Michigan and Maine, aided by U.S. consuls in Norway and Sweden, filled a ship with over four hundred Scandinavian immigrants who had signed two-year contracts at paltry wages. Recruiting agents advertised openly to lure American purchasers. In St. Louis, AEC official Thomas Souper tried to persuade "large corporations or special industrial interests to import in sufficient quantity the special kind of labor which they require." Promising he could get laborers of every stripe, Souper targeted railroads and mining companies as well as "manufacturers of iron and steel, machinists, boiler makers, ship and house builders, [and] manufacturers of all kinds." Such efforts paid off; employers throughout the country, including iron mogul Andrew Carnegie, engaged imported labor in the mid-1860s.[7]

American workers attacked the importation of foreign contract labor from its inception during the Civil War. Opposition intensified when employers imported laborers to break strikes. In 1864, St. Louis stove manufacturer Giles Filley refused demands of the Iron Molders' Union and imported twenty-five workers from Prussia on a one-year contract. The agreement barred the Prussians from joining the union, specified a low wage of two dollars a day, and allowed the company to deduct 25 percent of each worker's pay until the price of the overseas passage had been recouped. Union members in Missouri got wind of the scheme and alerted eastern molders to watch for the train carrying the "slaves of Mr. Filley." When the Prussians passed through Indianapolis, local workers intercepted them and informed them of the situation. Unswayed, the Prussians marched onward, and when the train reached St. Louis, members of the union and guards hired by Filley showed up to greet them. Siding with the striking molders, the Prussians broke their contracts, joined the union, and refused to work. At a victory celebration soon after, a molder flogged a "scab-covered horse," joking that he was teaching the obstinate "Filley" a lesson. Cruel punning aside, this early encounter between local workers and imported strikebreakers set the stage for later confrontations.[8]

After Lee surrendered at Appomattox in April 1865, the two armies demobilized, and the national labor shortage rapidly disappeared. With hands plentiful, employers began importing immigrants primarily to break strikes rather than to supplement their workforces. During the first peacetime summer, the Eagle Iron Works in Chicago engaged the American Emigrant Company to procure Belgians to break a strike. In 1865 and 1866, coal mine operators in Pennsylvania, West Virginia, and Illinois hired workers from England and Scotland to overcome local work stoppages, and in 1868, New York City builders imported workers from Canada to break a strike by bricklayers. Threats could be as powerful as reality. In June 1866, iron manufacturers in Pittsburgh warned striking workers that eight hundred puddlers were on their way from England. The contract labor law of 1864 gave tacit support to such schemes, and government officials gave support openly: in 1866, the U.S. commissioner of immigration declared importation a potent weapon employers should use to combat the "continued success of strikes by workmen of almost all kinds."[9]

Workers across the country repeatedly condemned importation in general and the AEC in particular. *Fincher's Trades' Review*, the major labor paper of the time, printed editorial after editorial on the subject in the mid 1860s. Other journals sympathetic to workers' interests, such as the *Detroit Union*, also denounced emigrant companies for "importing foreign labor" and urged workers to unite to "counteract the evil designs" of the importers. Criticizing importers' intentions "to fetch men as it were 'whole-sale' . . . [to] overcrowd the country with workmen," one Cleveland wage earner quoted in *Fincher's Trades' Review* condemned the "evil tendencies of the A. E. Co. to degrade our labor. . . . Let a gradual emigration go on, . . . but when capitalists seek to crush all spirit out of us by an overwhelming emigration, we have just cause for feeling alarmed."[10]

As early as 1864, labor leaders cautioned against denouncing the *imported* rather than the *importers*. "These [imported] men should not be spurned and treated as enemies," William H. Sylvis wrote, "because they are only the dupes of the wiley agents. We should rather seek to show them that they have been imposed upon. . . . Bring them to our standards, . . . and by their co-operation, we will diligently work for their as well as our good." President of the Iron

Molders' International Union, Sylvis was the foremost labor leader of the decade and director of the campaign against imported contract labor. He warned union officials abroad about ruses of the AEC, whose agents frequently appeared at the sites of European strikes to lure workers to the United States. Sylvis also attempted to negotiate agreements with union leaders in Europe to crack down on workers who signed contracts with American agents. Speaking out tirelessly against importation, Sylvis condemned the emigrant companies —"the promoters of this dirty work"—as "a combination of capitalists [seeking] to glut the market with foreign labor and break down wages." He also lashed out against the mainstream press for distorting his views and those of fellow workers. "Every effort has been made to convince the public," he wrote in 1867, that organized labor evinced "hostility to emigration generally. Nothing could be further from the truth." "The interests of labor are identical throughout the world," he said; all that separates workers in Europe from workers in America "[is] the water which divides us." Sylvis then stated what would become a guiding principle of the American labor movement: "We claim that our country is large enough for all. We care not who comes here. We are ready to give the hand of welcome to our fellows from all parts of the globe, but we are opposed to that kind of emigration that will reduce us and those who come here to starvation."[11]

Sylvis was not alone in this view. The *Workingman's Advocate*, which soon supplanted *Fincher's Trades' Review* as the nation's preeminent labor journal, also warned of press distortion. Workers, the *Advocate* observed in 1866, "are not opposed to encouraging immigration. The cause of labor is the same, and when the foreign laborer comes to our shores, he is as much identified with the workingman here as if he had been American born. The evil intended to be guarded against . . . is not immigration in general, but the system on which it is conducted, throwing emigration into the hands of capitalists, who take occasion to have them brought out, when it suits their own convenience and at the very nick of time perhaps that their workingmen are asking for an increase in wages."[12]

In her masterful study *American Industry and the European Immigrant, 1860–1885*, Charlotte Erickson has argued that imported contract labor actually accounted for very little of the postwar immigration to the United States. Expense, risk, and uncertainty kept employers from resorting to it frequently.[13] Erickson may well be correct, but she discounts the significance of the *threat* imported labor posed to American workers. Employers could intimidate workers merely by vowing to import foreign laborers. That importation was indeed utilized, however rarely, gave credence to manufacturers' warnings—and to workers' fears. Imported contract labor remained a powerful weapon that employers could threaten to unleash at any time. Consequently, opposition to imported contract labor remained at the top of the working-class agenda.

On August 20, 1866, sixty-five delegates from unions, trades assemblies, and workers' organizations gathered in Baltimore to found the National Labor Union (NLU). Conceived largely by Sylvis and editor Jonathan Fincher, the NLU represented the first major attempt to form a nationwide, working-class federation. Delegates discussed numerous issues and appointed a committee to visit President Andrew Johnson and present him with a list of grievances. Among those grievances was imported contract labor. Since manufacturers were protected by a tariff on imported *goods*, the committee told the president, workers deserved a law to protect them from imported *laborers*. "We desire protection," the committee leader said, "against foreign pauper labor imported against our interests, to reduce the price of labor."[14]

Continued reports of importation kept the issue on workers' minds, and at the second meeting of the NLU the following year, delegates roundly condemned the system. Alexander Scott, a Pittsburgh iron boiler, charged that manufacturers paid the American consul in Prussia ten thousand dollars to send one thousand men to replace striking ironworkers. Richard Trevellick, soon to be elected president of the NLU, noted "several cases" of importers inducing Europeans to emigrate by promising high wages. John Hinchcliffe of the American Miners' Association called such agents "a perfect pack of swindlers," explaining, "They deceive the men there, ill treat them on the passage, and cheat them when they arrive here." Delegates blasted American consuls for their complicity in the business and voted to send a representative to Europe to warn foreign workers to steer clear of importers.[15]

These protests eventually caught the ear of Congress. So did protests from the importers. Whereas workers sought a ban on contract labor, emigrant companies wanted greater federal protection. Company agents complained about the difficulty of tracking down absconding workers still under contract and lobbied for stiff fines and impounding the wages of fugitive laborers. When Congress balked at these proposals to strengthen the contract labor law of 1864, emigrant companies turned to state governments. The Connecticut legislature, which had chartered the AEC, passed a law authorizing importers to seize future wages of runaway workers until their debts were repaid. The law also permitted out-of-state employers to enforce their contracts in Connecticut courts. With state governments willing to step in, Congress backed off and then considered repeal. Some lawmakers had long found the contract labor law distasteful—"more monstrous," said one senator in 1866, "than the negro slavery that we have just abolished." To many Americans, the connection of contract labor to slavery created a powerful, frightening specter. When Congress passed the law in 1864, no connection to slavery had been made. As Senator Lot Morrill (R-Maine) recalled, it was "passed in the morning hour without attracting much attention, on the idea that it was entirely inoffensive." After Appomattox, however, the political climate changed radically; Morrill conceded that the contract labor law could "create an apprehension in the public mind that it was another species of slavery."[16]

As a result of the Civil War, American attitudes toward slavery underwent a fundamental transformation. Once an accepted, if controversial, institution, slavery now became associated with everything evil: subjection, barbarity, servility, despotism, and caste. It came to represent the antithesis of progress as well as of freedom. When the United States ratified the Thirteenth Amendment to the Constitution in 1865 abolishing slavery forever—an act considered unthinkable just five years earlier—few Americans, at least in the North, wanted to turn back the clock. If the Civil War meant anything to Americans black or white beyond the preservation of the Union, it meant the death of slavery, the triumph of freedom. But what did freedom mean? Definitions varied, but in large part freedom meant free labor: the right to work, to receive fair wages, and to make contracts enforceable in court. Freedom meant owning one's own muscles. On this everyone agreed. But did a person have a right to sign a contract selling his or her labor cheaply for years at a time to work in a place thousands of miles away when other workers were present to do the job? Herein lay a basic conflict between labor and capital in the postwar era: When did "free labor"—the right to sign a contract—cross the boundary into slavery? Would society allow individuals to sell their labor and their *freedom* for an extended period of time? Would society permit people to sell themselves into virtual slavery? After four years of war, one million casualties, and the emancipation of four million slaves, the answer was far from simple. To workers, the issues of contract labor and slavery would remain inseparable for years to come.[17]

When the Senate debated repeal of the contract labor law in 1866, Senator Morrill, chairman of the Commerce Committee, stated the matter plainly: "On what principle is it that this Government can enter into the business of importing foreign labor? The Senate will see at once that it is a novel feature in the transactions of this Government. It smacks so nearly of that trade which was African . . . that the committee was astonished that the Senate ever gave it a moment's consideration." Calling the act of 1864 the most "absurd" legislation he had ever seen, Morrill urged repeal—but he also made a crucial point. Importing contract labor was fine: "I have no objection to that. Any company has a right to import labor as well as anything else; but what have we to do with it? Why should we put our fingers in it? Why should we go to their aid and authorize agents to go all over Europe to import labor. . . ? I submit that it is not a very dignified business for the Government of the United States." Contract labor was legitimate, the senator argued, but government sponsorship was unseemly. With this vital distinction, Morrill spoke for an emerging Republican consensus. Nonetheless, he met resistance from members of his own party and many Democrats as well. Senators George H. Williams (R-Ore.), Edwin Morgan (R-N.Y.), and Reverdy Johnson (D-Md.) all defended the contract labor law of 1864, which, they said, encouraged immigration and protected newcomers from fraud and abuse. Employers with a direct financial stake in their workers, they added, would treat them better. Morrill dismissed such arguments as the cry of the old slaveholder. Senator John Conness (R-Calif.) went beyond Morrill, claiming that the "offensive" law of 1864 had subverted the ideals of the nation: "And now the mission that this great Republic is to go upon among the nations of the earth is to hunt up and hunt out the white men, to enable men who want their labor and can make money and profit and wealth out of it to make contracts with them in their impoverished condition, in their misfortunes, and then use the right arm of the law to compel their execution under the stars and stripes!"[18]

Despite the impassioned rhetoric, the Senate tabled the repeal bill. Little action followed in 1867. Rising costs of the bureau of immigration, though, coupled with difficulties of enforcing the law, eventually made Congress receptive to workers' protests. On March 30, 1868, Congress quietly repealed the contract labor law of 1864, tacking it onto a lengthy foreign appropriations bill.[19] In repealing the law, Congress removed its imprimatur for the importation of contract labor. Although no longer enjoying federal protection, however, importation was still enforceable under state and local laws. Imported contract labor thus remained legal, legitimate, and acceptable. Workers would spend the next seventeen years trying to persuade the federal government to *outlaw* imported contract labor. Along with eight-hour legislation, adamant opposition to foreign contract labor would unify organized labor for years— and this opposition would consistently inform workers' attitudes toward the Chinese. As the debates at the next NLU convention demonstrated, such opposition focused on the *nature* of immigration, not on its *nationality*.

Delegates to the National Labor Congress in 1868 unequivocally denounced immigrant companies that "bring the cheap labor of Europe" to America. They condemned state legislatures for protecting such companies and Congress for not outlawing them. At the convention's conclusion, former president J. C. C. Whaley reiterated Sylvis's earlier remarks that mainstream newspapers had promoted "a general misunderstanding" of the NLU's position toward immigration, a "misconstruction" that had distorted the organization's platform to people "throughout the country." It was not immigrants the NLU opposed but immigrant companies, Whaley said. The convention then adjourned for the year. Chinese immigration never once came up for discussion.[20]

As Elmer Clarence Sandmeyer and Alexander Saxton have shown, anti-Chinese hostility became a central factor uniting the labor movement in California in 1867. Among workers nationwide, however, it played no role whatsoever. In an era noteworthy for its relative absence of nativism, Americans of all stripes supported the nation's open-door policy and tradition. As the National Labor Congress's silence on Chinese labor and the lack of debate at working-class meetings and in the press east of the Rocky Mountains demonstrate, Chinese immigration remained dormant as a labor issue through 1868. The Burlingame mission that year reveals that it remained dormant as a national issue as well. In 1861, Lincoln appointed Representative Anson Burlingame (R-Mass.) minister to China. Once in Peking, Burlingame befriended the Chinese emperor and became a trusted confidant. When he announced his resignation in 1867, the emperor appointed him Chinese minister to the United States, and in 1868, the former congressman paid a state visit to his native country. Accompanied by numerous Chinese officials, Burlingame received enormous publicity, and his tour quickly turned into a triumphal procession. "The land of Confucius has greeted the land of Washington," he told an appreciative audience in Boston (that included Ralph Waldo Emerson). Americans everywhere heralded the trip as the dawn of a great new era in United States–China relations, anticipating, in Burlingame's words, that China "will come out of her seclusion and enter upon a course of trade, the importance of which and the amount of which no man can compute."[21]

The fabled China trade, with its images of untold wealth, attracted particular attention in Washington. While visiting the nation's capital, Burlingame and the Chinese met with President Johnson, his cabinet, and leading members of Congress. The press reported the encounters favorably and treated the Chinese with dignity and respect. Amid this atmosphere of friendship and goodwill, Burlingame negotiated a new treaty between the two nations. Guided by Secretary of State Seward, Burlingame composed an accord raising China to full diplomatic status and "an equal among the nations." Seward and Burlingame expected the treaty to open the Celestial Empire to increased American commerce and give the United States an upper hand over European nations. One clause in the treaty granted Chinese individuals the same right as people of other nations to emigrate freely to the United States. "I am glad,"

Figure 2.1. Nativism declined after the Civil War, and most Americans welcomed immigrants to the United States. Reflecting this national sentiment, cartoonist Thomas Nast invites people of all races, nationalities, and religions to "Uncle Sam's Thanksgiving Dinner" and gives everyone—white, black, American Indian, and Chinese—an equal seat at the table. Beneath the watchful gaze of Lincoln, Washington, and Grant, all feast around the centerpiece of democracy and equal rights. The traditional image of America as open to all, as a beacon of hope and a refuge for the poor and oppressed the world over, remained powerful and pervasive. (*Harper's Weekly*, November 20, 1869)

Burlingame declared at a banquet in his honor, "that while she [the United States] applies her [free-emigration] doctrines to the swarming millions of Europe, she is not afraid to apply them to the tawny race of Tamerlane and of Genghis Khan."[22]

On July 24, 1868, the Senate unanimously ratified the new treaty. Coming in a highly explosive period—two months after Johnson's impeachment trial, a few weeks after the Republican and Democratic nominating conventions, and four days before final passage of the Fourteenth Amendment—the Burlingame Treaty, as it came to be called, spawned a rare moment of bipartisan unity during the nation's first postwar presidential campaign. The Democratic *New York World* noted the treaty's "vast commercial importance," while the Republican *New York Herald* equated its impact with Columbus's voyage to America. Representative James G. Blaine (R-Maine), then completing his third term in Congress, lavished praise on his fellow Republican, calling Burlingame's diplomatic tour "the most important mission which China ever sent to

THE YOUNGEST INTRODUCING THE OLDEST.
AMERICA. "Brothers and Sisters, I am happy to present to you the Oldest Member of the Family, who desires our better acquaintance."

Figure 2.2. As Miss Columbia proudly presents China to the "family of nations," all of Europe (with the notable exception of the pope) bows in his honor. A satisfied Anson Burlingame sits quietly in the background flanked by the crates and goods that, thanks to his efforts, will soon start flowing across the Pacific. Original caption: "The Youngest Introducing the Oldest. America: 'Brothers and Sisters, I am happy to present to you the Oldest Member of the Family, who desires our better acquaintance.' " (*Harper's Weekly*, July 18, 1868)

Christian nations." The treaty signaled a major change for China and the Chinese government, which for years had discouraged emigration of its people, expressed little concern for their welfare abroad, and declined to establish diplomatic relations in foreign countries. In America, the immigration clause excited no concern. Politicians, newspaper editors, labor leaders, and workers didn't even mention it, nor did Republicans or Democrats at their nominating conventions that summer. A resolution against Chinese immigration that a California representative introduced in Congress earlier in the year went completely unnoticed. In 1868, Chinese immigration was not yet a national political issue.[23]

Events the following year would elevate Chinese labor to the working-class agenda, propel the issue to the national stage, and create the first Chinese "scare" in American history. The Chicago-based *Workingman's Advocate* sounded the tocsin on February 6, 1869.

> We warn workingmen that a new and dangerous foe looms up in the far west. Already our brothers of the Pacific have to meet it, and just as soon as the Pacific railroad is completed, and trade and travel begins to flow from the east across our continent, these Chinamen will begin to swarm through the rocky mountains, like devouring locusts and spread out over the country this side. Men who can work for a dollar a day . . . are a dangerous element in our country. We must not sleep until the foe is upon us, but commence to fight him now.
>
> In the name of the workingmen of our common country, we demand that our government . . . forbid another Chinaman to set foot upon our shores.

With this statement, *Workingman's Advocate* editor Andrew C. Cameron launched his campaign for Chinese exclusion. Prodding him was the imminent completion of the transcontinental railroad, which posed a dual threat: thousands of Chinese railroad laborers would soon be thrown out of work, and coast-to-coast travel would become fast and cheap. Without immediate action, Cameron feared, low-paid Chinese workers would flood the nation.[24]

If Cameron's editorial did not alarm workers in the East, direct threats from manufacturers and capitalists surely did. On May 10, 1869, laborers in Utah hammered in the final spike of the railroad (after unceremoniously whisking the Chinese away from view as photographers captured the historic moment). The same month, the Knights of St. Crispin, a one-year-old shoemakers union, conducted a series of strikes in Massachusetts. The convergence of these two events led employers to consider adapting modern methods of transportation to old tactics of strikebreaking. If Crispins persisted in demanding higher wages, threatened *Hide and Leather Interest and Industrial Review*, the shoe manufacturers' trade journal, then employers "can begin gradually filling the places of Crispins with workmen from other countries; French Canadians, French, Swedes, Germans, etc., are always available; and we think, now that the Pacific Railroad is open, that the appearance of forty or fifty pig-tailed Chinese in one of the New-England shoe factories would begin to open the eyes of the Crispins, and be most effectual in bringing them to their senses."[25]

Massachusetts Crispin leader Samuel P. Cummings dismissed the scheme. "The whole drift of this article" in *Hide and Leather*, he wrote, "is this: Crowd down your workmen if you can; but if they are strong enough to resist you, then import foreigners and pig-tailed Chinese, to take their places, and starve them into submission. Fortunately, for the good character of the State and the manufacturers, there are but few so lost to all sense of decency, as to try such an inhuman policy in these days of progress." Cummings overestimated the "good character" of manufacturers in Massachusetts and, despite "these days of progress," miscalculated the "decency" of employers elsewhere. Within weeks of the railroad's completion came widespread reports of employers forming emigrant agencies to import Chinese workers to the East. "Pennsylvania capitalists are talking about putting Chinese laborers into the coal mines," noted the *Cincinnati Commercial*. "The immediate reason urged is that they never strike or form combinations, and work cheaper." Pennsylvania representative Daniel J. Morrell, Radical Republican and vice president of the Emigrant Aid Society, wanted Chinese laborers in his Cambria Iron Works, and manufacturers in Boston, New York City, Philadelphia, and New Jersey also hoped to bring in Chinese laborers. In early July, the *New York Times* reprinted an article from the *San Francisco Chronicle* stating that forty-five thousand Chinese workers were about to descend on the South. China, one Harvard professor warned, "can supply labor for the house and field, for building railroads, for working in mines and factories, for every need on sea and land."[26]

Rumor threatened to become reality when thirty members of the Memphis, Tennessee, Chamber of Commerce gathered in June to plan a Chinese labor convention. Discussing business stagnation in the region, they highlighted the need of landowners and planters for "efficient and reliable labor." Since the Civil War, white planters had faced difficulties disciplining and maintaining a stable black workforce because former slaves demanded higher wages and greater say in setting labor conditions. The answer to the South's problems, the Chamber of Commerce believed, lay thousands of miles away across the Pacific. Rather than negotiate with blacks, better to bring in "the reliable, industrious and patient Chinaman" to intimidate them. "Better Shangee [Shanghai] than Timbuctoo!" rhapsodized the *Montgomery Mail*. "Better a few years of Confucian philosophy than a cycle of Ashantee feticism [sic]." The Chinese had many attractive qualities, a *Memphis Appeal* editorial noted, chief among them that they "are . . . easily controlled. . . . They are just the men, these Chinese, to take the place of the labor made so unreliable by Radical interference and manipulation." Louisiana planters had recently experimented with a handful of Chinese laborers imported from Cuba but hardly on the grand scale now envisioned. The meeting resolved that "all legitimate inducements shall be offered at once to encourage the emigration of Chinese laborers, in large numbers, direct from China, to supply the great demand now existing in the South." To publicize their aims, the men at the meeting organized a giant convention, inviting Tye Kim Orr, a Chinese missionary, and Cornelius Koopmanschap, the "great Chinese importer," to attend.[27]

Two weeks later, several hundred delegates representing planters, business leaders, and railroad companies descended on Memphis for the nation's first Chinese labor convention. Delegates hailed from nine southern states and California, and to lend prestige, former Confederate general Gideon J. Pillow attended and former Tennessee governor Isham Green Harris presided. Tye Kim Orr addressed the convention on the second day. This well-traveled Chinese Christian had preached the gospel in Latin America and established a Chinese colony in British Guiana before settling in Louisiana. Chinese workers, he claimed from firsthand experience, "can easily be procured through proper agents. They are easily managed, being patient, industrious, docile, tractable, and obedient."[28]

The next speaker was Cornelius Koopmanschap. This alliteratively named merchant was one of the more intriguing characters of the Gilded Age. Born in Holland in 1828, he emigrated to California during the gold rush and set up a business "importing flour and other provisions." He prospered, established a fleet of clipper ships, and entered the China trade in the 1850s. In 1861, he began "bringing over coolie laborers to San Francisco," later supplying several thousand to Central Pacific directors Leland Stanford and Chester Crocker to work on the transcontinental railroad. Stanford praised Koopmanschap highly, and by 1869 the Dutch immigrant, who claimed to have landed thirty thousand Chinese in California, was the nation's best-known importer of Chinese workers. With his "little leg-of-mutton whiskers," "round florid face," and "pearl-colored Derby hat," the stout, cigar-chomping Koopmanschap cut a sharp figure and stole the show at Memphis. He offered to import thousands of laborers direct from China for one hundred dollars a head. The Chinese would eagerly sign contracts, he said, for two years, five years, even eight years for a monthly wage of eight to twelve dollars—roughly thirty-five cents a day.[29]

Koopmanschap's schemes fired southern imaginations. The convention immediately made plans to organize the Mississippi Valley Immigration Labor Company with the aim of "bringing into the country the largest number of Chinese agricultural laborers in the shortest possible time." Delegates appointed a committee "to select a reliable agent" to go to China, bring back five hundred to one thousand immigrants, and distribute them throughout the South "to test their capacities and fitness for the labor required." As the convention's final report stated: "Two facts are patent—China has the labor that we need, and it can be procured to an unlimited extent. When the supply of this labor becomes a business, competition will of course spring up, and the expense of procuring it will be reduced to a minimum which must fall far below the expenses incident to our present labor system."[30]

Flush with optimism, delegates left Memphis envisioning the day when plantations, railroads, and infant industries throughout the South would be manned by quiet, compliant Chinese laborers. As soon as the convention closed, Koopmanschap left for New York and found that northerners also welcomed the prospect of millions of low-paid Chinese workers. The *New York Sun* predicted the Chinese would soon fill menial jobs in the nation's mines, swamps, and factories, as well as on the railroads and prairies. The *Times*, echoing prominent northern Republicans, opposed any schemes resembling slavery but liked cheap labor. After all, "the *class* of labor which these coolies performed is not intended for epicures to support themselves upon. At all events, we incline to think that repressive laws against the influx of cheap labor would be as hostile to the spirit of our institutions as they would be impracticable and unavailing."[31]

Prospects for a booming "coolie" trade seemed boundless until Treasury Secretary George S. Boutwell noted one small hitch: importing "coolies" was illegal. In a letter to the New Orleans collector of customs, Boutwell cited "An Act to Prohibit the 'Coolie Trade' by American Citizens in American Vessels," a law passed by Congress in 1862. This law stated that "no citizen . . . of the United States, or foreigner coming into or residing within the same, shall, for himself or for any other person whatsoever, . . . build, equip, load, or otherwise prepare, any ship or vessel . . . for the purpose of procuring from China . . . inhabitants or subjects of China, known as 'coolies,' to be transported to any foreign country, port, or place whatever, to be disposed of, or sold, or transferred, for any term of years or for any time whatever, as servants or apprentices, or to be held to service or labor."[32] Representative Thomas Dawes Eliot (R-Mass.) had drafted the law during the Civil War in the wake of numerous atrocities committed aboard American ships carrying Chinese "coolies" to Cuba.[33] On its face, the law clearly seemed to outlaw the importation of Chinese workers, but as advocates of imported labor soon realized, the law contained numerous loopholes. While it effectively prevented transporting "coolies" to foreign nations or places, it did not technically forbid transporting them to the United States. Nor did it forbid transporting "coolies" by rail once they had arrived in another country—say Canada or Mexico—by other means. Most important, the law never defined "coolie." What, indeed, was a "coolie"? The term, also spelled "cooly," derives from the ancient, Urdu-Hindustani word "kūlī," meaning "hire" or "hireling." Although its modern usage by Westerners dates back to at least the 1790s, Webster's *American Dictionary of the English Language* considered "coolie" a new term in the 1840s and defined it as an "East Indian porter or carrier," a definition the dictionary would maintain for years. Colloquially, however, "coolies" referred not just to East Indian but also to Chinese laborers, especially those transported in heavy numbers from Asia to Latin America during the nineteenth century to grow sugar, coffee, and other crops on large plantations. Many of these Chinese "coolies" signed long-term contracts for low wages to work halfway around the world. As Persia Crawford Campbell has related, speculators often hired "coolie brokers" to recruit illiterate Chinese men and induce them to sign contracts. Speculators then transported them on a grueling "middle passage" (under conditions approaching the African slave trade of preceding centuries) to Peru and Cuba and sold their contracts to the highest bidder. Were these "coolies" free men who voluntarily signed contracts or unfree men bound to service? The answer depended more on one's politics than on one's dictionary. In 1856, U.S. commissioner and minister to China Peter Parker called them "almost slaves" and urged legislation outlawing the "coolie traffic." But were all Chinese who signed contracts "coolies" and "almost slaves"? Could an impoverished Chinese man sign a contract and not be a "coolie"? Possibly, probably, but no one knew for sure. The vagueness of the language eviscerated the "anti-coolie" act of 1862. Although Americans who opposed the importation of Chinese frequently cited the law, it was virtually a dead letter from the day it passed.[34]

Yet the law did cause concern after the Memphis Convention, and delegate John Williams, a Louisiana businessman, hired a law firm to investigate the legality of importation. The firm concluded that the law referred to "an existing trade" in 1862 rather than the type the convention had just proposed. The firm also noted that the law lacked precision and that nothing in it prevented signing Chinese to labor contracts. The *New York Times* took a somewhat different approach. Conceding the illegality of the "coolie" trade but intoxicated by visions of China providing "untold millions" of laborers, the *Times* urged Congress to repeal the law if demand for "coolies" rose. Barring that, the *Times* suggested ways that Koopmanschap could evade the law and still supply the nation with Chinese workers.[35]

Widespread publicity generated by the Memphis Convention triggered a chain reaction of interest in importing Chinese workers. Southerners deluged Koopmanschap and George W. Gift, the man hired by the convention to go to China, with requests for laborers. Some planters ordered them for house servants, whereas others wanted them for fieldwork. Former Confederate general Nathan Bedford Forrest, president of the New Selma, Marion, and Memphis Railroad (and grand wizard of the Ku Klux Klan), subscribed five thousand dollars to procure a thousand workers from China to lay track across Tennessee. Northerners and midwesterners also showed enthusiasm. Manufacturers from Ohio and Missouri placed orders for Chinese workers, and

Chicago businessmen invited two Chinese traders to discuss similar ventures. Merchants Choy Chew and Sing Man accepted and visited cities further east in July and August. With excitement building in the Northeast, Koopmanschap "will employ all available vessels," the *New York Times* reported, "and his agents in China will be prepared to fill them with human freight as fast as they arrive." Businessman and former New York congressman Hiram Walbridge began planning a new fleet of steamships designed expressly to import "coolies" from China by way of the almost completed Suez Canal, while an Omaha contractor, fed up with strikes, suspended work in August and "determined to secure coolie or Chinese labor." Such labor would not be difficult to find. That summer, the *St. Louis Republican* carried the following advertisement:

CHINESE LABORERS—Parties wishing to employ large or small numbers of CHINESE LABORERS, may make the necessary arrangements for procuring gangs of the size required, delivered in any part of the country, by application to

KOOPMANSCHAAP [*sic*] & CO.
San Francisco, California.[36]

An American could scarcely pick up a newspaper in the summer of 1869 without reading about some new plan to import Chinese workers to the United States. They were coming south, they were coming north, they were coming east. They were coming to work on plantations and on railroads, in households and in factories. They were coming to replace blacks, they were coming to replace whites, and they were coming to break strikes. Labor reformer Robert W. Hume of Astoria, New York, placed workers on alert:

You sturdy tillers of the soil,
  Prepare to leave full soon;
For when John Chinaman comes in
  You'll find there is no room.
Like an Egyptian locust plague,
  Or like an eastern blight,
He'll swarm you out of all your fields,
  And seize them as his right.
Let the mechanics pack his traps,
  And ready make to flit;
He cannot live on rats and mice,
  And so he needs must quit.

Cheap, imported labor, Hume forecast, would undercut precisely what Union soldiers had fought and died for:

At the full cost of bloody war,
   We've garnered in a race;
One set of serfs of late we've freed,
   Another takes its place.
Come friends, we'll have to leave this land
   To nobles and to slaves;
For, if John Chinaman comes in,
   For us—there's only graves.

The connection to slavery remained central to workers' opposition to imported labor. "Koopmanschap," one critic quipped. "Koop-man-up it ought to be."[37]

Whether in verse or in pun, workers remained deadly serious in opposing schemes of importing Chinese workers. Labor poet Hume went even further. A lawyer and former abolitionist who also wrote for the *National Anti-Slavery Standard*, Hume embarked on a campaign in the pages of the *Workingman's Advocate* to persuade American workers to endorse Chinese exclusion. "We have no need of Chinese," he wrote. Working people must unite to "shut our ports to the Celestials."[38]

Hume's crusade, however, failed to catch fire. Despite encouragement from editor Andrew Cameron, the labor journal received little support from its readers. A few subscribers echoed Hume's anti-Chinese epithets but called only for a ban on importation. Some readers defended the Chinese. "We have in our nation American, European and African," wrote George Prindle of McGregor, Iowa. "Let Asia come also. . . . It becomes us as workingmen and women demanding our rights . . . to see to it that we lay not the hand of oppression upon man, woman or child, whether Asia, Africa, Europe or America gave them birth." Prindle dismissed any differences between Chinese and Americans. "Does he eat rats? We eat hogs. Are his vices bestial? Yes, and worse. But are ours less so? No!" Prindle also dismissed the cheap labor argument. "Have the Chinese lowered wages? So have the Germans and the women yet the Germans saved Missouri in the late rebellion of the slaveholders, and they and the women, together with the Asiatic, will yet save the cause of labor reform in the coming rebellion of the capitalists." This powerful vision of workers challenging "slaveholders" and "capitalists" would galvanize many American wage earners for years. As a subscriber from the Midwest observed, "Let all working men *be united* . . . [and] the influx of people from China, Ireland and Germany will then bless the nation."[39]

Even with threats of Chinese importation appearing almost daily in mid-1869, the first brief stabs at a campaign to restrict Chinese immigration fell flat among eastern workers. Labor leaders acknowledged as much when they

gathered in August for the fourth National Labor Congress. Chinese immigration came up for discussion for the first time in the Congress's history. "The
recent attempts of unprincipled and interested parties to revive the infamous
Coolie trade, which is, essentially, a revival of the slave system," declared acting
president Henry Lucker, a New York tailor, "is one which demands our earnest
and serious consideration. It is a question that effects [sic] all classes of society.
While we do not wish to array ourselves against legitimate or voluntary emigration, it must not be forgotten that there is a vast difference in the status of
the voluntary emigrant and the imported coolie."[40]

Lucker had stated the nub of the matter: immigration and importation were
two vitally different subjects. During the weeklong proceedings, California
delegates, along with Cameron, who chaired the Committee on Coolie Labor,
lobbied heavily to swing the convention against Chinese immigration. They
failed badly. Cameron's committee proposed three resolutions: (1) "while we
appreciate the benefits to be desired from voluntary emigration, we are opposed in TOTO to the importation of a servile race, bound to fulfill contracts
entered into on foreign soil"; (2) "rigid enforcement" of the "anti-coolie" act
of 1862; and (3) "voluntary Chinese emigrants ought to enjoy the protection of
the laws like other citizens." The convention urged reconsideration of the
resolutions and added three new members to the committee, including anti-
Chinese extremist Albert Winn of California and Crispin leader Samuel Cummings. The committee wrangled for another day and modified their recom-
mendations. They dropped the last two resolutions entirely. Only the first
remained, but the committee eliminated the reference to immigration. The
resolution read simply, "We are unalterably opposed to the importation of a
servile race, for the sole and only purpose of tampering with the labor of the
American workingmen." The resolutions were thus streamlined but their essence left intact. Only importation was condemned. The Congress approved. A
glum Robert Hume chastised delegates for refusing to denounce Chinese immigrants. "Our Labor Congress was not willing to sanction this course," he
observed. "Many good men, indeed, advocate their coming."[41]

Many "good men" in the labor movement would continue to advocate the
coming of Chinese immigrants. What American workers opposed, and had
opposed for years, was the importation of immigrants on contract, whether
from Europe, Canada, or Asia. The Chinese scare of 1869—sparked by the
Memphis Convention, Koopmanschap's appeals, and the barrage of threats to
procure workers directly from China—linked inextricably the issues of Chinese immigration and imported contract labor. Even amid the steady barrage
of threats, however, working people drew a distinct line between immigration
and importation, welcoming one, opposing the other. But workers had not

really been tested. Despite all the words and reports, 1869 produced only a scare, a series of rumors and threats. Little had actually happened. Would workers change their outlook when suddenly faced with "the appearance of forty or fifty pig-tailed Chinese" in their midst? Would efforts "to import Chinese Coolies," as a reporter at the National Labor Congress warned, "bring about revolutionary disturbances in the East"? The showdown was not far off. Within a year, a Massachusetts shoe manufacturer would carry through on the threat issued in *Hide and Leather* and import Chinese laborers to break a strike in New England. Labor and capital would soon go head to head in a battle for power, control, and a vision of American ideals.[42]

Before this confrontation took place, however, Congress tried to resolve the problem. Many Republicans in Washington still smarted from the connections people made between importation and slavery; a handful of westerners, meanwhile, now had a new agenda of their own. On December 6, 1869, Senator George H. Williams (R-Ore.) introduced a bill "to regulate the immigration of Chinese," and a week later Senator Henry Wilson (R-Mass.) introduced a bill "to regulate the importation of immigrants under labor contracts." Despite the difference in wording, both bills focused on importation and contract labor. As Williams's bill stated, "This act shall not be construed to deny to Chinamen free from any contract or obligation of service the right of voluntary immigration into the United States." Radical Republicans Jacob Howard (R-Mich.) and Samuel Pomeroy (R-Kans.) objected because it discriminated against the Chinese and threatened to hinder their immigration. Howard feared that it would prevent Chinese from signing contracts to emigrate; such contracts, he said, should be legal and inviolable. Countering this opposition, Senator William M. Stewart (R-Nev.) defended Williams's bill to "prohibit . . . the importation of Chinese; not . . . the immigration of Chinese, for I do not apprehend there is any danger in that direction." Stewart also urged legislation abolishing "unfair and discriminatory" taxes and laws against Chinese immigrants in California.[43]

The two bills languished in committee for months. On June 6, 1870, Senator Stewart introduced a compromise version to "prohibit contracts for servile labor" made in "any foreign country" for terms exceeding six months. By allowing contract labor for a brief period, Stewart aimed to please Republicans who defended the right to import workers from abroad. But he also hoped that such a short time frame would make imported labor unprofitable and thereby "break up that odious contract system." By directing the legislation at imported Chinese but not specifying the Chinese in the bill, Stewart—who defended the Chinese and urged no restriction on their immigration—hoped to satisfy both Radicals and workers. Without debate, the Senate remanded the bill to committee.[44]

Debate in the House reached a much more heated pitch. Representative Aaron A. Sargent (R-Calif.) introduced a similar anticontract labor law the same day as Stewart, but unlike the Nevada senator, he accompanied it with a vitriolic attack. "Chinamen, as a race, are addicted to all the nameless vices characteristic of the Asiatics," Sargent said. "Here are swarming millions of men, alien not alone to our blood and our language, but to our faith. They are idol worshipers . . . liv[ing] upon a lower plane . . . in the filthiest, meanest hovels, in unutterable stench." Other western representatives backed Sargent up. Calling the Chinese "willing slaves . . . imperialists . . . [and] polygamists," Thomas Fitch (R-Nev.) urged legislation to "stay the further influx of Chinese immigration." Samuel Axtell (D-Calif.) concurred, noting the Chinese were "pagans" unfit for citizenship. The House sent Sargent's bill to committee.[45]

In the Senate, Stewart made one more effort on June 17 to pass his bill, only to find opposition from fellow westerner Eugene Casserly (D-Calif.). Echoing his colleagues in the House, Casserly attacked the Chinese on racial and cultural grounds. Stewart's bill "totally failed" to solve the problem because it did *not* single out the Chinese, Casserly claimed, and he urged further debate. Stewart objected. "I would rather have the law general as to all foreigners, and not make any distinction," he said. "Let all come from any part of the world who choose to come voluntarily, but do not allow them to come in under servile labor contracts." Senator Charles Sumner (R-Mass.) endorsed Stewart's bill, as did several other Republicans. Yet they also agreed with Casserly to postpone the issue. Thus by mid-1870, Congress had failed to act on the importation of contract labor.[46]

With the first outbursts of anti-Chinese rhetoric in the nation's capital, the issues of Chinese immigration and imported contract labor opened widely for debate. But Washington's inability to resolve these issues left others to seize the initiative. The event that ignited the first labor-capital confrontation on the matter in the East and made "the Chinese question" a national issue for the first time occurred in a small mill town in the Berkshire Hills of New England. As the last days of spring approached in 1870, the nation's attention swiftly shifted from the halls of Congress to the streets of North Adams, Massachusetts.

> I don't object to their coming here. Let 'em come single-handed, like other emigrants, and take their chance. But they come banded together. That isn't right.
> —Unidentified Crispin,
> June 21, 1870

CHAPTER THREE

Yan-ki vs. Yan-kee

Americans React to Chinese Laborers in 1870

Labor relations at Calvin T. Sampson's ladies boot and shoe factory, one of thirty-eight mills in North Adams, Massachusetts, had been tense since 1868, when Sampson tried to break a strike by importing nonunion labor from Maine and Canada. The strikers, many of whom belonged to the Knights of St. Crispin, convinced the newcomers to join them, and the union prevailed. With anywhere from twenty thousand to forty thousand members, most of them native-, Irish-, or French Canadian–born, the Crispins were briefly one of the nation's largest and strongest unions. They struck a second time in 1870, and Sampson again imported strikebreakers, this time hiring Crispins from North Brookfield. When they arrived, the strikers met them at the train station and alerted them to the situation. Loyal to their union, the North Brookfield men refused to work, despite Sampson's offer of higher wages. An exasperated Sampson stormed off, vowing to destroy the union. That afternoon he set in operation the threat made in *Hide and Leather* the year before: he would import Chinese workers to break the strike.[1]

In May, Sampson's superintendent traveled to San Francisco and signed a three-year contract with Kwong, Chong, Wing and Company, a Chinese emigrant agency. The company agreed to provide "75 steady, active, and intelligent Chinamen" who would work eleven hours per day in spring and summer and ten and a half hours in fall and winter. Sampson would pay them twenty-three dollars a month—about ninety cents a day—for the first year, and twenty-six dollars a month for the second and third years, less than half the striking Crispins' wage. He would deduct twenty-five dollars from each worker's pay over the first six months "as a security . . . against a man's leaving before his time expires." Sampson agreed to pay traveling expenses from San Francisco to North Adams, "and if men work satisfactorily for three years or more they are to have a free passage back." The contract, Sampson noted, "was not made with the men personally, but was signed with Kwong, Chong, Wing & Co." He paid the emigrant agency seventy-five dollars for its services.[2]

As word of Sampson's scheme leaked out, the *Workingman's Advocate* intensified its yearlong campaign to rouse eastern workers. "Disguise it as we may," editor Andrew C. Cameron warned on June 11, "the time has come when the protest of the American workmen against the further introduction upon American soil of the beastly, idolatrous Mongolian race, must be heard; must say to their Legislators, thus far shalt thou come and *no further*, except at your peril." Cameron blamed the coming of the Chinese on the absence of protest from working people. He compared their complacency to that of "authorities, who, indifferent to the ravages of an epidemic in a neighboring city, waited for its appearance in their midst, before paying attention." With the issue at last forced, eastern workers could wait no longer. "They now must face the music."[3]

The response to the Chinese was swift and strong but not the one Cameron wanted. On June 13, hundreds of Crispins and roughly two thousand townsfolk—most of whom had never before seen an Asian person—gathered near the North Adams train depot to watch the "swarthy strangers" set foot on New England soil. "The streets were crowded with people," one reporter noted. "There had never been such excitement here as on that Monday evening." Roused by rumors of impending violence, Sampson had hired thirty extra policemen, joined the Chinese in Troy, New York, and armed them all with knives. When he disembarked in North Adams, he waved a pistol in the air and urged the crowd to make way. His precautions were a bit excessive. Although a few "hoots" and "taunting shouts" filled the air, "no general attack was made," the *Boston Advertiser* reported. "The Chinese were quite imperturbable, and did not even mind the appellations of wrath yelled into their ears from the wayside." The Crispins, the *Springfield Republican* noted, directed their "vociferous . . . abuse" not at the Chinese but at Sampson. Except for a rock-throwing incident—which the press blamed on rowdy boys—the "Chinese cobblers" marched peacefully through town in double file and arrived safely in Sampson's brick-walled factory a half hour later. Whether the seventy-five Chinese immigrants, most of them teenagers and some as young as fourteen, recognized the import of their journey to North Adams is unknown, for other than their names and ages no records remain. Peace in "the pleasant Berkshire village," however, did not last long. As an anonymous shoemaker scrawled on the factory wall, "No Scabs or Rats Admitted Here." It was an omen of the coming fury.[4]

Workers throughout the Northeast and Midwest mobilized at once, holding "grand mass meetings" of protest in town after town. "This new system of slavery has begun," railed iron molder Dugald Campbell on June 15 to a large gathering in Troy. "This is but the opening wedge. The capitalists have started the ball rolling and will keep it rolling over the continent if active measures to impede its progress are not at once taken by the workingmen." Alexander Troup, secretary of the National Typographical Union and a vice president of the National Labor Union, spoke next. "We have abolished the slavery of the black men, but these capitalists are endeavoring to resurrect it. The workingmen throughout the country should rise in a body and raise such a shout that its echo will reach Washington." Troup urged passage of Senator Stewart's bill in Congress. If enacted, a resolution adopted by the meeting stated, the bill would "make the importation of emigrants under labor contracts unlawful." The meeting's first resolution captured the essence of workers' protest: "We are inflexibly opposed to all attempts on the part of capitalists to cheapen and degrade American labor by the introduction of a servile class of laborers from China or elsewhere; while we at the same time, heartily welcome all voluntary emigrants from every clime, and pledge them our sympathy and encouragement in efforts to secure for themselves and their children homes on American soil."[5]

These words set the tone for similar meetings from the Atlantic to the Mississippi. A week later, three thousand to four thousand people gathered in North Adams for a mass meeting "in the open air." Hundreds of Crispins attended, the New York Herald reported, "and also their sympathizers employed in the woolen and cotton factories." Crispin leader Samuel P. Cummings spoke to an enthusiastic audience. Sampson, he declared, had imported Chinese workers "not to strike against the labor of North Adams alone, but to see if the experiment of Chinese labor can be carried out, and if it can, to strike against the laboring classes of the whole country." Cummings lashed out against the importation of contract labor and assailed Republican senators for not passing the bill in Congress, but he did not attack the Chinese. In fact, he urged organizing them into the Knights of St. Crispin. He praised them as good workers and even "eulogized John Chinaman as a gentleman far superior to Mr. Sampson." Spurred on by cries of "hear, hear," Cummings recoiled at having "to mention Sampson's name, but he did not wish to pollute his lips with it any oftener than possible, for it was such men as him who were their enemies, and whom they must protect themselves against." By rebuking the importer and not the imported, Cummings pinpointed the target of workers' anger. Working people must oppose importation, he counseled, but "to all men of whatever race and color . . . they should extend a hearty welcome."[6]

Cheering Cummings and uttering "loud groans for Sampson," North Adams workers evinced little hostility toward the Chinese, either collectively at the meeting or separately in quieter moments. In interviews later conducted by the Massachusetts Bureau of the Statistics of Labor, seven North Adams shoe-makers—at least three of them Crispins—gave their views on the event that had put their town on the map. Not one voiced antipathy toward the Chinese themselves, focusing instead on the issue of imported contract labor. As the *Springfield Republican* noted, "the general topic of discussion" among workers in North Adams was not the Chinese but "what the townsfolk call the 'slave question.' " The anti-Crispin *Albany Journal* conceded as much: "The working-men of North Adams . . . cast no blame on the Chinamen, but advise their enlightenment so that they may comprehend the value of their labor, and co-operate with their fellow-workmen in demanding remunerative wages." One local Crispin put it plainly: "I don't object to their coming here. Let 'em come single-handed, like other emigrants, and take their chance. But they come banded together. That isn't right."[7]

Workers beyond the Berkshires took their cue from their brethren in North Adams. The largest and most representative meeting took place on June 30 in Tompkins Square Park in New York City. Erecting three platforms, two for English speakers, one for German speakers, workers decorated these stands with American flags and, as newspapers loved to point out, dozens of Chinese lanterns painted red, white, and blue. Wage earners from virtually all the city's trades attended—bakers, barbers, bricklayers, cabinetmakers, carpenters, cigar makers, cigar packers, iron molders, painters, plasterers, printers, shoemakers, stair makers, tailors—and, as one paper noted, "a large number of sympathetic women."[8]

William Cashman of the Tailors' Union set the meeting's theme and tempo. "We will not let the monopolists and capitalists ride over us roughshod," he declared. "When the struggle for liberty began, the workingmen went to the front, and were then termed good citizens, but now that the question of cheap labor was involved they were no longer considered." The issue was not native versus newcomer but free versus unfree. "To the Chinaman as an emigrant there are no objections," Cashman said, "but when they are brought here in masses, and under contract, it was time something should be done." Plasterer John Ennis and bricklayer Richard Matthews made the same point. As an iron molder named Purdy summed up, workers opposed the importation of contract labor but "extended the right-hand of fellowship to all emigrants no matter what nationality."[9]

Speakers from the German stand delivered the identical message in a different language. "The Chinamen," said Adolph Douai, editor of the *Arbeiter-Union*, "had the same right as ourselves to emigrate to this country, but there are too many workingmen here without employment, and this importation of coolie labor is an insult to the workingmen." Cigar maker Conrad Kuhn agreed: "It would be foolish to argue against coolie immigration," he said in a speech tailored specially to his foreign-born audience, "as it would be to oppose German or Irish immigration." German orators took pains to make the same careful distinctions as those speaking in English. The "importation of coolies . . . ought to be forbidden," said cabinetmaker Fred Homrighausen, but "of course," he added, "no opposition could be made against the voluntary immigration of free Chinese to this country." Unrestricted immigration was a right "no free citizen could oppose."[10]

At meeting after meeting, workers repeated the themes voiced in Troy, North Adams, and New York City. In July, the Iron Molders' International Union met for its annual convention and adopted the same stand: pro-immigration, anti-importation. So did the Cigar Makers' International Union and the National Labor Bureau of Colored Men. Workers affirmed this stance at rallies throughout the summer in Albany, Boston, Cincinnati, Chicago, and Belleville, Illinois. After one such rally in Rochester, New York, a local newspaper commented: "In nearly all the meetings that have been held to protest against such importation, resolutions have been passed welcoming *bona fide* immigrants to our shores, and holding out to them the hospitable hand. This welcome has been offered not alone by capitalists and employers, but by the laborers who feel the most aggrieved. . . . It is not laborers and immigrants, but the importation of mere laboring machines that is objected to." As the *Cincinnati Gazette* noted, "Even the demagogues who have mounted this agitation do not propose prohibition [of immigration]. . . . The workingmen's meetings . . . ask only for a law forbidding labor contracts." The *Gazette*, a pro-exclusion Republican newspaper, ridiculed workers for making such a fine distinction between immigration and importation, calling their resolutions "absurd," "impotent," and a "humbug." These comments reflected the gulf of understanding between editors and working people.[11]

Robert Blissert of New York City put labor's position most ardently. "I have a horror of Slavery," the German-born tailor remarked at a meeting of the Workingmen's Association on July 21. "I believe I am like thousands of my countrymen whose kindred dyed the soil of America with their blood in putting down Slavery in the South. If Slavery should again be established, I am ready that my blood should be shed in Massachusetts or any other State to suppress it there." Importation, he added, "is even more . . . destructive" than slavery because "when a man is bought for three years [rather than a lifetime], the employer is bound to wring as much out of the slave as lies in his power, and then he can be cast away as a piece of useless machinery." It was importation Blissert opposed, not the Chinese: "The Chinaman is as welcome to me as men from Ireland, or Scotland, or England, or any other man who has sufficient energy to leave the land of his birth and desires to come here and cast his lot with the workingmen. As a workingman I will take his hand and say, 'Come along; we are both laborers, soldiers of the great army of labor. Let us fight the battle side by side.' "[12]

Throughout the summer the bulk of eastern workers whose voices can be rescued remained steadfast in their opposition to imported labor and support for voluntary immigration. What is remarkable about this stance and this solidarity is that it came from below, a below never considered, never understood, and barely even acknowledged by previous historians. In local meetings, countless speeches, spot interviews, and assorted letters, workers and their immediate leaders clearly stated their opposition to imported Chinese labor. Although occasionally lacing their comments with racism, workers persisted in welcoming all voluntary immigrants from China and elsewhere. Historians have at worst ignored and at best dismissed the distinction workers so painstakingly made between immigration and importation. Stuart Creighton Miller even described this distinction as "tortured reasoning."[13] Understanding this reasoning, however, is vital to understanding workers' attitudes and the origin of the Chinese Exclusion Act. Historians' failure to examine this key distinction is regrettable but unsurprising, because rank-and-file attitudes challenged those of national labor "leaders" who claimed to speak for them. Rank-and-file attitudes challenged those of Andrew Cameron, editor of the *Workingman's Advocate*, the nation's foremost labor journal, which since 1869 had staunchly advocated Chinese exclusion.

Rank-and-file attitudes also challenged those of labor sympathizer John Swinton, a former abolitionist and *New York Times* editorialist. In a full-page call to arms in the *New York Tribune*, Swinton deemed Chinese immigration "a question not only for to-day, but one which, if wrongly settled at this time, will be a disturbing question for ages." Calling the Chinese "inferior" and "depraved," he highlighted "their indecent and obscene, foul and mortifying vices." "Can we," he asked, "afford to admit the transfusion into the national veins of a blood more debased than any we have known?" Swinton urged immediate and total exclusion. It was a simple matter, he declared, of "the *roast rat* against the *roast beef*."[14]

This language and imagery remained unmatched in labor circles in the East for years to come. Swinton himself would later emerge as the nation's preeminent labor editor of the 1880s, proprietor of a radical newspaper that bore his name. But in 1870, Swinton stood at a crossroads, poised between pursuits as mainstream editorialist and budding labor activist. His anti-Chinese screed proved an ugly and ironic segue to his brilliant career: ugly because of its virulent racism; ironic because workers, for whom he intended it, largely dismissed his argument and disregarded his remedy.

In vying for leadership of the anti-Chinese movement, Cameron and Swinton had more impact on the National Labor Union (and future historians) than on workers at large. But even here their impact remained limited. In his opening address to the fifth National Labor Congress that August, president Richard Trevellick denounced importation but welcomed voluntary Chinese immigration. The committee on "coolie" labor, however, dominated by Californians, presented a vaguely worded anti-Chinese resolution. Alexander Troup, a speaker at the first protest meeting in Troy two months earlier, objected. "The distinction between immigration and importation must be clearly stated," he said. San Franciscan W. W. Delaney disagreed and urged the convention to oppose both. "Great confusion followed," a local reporter observed, as delegates began yelling at each other and talking out of order. "The gavel fell often, with direful clashing," and the convention postponed the question.[15]

When discussion resumed the next day, disorder reigned again. "Chinese coolies ought to be driven from the soil of America," a western delegate shouted, prompting President Trevellick, who had traveled the world over and seen Chinese immigrants firsthand in the Pacific islands, to note, "The marriage tie was not observed and the most shocking immorality prevailed among them." Former millwright Charles McLean of Boston dismissed these accusations, claiming, "In many things their customs were worthy of imitation." McLean, a Crispin leader, "was not in favor of denouncing the poor Chinamen," the *Workingman's Advocate* reported. "It was the heartless capitalist and monopolist he denounced. Let us adopt a resolution against importation, but not against immigration." McLean counseled delegates to allow the Chinese to "come and become citizens if they would. It was against the spirit of our institutions to forbid voluntary immigration." Peripatetic Crispin leader Cummings seconded McLean's statements and, with other delegates, defended both the Chinese and open immigration. But the issue continued to divide the convention, which again remanded it to committee.[16]

In the end, the NLU's resolution failed to make any distinction between immigration and importation. Delegates resolved only that "the presence in our country of Chinese laborers in large numbers is an evil entailing want and its consequent train of misery and crime on all other classes of the American people, and should be prevented, by legislation." Historians have long misread this resolution as a full-fledged endorsement of Chinese exclusion. Although indisputably anti-Chinese, the statement was purposefully ambiguous, a reflection of the NLU's vexation and inability to reach consensus. "The resolutions of the Labor Convention on Chinese emigration exemplify the difficulty of dealing with this question," the *Cincinnati Gazette* remarked. "The convention is not up to the point of declaring against the free emigration of the Chinese. Either its own moral sense is against this, or it thinks this will not be supported by the moral sense of the community."[17]

Although the NLU did *not* endorse exclusion, it stands out as the only labor body east of the Rockies that failed to distinguish plainly between immigration and importation. Trying to mollify delegates from both regions of the country —the East and the West—the Congress satisfied neither. Its shilly-shallying position suggests that the NLU, now in the throes of launching a new political party, hardly spoke for the majority of the nation's workers. This widening chasm between the organization's hierarchy and its constituents would no doubt contribute to the NLU's demise a few years later.

Just like the *Workingman's Advocate* and Swinton's article, the National Labor Union had scant impact on workers' attitudes regarding the Chinese. In contrast to Cameron and Swinton, working people supported Chinese immigration, and unlike the NLU, they stated their views clearly. By 1870, local chapters of the NLU had entered the political arena and begun running candidates for office. These chapters, such as the one in Massachusetts directed by Cummings, listened more closely to their constituents below than to their leaders above. A former Union soldier, the "indefatigable" Cummings was an effective orator— "sometimes eloquent," noted the *Workingman's Advocate*—and a superb political and union organizer. When he founded the Massachusetts Labor Reform Party in 1870, he was the most prominent Crispin leader in the nation. Called "the head and tail of Massachusetts laboring men and women" by the *New York Herald* and, despite differences over the Chinese issue, referred to affectionately by the *Workingman's Advocate* as "Our Sam," Cummings played the central role in spearheading the working-class uproar against importation in the summer of 1870. In September, he chaired the Massachusetts Labor Reform Party convention in Worcester and, with fellow delegates, drafted a platform that de-nounced importation "from China or elsewhere" and endorsed "voluntary emigrants from every clime."[18] To further emphasize this point, the convention nominated Wendell Phillips for governor. This eminent civil rights activist and former abolitionist had long defended both Chinese suffrage and unrestricted immigration. "We welcome every man of every race to our soil and to the protection of our laws," Phillips had recently written. "Every human being has the right to choose his residence just where he pleases on the planet. . . . The Chinese . . . will be a welcome and valuable addition to the mosaic of our Nationality. . . . But such immigration to be safe and helpful must be spontane-ous. . . . IMMIGRATION OF LABOR IS AN UNMIXED GOOD. IMPORTATION OF HUMAN FREIGHT IS AN UNMITIGATED EVIL." The *Workingman's Advocate* de-nounced Phillips for these statements. Nonetheless, delegates of the Mas-sachusetts Labor Reform Party backed them and nominated the "silver-tongued" abolitionist to head their ticket. So did their female counterparts, the Massachusetts Association of Working Women. Local labor leaders, such as Crispins Cummings and McLean, were evidently more attuned than Cameron and Swinton to the concerns of local workers. Despite pressure from above, workers in Massachusetts and throughout the East and Midwest remained firm and united in their stance favoring Chinese immigration and opposing impor-tation. This persistent solidarity on the issue and their defiance of both the National Labor Union and the *Workingman's Advocate* are noteworthy, espe-cially in light of other events during the summer of 1870.[19]

The North Adams incident ignited a chain reaction of interest in importing Chinese laborers comparable with that sparked by the Memphis Convention a year earlier. Within days of the Asian workers' appearance in the Berkshires, manufacturers descended on North Adams and flooded Sampson with re-quests for information. An "Oriental wave," as one journal put it, threatened to engulf the nation. The first shipment of two hundred Chinese laborers for the South arrived in New Orleans in June, and a second batch joined them on July 4. Meanwhile, a Tennessee railroad magnate wired Koopmanschap to send him fifteen hundred Chinese laborers. The Dutch-born entrepreneur dis-patched a trainload in August, and one thousand Chinese workers arrived in Alabama to lay track toward Chattanooga. Railroad directors in Virginia, West Virginia, and Pennsylvania placed orders, and Koopmanschap soon claimed that "eastern capitalists" had signed contracts for over two hundred thousand "coolies." Other importers jumped into the act. Julius Palmer opened a "Chi-nese immigration bureau" in Boston and was quickly swamped with orders. A similar agency opened in New York City.[20] For weeks, Sisson, Wallace, a Sacramento firm that had supplied Chinese workers to the Central Pacific Railroad, advertised itself as "agents for Chinese labor" in the *Trans-Continental*, a short-lived national newspaper.[21] Opportunities to procure Chinese workers seemed endless—and a slap at native wage earners. "FIRST INTRODUCTION OF CHINESE LABOR IN PRINTING," announced a notice in the *New York Sun*, "and Great Reduction of Prices in consequence." Employers in Massachusetts alone, the *Sun* predicted, would import twenty thousand Chinese within the year. By midsummer, Chinese contract laborers were working from New Orleans to New England, with requests pouring in from as far away as St. Louis, Toronto, and Washington, D.C.[22]

Employers played the Chinese card shrewdly. A railroad builder in upstate New York had trouble attracting laborers "at satisfactory prices," but after he invented a ruse that he had just signed a contract for one thousand Chinese, local workers accepted the lower wage. The *New York Tribune* hinted that capitalists could import Chinese laborers to intimidate the Irish, while a headline in the *New York Herald* deemed "A General Smashing Up of the Crispins Inevitable." With the issue of the day "Yan-ki vs. Yan-kee," as one cartoonist put it, the Chinese became the secret weapon employers had long dreamed of. "Every manufacturer in the country," the *Boston Advertiser* observed, "has felt to some extent the influence of trades unions, for which the most powerful enemy has now been discovered." The labor poet Robert Hume again picked up his pen to describe the impending state of affairs:

> "Hurrah!" cries the Factory King,
> "Now I'll screw my hands and make 'em sing!
>   'Gainst their Union prate
>   I'll shut my gate,
> When Chow-Chow's men from China I bring.["]

The poem became a reality in September when manufacturers in Fall River, Massachusetts, broke one of the largest and most bitter strikes in the region's history by threatening to import Chinese laborers.[23]

Many of these threats echoed those of the previous year, but suddenly the threats were backed up by action. Sampson's deed gave them substance, and other manufacturers aimed to follow in his footsteps. The North Adams incident scared workers, and the relentless barrage of threats fueled their anger throughout the summer. Mainstream, largely middle-class editors could sit comfortably in their chambers and dismiss the incident as trivial, lacking, in the words of the *Springfield Republican*, "any real importance." As protest erupted nationwide, the smug E. L. Godkin, editor of the *Nation*, wrote that "it

YAN-KI vs. YAN-KEE.

SHOWING THE DESCENT OF CELESTIAL CRISPINS UPON THE SHOEMAKERS OF THE BAY STATE, AND HOW THEY ROBBED THE NATIVE COBBLER OF HIS *ALL*.

Figure 3.1. Elfin Chinese laborers literally steal the food from the mouths of a shoemaker's family. Such racist portrayals of the North Adams incident took no account of the distinction workers made between immigration and importation. Note the "Celestial Crispin" ripping up a "trade prices" agreement, implying that manufacturers would no longer need to recognize union demands. Original caption: "Yan-ki vs. Yan-kee. Showing the Descent of Celestial Crispins upon the Shoemakers of the Bay State, and How They Robbed the Native Cobbler of his *All*." (*Punchinello*, July 23, 1870. Courtesy General Research Division, New York Public Library, Astor, Lenox, and Tilden Foundations)

is borrowing trouble for any of us to be worrying ourselves too much." Workers, however, believed otherwise. Their livelihood—not that of the middle classes—was at stake, and they took to the streets in protest. "Meetings must be held and voice given to the oppressed laboring men," one speaker implored at a rally in Cincinnati. "There is no better way of expressing ourselves than by the means of such assemblages as this." Many historians have dismissed workers' response to North Adams as "silly" and "exaggerated." To workers, however, the danger was genuine and immediate. Manufacturers could indeed import workers to break strikes, and they did. Manufacturers could indeed threaten to import workers to intimidate and undermine unions, and they did. North Adams served as the catalyst for working-class protest—not against Chinese immigration but against Chinese importation. In face of all the threats, strikebreaking incidents, and ongoing reports of importing Chinese laborers, it is truly remarkable that (non-Californian) workers maintained unity and neither compromised their ideals of open immigration nor succumbed to pressure from their so-called leaders.[24]

This rank-and-file solidarity is all the more notable when contrasted with the dissension the North Adams incident precipitated in other groups, particularly the Republican Party. At a Fourth of July celebration in Connecticut, Representative Benjamin F. Butler (R-Mass.) confronted newspaper editor and former Connecticut governor Joseph R. Hawley. "Is it not the theory of our government that we shall receive all who come to us animated by the love of liberty, and who desire to enjoy its sweets?" asked Butler, a onetime Democrat and Radical Republican ever angling for the workingman's vote. Certainly, Butler answered, but Americans must oppose schemes to bring workers here "by contract, or by force, as serfs" solely "to satisfy the avarice of men." Butler attacked the Chinese as "semi-barbarous strangers to our civilization," but he refused to bar them. "Let us not by any means," he concluded, "hinder or prohibit the voluntary coming to this country of all men who choose to add their labor, their energies and their industry in aid of our own."[25]

Hawley, an old antislavery crusader and founder of the state's Free-Soil and Republican Parties, also urged open immigration. "I don't know how to go to work to lock the doors of the United States," he said. "I wish the Chinese had a better education in regard to American institutions. I wish they could bring with them a better religion; but I believe they all can read. With our flag over me, and the New Testament in my hand, I say, Let them come!" Hawley urged "keeping open the gateways of the United States to the free access of all immigrating peoples." He also noted that he "could see no injury to any of our useful institutions by encouraging industrial immigration to our shores from every part of the earth." In this phrase lay the essential difference between Hawley and Butler: in "encouraging industrial immigration," Hawley offered tacit endorsement of imported labor. Unlike Butler and working people, the patrician former governor made no distinction between immigration and importation. Both should be permitted and encouraged. Hawley, incidentally, was closely connected to the American Emigrant Company and had edited the newspaper that served as its unofficial organ.[26]

The difference between Hawley and Butler—between support for and opposition to contract labor—threatened to divide the Republican Party. On the same day Hawley and Butler squared off in Connecticut, senators engaged in a lively debate in Washington. The debate had begun two days earlier when Senator Charles Sumner (R-Mass.) offered an amendment to strike the word "white" from a pending naturalization bill. The nation's first naturalization law, signed by George Washington in 1790, had restricted the right of naturalization—the process by which an immigrant becomes a citizen—to "any alien, being a free white person." Despite numerous modifications during the nineteenth century, this racist language remained in effect through the Civil War, preventing most Chinese immigrants from becoming citizens. On July 2, 1870, the Senate debated a new naturalization bill. This bill, originally drafted to prevent unnaturalized immigrants from voting, was aimed not at the Chinese but at the Irish, who, Republicans charged, Democrats fraudulently led to the polls before they became citizens. As the Senate's most prominent Radical and civil rights crusader, Sumner seized the moment to strike the word "white" from the nation's long-standing naturalization laws to make them apply equally to all—white, black, Chinese. Such provision would open the door to Chinese naturalization and citizenship and, opponents feared, provide an inducement to Chinese immigration. Sumner's amendment overshadowed the bill's original intent and threw the Senate into a ruckus. Amid this maelstrom, the recent protests by workers reverberated through the halls of the Capitol.[27]

"The country has just awakened to the question and to the enormous magnitude of the question, involving a possible immigration of many millions, involving another civilization, involving labor problems that no intellect can solve without study and without time," declared sometime Radical Oliver P. Morton (R-Ind.). "Are you now prepared to settle the Chinese problem, thus in advance inviting that immigration? I am not prepared to do it." Nor was moderate Republican John Sherman (R-Ohio). When debate resumed on July 4, he called Chinese naturalization "among the most grave and difficult propositions that have ever been submitted to Congress." To Lyman Trumbull (R-Ill.) the issue was less perplexing. As author of the Freedmen's Bureau and Civil Rights Acts of 1866, this Radical could not accept discrimination against the Chinese. "We have struck the word 'white' out of the naturalization laws so far as it applies to the Hottentot, to the pagan of Africa," he stated. "Now, is it proposed to deny the right of naturalization to the Chinaman, who is infinitely above the African in intelligence, in manhood, and in every respect?" Carl Schurz (R-Mo.) urged a compromise to naturalize Chinese immigrants who came to settle but not "birds of passage" who intended to return to China. Timothy O. Howe (R-Wisc.) suggested a religious test for immigrants that would bar naturalization to "any person born in a pagan country, unless . . . the applicant shall take and file an oath abjuring his belief in all forms of paganism." (This comment prompted the otherwise silent Democrats to criticize Republicans for subverting the First Amendment.) Most Radicals, however, were less conflicted; still guided by their belief in equal rights for all men, they backed Sumner's amendment.[28]

Sumner seemed taken aback by the tempest he had unleashed. He had introduced the measure three years earlier during the height of Radical Reconstruction, only to see George F. Edmunds (R-Vt.) bury it in committee. Sumner had reintroduced the measure in 1869, and now, he said, its time had come. Waving letters from southern blacks claiming they had been denied citizenship because of the word "white" in the naturalization laws, Sumner made an impassioned plea for racial justice. "I propose to strike out . . . a requirement disgraceful to this country and to this age," he stated, and for support, he recited the Declaration of Independence (a particularly apt occasion, he noted, it being the Fourth of July). This great document, Sumner observed, did not state that all *white* men are created equal but that *all* men are created equal.[29]

The Senate rejected Sumner's amendment, 22 to 23 (with 27 not voting), but then approved it, 27 to 22 (with 23 not voting). Reconsidering the amendment, the Senate again switched course and voted it down twice, 14 to 30 (with 28 not voting) and 12 to 26 (with 34 not voting). A similar amendment specifically allowing Chinese to be naturalized also lost, 9 to 31 (with 32 not voting), and the naturalization bill without the amendment finally passed, 33 to 8 (with 31 not voting).[30]

The closeness of the early votes reveals that many Republicans, Radical and moderate, were still driven by the ideals of equal rights and racial justice forged during the Civil War and embedded in law during Reconstruction. Citizenship and political rights, they believed, should be granted to all men and all male newcomers regardless of race. They were, however, becoming reluctant to fight for these rights. Radicals Henry Wilson (R-Mass.) and Hannibal Hamlin (R-Maine) both favored Sumner's amendment but voted against it because they feared it would jeopardize and delay passage of the bill as a whole. "We have consumed a great deal of time," Hamlin said. "I see no end to this debate. I want to be practical." And being "practical" meant rejecting Sumner's amendment. Senator Morton, the sometime Radical, pointed toward the future when he stripped the Declaration of Independence of any broader application. Naturalization, he said, was a question of "policy and expediency, and not a question of natural right." Roscoe Conkling (R-N.Y.) also pointed toward the future when he mocked the distinguished Senator Sumner for making "so much noise." The ideals of the Civil War no longer dictated policy nor commanded center stage. Unlike black suffrage, Chinese naturalization promised scant electoral benefits. With most of the Chinese congregated in the small states of California, Oregon, and Nevada, Republicans had little political incentive to push for Chinese citizenship. Without this pressure, many of the egalitarian principles that had inspired Radical Reconstruction began to wane.[31]

But they had by no means disappeared. Senator William M. Stewart (R-

Nev.) invoked this heritage repeatedly as he steered the debate away from naturalization to importation and immigration. "Is it not the duty of a humane Congress," he asked, "first to see that no more coolies are imported into this country under these contracts? Let us liberate them; and then when a Chinaman is naturalized, if that time should come, let him be naturalized because he is a freeman, and because he voluntarily chooses to become an adopted citizen." Still seething over the Senate's failure to vote on his contract labor bill, Stewart cited the demands of workers: "While I would protect anybody who comes to this country voluntarily in his right to labor and live . . . without distinction of race, or color, or anything else, I will not sanction any attempt, no matter how it may be glossed over, to introduce a system of slave labor in competition with free labor in this country; and you will find that the people of this country will not sanction it. The mechanics of Massachusetts will not sanction it." Stewart, praised in numerous labor meetings that summer, echoed workers' sentiments. "I want it distinctly understood now that my platform in regard to the Chinese is simply this: I would let those who choose to come here voluntarily do so . . . [but] I would prohibit all coolie contracts."[32]

Stewart's attitudes toward Chinese immigration had been formed both by Republican policy and by personal experience. Born in Wayne County, New York, in 1825, Stewart had been inspired as a young man by the antislavery congressman Joshua Giddings. He went west during the gold rush, studied law, and made a fortune litigating the Comstock Lode. As a frontier lawyer, he took pride in claiming to be the first person to introduce Chinese testimony (and interpreters) in court. He played a major role in bringing Nevada into the Union and became its first senator in 1864. Once in Washington, Stewart befriended abolitionist congressman Thaddeus Stevens, his next-door neighbor, and the two men frequently spent evenings together playing cards. A third hand found at the table was Mark Twain, whom Stewart hired as his secretary while the impoverished author struggled to finish his first book, *The Innocents Abroad*. With his silvery hair and long, flowing beard, Stewart, according to an observer, "was one of the most picturesque and rugged characters ever known in Washington." He supported the Civil Rights Act of 1866 and backed Johnson's impeachment two years later. He helped draft and steer the Fifteenth Amendment (enfranchising black men) through the Senate in 1869 and used all his leverage to make Nevada the first state to ratify it. Stewart's greatest moment came in May 1870 when he single-handedly guaranteed legal rights to all immigrants in the United States, whether from Asia or Europe. Just weeks before the arrival of the Chinese in North Adams and the Senate debate over Sumner's amendment to the naturalization bill, the House of Representatives passed a separate bill, an early version of the Civil Rights Act (also called the

Enforcement Act) of 1870. Prompted by Ku Klux Klan–sponsored violence in the South, this law aimed to safeguard black voting rights under the just-ratified Fifteenth Amendment. When the Civil Rights Act reached the Senate in late May, Stewart added a section providing that "all persons within the jurisdiction of the United States shall have . . . full and equal benefit of all laws." This clause, Stewart explained, "will protect Chinese aliens. . . . It is as solemn a duty as can be devolved upon this Congress to see that those people are protected, to see that they have the legal protection of the laws. . . . They, or any other aliens, who may come here are entitled to that protection." For the past twenty years, the Nevada Republican argued, Chinese immigrants had been subject to "barbarous and cruel laws," their fundamental rights "violated." As the act's sponsor, Stewart stated clearly why he had inserted this provision: "Justice and humanity and common decency require it," he said. "It is of more importance to the honor of this nation than all the rest of this bill." Although Stewart opposed suffrage for Chinese immigrants, the clause he drafted in the Civil Rights Act of 1870 proved to be the most momentous legislation on behalf of Chinese immigrants—and arguably on behalf of all immigrants—passed in the nineteenth century.[33]

Stewart's oratory on the contract labor bill on July 4 transformed the debate over naturalization into a forum on the Chinese—and race. "Mongolians, no matter how long they may stay in the United States, will never lose their identity as a peculiar and separate people," said Senator George H. Williams (R-Ore.). Their "besotted ignorance is only equaled by their moral debasement." A chief defender of the contract labor law of 1864, Williams had argued against its repeal. But when it came to the Chinese, race ruled everything. Chinese "immigration or importation," he said, will cause "inconceivable mischief." Only total exclusion could save the nation from this "influx of paganism and pollution to our shores." Williams, whom President Grant would shortly appoint attorney general, lampooned Sumner's argument: "Does the Declaration of Independence mean that Chinese coolies, that the Bushmen of south Africa, that the Hottentots, the Digger Indians, heathen, pagan, and cannibal, shall have equal political rights under this Government with citizens of the United States?" No, Williams scoffed, "that is the absurd and foolish interpretation."[34]

Senator Garrett Davis (D-Ky.) backed Williams's sentiments. "I am for opening the portals of our nation to all the European races," he said, "but I am for an embargo and total exclusion of all other races, and especially the Chinese race." (This unreconstructed southerner wanted to "eject the entire negro population" from the United States as well.) No other Democrat east of the Rockies participated in the debate, and except for Davis, the only senators

Figure 3.2. In 1870, Senator William M. Stewart (1825–1909) of Nevada drafted legislation insuring legal rights for all immigrants and strongly defended Chinese immigration. "Let those Chinamen who wish to come here voluntarily do so," he declared. "There is no question about their right to be here." (Courtesy Nevada Historical Society)

actively urging Chinese exclusion hailed from the West: Williams, Eugene Casserly (D-Calif.), and Henry Corbett (R-Ore.). Stewart remained steadfast. "Let those Chinamen who wish to come here voluntarily do so, and they shall be protected by the strong arm of the Government," he said. "There is no question about their right to be here." Fellow Nevada Republican senator James W. Nye lent him support: "To prevent Chinese immigration is as impossible as it is to prevent the rolling waves of the Pacific Ocean."[35]

Where did the Republican Party finally stand in 1870 on imported contract labor and the Chinese? Both everywhere and nowhere. Republicans recoiled at any hint of the revival of slavery and wanted all vestiges of the institution obliterated. At the same time, the party also clung to the ancient English tradition of free contract, the right of private individuals—employer and employee—to make any arrangement they chose, free from government interference. The North Adams incident suddenly placed these two principles at loggerheads, and Stewart's bill threatened to force a showdown. But the showdown never came because the Senate failed to vote on Stewart's bill. Although the Republican Party enjoyed the greatest Senate majority of all time (56 to 11) and could easily have passed the bill, party leaders declined to bring it to a vote.

Two reasons account for this: confusion and indifference. Importation vexed Republicans, and they preferred postponing a decision. As Senator Simon Cameron (R-Pa.) suggested, they should table the bill for a year and see what happens.[36] Republicans could well afford to ignore the demands of organized labor, which carried little weight in Washington and national affairs. With comfortable majorities in Congress and a popular general in the White House, Republicans had no interest in championing a controversial issue, especially one that could alienate important members of the manufacturing community. Avoiding the controversy seemed, from a political standpoint, the shrewd way out. Republicans were divided on importation but not racked by it. They could afford to wait and see how the political winds blew. As for immigration, Republicans evinced scant interest in tampering with the nation's traditional open-door policy. Although many voiced concerns regarding the impact of Chinese immigration and suggested limiting suffrage and political rights of Chinese immigrants, almost no one proposed closing the nation's gate or denying them legal protection. Both the ideals of the party and its complacent supremacy in national affairs precluded any move toward Chinese exclusion or immigration restriction in 1870.

Outside Congress, prominent Republican journals took various stands. The *Boston Commonwealth* and *Springfield Republican* endorsed the right of employers to import workers on contract. The *Cincinnati Gazette*, on the other hand, downplayed importation and urged total exclusion of Chinese immigrants. Most Republicans, however, while leaning toward support for importation, found the issue just as vexing as did their leaders in the Senate. The *New York Tribune* could not maintain a consistent position on even the significance of the issue. On June 18, the *Tribune* called the Chinese question "not worthy and . . . not destined to assume any grave political importance," but by month's end it deemed the issue "of paramount importance" and "one of the gravest questions of the age." In July, the *Tribune* again minimized it, noting that as "a political issue" it had "ridiculously failed." In these comments the *Tribune* found itself temporarily swayed by workers' protests, yet ultimately sympathetic to manufacturing interests and Republican indifference. But the issue was not simple. Questions of freedom and slavery and racial equality were not ones Republicans could dispose of easily in 1870.[37]

The people most torn over the issue of Chinese immigration and importation were former abolitionists. This daring group of idealists that had led the fight against slavery now found itself hopelessly divided. Some, such as Wendell Phillips, Frederick Douglass, and George W. Julian, echoed labor's stance opposing importation and favoring voluntary immigration. Most abolitionists, however, found themselves unable to think in class terms. They refused to

THE NEW PANDORA'S BOX.

Representative Manufacturer. (*springing open Chinese surprise box.*)—"THERE!—WHAT DO YOU THINK OF THAT LITTLE JOKER?"
Knight of St. Crispin.—"PSHAW! THAT'S A MEAN TRICK: WAIT TILL I OPEN *MY* BOX!"

Figure 3.3. In the "national game" of "capital vs. labor," the manufacturer unleashes his weapon of Chinese "cheap labor," while the Knight of St. Crispin threatens to stop him with a different weapon—the ballot box. In the 1870s, however, workers as a group exerted little power over Congress or national legislation, and a ban on imported contract labor would take years to pass. Note the class differences in attire, corpulence, pose, and even furniture. Original caption: "The New Pandora's Box. Representative Manufacturer (*springing open Chinese surprise box*): 'There!—What do you think of that little joker?' Knight of St. Crispin: 'Pshaw! That's a mean trick: wait till I open *my* box!'" (*Punchinello*, July 30, 1870. Courtesy General Research Division, New York Public Library, Astor, Lenox, and Tilden Foundations)

recognize any connection between contract labor and slavery. "Mr. Sampson," wrote William Lloyd Garrison, "simply asserted his unquestionable right as an employer, as against a brow-beating and exacting combination." Denouncing the Knights of St. Crispin as "dictatorial" and labor leaders as "political demagogues," the nation's most honored abolitionist defended the right to import foreign workers. Sampson's contract, Garrison declared, was made "in the usual manner, and under lawful conditions"; he saw no reason "why Chinamen should not be as freely induced to add their skill and labor to our capital stock."[38]

Reinforcing Garrison's views, Julia Ward Howe called workers' protests nothing more than "attempts made to avert competition . . . [which] would, if successful, dwarf and impoverish our country," while Lydia Maria Child deemed "the outcry about the Coolie trade" a far-fetched overreaction by the "monopoly of labor." On another end of the spectrum stood such abolitionists as Henry Blackwell and James M. Ashley (as well as the neolabor activist Robert Hume). Blackwell wanted no Chinese whether as imported laborers or free immigrants, writing that "Uncle Sam cannot afford to admit a horde of barbarous Asiatics." Ashley was even more direct. A former Ohio congressman, he had fought to abolish slavery in Washington, D.C., and introduced the first version of the Thirteenth Amendment to the Constitution. But Ashley's support for black freedom did not translate into sympathy for people of other races. As governor of Montana Territory, he urged the extermination of Native Americans and the exclusion of Chinese immigrants. "In Montana we want no more Chinamen or Indians or barbarians of any race;—we already have enough and to spare."[39]

Of the wide range of attitudes abolitionists expressed, Garrison's pro-importation stance garnered the most support. Why did antislavery veterans, many of whom had devoted their entire lives to emancipation, social justice, and racial equality, reveal such a profound lack of sympathy for workers and union demands? A simple explanation is that many workers were Irish, and "Sons of Erin" had gained notoriety for opposing emancipation and black advancement. On a deeper level, however, abolitionists could not bring themselves to support what was fast becoming known as "class legislation." They believed that the primary role of the state was to protect the political rights of individuals, not the economic interests of a class. As Lydia Maria Child remarked, "Money and labor ought to be left to regulate themselves." That government noninterference redounded in favor of capital did not bother abolitionists; such a laissez-faire approach, however, would make abolitionists largely irrelevant to the problems of the Gilded Age. Abolitionists were fading. With ratification of the Fifteenth Amendment in early 1870, their agenda had been nearly completed. Reflecting this fact, the *National Anti-Slavery Standard* changed its name that spring to the *National Standard*. The cause that had united a generation was won, and success spelled doom for a group unable to transfer their moral fervor to other issues. Abolitionists had recently split over women's rights, and their split over the Chinese issue further rent this aging band of reformers. They no longer spoke with a single voice on human rights or, even more specifically, on racial matters. Once the crusading vanguard for freedom and racial justice, abolitionists no longer served as the conscience of the nation.[40]

Other groups rushed to fill the void. As Eric Foner has written, "During Reconstruction the coalition which had fought the Civil War dissolved into its component elements, and strands of the free labor ideology were adopted by contending social classes, each for its own purposes." And one contending class, broadly speaking, was the working class. In the cacophony of voices in the Reconstruction era, workers claimed the free-labor legacy of the Civil War. Most northerners had fought the war to preserve the Union, but with emancipation the meaning of the war changed, and many former soldiers, including workers, took credit for having abolished slavery. As typographer Alexander Troup declared, workers had "shoulder[ed] the rifle to put down slavery" and would do it "once more" to prevent its reimposition. The importation of labor, while free from coercion and violence, presented clear-cut similarities to slavery: Large numbers of penniless foreigners were being transported thousands of miles to labor for a pittance. Furthermore, they were being used not simply as laborers but as weapons—as strikebreakers—against American citizens. At least that is how many workers saw it. Contrary to Alexander Saxton's claim that "not much of abolition rubbed off on them," the abolitionist movement—in which many workers had taken part—and the ideals of the Civil War had indeed affected both working-class ideology and working-class demands. East of the Rockies, workers clothed their protest not in the rhetoric of race versus race or native versus immigrant but in that of freedom versus slavery. For this ideal they had risked their lives, and for it they would continue to fight. The pro-immigration/anti-importation stance that eastern workers had formulated in broad terms in the 1860s they now—when confronted directly with the crisis sparked by North Adams—reiterated in specific terms regarding the Chinese in 1870. Whether workers would stick to this stance when faced with industrial depression, spreading unemployment, and rising tensions with capital would be the challenge of the coming decade.[41]

The Chinese have a perfect right, as well as any other foreigners, to migrate to this country if they wish to better their condition. But John Chinaman as an individual, and John Chinaman in gangs, bought and sold by greedy speculators, to break down the price of American labor, are quite different articles.
—Samuel Mason, Canton, Ohio, February 8, 1873

CHAPTER FOUR

All Sorts of Tricks

Defining Importation, 1871–1875

The arrival of Chinese workers in North Adams, Massachusetts, in 1870 was a seminal event in American history. It marked the first time that a manufacturer had transported Asian laborers to an industrial town east of the Rocky Mountains to break a strike. The widespread publicity and response it generated—ten journals sent reporters to North Adams, and newspapers everywhere reprinted their articles—made Chinese immigration a subject of intense national debate for the first time. As the *Springfield Republican* noted that fall, "The Chinese question . . . is being forced upon us with a rapidity that no one could have anticipated."[1]

Yet as the year came to a close, the issue receded from public view. Several reasons account for this. Despite their myriad threats, manufacturers seldom imported workers from Asia, and they never again imported Chinese laborers to New England to break a strike. Over the next five years they would be imported only a few times to any place east of the Rocky Mountains. Importing laborers from China was a daunting and expensive task, even with the assistance of an agent like Koopmanschap. Cost alone, however, cannot explain the reluctance of employers to import Chinese immigrants, for they could have easily mimicked Sampson and contracted Chinese directly from California at a nominal price. But few did. Some no doubt held the same racial views as other Americans and simply opposed the presence of Chinese immigrants. Most, though, were skeptical that the Chinese, with their different language and unknown abilities, could learn skilled trades quickly and adapt to the recent mechanization of American industries. Hence, employers could not risk alienating and losing large numbers of their employees. Importation could instantly turn an employer into a Sampson-like pariah—"what Judas was to Christianity, and what Jeff Davis was to the freedom of the slaves," as one worker put it. The numerous protest rallies of 1870 thus proved a partial success: while they had no effect on national legislation (Congress failed to outlaw importation), they had a decisive impact on employers. Fear of workers' reprisals kept most manufacturers from resorting to imported labor. One last crucial factor contributed to the absence of widescale importation: the nation's first major industrial depression. In 1873, a financial panic sent wages plummeting, and factory closings threw thousands out of work. Many unions disbanded as the depression wore on through the late 1870s. With a plentiful supply of domestic laborers hungry for work, employers had little need to look to China.[2]

In tracing the origin of the Chinese Exclusion Act, it is less important to assess blame than to study the process. Exclusion occurred at a particular moment—1882—for particular reasons. It did not occur in 1871 or 1873 or 1875 because neither congressmen nor their constituents nationwide (with the exception of California) had sufficient interest in such legislation. The only pressure on lawmakers east of the Rockies came from working people, but only on the subject of imported contract labor. A handful of legislators acknowledged their demands, and not a year passed between 1870 and 1875 in which members of Congress failed to present some bill to outlaw the practice. None of these bills ever came to a vote.[3]

Nor did one that Representative William Mungen (D-Ohio) introduced in 1871. In a long, blistering attack aimed at gaining publicity and shocking listeners, Mungen called the Chinese "a poor, miserable, dwarfish race of inferior beings" who were "docile, obedient . . . effeminate, pedantic, and . . . cowardly." Emphasizing the economic dangers of this "labor-crushing flood of Chinese and coolies," he cited Sampson's actions in North Adams as a precursor of capitalists' efforts "to turn the white laboring man or woman out of employment and install John Chinaman in his place . . . just as numerous corporations and capitalists have done, and as thousands of others are preparing to do." Unless Congress took immediate steps, he warned, "this Chinese immigration and importation . . . will beget a fatal war between labor and capital." Blurring the distinction between importation and immigration, Mungen argued that China was "a nation of abject slaves"—thus there could be no voluntary Chinese immigrants. Consequently, the bill he proposed to end "all further importation of Chinese" would, he said, result in "forbidding any Chinese to come to our country." Using the terms "importation" and "immigration" as synonyms, Mungen effectively ignored eastern workers' demands and helped transform the issue from a debate on foreign contract labor to one on Chinese immigration. And he did this, he said, for the American worker. Thus began a long, if sporadic, campaign—one that James G. Blaine would elevate to new heights eight years later—to convince eastern workers that they wanted something they did not say they wanted and at the same time to convince others that this was indeed what workers wanted.[4]

Rife with racist epithets and accusations that all Chinese immigrants were slaves, Mungen's speech in January 1871 offered everything an exclusionist could have wanted, except for one vital element: evidence. A prominent government official soon stepped in to rectify this omission. David H. Bailey had just been appointed U.S. consul to Hong Kong. As head of the consulate, one of his duties—as stipulated by the "anti-coolie" act of 1862—was to make sure that all "coolies" leaving China on American ships were free and voluntary immigrants.[5] He therefore undertook a four-month investigation of the "coolie trade." Bailey's 1871 report is a scathing indictment, describing in detail how importers scoured China to hoodwink unsuspecting peasants. "Men and boys are decoyed by all sorts of tricks, opiates, and illusory promises into the hands of the traders," he wrote. "Once in the clutches of these men-dealers . . . the stupefied cooly is overawed into making a contract." The contracts stipulated that the "cooly" work "for a series of years in a foreign country," and upon "faithful performance" of his duties, he would be brought back to China by his "purchaser." In making the contract, Bailey wrote, the immigrant "gives a mortgage on his wife and children" as collateral to insure compliance. Once signed, the "contract is sold by the dealer through his agents in the United States and elsewhere at a large advance, and is a source of great profit to capitalists, who have the means to buy and sell large numbers of men." This entire practice, Bailey concluded, "prostitutes everybody here, and thus far has prostrated every one who has stood up against it." Despite this macabre picture, Bailey reported "there is in reality free and voluntary emigration; but it is so surrounded, mixed up, and tainted with the virus of the coolie trade, as to require the utmost vigilance and scrutiny to separate the legitimate from the illegitimate emigration." The huge number of Chinese immigrants leaving on each ship, he explained, made it impossible to certify whether they left freely or under contract. Enforcement of the "anti-coolie" act thus became "a complete farce."[6]

Bailey offered various documents that, though far from conclusive, suggested an underground network in which Americans and Chinese conspired to import laborers to the United States. These dispatches seemed to offer convincing evidence of an ongoing "coolie trade" in which thousands of Chinese immigrants poured into the country as contract laborers. But were Bailey's reports valid? In the first modern account of Chinese immigration, Mary Roberts Coolidge dismissed the reports as "a mosaic of falsehood and misrepresentation." Bailey, she noted, didn't even speak Chinese. He invented this "misinformation" to cover up his own "mal-administration," she claimed, and he was accused by a successor of embezzlement. The historian George Anthony Peffer has cast doubt on these charges and defended Bailey's diligence. Whatever the consul's integrity, Coolidge's "exposé" of his alleged misdeeds neither validates nor invalidates his 1871 report. As one of the highest-ranking American officials in China from 1871 to 1879, Bailey had close contact with immigrants, shippers, and go-betweens and was the first consul to investigate Chinese immigration. He had, in effect, a monopoly on the "evidence." His firsthand reports assumed an official status, and as government documents, they offered strong support that the "coolie trade" thrived and prospered.[7]

Bailey thus provided the documentation Mungen had lacked. Anyone seeking justification to oppose the Chinese could now refrain from wild-eyed accusations and rely instead on sober government reports. Bailey's offerings dovetailed nicely with Mungen's charges. Mungen had presented a simple equation: immigration equals importation equals slavery. Bailey had distinguished between the first two but found them so entangled in practice that they could hardly be separated. If Chinese exclusion would eliminate these various abuses, it could even be seen as an act of humanity. Taken together, Mungen and Bailey offered workers (and anyone else) a convenient, principled argument against Chinese immigration.

Echoing this theme, Californian Albert Winn urged a Crispin convention meeting in New York City in April 1871—the same month Bailey issued his report—to endorse Chinese exclusion and stop "fiddling on the terms immigration and importation." So did the Workingman's Advocate, which reprinted Mungen's speech and maintained a steady barrage of anti-Chinese articles throughout the 1870s. In his single-minded campaign to rally workers behind the exclusionist banner, editor Andrew C. Cameron branded the Chinese "pestiferous vagabonds and yeleps" and called their immigration "the viper we are hugging to our bosoms." Accuracy became immaterial in the pursuit of his cause. In 1871, he misreported resolutions passed at a Crispin meeting, stating that workers had strongly opposed Chinese immigration, when, in fact, they had clearly distinguished between immigration and importation. But to Cameron, as to Mungen and to Winn, such distinctions were meaningless. As an 1874 editorial stated: "The *Advocate* has held for years . . . that there is no such thing as Chinese *emigrants*. It would be just as proper to say that the cured beef of Buenos Ayres [*sic*] *emigrated* to Great Britain, as to assert that the Coolies . . . are emigrants."[8]

Despite this ongoing assault from politicians, Californians, and the *Workingman's Advocate*, as well as repeated threats by manufacturers and employers to import Chinese laborers as strikebreakers during the early 1870s, eastern workers largely stuck by their original stance. "The presence in our country of imported *Chinese laborers* in large numbers, is an evil entailing want and crime," stated a resolution passed by the Michigan State Labor Union in 1873, "and [we demand] that the Congress of the United States prohibit the importation (not emigration) of coolies or other servile laborers." To many workers, importation and immigration were not terms lightly or interchangeably used. After a factory owner in Beaver Falls, Pennsylvania, imported Chinese laborers to break a strike in 1872, workers protested "their introduction into the United States, in the manner it is done," and petitioned Congress "to pass a law prohibiting any further importation of Chinese laborers under contracts made in China." As one Beaver Falls operative remarked, "We workingmen hold that Chinamen should come to America just as any other class of foreigners, and that buying them for a term of years is only Slavery in another form." Even as "pro-labor" politicians such as Mungen and labor editors such as Cameron argued that no difference existed between immigration and importation—or at least no difference worth fighting for—eastern workers continued to distinguish between the two. "The Chinese have a perfect right, as well as any other foreigners, to migrate to this country if they wish to better their condition," Samuel Mason of Canton, Ohio, wrote Cameron in 1873. "But John Chinaman as an individual, and John Chinaman in gangs, bought and sold by greedy speculators, to break down the price of American labor, are quite different articles." Three years after North Adams, eastern workers still defined immigration and importation as vitally different issues.[9]

That the Chinese seemed alien—a different race, a different religion, a different culture—made their importation particularly odious, but importation of *any* foreign laborers remained an abiding concern of working people. When leaders of the Iron Molders' International Union suspected that "unscrupulous employers" in the United States had approached potential strikebreakers in Britain, union president William Saffin contacted iron molders in England, Scotland, Ireland, and Wales to coordinate efforts against importation. Molders emigrating from one country to another, Saffin suggested in 1872, ought to be permitted to join the sister union overseas without restrictions. The only condition Saffin required was that British iron molders "not enter into written contracts to work in any foundry in the United States or Canadas, previous to their arrival in either country."[10]

Such international cooperation among workers could thus put an end to importation where governments failed to act. During a strike at a Rome, Georgia, iron foundry in October 1872, a company director sailed for Scotland to recruit workers. He advertised in Glasgow, assuring prospective recruits that at his foundry in Georgia there was no strike, no trouble, "only a scarcity of hands." Twenty-two workers signed up and embarked for America, many of them accompanied by their families. When Georgia workers informed them of the situation upon their arrival, however, the Scots honored the strike and refused to work. Despite entreaties from the director, they "would not scab," and the company soon gave in. Such events inspired the Iron Molders' International Union in its campaign against imported labor, and the union's journal regularly publicized the issue. As one editorial in 1874 observed: "Hundreds of thousands of men and families have been induced to come from Europe to this country by the false statements of interested parties, and the poor emigrant has no redress. Even now, when industry is paralyzed, and tens of thousands of mechanics and laborers out of employment, the emigrant agencies in Europe, sustained by American capitalists, are in full blast, and every vessel arriving from foreign ports, swells the list of victims to unscrupulous capital's false pretenses."[11]

Just as this editorial was being typeset, the importation of foreign workers provoked violence in western Pennsylvania. Seeking to break a strike by miners in September 1874, mine owners ordered three hundred laborers from the recently established New York Italian Labor Company, which for months had been supplying employers with Italian immigrants willing to work "at panic prices"—about two hundred to three hundred dollars a year. The striking miners learned of the plan and posted handbills at the mines threatening "fatal vengeance" against any scabs. When the Italian laborers—armed with muskets and knives and protected by special police—disembarked from their train, the miners greeted them with gunfire. By nightfall several Italians lay dead. The parallels to North Adams are eerie. In both cases employers imported foreign-born laborers en masse to break a strike. In both cases employers braced for violence, arming the strikebreakers and adding extra police. Even the contracts were similar in terms of accommodations and paltry wages. "The same system of contracts that has been so much talked of in the coolie system, is in full vogue with the Italians," the *Iron Molders' Journal* observed. "They belong, body and soul, to contractors in New York city. They are not free agents, and are as much slaves as any that existed twelve years ago."[12]

From Pennsylvania to Illinois, mine owners frequently imported outside laborers to break strikes during the 1870s, pitting one ethnic or racial group against another. "If the Italians are not found to answer the purpose Swedes will be tried," the *Allegheny Mail* noted, "and if they fail colored men will be set to work." In addition to Italians, Scandinavians, and southern blacks, owners imported Hungarians, Poles, and Belgians both to break strikes and, as one labor newspaper put it, to "whip the miners into the employers' traces." Modern transportation was making the world a smaller place, facilitating movement across states and across oceans. "With but ten days distance apart by steam, and but a few minutes by telegraph," union leader William H. Sylvis had noted a few years earlier, "it is an easy matter for capitalists and chartered emigrant societies to arrange an exodus of labor from one country to another, to carry out schemes of oppression." Improved transit would make such "schemes of oppression" only easier, quicker, and cheaper. A world of peasants and poor appeared ripe for the picking. Imported labor posed a legitimate threat to workers in the 1870s. Whether from China, Italy, or elsewhere, importation—"this villainous system"—remained importation. It was not, in workers' minds, immigration.[13]

Words matter, and workers chose them carefully. Even the National Labor Union, the outstanding example of ambiguity on the issue in 1870, eventually endorsed the position long championed by eastern workers—but not until it was too late. At its 1871 convention, delegates adopted with little debate the identical fuzzy resolution adopted the preceding year. In 1872, however, NLU leaders resolved to enter the presidential campaign, and the convention nominated a candidate to run on the National Labor Reform ticket. As part of their campaign strategy, delegates revised their language on the Chinese issue. The only Chinese laborers to which they objected, the party platform read, were those "imported by capitalists." The ambiguous wording was gone. A few mainstream newspapers misread the platform, claiming that it endorsed Chinese exclusion. Such a conclusion was quickly refuted. "The Labor Reformers do not object to the Chinese as emigrants," the *Hartford Labor Journal* remarked, "but they do object to any system that perpetuates slavery in its worst form."[14]

The National Labor Union had inched closer to the position of its targeted constituency, but at this point it didn't much matter. When its candidate,

Supreme Court justice David Davis, withdrew from the presidential race during the summer of 1872, the National Labor Reform Party collapsed and the NLU disbanded. Resurrecting the organization the following year, the newly christened Industrial Congress met in 1873 and adopted a platform more in line with workers' views: "that as a Congress of Laboring Men, we would welcome to our shores all emigration, as skilled workingmen or laborers; that our country is a home for the oppressed of all climes, but that we emphatically protest against the importation of laborers to serve a term of years for a fixed price." Delegates never endorsed Chinese exclusion. At the next two annual meetings, delegates passed nearly the identical resolution, demanding "passage of a national law" to make the "importation of foreign laborers under contracts . . . a penal offense." With that, the Industrial Congress passed out of existence in 1875.[15]

By any measure one chooses to use—scattered orations, petitions of protest, assorted letters, or formal resolutions—the message of working people east of the Rockies remained consistent during the early 1870s. Despite speeches by politicians, reports by government officials, and appeals by the nation's foremost labor editor, eastern workers refused to join (let alone lead) the movement for Chinese exclusion. These were not simply the views of a handful of socialists or radicals but ideas carefully expressed by a great variety of American wage earners from the Atlantic to the Mississippi. Vehemently denouncing importation and repeatedly urging Congress to ban contract labor from abroad, these workers continually shied away from any demand for restriction of immigration. The politics of exclusion was not of their making, nor did such a policy easily gain their sanction.

One reason workers in the West voiced such different attitudes toward Chinese immigration from those of workers elsewhere in the nation may simply be numbers. Hardly any Chinese lived east of the Rockies in the late nineteenth century. Of the 63,254 Chinese counted by the census in 1870, 62,864 (99.4 percent) lived in the West. A mere 390 lived east of the Rockies, and one-quarter of these worked in Sampson's factory in North Adams. No northeastern state counted more Chinese than Massachusetts, and with the U.S. population east of the Rockies just above 37.7 million, the Chinese in this section composed a minuscule .001 percent. In the West, the Chinese composed 5.1 percent of the population (and 8.5 percent of California's). Their numbers grew during the 1870s, and the 1880 census counted 105,465 Chinese, of whom 102,102 lived in the West, composing 5.8 percent of the section's population (and 8.7 percent of California's). In the East, the Chinese numbered 3,363 in 1880, a virtually invisible .007 percent of the section's 48.4 million people. Most Americans in the nineteenth century lived their entire lives without ever setting eyes on a person from China, and many eastern workers no doubt welcomed and accepted Chinese immigration simply because the number of Chinese immigrants in their region remained so small. Although compelling, this explanation fails to account for the racist policies long practiced by northerners against other groups who also constituted a tiny fraction of the population, such as blacks and American Indians. In the northern and midwestern states that fought the Confederacy, blacks accounted for just 1.5 percent of the population in 1870, and Indians, just .2 percent. Despite these tiny numbers, however, many northern and midwestern states consistently denied blacks political and civil rights through the Civil War, and some, such as Illinois and Indiana, tried to exclude blacks entirely from their borders. Policies against Indians were similarly discriminatory. When it came to the few blacks and Indians within their states, many northerners acted on their prejudices. But not when it came to the Chinese. Thus numbers alone cannot fully explain the tolerant attitudes eastern workers voiced toward Chinese immigrants.[16]

Both self-interest and idealism dictated workers' attitudes on Chinese immigration. As John Higham has pointed out, many American workers were themselves foreign-born and remembered well the Know-Nothing hysteria of the 1840s and 1850s.[17] With anti-Irish sentiment still prevalent, most workers wanted little to do with any new anti-immigrant movement that could threaten their own status and livelihood in the United States or precipitate the closing of the nation's doors to their own compatriots. Many immigrant workers maintained loyalties to their native country and had friends and relatives eager to emigrate; political upheavals in Ireland and Germany in the 1870s further made immigrant workers in the East determined to keep open the country's gates. This connection to Europe proved weaker in California, where both geographically and psychologically the Old World was more distant, literally half a world away. Oriented more toward the Pacific than toward the Atlantic, westerners had greater reason to focus on Asia than on Europe. In the East, however, where thousands of Europeans arrived on American shores every week, workers recognized that sanctions against Chinese immigrants could easily lead to sanctions against other immigrants. Who would be next? In an age when travelers needed neither passports nor papers to cross national borders, immigrants wanted freedom to travel back and forth between Europe and America. Erecting barriers could only hinder such mobility.

This crude self-interest merged with broader ideals. Despite the resurgence of nationalism during the Civil War, many wage earners viewed themselves as part of a larger community with other workers throughout the world. The emphasis on equality and political rights during Reconstruction generated efforts to overcome differences of color and nationality, and several unions added the word "international" to their names and established contact with union leaders abroad. The vision of "universal brotherhood" in such fledgling working-class organizations as the Knights of Labor further inspired workers in the East to transcend the ancient barriers of race and ethnicity. Racism and bigotry still surfaced, of course, especially during labor disputes involving workers of different groups, and many historians have emphasized the centrality of race to white working-class identity in the nineteenth century. "Working class formation and the systematic development of a sense of whiteness went hand in hand for the U.S. white working class," David Roediger has argued, and by the 1860s, "the importance of a sense of whiteness to the white U.S. worker was a long-established fact, not only politically but culturally as well." In combining separate concepts—such as thought and action—into a single construct, such generalizations on "a sense of whiteness" mask far more than they reveal about working-class racism. Although racism pervaded American society in the nineteenth century—and, as Roediger notes, a belief in "white supremacy was widely shared"—it is wrong to assume that Americans, whether working-class or not, therefore advocated racist policies. Racist thought and racist action are two vitally different things; however strong workers' "sense of whiteness," it did not automatically lead them to support racial acts or racial legislation against nonwhites. Contrary to Roediger's claim that "outside California the anti-Chinese movement won tremendous working-class response in areas such as . . . Massachusetts," workers in the Bay State and beyond clearly distinguished between immigration and importation in the early 1870s, distancing themselves from the anti-Chinese cries of the West. Racism and Chinese exclusion were separable issues, and eastern workers consistently separated them. "Whiteness" was just one of many factors shaping workers' sensibilities and actions in the late 1800s, and while racism remained a potent source of conflict that could be tapped—by employers, by union leaders, by politicians—in periods of unrest, ideals too remained a potent force shaping working-class ideology. The ideals of free labor, free movement, and freedom remained a guiding force among many workers, one that immigration restriction would have undercut. The ideals of equal rights, equal opportunity, and universal brotherhood also remained a guiding force. As one Irish American wage earner wrote the *Boston Pilot* in 1878 in rejecting westerners' calls for Chinese exclusion, "Not many years ago a similar war-cry, 'No Irish need apply,' was echoed and re-echoed throughout America by bigots as blind, ungenerous and intolerant . . . as any in the world." Workers had ample reason to keep the doors of the nation open to all. To them, America ought to remain, as they often said, "an asylum for the oppressed of every clime."[18]

Eastern workers stated this point again and again. Historians can read any number of sinister meanings into the words workers used, but the key to interpreting their message lies in understanding the context of their protests and the dangers they recognized. Whether faced with Chinese in North Adams, Scots in Georgia, or Italians in Pennsylvania, eastern workers identified importation, *not* immigration, as the evil to be guarded against—and they said so. Although they could have combined the two issues, workers repeatedly took pains to keep them separate and distinct. Historians should at last accept them at their word.

After stealing the spotlight in 1870, the Chinese issue receded to the background for the next five years. The period from 1871 to 1875 represented an "incubation period" for the issue on a national level. Open immigration had been the nation's creed since its founding, and few people saw any need for change. Those who did lived mainly in the West, and their legislators—particularly Senator Aaron A. Sargent (R-Calif.) and Representative Horace F. Page (R-Calif.)—pleaded their case in Congress with vicious anti-Chinese oratory in the early 1870s. Although both lawmakers would ultimately play key roles in securing the Chinese Exclusion Act, their efforts at the time excited little notice. Anti-Chinese politics failed to resonate nationwide. "The matter is of very great local importance," Sargent observed in 1874, "and perhaps it is to be regretted that it is so local in its character that its importance cannot be fully estimated in other parts of the country."[19]

California remained the hotbed of anti-Chinese politics. Both parties there urged exclusion in the early 1870s, and a candidate could not be elected governor without advocating immigration restriction. Numerous historians have related the combined efforts in the 1850s and 1860s of California miners, workers, politicians, and small manufacturers to ban Chinese immigration. By the early 1870s, merchants and manufacturers on the West Coast took a commanding role in marshaling anti-Chinese opinion. "The present movement . . . has not been produced by any effort of the working classes, nor is it undertaken for their benefit," the *San Francisco Examiner* observed in 1873, but "has been commenced by our capitalists, to protect themselves against Chinese capitalists who have greater advantages for employing cheap labor." When local carpenters circulated an anti-Chinese petition that year, they found that most signers were not workers but businessmen. As Ira B. Cross and Alexander Saxton have shown, support for immigration restriction penetrated every class in California by the mid-1870s, and Golden State voters of all stripes rallied to the anti-Chinese banner.[20]

In 1874, California's anti-Chinese crusade won over an unlikely ally: the president of the United States. In his annual message on December 7, Ulysses S. Grant indicated that he took seriously Consul Bailey's 1871 report: "[It is] a generally conceded fact—that the great proportion of the Chinese immigrants who come to our shores do not come voluntarily . . . but come under contracts with headmen, who own them almost absolutely." The president was not advocating Chinese exclusion but professing the belief that virtually all Chinese were imported by force. Scarcely any emigrated freely, and females, he claimed, were "brought for shameful purposes, to the disgrace of the communities where settled and to the great demoralization of the youth of those localities." Reports of Chinese prostitution rings had become common fare in the daily press, but efforts to crack down on them had been no more successful than enforcement of the "anti-coolie" act of 1862. Grant's message, however, combined the issues of imported Chinese laborers and prostitutes and spurred action in Congress. Representative Page drafted a bill outlawing "the importation . . . of women for the purposes of prostitution," which singled out those from "China, Japan, or any Oriental country." Such women could no longer emigrate to the United States "for lewd and immoral purposes." Though the bill restated sections of the "anti-coolie" act, contract labor from China remained legal as long as laborers were not coerced. With little debate, Congress passed the Page Act, as it came to be called, and Grant signed it into law on March 3, 1875.[21]

Thus after more than five years of agitation, Congress could come up with nothing stronger than a pallid act to ban Asian prostitutes from the United States. The demands of eastern workers—for an end to imported contract labor—and the demands of Californians—for an end to Chinese immigration—remained unmet. Neither group exerted much pressure on lawmakers, and Congress felt no compulsion to act. Dominated by local issues, eastern workers remained politically fragmented, and whatever muscle they might have flexed in Washington as a voting bloc dissipated with the electoral fiasco of the National Labor Reform Party in 1872. Without a stronger organization to pressure Congress, a ban on imported contract labor would never come to pass. Nor was the influence of California much greater. Located three thousand miles from the nation's main centers of power, California had scant impact on national legislation. Its lawmakers commanded neither authority nor prestige in Washington, and the state's meager population (582,000 in 1870) ranked it among the nation's smallest. With an overwhelming Republican majority in Congress, California's six electoral votes (out of 352) seemed paltry. National politicians had little incentive to trouble themselves with California—or Chinese immigration—in the early 1870s. Furthermore, while

California's two senators pushed for exclusion during the first half of the decade, the senators from neighboring Nevada (where the Chinese composed 5.4 percent of the population) urged open immigration.[22] Chinese exclusion thus remained an issue without a national constituency in the early 1870s, and without a constituency it had few advocates.

But American politics was changing. Lincoln's victory in the "critical election" of 1860 had inaugurated a political realignment, which scholars have labeled the third party system. Historians have observed that such major realignments (and party systems) have occurred with some regularity every generation. The third party system (which followed the first and second party systems, inaugurated, respectively, by the "critical elections" of 1800 and 1828) was marked by the emergence of the Republican Party and the parity it achieved over the next three decades with the Democrats in presidential elections. This third party system lasted until 1896, when another "critical election," marked by a huge Republican victory, ushered in the fourth party system, which itself would endure until 1932. Some of these major political realignments stemmed from significant events, such as the sectional crisis in 1860 and the depression in 1932, when voters faced distinct choices for president. While the theories behind these "critical elections" and party systems are based largely on voting returns and the consequent emergence or entrenchment of political parties, less attention has been paid to the role of political issues—or lack of issues—in perpetuating each system. In terms of issues, the election of 1872 signaled the end of an era. In the four previous elections, the Republican and Democratic Parties had offered voters genuine choices on vital issues. In 1856 and 1860, positions on the extension of slavery clearly demarcated the two major parties. The election of 1864 was nothing less than a referendum on emancipation and the war itself. The 1868 campaign focused on Radical Reconstruction and the rights of former slaves. Democrats resorted to race baiting and Ku Klux Klan–sponsored violence, both of which Republicans condemned. During each of these four elections, Republicans and Democrats provided vastly different platforms that focused on real issues, including slavery, freedom, civil rights, and equality. Voters had clear and important choices to make.[23]

In 1872, this was no longer the case. The bizarre presidential campaign that year began with the Republicans splitting in two. Believing the party had fallen prey to machine politicians and corrupt office seekers, Missouri senator Carl Schurz and others broke away. Liberal Republicans, as these self-styled reformers called themselves, championed civil service reform and sectional reconciliation as well as tariff reduction, reduced federal protection for blacks, and less government intervention in the economy. As David Montgomery and Eric Foner have pointed out, a key impulse propelling Liberal Republican leaders was the fear of an active, powerful state—especially one that men of "property and enterprise," in the words of Senator Schurz, could not dominate. Although many such men had favored enhanced federal powers to prosecute the war and protect the rights of southern freedmen during Reconstruction, they now recoiled at the growing influence of Washington. As *Nation* editor E. L. Godkin said: "The government must get out of the 'protective' business and the 'subsidy' business and the 'improvement' business and the 'development' business. It must let trade, and commerce, and manufacturers, and steamboats, and railroads, and telegraphs alone. It cannot touch them without breeding corruption." A stark antidemocratic strand ran through Liberal thinking; foremost among their concerns was that a strong central government elected by workers and immigrants would legislate on such matters as eight-hour laws and inflationary greenbacks—and the importation of contract labor. These fears drove Liberals away from the Republican Party in 1872. Many hoped that the new party would attract the "best men" who would purify the political system and unite the "natural" leaders of the country. For president they nominated *New York Tribune* editor Horace Greeley, the iconoclastic abolitionist and reformer lately reborn a conservative. Although the choice dismayed many in the new party, Liberals hoped that Greeley would appeal to aging abolitionists as well as to those fed up with racial conflicts in the South and the scandal-ridden Grant administration in Washington.[24]

In one of the campaign's more extraordinary developments, the Democrats also nominated Greeley for president. Losers of three elections in a row, the old party of Confederates and Copperheads sought to put the past behind it. In what was called their "new departure," the Democrats accepted all three recent constitutional amendments—emancipation, black citizenship, and black male suffrage—as the law of the land and abandoned overt appeals to racism. Notwithstanding Greeley's lifetime of attacks on Democrats (he once called them "murderers, adulterers, drunkards, cowards, liars, thieves"), party leaders found the old abolitionist's postwar conservatism attractive, and in their anything-to-beat-Grant strategy, they formed an unlikely coalition with the Liberals. Amid this slew of twists and turnarounds, Republicans dutifully nominated Grant for a second term.[25]

Despite the Liberals' genuine grievances and political differences with the Republican Party, neither principles nor ideas mattered much during the campaign. The Liberal platform, which Democrats adopted for their own, varied little from that of the Republicans. All three parties endorsed equal rights and the recent amendments to the Constitution. All three praised Union soldiers, favored amnesty for former rebels, and urged civil service reform. The main difference in the platforms was that Republicans favored abolition of the franking privilege for members of Congress. They also paid lip service to women's rights. When it came to issues, it mattered less and less whether one was a Democrat or a Republican: after a decade of cataclysmic conflicts and polar positions, the parties found little on which to openly disagree.[26]

As a result, the 1872 canvass focused more on personalities than on platforms. Greeley undertook a breakneck campaign tour and made a series of intemperate comments that offended nearly everyone. The unassuming Grant, meanwhile, sat quietly in the White House doing nothing. In a contest of personalities—the crackpot editor versus the somber general—the need for issues diminished. It comes as no surprise, therefore, that Chinese immigration and imported contract labor played no role in the presidential election of 1872. Politicians had no reason to inject new issues and risk losing votes. The old issues, though fading, provided the little substance that was needed. Republican strategists felt confident with a stand-pat candidate, and the squeaky-voiced, much-heckled Greeley practically self-destructed. Grant won in a landslide, and the Republicans swept Congress, capturing the House, 194 to 92, and the Senate, 49 to 19.[27]

Despite this huge victory, Republicans had reason to worry. An influential segment of their party had defected. The coalitions forged during the Civil War and Reconstruction had shattered, and Democrats raced to pick up the pieces. In accepting the elevation of blacks to citizenship and suffrage, Democrats had at last come to terms with the results of the war. Significant partisan differences still remained—over federal intervention in the South and enforcement of civil rights—but even these would soon disappear. After a turbulent era marked by divergence on fundamental issues, the nation's two great parties were entering an era of convergence. Racial politics fell into eclipse, at least temporarily. The issues that had long defined the Republican Party—free soil, preservation of the Union, emancipation, equal rights—no longer racked the nation. As John Sproat has noted, "The events in 1872 marked the end of the old Republican coalition of the Civil War years."[28] Victory had shorn the party of its purpose (much as it had the abolitionists), and the glorious achievements of the past said little about the future. Republicans could still wave the bloody shirt (to remind voters that Democrats had started the war), but Democrats could take the higher road of sectional reconciliation.

This slow demise of Civil War partisanship would dramatically alter national politics. As party leaders knew, Republican dominance rested on shaky supports, and when the panic on Wall Street in 1873 ushered in a major depression, the party foundation crumbled. In one of the most stunning electoral reverses in history, Democrats regained the House in 1874 by a hefty 169 to 109 margin. The depression only deepened the following year, and as the United States approached its centennial, more than half the nation's railroads faced bankruptcy. Iron production plummeted, factory closings soared, and unemployed workers roamed from town to town looking for jobs. The "tramp" problem grabbed headlines as labor unrest exploded nationwide. The vanishing of Civil War issues, coupled with hard times, offered Democrats their first real chance in a generation to capture the White House. Politicians of both parties knew that the election of 1876 would be the first closely fought contest in recent memory. As Walter Dean Burnham has observed, the eighteen-year period beginning in 1874 "was precisely one in which—uniquely in a hundred and forty years of electoral history—there was in fact no national majority for either party."[29] Consequently, politicians scrambled for every available electoral vote, even those of tiny California and Oregon. In the political vacuum caused by the fading of the war, both parties would need to redefine themselves by identifying with new issues. Anything to swing a vote—or swing a state—would be considered. Racial politics, which had proved effective in the past, would be resurrected. The politics would not be white versus black, however, but "Caucasian" versus Chinese. The upcoming election would make 1876 the year that Chinese immigration became a presidential political issue for the first time.

CHAPTER FIVE

To Overcome the Apathy of National Legislators

The Presidential Campaign of 1876

On an early summer day in 1876, Philip Augustine Roach entered the stately residence of Samuel J. Tilden near Gramercy Park in Manhattan. Roach had long served as a California state senator and editor of the *San Francisco Examiner*. Tilden, the governor of New York, was on the verge of being nominated for president at the Democratic National Convention less than a week away. After a private conversation they were joined by Democratic leader Manton Marble, editor of the *New York World*. Roach's message was simple and direct: he wanted Tilden and the Democratic Party to adopt the issue of Chinese exclusion for the presidential campaign. "Treat this question well," Roach advised Marble, "and Mr. Tilden can get, as he desires, the Pacific Delegation." Chinese exclusion, Roach explained, was an ideal campaign issue: "Properly treated [it] will rally the workingman to our support where the mongolians have secured a lodgment." Tilden accepted the advice; Marble then drafted an anti-Chinese resolution that would shortly appear in the party's platform.

"And thus commenced in Mr. Tilden's own studio," Roach later noted, "the action which made opposition to Coolieism a national Democratic issue."[1]

This meeting, and the year 1876 itself, marked a turning point in the anti-Chinese movement. After years as a local issue in the West that had drawn only sporadic interest in the East, politicians attempted to portray Chinese immigration as a national emergency. With little instigation from any group east of the Rocky Mountains, politicians seized—one might say created and refashioned—the issue of Chinese exclusion in the quest for votes. Republicans had actually taken the initiative, but Democrats quickly caught up and pushed the issue more vigorously. Both parties wrote anti-Chinese planks into their national platforms in 1876, and many a politician jockeyed, in Roach's words, "to set himself right on the Chinese question."[2] Such posturing, however, yielded few rewards. Despite politicians' efforts, they could not make Chinese immigration a matter of national importance to workers or to voters in the East. Chinese immigration remained in the background, overshadowed by the dying embers of Reconstruction. The time and the purpose for such an issue had not yet arrived and would not arrive until major class conflicts erupted across the nation. That time was coming. Social upheavals of the late 1870s would not only bloody workers and soldiers but would also shock the country and provide the ammunition politicians needed to buttress the arguments of their crusade to restrict Chinese immigration. The centennial year set the stage for that crusade.

The winter of 1875–76 gave little indication that Chinese immigration would become a national political issue, much less a plank of each party's platform. Two years of depression had produced no resurgence of prewar nativism or antiforeigner sentiment. On Washington's Birthday in 1876, the Order of United American Mechanics met in New York City. Founded in 1845 by masters and journeymen, this fiercely xenophobic, cross-class organization had advocated anti-immigrant legislation, temperance reform, and harmony between employer and employee, all strands that would find their way into the Know-Nothing movement and the Republican Party. The Order's evolution during the 1860s and 1870s is largely unknown, but the New York meeting suggests a change in direction. One speaker lavished praise on "foreigners who had done so much in behalf of liberty," while another lauded the French, Italian, Irish, and German immigrant for coming to America to seek the "manhood which he could not find at home." Saluting "religious equality, political equality and social equality, all of which . . . meant true Americanism," the latter orator stated: "All religions must be tolerated so long as they did not cross that of another. The Chinaman had just as much right to his peculiar kind of worship as anybody else."[3] Popular nativism, it appears, had, at least momentarily, done an about-face. Support for foreigners—even Chinese—could earn plaudits in the East.

California politicians, however, were gearing up for a major assault on the rest of the nation. In March, the California State Republican Committee demanded modification of the Burlingame Treaty of 1868 to permit the restriction of Chinese immigration. The Democrats at once tried to steal their thunder. San Francisco mayor Andrew Jackson Bryant issued a statement on the "evils" of Chinese immigration and directed the city's Board of Supervisors to draft a list of grievances for a giant public rally. The mayor wanted the grievances taken to Washington and a million copies circulated throughout the country. The Board of Supervisors lined up prominent speakers and, to emphasize the issue's widespread appeal, "urgently recommended that the people in every town, village and hamlet throughout the Coast" hold similar meetings.[4]

The day of the rallies proved a rousing success. On April 5, 1876, some twenty-five thousand people—the largest gathering the Pacific Coast had ever seen—assembled in San Francisco to hear the state's leading citizens viciously denounce the Chinese and sign a petition to be delivered to Congress. The governor, lieutenant governor, and a former governor, as well as numerous other officials and businesspeople, including State Senator Philip Roach, all called for an end to Chinese immigration. "We must do it," Governor William Irwin told the cheering crowd, "by urging a sufficient number of members of Congress, and by urging the Executive Department . . . [to] secure a modification of our treaty relations with the Chinese Empire." To assure success, the governor stated, the West Coast must rouse "public opinion on the other side of the continent."[5]

The State Senate had the same idea. Two days before the rallies, California lawmakers authorized an investigation of the impact of Chinese immigration on the Pacific Coast. They aimed to determine "the effect their presence has upon the social and political condition of the State" and then to recommend the "means of exclusion." Confident of the conclusions investigators would reach, legislators resolved that the report be sent to all the "leading newspapers of the United States," as well as five each to every member of Congress. Stirring public opinion in the East and Midwest remained the underlying goal. From April to June, lawmakers held fifteen sessions and interviewed sixty witnesses; they later adopted a report and issued a memorial calling the Chinese slaves and "pariahs," the "dregs of the population." The State Senate urged Congress to repeal the Burlingame Treaty and limit the number of incoming Chinese immigrants to ten per ship.[6]

The Chinese in San Francisco opposed these actions vigorously. In a memorial sent to President Grant shortly after the April rallies, seven Chinese community leaders argued, "The Anti-Chinese Crusade, started by sectarian fanaticism, encouraged by personal prejudice and ambition for political capital, has already culminated in personal attack, abuse, and incendiarism against the inoffensive Chinese." Rebutting attacks on their religious, culinary, and sartorial customs, one defender added: "It will be a sad day, indeed, for this great Republic when it shall prescribe personal qualities of this kind as conditions to immigration. America will again become a wild then, and her great boast as 'The Land of the Free' will be no more."[7]

Such protests had little effect in stopping the anti-Chinese onslaught. Politicians up and down the coast continued to denounce the Chinese, and in June, the San Francisco Board of Supervisors even passed a law—the so-called queue ordinance—to inhibit the Chinese hairstyle in hopes it would check immigration.[8] But such piecemeal efforts were ineffective, and politicians knew it. Their only real hope for immigration restriction lay with the federal government. It was no accident that the mass meetings and the State Senate investigation occurred when they did. The national nominating conventions were around the corner—if Washington was to respond, this was the time. "We are on the eve of a presidential election," Mayor Bryant proclaimed in March, "and both parties are looking toward this coast for aid." As the San Francisco Bulletin noted, "The session of Congress preceding a Presidential election is the most promising. The Democratic House . . . will not be disposed to throw away the votes of the Pacific States. . . . The Republican Senate will be likely to be swayed by precisely the same motive." In dangling the bait of electoral votes, California hoped to lure politicians thousands of miles away to its cause. To publicize this bait and the sentiment of the Pacific Coast, Californians continued holding huge anti-Chinese meetings throughout the spring. To top everything off, the San Francisco Board of Supervisors authorized a delegation to deliver the mass meeting's list of grievances to Congress and spur anti-Chinese hostility throughout the East. The delegation consisted of three politicians: Frank Pixley, Mark McDonald, and the distinguished statesman Philip A. Roach.[9]

Philip Augustine Roach was born in Ireland in 1820. His family moved to New York in 1822, and at age fourteen he became a clerk in a large importing house and began his career as a merchant. A man of varied interests, Roach served briefly as editor of the *Vicksburg Sentinel* and later studied at the University of Paris. President James K. Polk appointed him U.S. consul to Portugal in 1846, but he resigned three years later to head for California. Settling in Monterey, the forty-niner quickly became, in the words of the *New York Times*, "one of the best known and most universally respected citizens on the Pacific coast." He helped frame California's first constitution and was elected judge and then mayor of Monterey. As a state senator in 1852, Roach wrote one of the earliest reports denouncing the Chinese. After leaving office, he held numerous titles and in 1867 bought an interest in the *San Francisco Examiner*. He wrote editorials for the newspaper for the next seven years and was reelected to the State Senate in 1873. Well connected with politicians and men of commerce and possessed of "gentleman-like instincts" and a fine speaking voice, this lace-curtain Irish immigrant was an ideal choice to lead the city's anti-Chinese delegation.[10]

Roach embarked on his trip east in May. He stopped first in Chicago where he engaged a lecture hall and distributed five thousand handbills around the city. Five hundred people showed up to hear him attack the "coolie system" as "slavery and peonage." He described in detail how the Chinese "drove out competition" in every trade. "Thousands of Spanish and American cigar-makers were thrown out of work by the Chinaman," he said. So were fishers, servants, and shoemakers. "The Chinaman worked longer and cheaper than the white man" and thus crowded out "honest labor." They "brought diseases with them" and were "fearful liars . . . opposed to the manners and customs of the [American] people." Emphasizing Chinese prostitution, vice, and criminality, Roach urged his listeners to support his mission to end Chinese immigration.[11]

A week later the *Workingman's Advocate* reported that Roach's lecture "was well received." But apparently not well enough. The Californian "had hoped for a larger audience," he said, and his Chicago lecture was his last. Switching tactics, Roach appealed to the press rather than face large audiences, and as he traveled on to Philadelphia, New York, and other big cities, he spoke mainly to reporters. His new strategy was to grant interviews, provide copy, and, as his colleague Frank Pixley hoped, "enlist leading journals in our cause." Pixley, former attorney general of California, also urged newspapers back home to step up the pressure: "The press should cry aloud and no public opportunity should be allowed to pass without pushing this question." Pixley's message got through. The *Nation*, for example, printed a venomous anti-Chinese letter while Roach was in town, prompting editor E. L. Godkin to worry about the "influx of a horde of barbarians" into the United States: "The picture drawn by Fourth-of-July orators of the welcome which the United States offers the 'poor and oppressed of every land,' is somewhat out of date." Roach's strategy was working. His deliberate, well-planned campaign rolled along smoothly, pro-

Figure 5.1. Forty-niner, mayor of Monterey, and longtime state senator, Philip A. Roach (1820–89) was one of California's most distinguished citizens of the nineteenth century. As both an editorialist and politician, he spearheaded the state's anti-Chinese movement after the Civil War. In 1876, he led a delegation east to alert the country to the "dangers" of Chinese immigration and convince Democrats to adopt the issue nationally in the presidential campaign. "Properly treated," Roach advised, "[it] will rally the workingman to our support where the mongolians have secured a lodgment." (Courtesy California Historical Society, FN-31042)

pelled by the same rhetorical approach he had set out in Chicago: while ostensibly aiming his message to working people, he tailored his arguments to be acceptable to all segments of society.[12]

Venturing beyond the editorial rooms of the press, Roach made his most publicized appearance in New York City, where he was feted by the Associated Pioneers of the Territorial Days of California. Numerous "prominent citizens" attended the full-dress banquet and delivered testimonials to the New York boy who had made good. Those that could not attend, such as General William T. Sherman and former crony Mark Twain, sent congratulatory letters. One speaker praised Roach for alerting the East to the "dangers" of Chinese immigration and saluted him for his efforts "to exclude this useless addition to our population." Roach had made a hit. A week later, the "Pioneer of California" got a sympathetic hearing from the Connecticut legislature in Hartford. Roach's audience extended well beyond labor circles.[13]

Though Roach received favorable publicity everywhere, he made his biggest sensation in Washington, where he hammered out his message directly to President Grant and his cabinet. He also met with influential senators and testified before the Foreign Relations Committee, presenting the list of grievances endorsed two months earlier by the San Francisco mass meeting. Pixley testified with him, as well as to the House Committee on Foreign Affairs. Pixley also met with Grant three times, stressing the dangers of Chinese immigration. "I have found no public man (not from our coast) who is more alive to the importance of the subject or more anxious to give us prompt relief," Pixley wrote. He claimed that the president, the attorney general, and several other cabinet members "agree upon one point, viz: The necessity of qualifying those clauses of the Burlingame treaty that now permit unlimited emigration."[14]

Despite their immediate impact, Roach and Pixley comprised but a fraction of the anti-Chinese onslaught during the spring of 1876. West Coast congressmen also joined the crusade. In April, the House of Representatives adopted a resolution submitted by Horace F. Page (R-Calif.) requesting the president to open treaty negotiations with China. In the Senate, Aaron A. Sargent (R-Calif.) offered a similar resolution and asked if he might make a few comments. His colleagues consented, and on May 1, less than a month after the wave of anti-Chinese meetings had swept California, as the State Senate was conducting its investigation and on the eve of Roach and Pixley's visit east, Sargent launched into one of the most venomous anti-Chinese attacks the Senate had ever heard.[15]

"The emigration of Chinese is not like that of Europeans who seek our shores voluntarily to become citizens," he said. "They are *quasi* slaves" with whom free workers could not compete. San Francisco was becoming "a purely Asiatic city," he warned, replete with hidden opium dens and "plague-breeding nuisances." Sargent compared such scenes to Tom-all-alone's, the famous slum in Dickens's *Bleak House*, but claimed that nothing the novelist had depicted approached the squalor of Chinatown. "Even his pen would fail to do justice to the Chinese alleys in San Francisco . . . reeking with the slime of nastiness." Unless stopped immediately, the Chinese would bring havoc everywhere they settled. Seeking to nationalize the issue, he declared: "If a community is built up by such industry, it is not as a New England or western village is built up. It is Foo Chow, and not Cedar Rapids; it is Donovan Alley [part of the fledgling Chinese community in Manhattan], and not Broadway; it is the hovel and not the home; the joss-house and not the church; it is not republican; it is not civilization."[16]

A native of Massachusetts and, like Roach, a forty-niner, Sargent had been a Radical Republican and staunch defender of civil rights. (He was also the Senate's foremost advocate of woman suffrage.) But now, he confessed, he was no longer blinded by the ideals of his youth. He urged fellow senators to abandon the "humanist view" of equality forged in the fires of Civil War and

Figure 5.2. As a representative and a senator throughout the 1870s, Aaron A. Sargent (1827–87) of California was the leading anti-Chinese crusader in Congress. "Here are swarming millions of men, alien not alone to our blood and our language, but to our faith," he said. "Chinamen, as a race, are addicted to all the nameless vices characteristic of the Asiatics. . . . There can be no remedy but general exclusion." (Courtesy Bancroft Library, University of California, Berkeley)

emancipation. Lawmakers during Reconstruction, he said, had been "too emotional" when dealing with racial problems: in seeking to promote human equality, "we looked too much to the sentimental side." But those days were over. It was time now for Congress to act. "There can be no remedy," he concluded, "but general exclusion."[17]

The senator's words fell on a rapt audience. "Sargent's speech . . . has excited much interest here," a reporter noted. "Congressional sentiment on the question is awakened under such efforts and discussion[s] by the California Press . . . have seemed to startle the public mind into a more careful examination and review of the whole subject." To bolster his case, Sargent submitted the anti-Chinese petition—"in two large bound volumes"—signed at the San Francisco mass meeting, he claimed, by "nearly twenty thousand" people, including "lawyers . . . merchants . . . bankers, and clergymen." Two weeks later, Representative William Piper (D-Calif.) and Senator John H. Mitchell (R-Ore.) continued the fusillade. Contrasting the "superior Anglo-American" race with "the semi-civilized yellow race, the savage African, and the perishing red man," Piper dismissed the Chinese as "atheists" who "use praying-machines and expend immense sums . . . in purchase of idols in which they do not believe." Echoing Sargent, Piper and Mitchell noted but minimized the distinction between immigration and importation, and they urged two immediate steps: an investigation into the matter, and a new treaty with China. These were only preludes, however, to their demand for the "absolute prohibition of the Chinese immigration."[18]

This four-pronged attack orchestrated by western politicians—anti-Chinese demonstrations on the Pacific Coast, the California State Senate investigation, the Roach delegation east, and didactic orations in Congress—bore instant fruit not in Washington but in Cincinnati, where on June 14 (the same day San Francisco passed its queue ordinance), Republicans gathered for their national convention. The leading candidate, former House Speaker James G. Blaine, seemed destined for the nomination until allegations surfaced that he had accepted bribes from railroad companies. The popular Maine Republican had never commented publicly on Chinese immigration, nor had the subject ever made its way into a major party's national campaign platform. But on the convention's opening day, Joseph R. Hawley—the former Connecticut governor who had endorsed importation and immigration in his debate with Ben Butler on July 4, 1870—presented the resolutions he and the platform committee had framed: "It is the immediate duty of Congress fully to investigate the effects of the immigration and importation of Mongolians on the moral and material interests of the country."[19]

A debate erupted that lasted nearly an hour. Calling the plank "discrimination of race," Massachusetts delegate Edward L. Pierce wanted it stricken from the platform. "I denounce . . . that resolution as a departure from the life and memory of Abraham Lincoln," he said. "I denounce it as a departure from every Republican platform adopted by every Republican national convention." Pierce labeled it anti-Christian and against the Declaration of Independence. "It is not," he said, "the doctrine of New England." Defending the resolution, Nevada senator John P. Jones described the Chinese as a "brutalized people" whose "very language . . . has degenerated into a libidinous slang." Put to a vote, the measure passed easily, 532 to 215 (71 percent in favor). Westerners approved overwhelmingly, 42 to 2, but the vast majority of support came from the East. All 58 Pennsylvanians voted in favor, and the combined vote from the Northeast and Midwest was 325 to 133 (71 percent in favor)—the same proportion as the convention at large. And although the anti-Chinese plank may not have been "the doctrine of New England," delegates from the five states split almost evenly. In the end, the *San Francisco Alta California* noted, the resolution was "adopted amid loud cheers." The *New York Tribune* called it "a necessary tub thrown to the anti-Chinese whale on the Pacific coast, without which the delegates from the States on that coast were fearful that they could give the Republican nominee no electoral votes." True enough. But as the *New York Witness* commented, "The Republican party, as represented by the Cincinnati Convention, regards the Chinaman as the Democratic party does the African, namely, to be excluded from equal opportunities with the white man." The ideals of the Civil War—the very basis of Reconstruction—were indeed fading: principle could be sacrificed in pursuit of the presidency. Republican politicians were learning to play the politics of anti-Chinese racism.[20]

It was one week later that Philip Roach met in New York City with Governor Tilden and Manton Marble. Spurred by the Republican action, Roach pressed them to insert an even stronger plank into the Democratic platform. So did Andrew Bryant. "I desire respectfully," the San Francisco mayor wrote Marble, "to call your attention to the *necessity* of having engrafted in the Democratic Platform . . . strong and unequivocal Anti-Chinese Resolutions." At the Democratic Convention, which opened on June 27, western delegates reinforced these efforts. Former California senator John S. Hager and his colleague J. L. English emphasized that "our delegation is united" on placing an anti-Chinese plank in the platform and that their choice for a candidate "will be in some measure guided . . . by the all-important Mongolian question." They were not disappointed. Denouncing the policy that "tolerates the revival of the coolie-trade in Mongolian women for immoral purposes, and Mongolian men held to perform servile labor contracts," the Democratic Party resolved to "demand such modification of the treaty with the Chinese Empire, or such legislation within constitutional limitations, as shall prevent further importation or immigration of the Mongolian race." Delegates greeted the plank with shouts of " 'Good!' 'Bully!' and cheers."[21]

Both parties were now on record in favor of some measure hostile to Chinese immigration. The momentum from the national conventions propelled Congress to act. On July 6, the Senate passed a resolution pledging to "investigate the character, extent, and effect of Chinese immigration to this country." Republicans could now claim they were already making good on their campaign promises. The House passed the same resolution, 186 to 14, and the two branches created a joint committee to investigate Chinese immigration. This committee, authorized a few days after the country's one hundredth birthday, would begin its hearings in San Francisco in the fall.[22]

Western politicians had scored their first victory. Coming from virtually nowhere, they had turned a local concern into a national issue in a mere few months. Pixley himself stated that upon his arrival in the East in May, he had "found great ignorance and great indifference about the Chinese matter in Washington." The *San Francisco Chronicle* agreed and banked on Roach, Pixley, and western congressmen "to overcome the apathy with which national legislators . . . regard the whole subject." After the Republicans had adopted their platform, the *Chronicle* called the anti-Chinese plank "all that the people of this coast could have reasonably expected in the present state of the agitation of that question. The whole subject is new to the people of the East." Harping on this "newness," the *Chronicle* added, "The people of the East know absolutely nothing of the blight and curse caused by the influx of hordes of Asiatics." But they found out soon. Thanks to Roach and his delegation, journals that had scarcely considered the subject before—the *Philadelphia Public Ledger*, the *New York Herald*, and the *St. Louis Republican*, to name but a few— began urging modification of the Burlingame Treaty to restrict Chinese immigration. "Public sentiment is turning our way," Pixley observed during his tour, "and will, I think, eventuate in public sentiment adverse to Chinese emigration." Even newspapers that Roach and Pixley could not convince to endorse exclusion proved amenable to their cause. The staunchly Republican *St. Louis Globe-Democrat*, for example, opposed any revisions to the Burlingame Treaty but nevertheless labeled Chinese immigrants "soulless, conscienceless, alien heathens . . . the outcasts of . . . [a] stunted civilization." However, the newspaper concluded, the problem should be left to Californians to resolve. Roach and company would have been happy to oblige.[23]

By midyear, the avalanche of publicity against the Chinese appeared to have succeeded. Roach and Pixley "have gone home," the *New York World* noted on August 1, "well satisfied with the result of their missionary labors." *World* editor Manton Marble had helped draft the Democratic platform and had been the individual singled out by Roach to foment anti-Chinese feeling and so create a national political issue. "The whole sentiment of the East," the *World* continued, "has suddenly grown sober and serious in regard to the Mongolian question."[24]

But had it? Despite Roach's entreaties, the *World* had not jumped onto, let alone tried to steer, the anti-Chinese bandwagon. "The present anti-Mongolian crusade is as undesirable as it is unjust," the *World* had editorialized in June. "The anti-Chinese agitation on the Pacific coast has in all likelihood been given more prominence than it deserved." The *World* even assailed the anti-Chinese plank in the Republican platform for its "vicious spirit" of "race prejudice." But it was that week that Roach visited Marble at Tilden's home, and thereafter his editorials became more muted. Though endorsing the Democratic platform, the paper virtually ignored the anti-Chinese plank (which Marble himself had helped draft). The *World* acknowledged eastern ignorance of the subject and in July published an article on "degraded Chinese women." This was the extent of its anti-Chinese crusade. The *World*'s editorial on August 1 was the last to mention the subject for the rest of the campaign.[25]

The flurry of anti-Chinese activity during the spring had evoked momentary support, but once Congress pledged action and the California delegation returned home, the issue died of apathy east of the Rockies. Anti-Chinese propaganda had a short shelf life and if not repackaged by politicians or reinvigorated by the press, it disappeared from public view. Party literature and stump speakers ignored the issue, and neither candidate—Ohio governor Rutherford B. Hayes, who triumphed over the scandal-tainted Blaine for the Republican nomination, or Democrat Samuel Tilden—mentioned the Chinese once the campaign got under way. Even the opening of the congressional investigation in San Francisco in October created few ripples. As *Scribner's Monthly* noted that fall, easterners displayed "marked indifference" toward the Chinese question. Politicians realized that the issue could galvanize voters in the West but that it carried little appeal in the East, and despite countless opportunities throughout the campaign to make political capital on the Chinese, neither Democrats nor Republicans east of the Rockies raised the issue. As the *New York Herald* observed, "The democrats may gain a few votes in California by the strong declaration in their platform against the Chinamen, but elsewhere the question has no interest."[26]

This same pattern—initial excitement in the spring followed by utter apathy in the fall—can also be found among workers. In the wake of the West Coast anti-Chinese agitation in April, the labor press responded at once. Three pro-labor newspapers—the *National Labor Tribune* (Pittsburgh), *Workingman's Map* (Indianapolis), and *Irish World* (New York)—echoed the mainstream press with anti-Chinese editorials urging modification of the Burlingame Treaty. One labor convention in Pittsburgh passed a resolution to this effect. These actions made it seem as though the anti-Chinese movement was picking up steam, but as dramatically as it had appeared, it stopped: efforts to whip up anti-Chinese hatred ultimately fell flat. In Indiana, for example, the *Workingman's Map* urged workers to hold a mass meeting and organize a boycott against Chinese laundries. Nothing happened. "It is very singular," a subscriber later wrote, "that the horney-handed washwomen do not make a crusade on the Chinese in this city." The *Map* renewed the call for a boycott but to no avail. The anti-Chinese campaign made no observable headway among workers, and the *Workingman's Advocate* conceded as much. Despite his herculean efforts against the Chinese for the past seven years, editor Andrew C. Cameron ruefully admitted in 1876 the "apparent apathy which now prevails on this important subject." One can only speculate how Cameron felt when a Philadelphia cigar makers union admitted thirty new members that fall, with "Americans, Englishmen, Germans, Spaniards, Cubans, and even Chinamen present at the meeting."[27]

To many workers, the Chinese had become the symbol of the problem but not the problem itself. At a meeting of the Boston Eight-Hour League in May, the three luminaries of the New England labor movement—George Gunton, Ira Steward, and George McNeill—addressed this matter. Gunton emphasized that the "economical" lifestyle of the Chinese drained the American economy, while Steward warned of the "the vast reservoir of cheap labor—millions of six cent a day Chinamen" who could at any time venture eastward, but neither speaker advocated exclusion or immigration restriction as a solution. "Nothing will save us," Steward said, "but the statesmanship that can make labor dearer everywhere." McNeill likewise warned of the dangers not of *Chinese* labor but of *cheap* labor. All labor must rise together, he said: "Our platform is the platform of *Labor*;—not the labor of Massachusetts, not the labor of New England, not even the labor of the United States. We do not want any man on our platform who does not propose to benefit the labor of the whole world, no matter, whether he be German, Irish, Chinese, or Japanese." Reflecting these distinctions, the platform adopted by the league urged workers "everywhere" to read Senator Sargent's recent speech not to foment hostility toward the Chinese but to learn "of the terrors of *cheap* labor." The Eight-Hour League framed the issue not in terms of ethnic hatred but on the basis of economics and politics. As one resolution stated, "The most highly paid labor the world ever saw, was necessary to make a Republican form of government possible; and confidence in the Republic falls, when wages fall." Therefore, "the question is not narrowed to a conflict between Chinese and American laborers, but is between the *cheap* labor and the *dear* labor of the whole world."[28]

The newly founded *Socialist* (New York) took these sentiments a step further. "We do not object to the Chinaman as a Chinaman," an editorial stated in June, the same month the Republican and Democratic conventions met, "but we object to him as a coolie, the same as we would object to a French, English, or German, if he comes to this country under the same economic conditions. We object to the system, and not to the man; as we objected to slavery, and not to the negro." Although the *Socialist* printed numerous letters from California subscribers denouncing the Chinese, it also printed letters from easterners defending them, and editorials criticized western workers for their involvement in the anti-Chinese movement. "Organize and agitate for the abolition of the coolie system, and when that is achieved, agitate for the abolition of the capitalist," the *Socialist* advised workers in the West. "The coolie is a slave, the wage laborer is a slave, and the capitalist in both cases is a slave-holder. Organize, organize, organize, but, *don't kill the coolie!*"[29]

The extremes within the labor press—between, for example, the *Workingman's Map* and the *Socialist*—coupled with the equivocal attitudes expressed by labor leaders, illustrate that when it came to Chinese immigration, organized labor was neither much ahead nor much behind the rest of society. Even during the peak period of western agitation, most workers paid the issue no heed. An exhaustive search of labor meetings throughout the East and Midwest from March to June reveals that the issue seldom surfaced, and for the remainder of the presidential campaign it completely disappeared from organized labor's agenda. This same lack of interest is reflected in the two fledgling pro-labor political parties of the period: the Greenback-Labor Party and the Workingmen's Party of the United States. Organized in 1875, the Greenback-Labor Party included middle-class reformers, agrarian business leaders, and pro-labor activists. Their major demand was for the government to reissue large amounts of paper money—greenbacks—to increase the nation's currency supply. Greenbacks had helped the North finance the Civil War, and their large-scale reintroduction, Greenbackers argued, would raise wages, wrest financial power from "monopolists and bondholders," and return the economy to the people. Opponents ridiculed the "rag" money idea as inflationary and unworkable, but in the depths of the depression currency reform drew adherents, and Greenback clubs sprang up in many states. Greenbackers quickly became the largest third party of the decade and would soon mount forceful challenges to Democrats and Republicans. While greenbacks remained the party's raison d'être, leaders tried to boost membership by advocating pro-labor measures, such as eight-hour legislation and a national bureau of labor statistics, and organizers included former National Labor Union officials Richard Trevellick, Alexander Troup, John Hinchcliffe, and Robert Schilling. The Greenback-Labor Party would ultimately play a role in the anti-Chinese movement, but in its early days the issue held no prominence. At county and state conventions during the centennial year, the issue failed to surface, and neither the party platform nor its presidential candidate, eighty-five-year-old inventor Peter Cooper, ever raised the issue. Unlike Republicans and Democrats, Greenbackers remained mum. For a party reaching out to workers, anti-Chinese politics was not the trick.[30]

If mainstream politicians criticized Greenbackers from the right, Socialists did so from the left. Currency reform would provide workers few tangible benefits, Socialists argued, and in July 1876, they organized their own party, the Workingmen's Party of the United States. Modeling itself after the recently collapsed International Workingmen's Association, this new socialist party claimed thousands of German- and English-speaking members and ran candidates in numerous states. The Workingmen's platform made no mention of Chinese immigration or exclusion. In the centennial year, immigration restriction was not an issue with which a self-proclaimed national workers' party chose to be identified.[31]

It is impossible to know exactly what workers spoke about on the job, at home, at their neighborhood taverns, or in private conversations. Even for official gatherings we are dependent on scattered reports and secondhand observations. Nonetheless, it is curious that all the scare tactics used by congressmen, western leaders, and the labor press had so little observable effect on working people east of the Rockies. The massive bombardment of anti-Chinese rhetoric made a strong, sudden impact on everyone in the East, and then fell with a thud. From offhand comments to formal platforms, the evidence reveals scant interest among workers in Chinese immigration restriction. Sparks that could have set off major confrontations or protests—a fistfight in June between a white man and two Chinese launderers in lower Manhattan, rumors during the spring that Chinese laborers had been imported to work on the Long Island Railroad, the naturalization of seven Chinese in the fall so they could vote in the election, or a tour in October by two Chinese officials from the Philadelphia Centennial Exposition to schools and factories in New York— simply extinguished themselves without causing an uproar. Had workers sought an impetus to mobilize anti-Chinese sentiment or needed a catalyst to urge hostile legislation, any of these incidents could have sufficed. But nothing happened. The first wave of anti-Chinese activity crested early in the East without engulfing working people.[32]

Politicians, however, were another matter. The hunt for votes in the West had made Chinese immigration an important issue to national office seekers and their political parties. As everyone had predicted, the election of 1876 proved extremely close: Rutherford B. Hayes carried California by a slim twenty-eight hundred ballots, and without the state's six electoral votes, he would have lost the race, and Republicans, the White House. "California," the *Chicago Times* noted, "would never have given him her vote if there had not been an anti-Chinese plank in the Cincinnati platform." Both the Republican and Democratic platforms revealed the growing significance of the Chinese issue, even though eastern politicians had not yet learned to manipulate their local constituencies with it. The centennial year showed that Chinese immigration could spark excitement but that such excitement was neither indigenous nor self-sustaining. It would need careful nurturance to be successfully exploited. Recognizing that workers in the East and Midwest exhibited little interest in Chinese immigration, politicians did not trumpet the issue in their name. Realizing that class disputes still took a backseat to sectional disputes, politicians kept the issue in abeyance. But politicians also recognized the underlying racism pervading American society and that a handy issue might be theirs for the taking. To politicians, 1876 served as a trial run, during which they laid the groundwork for future campaigns. With class tensions approaching the breaking point throughout the country, politicians would simply have to follow the lead of an "old toiler" from California who pleaded with eastern wage earners to "arouse yourselves from your lethargy." Workers had not responded, but politicians were beginning to. The explosion of class conflict in 1877 would provide politicians with the volatile climate necessary to transform Chinese immigration from a regional concern into a sustained national issue.[33]

The time has evidently come when the Chinese question has grown to such an importance as to demand from Congress a more careful examination than it has heretofore received.
—*New York Tribune*,
November 30, 1877

CHAPTER SIX

The Reign of Terror to Come

Uprising and Red Scare, 1877–1878

At a St. Patrick's Day banquet in Hartford, Connecticut, in 1877, an Irishman proposed a toast to "China and Ireland—The two ancient nations." Yung Wing, director of the Chinese Educational Mission, a school for Chinese boys located in Hartford, saluted the revelers: "I would simply say that however the two people may now differ in manners and customs, in politics and religion, the day, I hope, is not far distant when these differences will vanish before the light of knowledge and truth, as the *two races progress in Christian education and civilization.*" The celebrants warmly greeted these sentiments, the *Irish World* noted, and the spirit of merrymaking carried on late into the evening.[1]

Such tributes to interethnic unity existed but seldom received headlines in early 1877, as most newspapers focused on the unresolved presidential election. Samuel Tilden had carried the popular vote and seemed to have edged out Rutherford B. Hayes in the electoral count as well, but disputed returns from four states prevented either candidate from securing a majority, throwing the election into Congress. After three months of bitter partisan fury, Congress remained deadlocked, and in late February, as Grant's term neared its end, the president still lacked a successor. On March 2, just hours before Inauguration Day, a mix of political deals—chief among them an end to Reconstruction—finally awarded the White House to Hayes by a single electoral vote. The crisis had passed, but charges of conniving and corruption would dog Hayes, who had promised to serve just one term, throughout his presidency. "Rutherfraud" became a popular sobriquet.[2]

On February 28, at the peak of the electoral controversy, Congress released its report on Chinese immigration. The committee had held seventeen sessions in San Francisco and had taken testimony from 128 manufacturers, ministers, public officials, and workers, who answered a series of questions loaded against the Chinese. "What is the condition of their health and their habits of cleanliness and sanitary regulations?" read one. "Do they prevent the immigration of white labor to this coast from Europe and from the eastern states?" read a second. Philip Roach, Frank Pixley, and Mayor Andrew Bryant testified and questioned witnesses, while leaders of the Anti-Chinese Union and three local "anti-coolie" clubs observed the proceedings. No Chinese testified. Although numerous witnesses defended the Chinese, many others attacked them, recycling the familiar charges of immorality, nonassimilation, and cheap labor. "Chinese immigration involves sordid wages, no public schools, and the absence of the family," chairman Aaron A. Sargent (R-Calif.) wrote in the committee's majority report. A "revolting" and "pernicious" people who pose "a continual menace" to American society, "they are cruel and indifferent to their sick . . . have no knowledge of or appreciation for our institutions," and lack "sufficient brain capacity . . . for self-government." Sargent's hostile report recommended both modification of the Burlingame Treaty and legislation "to restrain the great influx of Asiatics to this country." Two minority reports emerged. One, written by Representative Edwin R. Meade (D-N.Y.), varied little from Sargent's, but the second, by Senator Oliver P. Morton (R-Ind.), differed sharply. Deploring the racial prejudice in California, Morton urged open immigration. His report, however, gathered from his private papers, appeared posthumously almost a year later, and critics challenged its authenticity. Despite the official nature of the inquiry and more than twelve hundred pages of testimony, the congressional investigation had limited impact. Witnesses offered little that was new, and their undisguised prejudice robbed the investigation of its claim to objectivity. Even those sympathetic to the Chinese, such as railroad magnate Charles Crocker, who had hired some ten thousand of them to build the transcontinental railroad, remarked: "I preferred white labor. . . . I believe that white population is better for the country than Chinese population. . . . I want to be on record as saying that the white immigrant is worth more to the country than any other." The poor timing of the report's release further dampened its effect.[3]

A brutal massacre two weeks later captured more headlines than all the pages of testimony released by Congress. On March 13, armed white men in Chico, California, stormed a cabin where Chinese workers were resting. Without provocation, the whites opened fire, then threw oil on the bodies and set the cabin ablaze. Editorials of outrage deploring the "Chico Massacre" appeared everywhere, but even this grisly episode—one of many involving white violence against Chinese immigrants in the nineteenth century—receded quickly from the spotlight. The anti-Chinese movement remained stalled and localized in the West. The newly elected Congress would not convene until the end of the year, and with 1877 an off year for elections, politicians had little interest in raising the issue.[4]

Nor did workers. With the United States entrenched in its fourth year of depression, their suffering and frustration—and inflammatory rhetoric—mounted throughout the winter. In Scranton, Pennsylvania, hungry workers marched through a snowstorm, demanding "bread or blood," "relief or riot." The *New York Herald* quoted an unemployed laborer saying that a workers' revolution was a distinct possibility, and the *New York Labor Standard* observed that "in every State of the Union men are out of employment by thousands. The poorhouses and prisons are full to overflowing; . . . an army of tramps, homeless and desperate, wander back and forth through all the land, while our cities swarm with the destitute and starving." Such widespread misery prompted Henry George to write *Progress and Poverty*, the masterpiece that posed the nation's fundamental economic question of the late nineteenth century: How in a land of such wealth could so much poverty exist? George's 1879 treatise proposed a new taxation policy on urban land as the solution, but such a remedy offered little immediate relief for the unemployed. Labor violence erupted sporadically throughout the depression: in Pennsylvania in 1874, in Indiana in 1875, and in New York in May 1877. Nothing, however, prepared the country for the labor uprising that broke out in the summer of 1877 when railroad workers sparked the first nationwide general strike in American history. It began in Martinsburg, West Virginia, on July 16 when workers blocked a train from passing through town until the company rescinded a wage cut. The company refused, and the governor sent the militia to disperse the striking workers. Backed by the community, however, the strikers resisted and scattered the soldiers. This momentary victory ignited similar revolts in Buffalo, Pittsburgh, Chicago, and smaller towns across the country. Workers everywhere walked off the job, and in some cities business practically stopped. As the strike spread through the Midwest and into the South, governors called out state militia, and when local soldiers could not quell the uprising, President Hayes sent in federal troops. From Boston to St. Louis, from Newark to Baltimore, workers in city after city gathered by the thousands to support the strikers and denounce government repression. Never before had the United States witnessed such an outpouring of revolutionary rhetoric and proletarian protest, as laborers demanded jobs, justice, and bread. "We are," Albert Parsons told a desperate crowd of twenty thousand in Chicago, "the grand army of starvation."[5]

Fears of revolution and anarchy dominated headlines for the rest of the month. "The Reign of Mob Law," trumpeted the *New York Times* on July 25. "Thieves and Ruffians Still Leading the Strikes." "Pittsburgh Sacked," the *New York World* noted, "in the hands of men dominated by the devilish spirit of Communism." The *New York Herald* urged soldiers to shoot into the crowd; even the generally pro-labor *New York Sun* urged "a diet of lead for the hungry strikers." And the sanctimonious Brooklyn minister Henry Ward Beecher earned the everlasting enmity of workers everywhere by declaring that a man unable to survive on bread and water and a dollar a day wasn't fit to live. By month's end, more than a hundred people were dead and millions of dollars of property lay in ruins.[6]

The railroad strike was the most significant national event of the decade. It bared for all to see the deepening social divisions that Americans had been denying for years, and violently jolted the nation into the Gilded Age of working-class radicalism, federal military intervention, and widespread red-baiting. A watershed coming at the end of Reconstruction, the strike symbolically marked the close of the Civil War era. Some of the troops that were used to suppress the strike, in fact, had just been withdrawn from the South by Hayes as part of the deal for the presidency. But politics aside, the preindustrial world of artisans and journeymen had practically vanished, making way for a new world of massive corporate enterprise, heavily capitalized industry, and endless confrontations between labor and capital.

An indirect result of the labor uprising of 1877 was the Chinese Exclusion Act. Although workers would continue to express only minimal interest in immigration restriction, other groups would begin to see it as a solution for the nation's industrial problems. Class tensions remained high for the next twelve months as politicians, editors, and clergy voiced fears of an armed proletariat poised for revolution. This atmosphere of violence and uncertainty breathed new life into the anti-Chinese movement among those seeking to eliminate or defuse class tensions.

The major reforms sought by organized labor during the 1870s all shared one common feature: the need for government intervention. Whether public works programs, nationalization of railroads, a federal bureau of labor statistics, or the abolition of imported contract labor, each predicated a large, active state for implementation. The Civil War had witnessed the peak of government intervention in national and local affairs. In issuing greenbacks, drafting soldiers, liberating slaves, and pursuing reconstruction, the federal government had assumed unprecedented powers. The rise of an active state, however, frightened many Americans, who recoiled at the prospect of an all-powerful government. What might such a government do if controlled by the "communistic," working-class "rabble"? Workers, after all, composed a large percentage of the nation's voters. Fear of an active state contributed to the collapse of Reconstruction and underlay much of the Liberal Republican bolt of the early 1870s. But if Republicans (and Democrats) could begin preaching a small-government, laissez-faire philosophy, they still could not ignore the class divisions renting society. Something had to be done to mollify workers. From this crucible of political stagnation and labor violence, Chinese exclusion emerged as a savior to leaders in Washington. After 1877, politicians would increasingly appropriate the issue of Chinese exclusion and couch it in the language of a class imperative. Chinese exclusion served as a panacea for a complex web of problems, with politicians striving to turn a regional, cross-class issue into a national, working-class demand. Although immigration restriction offered scant relief and appealed to few wage earners, politicians seized it, amid the clamor for government retrenchment, as an easy solution with which they could pose as defenders of working people everywhere. As a result of the national railroad strike, Chinese exclusion would find new champions in the highest echelons of government.

Though this process would take time, the labor uprising also had the more immediate effect of invigorating the anti-Chinese movement in the West. In late July, workers in San Francisco held a mass meeting to express support for strikers back east. Near the end of the evening, members of an "anti-coolie" club barged in and commandeered the audience. With cries of "On to Chinatown," gangs of men and boys began roaming the city and quickly demolished twenty Chinese laundries and buildings, the most serious disturbance in San Francisco history. The rampage continued the next day, when "hoodlums," as the rioters were called, attempted to burn the docks and ships of the Pacific Mail Steamship company, the main transporter of Chinese immigrants. With assistance from the U.S. Navy, a vigilante-style group of four thousand volunteers battled the hoodlums, and a third day of violence left four men dead and fourteen wounded. With this, the riots finally ended. But California workingmen's meetings did not.[7]

In August, San Francisco workers and sympathizers began meeting on a large open space near City Hall called the "sandlots." Amid the glow of bonfires and torches, sandlot speakers rabidly denounced corporations, monopolies, and the Chinese. In September and October, the group organized itself into the Workingmen's Party of California and elected Denis Kearney president. The sandlots' most fiery orator, Kearney rallied supporters with the cry "The Chinese Must Go" and threatened violence to achieve this end. Kearney's appeal proved magnetic, and egged on by the press, sandlot audiences grew rapidly, embracing all segments of society. "Clerks and the better class of citizens now began to attend his meetings," the eminent observer Lord Bryce wrote, and the Workingmen's Party soon became an important factor in California politics.[8]

The labor uprising of 1877 breathed new life into the anti-Chinese movement in California and galvanized workers nationwide. As news from San Francisco filtered east throughout the summer, numerous strikes broke out in city after city. The most significant of these, and one that directly raised the subject of Chinese labor, occurred in New York City when cigar makers struck to abolish the tenement house system. The cigar-making industry had been one of the hardest hit by the depression. Manufacturers had slashed wages during the past two years and fired thousands of workers; earlier in the decade, they had introduced a wooden mold to speed up production, which also led to the deskilling of jobs and consequent hiring of immigrants, women, and minors. "About one-third of the cigar operatives," the New York Tribune noted, "are young children." Many of these children lived and worked with their parents (and grandparents) in squalid tenement house factories owned by landlord employers. Preparing tobacco and rolling cigars for up to sixteen hours a day, they were among the city's most exploited laborers. By 1877 union membership had declined from four thousand to a mere five hundred, but the national railroad strike spurred labor militancy. After two small strikes by organized cigar makers, tenement house workers walked out en masse in October 1877. Samuel Gompers, the twenty-seven-year-old president of the local, initially decried this "reckless precipitate action" taken without approval of the union's executive committee, but he soon followed the strikers' lead. Higher wages and abolition of the tenement house system became everyone's rallying cry.[9]

Cigar makers picketed the major companies and held strategy sessions twice a day. Boisterous rallies conducted in English, German, and Czech became commonplace events supported by all the city's trades. By late October, fifteen thousand cigar makers had joined the walkout. Adolph Strasser, president of the Cigar Makers' International Union, organized a nationwide campaign to raise funds, and up to five hundred dollars arrived daily from workers across the country. Cigar makers distributed small cash benefits to strikers and set up "relief kitchens" to provide food, fuel, and medical assistance. Manufacturers, however, refused to budge. They defended the tenement house system and retaliated by instituting lockouts and evicting workers from their homes. "The distress that followed was appalling," Gompers later wrote, as employers threw impoverished families onto the street.[10]

One of the strike's notable features was its diversity and solidarity. Women played key roles in the walkout, appearing at every meeting, marching on every picket line, and suffering repeated arrests for strike activity. The walkout had a genuinely international flavor. Although primarily German-, Bohemian-, and native-born, strikers included Cuban, Spanish, and Chinese workers. Labor journals highlighted this ethnic cohesiveness. "Even CHINAMEN," the *New York Labor Standard* observed, "have asserted their manhood in this strike and have risen to the dignity of the American trade unionists." Demanding higher wages, four Chinese cigar makers joined their coworkers in marching out of the factory of Wangler and Hahn. Another walked out at Jacoby's establishment. These may have been among the Chinese who applied for relief from the strike committee and, for reasons not explained, received an extra dollar in rations. In a double-edged compliment, the *Labor Standard* remarked that in joining the strike, the Chinese "showed themselves capable of *real* civilization." The striking Chinese were also a source for inspiration, emboldening workers in other states. As a potter in Trenton, New Jersey, observed, "The numbers who have joined the great uprising of the cigarmakers, the rapidity with which the movement is spreading, and the fact that both sexes, and even the Chinamen have asserted their rights, affords ample evidence that . . . their demands are moderate and just."[11]

But the strike had an ugly side as well. Rumors swirled that manufacturers had wired California for Chinese laborers. "Holtzman & Deutsenberger," the *Tribune* noted on October 19, "will employ Chinese if the old workmen do not return to work." An unnamed "San Francisco firm," the report continued, "had promised from 200 to 400 Chinese. The news caused great excitement among the strikers." And with good reason, for after the shoe industry, cigar making was the trade hardest hit by Chinese laborers in the West. Chinese often underbid white workers in San Francisco and in some cigar factories completely dominated the labor force. In early November, the *Herald* claimed that the rumor of imported Chinese workers "is fully confirmed" and that Straiton and Storm, one of the city's largest manufacturers, planned to spend forty thousand dollars "on the experiment." Straiton and Storm, the *Herald* added, had hired three hundred Chinese workers on a one-year contract: "It is not so much a question of prices as whether or not they shall have control of their own shops, since they cannot get non-union men, they will engage experienced Chinese workmen, any number of whom can be had in San Francisco." Some workers dismissed the report. The *Cigar Makers' Official Journal*, the union's mouthpiece, called the threat "ridiculous," nothing more than a "scarecrow" to frighten strikers, while union president Strasser commented that he "did not fear any incursion in this city of Chinese workmen."[12]

Rumors persisted, however, and the specter loomed of a second North Adams. Manufacturers exploited these rumors to drive a wedge between strikers. One employer hired a Chinese immigrant merely "to walk in and out of his factory, endeavoring to make the pickets believe that the Chinaman had already arrived from San Francisco," while another hired several scabs, dressed them "as Chinamen," and made them wear queues. The *Cigar Makers' Official Journal* discovered the latter ruse and printed their identities. "Let them be branded indelibly," the *Journal* declared. Manufacturers' ploys, rumors, and threats paid off. Strikers began calling scabs "Chinamen." In the yard of one shop, workers hanged a scab in effigy bearing the label, "So we will serve every Chinaman." And when one family broke ranks and returned to a tenement house, "they were saluted with cries of 'Chinamen.'"[13]

Manufacturers had rediscovered a potent weapon to intimidate workers: the exploitation of racial and ethnic tensions. But traditional methods of crushing resistance remained more effective. With the onset of winter, manufacturers expanded the lockout and fired key workers. These actions, Gompers wrote, broke "the financial backbone of the strike," and after 107 days, the strike collapsed in January 1878. "It was," Gompers recalled more than forty years later, "a wonderful fight" filled with "heroic sacrifices." He labeled it "the great strike" and "an important turning-point in the history of the Cigarmakers' Union." In enumerating the strike's accomplishments—tighter organization, centralized leadership, and authorized benefits—Gompers omitted the ethnic infighting and ethnic solidarity. A lifetime of union struggles may well have chastened him, but at the time, ethnic cohesiveness—or lack thereof—was one of the key lessons the strike taught. Shortly afterward, the *Cigar Makers' Official Journal* noted that a Philadelphia local composed of Cubans, Spaniards, Chinese, and blacks waged a successful strike, only because "appeals to national prejudices . . . were in vain."[14]

The great cigar makers' strike of 1877–78 had shown both the strength and fragility of interethnic and interracial unity. When exacerbated by manufacturers' threats and race-baiting tactics, anti-Chinese sentiment could emerge. Otherwise it remained dormant, nascent, checked. Despite the myriad tensions and ongoing threats to import Chinese laborers during the strike, no cries surfaced for immigration restriction or Chinese exclusion. "There is perhaps no other trade which embraces such a mixed element," the *Cigar*

Makers' Official Journal noted. The heterogeneous union "invites all cigar-makers, skilled or unskilled without any distinction of color, sex, nationality or creed to rally under its banner." Recounting the strike's highlights, the *New York Labor Standard* observed, "That was a glorious moment for labor when Bohemians, Germans, English, and even Chinese, clung to each other for support and learned that in union only is there strength."[15]

The strike by cigar makers had a lasting impact on workers' attitudes toward Chinese immigration. Despite growing pressure from sandlotters, Kearneyites, and westerners, the "glorious moment" of clinging "to each other for support" checked the growth of the anti-Chinese movement in the East. But headway was being made, and as a survey of the labor press reveals, contrary views began to surface. The *Labor Standard* remained steadfast against exclusion. "The cry that the 'Chinese must go' is both narrow and unjust," the New York weekly declared on June 30, 1878. "It represents no broad or universal principle," resembling instead the old nativist cry of the Know-Nothings, which was "intolerant, silly, and shameful." The collapse of the Know-Nothings in the 1850s taught a lesson. "In our day we must commit no such blunders," the *Labor Standard* continued, "we have no right to raise a cry against any class of human beings because of their nationality." Importation remained the enemy, whether conducted "from Europe or Asia," and the journal denounced as "wild and unwise" the anti-Chinese crusade of the sandlotters in San Francisco. Despite its stated opposition, the *Labor Standard* began to use the newly popularized verb "Chineize"—meaning to lower wages and tame workers—and devoted considerable space to western correspondents critical of Chinese immigration. Letters from subscribers east of the Rockies scarcely ever raised the subject, however, and when they did they couched it in the context of importation rather than race or nationality. As "A Factory Slave" argued in linking Calvin Sampson in North Adams to cigar manufacturers in New York City, workers required "international" solutions to their problems: "No better evidence is needed of this fact than the way capitalists import workmen from one locality and even one country to another in order to thwart the objects of workmen everywhere in improving their condition."[16]

Other eastern labor journals, such as the *Socialist* of Detroit and the *National Socialist* of Cincinnati, showed greater diversity of opinion. They printed occasional articles on the "evils" caused by Chinese laborers, including a harsh indictment from a Philadelphian who quoted heavily from the recent congressional investigation. Brief but equally hostile articles also appeared, prompting one subscriber, B. E. G. Jewett of Evansville, Indiana, to upbraid his fellow workers: "In the first place . . . cease to combat the Chinamen as a class. . . . The Chinamen coming here of his own accord and at his own expense of accumulated earnings, has as much right here as you or any German, Russ, Switzer, Frank, Turk, Pole, Irish or Ethiopian in the land; . . . they shall NOT be debarred that privilege [sic]."[17]

By 1878, a debate of sorts had emerged within the labor press on Chinese immigration. While exclusion sentiment remained largely localized on the West Coast, some had begun to creep eastward, but still not much. At the first official gathering of the still-secret Knights of Labor in January, delegates raised more than a dozen issues of concern to workers, from the eight-hour day to the abolition of contract labor. Chinese immigration was not among them. Five months later, some twenty thousand workers gathered in Chicago at a massive demonstration sponsored by the Amalgamated Trades and Labor Unions. The nation's most prominent labor leaders delivered speeches, including eight-hours advocate George McNeill. "The present workingmen's movement was for all, without distinction of race, color, nationality, politics, or religion," he told the audience. "It mattered nothing . . . whether a man was born in Africa or China, in Europe or America." When he added that he "wanted Chinamen in America, if they would work for American wages," the crowd applauded. "They [the working people] did not want to keep the Chinamen out," McNeill declared, "but they wanted to do away with the Six Companies so that men should not be able to work in America for wages contracted on foreign soil." This concluding sentence, the *Chicago Times* noted, received "great cheering."[18]

Although eastern workers remained generally sympathetic, though largely indifferent, to Chinese immigration, more powerful forces in the East began airing hostility. A few weeks before the strike by cigar makers broke out, Edwin R. Meade, the former New York representative who had written a minority report for the congressional investigation of Chinese immigration, delivered a paper at the annual meeting of the American Social Science Association in Saratoga, New York. This twelve-year-old organization of middle-class humanitarians, patrician reformers, and Republican intellectuals gathered regularly to discuss current events and social problems and to suggest ameliorative actions. Meade's topic at the September 1877 gathering was Chinese immigration. Attacking the Chinese on moral, economic, and racial grounds, the former congressman recommended total exclusion. A Dr. Harris agreed, adding that the Chinese propagated disease, whereas a Rev. Fessenden of Connecticut dissented, noting that several Chinese students were attending Yale. Other members favored Chinese immigration yet not without qualification, one man noting that the issue "require[s] careful investigation." Franklin B. Sanborn, aging abolitionist and the association's founder, considered the question moot because the Chinese "were not an emigrating people," but economist and former Liberal Republican David A. Wells was less sanguine. He feared the impact of large numbers of Chinese immigrants who would not conform to American ways. "A stone in the stomach of the body-politic," Wells remarked, "which will neither digest nor assimilate." In time, he said, "they would have . . . to get out of our way."[19]

Other prominent intellectuals added their voices to the cry for restriction. "I confess to a very deep-seated dread of this influx of Asiatics," wrote Andrew White, president of Cornell University, while the Rev. Charles Hodge, president of Princeton, called "the evil . . . so great" that "something surely ought to be done." After pondering "closer relations with our pig-tailed brethren," poet and editor William Cullen Bryant remarked, "I do not contemplate it with any pleasure; I prefer the Caucasian race." In January 1878, the conservative *North American Review*, the nation's oldest magazine, published an article hysterically denouncing the Chinese. Centuries of "savage life" had taught them to survive in meager surroundings, the author M. J. Dee argued, enabling "the Chinaman [to] live and accumulate a surplus where the Caucasian would starve." Attempting to place the issue of Chinese immigration on a strictly scientific basis, Dee invoked both Malthusian economics and Social Darwinism: "His miserable little figure, his pinched and wretched way of living, his slavish and tireless industry, . . . his capacity to live in swarms in wretched dens where the white man would rot . . . all these make him a most formidable rival for ultimate survival as the fittest, not only in America, but wherever he may find a footing." By using cold, hard "facts," Dee showed how modern science could supply a strong, "objective" argument for Chinese exclusion. As remarks by the American Social Science Association, university presidents, and the *North American Review* reveal, Chinese immigration was becoming an issue on which "respectable" opinion could disagree. The educated "best men" of society could oppose the Chinese as emphatically as could anyone.[20]

While eastern patricians debated the issue at conferences and in journals, Californians again seized the offensive. Sandlot meetings became increasingly vicious as the autumn of 1877 progressed. "Before you and before the world," Denis Kearney proclaimed that October, "we declare that the Chinaman must leave our shores. We declare that white men, and women, and boys, and girls, cannot live as the people of the great republic should and compete with the single Chinese coolie in the labor market. . . . Death is preferable to an American to life on a par with the Chinaman." Kearney inveighed listeners to hang government officials, burn the mansions of the rich, and "cut the capitalists to pieces." At a massive Thanksgiving Day demonstration, speakers, resolutions, and banners called for an end to Chinese immigration. One image portrayed Uncle Sam beside a Chinese immigrant. "The Mongol bore a broadsword, [labeled] 'The industries of the United States,'" the *San Francisco Chronicle* noted, "while his queue was coiled like a boa constrictor around poor Uncle Sam, who was gasping for breath." Another showed a scale with the United States on one side, China on the other, with the caption, "The Press our lever and public opinion our fulcrum."[21]

Concurrent with these events, Governor William Irwin delivered a strong speech raising the fear of Asian civilization overrunning America, and Representative Horace F. Page (R-Calif.) wrote a lengthy letter to President Hayes urging immediate action. The State Senate sent a memorial to Congress demanding Chinese exclusion—a stance, the document claimed, supported by all Californians. Even the *New York Tribune* conceded the issue's broad popularity on the Pacific Coast. "Eastern tourists, visiting California," the staunch Republican journal noted in November, "have . . . seldom failed to return strongly impressed with the unanimity of sentiment upon the subject which they found to exist there, and with the arguments of people, whose intelligence raised them above a vulgar hatred of an inferior race." These developments led the *Tribune*, largely sympathetic to Chinese immigration, to rethink its position: "The time has evidently come when the Chinese question has grown to such an importance as to demand from Congress a more careful examination than it has heretofore received. . . . If Chinese labor is a tithe of the evil it is pictured to be, then it is time that the fact was known to the whole country, and a remedy found and applied."[22]

Three weeks later, as the strike by cigar makers reached its peak in New York City, the *Tribune* highlighted a visit to Washington, D.C., by Darius Ogden Mills, former president of the Bank of California. The banker met with "several leading public men" who questioned him on the Chinese. Mills praised the Asian immigrants. "They are industrious and peaceable," he said, and they work cheap. But he admitted they presented a problem. "It might be well," he said, "for Congress to check temporarily the flow of Chinese emigration." Despite this comment, the *Tribune* editorialized that Mills was "strongly in favor of the Chinese."[23] Perhaps so, but the difference between pro- and anti-Chinese attitudes was becoming increasingly murky.

This series of events—sandlot meetings in San Francisco, efforts by California politicians, and increasing doubts among the influential in the East— approached a climax during the winter of 1877–78 as the 45th Congress convened in Washington. "The delegates from the Pacific Coast," one journal reported, "declare their intention of forcing legislation on the Chinese question during the coming session." Indeed, during the opening weeks of the new Congress, lawmakers introduced a dozen different anti-Chinese bills, most of which called for immigration restriction or outright exclusion. At a cabinet meeting on January 18, 1878, the executive branch seized the initiative. "The President is of opinion," the *Chicago Times* reported, "that a great influx of Chinese immigrants to this country is impolitic and ought to be restricted." Hayes suggested renegotiating the Burlingame Treaty so as to allow the United States to limit Chinese immigration.[24]

In February, a House committee recommended that Hayes open treaty negotiations with China, and in March, Aaron A. Sargent urged the Senate to concur. In a long, vicious speech against the Chinese, the California Republican capitulated much of what he had said two years earlier, only now his statements were cloaked with the authority of a congressional investigation (which he himself had led). Two months later, Senator Timothy O. Howe (R-Wisc.) submitted a resolution calling for a new treaty so that "the unrestricted emigration to this country from China might wisely be modified." Senator Hannibal Hamlin (R-Maine), the former vice president, drafted the wording. The resolution passed the Senate on May 25 and the House on June 17. Thus by the spring of 1878, both the executive branch and the legislative branch of the federal government had committed themselves to the restriction of Chinese immigration.[25]

This commitment by the president and by Congress marked a milestone in the anti-Chinese movement. The unceasing agitation on the West Coast had at last succeeded in winning over a powerful ally: the federal government. The westerners' success stemmed not only from their decade-long persistence but from the convergence of two unexpected events—a red scare and a growing third party—made possible by the ongoing depression and the continuing specter of class conflict. The period following the national railroad strike was an unusual one in American history. The labor uprising had propelled the nation into a new era, posing problems many Americans neither understood nor anticipated. Class conflict had long been considered a European phenomenon, not one that existed in a free, expanding, egalitarian republic. The violence of July 1877, however, brutally called these assumptions into question, and the press responded with uncharacteristic vigor. After years of little more than scattered articles on labor activity, newspapers suddenly teemed with reports of union meetings, radical speeches, and interviews with common workers. The "labor question" entered the national arena turbulently, and Americans searched for answers and explanations. This heightened interest in the "labor question" had an unexpected consequence: the first red scare in

American history. Unlike later red scares, which have been well documented, the red scare of 1878 has received little attention. Perhaps because no one was killed, few were arrested, and no publications were suppressed, this episode has escaped notice. But in the spring of 1878 it was the dominant topic of conversation, as fears of a communist uprising electrified the nation.

The red scare originated in Chicago. Following the election of Socialist Frank Stauber to the City Council in April, the *Tribune* and *Inter-Ocean* published articles on "the dangers of communism." Alarmed by "the recent performances of the Commune," the *Inter-Ocean* reported, citizens had contacted the military to learn if "the city could depend on the army in case of trouble with the Communists." Reports of armed Socialists drilling on vacant lots fueled fears, and with the uprising of the previous summer still fresh in people's minds, both newspapers urged reinforcement of the local militia. "There is distrust, dissatisfaction, discontent about us everywhere," the *Inter-Ocean* warned. Rumor and fear spread the hysteria to other cities, with newspapers reporting Socialists armed and carrying out maneuvers in St. Louis, Cincinnati, Cleveland, and New York. Further north, labor violence racked Montreal and Quebec. Washington buzzed as politicians talked of "communist . . . mischief" racing across the country, and many fixed on June 16 as the date for the uprising to begin. The press brimmed with anticommunist editorials and articles. The *New York Herald* and *World* blamed foreign-born radicals. "They are the reddest of Red Republicans," the *World* wrote, "professional revolutionists . . . implacable enemies to the republican form of government . . . [who] maintain correspondence with communists all over the world. . . . To them the Tompkins square meetings were mere child's play, and the outbreak of the railroad strikers of last year but a mild warning of the reign of terror to come." Pro-labor journals were no less frightened. "Communistic movement of alarming proportions has been inaugurated," the *Boston Globe* noted. It was planning "hostilities against law and order . . . [and] having for an object a grand division of property, irrespective of ownership." The *Globe* printed reports of communist activity in Chicago, Pittsburgh, St. Louis, and San Francisco, as well as in such small towns as Omaha, Parkersburg, West Virginia, and Brownsville, Texas. Revolutionists, it seemed, were everywhere. As the *New York Herald* commented in June, "We find the rural press laden with articles on Communists and the terrible, awful, gigantic fee-to-fum that is to upset society in a few days."[26]

Radicals and workers dismissed the rumors. In interviews, Chicago Socialists "ridicule[d] the idea of any uprising by their people," calling such charges "absurd" and "senseless verbiage." Albert Parsons deemed the red scare a capitalist ruse designed to expand the military. He had a point. Major William

Frew of Standard Oil in Pittsburgh called for five hundred troops in case of labor unrest, while Chicago merchants demanded the army be bolstered with one hundred thousand new recruits. General William T. Sherman, however, the nation's top military officer, assured citizens that the army was prepared for any emergency. Nothing, of course, happened. On June 16, the date of the expected uprising, America's cities remained calm. No violence erupted, no revolution broke out. Three days later, however, Denis Kearney's Working-men's Party won fifty-one seats—one-third of the total—in the election of delegates to the California state constitutional convention. The prospect of "communists" rewriting a government charter sent shock waves through the eastern press and reinvigorated the red scare.[27]

Amid this atmosphere of tension and uncertainty, the Greenback-Labor Party began showing remarkable growth. Polling 187,000 votes in 1877 (double the previous year), Greenbackers predicted that the next congressional elections would catapult them to power. They generated enormous enthusiasm in early 1878, and Greenback journals sprouted up everywhere. Nicknamed the "rag baby"—an allusion to paper money—the Greenbackers threatened the established parties. Although an entrenched two-party system had existed for more than half a century, the Republican Party was less than a generation old, its longevity by no means assured. As Greenbackers liked to point out, the Republican Party had already achieved its goals—emancipation, union, and reconstruction—and was destined to die out soon. The Greenbackers, on the other hand, with such modern issues as finance and currency reform, signaled the wave of the future. Even the ridicule they encountered evoked the abuse Republicans had faced in the 1850s and reinforced their sense of mission. In an era distinguished by elections decided by razor-thin margins, the Greenback-ers posed a genuine threat: whether as a potential second-party replacement or simply a nettlesome third-party power broker, the Greenbackers presented a viable alternative in a period of massive economic dislocation and great social unrest.[28]

At a convention in Toledo, Ohio, in February 1878, Greenbackers adopted a series of resolutions that would become the party's rallying cry for the next two years. The "Toledo platform" endorsed greenbacks, eight-hour legislation, abolition of prison labor, a graduated income tax, state and national bureaus of labor statistics, and "the full employment of labor." One plank focused on the Chinese: "The importation of servile labor into the United States from China is a problem of the most serious importance, and we recommend legislation looking to its suppression." By adopting these pro-labor planks, Greenbackers hoped to lure Democratic and Republican workers loath to align with the more radical Socialist or Workingmen's Parties. Key organizers included prominent trade unionists Robert Blissert, John Ennis, and George Blair, as well as Knights of Labor leader Terence V. Powderly, who in February 1878 was elected mayor of Scranton, Pennsylvania, on the Greenback ticket. Samuel Gompers had voted the Greenback slate in 1876 and claimed (with just a bit of exaggeration) that he was followed by "practically all the wage-earners of New York." As the *Greenback Standard* of Oshkosh, Wisconsin, noted in 1878, "[This] party is composed of two elements—currency reformers, and rights of labor advocates." Neither of these "two elements" displayed much interest in the Chinese issue. That spring, on one of the rare occasions when the subject arose, Samuel F. Cary, the Greenbackers' vice presidential candidate in 1876, echoed eastern workers, noting that the party "demands that while this country shall continue to be an asylum for the oppressed of all lands, and give equal protection to all emigrants, the *importation* of servile labor shall be prohibited and the offence be severely punished." Greenback strategy seemed to be working: the party swept numerous local offices in the spring of 1878 and fielded candidates for the upcoming congressional elections in thirty-one states. The Greenback threat was real—in fact, in 1878, it was at its peak. Mainstream politicians needed a way to steal their thunder. Mass circulation of paper money, eight-hour legislation, and other reforms remained an apostasy to most lawmakers. Chinese immigration restriction, however, offered an alternative. Eliminating the distinction between immigration and importation, politicians would fashion an issue to rally voters and perhaps defuse the Greenback frenzy.[29]

The convergence of the red scare and Greenback fervor in the spring of 1878 provided a one-two punch propelling politicians to take immediate action. On June 17, the day after the labor uprising was supposed to have occured, Congress adopted its joint resolution urging President Hayes to open treaty negotiations to enable the restriction of Chinese immigration. Two days later, the House authorized an investigation to determine the causes of the depression and pinpoint the demands of American workers. Neither action received much attention, but on July 1, twelve days after Denis Kearney's Workingmen's Party of California scored victories statewide, West Coast congressmen met with the president to discuss Chinese immigration. Hayes promised them that he would promptly open negotiations with China, and the imminent arrival in Washington of the first permanent Chinese legation to the United States would facilitate the process. Secretary of State William M. Evarts seconded the president's motion, acknowledging the need "to check the immigration to our shores of the uncounted millions of Chinese aliens." The secretary of state, the

San Francisco Alta California reported, said that "he was not only willing, but patriotically desirous to aid in erecting proper barriers against this threatening incursion."[30]

The wheels of government had begun to turn. Unprovoked by the demands of organized labor and working people east of the Rocky Mountains, the federal government had set a new national agenda. Exclusion was not yet inevitable, but the direction of American immigration policy was clear. Still, the subject was hardly closed. In fact, eastern workers were on the eve of their greatest challenge on the issue of Chinese immigration and whether to make the cause their own. With the red scare still heavy on people's minds, Denis Kearney, the walking embodiment of the anti-Chinese movement, announced he was coming east to rally workers to back Chinese exclusion.

> The man who would propose
> to dump into the sea the
> people of any nationality, to
> improve the existing state of
> things, has too poor a head,
> and too weak a heart to be a
> leader of the masses.
> —"A Mechanic," *New York
> Witness*, August 15, 1878

CHAPTER SEVEN

An Unduly Inflated Sack of Very Bad Gas

Denis Kearney Comes East, 1878

Denis Kearney left California on July 21, 1878. A self-proclaimed working-class leader and the nation's foremost anti-Chinese agitator, Kearney embarked for the East with three goals: to convince workers to form a workingmen's party, to campaign for Benjamin F. Butler, and to publicize the "dangers" of Chinese immigration. No visit by a West Coast citizen had ever received more publicity or aroused more excitement. The eastern press heralded his arrival as a momentous occasion; indeed, the young Irish immigrant became *the* event of the summer of 1878. Reporters followed his every move and printed every word he uttered. On ground fertilized by Philip Roach, Aaron Sargent, and other western politicians come east, Denis Kearney aimed to raise a harvest of anti-Chinese sentiment. He gave speeches in Massachusetts and then toured the Midwest. Crowds flocked to hear him in Indianapolis, Chicago, St. Louis, Bloomington, Cincinnati, and Columbus. He visited Washington, where he gained an audience with the president, and he later spoke in Philadelphia, Newark, Jersey City, Brooklyn, Troy, Baltimore, and New York City, where, one newspaper claimed, he drew the largest crowd since the Civil War. Returning to Massachusetts in September, he planned to start a newspaper, organize a workingmen's convention, and speak throughout the state. By the time he left for California in November, the "Anti-Chinese Man" had addressed more than one hundred thousand people, and his audience through the newspapers reached well into the millions. Whether he was loved or hated, press attention turned Denis Kearney into a household name.[1]

But something peculiar began to happen midway through his tour. Crowds, which had numbered in the thousands during the summer, diminished markedly in the fall. He was hooted off the stage in September and pelted with rotten eggs and tomatoes in October. The Workingmen's Party of Boston turned openly hostile, forcing Kearney, "a laughing stock," to go home.[2]

At first glance, the impact of Kearney's four-month swing across the East and Midwest appears obvious and clear-cut. Workers and labor leaders seem to have swarmed to his speeches and warmly applauded his anti-Chinese rhetoric, whereas the middle and professional classes shunned him and mainstream editors denounced him. Kearney's visit thus appears to have demarcated the basic class boundaries of the Gilded Age. On closer examination, however, a more ambiguous picture emerges. Labor response to Kearney fits into no neat box. Workers' attitudes toward him ran from general acceptance to complete disavowal. Attitudes toward the Chinese and immigration restriction proved equally diverse, and middle-class opinion demonstrated similar variations. Though few members of the middle and upper classes openly praised Kearney, many anonymously applauded his anti-Chinese message. An analysis of Kearney's eastern tour reveals the difficulty of accurately gauging public opinion; it also reveals the obstacles historians face in understanding the thoughts and positions held by different classes of people. Such analysis further reveals the critical distinction between public opinion and people's *perception* of public opinion. The key legacy of Kearney's visit was not that he galvanized workers against the Chinese but that he succeeded in making some politicians and segments of the press think that he had. Perhaps more important, he helped cement Chinese exclusion as a cross-class (or nonclass) movement. Editors branded Kearney a demagogue, a rabble-rouser, a "brutal, ignorant, blaspheming ruffian."[3] But condemn him as they did, politicians would soon outdo him. Within days of Kearney's return to the sandlots of San Francisco, Congress would begin drafting its first law to restrict Chinese immigration.

Denis Kearney was born in County Cork, Ireland, in 1847. The second of seven sons, he left home after his father's death and went to sea at age eleven. A sailor, first mate, and later captain, Kearney sailed on the clipper ship *Shooting Star* and, while still a teenager, "circumnavigated the globe and visited many parts of the earths [*sic*] surface." He married in 1870 and settled in San Francisco in 1872. He purchased a draying, or trucking, business and, after becoming an American citizen, cast his first ballot for Rutherford B. Hayes. Kearney had little schooling but considered himself "a great reader," particularly of Darwin and Spencer. He neither drank nor smoked and was, according to economist Henry George, temperate in everything but speech. He attended a club known as the Lyceum of Self-Culture and by participating in weekly debates learned to speak in public. In his early days he defended Chinese immigration and attacked both organized religion and working-class lethargy. Even later, when he became "the workingmen's advocate," he remained critical of unions and frequently denounced strikes.[4]

Kearney cut his political teeth in 1877 when, as a member of the Draymen and Teamsters' Union, he challenged the city-backed carting monopoly. He burst into prominence a few months later in the wake of the national railroad strike. On the sandlots of San Francisco, he addressed—some said "harangued"— listeners on problems plaguing the city. A "ready and forcible speaker," Kearney emerged as the leader of both the sandlots and the Workingmen's Party of California around the rallying cry "The Chinese Must Go." Meetings began and ended with this benediction, and orations highlighted the alleged evils of Chinese immigration. "Every speech and every document written by me," Kearney later wrote the English historian Lord Bryce, "ended with the words, 'And whatever happens the Chinese must go.'" In spite of his frequent arrests for "incendiary language," friends and enemies considered him the head and tail of the anti-Chinese groundswell, "the master spirit of the movement." His admirers, one contemporary observed, compared him to "Napoleon, to Caesar, and to Christ." To his enemies he was more like the devil. When the Workingmen's Party swept local offices in the spring of 1878, Kearney foresaw uniting wage earners across the nation into one grand political party that would include workers, Greenbackers, and Socialists. The party's chief aims, he declared, would be to elect workingmen and rid the country of both "capitalist bondholders" and Chinese immigrants. With these goals in mind, Denis Kearney, just thirty-one years old, arrived in Boston on July 28, 1878.[5]

"It is evident from several indications," the *Boston Journal* noted as Kearney crossed the continent, "that the workingmen of this State are by no means united in welcoming Kearney on his forthcoming visit. Many of them have no sympathy with his anti-Chinese policy, they dislike his open Communistic principles and will not endure his conceited intolerance." Despite such disclaimers, every newspaper touted his arrival, turning Kearney into a star attraction. As the *Journal* predicted, "He is likely to be the sensation of the hour when he comes, and crowds will gather at his public appearances." Thousands, indeed, packed Faneuil Hall on August 5 to hear his first speech, and thousands more had to be turned away. "Not one-fourth of the crowd," the *New York Times* noted, "could gain entrance." His Celtic origins no doubt helped swell attendance in heavily Irish Boston and vicinity, as huge audiences turned out in Marblehead, Lynn, Lowell, and Brighton.[6]

Kearney's style and appearance varied little from speech to speech. "He dresses," the *New York Tribune* reported, "just like his class," in a dark, rough jacket, a blue or checked muslin shirt, and a short silk cravat tied in a sailor's knot. One of his trademarks was, after speaking and getting hot, to throw off his coat dramatically and unbutton his collar, gestures that always provoked a storm of applause. Then he would stand, "with his thumbs in the arm-holes of his vest," waiting for the ovation to subside. As he spoke, the former seaman would march frenetically up and down the platform, "as though pacing the deck of a vessel." He was of medium height, sporting a ruddy complexion and "negative-colored" mustache. Tony Hart, of the musical combination Harrigan and Hart, who happened to meet the Californian on his cross-country trip, described him as "round-headed," with a "half-inch forehead, terrier mouth, and a brogue that you could cut." The *Tribune* called him "just an average bullet-headed Irishman" but defended his elocution: "[He] uses perfectly good grammar, and except in his abusive phrases, employs well-chosen words, and has a straightforward English pronunciation, with a few lingering traces of his early education in such words as 'pul-pit' 'col-yume,' (column) and here and there an insignificant slip or two." Brogue or not, Kearney spoke clearly, carefully, and deliberately. When he wanted to stress a point, he would stop abruptly, raise his right hand, and "hurl it toward the audience, as though he were throwing a stone." The emphasized words he "forcibly . . . ejected like hot shot from a battery." By using language like "a missile," the "Illustrious Drayman" entranced his audiences and stirred them to applause. "Mr. Kearney has power," the *Boston Globe* concluded, "and his power is of that kind which to be appreciated must be seen and heard. It cannot be properly described."[7]

Kearney used strong language to provoke response, and his phrases, like his gestures, varied little from place to place. Usually lasting one to two hours, his addresses covered four general topics: contempt for the press, contempt for capitalists, contempt for politicians, and contempt for the Chinese. "Fellow workingmen and women of Boston," he began his first speech. "On behalf of the workingmen of the Pacific coast I thank you for this enthusiastic reception." Then he launched into attack:

First and foremost I will pay my respects to the newspapers. (Clapping. Mr. Kearney here called for order, there being much excitement, and then proceeded.) . . . The newspapers, from the earliest history of printing, have been run in the interest—take it down reporters—of cut-throats, political bilks (applause), daylight thieves and midnight assassins. A newspaper is an enterprise like all other business enterprises. For the reporters of the press I have great respect. (Applause and laughter.) The reporters of the newspapers are workingmen, like ourselves—working for bread and butter. (A voice, "That's so.") But for the villainous, serpent-like, slimy imps of hell that run these newspapers, I have the utmost contempt.[8]

Kearney denounced any newspaper that criticized him. At Marblehead and Lynn, mention of the *Boston Herald* drew hisses. "I now propose three groans for that slimy sheet," and a trio of groans resounded. In New York, he ripped up a newspaper onstage to the delight of the crowd. The editor of the *New York Tribune* ("the organ of the plunderers"), he declared, "is not fit to tie the shoestrings of Denis Kearney." In Cincinnati, he simply bemoaned "the lying, venial, venereal press of the United States." And as always, he lambasted "an old prostitute known as the Associated Press"—that "villainous, thieving, infamous band of scalawags that are aiming to control public opinion."[9]

Denunciations of the press, "the subsidized, contemptible, slimy tool of the money power," provided a lead-in to more despicable foes—monopolists and capitalists. This group included "bank smashers, railroad thieves, and political bummers." Workers, he exclaimed, must "tear the masks from off these tyrants, these lecherous bondholders, these political thieves (laughter and applause) and railroad robbers, when they do that they will find that they are swine, hogs (laughter) possessed of devils (renewed laughter), and then we will drive them into the sea. (Prolonged laughter and applause.)" In Newark, he denounced the "capitalistic vagabonds" as "blood-sucking vampires." In Cincinnati, they were "cowardly whelps," both "leprous" and "lecherous." When newspapers accused him of mispronouncing the latter term, he laughed and heaped more abuse on the "leecherous bondholder[s]"—"spell it with two ee's, if you please," he requested—"and their lickspittles."[10]

This last category—"lickspittles"—included the bar, the university, and the pulpit. As he told a crowd, "Legal pirates—you will excuse me for being . . . down on lawyers—I am down on them from principle; I look upon them as a set of garroters of humanity." In one speech he purposely used the terms "lawyer" and "liar" interchangeably. Professors he dismissed as "college con-

THE PROGRESS OF ONE OF KEARNEY'S SPEECHES.—HOW HE COOLS HIS TISSUES.

Figure 7.1. Cartoonists went wild lampooning Denis Kearney. Here, his habit of taking off his jacket is carried to the extreme to reveal the savage underneath. Note the hat beside him, which Kearney always passed around at the conclusion of his speeches. Original caption: "The Progress of One of Kearney's Speeches.—How He Cools His Tissues." Captions below individual panels: (top, left) "Kearney Commences. 'I propose to hurl vituperation like thunderbolts!'" (top, center) "He Warms to the Subject. 'The slimy imps of hell!'" (top, right) "He Gets Warmer. 'The blood sucking vampires of hell!'" (bottom, left) "He Grows Hotter. 'The first man that opposes us will be hung; and after he is hung his body will be roasted!'" (bottom, center) "And Hotter! 'The hell-bound, crop-eared festering crew of whiskey-drinking bummers who edit the loathsome filthy sheets!'" (bottom, right) "Grand Finale. 'I would go further, only for the mock-modesty of modern civilization!'" (*Puck*, September 11, 1878)

sumptives" who lectured to "bandbox gentlemen." Through the person of Henry Ward Beecher, Kearney attacked the upper-class clergy and congregation. "They use money that they steal from the people to hire this bread and water Beecher to preach to them from velvet cushions," he railed. "Who are the men that he preaches to? A dirty lot of prosperous, fat, lazy gamblers, [and] thieving rascals. (Laughter.) . . . There would be no desolate households if Beecher had dined on bread and water. . . . Oh, you hoary headed vampire, we are going to give you all the hell you want right here."[11]

Kearney did not normally preach violence. He relied instead on the ballot box as a remedy for workers' problems, though force might be necessary to keep elections clean and politicians honest. He urged listeners to "take the life of any man . . . who attempts to debar the voters from exercising their right of suffrage." Public officials who broke their promises deserved swift reprisals. "Shoot the first man that goes back on you after you have elected him intelligently," he said, "see that you hunt him down and shoot him. (Cheers.) Moreover, see that you roast him afterward. (Cheers.) And if he goes to Europe —goes to Paris—or if he goes to the Springs, see that you watch him, and follow him, and shoot him there. (Cheers and laughter.)" Oppression and suffering justified murder and plunder: "Before I starve in a country like this, I will cut a man's throat and take whatever he has got." Kearney advised workers to organize—not into labor unions but into one great political party. The solution he preached everywhere was for "honest workingmen"—"eight-tenths of the American people"—to unite behind his organization. "I say we must oppose everything," he said in Cincinnati. "The Workingmen's party must win, if it has to wade knee deep in blood and perish in battle. (Applause, laughter, and hisses.) The workingmen of this country must win though hell boil over. (Laughter, applause, and hisses.)"[12]

Kearney's main piece of advice, indeed the phrase that became associated with him, was "Pool your issues." By this he meant that all workers—Greenbackers, Socialists, and laborers of every persuasion—should drop their differences and unite in one "solid phalanx" at the ballot box. "You must forget that you are Irishmen, Englishmen or Scotchmen," he told crowd after crowd, "that you are Catholic or Protestant, Spiritualists or Atheists." You must "put all your issues into one pot, . . . screw a cover on it, and tie it so tightly that nobody could lift it" until you "elect workingmen to office." Precisely what issues Kearney wanted workers to pool he never spelled out. In Cincinnati, labor leaders asked what he meant by the slogan. " 'Knock the first man down who disagrees with you,' " he told them, " 'capture the State.' 'But,' " asked one of the labor leaders, " 'suppose you are asked some plan or reason for pooling issues?' 'D—n such conundrums,' " Kearney retorted, " 'the people are starving; aint that enough?' " For many it was not. "In God's name," one newspaper pleaded, give us some ideas, "propose *something*." But Kearney refused, offering neither programs nor solutions.[13]

Despite such vagueness, every Kearney speech was clear on one point: supporting Representative Benjamin F. Butler for governor of Massachusetts. The iconoclastic congressman from Lowell—a Democrat in the 1850s, a Civil War general and Radical Republican in the 1860s—had always courted a labor constituency. Despite, or perhaps because of, his popularity, patrician Republicans had never trusted him and repeatedly accused him of corruption, demagoguery, and opportunism. In 1878, Butler renounced the Republican Party and revealed that, if offered, he would accept the Greenback-Labor nomination for governor. A walking source of controversy, Butler was one of the few House members recognized nationwide, able to make headlines wherever he went.[14]

Hoping to cement an alliance among workers and Greenbackers—with Butler and himself at the helm—Kearney invoked the congressman's name to resounding cheers in city after city. The "chivalrous Butler," he proclaimed, "the gallant, the gifted, the glorious. We hope that he will receive the reward from the workingmen of Massachusetts he so justly merits for his bold and unspoken action on behalf of down-trodden humanity." Many charged that, if elected, Butler would use the governorship as a springboard to the presidency and that he had brought Kearney east to campaign for him. Although false, this latter charge would hound Butler throughout the campaign.[15]

And then came the Chinese. As Kearney remarked on his cross-country journey, "My chief mission here is to secure the expulsion of Chinese labor from California." In speech after speech, Kearney described the "putrid carcasses" of the Chinese, their crowded living arrangements, their diet of "rice and rats." The Pacific Coast is "cursed with parasites from China," he said in New York, and "used as a weapon by the grinding, grasping capitalists . . . to oppress the poor laboring men. . . . But let me tell you here to-night, that the laboring men of California . . . have captured the State, and they are going to take care of the Asiatic leper. (Cheers.)" He urged listeners to back him, shouting on Boston Common: "These leprous Chinamen are about the meanest creatures that God Almighty ever put breath into. (Applause.) The question is: 'Are the Chinamen to occupy this country (cries of "No!") or the white man?' (Shouts 'We alone,') and will you assist us in ridding this country of the moonlight lepers? (Applause and exclamation of approval.) All in favor of the Chinamen hold up their hands. (Hisses and no hands.) All in favor of the white man, up hands. (Applause and all hands up.)"[16]

After regaling listeners with anti-Chinese rhetoric, Kearney concluded his rallies with resolutions for the crowd to endorse. In Ohio, he spoke for an hour, and then declared "that the workingmen of Cincinnati, in mass meeting assembled, to the number of 6,000, after a full intellectual and moral consideration, unequivocally indorse the motto of the California workingmen, 'The Chinese must go,' and will defend our country with our lives, our fortunes and our sacred honor." Cheers or raised hands signified approval. In Lowell, Marblehead, and Boston, the resolutions received "great applause." In New York, Kearney read his resolution and demanded: "All in favor signify it by saying Aye. (Large numbers responded by upraised hands.) All opposed—(no re-

Figure 7.2. Steering the twin horses "Labor Reform" and "Greenbacks," drayman Denis Kearney carries candidate Ben Butler toward the Massachusetts governorship—en route to the White House. Butler sits in back nursing the "rag baby," a symbol of the infant Greenback-Labor Party. Original caption: "Up Hill Work for the California Drayman." (*New York Graphic*, August 20, 1878. Courtesy General Research Division, New York Public Library, Astor, Lenox, and Tilden Foundations)

sponse)." Thus, Kearney concluded, "It is carried unanimously." In Jersey City, one newspaper reported, "Mr. Kearney read a resolution that the meeting heartily approved the California cry of, 'The Chinese must go!' It was carried with only a few dissenting voices." The workingmen of the East, Kearney claimed, were fully behind him. Chinese exclusion, it appeared, was endorsed by workers everywhere he went.[17]

The press had a field day excoriating Kearney. "He is simply a blatant booby," the *Boston Transcript* stated, "with a profane and bullying rigmarole of epithets." Exhibiting "unblushing blackguardism," his "only talent," the *Philadelphia Inquirer* charged, "is the Billingsgate fishwife's talent for vituperation, and [his] head is as empty of ideas as his mouth is full of oaths and ribaldry." Party affiliation mattered little. The Republican *New York Times* called Kearney an "eminent blatherskite," while the Democratic *Chicago Times* called him a "flatulent little brat." The Greenback press also lampooned him. "Kearney's ideas are of the pig, piggy," noted *Pomeroy's Illustrated Democrat.* "The medicine he prescribes comes in such a mass of mental manure that it turns the stomach before it is swallowed." Practically every detractor called him a communist. The *Nation* compared him to a "naked Bushman," labeling him "the lowest type of demagogue that has yet appeared in history." To *Harper's Weekly* he was "harmless slime," to the *Pottsville (Pennsylvania) Miner's Journal*, "a dangerous fire-brand," and although the *New York Tribune* lavished column after column on his tour, it called him a "particularly stupid and uninteresting creature" who appealed only "to those who like profanity, indecency, and coarse, vulgar and savage brutishness." Even the Irish American press attacked Kearney. The *Boston Pilot* disavowed him as dangerous, empty-headed, and lacking ideas, while the *New York Irish-American* condemned the "foul-mouthed demagogue" and his "tirades of the wildest and most indecent abuse."[18]

Pilloried and ridiculed, Kearney became the press's number one whipping boy. The unceasing attacks from editors, however, ultimately differed little from the epithets Kearney hurled at them—a fact pro-labor newspapers noted. "The daily press," the *New York Labor Standard* observed, "as usual, denounce Mr. Kearney's speech as vulgar and profane, yet in their editorial columns use worse language to denounce the leaders of the labor movement." The *Irish World* was more direct. "After all, in the employment of adjectives, Kearney only borrows from the corrupt press itself. Who flings about nicknames and abusive epithets nearly so profusely as they do?" While conceding that Kearney was "rude," "crude," and a "simple plebeian," the *Irish World* pointed out the root of the attacks on him: "It is not Kearney himself his calumniators hate—it is the Labor movement. Keep this in mind: *It is the Labor cause they want to stab through him!*"[19]

Criticisms of Kearney extended well beyond the press. Senator James G. Blaine (R-Maine) called him "an unduly inflated sack of very bad gas," while Ch'en Lan-pin, the newly appointed Chinese minister to the United States, termed his speeches "thoroughly insulting" and "libelous." Clergy denounced the "Kalifornia Kommunist" to their congregations; even phrenologists got into the act. A "Professor" P. Graham, "a man with a Scotch accent," gave a lecture in September at New York's Science Hall at which he displayed pictures of Kearney's head. "That head," he stated, "does not exhibit one inch and a quarter of moral brain." The phrenologist compared his subject with a murderer, adding that Kearney possessed a "forehead no higher than an African baboon's and a pair of ears as large as any average sized donkey's." Furthermore, his brain size approximated that of a parrot. " 'Heaven help us,' cried the orator, gazing in horror at his own drawing, 'from the working classes that can be influenced by such a head as that.' "[20]

The phrenologist's cry poses two key questions: What was Kearney's influence on "the working classes," and what effect did his presence actually have? The class-based nature of Kearney's rhetoric and the often enthusiastic responses of his listeners suggest that he and his message "the Chinese must go" were popular with workers in the East and Midwest. Indeed, pro-labor newspapers, such as the *Boston Globe* and the more radical *Irish World*, praised Kearney as the "champion of the workingmen," and some labor advocates welcomed him warmly. Uriah Stephens, founder of the Knights of Labor, considered him "solid," and in a letter to Terence V. Powderly, he expressed his hopes that Kearney would "be favorably launched as an element in the Labor Movement on the Atlantic Slope." Greenbackers, as well as such Socialists as Peter J. McGuire and Albert Parsons, crowded the stage when he spoke.[21] Such support, however, masks the divisiveness Kearney's visit caused within these groups. Rather than make assumptions based on outward appearances, we must ask other questions: Who actually attended Kearney's rallies? Why did they attend? What can be said about individuals' true thoughts based on their participation in a crowd? And how did workers ultimately respond to Kearney and his message? Although some answers must remain speculative, further inquiry reveals that appearances can be deceiving: what occurred on the surface differed sharply from what went on below.

The makeup of Kearney's audiences can be gleaned from the brief descriptions reporters supplied. While admittedly impressionistic, these accounts suggest that Kearney's appeal crossed class lines and, when buttressed with other evidence, reveal that labor leaders and workers held very mixed opinions of Kearney and his anti-Chinese message. Some audiences consisted largely of workers. The Newark crowd "was mainly composed of Irish and German laborers," the *New York Sun* noted, with "no conspicuous citizens of Newark in the park at any time in the evening." On the following night in Jersey City, the audience "was made up largely of workingmen," the *New York Tribune* reported, "but on the edge of the crowd were here and there a few well-dressed men." Kearney's audiences in the industrial cities near Boston were also heavily working-class. Shoemakers turned out en masse to greet him in Lynn; when he spoke in Marblehead, about two thousand "New England mechanics, intelligent, thinking men," attended, and "every seat in the hall was filled by horny-fisted Marbleheaders."[22]

Elsewhere audience composition was not clear and, in fact, became a subject of dispute. On Boston Common, the *Globe* noted the "throng of intelligent and earnest-faced workingmen" and called the occasion "a workingmen's meeting in every sense of the word," whereas the *Boston Transcript* insisted "there was a liberal sprinkling of men who might be workmen of a higher order; either mechanics, business or professional men." The *New York Sun* reinforced this account: "It was a noticeable fact that many well-dressed and aristocratic-looking men were present."[23]

Accounts of the Faneuil Hall meeting also conflict. A *Tribune* correspondent considered the meeting "no doubt" all "workingmen." Both the *Sun* and the *Globe*, however, in nearly identical language, recognized "here and there the face of a well-known business man." The *Irish World* stated more directly, "Business and professional men were there in respectable numbers." The *Globe* had the last word: "It is but fair to say that the audience was a representative, orderly and well-behaved assemblage of American citizens, far above the average crowd that congregates to a political speech-making in the campaign season."[24]

Here a possible explanation emerges. Pro-Kearney newspapers, such as the *Boston Globe* and *Irish World*, stressed the middle- and upper-class attendance to demonstrate Kearney's broad-based appeal, whereas anti-Kearney newspapers, such as the *New York Tribune*, downplayed it to reinforce the belief that Kearney attracted only the working classes. This theory, however, does not hold up, as the anti-Kearney *Transcript* noted that one of his crowds in Boston "included some of the best known citizens." Nor does the theory hold true for New York City. At Union Square on September 6, Kearney attracted the biggest audience of his trip. The hostile *New York Times* estimated the crowd at fifteen to twenty thousand, whereas friendly papers claimed a turnout of forty to fifty thousand. Regardless of number, the question remains: Who were these thousands that cheered Kearney and "unanimously" endorsed his resolutions? "At least half the crowd—" the *Irish World* wrote, "judging from their dress and appearance—was composed of business or professional men." The *New York Sun*, an anti-Kearney but generally pro-labor newspaper (Kearney himself called it "pretty independent"), gave the same breakdown: half working-class, half business and professional. The *Tribune* broke its working-classes-only tradition and gave a cross-class portrait that complemented those of the *Irish World* and *Sun*: "Workingmen . . . did not form the main proportion of the throng, as was perhaps expected." Rather, the *Tribune* wrote, the crowd consisted of "representatives of all classes of society—mechanics, clerks, cartmen, merchants, etc." Furthermore, the *Tribune* noted "a knot of gentlemen" watching the speech from the posh Everett House across the square with a "number of ladies" on the balcony. Descriptions of audiences in other cities also stressed the mixed, "motley" nature of Kearney's gatherings. Listeners in Washington included "a great throng of well-dressed clerks," one paper noted, and the "proportion of laboring men present was comparatively small." Kearney's crowds, the *Indianapolis Sun* observed, were "composed of all classes." Such evidence, of various gatherings and from newspapers that differed tremendously in their opinions of Kearney, points to the cross-class nature of his audiences. Kearney's appeal well transcended the working classes.[25]

That Kearney attracted large, diverse crowds should really not be too surprising. The man received such enormous advance publicity that easterners of all stripes couldn't help but be drawn. "His name," noted the *Portland (Maine) Eastern Argus*, "is mentioned more times in the columns of the seven Boston daily papers than that of any other man that ever lived." Newspapers across the political spectrum showered attention on him, turning "a big blustering schoolboy" into a national celebrity. As the *Chicago Times* observed, "Every newspaper in the land teemed with his name." Like a president whose every action is noted and discussed, Kearney, "this new-fledged wonder of the Pacific slope," became a magnet for journalists. "Wherever he went," wrote Henry George, "a retinue of reporters and correspondents" followed him so that Kearney could "rise every morning to find the newspapers filled with him." As a consequence, this "rude, uncultured drayman" came "to be known and talked about, not merely through the whole country, but over the world!" Kearney's dramatic style and incendiary language—"Swears Like a Pirate," blared one headline—only enhanced his appeal. "Now, as in the days of the apostle," the *Philadelphia Inquirer* remarked, "people are as ever anxious to see and hear some new thing, and among orators Mr. Kearney is indeed a peculiarly new thing."[26]

Curiosity was no doubt a major factor in drawing crowds. So was amusement. "It is as good as a circus to attend a Kearney meeting," one detractor observed. "Dennis is the manager, clown, and the whole show combined." With noisy parades, brass bands, and male trios, a Kearney rally was novel entertainment for a quiet summer evening. And it was free (although Kearney did pass around a hat after each speech). Theater and concert halls could hardly compete with the excitement of a compelling, never-before-seen speaker. "He was circus and clown combined," the *Boston Transcript* noted disparagingly, "and the attraction proved great enough to hold the spectators pretty well together."[27]

Spectators also became part of the act, erupting in "roars of deafening applause" at some points, "derisive and slanderous epithets" at others. Hecklers showed up to razz Kearney, and he razzed them right back to the delight of the audience. His speeches resembled a modern-day sporting event, unimaginable without a lusty, volatile crowd cheering, hooting, and booing. Like a boxer, Kearney gave abuse and took abuse, swinging and jabbing, trying to draw blood. In Boston, the audience "shouted and yelled its applause at every mention of the word 'hell,' or 'thief,' or 'villain,' or 'bondholder,'" the *Tribune* reported, "and were always ready with a horse laugh for anything that savored of rowdyism." Toward the end of one speech, the *Transcript* noted, "the laughter began to predominate over the applause, and people listened and thought it fun, getting amusement not only out of what was said, but out of the speaker's manner of saying it." As the *Cincinnati Enquirer* observed, "Save when he talked of 'shooting 'em,' of 'wading in blood up to our knees,' and of 'hell boiling over,' he did not seem to be making a hit." Curiosity, amusement, and participation all contributed to the swelling of Kearney's audiences. For many listeners, his speeches also proved something of a catharsis. "It may be nearer the mark to suggest," the *New York World* pointed out, "that men go to his meetings and applaud because they like to hear their betters abused and listen to flattering schemes for a change in society which shall put down the mighty from their seats and exalt them of low degree."[28]

As Kearney rallies were more entertainment than discourse, more political theater than political discussion, the meaning of crowd reactions remains open to conjecture. Does a momentary response by listeners actually indicate sincere agreement? As one observer at the New York rally noted, applauding Kearney's resolutions was part of the fun: "The voting on every proposition submitted by Kearney was almost unanimous, many who had no sympathy whatever with his views holding up both hands, or loudly exclaiming 'Aye,' and then laughing as the result was announced by the speaker as unanimous." The fact that Kearney declared every resolution everywhere he spoke as passing unanimously reveals more about him than about the true sentiments of his listeners. Kearney was simply not a person who could tolerate opposition. Like an evangelist, his goal was to stir a crowd, and doubtless many people showed up purely for the sake of cheering. As the *Boston Journal* noted, some people "turned away disgusted at his violent harangue," whereas others "were prepared to applaud indiscriminately his every utterance." The substance of his utterances may well have been secondary. The extreme nature of Kearney's speeches and resolutions also challenges credibility that his listeners fully endorsed them. In Washington, for example, a police captain attempted to prevent Kearney from speaking, but Kearney prevailed. Referring to this incident the next night in Philadelphia, Kearney offered the following resolution: "That we recognize Kearney's action on that occasion as one of the noblest examples of heroism in ancient or modern history, and worthy of public recognition at the hands of a free people." The crowd, needless to say, "unanimously" approved. Was this an honest gauge of his listeners' opinions? Or was it more the result of a riveting speaker driving a crowd to a frenzy? To understand Kearney's genuine impact, we must look beyond the temporary crowd reactions to his tirades and analyze instead the response to his *tour*.[29]

Despite his image as the "workingman's friend," Denis Kearney provoked vast dissension among Greenbackers, labor leaders, and workers. In Pennsylvania, "there was a noticeable lack of anything like enthusiasm" among

Greenback-Labor organizers "in regard to his appearance," a reporter noted in late August, and the consensus was "in the interest of as much quiet as possible." After interviewing working-class organizers, the reporter explained: "Further conversation with the Labor men developed a feeling of disapproval of the agitators' [sic] coming to Philadelphia." Many Greenbackers outright opposed his presence. The party's gubernatorial candidate assailed him, and the state chairman purposely left town to avoid him. As Mayor Terence Powderly of Scranton remarked, "I am disgusted with Kearney." Plans once afoot to take Kearney to the coal regions were quickly abandoned as Greenbackers everywhere turned their backs on him. "His rhetorical extravagances," the *Washington Star* explained, "have convinced the more reflecting men of the greenback party that they will lose more than they will gain by him, while many of the workingmen who were disposed to look upon him as the man for the times, have come to the conclusion that he is a good man to have as little to do with as possible." The venerable Peter Cooper, the party's presidential candidate in 1876, refused Kearney permission to speak in Cooper Union (which he himself had founded) as originally planned, and other Greenback leaders tried to keep him from speaking in New York altogether. (Perhaps Kearney's dismissal of Cooper as "an old granny" had been too much for the eighty-seven-year-old Greenback patriarch to take.) A poet for the pro-Greenback *Indianapolis Sun* captured the party's general repugnance to Kearney and the failure of his message to resonate this side of the Rockies:

But your high saisoned spaich
It can only annoy,
For the Aist aint the West
Be a jugfull, me bhoy.[30]

Kearney was a political man rather than a workingman, and his antiunion attitude frustrated workers and labor reformers. In Washington, D.C., the National Workingmen's Assembly—the city's central labor organization—wanted nothing to do with him. "I did not know that he was coming," said J. F. Clarkson of the Pressmen's union the day Kearney arrived, "and he certainly did not come on the invitation of the assembly." Workers elsewhere kept their distance. In Indianapolis, one newspaper noted, "it was thought all the labor organizations of the city would fall in at the court house" for the parade to honor Kearney, but not more than seventy people showed up, and in Chicago, labor organizations "did nothing unitedly" to generate interest in his appearance. This is particularly surprising because the city's shoemakers were on strike, and rumors abounded that employers planned to import Chinese laborers from San Francisco. Consequently, the correspondent to the *New York*

Herald reported with what must have been puzzlement, "For some reason the trades unions of Chicago have not entered into Mr. Kearney's mission here with that spontaneity of enthusiasm which was probably looked for."[31]

While these responses indicate a growing dissatisfaction with Kearney, they do not provide explicit *reasons* for this dissatisfaction. Was it Kearney's incendiary language they opposed, his antiunionism, his presumed lack of ideas, or his crusade against the Chinese? Judging by the various criticisms of diverse labor organizations, Socialists, and individual workers, all these reasons contributed, but the Chinese issue was singled out prominently. Peter J. McGuire, the Socialistic Labor Party's top organizer, criticized Kearney for taking "diametrically opposite views from those of the Socialists about trades-unions." Even though McGuire shared the platform with Kearney in Boston and Indianapolis, he assailed his views on the Chinese. "The course Mr. Kearney wishes the people to adopt in relation to Chinese immigration is opposed to the first principle of socialism," he explained. "I do not believe the Chinese should come here as vassals already formed to other men, but if they come voluntarily to make this country a home, I do not see how we can prevent them and allow people of other nations to come." Sam Goldwater, who would shortly become president of the Chicago Trade and Labor Council, explained his dissatisfaction with Kearney. "I don't see what use he can be to the laboring men," the Polish-born cigar maker said. "Why, I know 7-year-old boys that know more, or at least as much, about the labor question as he does." Calling Kearney's ideas "all nonsense and bosh," Goldwater recounted his conversation with the drayman: "I tried to get him to talk about some other place than California, and to get him off the local Chinese question there. . . . I asked him how it was that times were hard in England, in Ireland, in Russia, in Germany, in Poland, where there was no Chinese, but he had nothing to say; in fact he couldn't say anything about it at all. . . . He quickly ended the talk with a remark like this: 'Oh, if you are for the Chinese I can't argue with you; you can go to hell.' " From the *Voice of Labor* in Missouri to the *Volkszeitung* in Ohio to the *Labor Standard* in Massachusetts, the radical, Socialist press condemned Kearney's "ridiculous manner" and warned workers not to get sucked in by his racist message. At a labor rally in Washington, a speaker cautioned listeners "against believing in those who travel about the country professing to be the friends of the workingmen, but who only appeal to their prejudices, and do nothing to benefit them." Many labor leaders and radicals maintained confidence that such appeals "to their prejudices" would be in vain. "Mr. Kearney . . . has not got the hang of things here yet," Brooklyn Socialist Justus Schwab commented. "The ways of the people out on the Pacific slope differ greatly from those in the Atlantic States." As New York City jewelry worker Hugh McGregor remarked on Kearney's crusade against the Chinese, "We doubt whether he can interest the Eastern workingmen upon that subject."[32]

The outlook of prominent Greenbackers, labor leaders, and Socialists on Kearney is clear: although welcomed in some places as a forceful speaker who could rivet a crowd, many remained skeptical of his abilities, fearful of his message, and leery of his race baiting. These groups, however, remained few in number and can hardly be considered representative of American workers. A more accurate gauge of working-class sentiment can be found by surveying letters and comments in various newspapers from individuals identifying themselves as "Toil," "A Workingman," and the like. "Mechanic," for example, condemned Kearney in the New York Tribune as a "flimsy fraud" who could "only bungle and rave and tear his English into smithereens giving us his views." A like-minded writer to the New York Sun simply urged Kearney to "close his mouth" and stop breeding dissension: "Workingmen are composed of all creeds and nationalities, and for a so-called representative to denounce any one wing of that body shows an utter disregard of self-respect." "He has been blinded by the Chinese question," a "Mechanic" wrote to the New York Witness. "The man who would propose to dump into the sea the people of any nationality, to improve the existing state of things, has too poor a head, and too weak a heart to be a leader of the masses." An unnamed foundry worker who had attended Kearney's speech in St. Louis with "great hopes" told a reporter: "His thoughts are not connected . . . and there is no logic in any of his arguments. . . . The crowd, or the intelligent portion of it, last night were thoroughly disgusted with him. His views upon Chinese emigration will never be seconded by the people here."[33]

Such views, of course, could be expected in a mainstream press seeking to marginalize the "mountebank drayman." Their validity would be suspect if not supported by other sources. The Boston Pilot presents an interesting case. This leading Irish Catholic weekly had subscribers throughout the country. Echoing the mainstream press, the Pilot denounced Kearney as a vacuous rabble-rouser, and letters seconded this opinion. As one irate reader remarked, "He is no workingman's friend." What is noteworthy, however, is that for years the Pilot had opposed Chinese immigration, and thus its editorials attacking Kearney made no mention of his anti-Chinese stance. Its readers did. Criticizing Kearney for his "cheap rhetoric" and lack of argument, "An Irish Workman" wrote: "It is not enough to say, for instance, 'The Chinese must go.' . . . For one workingman I should hate to give up my situation to a Chinaman or anybody else who offered to do my work as well for a fourth of my wages. Yet the proposition to drive the Chinaman into or beyond the Pacific is so shocking to every preconceived idea of justice or wisdom, so hostile to the glorious traditions of this free land, that I want something more than Mr. Kearney's key-note before I join what is at best a cry for proscription." Kearney, he concluded, should rely on "reason and not prejudice." Another subscriber, "O'Brien" from Port Huron, Michigan, warned, "He is organizing a Know-Nothing sentiment on the Chinese question, which if carried a trifle farther, may embrace all foreigners."[34]

However vehement the sentiments expressed in these anti-Kearney letters, they still remain too scattered to be accepted as the voice of labor. The final judgment on Kearney and his anti-Chinese agitation must ultimately be left to ordinary workers. They made their judgment known partly with their pen and partly with their bodies. In the end workers just stopped coming to hear him speak. And those that showed up came to laugh and to jeer.

One method of discerning the distinctions workers made between Kearney and the Chinese issue is by examining the countless placards, banners, and transparencies workers carried to his rallies. Greeting him in Boston on his arrival were such slogans as "Equal rights for all; the land must be free; down with monopoly." Other mottoes (inscribed "in roughly drawn letters," the *New York Times* noted) included "The people cannot be put down; tyrants tried that for thousands of years" and "The contract system must be abolished." Workers chose these slogans and paraded them everywhere Kearney spoke. "Labor to the Rescue," blared one in Brooklyn. "We've Burst Our Bonds," trumpeted another. "No Monopoly, No Usury," "Earth is man's and the fullness thereof," and "God help the poor, the Government helps the rich," read still more. Similar messages appeared in other languages. "Nicht herrenmehr und nicht mehrknechte dis arbeit fruct sie jedermann" ["No more lords, no more serfs, this work benefits everyone"], said one of several German banners in Indianapolis. And in a language no one could fail to understand, a banner featured a cartoon of "a fat bondholder swinging from a lamp post" and was captioned, "Sure cure for corrupt officials: Kearney has come." Workers knew well beforehand the substance of a Kearney speech, the subjects he would raise, and the subjects he would denounce. They had plenty of time to devise mottoes and create slogans. In all the placards and banners that workers carried or that hung on platforms when Kearney spoke, not one mentioned Chinese immigration or portrayed a Chinese immigrant. Of the hundreds of banners Kearney's visit inspired, the evidence suggests that none of them reinforced the sentiments for which the "Chinese bouncer" was best known.[35]

Workers did not jump onto the anti-Chinese bandwagon; soon they were not even jumping onto Kearney's bandwagon. After his monthlong tour of the Midwest and Atlantic coast, Kearney returned to Massachusetts in mid-September. Confident of his popularity, he planned to campaign for Butler and the entire Greenback slate. He altered his strategy, however, when he discovered that the state's Greenback platform failed to mention Chinese immigration. "Why this omission and procrastination?" he complained. "To me it savors too much of compromise, as though some conniving was going on behind the scenes." Although praising Butler, Kearney accused the Greenbackers of selling out to the Democrats. He denounced the "high-feathered bards" who ran the party and threatened to organize a rival faction. He called for a Workingmen's convention to meet in Boston in October, announced plans to start a campaign newspaper, and vowed to "stump the State" to assure victory. As it worked out, however, no such convention ever met, no copies of his newspaper made it off the press, and Kearney scarcely left the Boston area for the next six weeks. Perhaps most significant, the few times he tried to speak, crowds turned sharply against him.[36]

"I don't want to hear you," a listener yelled to him during a speech in Worcester in September. "You can go plumb to hell," Kearney shot back. Attempting to speak in Boston a week later, Kearney "was hustled off the stage." In October, he tried to stir a crowd in East Boston, but instead, the crowd heckled him and attacked him. "He was pelted with potatoes and onions," the *Transcript* noted. Another witness reported "rotten tomatoes" being flung at him. The event became more ludicrous when some boys began burning gunpowder beneath the stand from which Kearney was speaking. The explosions and bright lights finally silenced the orator. "Mr. Kearney said he was obliged to stop," the *Globe* reported tersely, "because of noise on the outskirts of the crowd." The next night in Brookline his speech "fell very flat," and he was "interrupted several times by derisive cries and yells." He was also interrupted by people who hurled eggs, turnips, and "other missiles." The evening became a "complete fiasco" when Kearney shouted that someone ought to "take a pistol and shoot" whoever had struck him. The following night's speech in South Boston was more peaceful, but only because much of the crowd drifted away "after listening to him for a few minutes." An anonymous poet-punster captured this burgeoning discontent:

And then with one accord the crowd,
With cheers hilarious, curses loud,
And heer a sneer and there a cough
Looked once at DIN, and then walked off.[37]

Such embarrassing confrontations convinced Kearney to curtail his schedule. Limiting his appearances, however, did little to boost his popularity. As the *New York World* noted, Kearney had become "too dismal to attract audiences." His speeches in the fall, though, reveal a slight but significant change in content: Kearney no longer attacked the Chinese. After his speech in Brookline on October 2, Chinese immigration disappeared from his repertoire. "The Chinese must go" would not rouse crowds in Massachusetts and would no longer be Kearney's battle cry in the East. As one observer noted, "The workingmen of this State . . . have no sympathy with his anti-Chinese policy."[38]

Declining popularity turned the drayman of California into a political liability in Massachusetts. "Kearney," the *Transcript* noted, "having reached that point where he is jeered by his own diminished gatherings of motley idlers, is no longer dangerous to anybody but Butler." Fearing the adverse impact of Kearney on the campaign, the *Pittsfield Sun* observed that "the Butler men are prepared to 'shut down' on Dennis, and will issue . . . a proclamation disavowing any connection with the sand lot speaker's issues." Both the speaker and his "issues"—anti-Chinese agitation foremost among them—posed a danger to Butler; while he made no such "proclamation," he did try to confine Kearney to Boston. When Kearney ventured to Springfield, "Butler men . . . gave him the cold shoulder," and he left town as quickly as he had arrived. "Dennis," a local paper noted, "seems to have been pretty thoroughly frozen out here." Political realities, however, forced Butler to walk a fine line: he desperately wanted the handful of votes Kearney might bring him but not the negative publicity that followed him. "I neither criticize nor condemn him," the Lowell congressman remarked. Butler had received the endorsements of Peter Cooper and Wendell Phillips, and with a fair shot of capturing the governor's mansion, he embarked on a whirlwind tour to rally the "Tribe of Benjamin." Cringing at the prospect of a Butler victory, Republicans accused him of embracing "Kearneyism" and "Communism" and imported their biggest guns—James Blaine, James Garfield, and Carl Schurz—to campaign against him. A Butler victory, they feared, would place the Greenbacker in a strong position to mount a third-party challenge for the White House in 1880. And what office might a Butler administration owe to Kearney? "General of the Army is good enough for me," the "doughty Dennis" remarked. All this became too much for Butler, and in the final week of the campaign he at last criticized Kearney openly. Despite this turnaround, Kearney recognized that a Greenback victory in one of the nation's leading industrial states would boost party fortunes—and his own—nationwide, and he championed Butler to the campaign's closing day. "If our candidate is defeated," he declared, "we Workingmen . . . shall then unfurl the red flag of revolution, kill and destroy millions of capital and free the people from tyranny." The excitement and publicity produced a heavy turnout on election day. Butler polled 109,435 votes to the Republican's 134,725 and the Democrat's 10,162. Butler had done remarkably well for a third-party candidate. Still, he lost.[39]

The election itself did not spell Kearney's final demise. He brought that on himself a week later when he tried to manipulate the mayoral nomination of the Workingmen's Party of Boston. While addressing the party's convention, the assembly showered him with boos and hisses. "Several delegates went so far as to shake their fists in Kearney's face, inquiring why he should come here meddling with the politics of the city." Kearney tried to continue speaking but, the *Globe* reported, "the audience . . . was in no mood for listening." Then someone "turned the gas off in his face," darkening the room. During this "scene of confusion," the chairman and secretary left the hall while "a portion of the audience crowded on to the platform, some blaming Kearney and others offering advice to the sand-lot orator to keep out of this business altogether." The meeting quickly dissolved, but not without further attacks. "The workingmen denounced him," the *New York World* noted, and told him "that he was not a true representative of labor." They refused to "be dictated to by him" and asked him to leave. Kearney "departed completely discomfited."[40]

Kearney's stock had never been lower. The Workingmen met again the next night, and although not present, he was nonetheless the object of discussion. One newly elected legislator "deprecated the disgraceful proceedings of the [previous] meeting and was particularly severe on Dennis Kearney, whom he considered as the principal cause of discord." Another speaker remarked that "if he had been a hireling of the republicans to throw apples of discord into the ranks of the workingmen, he could not have done his work better." This speaker concluded: "Let him go back to California. The workingmen here repudiate him."[41]

Kearney heeded the advice. Claiming he was needed by workers in San Francisco, Kearney announced he would leave Massachusetts, but he promised a "farewell speech." On November 17, he spoke in Boston's Independence Square. He denounced the Democrats and Republicans, and he denounced those who had denounced him. The speech differed little from those he had made in the past two months. He did not mention the Chinese. The crowd seemed little interested in what he had to say, and the *Globe*, so long his champion and cheerleader, did not dispute the fact: "During the speech, which occupied about an hour, the large crowd . . . were exceedingly quiet, and only a few interruptions were made. No enthusiasm was evinced and the whole speech fell flat. . . . At the close the large crowd quickly dispersed." Kearney left town two days later. His four-month tour was over.[42]

From the abuse heaped on Kearney by the mainstream press during the summer, one would have expected smug editorials of satisfaction upon his ignominious departure in the autumn. In a sense vindicated by the thorough rejection of Kearney by most everyone, editorialists could have congratulated themselves for predicting his demise. This, however, was not the case. Few newspapers noted his leaving. In fact, readers would have been hard pressed to know that Kearney was still in the East in October and November. After initially receiving an avalanche of publicity, "the Great Agitator" practically dropped out of view in mid-September. Kearney, the *Pittsfield Sun* reported, was little more than "a seven day sensation" who "passes out of memory as he goes out of sight." After his tour of the Midwest, journalists no longer considered him newsworthy. "Poor Kearney!" rhapsodized the *Philadelphia Times* in late September. "But a brief fortnight ago he was made bright and glorious by display heads in big type leading column-long articles—and now he is stuck away in odd corners in three-line agate type." Newspapers that had delighted in ridiculing him virtually stopped mentioning his name. One has to comb the back pages of the daily papers painstakingly to find the slightest reference to his whereabouts. Even the *Boston Globe* disposed of Kearney's speeches in brief paragraphs and single sentences. While Butler's campaign for governor received nationwide publicity—and was branded with "Kearneyism"—Kearney himself received scant notice. Like a "shooting star," ironically the name of the clipper ship he once sailed, Kearney shone brightly and fizzled quickly, or as one newspaper observed, having "risen like a rocket in the West . . . he falls like a stick in the East." No longer attracting crowds, Kearney no longer attracted headlines. As far as the public knew, he had disappeared.[43]

Kearney's near banishment from the newspapers divided his tour neatly into two parts: the first eight weeks heralding his advent and describing his rallies, and the last eight weeks slighting his speeches and ignoring his downfall. This shift in coverage had significant consequences. Readers east of the Rockies received a full account of Kearney's diatribes in August and September, the often tumultuous crowds that greeted him, and the enthusiastic approvals of his resolutions, but they received scarcely any hint of his decline, his humiliation in October, and his repudiation in November. In addition, the cross-class composition of the crowds received only the briefest of notices—seldom more than a sentence or two—whereas Kearney's violent class-based rhetoric dominated reports. Objections by individual workers to Kearney and his anti-Chinese epithets were no more than whispers next to the "thunders of applause" early crowds gave him.[44] Thus the message most readers got differed markedly from the reactions many workers evinced. Whereas working-class opinion revealed deep divisions and ultimate rejection of Kearney, the press-created *perception* of working-class opinion showed general approval. The image of cheering working-class crowds was implanted in people's minds far more saliently than was that of well-dressed spectators, egg-throwing critics, or disgusted workers. This disparity would have serious repercussions in the months to come.

Kearney was not the only show in town in the summer of 1878. Workers had another forum far removed from the noisy streets and open-air meetings in which to express their grievances. In June, the House of Representatives had appointed a committee to investigate the causes of the depression in which the country had been mired for five years. Chaired by Abram Hewitt (D-N.Y.), the committee held sessions in New York, Scranton, and Washington, D.C. The Hewitt Committee, as people called it, heard testimony from over seventy witnesses, offering workers a unique opportunity to inform Congress directly of their viewpoints, their complaints, and their demands. Here they could tell their representatives in the federal government exactly what they wanted. A better, more official forum could hardly be imagined.[45]

Only two labor leaders mentioned Chinese immigration: Adolph Douai and Adolph Strasser. Editor of the *Arbeiter-Union*, Douai had been one of the many speakers at the New York City rally in Tompkins Square Park in 1870 to denounce imported contract labor but welcome Chinese immigrants. Near the end of his testimony on August 2, 1878, one congressman asked Douai if he favored the restriction of Chinese immigration:

DOUAI: We would not restrict anyone. . . . We demand that Chinese emigration under contract ought to be stopped immediately.
HEWITT: Not otherwise?
DOUAI: Not otherwise.[46]

Adolph Strasser, who had just led New York City cigar makers through the "great strike" against tenement house labor, was president of the Cigar Makers' International Union. With the exception of shoemaking, the cigar industry was the trade most threatened by Chinese laborers, who had made major inroads in the workforce in California. No one knew this better than Strasser. He testified before the Hewitt Committee on August 5, the exact same day Kearney spoke at Faneuil Hall in Boston. Strasser's message, however, differed sharply. In a lengthy statement filled with charts and statistics, Strasser described the cigar industry in detail. He mentioned the Chinese just once, as little more than an afterthought. Hewitt, however, picked up on this. "Would you," the congressman asked, "prohibit coolies from being employed in the manufacture of cigars?" Strasser replied: "I am not opposed to the Chinaman, or any nationality; but I am opposed that John Chinaman or any one else should be imported here as a coolie under contract. I don't agree that the Chinaman must go. I cannot agree with that, because you might as well say that some one else must go. That is wrong; I cannot agree to that. I am not in favor of that; but I am in favor not to tolerate the direct importation of coolies by contract."[47]

Hewitt continued on the same line of questioning:

HEWITT: Suppose a silk merchant wanted to get people [from France] to work in his factory, would you oppose his employing them under a contract for five years?

STRASSER: I would.

HEWITT: You think he should not be allowed to introduce skilled operatives into this country?

STRASSER: No, I am in favor of that, but opposed to their being brought here as slaves. . . .

HEWITT: Would you make a law in regard to contracts made in China between Chinese?

STRASSER: I don't suppose our jurisdiction goes over to China; I suppose the question is superfluous.

HEWITT: You say you would not tolerate such contracts; but the contracts are made in China?

STRASSER: I am only opposed to bringing them here under contract.

HEWITT: You would not allow Chinamen to be brought here under contract?

STRASSER: Yes, sir.

HEWITT: Would you object to Frenchmen being brought here under contract to introduce the silk business?

STRASSER: Yes, sir.

HEWITT: You won't allow any one to be brought here under contract?

STRASSER: I am opposed to it.

Hammering away at Strasser, Hewitt finally became exasperated and asked him at last what limits he wanted placed on the employment of foreigners in the United States. "I am not proposing any limits," the cigar maker responded. "I don't care if 500 Chinamen came to this country on their own hook. I don't oppose them or anyone else."[48]

Cigar makers responded favorably to Strasser's testimony, which the union's journal reprinted. "Your interview with the Hewitt Congressional Committee

Figure 7.3. President of the Cigar Makers' International Union, Adolph Strasser (1844–1939) led New York City cigar makers through the "great strike" of 1877–78, a strike marked by boisterous rallies, devastating lockouts, and threats to import Chinese laborers. In August 1878, Strasser testified before the Hewitt Committee. Asked his views on immigration restriction, Strasser replied: "I am not proposing any limits. I don't care if 500 Chinamen came to this country on their own hook. I don't oppose them or anyone else." (Courtesy George Meany Memorial Archives)

meets with general approval among the craft," the Detroit correspondent wrote. "We agree individually," added the Massachusetts correspondent, "in approving the remarks of the International President before the Congressional Committee." The Hewitt Committee itself commended the cigar maker. "So clear was the statement of Mr. Strasser," one newspaper noted, "that the Committee thanked him for the manner in which he had presented it."[49]

Despite these words of support, most everyone else criticized the Hewitt Committee and denounced the witnesses as "loafers," "crazy idealists," and "crack-brained idiots." For once, Denis Kearney agreed, condemning the testifiers as "simpletons . . . more fit to be in a lunatic asylum than representing labor." Only the *New York Dispatch*, which dismissed the bulk of the hearings as offering "very little that is of the slightest importance," singled out Strasser for commendation. "In the other trades there are men as painstaking and sensible as Mr. Strasser, and to these the Congressional Committee should give its time. . . . The real workingmen have discussed the things which affect their trades, and they are likely to have special knowledge of the way in which their trades can be benefitted by changing certain laws." Such reactions were unusual. While most newspapers printed excerpts of the testimony, several misquoted Strasser and Douai and ignored their comments on Chinese immigration. Their words, and those of their fellow workers, simply drifted away into history.[50]

During the summer of 1878, Adolph Strasser and Adolph Douai spoke clearly and forcefully on their attitudes toward Chinese immigration. So did cigar maker Sam Goldwater, "O'Brien," "An Irish Workman," an anonymous St. Louis foundry worker, and countless other laborers whose voices can be rescued from the past. But these individuals received few headlines in the summer of 1878, their voices drowned out by the roaring rhetoric of Denis Kearney and the inflated attention he received. The electrifying speaker and pulsating audience became front-page stories, far more thrilling than dry testimony before Congress, handmade banners hung from podiums, and assorted interviews and letters to the editor.

Denis Kearney fits into a long American tradition of charismatic orators who blended a vibrant populism with vicious racism. Like Mike Walsh in the 1840s and Tom Watson at the turn of the century, Kearney gained notoriety by spouting class-conscious, anticapitalist, racist rhetoric. Although Kearney would soon disappear from public view (and die in obscurity in 1907), his meteoric career would have effects at least as great as those of Walsh or Watson. The "shouting drayman" blazed a trail that others would tread long after his demise. Few were aware of this in the autumn of 1878, however, when Kearney left Boston "a laughing stock." Interviewed in late November, Senator Aaron A. Sargent called Kearney's trip east "a complete failure." In some respects, the California Republican was right, as people of all persuasions repudiated the "Howling Hoodlum." But in one crucial respect, Kearney was a dazzling success. He showed that a forceful speaker could stir a crowd to its feet in the East by mouthing virulent, racist, anti-Chinese epithets. No matter that the crowd embraced many classes and segments of society. No matter that people came to laugh and to shout. No matter that numerous workers and labor leaders had renounced Kearney and his anti-Chinese message. To people trying to gauge public opinion, the spontaneous agitation of the "rabble" carried more weight than all the scattered voices from the working-class community that rose up in protest. The divergence between public opinion and perceptions of public opinion would have tragic consequences in the years to come. It would lead both to the exclusion of an entire race of people from the United States and to the pillorying and blaming of one class of society as the culprit for this exclusion, a class that in reality expressed a quite different view of the issue.[51]

After years of only sporadic interest, politicians began viewing Chinese immigration in a new light. Politicians, after all, are one group of society especially interested in public opinion. Their power and their jobs, in effect, depend on it. One politician concerned with public opinion in 1878 was President Rutherford B. Hayes. In a meeting with Kearney on August 28—"DENNY AND RUTHY," one headline blared—Hayes discussed Chinese immigration, assuring the sandlot orator, "I think Congress next winter will come to a definite conclusion favorable to your people on this question."[52]

The politician most concerned with public opinion in 1878 was James Blaine, senator from Maine and the leading contender for the presidential nomination in 1880. A former Radical Republican and staunch defender of civil rights, Blaine had never yet commented publicly on Chinese immigration. One might have expected him to defend the Chinese, as he had defended blacks, as human beings entitled to equal rights and political privileges. Indeed it was Blaine who had dismissed Kearney in September as "an unduly inflated sack of very bad gas." But that summer the Maine Republican read the newspapers and recognized the appeal that Chinese exclusion seemed to have among workers. Disregarding, or maybe not noticing, the diversity of working-class opinion, Blaine seized on the issue with a sudden fervor.

In December, as Kearney returned to the sandlots in San Francisco, Senator Blaine attended a dinner party in Washington with southern Democrats and northern Republicans. For the first time, the *San Francisco Chronicle* reported, Blaine "took strong and decided grounds against Chinese immigration. 'A people who eat beef and bread and who drink beer,'" the Maine senator quipped, "'cannot labor alongside of those who live on rice, and if the experiment is attempted on a large scale the American laborer will have to drop his knife and fork and take up the chop-sticks.'" Blaine's language was not as vulgar as Kearney's, but it would be soon. His conversion would prove one of the major factors in the exclusion of Chinese immigrants from the United States. Others were converting as well. As the *Chronicle* noted in December 1878, "The Chinese question has of late excited a great deal more interest among public men at the Capital than it has ever before been possible to arouse."[53] Kearney's message had gotten through to the most unexpected of listeners.

CHAPTER EIGHT

Rolling in the Dirt

The Fifteen Passenger Bill of 1879

No man hungered more for the presidency in the Gilded Age than James Gillespie Blaine. As Speaker of the House from 1869 to 1875, senator from 1876 to 1881, and twice secretary of state, the Maine Republican was the era's pre-eminent politician, the consummate Washington insider who dictated party policy and a spellbinding orator who electrified crowds. The "mere magic of his presence," one fawning biographer wrote, could inspire "cries of frantic enthusiasm." Patrician businessman Chauncey Depew called him the "most versatile and capable" speaker he had ever heard, "always ready" and "brilliantly effective. In a few sentences he . . . captured his audience and held them enthralled." The gruff Thaddeus Stevens remarked on "the magnetic manner of my friend from Maine," and indeed, almost everyone has employed the term "magnetism" when trying to describe Blaine's appeal. Magnetism can either attract or repel. "There has probably never been a man in our history upon whom so few people have looked with indifference," wrote his colleague, Senator George Frisbie Hoar. "He was born to be loved or hated. Nobody occupied a middle ground as to him." What was it about Blaine that provoked such extreme reactions? As a legislator he had many admirable qualities. Born in 1830, he started out as an antislavery Whig editor, converted early to Republicanism, and at age twenty-six was one of the youngest delegates to the party's first nominating convention. He became a fierce Lincoln partisan during the war and an early advocate of black suffrage and Radical Reconstruction. As Speaker, he called Representative Joseph H. Rainey of South Carolina to chair proceedings in the House, marking the first time a black man presided over Congress.[1]

Symbolism aside, no one ever accused Blaine of being an idealist. He had little interest in altruism or abstract principles. He used his office for private gain, accepted gifts from financier Jay Cooke, and was implicated in the Crédit Mobilier scandal. The taint of corruption followed Blaine throughout his career. But if Blaine amassed a fortune in politics, he was no more corrupt than many a Gilded Age politician. What separated him from his contemporaries was his mastery of machine politics and his undisguised ambition for higher office. In an age when the office—at least the presidency—was supposed to seek the man, Blaine openly lusted for the White House. As fellow senator Zachariah Chandler put it, the Maine Republican suffered from the "incurable disease of presidential fever." And Blaine himself confided to his wife, "When I want a thing, I want it dreadfully." This craving for the presidency made even his closest associates wary. "I like Blaine—always have—yet there is an element in him which I distrust," his friend James Garfield wrote in his diary. Many people distrusted Blaine—the New York Times called him an "utter scoundrel"—but no one questioned his abilities, his influence, or his devoted following of "Blainiacs." The Plumed Knight, as his admirers called him, never forgot a name or a face, and even detractors acknowledged his infectious charm. Blaine's charismatic appeal and dual nature became legendary: "This man had two paths that he walked," one keen observer remarked, "one in the daylight that was straight, one in the dark that was twisted as a ram's horn." To understand James Blaine one must bear in mind that virtually every speech he made and every word he uttered were designed to land himself at the finish line on the path to the White House. After narrowly losing the Republican nomination in 1876, he would be the front-runner at every convention for the next twelve years. Possessing superb political instincts, the Plumed Knight cast his shadow over every Republican of his generation. "He had a keen sense of the public's wants," one biographer noted, and the "ability to recognize the leading topic of the moment." In the winter of 1878–79, the leading topic was Chinese immigration. James Blaine would have sold his soul to be president, but as that was not possible, he sold out the Chinese instead.[2]

On January 14, 1878, long before the red scare and Greenback agitation in the spring, long before Kearney's swing east in the summer and fall, and long before Senator Blaine's offhand comments at a dinner party in the winter, Thomas Wren (R-Nev.) introduced a bill in the House of Representatives to restrict Chinese immigration. It was referred to committee, where it languished for one year. As 1879 dawned, however, and the 45th Congress gathered for its final session, the issue had gained new momentum and the House considered the measure in January. The Fifteen Passenger Bill, as it was popularly called, limited the number of Chinese passengers permitted on any ship coming to the United States to fifteen. Violation would make the ship's captain liable to six months in prison and a fine of one hundred dollars for each Chinese passenger exceeding fifteen. Set to become effective on July 1, 1879, the measure had one major loophole: it covered only entry by sea. Chinese immigrants would still be free to sail to Canada or Mexico, then cross into the United States. Nonetheless, the Fifteen Passenger Bill was the first immigration restriction law aimed at a particular nationality ever drafted, debated, and passed by Congress.[3]

The House committee issued a brief report accompanying the bill. Recounting the history of congressional efforts to restrict entry of the Chinese, it stressed their "sordid, selfish, immoral, and non-amalgamating habits" as well as "the almost unanimous sentiment of the people of the Pacific slope" that Chinese immigration was "a great evil." Representative Horace F. Page (R-Calif.) delivered the main address. Author of the Page Act of 1875 (which restricted immigration of Asian prostitutes) and a Republican for twenty years, the California congressman recognized "the guaranteed rights of all, without regard to race, color, or previous condition"—except when it came to the Chinese. These "filthy . . . aliens," Page said, "are unfitted by education, habits, religious superstition, and by their inborn prejudices to assume any of the duties" of American citizenship. After exhibiting his own prejudice, Page argued that immigrants from Asia "retard desirable immigration from Europe." America welcomed newcomers, he said, but the "immigration sought has always been Caucasian." While noting that the Chinese "inspire a profound irritation and discontent among all citizens of all classes," Page advocated the bill specifically "in the interest of the workingmen of our own section and of our whole land . . . in order to bring relief to the workingmen of the country." To demonstrate the bill's national appeal, Democrat Albert Willis of Kentucky delivered a similarly vitriolic speech dripping with racism, but he too favored the bill as a means of helping the "laboring-men who comprise four-fifths of our population." Workers, these two politicians argued, would gain from restricting Chinese immigration.[4]

Figure 8.1. Republican James G. Blaine of Maine (1830–93) was the preeminent statesman of his generation. Speaker of the House, senator, and twice secretary of state, the White House was the one prize that forever eluded him. His conversion to the anti-Chinese banner marked the turning point in the crusade against Chinese immigration. (Theron Clark Crawford, *James G. Blaine: A Study of His Life and Career from the Standpoint of a Personal Witness of the Principal Events in His History* [Philadelphia, 1893])

The Fifteen Passenger Bill inspired virtually no debate in the House. George Robinson (R-Mass.) dismissed it as "cheap nostrums," but only two members spoke at any length against it. In a highly partisan speech, Martin Townsend (R-N.Y.) attacked the bill as a modern version of Know-Nothingism, while Augustus Hardenbergh (D-N.J.) called it an affront to American ideals and the tradition that "this continent, dedicated to freedom and progress, will extend its arms to every race. . . . I cannot . . . consent . . . that any single portion of my country shall close its ports to the oppressed of earth, from whatever clime they come or beneath whatever skies they may chance to have been born." A few legislators suggested modifications to soften the measure. Joseph G. Cannon (R-Ill.), later to become the autocratic Speaker of the House, urged excepting Chinese students, travelers, and diplomats from the bill's provisions. Omar Conger (R-Mich.) urged exempting Chinese shipwrecked at sea, and James A. Garfield (R-Ohio), calling the act a violation of the Burlingame Treaty, recommended delaying its effective date until "due notice has been given to China." But the Speaker rejected these demands and quickly brought the bill to a vote.[5]

On January 28, 1879, the House of Representatives passed the Fifteen Passenger Bill, 155 to 72 (with 61 not voting). As Representative Townsend remarked, "Kearney was [now] represented in the national halls." Democrats, the majority party, endorsed the measure overwhelmingly, 104 to 16 (with 31 not voting), while Republicans split, 51 to 56 (with 30 not voting). The breakdown of the vote largely supported the claim by the *New York Times* "that the Democratic House is entitled to the credit of passing the bill." The *Times*, however, overlooked the fact that Republicans contributed a substantial number of votes, and had party members united against the bill they could have easily defeated it. If 42 Republican supporters (or fewer if those not voting had cast ballots against it) had switched their votes, the bill would have lost. Most significant, just 56 of the party's 137 members opposed the bill. Twelve of the 30 nonvoting Republicans were paired either with Democrats or fellow Republicans; of these twelve, one stated support for the bill, two stated opposition. Adding these opponents of the measure to the total, only 58—a mere 42 percent—of House Republicans went on record against the Fifteen Passenger Bill. It was hardly a ringing endorsement for Chinese immigration.[6]

The press practically ignored the House vote, waiting for the real showdown in the Senate. With an edge of thirty-nine votes to thirty-seven, Republicans could control the Senate calendar and take fuller responsibility for the bill's outcome. Debate began on February 13 and raged for three days, revealing clearly the competing factions in the Republican Party, split between the ideals of the past and the realities of the present. Democrats too showed considerable conflict, further indicating that Republicans no longer held a monopoly on principle. The only group united, as it had been for years, was the West Coast, irrespective of party. To Aaron A. Sargent, the California Republican who had led the battle cry in 1876, belonged the honor of introducing the bill and delivering the keynote address. From his opening sentence, he downplayed the pathbreaking nature of closing the gates of the United States. "There is nothing novel or strange in the legislation proposed," he said, "except that it is directed to one people instead of to all peoples." That, of course, was the entire point. The legislation was directed at one people—the Chinese—a people, he said, that all others—the English, the Dutch, the French—despised. Even "the Hindoos and other Asiatic races which we have been disposed to consider in the lowest scale of humanity will not associate with the Chinese." Such sentiment, Sargent argued, was universal: "Wherever they go there is this same feeling with regard to them, this same attempt to void them from the public stomach. . . . Was it the design of the founders of this Government that we should be a mere slop-pail into which all the dregs of humanity should be poured?"[7]

Sargent was a Republican, proud of his party's past: "I have no sympathy with agrarian notions; I believe in the rights of property; I believe in peace and order; I have no sympathy with Kearneyism; I am speaking in no such interest." Like Page and Willis, he claimed to speak for the working classes. The Chinese had "invaded . . . every avocation except the newspaper and the law," and as a result American laborers were perched on the brink of starvation. The Chinese immigrant "can live on a dead rat and a few handfuls of rice" and "work for ten cents a day. . . . How can the American laborer compete with that?" Recalling the recent "labor riots," he advised his colleagues that "these considerations . . . should go to every Senator's mind." If the restriction of Chinese immigration could buy a few more years of labor peace, it would be a small price to pay.[8]

Fellow western senators hammered home the same message. "The discontent of labor is a powerful factor in our society and politics, to-day," said Newton Booth (R-Calif.). "Its suffering is real," and if Chinese immigration continued unabated, "the discontent of labor will take the form of violent anger or sullen despair" and "become an element of revolution." To invite such immigration, added John P. Jones (R-Nev.), "is to invite disorder, commotion, and massacre." Public order required restriction. "It is of very little consequence," Jones said, distorting the demands of organized labor, "whether the Chinese in this country are called slaves or freemen." To most workers, this was indeed the essential difference, but to western senators it hardly mattered. "The strikes of white laborers may be annoying," Jones continued, "but their training and traditions, hopes and family ties, make them upholders of law and the ready, sturdy defenders of the Government against its enemies, foreign and domestic." In arguments eerily foreshadowing the World War II internment of Japanese Americans two generations later, Jones charged that an "alien race . . . among us . . . would swell the ranks of any invasion. . . . We should be liable always to insurrection and compelled constantly to be on our guard against it."[9]

To western senators, however, fears of working-class rebellion paled beside the exigencies of race. "As statesmen, looking before and after, we cannot ignore the fact of race antipathies," Senator Booth said. "The darkest passages of human history have been enacted when alien races have been brought into contact." Conjuring up images of forced racial mingling, western senators used Chinese immigration to evoke the recent failure of Reconstruction, an issue many Republicans now wanted to shed. "We want no more mixture of races," Senator La Fayette Grover (D-Ore.) said. "No strong nation was ever born of mongrel races of men." Describing "the contaminating, corroding, and destructive effects of the . . . Asiatic barbarians," Senator John H. Mitchell (R-Ore.) compared Chinese immigration to a "great anaconda" squeezing the life out of American civilization. As Senator Jones concluded in his most chilling metaphor, "We oppose their coming because our sturdy Aryan tree will wither in root, trunk, and branch, if this noxious vine be permitted to entwine itself around it."[10]

The rhetoric of these western senators exceeded anything uttered by Kearney on his recent eastern tour. Although legislators consciously sought to distance themselves from the "sandlot orator" and his "hoodlum audience," their message was exactly the same: the Chinese must go. This message, of course, was nothing new. For the past decade, western politicians had argued in Washington for a restriction of Chinese immigration, and the racist images they invoked in their advocacy of the Fifteen Passenger Bill were common fare by the late 1870s. Only the *magnitude* of the anti-Chinese onslaught was new, as westerners unleashed every thunderbolt in their arsenal in an effort to convert their eastern colleagues. Long accustomed to hearing such attacks from western politicians, no one in the East was really surprised by the intensity of their comments. They were to be expected; they were to be endured. Senators from east of the Rockies had themselves largely avoided debate on the issue during the 1870s. They had heeded westerners' cries so far as approving an investigation and supporting renegotiation of the Burlingame Treaty, but their involvement had been passive, not active. Before Kearney's tour in 1878, eastern senators had been passengers rather than drivers of the vehicle of Chinese exclusion. In the winter of 1879 this suddenly changed. James Blaine himself stepped forward to grab the reins.

On February 14, the Plumed Knight took center stage on the Senate floor as he delivered his first speech ever on Chinese immigration. The Fifteen Passenger Bill, Blaine said, "divides itself naturally into two parts, one of form and one of great substance. The one of form is whether we may rightfully adopt this mode of terminating the [Burlingame] treaty. . . . The second and graver question is whether it is desirable to exclude Chinese immigration from this country." Blaine wasted little time on the first part. The United States had every right to break a treaty, he argued, and besides, China had violated the treaty numerous times. So much for form. Blaine emphasized the "second and graver" part of the issue, "whether we will have for the Pacific coast the civilization of Christ or the civilization of Confucius" and whether the U.S. government should assist "the free American laborer" or "the servile laborer from China." As "political and social pariahs," Blaine warned, "the swarming coolies of Shanghai" and "the vast . . . incalculable hordes in China" threatened to "throttle and impair the prosperity of . . . the United States. . . . The Asiatic cannot go on with our population and make a homogeneous element. The idea of comparing European immigration with an immigration that has no regard to family, that does not recognize the relation of husband and wife, that does not observe the tie of parent and child, that does not have in the slightest degree the ennobling and the civilizing influences of the hearth-stone and the fireside!" Blaine concluded, "I am opposed to the Chinese coming here; I am opposed to making them citizens; I am opposed to making them voters."[11]

It was neither the substance nor the style of Blaine's rhetoric that was new. It was the source. No longer coming from just the sandlots of San Francisco or the Senator Sargents of the West Coast, the message came now from the most powerful statesman in Congress: the Chinese must go. And just in case anyone failed to hear his speech, Blaine publicized his views in a lengthy letter to the *New York Tribune*. Using such adjectives as "vicious," "odious," "abominable," "dangerous," and "revolting" to describe Chinese immigration, he claimed that nothing in all history could compare with "the atrocious nastiness" of San Francisco's Chinatown, except perhaps the "feculence and foulness of Sodom and Gomorrah." Because the Chinese bred "plague" and "pestilence" wherever they went, they would "physically contaminate" and "morally corrupt" the nation. Enumerating ten distinct reasons for the restriction of Chinese immigration, Blaine focused on the one he considered central: the need to help the working classes. Seizing his western colleagues' theme of class and the need to help the *American*—not just *western*—worker, Blaine nationalized the issue. Workers, he said, both demanded and deserved anti-Chinese legislation: "I feel and know that I am pleading the cause of the free American laborer and of his children and of his children's children." No matter that "the free American laborer" had for years distinguished between voluntary and imported Chinese immigrants. No matter that "the free American laborer" had for years welcomed open immigration. No matter that "the free American laborer" east of the Rockies had repudiated Kearney and his cry, "the Chinese must go." Blaine cared little about the exact demands of workers. But Blaine did care about law and order, and he did care about labor unrest, particularly the bloody railroad strike of 1877 and the threatened uprising of 1878. "Discontent among unemployed thousands has already manifested a spirit of violence," he warned, "and but recently arrested travel between the Atlantic and the Mississippi by armed mobs which defied the States and commanded great . . . railways to cease operations." The long depression, railroad strike, and red scare had put class tensions at center stage, and Blaine invoked these tensions to legitimize the cry for Chinese exclusion.[12]

As if class conflict weren't enough, Blaine added, the South remained racked by racial conflict. "I supposed if there was any people in the world that had a race trouble on hand it was ourselves. I supposed if the admonitions of our

Figure 8.2. Comparing white treachery against Native Americans in the past to possible Chinese treachery against whites in the future—*if* Chinese immigration remained unchecked—this cartoon ominously invoked the nation's heritage to justify Chinese exclusion. It also helped illustrate Senator James G. Blaine's prediction that "either the Anglo-

own history were anything to us we should regard the race trouble as the one thing to be dreaded and the one thing to be avoided." And here was a chance to avoid a new "race trouble." With revolutionary disturbances brewing and race problems rife, the military was stretched to its limits preserving the peace. "Practical statesmanship," Blaine concluded, "would suggest that the Government of the United States has its hands full." Herein Blaine stated the nub of the problem. Labor militancy frightened politicians of every stripe. Race differences had recently torn the country in two and precipitated civil war. Now class differences threatened to do the same. "I think it is a good deal cheaper . . . to avoid the trouble by preventing the immigration," Blaine said. "You must deal with things as you find them." To Blaine, the primary goal of statesmanship—or of "practical" statesmanship—was to preserve order rather than to serve justice. The U.S. government did indeed have "its hands full"—and Chinese immigration restriction presented an easy, simple "solution." Blaine's argument was masterly. Pitting class against class and race against race, he effectively killed two birds with one stone: he could now pose as the champion of peace and order and claim all the while he was on the side of the working person. As the Maine Republican declared, "[I speak] in defense and advocacy of the interests of the laboring classes." Blaine's conversion to the exclusionist banner marked the key turning point in the anti-Chinese movement. As the most influential Republican in the country (with the possible exception of lame-duck president Rutherford B. Hayes), Blaine elevated the Chinese issue nationally in a way no other individual—whether in the Senate, in Sacramento, in San Francisco, or in the sandlots—ever could have, and he single-handedly raised the politics of race to a new level. Whereas Denis Kearney could be dismissed as a mindless demagogue, James Blaine was running for president. And therein lay the difference.[13]

The presidential election of 1876, when measured by popular vote, proved the closest in over thirty years, and the electoral vote, 185 to 184, remains the closest in American history. Blaine knew that the election of 1880—which he hoped to win—could be just as close. He also knew that three of the closest battles had taken place in the West. Hayes had won California by less than three thousand votes—a slim 1.8 percent—and had carried Oregon and Nevada by just over

Saxon race will possess the Pacific slope or the Mongolians will possess it." Original caption: "Will History Repeat Itself? Eastward the Star of China takes its way!—Population of the United States, 40,000,000; of China 400,000,000." (*McGee's Illustrated Weekly*, March 6, 1880)

one thousand votes each. With the parties almost evenly divided in the West, Blaine knew that an extreme anti-Chinese stance could make the difference. "The local troubles on the Pacific slope have caught his eye and aroused his ambition," one observer remarked. "He imagines that they will be exactly the hobby-horse that will carry him to the Presidential chair." Blaine hoped that such a stance would first secure him his party's nomination by guaranteeing support from western delegates at the 1880 national convention. "Mr. Blaine made no secret . . . of his anxiety to have it known, and well and widely known on the Pacific coast, that he opposed Chinese immigration," the *Utica Herald* noted. "He was weaker there in 1876 than in any other republican community not ruled by a well-drilled machine."[14]

Blaine's sudden embrace of anti-Chinese politics had another aim. In November 1878, thirty-seven of the nation's thirty-eight states had elected their representatives to the 46th Congress, which would convene in December 1879. California, however, alone among all states, elected its congressional delegation in odd-numbered years and would choose its members to the 46th Congress in September 1879. If Blaine and the Republican Party could take credit for the Fifteen Passenger Bill, it might swing this upcoming congressional election—just seven months away—to the Republicans. Such a victory could be vital in the next presidential contest if, as many politicians predicted, the closeness of the electoral vote prevented any candidate from claiming a majority and threw the election into Congress. Such a possibility was not far fetched. It had just happened in 1876, and the rise of the Greenback-Labor Party had suddenly complicated the electoral equation. Receiving more than a million votes in 1878, Greenbackers had captured fourteen seats in the new Congress. Their success stunned almost everyone, and their popularity seemed to be waxing. George C. Gorham, secretary of the Senate and chairman of the Republican Congressional Committee, confided to Blaine that Greenback success was creating "a good deal of panic" and could spell "disaster" for Republicans. Although aiming his net around California, Blaine hoped that with Chinese exclusion he could also snare votes of workers nationwide—whose "cause . . . I am pleading"—and thereby solidify his own support and derail the Greenbackers.[15]

Blaine and fellow politicians had one final concern if the election of 1880 ended up in Congress. According to the Constitution, each state delegation in the House of Representatives regardless of size casts a single vote for president. By early 1879, Blaine knew that a party vote by state in 1880—not counting California or Indiana—would yield a balance of eighteen to eighteen in the House. Indiana's thirteen-seat delegation divided evenly—six Democrats to six Republicans—with one Greenbacker. This lone Greenbacker could thus become "kingmaker" if the election ended up in the House. Unless, of course, one party carried California. If Blaine could swing Golden State voters to the Republican column, then he (or at least his party) might then capture the presidency in 1880. California's four-seat House delegation potentially held the key to the White House. As the *New York World* sneered, "If the [Fifteen Passenger] bill had been entitled 'a bill to bag the Congressional representation from California in September, 1879,' it would have been exactly and honestly described."[16]

Blaine thus had three goals in championing Chinese exclusion: influencing the California election; swinging western delegates at the Republican Convention; and, with workingmen's votes nationwide, winning the presidency. Blaine would fulfill two of these goals, but the final and most critical one would forever elude him. Nonetheless, he had, with one single oration (and letter) thrust himself in the forefront of the anti-Chinese movement, and his views became known everywhere. As a verse to one of the year's most popular songs went, "All Chinese must emigrate, and go back home again, / And when I'm there in Washington I'll stick to Senator Blaine."[17] The Plumed Knight took a calculated gamble that his exploitation of racial and class fears would carry him into the White House. As the *New York Sun* observed just after his speech: "Every step which Mr. Blaine takes in politics has reference to his personal ambition to be President of the United States. It is one of the painful consequences of his record that he cannot cast a vote or take sides upon any important question without having the sincerity of his motive disputed."[18]

Blaine never admitted any ulterior motive for supporting the Fifteen Passenger Bill, but the evidence is overwhelming. In his otherwise skimpy collection of personal papers, Blaine devoted meticulous attention to gauging reaction to his anti-Chinese effusions. In a scrapbook, he carefully preserved dozens of clippings from editorials around the country commenting on his newfound opposition to Chinese immigration. No journal was too obscure to escape his notice, from the *Auburn (New York) Advertiser* (anti) to the *Rockford (Illinois) Free Press* (pro). Blaine also preserved numerous speeches and letters remarking on his address and a congratulatory telegram from the governor of Nevada. In a day before public opinion polls, press reaction was the closest way to measure popular approval. On no other issue did Blaine track political effects so assiduously. This alone suggests the impetus behind his actions. The subject of Chinese immigration scarcely ever appears in his correspondence before 1879, and if he truly cared about imported Chinese labor, immigration, and the Burlingame Treaty, "why," asked the *New York World*, "did not the country hear from Mr. Blaine about this between 1868 and 1875," when he was Speaker of the House? The answer, quite obviously, was that Blaine did not then consider the issue a vote-getting ploy. But he did now. And with the presidency within his grasp, no position was too low to adopt. As the *World* noted, "Senator Blaine has made himself the showman in behalf of the anti-Chinese movement." To the rhythm of "John Anderson," an unnamed poet put the matter simply:

> John Chinaman, my Josh John,
>   Jem Blaine, in tones terrific,
> Pitched to command the suffrages
>   Next year from the Pacific,
> Cries out: "My friend, the black man,
>   Knows well I love his race;
> But I loathe the voteless aspect
>   Of a copper-colored face."

Despite the press's emphasis on California, Blaine had also pitched his cry to the rest of the country. His decision to showcase his anti-Chinese message in the high-profile *New York Tribune*—rather than in a western paper—illustrated his desire to reach the widest possible audience. "None knew better than he," one biographer observed, "how to use the channels of the newspapers for creating impressions upon the public mind." By stressing that workers nation-wide demanded such legislation and by prominently placing the working person at the core of his constituency, Blaine placed himself in a distinct category of presidential aspirants.[19]

Blaine, of course, was not the only man itching to be president. Two leading Democratic contenders sat with him in the Senate: Thomas F. Bayard and Allan G. Thurman. Scion of a distinguished Delaware family, Bayard was the only Democrat south of Pennsylvania with both a national reputation and a realistic chance for higher office. To capture the presidency, he too would need western votes, and leading Democrats in California urged him to support the Fifteen Passenger Bill. "The treatment of this question by a Democrat of your promi-nence," wrote Philip Roach, "would help our party in the next Presidential contest." Roach, an advocate of Chinese exclusion for some twenty-five years, had met privately with Bayard during his anti-Chinese tour of the East in 1876. Now, he advised the senator, the stakes had risen—the presidency was on the line. George Gorham, the high-ranking Washington insider (and Blaine confi-dant), he wrote, "will see that the Chinese baby is properly nursed so as to give the Congressional election in this State to the Republicans." As if this weren't bad enough, "here Kearney has carried off two-thirds of our party by his cry 'the Chinese must go.'" If Democrats were to have any chance of carrying Califor-nia—and thereby the nation—they had to trumpet the issue loudly. "You are in a

Figure 8.3. At "Kearney's Senatorial Restaurant," Senators Thurman, Bayard, and Blaine feast on "hoodlum stew." Like Esau in the Bible, they have sold their birthright—American principles—for a "mess of (sandlot) pottage." Of the three presidential hopefuls, Blaine takes the biggest mouthful. A nauseated Confucius observes, "How can Christians stomach such dirt?" Original caption: "A Matter of Taste. Confucius: 'How can Christians stomach such dirt?'" (*Harper's Weekly*, March 15, 1879)

position to direct public attention," Roach remarked. "I think you can treat this question in a manner to convince the masses that their relief will be secured only by electing a Democratic President and adhering to Democratic principles." Former senator Eugene Casserly, who had urged Chinese exclusion back in 1870, was more blunt. "California intensely unanimous for Chinese . . . bill," he telegraphed Bayard, "hear cry of whole people. Fail us not."[20]

Bayard had no intention of failing. A lifelong opponent of civil rights and black equality, Bayard favored the Fifteen Passenger Bill, and his opposition to Chinese immigration dovetailed easily with his racist proclivities. "I am a strong believer in blood and race," he had noted recently, "and am convinced that the downfall of a man or nation is near at hand when a disregard for such facts is permitted. . . . All over this broad land we should watch and combat the stealthy step towards Mongolianism." In backing the bill, a disillusioned supporter remarked, Bayard was now "on the side of the hoodlums & scalawags of the Pacific Coast."[21]

Bayard's colleague Allan Thurman also had his eye on the White House—

and was also "on the side of the hoodlums & scalawags." Thurman had served in the Senate since 1869 and, like Blaine and Bayard, had scarcely ever uttered a word about Chinese immigration. In one address in 1870, the Ohio Democrat had endorsed the distinction eastern workers made between immigration and importation. But in 1879 this distinction no longer mattered. The Chinese are not a "desirable population," he said. Chinese immigration "is a pernicious evil that we want to get rid of. . . . We want no more mixture of . . . races in this country."[22]

This sudden embrace of anti-Chinese politics surprised no one. As the *New York Times* noted, "The Senate is well-known to be painfully overcrowded just now with people who have Presidential aspirations." Despite all the oratory heard in Congress, a Washington correspondent observed, winning western votes "is, in fact, almost the only argument that has been used in private at any stage of the movement." Furthermore, the reporter added, "there has probably never been a bill before Congress where all the parties interested in pushing it so readily and unblushingly admitted that the reasons addressed to the public were mere claptrap, while the real move was one to secure party supremacy." Claptrap or not, of the three presidential aspirants in the Senate, Blaine alone couched the bill in class terms, hoping it would solidify Republican strength nationwide. But everyone played the race card. For Democrats, the *Cincinnati Gazette* noted, this was par for the course. They had been playing racial politics for years and had never voiced allegiance to higher ideals. But for Republicans to engage in "such baseness" was distressing. "Republicans only roll in the dirt for nothing," the *Gazette* declared, "when they strive with the Democrats in such dirty work."[23]

Not all Republicans rolled in the dirt. A select handful led by Hannibal Hamlin (R-Maine) stood up in the Senate against the Fifteen Passenger Bill. "I know the power of prejudice," the party patriarch said. "I know how it holds with grappled hooks of steel." Almost seventy, Hamlin was the oldest Republican in the Senate and one of the few to have served before the Civil War. As Lincoln's first vice president, he had been an early advocate of emancipation and a loyal member of the party's Radical wing. To Hamlin, truly a generation removed from his fellow senator from Maine, James Blaine, defending Chinese immigration seemed a logical extension of the Republican Party's heritage of free soil and equal rights. Racial prejudice, he said, must be confronted and overcome to achieve America's promise of "human liberty and the rights of man . . . principles deep imbedded in the foundations of our Government." And now, with the arrival of a few Chinese, he asked, ought these principles, these traditions—"as 'the home of the free,' where the outcast of every nation, where the child of every creed and of every clime could breathe our free air"—

be reversed? "I am as indifferent to all the danger that shall come away down into the stillness of ages from the immigration of the Chinese. Treat them . . . like Christians, and they will become good American citizens." Hamlin's oratory stirred applause from the gallery. "I have convictions upon this question," he said, "and they are deep in my heart."[24]

Clad in his customary "full dress suit of black" and with his face bearing "faint reminiscent outlines of [Daniel] Webster's," Hamlin's appearance seemed as outdated as his ideals. "I regret that every man of every creed and of every clime may not come here," he said. Ban the Chinese today and who will be next? Catholics? Southern Europeans? "I know not where it may end. . . . We are hurrying on now to do an act at which I fear in after-time the men who do it will blush, and he who writes the history of the day will read it with amazement and astonishment." Calling immigration restriction one of the most "far-reaching" issues the Senate had ever debated, Hamlin left no doubt as to where he stood: "I shall vote against the measure, and I leave that vote the last legacy to my children that they may esteem it the brightest act of my life."[25]

Hamlin was not the only senator to invoke the nation's heritage of open immigration and equal rights. The great mission of America, said George Frisbie Hoar (R-Mass.), is to live out "the truth, that wherever God has placed in a human frame a human soul, that which he so created is the equal of every other like creature on the face of the earth,—equal, among other things, in the right to go everywhere on this globe." Equal rights had been at the root of the Civil War, Hoar said, and were now carved in stone by "the three great amendments to the Constitution blazing like three stars in front of our history." For most Republicans, whether pro- or anti-Chinese, the lessons of the Civil War and Reconstruction remained the focal point of the debate. Senator Stanley Matthews (R-Ohio) argued that it was not "the presence of the black man on this continent that brought in upon us all this woe, it was his presence here as a slave." The Civil War had taught America that the twin evils of slavery and inequality must be abolished. God made all people "of one blood . . . and the same destiny," Matthews said. "Do right; treat every man, white or black, copper-colored or whatever, as you would be done by yourself in like circumstances." The right of emigration belonged to "all humanity," Henry L. Dawes (R-Mass.) intoned, and opposition to the Chinese stemmed purely from racial prejudice—a prejudice the Republican Party stood pledged to eradicate. "The political organization which I am proud to belong to," Dawes declared, "was summoned into existence for the very purpose of vindicating the equality of the human race upon this continent in all political rights."[26]

Passage of a century has dulled neither the passion nor the eloquence of the ideals stated by these senators. Their pleas for racial equality and human rights

Figure 8.4. In spearheading the fight against the Fifteen Passenger Bill, aging abolitionist senator Hannibal Hamlin of Maine (1809–91) spoke eloquently in defense of the Chinese and America's open-door tradition. "I know the power of prejudice," he said, "how it holds with grappled hooks of steel." The former vice president, however, revealed prejudices of his own and quietly assisted the effort to restrict Chinese immigration. (Courtesy Collections of the Maine Historical Society)

still shine brightly more than a hundred years later, testifying to the enduring power of ideas (and ideals) to influence people's judgments. A generation schooled in the ideology of Republicanism and equal rights could not easily cast this ideology aside when confronted by new problems. The same Republican ideology that had inspired emancipation and civil rights provided a basis for defending Chinese immigration. It was no coincidence that Senator Hoar, while acting as pro tem during the debate, invited Senator Blanche K. Bruce (R-Miss.) to chair the proceedings, marking the first time a black man ever presided over the Senate. In both symbolic acts and national legislation, the cause of racial justice still remained a vital force uniting a remnant of the abolitionist wing of the Republican Party. Their tributes to human equality— especially when contrasted with their opponents' visceral appeals to prejudice —provide strong evidence that the nation, or at least a portion of it, had indeed progressed since the days of slavery. And as Senator Hoar remarked, "I do not wish to go back."[27]

As noble as these tributes were, however, they do not tell the whole story. A deeper analysis of the position of these Republicans reveals prejudices of a different nature; underneath the umbrella of humanitarianism and equal rights lurked attitudes of indifference and even hostility to the Chinese as well as powerful fears of the working classes. Senator Hamlin provides a prime example. "I am a little inclined to think," the Republican patriarch said, "that if all the Chinamen in our land had the ballot in their hands to-day we should not have heard a word of this Chinese question here. I think that is a key to a solution of the whole question. I am willing to admit them to naturalization." Despite these avowals, Hamlin had been one of the leading senators to vote against Chinese naturalization (and suffrage) nine years earlier in the great Senate debate of 1870. When pressed on this point by Blaine, Hamlin conceded the fact. He had opposed naturalizing the Chinese, he said, because he feared admitting "another element and another class" who were yet "to be assimi-lated." Granting suffrage to blacks had been difficult, Hamlin recalled, and "I thought we might postpone for a limited period when we should bring in the Chinaman and give to him the ballot." In the following years, however, neither Hamlin nor his colleagues had introduced any measure aimed at enfranchising the Chinese. Such a law—especially the one in 1870—might indeed have influenced the course of anti-Chinese politics and prevented forever the consideration of Chinese exclusion. But by 1879 it was too late, and the Chinese lacked the power of the ballot box. By failing to act on their professed ideals during the past decade, even these Republicans had belied their party's heritage.[28]

A principled defense of Chinese immigration could be a thinly disguised slap at others. Hamlin attributed the Fifteen Passenger Bill "to your Dennis Kearneys and to your unnaturalized Englishmen." Why single out one nationality, he asked, when all immigrants have "as much to revolt us as . . . the Chinese"? He cited, for instance, the Irish ("unnaturalized Englishmen") and "the lazzaroni that swarm the coasts of the Mediterranean." He then noted various shortcomings of the Chinese: "their system of prejudices," their "want of religion," their slowness to assimilate. These were serious problems, Hamlin acknowledged, and if the Chinese threatened to cause "imminent peril" and "overrun our country," he would certainly consider restrictive legislation. Only not yet.[29]

While Hamlin defended open immigration, he paradoxically also defended Chinese immigration restriction. During his speech, in fact, he trumpeted his own role in furthering the anti-Chinese agenda. As chairman of the Foreign Relations Committee, he took personal credit for having drafted the 1878 resolution urging renegotiation of the Burlingame Treaty so as to allow restriction of Chinese immigration. He now asked his colleagues to have "a little . . . patience" and let such negotiations proceed: "If we would only wait a fair and reasonable

THIS CHINESE QUESTION WOULD BE SETTLED IF THE CHINEE, CHINEE, WOULD VOTEE! VOTEE!! VOTEE!!!

Figure 8.5. In 1870, the Senate had debated granting the right of naturalization (and suffrage) to Chinese immigrants. Had such a measure passed, politicians and party bosses might have embraced—rather than attacked—Chinese immigrants and wiped out any prospect of Chinese exclusion. Original caption: "The Chinese Question Would Be Settled If the Chinee, Chinee, Would Votee! Votee!! Votee!!!" (*Puck*, March 12, 1879)

time, . . . we should reach a solution of this question under that resolution that would be satisfactory to our friends on the Pacific slope, as well as to the people of the whole Union." Ideals, evidently, were open to compromise.[30]

Hamlin thus stated what was to him the fundamental issue: the Fifteen Passenger Bill violated the Burlingame Treaty. First modify the treaty, he said, *then* pass the law. Hamlin spent the better part of his speech arguing that treaties were solemn international pacts from which neither party could arbitrarily withdraw. A fifteen passenger law, he warned, would sully "our . . . national honor" and could lead China to consider the Burlingame Treaty nullified. Hamlin feared the dire effects of such an action. "There is here a great question of commercial intercourse," he said, noting that under the treaty, exports to China had tripled during the 1870s. Who is to say, he asked, that if the United States limited to fifteen the number of Chinese passengers on each ship from Asia to America, China may not turn around and limit to fifteen the number of barrels of flour on each ship from America to Asia? "Oh, I cannot bear to see a stop put to the untold millions of commerce that shall roll to our shores," Hamlin concluded. "I cannot bear to see that uncounted commerce that shall go from us to them interfered with."[31]

Money and "national honor"—the two issues became inextricable—lay at the heart of the Republican opposition. Every Republican who spoke against the Fifteen Passenger Bill emphasized the Burlingame Treaty as the major stumbling block. Senators Timothy O. Howe (R-Wisc.), Samuel J. R. McMillan (R-Minn.), and George F. Edmunds (R-Vt.) all cited the treaty as their only obstacle. They never once mentioned equality, justice, or America's open-door tradition. Nor did Senator Bainbridge Wadleigh (R-N.H.), who noted that "leading manufacturers" had recently told him that the United States was gaining more of the cotton market in China at the expense of Great Britain. Overturning the treaty might harm this trade.[32]

Republicans such as Hamlin who mentioned racial equality and the nation's open-door tradition made it plain where their beliefs and priorities lay. Senator Dawes, though preaching equal rights, stressed the moral and intellectual superiority of "the Anglo-Saxon." Matthews, meanwhile, called the Chinese "pagans and heathens." Restrict them if you will, he said, but do it properly; diplomacy would "accomplish all the beneficial results" intended by the legislation and take only a "few months longer." Nothing less than "the commerce of this nation is at stake," he said. Hoar also spoke reverently of the Burlingame Treaty—"upon which very large commercial and business interests depend"— and feared that the bill would "overthrow by a single blow every right to the commerce which the merchants of the United States have . . . with China." Enumerating the reasons he opposed the bill, Hoar emphasized first the violation of the treaty and second the potential harm to commerce. The rights of man came last. "Republicans," Abraham Lincoln had once said, "are for both the man and the dollar, but in case of conflict the man before the dollar." For opponents of the Fifteen Passenger Bill of 1879, these two causes—the man and the dollar—still converged neatly, but it had become evident that even among the graying abolitionist wing of the Republican Party, Lincoln's dictum had been reversed.[33]

That the Republican opposition cared less about limiting Chinese immigration than about overturning a treaty and obstructing trade was further made evident by the methods senators sought to modify the legislation. On February 14, Senator Matthews proposed an amendment urging the president to renegotiate the immigration clause of the Burlingame Treaty, and if, by January 1, 1880, the president had not submitted the new treaty to the Senate, the

United States would then declare the old treaty void. Senator Roscoe Conkling (R-N.Y.) suggested that if by the end of the year China refused to revise the treaty's immigration clause—which he labeled "unsatisfactory" and "pernicious"—the United States would then consider that clause of the treaty void and proceed to pass laws to "regulate or prevent the migration or importation" of Chinese subjects. Conkling claimed his amendment was more specific and would abrogate only a single clause rather than the entire treaty. Matthews agreed and withdrew his amendment.[34]

The Conkling amendment dominated the debate for the next two days, during which senators discussed the merits of forcing diplomatic negotiations on China to restrict immigration or simply restricting it by legislative fiat. Favoring the latter, Thurman called the Conkling amendment "rude" and "bullying," while others, such as Edmunds and David Davis (D-Ill.), deemed diplomacy preferable and the amendment appropriate. Senator Blaine listened to his colleagues in astonishment. The only difference between the original bill and the Conkling amendment, he said, was timing. Either the United States stops immigration now or tells the emperor of China that if he doesn't negotiate a new treaty immediately, the United States will stop immigration in a year. The United States was indeed bullying: "Shaking the American fist in his face, 'I want you [the emperor of China] . . . to understand that whether you consent or not, we will undertake to declare, through our legislative power that this thing is to be at an end.' . . . That is all the difference." Blaine was right. The main distinction *was* timing—but some senators considered this crucial. When breaking a contract, Howe said, "it is . . . far preferable to give a few days of grace" to the other party. This makes for "a politer way . . . of reaching that end." Hamlin agreed. The amendment was indeed "politer," and he backed it because it set a definite period—ten months—for negotiation.[35]

On February 15, the Senate twice rejected the Conkling amendment, 31 to 34 (with 10 not voting) and 31 to 33 (with 11 not voting). Politeness, apparently, was not persuasive. The significance of the Conkling amendment lies not in the closeness of the votes but in the substance of the dispute. Senators debated the *method* of Chinese immigration restriction—diplomacy versus legislation —rather than restriction itself. The ethics of overriding a treaty outweighed the ethics of proscribing an entire race of people from the United States. It was the means and not the ends on which senators clashed: in the ornate halls of the Capitol, most Republican and Democratic lawmakers had reached consensus in favor of limiting the immigration of the Chinese people.[36]

The final vote proved almost an anticlimax. Late in the afternoon on February 15, the Senate passed the Fifteen Passenger Bill with a few minor amendments, 39 to 27 (with 9 not voting). Democrats supported the bill 21 to 10 (with

Figure 8.6. With the Fifteen Passenger Bill in hand, a demagogue stands by the "golden gates," locked by the "hoodlum" Congress against the Chinese. The Burlingame Treaty lies underfoot, broken with a mallet of "bad faith," while the American version of the Great Wall of China stands behind, inscribed with the names of Blaine and leading senators. Original caption: "The Demagogues' Triumph." (*Puck*, February 26, 1879)

THE DEMAGOGUES' TRIUMPH.

6 not voting), while Republicans supported it 18 to 17 (with 3 not voting). The Fifteen Passenger Bill thus received a bipartisan majority in what one critic labeled "the Hoodlum Congress." As the *Chicago Tribune* remarked, "Altogether Mr. Denny Kearney has triumphed."[37]

On February 22, the House approved the Senate version.[38] Only the president's signature now lay in the way of Chinese immigration restriction. Would Hayes sign or veto the bill? Over the past year he had given contradictory signals, favoring restriction but seeming to prefer a diplomatic approach. Because no one was sure what he would do, the last two weeks of February witnessed intense lobbying from the press and the people across the country.

This frenetic activity focused enormous attention on Chinese immigration—the most since North Adams in 1870—and made the Fifteen Passenger Bill the most regionally divisive issue since the Civil War. The West mobilized at once. "Never in any community was there more unanimity of opinion than that which prevails on this coast adverse to the inroads of the Chinese," the San Francisco Chamber of Commerce asserted. "It pervades every class, trade and occupation." Indicative of this "unanimity," the *Washington Star* noted that every western member of Congress had "received at least a bushel of telegrams from citizens of his state, ministers, doctors, lawyers, merchants—men of all professions, in fact—urging him to use his every effort to induce the President to sign the bill." The western press kept the momentum at full throttle. "The bill carries mercies and blessings to generations yet unborn," declared the *Virginia City (Nevada) Enterprise*, which called passage of the legislation the greatest event "since the day when the guns of rebellion grew still." Politician after politician in the West lined up behind the bill, from governors and state lawmakers to mayors and city trustees. Delegates to the California constitutional convention, just putting the finishing touches on the new charter, interrupted proceedings to issue a unanimous appeal for Hayes's signature. Clergy also jumped into the act. Baptists and Methodists urged approval, and at an ecumenical meeting in San Francisco, Presbyterians, Episcopalians, Catholics, and Jews united in support.[39]

Merchants played a prominent role in this agitation. The San Francisco Chamber of Commerce, Portland Board of Trade, and Oakland Merchants' Exchange held special meetings to endorse the bill. All 250 members of the Chamber of Commerce supported it, noted director George C. Perkins (soon to be California's next governor), who then asked the mayor to organize a mass meeting. On February 27, more than ten thousand San Franciscans gathered to hear such luminaries as Mayor Andrew Bryant, Governor William Irwin, and Philip Roach denounce Chinese immigration and demand the president's signature. "The platform seats were occupied by leading merchants and professional men of the city," the *New York Herald* observed, "and three-fourths of the audience were . . . substantial citizens, while the working men were largely represented." A separate labor meeting also backed the legislation, although Denis Kearney considered the bill weak and designed only for political purposes. The most extreme statements came neither from Kearney nor the "hoodlums," however, but from the *Daily Stock Report* of San Francisco, the region's oldest financial journal. Failure to sign the bill, the *Stock Report* claimed, could lead California to "sever our connection with the national confederation. . . . Already such a dread possibility as secession from the union . . . is broadly talked of in high circles." Less than fifteen years after the Civil War, secession remained the most incendiary word in political discourse. While sandlotters could be dismissed as demagogues—and the state mocked as "Kearneyfornee"—the sober *Daily Stock Report* acted as a mouthpiece for the Pacific Coast's financial leaders. Preaching secession was a surefire method of alarming the rest of the nation. As a poet for the *New York Sun* wrote:

We're tired of waiting for your dictating,
　　For that man Hayes to say Yes or No;

The Chinese question spoils our digestion,
　　We find your ways too airy and slow;
So now, without a doubt, we'll to the right about
　　Send every heathen that wears a queue,
Though it's our impression it will take secession
　　To make you see it in the light we do.

Easterners could wax poetic, but westerners remained dead serious. " 'The Chinese must go,' is not the vulgar *patois* of the sand-lots," a local minister observed. "It is the epigram of the will of California . . . the watchword of the guard at the Golden Gate." During the last two weeks of February, Californians unleashed every weapon in their arsenal—meetings, resolutions, demonstrations, telegrams, editorials, letters, and outright threats of treason—to pressure Hayes to sign the Fifteen Passenger Bill and thereby close the "Golden Gate."[40]

The reaction in the East stood in total contrast to that in the West. East of the Rockies the press and the public heaped nothing but abuse on the bill. Republican journals called it "crude and objectionable," "a discredit and a degradation," and Democratic papers reacted with similar outrage. The *Brooklyn Eagle* denounced the bill's "Know-Nothing spirit" and, picking apart Blaine's *New York Tribune* letter paragraph by paragraph, scolded Congress for "pandering to the un-American brutality of the Pacific slope." The *New York World* called it a "scandalous act" and a "villainy," while the *Louisville Courier-Journal* dismissed the "buncombe bill" as "a weak concession to vagabonds and vagabondage." As the *Poughkeepsie Eagle* observed, "nine-tenths of the respectable newspapers of both parties" opposed the bill. Belying the common belief that the Irish united behind Chinese exclusion, the *New York Irish-American* condemned the bill as "un-Democratic" and "a step of the most serious significance taken away from that principle of human brotherhood which is the vital element in popular government." The *Cincinnati Commercial* put it best: "Congress is an ass."[41]

This sudden wave of antibill sentiment must not mask a crucial point: it was possible to oppose both the Fifteen Passenger Bill *and* Chinese immigration at the same time. In fact, the arguments marshaled against the bill demonstrated clearly that Chinese exclusion would ultimately prevail. The arguments also revealed the nation's retreat from the ideals of the Civil War and Reconstruction. The *Chicago Times* opposed the bill but dismissed the equal rights argument as "nonsense" and "antique flummery." And the notion of "America being the refuge of the oppressed of all lands," the *Cincinnati Enquirer* added, was nothing but "flimsy flapdoodle." Such mockery might have been expected from Democratic organs, but Republicans mouthed similar comments. The

Chicago Tribune, once a staunch Radical Republican journal, savaged the bill's detractors for clinging to their equal rights ideology—a vestige of their "maudlin, unpractical, dishwater sentimentality." The *Nation* called the bill "absolutely indefensible" but made clear that "in saying all this we are not disposed to pooh-pooh the arguments of Senator Sargent in support of the bill."[42]

Such was the verdict of virtually every Republican journal regardless of its views on Chinese immigration, equal rights, or the nation's open-door tradition. The virulently anti-Chinese *Cincinnati Gazette* stood on one extreme. "We have never advocated the unrestricted influx of Chinamen to our shores," the *Gazette* noted. Indeed, in the aftermath of North Adams in 1870, the *Gazette* advocated Chinese exclusion and chastised workers for not adopting this position. The passage of nine years had not altered the newspaper's stance. Despite its long track record of anti-Chinese editorials, however, the *Gazette* condemned the "hoodlum bill" as "a stain of dishonor upon our national faith" that would "unquestionably unsettle all American interests in China."[43]

Republican journals that had long championed equal rights and the nation's open-door heritage ultimately took the same position, if perhaps with a touch more regret. The *New York Tribune* recognized that enactment of the bill would "belie the principles of the past century. . . . Why should a nation which did not shrink from three millions of negroes, get into a panic over a paltry one hundred thousand Mongolians?" Why indeed? The *Tribune* couldn't say. But it clearly did not welcome the "Mongolians" and acknowledged that Blaine's letter denouncing them was "clear, concise, admirably stated, full of facts, and amply backed by authorities." Restriction might eventually be justified, the *Tribune* conceded, but it should be accomplished "deliberately and decently," rather than in the "cowardly and unmanly fashion" proposed. Again, it was the *method* that rankled more than the goal. Instead of acting in "hot haste," the United States should "comply with the usual diplomatic formalities." The nation's ideals, evidently, like the treaty itself, lay open to modification. And at the root of the issue lay not the man but the dollar. The Burlingame Treaty "is to be abrogated," the *Tribune* regretted, "just at a time when American influence seemed about to secure greatly increased advantages for the commerce and industries of this country."[44]

The *New York Times* also condemned the bill as "needless and dishonorable" and paid lip service to the nation's long-cherished ideals. "The equality in rights of all men is the corner-stone upon which the American Republic rests," the *Times* stated; the bill's enactment "would violate all the principles upon which our Government is founded." Despite these sentiments, the *Times* hardly defended the Chinese, calling them "an avaricious people" unlike those "of any civilized country." Their immigration was "objectionable" and filled with "evils." Just in case anyone accused the paper of being pro-Chinese, the editor insisted that "it is grossly unjust to say that those who have opposed the bill to restrict Chinese immigration necessarily favor, or are indifferent to, the immigration of the Chinese." The *Times* deemed it "lamentable" that a diplomatic solution to limit Chinese immigration had not been achieved and concluded that "a remedy of some sort should be sought." So much for the "equality in rights of all men" and the principles of the nation.[45]

With visions of dollars dancing before Republican eyes, the nation's heritage retreated to the periphery. All told, the Fifteen Passenger Bill elicited three basic responses in the Republican Party. The first response, highlighted by Blaine, emphasized the evils of Chinese immigration and urged immediate restriction. The second response, represented by Conkling, acknowledged the evils of Chinese immigration and urged eventual restriction, within a year. The third response, epitomized by Hamlin, questioned the evils of Chinese immigration but stressed treaty and trade as the dominant issues and accepted the need for restriction. Whichever path Republicans chose to walk, the stumbling blocks of equal rights and the nation's open-door tradition appeared as little more than pebbles lying along the wayside. They could be seen but they could be ignored. And they could be trampled upon. The *Boston Post* put it squarely: "John Chinaman will not have visited the country for nothing if it proves that he has succeeded in taking down the towering pretensions of the Republican party on the subject of races. All thoughtful men knew it would come sooner or later, and the Mongolian can claim to have fulfilled his mission in the West."[46]

The press was the most visible expositor of public opinion but by no means the only one. Business leaders, ministers, and public figures rushed to make their views known in an effort to influence the president's decision. Leading merchants in the Northeast strongly criticized the bill as "a base act of international treachery" that "would be very detrimental to our commercial interests." One New York businessman complained that "just when the good results of the Burlingame treaty were unfolding themselves, the American Congress deliberately puts a check upon them." Merchants considered the Burlingame Treaty *their* treaty, wrung by the United States from a reluctant China, "proclaimed," in the words of merchant Abiel Abbot Low, "at the cannon's mouth." And now, because of the ill-conceived schemes of politicians, this commerce suddenly seemed in jeopardy. To disseminate their views more widely, J. P. Morgan, Levi P. Morton, Seth Low (merchant Low's son), and other leading bankers and businesspeople organized meetings at the Chambers of Commerce in New York and Philadelphia to protest the dangers to trade. Just as workers had been motivated by their own economic interests to urge a ban on imported contract labor, so merchants were motivated by their economic interests against a threatened loss of business. As one merchant warned, "The one hope for the salvation of American commerce with China lies in the Presidential veto."[47]

Most of the nation's religious leaders echoed the call of capital in fearing the effects of a violated treaty. They cared less about saving commercial rights, though, than they did about saving souls. The bill would "seriously interfere with missionary operations in the Celestial Empire," the *Methodist* (Baltimore) noted, "now in so hopeful a condition." Warning that it would impede the conversion of Chinese to Christianity, the American Missionary Association and ministers of numerous faiths denounced the bill. So did Rev. Henry Ward Beecher, the nation's most prominent pastor. Sounding more like a merchant than a minister, however, Beecher stressed the nation's honor and international obligations. Denying "any personal liking" for the Chinese, he attacked the bill to prevent "plac[ing] you and me and our posterity in the position of treaty-breakers." Though a few eastern ministers cited the familiar grounds of Chinese immorality and irreligion, the majority aligned with both the press and capital and urged a veto.[48]

A variety of public figures also spoke out against the bill. Venerable Republican Thurlow Weed, then in his eighty-second year, defended the Chinese and recommended a veto, as did former abolitionist William Lloyd Garrison, American and Foreign Anti-Slavery Society president Henry Highland Garnet, *Atlantic Monthly* editor William Dean Howells, showman P. T. Barnum (then a Connecticut state legislator), and *Harper's Weekly* editor and civil service reformer George William Curtis, who found it astounding "that the Republican party should be the first to shut the gates of America on mankind." Also urging a veto were Theodore Woolsey, former president of Yale University, and the entire Yale faculty, which signed a petition drafted by Professor S. Wells Williams. A noted scholar of the Orient who had helped negotiate the Burlingame Treaty and served twenty-one years as secretary of the U.S. legation in China, Williams had long opposed banning Chinese immigrants but remarked, "I myself should not like to have them come in droves. . . . We don't want them."[49]

Amid this rising clamor in the East, one group remained noticeably silent: workers. The labor press barely acknowledged the pending legislation. The *Cigar Makers' Official Journal* ignored the Fifteen Passenger Bill entirely, while the *Paterson Labor Standard* dismissed it in two sentences, taking no stand whatsoever. The *National Labor Tribune* (Pittsburgh) uttered scarcely a word more. The *Socialist* (Chicago) and the newly rechristened *Irish World and American Industrial Liberator* (New York) supported the bill but with little gusto. "It is the infamous system that permits the importation of Coolies (slaves) and the importers of them that we contend against," the *Socialist* stated. "This explanation we deem necessary in order to prevent mistakes." Also decrying importation, the *Irish World and American Industrial Liberator* added, "It is truly a pitiable sight to see grave and reverend Senators . . . loading their debates with race-bigotry."[50] Even with the government on the brink of passing the Fifteen Passenger Bill, the labor press—when it bothered to comment on the legislation at all—continued to frame the issue around importation rather than immigration.

Some labor leaders no doubt greeted the bill with reluctant approval, but few expressed interest in it, even when actively lobbying for other legislation. Since the great strike of 1877–78, cigar makers had fought for a federal law to abolish tenement house labor, and during the winter a Senate committee approved such a measure and sent it to the full Senate. To urge passage, cigar makers launched a nationwide lobbying drive. On February 11 and 15—the same week that senators debated the Fifteen Passenger Bill—cigar makers held mass meetings in New York, and cigar makers from Boston to Detroit held similar meetings a week later. Enlisting aid from workers in other trades, cigar makers organized a letter-writing campaign and petitioned individual congressmen. Union president Adolph Strasser even traveled to Washington to lobby senators personally. Amid all this agitation and all these efforts to influence legislation in Congress, the Fifteen Passenger Bill never came up for consideration. Although cigar makers and fellow workers could easily have injected such a reference at any of their numerous meetings, they did not. Although Strasser could have touted it to Congress or the president, no evidence suggests that he did. Nor was Strasser the only labor lobbyist in Washington. Samuel Hunt, head of the Boston Navy Yard workers, was also in the nation's capital in February urging Congress to enact a new eight-hour law. In addition, other labor groups pressured Congress for various legislation. And yet in all the speeches, all the lobbying, and all the agitation, Chinese immigration remained unmentioned. Nor did the issue come up in St. Louis during the annual four-day convention of the Knights of Labor in January. Although grabbing headlines and causing tumult nationwide in the opening months of 1879, the Fifteen Passenger Bill remained conspicuous for its near absence in working-class circles. In labor meeting after labor meeting during the key weeks of congressional debate, the issue failed to surface.[51]

But not completely. Existing evidence indicates that the issue came up at least twice among workers east of the Rockies. On February 23, the Cincinnati Trades and Labor Assembly endorsed the bill. Workers revealed serious misgivings, however, at its failure to tackle importation. The National Workingmen's Assembly in Washington also endorsed the measure. Having never said a word about the legislation as it passed from committee to the full House and then to the Senate, the association at last urged the president to sign the bill, "as it is the only means that will prevent a terrible calamity and the annihilation of the Chinese on the Pacific coast." Thus two labor organizations did indeed take a stand in favor of the Fifteen Passenger Bill, but with neither the vigor nor the venom voiced by Senator Blaine and his colleagues. As Greenback leader Solon Chase colorfully noted, the Maine Republican "tried to make the 'Heathen Chinee' an issue. All of which went to show that Blaine was 'barking up the tree on which there was no coon.'" To the mass of American workers, in whose behalf Blaine demanded the legislation, Chinese immigration remained a side issue at best, as barren as an empty tree.[52]

Assessing working-class opinion is fraught with danger, however, for labor seldom spoke with a unified voice. A couple of these voices, as noted, sang out in support of the Fifteen Passenger Bill, but from the great chorus of workers and labor leaders east of the Rockies came a deafening silence. At the very moment of peak interest in Chinese immigration restriction, workers responded with one great yawn, and as the first immigration restriction measure sailed through Congress in 1879, workers expended little wind to help it through. A few critics bemoaned this indifference. "The workingmen of Australia are wiser than those of the United States," the *Cincinnati Enquirer* observed. "They are forming Anti-Chinese Leagues, and inaugurating a general crusade against the employment of Chinese." Why, the *Enquirer* wondered, were American workers so apathetic? As the *San Francisco Chronicle* explained, "They [the workingmen] are just beginning to study the problem in the east." Anti-Chinese crusaders made the same observation. "How much persuasion is necessary," asked a western correspondent for the *Socialist*, "to induce the New England workingman to interest himself about the Chinese question?" Apparently, a great deal more, he concluded; "working people are so extremely dull and slow." Even as politicians such as Blaine argued for immigration restriction in the name of the American laborer, workers in the East revealed little desire to embrace anti-immigration legislation or practice the politics of race. As machinist Thomas J. Morgan, leader of the Chicago Trade and Labor Council, remarked in testimony before the Illinois legislature in March, "The Chinese should have the same right to come here as any other nationality, but . . . the whole affair had been given a greater importance than it deserved."[53]

In the evaluation of working-class attitudes toward Chinese immigration, it is essential to distinguish between working-class opinion and the *perception* of working-class opinion. Just as with Kearney's tour a half year earlier, a crucial disparity emerged between the two, a disparity illustrated by the *Cincinnati Enquirer*. Although this rabidly pro-exclusion journal acknowledged workers' lack of awareness on the issue, the *Enquirer* nonetheless concluded that the

Fifteen Passenger Bill "is a measure in the interest of the working classes." Therefore, the *Enquirer* assumed, workers *should* want it, exclaiming, "It is high time that the workingmen, the class most nearly affected by Chinese cheap labor, were taking action in their own defense."[54]

The *New York Tribune* also assumed that workers supported the bill and then blamed the anti-Chinese agitation on "such persons as seek through trades-unions and organized strikes to create an antagonism between labor and capital. . . . This opposition has not been shown generally by persons of American birth." The *Tribune* blamed anti-Chinese sentiment on European immigrants or, to be more precise, the Irish and "the ignorant." So did the *Cleveland Herald*, which argued that the legislation originated not with politicians but "with a class of men who are themselves foreigners."[55] This attitude meshed neatly with Hannibal Hamlin's assertion in the Senate that "unnaturalized Englishmen"—that is, the Irish—were the ringleaders of the anti-Chinese movement. It also reinforced Senator Blaine's contention that the bill was being passed to satisfy "the free American laborer." Politicians and the press converged in distorting working-class demands; then, in the hopes of gaining votes, politicians made this distorted demand their own. Although few eastern workers had ever voiced such a demand, national politicians now advocated closing the nation's gates on Chinese immigrants in workers' names. And the eastern press, which "utterly regardless of political affinities" opposed the Fifteen Passenger Bill, nevertheless sympathized with immigration restriction. A handful of workers, meanwhile, went along, but the great majority simply looked the other way.

And what finally became of the Fifteen Passenger Bill? The White House had long since indicated its support for restricting Chinese immigration. At a well-publicized meeting on January 3, when the bill was still in committee, the majority of Hayes's cabinet recommended limiting Chinese immigration. Most cabinet members, in fact, urged a complete ban on immigration, arguing that "immigration of all kinds had been overdone in this country, and that in the future it would be a good policy to discourage it from all sources." Chinese exclusion would thus ease the way for the exclusion of other immigrants. Only Attorney General George Devens spoke in favor of the Chinese. After considering various options, the president instructed Secretary of State William M. Evarts to "open formal negotiations with the Chinese government for modification of the Burlingame Treaty, with a view to placing restrictions upon Chinese immigration to this country."[56]

The executive branch had thus chosen to limit Chinese immigration through diplomatic channels. But just as Evarts began contacting Chinese officials in Washington, Congress rushed ahead with the Fifteen Passenger Bill, upsetting the White House plan. At a meeting with the secretary of state, Ch'en Lan-pin and Yung Wing, the top two diplomats in the recently established Chinese legation to the United States, criticized the measure as "offensive" and "insulting," and at the next cabinet session, Evarts urged Hayes to veto the bill. Though the secretary of state favored restriction of Chinese immigration, he warned that the measure "was clearly a breach of faith," which would embarrass the nation, threaten commerce, and undercut the authority of the executive branch. Evarts and fellow cabinet members reflected the views of the Republican press.[57]

Hayes took the advice to heart. "Both houses have passed a bill intended to prevent the Chinese from coming to this Country in large numbers," the president confided in his diary on February 20. "I am satisfied the present Chinese labor invasion—(it is not in any proper sense immigration—women and children do not come) is pernicious and should be discouraged. Our experience in dealing with the weaker races—the negroes and indians for example is not encouraging. We shall oppress the Chinamen, and their presence will make hoodlums or vagabonds of their oppressors. I therefore would consider with favor measures to discourage the Chinese from coming to our shores. But I suspect that this bill is inconsistent with our treaty obligations. I must carefully examine it. If it violates the national faith I must decline to approve it." A week later, the president noted that the Chinese population was "hateful" and "cannot safely be admitted into the bosom of our American Society." The distance between the sandlots and the White House was far shorter than anyone cared to acknowledge.[58]

While Hayes pondered the issue in his diary, the storm over the bill swirled across the country, and letters, telegrams, and petitions poured into the White House. The president, one newspaper reported, "has received more advice, with reference to the action he should take on the bill, than upon any subject that has yet come before him. . . . The only opposition to a veto comes from the Pacific Coast." Leaning toward a veto but still undecided, Hayes called Evarts for one last consultation. He also invited Representative James Garfield. The three of them "had a full conversation" about the bill, the prominent Ohio congressman wrote in his diary. Sentiment against the measure, he remarked, was "growing very strong." To the president, Garfield stressed the "iniquity of its provision" and, seconding Evarts, urged a veto.[59]

Evarts, Garfield, and the views of prominent Republicans ultimately determined the president's action. On March 1, 1879, Hayes vetoed the Fifteen Passenger Bill. In his veto message (drafted by Evarts), the president objected to the bill for all the familiar reasons. It would unconstitutionally abrogate the Burlingame Treaty, threaten American "merchants or missionaries" in China, and "endanger . . . the growing commerce and prosperity" of the two nations. Only once in his three-thousand-word message did Hayes address human rights, equality, or justice. Citing "the American doctrines of free migration to and fro among the peoples and races of the earth," he conceded, "Up to this time our uncovenanted hospitality to immigration, our fearless liberality of citizenship, our equal and comprehensive justice to all inhabitants . . . our civil freedom and our religious toleration had made all comers welcome." But once he acknowledged these ideals, Hayes felt free to shove them aside because "the very grave discontents of the people of the Pacific States . . . deserv[e] the most serious attention of the people of the whole country." Hayes recommended "more careful methods" be used—such as negotiating a new treaty—to keep the Chinese out. By using such methods, Americans could protect "ourselves against a larger and more rapid infusion of this foreign race than our system of industry and society can take up and assimilate with ease and safety." It was the means of Chinese exclusion and not the ends to which the president objected.[60]

The Fifteen Passenger Bill proved a major advance for the anti-Chinese movement. Although the measure failed, the debate revealed that the days of unrestricted Chinese immigration (and hence of unrestricted immigration in general) were numbered. Only a legal technicality—a treaty—lay in the way of restriction, and no one voiced any reservation about modifying it. Defending Chinese immigration offered little reward. "The feeling in favor of the Chinese will not help carry a State any-where," the *Cincinnati Enquirer* noted. "The States that lie east of the Rocky Mountains that are Republican will remain so, Chinese or no Chinese. The Chinese question will neither hurt nor help in any of those States; but it will hurt in California, Oregon and Nevada." Therein lay the reason for Chinese exclusion. In a national political system almost perfectly balanced between the two major parties, a single issue and a single state could mean the difference between defeat and victory. No one knew this better than the nation's most influential Republican, who shrewdly seized the issue, hoping it would catapult him into the White House. With virtually no Chinese voters and few ardent sympathizers, Senator Blaine had taken an astute political gamble. Overnight he became the most powerful man in the nation to champion Chinese exclusion. His embrace of the politics of race made exclusion acceptable. "Blaine's letter on the Chinese has changed the tune of denunciation among the Republicans in this vicinity," one New England journal observed. "They have more respect for Blaine's position."[61]

Blaine, indeed, made Chinese exclusion respectable. But he did not make it inevitable. Many Republicans, after all, criticized him and opposed the bill.

"Senator Blaine has made a great mistake in his advocacy of it," Garfield wrote in his diary on February 24. "At the same time," the future president added, "I am anxious to see some legislation that shall prevent the overflow of Chinese into this country."[62] Only when such solid conservatives as Garfield, Hayes, and Evarts voiced such sentiments did Chinese exclusion become inevitable. Only when scores of Republicans across the country echoed these opinions did Chinese exclusion become a fait accompli. By mainly attacking the bill for its violation of a treaty and not for its violation of human rights and justice, Republicans had pretty much conceded the issue. And when aging abolitionist senators such as Hannibal Hamlin devoted the bulk of their energies to defending the rights of commerce rather than the rights of the Chinese, little doubt remained as to which direction the country was heading. People could justifiably accuse Blaine of playing politics. They could just as rightfully accuse the Republican Party of abandoning its ideals of equal rights and racial justice. The party that had once fought for emancipation and the inclusion of blacks in the American political system now took a commanding role in exploiting racial tensions and endorsing the exclusion of Chinese from the United States. In so doing, the Republican Party ultimately made Chinese exclusion inevitable.

Both Elmer Clarence Sandmeyer and Alexander Saxton have argued that 1879 marked a "turning point" in the national effort to ban Chinese immigrants. While this is correct, 1876 (when both parties adopted anti-Chinese planks) and 1878 (when the Senate urged renegotiation of the Burlingame Treaty to restrict Chinese immigration) also marked turning points in the national effort toward exclusion. What distinguished 1879 from earlier years was not just the overwhelming approval by both houses of Congress but the arguments marshaled by leading congressmen—especially Senator Blaine. In arguing that Chinese exclusion would benefit workers nationwide and defuse class tensions throughout the country, Blaine had struck a powerful chord in American society. His stature helped make Chinese exclusion a legitimate battle cry and, in "pleading the cause of the free American laborer and of his children and of his children's children," an act of farseeing statesmanship.[63]

The irony of this political transformation did not go unnoticed. "A few years ago," remarked the *Daily Advance*, an obscure Cleveland labor journal, "when labor reformers demanded the prohibition of the IMPORTATION of Chinese laborers (not their free immigration mind you) a howl went up in the columns of the monopoly press from one end of the country to the other." And now immigration restriction had become all the rage in Congress. "Well," the *Advance* concluded, "the world does move."[64]

CHAPTER NINE

An Earthquake of Excitement

California and the Exodus East, 1879–1880

On March 3, 1879, two days after Hayes vetoed the Fifteen Passenger Bill, the California state constitutional convention completed its labors, thereby shifting the momentum for Chinese exclusion from Washington to the West. Backed by the Workingmen's Party, whose members made up one-third of the convention's delegates, and by Denis Kearney, who delivered more than one hundred speeches in support, the new state constitution won approval from voters two months later, 77,959 to 67,134. The hand of the Workingmen seemed evident: the document was one of the most pro-labor charters in the nation. The California constitution mandated an eight-hour day for all public works, abolished contract prison labor as of 1882, and prevented foreclosure on small farms. It empowered the state government to regulate corporations and railroads, limit utility and telegraph rates, and enact an income tax and mechanic's lien law. A combination of both radical and racist doctrines, the constitution also featured a series of anti-Chinese clauses. It forbade the employment of Chinese workers by corporations and on public works and declared void "all contracts for coolie labor." It also authorized the legislature to set boundaries for Chinese neighborhoods, relocate Chinese residents beyond city and town lines, and "discourage their immigration by all means within its power."[1]

In *The Indispensable Enemy*, Alexander Saxton echoes Henry George in arguing that the California constitution was actually a very moderate charter, "no more radical in most of its aspects than other new state constitutions of the period." A real "workingmen's" constitution, Saxton contends, would have included an eight-hour day for *private* employees and a bureau of labor statistics. The so-called radical features, he says, were nothing more than the "Granger program," which Workingmen's Party delegates supported but did not formulate themselves. Saxton, however, never examines the swift and overwhelmingly positive response to the new constitution from workers and labor leaders across the country, as well as the uniformly negative response from most other segments of society. Within days of its passage, wage earners from Boston to Chicago held mass meetings to celebrate the new charter and the apparent achievement of the Workingmen's Party of California. These meetings also signaled the resurrection of Denis Kearney in the East. Laughed out of the region just a half year earlier, he now became a symbol of labor triumphant, the champion workingman slaying the dragon capital. Whatever his faults, he had spearheaded the drive for ratification; how many labor activists, after all, could boast of such a triumph as the adoption of a new constitution?[2]

At these eastern meetings, speakers praised Kearney and the numerous pro-labor clauses in the new charter, which they viewed as a blueprint for their own states. Workers balked only at the sections aimed at Chinese immigration. Endorsing most of the constitution clause by clause, workers in New York City "condemned the importation of Chinamen" but elaborated no further on the issue. A second meeting saluting the new charter ignored the Chinese entirely. Spurred by the success of their western brethren, the city's labor leaders considered forming a new workingmen's party in the East. Just in case anyone questioned their goals, a notice advertising the meeting stated, "A New Constitution for New York on the California plan (without Chinese clause . . .)." Boston workers also celebrated "the great triumph in California" yet, like their New York brethren, pointedly rejected the anti-Chinese sections. As the *Boston Globe* observed, "It is unlikely that the mass of workingmen here can be brought to unite in any very decided protest against the Chinese."[3]

But in Chicago workers broke with tradition. At a meeting called by the Trade and Labor Council in May, workers came out for Chinese exclusion. After praising "Denis Kearney and the brave band of Labor-agitators . . . upon their manful fight and their glorious victory," the meeting resolved: "That in

VOL. V.—No. 114. MAY 14, 1879. Price, 10 Cents.

"What fools these Mortals be!"
MIDSUMMER-NIGHT'S DREAM

Puck

PUBLISHED BY
KEPPLER & SCHWARZMANN.

NEW YORK
TRADE MARK REGISTERED 1878

OFFICE No. 21-23 WARREN ST.

NEW CONSTITUTION

SAVINGS BANK

$1000

$1000

$1000

$100

CALIFORNIA'S NEW CONSTITUTION.

Figure 9.1. In this nightmarish vision, California's new constitution wreaks havoc on the Golden State, forcing everyone to escape its clutches: the capitalist, the Chinese immigrant, the honest workingman, and even capital itself. Few illustrations better capture the class tensions of the era. While eastern workers celebrated the new charter—with specific reservations on the anti-Chinese clauses—most other segments of society recoiled in terror from its specter of revolution and devastation. Note that the monster, with its upturned hair and bristly mustache, bears a passing resemblance to Denis Kearney. (*Puck*, May 14, 1879)

answer to the California war-cry of 'The Chinese must go,' we echo the universal watchword of American workingmen: 'Not only the Chinese, but Chinese institutions must go.'" At last, after years of lobbying by western activists, the sweeping approval of Chinese immigration restriction by Congress, the support for restriction by the president and his cabinet, and the adoption of an anti-Chinese state constitution, a labor body east of the Rocky Mountains came out unequivocally against Chinese immigration. The pro-immigration/anti-importation consensus that had largely prevailed among eastern workers for more than a decade finally showed signs of cracking. Energized by California and influenced by the recent political discourse and growing national acceptance of immigration restriction, a segment of the labor movement openly embraced Chinese exclusion. This group would remain small and localized, but it would remain. As the city with one of the nation's most active and best-organized working-class populations, Chicago marked an important advance for the anti-Chinese movement. And yet, workers dropped the issue almost immediately. At dozens of labor gatherings from Boston to Chicago in the following months for which records exist, Chinese immigration vanished from the working-class agenda, as it had so often in the past.[4]

California remained the most explosive and unpredictable state in the country, and the congressional election scheduled for September 3, 1879—the one Blaine had had his eye on seven months earlier—assured that the Chinese issue would remain in the national spotlight. The three-way aspect of the race, with the Workingmen's Party posing a formidable challenge, promised a suspenseful campaign, and a referendum on Chinese immigration insured a heavy turnout. In addition to the four coveted House seats, every major office was up for grabs. As if to illustrate the volatility of California politics, a prominent newspaper editor in San Francisco shot the Workingmen's mayoral candidate just days before the election, and a mob gathered for revenge, awaiting only Kearney's command to lynch the gunman. Such antics catapulted the California campaign to front pages across the country.

Three weeks before election day, however, the Chinese issue took center stage when a congressional committee met in San Francisco. This committee, successor to the Hewitt Committee of 1878, had expanded its mission to investigate not just the causes of the depression but also the effects of Chinese immigration. The "Congressional Hard Times Committee," as some nicknamed it, convened on August 15, and the bulk of the witnesses came from the ranks of the rich and powerful: merchants, manufacturers, attorneys, and publishers. They were balanced by just a handful of workers, consisting of a shoemaker, a lather, a miner, and a "street peddler." Practically everyone urged exclusion. "If the Chinese immigration continues," one businessman testified, "we will have to leave or fight." Several manufacturers feared they would go out of business because "Chinamen work cheaper for other Chinamen than they do for white men." Citing biology, one shirt manufacturer claimed that "Chinamen can beat the Irish with the grub-ax and spade and shovel and digging in mud. They stand the stooping position best." The most revealing testimony came from those who had switched sides. Loring Pickering, publisher of the *Evening Bulletin* and the *Morning Call*, noted that "seven or eight years ago there was hardly anybody in my own office who did not say, 'Let the Chinese come. Give everybody a chance'; but I do not think there is one there now who will say so. They find that the Chinese are eating up everything." Clothing merchant and manufacturer John Schaefer warned that without resolute action, the Chinese would "overrun" and "ruin" the United States by 1930. "I have always been a steady Republican," he noted, "but this idea of wanting to sell out (as I may say) our country and homes to the Chinese goes against my grain." Testifiers emphasized both the importance of the issue and the breadth of its support, prompting a request for clarification from one congressman who thought the conflict "only between the white laborer and the Chinaman. I want to know if the rest of this community is in harmony on the Chinese question?" "I think it is pretty much a unanimous thing," replied T. B. Shannon, collector of the Port of San Francisco. "You mean to say," asked a second congressman, "that there is no class of American citizens in this city favorable to Chinese immigration?" Shannon answered, "I do not know of any; if there is, I do not know of it." As merchant John Schaefer summed up, "I do not know one white man to-day who is in favor of Chinese coming here."[5]

Only two of the twenty-eight Californians who testified defended Chinese immigration. Patrick J. Healy, an Irish-born shoemaker, praised the Chinese highly and urged continuing the policy of open immigration, and Rev. Otis Gibson, one of the state's most prominent Methodist ministers and missionaries, argued that the Chinese were good for American industry. Although the Chinese had many base qualities, Gibson argued, they were no worse than "the worst classes" of immigrants from Europe, and he proposed restricting immigration from both continents, Asia and Europe. Healy and Gibson aside, the view of most testifiers was clear: the Chinese must go. Whether California voters held the same view would be answered by the referendum on September 3.[6]

Four days after the congressional committee closed up shop on August 19, however, an assassination attempt on mayoral candidate Isaac Kalloch eclipsed the issue of Chinese immigration. A Baptist minister, Kalloch was a colorful character who, like Rev. Henry Ward Beecher, had been charged with adultery years earlier. After successful stints as a lawyer and rancher in Kansas, Kalloch settled in San Francisco and began preaching at the Metropolitan Temple, the largest Baptist church building in the nation. Attacking the pretensions of the rich and the infallibility of the Bible, Kalloch won a loyal working-class audience, and the Workingmen's Party nominated him for mayor in 1879. Blasted, like Kearney, as a demagogue ("pestiferous agitators," one local clergyman said, lumping the two together), such attacks only made him dearer to the city's working-class voters. During the campaign, Kalloch and Charles De Young, editor of the *San Francisco Chronicle* (the most widely read newspaper in the West), exchanged verbal attacks. De Young published the old allegations of Kalloch's adultery and charged him with seducing minors and retaining a mistress. Kalloch, in return, called De Young's mother a "whore." In revenge for this slight, De Young armed himself, rode to the Metropolitan Temple, and, finding Kalloch in the street, shot him twice. With Kalloch bleeding profusely, the police took De Young into custody. The response among workers was electric. "The news spread like fire," one observer noted; "men left their stores, their shops, and work benches; a universal cry went up for the life of the assassin De Young." Crowds marched to City Hall to prevent De Young's escape, and twenty thousand people—"many . . . carrying rifles and shotguns"—gathered on the sandlots. "The cry for vengeance was so loud and deep that it could not be ignored." Workers' militia companies fetched arms and "held themselves in readiness for any emergency." Threats of "mob rule" and a working-class uprising reawakened fears of 1877, and the commander of the state militia telegraphed the secretary of war that "the city of San Francisco is threatened with riot . . . it is necessary to have ammunition at once." Washington moved swiftly, rushing the navy into port, placing the army on alert, and authorizing shipment of fifty thousand cartridges. The *Boston Pilot* compared the scene to the "Reign of Terror" in the French Revolution. "The police," wrote the *Irish World and American Industrial Liberator*, "massed themselves at the City Hall behind Gattling [*sic*] guns in terror."[7]

With the city on the verge of explosion, Denis Kearney cut short a trip to Vallejo and returned home. An "immense crowd" met him at the wharf with a "tumultuous greeting." Kearney directed everyone to the sandlots, where the crowd reassembled ten minutes later, prepared for battle. Kearney spoke briefly. Forbidding violence, he counseled patience and instructed workers to lay down their arms and disperse quietly. His words had a powerful effect. "One hour afterwards," a reporter noted, "the streets were clear, order reigned, and the city saved from the terrible consequences of a riot." With the Workingmen on the brink of electoral victory, Kearney wanted no violence to mar the campaign. His speech defused the crowd's fury, and San Francisco remained calm for the next week. It was Kearney's finest hour.[8]

Kearney's actions met with success at the polls. Kalloch survived his wounds and became mayor, and the Workingmen's Party elected seventeen assemblymen, eleven senators, and the chief justice and five associate justices of the Supreme Court.[9] Despite this fine showing, Republicans captured three of the four congressional seats, thus assuring a Republican majority (by state) should the 1880 presidential election be decided in the House. Blaine's efforts had paid off: whatever their differences on local issues, Californians felt comfortable that Republicans would see to their needs on national matters. And the results of the referendum left no doubt as to where the state stood on Chinese immigration: 883 (.6 percent) in favor, 154,638 (99.4 percent) opposed. A nearly unanimous verdict, it may have been the most lopsided election in American history. The same sentiment voiced in California by workers and by the wealthy, on the sandlots and in Sacramento, and in chorus before Congress was voiced in unison at the voting booth. James Blaine had won the first round of the presidential sweepstakes of 1880.[10]

Kearney and the Workingmen also emerged as winners. The new party had proved itself a force to be reckoned with, and Greenbackers in the East reached out in support. "We regard the workingmen's party of California as a sister organization," a New York Greenback convention resolved on the eve of the election, "and extend to it both hands of fellowship, believing that they, like ourselves, are arrayed against our common enemy—corporate monopolies, enjoying special privileges at the expense of impoverished labor." Eastern Greenbackers hoped to capitalize on the California Workingmen's success by merging forces with them and guiding them toward Greenback principles. The key to transforming the Workingmen into Greenbackers, they believed, lay in converting Denis Kearney, whose hold on western workers might translate into votes. And Kearney was becoming respectable: in his new role as peacemaker, he achieved a certain legitimacy. Even the staid *New York Tribune* commended him for maintaining order after the Kalloch shooting. The Greenbackers now treated him as one of their own. The *National View*, the party's new journal, praised Kearney's "wisdom and courage," while Greenbackers in New York lauded "the prudent and masterly manner in which he prevented bloodshed at a time when all admitted he had the destiny of property interests within his grasp." Flattered by the attention, Kearney reciprocated, predicting that the Greenbackers would sweep the presidency in 1880. With the alluring prospect of winning California, Greenbackers invited Kearney to a high-level planning conference in Washington to discuss the 1880 campaign. The chance of playing a role in national politics proved irresistible to the "Howling Hoodlum," and in December he embarked for the nation's capital for his second tour of the East.[11]

Interviewed en route, Kearney identified himself as a Greenbacker, promising to support "any man who agrees with the Western sentiment on finance." The "Chinese question" was also important, he said, but sounding more and more like a convert, he announced he would speak in the East "in favor of the greenback movement," adding, "The financial problem will be the great issue of the next election." In January 1880, Kearney attended the Greenback-Labor conference in Washington where leaders officially planned the party's nominating convention for June and appointed the "sandlot orator" one of the conference's several vice presidents. Kearney objected that too many people had received this title but was overruled. In a brief speech, he stressed he was a Greenbacker and urged thorough organization for the upcoming campaign. He reveled in denouncing the two major parties, calling the Republicans "iron-hoofed scoundrels who were shod in hell" and the Democrats "tools of these scoundrels." It was standard Kearney fare, except for one thing: he did not denounce Chinese immigration.[12]

Nor did Kearney raise the subject at his single appearance in New York City on January 16 or at his two appearances in Chicago later in the month. The Chinese issue, novel and ultimately unpopular during his visit in 1878, went unmentioned in 1880; as Kearney had dropped it at the end of his first tour, so he dropped it entirely from his second. No race baiting passed his lips. Despite his resurrection in the East in the wake of the new California constitution, workers remained suspicious of Kearney and divided over his visit. The National Workingmen's Assembly in Washington never acknowledged his presence, and his appearance in Chicago caused dissension. Gone were the processions that had greeted his arrival in 1878; gone were the resolutions for his listeners to "unanimously" endorse. Gone was the fanfare, gone was the enthusiasm, gone was the publicity. Both the labor and mainstream press all but ignored him. Kearney was old news, and while his invective hadn't changed much since his first tour—in New York, he called railroad baron Jay Gould "the lean, lantern-jawed, lopsided pelican . . . and shark snouted cormorant . . . who crawls through Wall street, crunching the bones of his victims"—the political climate had. The return of prosperity in the closing year of the decade, coupled with Congress's commitment to Chinese immigration restriction, had created a new atmosphere. No longer was the nation—outside of California—convulsed by the fear of revolution; no longer was Kearney deemed the spark that could ignite insurrection. No red scare saturated the press, and no threat of a labor uprising hovered over the nation. Without a political hurricane, Kearney was simply hot air. Consequently, his tour of 1880 received none of the attention from the press or the public that had greeted his first tour sixteen months earlier. The arrival in the United States of Irish nationalist Charles Stewart Parnell completely eclipsed Kearney's presence and further reduced the once-feared "mountebank drayman" to a sideshow attraction.[13]

In California, on the other hand, where Workingmen now controlled many state and local offices, Kearney still commanded attention. Returning home in February, he lobbied Sacramento for anti-Chinese legislation, while the newly inaugurated Mayor Kalloch persuaded San Francisco's Board of Health to investigate problems in Chinatown. The board issued an adverse report calling Chinatown a "nuisance" that must be "abated." Exactly how and by whom, however, remained unclear. When the Board of Supervisors failed to act, "hoodlums" seized the initiative, marching to factories around the city and demanding employers dismiss all Chinese laborers. A few actually complied. Elated by events, Kearney shuttled back to San Francisco, where fellow sandlotters spoke openly of hanging manufacturers and burning down the city. Tensions rapidly escalated to the level of the preceding August. Rumors of assassination and revolution filled the air, and the rumors traveled east. "An earthquake of excitement is heaving beneath this city," a California minister wrote to the *Cincinnati Enquirer*, "and threatening to engulf the Chinese, and popular indignation may storm our pavements with the blood of unreasoning vengeance." As the *St. Louis Post-Dispatch* observed: "The agitation which was begun and carried on for a long time ostensibly for the discouragement of Chinese immigration has degenerated into a carnival of impudent, blasphemous threatenings against life and property and vilifications of private character, until it has become the scandal of the time and brought dishonor upon American civilization. So long as its agitation was confined to its original purpose it proceeded without objection, for the people of California recognized the evils of Chinese immigration and united to oppose it by lawful means." Just as congressmen dealing with the issue of Chinese immigration wrangled over the method (legislation versus treaty revision) and not the goal (restriction), Californians differed over the means (violence versus nonviolence) and not the ends (exclusion). And Kearney made the most of it. Shedding his new image as a man of restraint, he now prepared for martyrdom. He inflamed his rhetoric, accelerated his attacks, and proposed building a gallows on the sandlots. "If I hear of any man plotting to kill me," he cried, "I will kill him so help me God." The old Kearney was back. But soon he would be behind bars. For uttering those words, Kearney was arrested.[14]

The resolutions to demolish Chinatown, accompanied by official notices that all Chinese residents would be evicted within thirty days, impelled Chinese diplomat Yung Wing to complain to Secretary of State William M. Evarts that his countrymen lived in dread "of being driven from their homes to starve in the streets." Evarts declined to intervene—"Keeping peace within their own borders rested with the respective state governments," he told Yung—enabling the powder keg atmosphere in San Francisco to spark the first general exodus of Chinese workers from California. They began heading east over the Rockies by rail in February 1880. "Two car-loads of Chinamen" passed through St. Louis, one newspaper reported, and more Chinese followed a few days later. They fanned out across the North, heading for cities in Illinois, Ohio, Pennsylvania, and New York. About seventy-five Chinese landed in Jersey City, New Jersey, and it appeared many more would be following. The *New York Star* predicted that six hundred Chinese were crossing the country; the *Herald* put the figure much higher. Even the conservative *New York Times* claimed the Chinese were coming en masse.[15]

This looming wave of migration aroused the interest of wealthy society women in the East. To them the newcomers represented a solution to a vexing problem: the Chinese would "supplant . . . the incompetent order of servants who have so long cursed our cities." For several weeks, a flurry of letters in the *New York Herald* attacking Irish, German, Mexican, and black domestics trumpeted the Chinese as welcome replacements. Ladies associations descended on Mott Street, the heart of New York's Chinatown, "in quest of Chinese servants." Foreseeing a vast market for Chinese laborers in the East, Mrs. Timothy

Figure 9.2. The first Chinese graduate of an American college (Yale, 1854), Yung Wing (1828–1912) directed the Chinese Educational Mission in Connecticut in the 1870s and served as associate Chinese minister to the United States from 1878 to 1881. Yung denounced immigration restriction to the secretary of state and spoke out repeatedly on abuses committed against Chinese immigrants in California. Despite impassioned pleas on behalf of his compatriots who were "being driven from their homes to starve in the streets," Yung's protests fell on deaf ears in Washington. (Courtesy Connecticut Historical Society, Hartford)

Sargent, a leading advocate of the scheme, planned to open a Chinese Aid and Emigration Society in Manhattan. "We are just on the verge of flooding New York and its suburbs with Chinese," she told a reporter, while a colleague proposed having "all the hotels at Lake George hire Chinese domestics for the coming season." *Puck* featured a cartoon showing wealthy society women welcoming Chinese immigrants to New York as a displaced and disgruntled Irish domestic remarks, "Dinnis Kearney will see me roighted, ye Haythin Chinee!" Sargent, meanwhile, claimed to be "receiving hundreds of letters daily from manufacturers and others who were anxious to preclude all possibility of strikes by the employment of cheap and reliable Chinese workmen. . . . Any one who has had dealings with the Celestials knows perfectly well that they are infinitely superior to the average white laborer." Sargent listed some of the applicants who had contacted her: bonnet-making, chair-making, and box-making firms; textile manufacturers in Massachusetts; corporations in Long Island; and the Jockey Club race course near Coney Island. "It is likely," she said, "that 5,000 Chinamen will be brought East to engage in various labors." And this was only the beginning. "It will be an easy matter to secure special rates and pay the fares of 100 or 200 at a time, as the case may be." With sufficient capital, she concluded, "the Mongolians will fairly swarm here. Their neatness and economy will soon win them favors in the cultured East, and the time is not far off when New York manufacturers will be glad to send to China direct for recruits to their workshops." Sargent pulled no punches: "The Chinese wave was advancing . . . and incompetence would be swept away from the workshops and factories to make room for the industrious little brown people."[16]

The importation of "servile" labor—precisely the issue workers had protested for the past decade and a half—was suddenly being advocated openly, and similar plots and threats reinforced Sargent's scheme. The same week she introduced her plan, Gifford Parker, a businessman long engaged in trade with China, delivered a lecture in New York City. Praising the Chinese for their "many excellent traits," he described their method of entry: in exchange for passage to America, the Chinese agreed to work five years for a contractor, and once in San Francisco, they headed straight for Chinatown, where "they remained until they were sublet at from $30 to $40 a month each." Sam Quong, a newly arrived immigrant, told a *New York Times* reporter virtually the same item: that the Chinese were imported to America under contracts for several years. In Mississippi, the *New York Herald* reported, planter Henry Scharrett had contacted agents in San Francisco and planned to import Chinese laborers "in a few weeks." And, finally, in the most elaborate scenario of all, employers in the South and West were plotting a cross-country labor exchange. During the preceding year, large numbers of blacks known as Exodusters had migrated to Kansas and other midwestern states, prompting leading citizens in California, one observer noted, to consider schemes "to bring negroes here to replace the Chinese who are to be thrown out of employment" and "to replace the departing hordes of negroes in the south, with the *practically* expelled Chinese labour here."[17]

The ghost of Koopmanschap hovered ominously. Each day seemed to bring a new charge, a new rumor of what one magazine labeled "the Chinese Invasion."[18] People from different backgrounds—Sargent, Parker, Quong, Scharrett—were saying essentially the same thing. There may have been little truth to their statements, but no one could be sure, and in the end it really didn't matter. The fact was, such claims were being made, by the high and by the lowly, independently and simultaneously. They were receiving wide notice, and they weren't being denied. The message to workers was clear: *You are replaceable, and your replacements are ready*. And one indisputable fact lent support to all the rumors: hundreds of Chinese were indeed crossing the plains and coming east.

Figure 9.3. In one of the most insidious cartoons of the period, a "locust horde" of Chinese immigrants swarms over the nation, poised to gobble up working-class jobs. The approaching storm cloud forms an outline of the United States. Original caption: "The Chinese Plague. Farmer Knickerbocker: 'What shall I do with this darn'd locust horde? They'll eat up all my labor crop! [the heads of wheat bear the names of threatened occupations—shoemakers, cigar makers, common laborers, factory hands, housemaids, etc.]' " (*McGee's Illustrated Weekly*, April 3, 1880)

THE CHINESE PLAGUE.—Page 806.

Farmer Knickerbocker.—What shall I do with this darn'd locust horde? They'll eat up all my labor crop!

The Chinese scares of 1869 and 1870 seemed to be repeating themselves, and workers, many felt, had no one to blame but themselves. By being both lazy and greedy and by striking one time too many, they alone had precipitated the Chinese influx. Employers had no choice but to seek other labor.

This explosive combination of threats and reality led to the first full-blown, working-class, anti-Chinese meeting east of the Rockies. On March 15, workers, Socialists, and members of the Chicago Trade and Labor Council gathered to denounce Chinese immigration. "America could not afford to let her workingmen become the victims of cooly ignorance and contagion," printer P. H. McLogan declared, nor be placed "in degrading competition with the Mongolian locusts who would devour the prosperity of the land." A. B. Adair spoke in a similar vein: "When Kearney and his followers said 'The Chinese must go,' it was not intended they should leave San Francisco to curse with their presence cities further eastward. It was intended that they should return whence they came, and back they must go before the force of American public opinion." Images of doom and terror dominated the meeting. Workers should boot the Chinese out of the city, one speaker railed, and "drive them to New York—to the jumping-off place. If they do not go into the sea they would make them take the river. (Cheers and laughter.)" The meeting endorsed three anti-Chi-

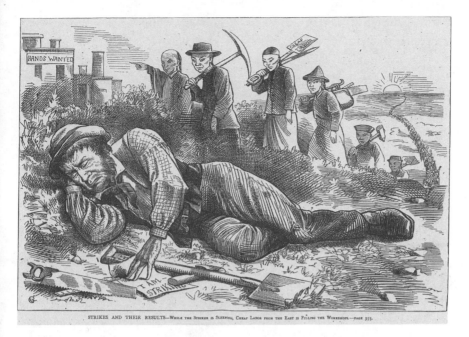

STRIKES AND THEIR RESULTS—While the Striker is Sleeping, Cheap Labor from the East is Filling the Workshops.—page 355.

Figure 9.4. As the Irish worker sleeps, an endless stream of Chinese immigrants marches east across the country. The different tools and variety of hats suggest the many jobs the Chinese could fill. Original caption: "Strikes and Their Results—While the Striker Is Sleeping, Cheap Labor from the East Is Filling the Workshops." (*McGee's Illustrated Weekly*, April 24, 1880)

nese resolutions and then adjourned with leaders planning to hold a second anti-Chinese meeting later in the month.[19]

Finally, four years after Aaron Sargent had condemned Chinese immigration on the Senate floor and both major parties had written anti-Chinese clauses into their national platforms, two years after the president and Congress had pledged to renegotiate the Burlingame Treaty so as to limit Chinese immigration, and one year after James Blaine had led a bipartisan majority of senators to support Chinese immigration restriction, workers east of the Rocky Mountains held their first meeting to demand Chinese exclusion. For ten years most workers in the East had carefully emphasized the distinction between immigration and importation; for ten years their distinctions had fallen on deaf ears. At last, in March 1880, almost ten full years after North Adams, workers in Chicago crossed the line—as they had momentarily one year earlier—from anti-importation to anti-immigration. Historians need look no further to find proof of Chinese exclusion sentiment among organized labor. Historians would err, however, in concluding that such sentiment was either predominant or broad based. The Chicago meeting of March 15, like the May meeting of 1879, stands out as both a groundbreaking event and a notable exception. It was never followed up: despite plans, no second meeting took place. A few days after the March meeting, organizers wired their brethren on the East Coast to urge that "a simultaneous meeting of protest against Chinese cheap labor [be] held in New York." Labor leaders in the nation's largest city demurred. Although anti-Chinese dispatches poured in from Chicago, "they have not," a reporter noted, "elicited a favorable response. The trades unions feel that with the present strikes on their hands they have enough to do without agitating the Chinese question."[20]

New York was indeed reeling from a wave of strikes and union activity in the early months of 1880. With the return of prosperity, city workers began organizing new trades, inspiring a strike wave that rippled across the nation. Even as Chinese laborers began arriving from California, workers continued striking, indifferent to the threats of large-scale importation blazing through the press and the cries emanating from Chicago. "The Mongolian is taking his queue and going Eastward," the *Chicago News* quipped. "Will New York evoke a Denis Kearney?" The answer, in a word, was no. Scarcely any protest emerged. And on the one occasion when the subject of Chinese immigration arose, working-class response contrasted sharply with that expressed in Chicago. Employer response also challenges the popular wisdom of who feared and who didn't fear Chinese immigration.[21]

The main strike of the season occurred in the piano-making industry in New York when Steinway employees, demanding a wage hike, walked off the job in February. Eighteen other piano firms then instituted a lockout on March 15—the same day of Chicago's anti-Chinese meeting—throwing four thousand piano makers out of work. The next day, "young Mr. Haines" of Haines Brothers piano factory announced he had been approached "by parties representing capitalists of the Pacific coast," who had informed him he could have as many Chinese workers as he wanted, at fifty to seventy-five cents a day. Haines mentioned the proposal to fellow manufacturers. Their response was immediate and unanimous. "I don't want to bother with a lot of Chinese," one said. "I hate 'em worse than the devil!" This position, the *New York Times* remarked, "was reiterated by others." A second manufacturer feared the social effects of introducing a new race. "We'll be getting so many Chinamen," he said, "that the amalgamation will become serious." And a third manufacturer simply said, "I'm dead against the mixture." As one Steinway executive commented, "We don't want any Chinese, and won't have them at any price."[22]

Sticking to their demands for higher wages, the piano makers dismissed the rumor without a worry. "The men affect to treat the story . . . to employ cheap Chinese labor with great indifference," the *New York Sun* reported. The proposal "was much talked of among the men," the *Times* added, "but no one seemed to be at all alarmed." Workers were amused instead. "The Chinese!" exclaimed one. "Why we've all had a good laugh over that." And another worker remarked with a swagger, "The Chinese will be good for washing their dirty aprons and cleaning the glue from the handles of their tools." The contrast between manufacturers and workers could not have been more stark: employers, as this one incident makes clear, feared and loathed the Chinese far more than their employees. Even as the Chinese began arriving in the East and Chicago labor leaders advised agitating against them, little opposition or hostility surfaced. New York evoked no Denis Kearney.[23]

Events in California, though, sparked one last round of protest meetings in the East. Just as the strike by piano makers reached its climax in the spring, a San Francisco judge convicted Denis Kearney of using "vulgar and threatening language" when he vowed (despite qualifiers) to murder his enemies. For this misdemeanor, the judge sentenced him to six months in prison and fined him one thousand dollars. In April, Kearney went to jail. Newspapers everywhere denounced the harsh sentence, and workers in the Northeast held large "indignation meetings." Orators at these gatherings focused on free speech—a freedom Kearney had been denied—but consciously distanced themselves from Kearney's crusade. As William G. H. Smart, who chaired the assembly in Boston, remarked, "The meeting was composed of persons who agreed in regard to the protest against Kearney's imprisonment, but did not coincide in sentiment as to the objects or methods of his agitation." Workers and labor leaders in New York City also did not "coincide" with the "objects or methods" of Kearney's "agitation." Tailor Robert Blissert, founder of the New York Central Labor Union, opened his speech by explaining that "he did not agree with all of Dennis Kearney's doctrines. He was not opposed to Chinese immigration." Blissert, one of the labor leaders who had boldly welcomed Chinese immigrants in 1870, welcomed them still: "He did not think it right to forbid any of God's creatures from coming to America," the *Irish World and American Industrial Liberator* reported. "What [Blissert] opposed was the Importation of Slaves. (Applause.)"[24]

Few individuals possessed a more mercurial image among workers than Denis Kearney. Up one moment, down the next, Kearney could arouse strong passions among his constituents. Yet even when defending him, most workers in the East took great pains to dissociate themselves from his notorious cry, "The Chinese must go." Pressure had been building for years. Even more than Roach's tour in 1876, Kearney's tour in 1878, and the California Workingmen's victories in 1879, the events of early 1880—Kearney's second visit, the Chinese exodus, the importation scare, the strike by piano makers, Kearney's imprisonment—could well have ignited a firestorm of anti-Chinese hysteria in the East. But they didn't. Although Chinese immigrants were crossing the Rockies by the hundreds for the first time and plans to import thousands echoed everywhere, the labor movement remained on the sidelines, observing rather than acting. Despite all the threats and actions, few workers—those in Chicago being the notable exception—broke ranks. Eastern workers' views on Chinese immigration, had anyone bothered to look or listen carefully, had proved remarkably consistent for more than ten full years.

Anti-Chinese sentiment in the East was like a wave on a beach: it did not run deep, and it receded quickly. And without a generating force, such as California or Congress, it subsided almost entirely. Seldom initiating, Eastern workers acted—or reacted—only when prodded. The events of 1879 and 1880 illustrate this decade-old pattern, as most workers, when they considered the issue at all, continued to frame it around importation, not immigration, even highlighting episodes of white-Chinese cooperation. In a reprise of the great strike by New York City cigar makers in 1877–78, white and Chinese cigar makers in St. Louis went on strike together in late 1879—and won. And in February 1880, just as the Chinese exodus to the East had begun, white and Chinese workers emerged victorious in a strike at a Mount Vernon, New Jersey, shirt factory. "As soon as the Chinaman understands that the white people will stand by him, he will stand up for his wages," the *Fall River Labor Standard* observed. "Bread and butter is alike to all nationalities."[25]

The momentum for Chinese exclusion continued to come—as it had for years—from Washington and from the West. National politicians and party leaders were again gearing up to promote the issue in pursuit of the presidency. Within days of the final Kearney-inspired protest meetings in the East in May 1880, all three political conventions—Republican, Democratic, and Greenback —would meet to choose their candidates. Although Senator Blaine remained the Republican favorite, no one knew for sure who the nominees would be. But on the restriction of Chinese immigration there was little disagreement among the two major parties. The bipartisan consensus expressed in the two platforms of 1876 and the vote on the Fifteen Passenger Bill of 1879 had grown only stronger in the intervening years and months. Workers' indifference no longer mattered. As the politicians and platforms would soon make clear, Chinese exclusion was only a matter of time. The issue would play an exciting and thoroughly unexpected role in the coming campaign, and the presidential election of 1880 would result in a resounding victory for bigotry.

CHAPTER TEN

No Material Difference

The Presidential Campaign of 1880

Ever since he narrowly lost the Republican nomination in 1876, James Blaine had been carefully plotting his course for the White House. For four years the charismatic senator from Maine lined up votes and positioned himself for the 1880 campaign. Spearheading the Fifteen Passenger Bill in February 1879 formed a key part of his grand strategy and made his stance toward Chinese immigration better known than that of any other American, save Kearney. Republican victories in the California congressional elections the following September seemed a good omen, and his party rallied behind him in the West. "Blaine is the man . . . nearest the hearts of the people on the Pacific coast," proclaimed Nevada governor Jonathan Kinkead on the eve of the Republican National Convention in 1880. "His record on the Chinese question has given him a place in the affection of our people that can not be filled by any other republican in the nation." The California delegation was "solid for Blaine," the state's governor noted, and so were the delegations from Nevada, Oregon, Washington, and Wyoming. "They were for Blaine 'first, last, and all the time,' "

185

one Golden State delegate declared, "and would vote and shout for the 'gallant knight' so long as his name was kept before the convention." California delegates did indeed stay loyal to the "gallant knight" until the very end. By shrewdly embracing the politics of race, Blaine showed how the West could be won.[1]

Blaine would likely have carried the Republican nomination on the first ballot were it not for the return of Ulysses S. Grant, who for the past two years had been abroad on a highly publicized tour of the world. Accompanied by *New York Herald* reporter John Russell Young, the former president's travels received wide coverage in the American press, keeping him constantly in the news but far removed from political controversy. Well before the old general set foot again on American soil, Republicans began talking of nominating him for a third term in the White House. When he sailed into San Francisco in September 1879—just two weeks after the California election—he received a tumultuous welcome, and the fanfare followed him everywhere. For the next four months, Grant toured the nation in royal fashion, as crowds and dignitaries turned out to greet the "hero of Appomattox." This outpouring of sentiment gave Grant an aura of invincibility, and by early 1880, he emerged as the major challenger to Blaine.[2]

During his eight years as president, Grant had never said much regarding Chinese immigration. The few times he addressed the subject, in his annual message in 1874 and in meetings with the Roach delegation in 1876, he indicated his willingness to restrict Chinese immigration. At the time, though, the issue played a small role in national politics. But Blaine raised the stakes in 1879, and Grant made sure to match his ante. "The trouble about your countrymen coming to America," Grant told Chinese leader Li Hung-chang in Tientsin in June 1879, "is that they . . . do not come of their own free will. . . . Their labor is not their own, but the property of capitalists." Here Grant sounded much like labor leaders Adolph Strasser and Robert Blissert. "If you can stop the slavery feature, then emigration from China is like emigration from other countries." But, unlike Strasser and Blissert, Grant did not dwell on this distinction. The problem was that the "Chinamen [were] coming too rapidly," he said, "coming so as to glut the labor market." To solve this, the former president suggested, "emigration might be stopped for a period—for three or five years." After all, he said, "the complaint [against the Chinese] comes from good people, and should be considered." Loath to insult his host, Grant insisted that he himself had not come up with the solution of immigration restriction; rather, he had relied on others for advice. "I have," he admitted, "no ideas of my own on the subject." Critics might have charged that Grant, never known as a great thinker, had few ideas of his own on *any* subject (except, perhaps, military affairs). Still, the fact remained that as Grant's ship sailed into San Francisco harbor at summer's end in 1879, the old general had gone on record in favor of a three- to five-year ban on Chinese immigration to ease the "glut" in the "labor market," and he had engaged in preliminary negotiations with China. Although far less zealous than the "magnetic man from Maine," Grant too could press the anti-Chinese button and claim it would help the workingman.[3]

The election of 1880 is remembered chiefly for two reasons: it introduced the issue of the tariff, which would dominate presidential campaigns for the rest of the Gilded Age, and it marked the emergence of a pro-Democratic "solid South," which would shape national political strategy for the next century. Less well known is the role played by Chinese immigration. As the campaign unfolded, party leaders lifted racial politics to new heights. Because Republicans and Democrats considered the volatile Pacific Coast vote essential for victory, both parties made anti-Chinese bigotry central to their western strategy, much as they had in 1876. But with the election still tight in October, politicians desperate for an issue and desperate for votes applied the identical strategy for winning the East. The same racial politics that lured western voters might also lure easterners, and in the campaign's final days, party leaders catapulted Chinese immigration to the top of the national agenda, effectively reducing the contest to which party could "out-Chinese" the other. With racial appeals providing major ammunition for both sides, party leaders ensured that, no matter which candidate won, the Chinese would lose. Although one historian has dismissed the election of 1880 as "one of the most insignificant in United States history," the campaign's amazing climax would elevate the politics of race to its zenith.[4]

Few, however, could have predicted this bizarre turn of events early in the canvass, least of all James Blaine. As Republicans gathered to open their convention in Chicago on June 2, 1880, his detractors raked up all the old allegations of corruption and deftly branded him with the mark of Kearney. The contest between Blaine and Grant promised to be exciting. With 756 delegates, the convention was the party's largest to date; even royalty was present in the person of Prince Leopold of England, who from his seat on the platform "watched all the proceedings with keen interest." He and fifteen thousand spectators witnessed a good show, as delegates maneuvered and battled for an entire week. It was the liveliest and longest slugfest in the party's history.[5]

While the Blaine and Grant camps marshaled forces, the platform committee drafted resolutions. Four years earlier the Republican platform had called for an investigation into Chinese immigration and nothing more. By 1880

THE "*MAGNETIC*" BLAINE, OR, A VERY HEAVY "**LOAD**"-stone FOR THE REPUBLICAN PARTY TO CARRY.

Figure 10.1. In his quest for the presidency, the "magnetic" Blaine attracts many unsavory issues—and one unsavory convict. Original caption: "The '*Magnetic*' Blaine; or, a Very Heavy 'Load'-stone for the Republican Party to Carry." (*Harper's Weekly*, May 8, 1880)

Republicans prepared to go further. Judge D. O. Payne, the lone Californian on the committee, introduced a "strongly worded" anti-Chinese resolution, which eastern Republicans found too harsh. Then "a war of words" erupted, the *Chicago Tribune* reported, and the committee spent hours discussing a compromise. When debate raged past midnight, delegates referred the matter to a subcommittee. Emory Storrs of Illinois urged the subcommittee to "draw it mild," but Judge Payne insisted on a bold anti-Chinese statement: "The Pacific slopers must be placated," he said, "or the party would go to the bow-wows by lightning express." There was no mention of winning workers' votes nationwide. Western politicians such as Payne knew that the Chinese issue had captured a region, not a class.[6]

Expediency superseded principle, and Payne's view prevailed. On June 5, former attorney general Edwards Pierrepont read the finished platform to the convention: "Regarding the unrestricted immigration of the Chinese as a matter of grave concernment, . . . the Republican party . . . would limit and restrict that immigration by the enactment of such just, humane and reasonable laws and treaties as will produce that result." The resolution received thunderous applause. Coming after a bruising fight over voting rules and before the final struggle over the nomination, the platform produced a rare moment of unity at the fractious convention. Restriction of Chinese immigration had become a reliable rallying point for the nation's ruling party.[7]

Outside the convention, Republican response was mixed. The *New York Times* called the anti-Chinese plank an "ambiguous and half-hearted resolution . . . conspicuous for its maladroitness and its obvious spirit of buncombe." Muting its criticism, the *Philadelphia Press* noted that the plank "does not represent the views of the mass of Eastern Republicans" but claimed few would mind "that this moderate and temperate provision was added." Restriction of Chinese immigration—once associated with sandlot "hoodlums"—had passed into the mainstream. As the *New York Tribune* declared, the anti-Chinese plank "give[s] fresh emphasis to the views which are well known to prevail among Republicans." Although editorials reflected the range of attitudes Republicans held regarding Chinese immigration, party policy was now clear and direct: the Chinese must go. Democrats appreciated this political pandering. "And so the Republican party adopts an Anti-Chinese plank in its platform, and declares that Congress should restrict that immigration," the *Boston Pilot* observed. "There is no trick too dark for politicians to keep office, nor any policy so virtuous that demagogues may not claim it as their own."[8]

Quibbles over the platform receded as balloting for the nomination commenced on June 7. As expected, western delegates overwhelmingly backed Blaine. Seconding his nomination, in fact, was none other than Frank Pixley, the former California attorney general who had accompanied Roach on his eastern tour in 1876. "Blaine's view on the Chinese question captured the people of the Pacific slope," Pixley remarked, "and therefore they wanted him as the chief executive of the nation." Despite western support, Blaine trailed Grant on the first ballot, 304 to 284, with 168 votes split among four minor candidates. The second ballot yielded little change, and delegates voted again. And again. Ballot followed ballot throughout the day with neither candidate mustering the 379 votes needed for victory. After twenty-eight nearly identical ballots, the convention adjourned, and in private hotel suites throughout the night, Blaine and Grant factions discussed deals. Neither side budged, and the convention gathered again the next morning. Still deadlocked, Grant gained support on the early ballots but not enough to win. Exhausted delegates considered alternatives, and on the thirty-fourth ballot a breakthrough occurred. Sixteen Wisconsin delegates switched their votes from Blaine to a dark horse, James A. Garfield—Civil War general, nine-term representative, and senator-elect from Ohio. The response was electric. The next ballot tripled Garfield's total, and the one after gave him 399 votes to Grant's 306 and Blaine's 42.[9]

Garfield's nomination stunned the nation and delighted most delegates. To appease the Grant wing and help secure victory in the Empire State, Republicans chose for vice president Chester A. Arthur, a New York politician and avid supporter of the former president. "The result of the Convention," the defeated Blaine later wrote, "was generally accepted as a happy issue of the long contest."[10] Happiness aside, several points deserve notice. The only state whose delegation stood unanimously by Blaine to the end was California, reaffirming that the key to the Maine senator's popularity in the West was his anti-Chinese stance. Otherwise, Blaine delegates deserted en masse for Garfield on the final ballot. Garfield owed his nomination to Blaine's supporters and thus had a debt to pay the Plumed Knight. He would later appoint Blaine secretary of state, but not before asking his advice on the Chinese question.

While Garfield and his aides began mapping strategies for the fall campaign, Democrats gathered in Cincinnati on June 22 to choose their nominee. The front-runner, former candidate Samuel J. Tilden, had withdrawn from consideration just days before the convention, leaving the field wide open. Delegates braced for a fight but showed little of the rancor that had racked the Republicans. Senators Thomas F. Bayard and Allan G. Thurman, advocates of the Fifteen Passenger Bill, had ardent supporters—as well as opponents. On the first two ballots, Bayard ran second and Thurman fourth. Neither could command a majority, and on the third ballot delegates turned to Winfield Scott Hancock, the most forgotten candidate of the Gilded Age. A Civil War general as was Garfield, Hancock had distinguished himself at Gettysburg; as a war Democrat, a rare breed, he had won plaudits for his gallantry in battle. During Reconstruction he served ably as military commander in Louisiana and Texas, and as early as 1868 Democrats had considered him presidential material. With a military record appealing to both North and South, the statesman-general cultivated an image of sectional healer and national unifier, capable of burying the "bloody shirt" forever. That he had never held elective office presented no problem; in fact, it was a distinct asset. He had no enemies, and his political inexperience meant he had taken few positions that could offend. Like General Washington, partisans claimed, he was a man above politics. Untainted by corruption, Hancock the war hero was a strong and viable candidate who posed a genuine threat to Garfield.[11]

To enhance Hancock's stature on the Pacific Coast, western delegates at the Democratic convention demanded a strong anti-Chinese plank, but just as with their Republican counterparts, a sectional split emerged. "The Chinese plank . . . brought to light the differences of opinion," the *Chicago Times* reported, "and occasioned a good deal of debate." As with the Republicans, however, western delegates prevailed. Calling for "amendment of the Bur-

Figure 10.2. With James Garfield on the left and Winfield Scott Hancock on the right, Chinese immigration is effectively nailed by the Republican and Democratic Parties. No illustration better captures the politics of Chinese exclusion in the Gilded Age. Original caption: "Where Both Platforms Agree—No Vote—No Use to Either Party." (*Puck*, July 14, 1880)

lingame Treaty," the Democratic platform stated tersely: "No more Chinese immigration, except for travel, education, and foreign commerce, and that even carefully guarded." Both parties thus made the restriction of Chinese immigration a centerpiece of their platforms, with only the slightest of differences. As the *Times* noted, "The Cincinnati party . . . strike hands with the Chicago party to restrict the immigration of Chinamen." The *New York Herald* was more nuanced: "Even on the wretched Chinese question, where both platforms are, in our opinion, bad and un-American, the republicans halt and shuffle, while the democrats are outspoken. Mr. Facing-both-ways, who was evidently the author of the republican platform, tells John Chinaman that he must go—but he tells him with a snivel; he puts his arm lovingly around John before he stabs him; the democrat bluntly, but definitely, tells him he shall not come here." Few others wasted words on these distinctions, most deeming the two planks interchangeable. As the *San Francisco Alta California* observed, there was "no material difference" between the two sides. *Puck* captured this view best in a cover illustration showing Garfield and Hancock nailing a Chinese immigrant between two identical Chinese planks, with both candidates impervious to the pleading immigrant's cries and outstretched arms. No image more vividly depicts the political usage of the Chinese issue in the Gilded Age. "Both the old parties have attempted to steal Denis Kearney's thunder, 'the Chinese must go!'" the Greenback *Oshkosh Standard* scoffed. "What 'blatherskites' these old parties are getting to be, anyway."[12]

The Greenbackers also prepared for their national convention, and at meetings throughout the spring members chose delegates and debated platform planks. At only a few of these local gatherings did members discuss Chinese immigration. One or two meetings endorsed strong (but imprecise) anti-Chinese resolutions, yet not without a battle. Pennsylvania Greenbackers struggled for four hours in "protracted deliberation" over the issue, while New Yorkers engaged in a lively floor fight. Greenbackers held a range of views toward Chinese immigration and, fearing its divisiveness on the young party's tenuous unity, tried to sidestep and downplay the issue. Those who could not played it safe, such as the three hundred Greenbackers who gathered for a preliminary national convention in St. Louis in March. They simply decried "the importation of servile labor" without mentioning the Chinese by name. The Greenbackers who met for their national convention in Chicago, however, would not have the luxury of dancing around the issue. Denis Kearney, just released from prison, promised to attend.[13]

Less than twenty-four hours after the Republican convention adjourned, one thousand Greenback delegates (and ten thousand supporters) crowded into the same hall on June 9 to nominate a candidate for president. After a few opening speeches, Kearney initiated the first of many disruptions when he protested a motion permitting Susan B. Anthony to address the convention. Finding no supporters, Kearney "fought it alone and single-handed," shouting, "I insist upon this Convention proceeding to business and referring all this woman suffrage matter to a committee consisting of the daughters of Eve, to report back . . . here fifty years from to-day." Delegates voted overwhelmingly to let Anthony speak, and a furious Kearney stormed out of the room, muttering, "I didn't . . . travel over 2,614 miles to waste away my time." Kearney's antics polarized the convention. When a delegate later proposed that Kearney be invited to speak, the motion was met with "cheers and cries of 'No.'" The motion, however, prevailed.[14]

Kearney relished the moment. Denouncing Republicans as "beggars . . . robbers . . . pimp[s] [and] nincompoops," he attacked Garfield as a "coward" who lacked convictions. He then turned to his favorite topic. Having carefully bottled up his anti-Chinese rhetoric on his tour in January, Kearney could contain himself no longer. "There are five hundred millions in China," he said.

"Why, my friends, if this Chinese immigration is not prohibited now and forever, they can build a raft and send them over across the Pacific one hundred thousand every year." As Roach had used the Chinese issue to lure Democrats and Blaine had used it to lure Republicans, now Kearney used it to try to lure Greenbackers. Part demagogue, part politico, Kearney had difficulty separating the two and even more difficulty suppressing either. His recent arrest and jail term reinvigorated his anti-Chinese sensibilities, and at the Greenback convention Kearney let loose, nullifying his short-lived career as peacemaker. "The Chinese must go," he thundered, "even if we are to deluge the state of California in blood."[15]

Kearney set off more fireworks the next day when, in response to Anthony's speech, the convention seemed poised to adopt a resolution in favor of woman suffrage. Kearney objected, and a heated exchange erupted between him and feminist Sara Andrews Spencer. Kearney remarked that his wife had instructed him to oppose any such plank, warning that if he didn't, "instead of greeting him with a kiss [when he returned home] she would greet him with a flat-iron." Spencer quipped that she was "glad to know who . . . wore the breeches in Kearney's household." Assailing "the shrieking sisterhood," Kearney then retreated, taking refuge on the reporters platform. This hardly quelled the discord. The chaos became so great that Richard Trevellick, the convention's chairman, lost his temper. "You are worse than a pack of geese," he exclaimed. "You are all talking at once. Absolutely, you are as bad as the republican convention," at which point Kearney retorted, "If the chair would use less gas himself there would be less gas on the floor." Trevellick, the former president of the National Labor Union, commented caustically, "That fellow can't bull dose anybody here, although he may in California."[16]

After restoring order, the Greenbackers adopted a platform favoring woman suffrage, a national bureau of labor statistics, factory inspection, and enforcement of the national eight-hour law, and opposing child labor and contract labor. In addressing these issues, the Greenbackers clearly distinguished themselves from the two major parties. They also distinguished themselves by the language they used regarding the Chinese: "Slavery being simply cheap labor, and cheap labor being simply slavery, the importation of Chinese serfs necessarily tends to brutalize and degrade American labor; therefore, immediate steps should be taken to abrogate the Burlingame treaty." Like the Republicans and Democrats, Greenbackers expressed hostility toward Chinese laborers, but —alone of the three parties—stressed importation not immigration. Iowa representative James B. Weaver, whom the Greenbackers nominated for president, reinforced this point. "The immigration of persons from foreign countries, seeking homes and desiring to become citizens of the United States, should be encouraged," he declared in accepting the nomination, "but the importation of Chinese servile laborers should be prohibited by stringent laws."[17]

Like many workers, Weaver carefully separated immigration from importation—a stance that no doubt contributed to the Greenbackers' dismal showing in the West, where voters deserted the party in November. To Californians, the plank was simply too mild. The Greenback platform, of course, was by no means a pro-Chinese document. With references to "serfs" and "slavery" and a denunciation of the Burlingame Treaty, the platform could easily have been interpreted as a call for immigration restriction, and the fact that Kearney endorsed the platform lent credence to this view. Yet there remained ambiguity, and it is this very ambiguity that is crucial. Indeed, ambiguity is precisely what the Greenbackers wanted. Trying to be all things to all people, the Greenback platform was purposefully vague. Voters could construe the Chinese plank however they wanted: to those who discerned a difference between immigration and importation, it could mean one thing; to those who found the two synonymous, it could mean another. The Greenbackers miscalculated badly, though—1880 was not the year for ambiguity. The distinction between immigration and importation, long championed by working people in the East, was becoming anachronistic, a relic of a bygone era.

Mainstream politicians had little use for this distinction or for ambiguity. Immigration restriction was easier, simpler, and less confusing; restriction, thanks to Democratic and Republican leaders, was now on the tip of everyone's tongue. Moving to place Garfield squarely in the anti-immigration camp, the *Chicago Tribune* reprinted an interview he had given a year and a half earlier on the eve of the debate over the Fifteen Passenger Bill. "It is believed . . . that the idea of conquest has once again taken possession of the Chinese mind," Garfield reportedly said, "and that the great Buddhistic family of Asiatic races can be leagued for . . . a descent upon the Pacific coast of the United States. Such a movement means the possible wiping out of Caucasian civilization." Comparing the Chinese to "locusts" and "grasshoppers," the future president concluded: "Once started, where would they stop? Civilization would retire before them as from a plague." Despite these reputed sentiments, Garfield had opposed the Fifteen Passenger Bill; like many Republicans, he had cited treaty violations as the reason rather than sympathy for the Chinese. Nonetheless, his position was several notches milder than was Blaine's.[18]

As a consequence, California Republicans flooded Garfield with letters urging firm opposition to Chinese immigration. "It is *very* important that you define your views on the Chinese question as soon as possible," Oakland district attorney E. M. Gibson wrote him the day after he was nominated, "and in so doing you must be especially carefull [*sic*], as there is strong and almost universal antipathy to the Chinese on this coast." California buzzed with excitement. "Your nomination was hardly announced on the bulletin boards," another westerner wrote, "before the inquiry, 'How is he on the Chinese question.' Thus has this point been discussed, during the past 24 hours." Reminding Garfield "that no candidate can carry the Pacific States except [if] he is somewhat *clear* and *definite* on the Chinese question," this supporter warned, "the whole danger in Nov. *may* exist *right here*." Recently retired senator Aaron A. Sargent, Representative Horace F. Page, and Republican leader George C. Gorham also urged Garfield to declare himself strongly in favor of restriction. The party platform was "not sufficiently positive and explicit," Page wrote the nominee. "Knowing that your own sentiments are in sympathy with us in this matter, may we ask you to state your views in your letter of acceptance so clearly as to remove this anxiety."[19]

In an era when presidential candidates never addressed the conventions that nominated them, the letter of acceptance assumed tremendous importance. The letter was the candidate's personal statement that spelled out the goals and priorities he would pursue if elected. Comparable to a modern-day acceptance speech, the letter became the most important document of a Gilded Age campaign. As the direct expression of the candidate himself rather than a vague set of principles drawn up by party leaders, the letter overshadowed the party platform. As one newspaper remarked, "Letters of acceptance by candidates have become the real platform of parties."[20] The fact that presidential candidates in the nineteenth century seldom campaigned actively for office further focused attention on the letter. Candidates normally took several weeks to compose it, which provided time enough to hear from constituents and advisers alike.

Western Republicans thus lobbied Garfield in June, urging him to stress immigration restriction in his letter. Garfield also heard from easterners, including constituents in the labor movement. Of these, only John Fehrenbatch of Ohio mentioned the Chinese issue. A former president of the Machinists' and Blacksmiths' International Union, Fehrenbatch had helped organize the Industrial Congresses (the successors to the annual meetings of the National Labor Union) in the early 1870s. He later threw in his lot with the Republican Party but maintained close ties to workers, frequently attending meetings of the Trades and Labor Assembly in Cincinnati. "The members of this organization," he informed Garfield on June 16, "are without a single exception utterly opposed to the importation of Chinese." The "matter is very seriously discussed" among the six thousand members, he wrote. "Your enemies have been and are now doing their level best to misrepresent your position. . . . I have been fighting all reports of a detrimental nature on the subject, asking them to judge you by your letter of acceptance. . . . Hence they are on the tiptoe of expectation, anxiously awaiting the advent of that all-important document." Fehrenbatch then made his pitch. Having conversed with numerous workers and labor leaders in Cincinnati, he suggested the best course Garfield could follow to gain the workingman's vote: "My advice is this: While I would not oppose the voluntary immigration of any class of people, I would take a decided stand against the *importation* of the Chinese." Of the thousands of constituents Garfield heard from, Fehrenbatch was the only one to stress this distinction, and to bolster his argument, the former machinist added, "What is true of Cincinnati, is true of every large city in the north."[21]

Garfield listened to all the advice carefully. He even had his private secretary collate the suggestions that poured in from around the country. The dominant influence on Garfield's letter of acceptance, however, came from two colleagues: James Blaine and Secretary of State William M. Evarts. Blaine's position came as no surprise. Noting that "the three Pacific states will be largely if not entirely controlled by it [the Chinese issue]," the perennial candidate implored Garfield to favor restriction but added that it would be preferable that "you should clothe the proposition in your own language than that you should take any phrase of mine." The Plumed Knight would not personally get to reap the rewards of the anti-Chinese seeds he had so meticulously sown.[22]

But his party would, and William Evarts made sure of it. The advice of the secretary of state to Garfield was more precise than Blaine's—and more illuminating. His advice, however, can be understood only in light of his background and ambitions. Scion of a distinguished New England family (his grandfather was Roger Sherman), William Maxwell Evarts had been graduated from Yale University and Harvard Law School. Such impeccable credentials and a keen intellect enabled him to rise quickly to the top of his profession. He served as chief counsel for President Johnson during his impeachment trial in 1868, for which efforts Johnson appointed him attorney general. Evarts later defended Rev. Henry Ward Beecher at his famous adultery trial and served as lead counsel for the Republican Party during the Hayes-Tilden election dispute. Known for his sharp wit and habit of couching his ideas in "sentences as long as the English language can supply," Evarts in his frock coat and top hat reigned over the American legal profession for the last third of the nineteenth century. An early convert to the Republican Party, he helped found the New York City Bar Association and served as president for nine years. It had thus come as little surprise when Hayes appointed him secretary of state in 1877. Strongly influenced by his mentor, William H. Seward (Evarts had chaired the New York delegation for Seward at the 1860 Republican convention and placed his name in nomination), and possessing close ties to the financial community,

Evarts prepared the groundwork for the nation's aggressive expansionism and rise as an imperialist power at the end of the century. The "vast resources of our country need an outlet," he declared in 1877. "It is for us to enter the harvest-field and reap it."[23]

Evarts was true to his word. As secretary of state he oversaw massive U.S. investment in Latin America and threatened military force to insure U.S. control of the interoceanic canal being built by France in present-day Panama. Evarts looked west as much as south in his vision of an American commercial empire. There beyond the setting sun lay Asia with a billion potential consumers. Efforts to secure this market dominated Evarts's tenure in Washington. Through diplomatic channels, he attempted to extend American merchants' foothold in Asia, lower international duties, and keep European powers at bay. Securing China and Japan within the American sphere of influence, Evarts hoped, would be the capstone of his career and would, as one colleague remarked, "be known in history as the 'Evarts doctrine.' "[24]

This was Evarts's grand plan, and in his efforts to implement it he played a major behind-the-scenes role in the contest over Chinese immigration. As early as 1878 he had assured western members of Congress that he favored immigration restriction. Like many Republicans, however, he feared anything that might conflict with the Burlingame Treaty and jeopardize commerce with China. He thus urged Hayes to reject the Fifteen Passenger Bill and drafted the president's veto message. Immediately following this action, Evarts authorized George F. Seward, U.S. minister to China (and nephew of the former secretary of state), to open discussions in Peking regarding treaty negotiations and immigration. Democrats, however, angered by the president's veto, retaliated by drawing up articles of impeachment against Seward based on rumors he had abused his office through bribery and fraud. The impeachment failed, but the allegations undermined Seward's authority and forced Evarts to dismiss him later in the year. By laying the Hayes administration open to charges that it was dawdling on treaty negotiations, the Seward imbroglio precipitated two important developments: Evarts's well-publicized appointment of a new treaty commission to China in 1880 (discussed in the next chapter), and Evarts's unpublicized appointment of a secret agent to gather inside political information on the West Coast.[25]

Evarts's ties to the Republican Party were no less important than his ties to the financial community. These ties overlapped, and indeed, the success of one often depended on the other. With the ratification of California's constitution in May 1879, Evarts became alarmed that the growing anti-Chinese activity in the West would threaten Republican prospects and trade with China. He therefore hired a secret agent named Beverley Tucker to go west on an undercover mission. Tucker is a rather shadowy figure. Born into a leading Virginia family, he became a Confederate arms dealer who was later implicated (despite his fervent denials) in the plot to assassinate Lincoln. After the war he formed connections with the ruling Republican hierarchy, counting among his friends Blaine, Garfield, and Evarts. A master of intrigue, the fifty-nine-year-old Washington insider seemed well suited for a spy mission. In August 1879, Evarts sent him to California to scrutinize the statewide election—the first under the new constitution—and gauge the intensity of anti-Chinese sentiment. More important, he wanted Tucker to determine what other issues Republicans could raise in the coming presidential campaign that would attract western voters. Fearing the disruptive impact of the Greenback and Workingmen's Parties, Evarts wanted Tucker to test the popularity of commercial expansionism as a political issue. Evarts also wanted to know the Chinese government's attitude toward negotiating a new treaty and instructed Tucker to meet with Chinese officials in San Francisco. He further instructed Tucker to meet with confidants of Grant (whose arrival from Asia was imminent) to discover what the former president had learned from diplomats in China. Evarts wanted to keep tabs on Grant, whom he disliked and who he rightly suspected wanted to run again for president. Such was Tucker's assignment. All told, it was a tall order.[26]

Tucker took to the mission with a gusto. Arriving on the eve of the Kalloch shooting, he promptly began meeting with myriad officials and sending back dispatches marked "personal" to the secretary of state. "In view of your desire to be *fully informed* upon the Chinese question," he wrote Evarts, "this Chinese question right here is assuming most alarming proportions. A blind fatuity— an unreasoning spirit, amounting almost to madness—seems to have seized upon the mass of people here on this subject—and hence, any movement, from any quarter in alleviation of this curse, as they call it, is regarded most favorably." Tucker then suggested "*new, live issues*" that could expand the base of the Republican Party. Building an interoceanic canal would gain votes. So would buying the Hawaiian Islands. If the Republicans could turn the purchase of Hawaii into a political issue, Tucker wrote, "it would be a very popular one, for a presidential canvass." Expanding trade with China and Mexico could also win votes. These two countries "furnished a wide & fruitful field for the exercise of a grand diplomacy," he explained, stroking Evarts's ego, "which in *your hands* permit me to say, would electrify the country. . . . Depend upon it, my dear sir, that it is the line of an elevated patriotism, which will touch the popular heart of the whole nation." Profits and politics went hand in hand. Evarts had now heard what he hoped to hear: imperialism could win votes.[27]

As instructed, Tucker met with Chinese diplomats and Grant confidants, all

Figure 10.3. One of the most prominent lawyers of the nineteenth century, Secretary of State William M. Evarts (1818–1901) played a central, if largely secret, role in the effort to restrict Chinese immigration. (Photograph by Clover Adams, Courtesy Massachusetts Historical Society)

the while concealing the motive of his mission. "I have been vigilantly on the *qui vive* concerning the confidential matter entrusted to me," he wrote, "and am happy to say, I can see, or hear of, nothing that gives ground for so much as a suspicion." The Chinese government, he told Evarts, was willing to issue an "imperial edict" that would stop emigration to the United States. Such an edict could be issued "without the necessity of a *new treaty*," Tucker noted; all that was necessary was a request from the secretary of state. Then Tucker mysteriously added, "Of course all this *you* know already, & more that has not reached the public channels, but it is in respect of the *political* significance of this movement, voluntary or semi-official of Genl Grant, that I desire to post you." These comments indicate that Evarts presumably knew he could quietly and quickly ask China to close off emigration. Why then did the secretary of state not take this simple diplomatic step toward Chinese exclusion? Perhaps he doubted its efficacy. But, more likely, he decided that the quiet approach would not yield the political capital Republicans desired. Better to keep the issue in the public eye and exploit it during the presidential campaign—which is precisely what Evarts did. He appointed a treaty commission in March 1880, had them set sail for China in June, and directed them to commence negotiating a new treaty in the fall—all timed in accordance with the presidential canvass. The Republicans could thus actively portray their commitment in appropriate, legal fashion to restricting Chinese immigration. They could also campaign on commercial expansionism. Tucker had done his job and done it well. The politics of exclusion, if played correctly, could yield valuable electoral rewards.[28]

Garfield was a personal friend of Evarts and greatly respected his judgment. Before penning his letter of acceptance, he studied Evarts's advice on how to frame the issue. "The movement of the Chinese to our Pacific coast partakes but little of the qualities of such an emigration from their home, or such an accession to our community," the secretary of state wrote the Republican nominee in early July. "Neither in motives, nor in purposes . . . does this movement exhibit the familiar and acceptable traits of immigration aiming at transfusion with our society. It partakes too much of the nature of invasion not to be looked upon with solicitude." Evarts then highlighted the treaty negotiations "in progress." The accord would lead to an "incalculable extension of reciprocal trade, and immense development of markets for the interchange of products and manufactures. . . . Should, as is not to be anticipated, these negotiations fail, it will pertain to domestic legislation to redress the evils already felt and repel their increase, by such restrictions and regulations and permanent interests of the country, and maintain upon the surest foundations the freedom and dignity of labor."[29]

Garfield followed Evarts's advice carefully and copied parts of it word for word. On July 12, 1880, the candidate issued his letter of acceptance. The section on Chinese immigration took up nearly one-sixth of the text.

> The recent movement of the Chinese to our Pacific coast, partakes but little of the qualities of such an immigration, either in its purposes or its results. It is too much like an importation to be welcomed without restriction; too much like an invasion to be looked upon without solicitude. . . . Recognizing the gravity of this subject, the present Administration, supported by Congress, has sent to China a Commission of distinguished citizens, for the purpose of securing such a modification of the existing treaty, as will prevent the evils likely to arise from the present situation. It is confidently believed that these diplomatic negotiations will be successful without the loss of commercial intercourse between the two Powers, which promises a great increase of reciprocal trade and the enlargement of our markets. Should these efforts fail, it will be the duty of Congress to mitigate the evils already felt, and prevent their increase by such restrictions as . . . will place

upon a sure foundation the peace of our communities and the freedom and dignity of labor.[30]

Party leaders instantly recognized the document's import and origins. "General Garfields [sic] letter makes him a strong candidate," the aged Thurlow Weed confided to Evarts. "I suspected that he drew his Chinese inspiration from you." Garfield's letter was a hit practically everywhere. Although somewhat convoluted (thanks to copying Evarts's laborious style), it squarely favored restriction of Chinese immigration. "His views on . . . the Chinese question . . . will be endorsed by every intelligent person who has given the subject . . . thoughtful study," the *Cleveland Leader* stated, while an enthusiastic *New York Tribune* saluted the candidate for his "manly frankness" and "excellent wisdom." "The Chinese question is deftly handled," the *Cincinnati Commercial* added, and should gain enough votes on the Pacific Coast to give "the republicans of the sundown land a living chance." After perusing the western press, a confident Garfield jotted in his diary, "Reports from California indicate that my letter of acceptance has been well received there by the better class of citizens." Evidently it was not the *working* class in California that concerned him. Garfield's letter carried wide appeal. Still, as the *New York Herald* remarked, "He assents to the proscription of the Chinese, in language adapted to propitiate the hoodlums of the Pacific coast." And, the *Herald* could have added, the secretary of state as well.[31]

Two weeks later, Winfield Scott Hancock issued his letter of acceptance. It made no reference to Chinese immigration. Perhaps he presumed that western voters would be satisfied with the Democratic platform. Perhaps he presumed that the brief mention of the subject in his running mate's letter of acceptance was sufficient to win the West. Or perhaps Hancock simply didn't care about the issue. Whatever the case, the omission left open room for speculation. "It will be noticed that he makes no reference to the Chinese question," the *Washington Star* observed, "and that the report afloat that he would undertake to out-bid General Garfield for the anti-Chinese vote had no foundation." The *Chicago Times* had its own opinion: "General Hancock purposes to welcome them [the Chinese] to the United States if they come as free as Irish and German immigrants." Did Hancock thus share the view of many workers? If so, there is no further evidence. The Democratic candidate made no public comment on the subject throughout the campaign.[32]

Hancock's silence became a rallying point for Republicans in the West. The omission was no "mere oversight," the *San Francisco Chronicle* noted, and "must be regarded as significant." Democrats were at "their wit's end," the *Chronicle* added, trying "to excuse the total ignoring of this important subject by the Presidential standard-bearer." On one occasion the *Chronicle* printed the two candidates' clauses on the Chinese question side by side—the Democratic side obviously being blank. The empty space spoke volumes: "It will be noticed that Hancock's views on the subject are rather obscure. But that may be a merit, for when a man says nothing he can't be picked up."[33]

Republicans had various explanations for Hancock's silence, the main one being that the Democrats were the original party of slavery and servile labor and thus condoned Chinese immigration. More specifically, they charged that Hancock feared offending powerful southern interests who, like Mississippi planter Henry Scharrett, were considering hiring Chinese laborers to replace the thousands of black workers then migrating to the Midwest. Southerners were on the verge of importing thousands of Chinese laborers from Cuba, the *Chronicle* claimed: "Any man who looks to Hancock or the Democratic party to put a check on Chinese coolieism in America is a fool." As a consequence, one reporter noted, many western Democrats who had vowed to support their party's candidate "are now on the fence." And Republicans tried their best to yank them over. Just as Evarts had hoped, the Republican press lavishly publicized the Chinese Commission en route to Peking, and the arrival of President Hayes in California provided the final touch. In September 1880, Hayes became the first sitting president to visit the West Coast. Though he repeatedly denied political motives, he expressed confidence that the new treaty with China would lead to restriction. "I hope, and think the Commission will accomplish something satisfactory to all parties in every section of the country," the president remarked. His meaning was obvious, and westerners cheered him lustily.[34]

While Chinese immigration proved a live issue in the West, permeating the entire campaign, the subject remained dormant in the East. As the *Chicago Times* noted, "The Chinese [issue] is not the burning question throughout the union that it is in California." But the East and Midwest were in for a big surprise. On October 12, gubernatorial elections took place in Ohio and Indiana, two states evenly balanced between Republicans and Democrats. In 1876, Hayes had carried Ohio by 1.1 percent and Tilden had carried Indiana by 1.2 percent. Politicians considered the October contests in these two bellwethers a testing ground for the upcoming election and indicative of party strength in the North. Money poured in to both states, and Republicans went so far as to hire Pinkerton detectives to spy on Democratic operations. Such efforts paid off; Republicans handily won Ohio, Garfield's home state, and eked out a slim victory in Indiana. These triumphs, Garfield wrote, "ought to be decisive of the contest" in November. Fearing the same, Democrats searched for an issue to turn the election around, an issue that could be manipulated to their advantage. The issue they seized was Chinese immigration.[35]

Politicians knew well that both Roach's tour in 1876 and Kearney's tour in 1878 had failed to generate sustained interest in the issue of Chinese immigration. Politicians also knew, however, that the issue could excite momentary enthusiasm. For several weeks, Roach had received accolades in New York, Connecticut, and Washington, D.C., for his opposition to Chinese immigration, and Kearney, similarly, had inspired massive turnouts in the early weeks of his tour. Easterners had an extremely short attention span on this issue—but an attention span nonetheless. And the recent Chinese scare in the spring had again focused attention on Chinese immigration. No matter that the great majority of workers feared importation rather than immigration. No matter that workers had been consistent, articulate, and adamant on this point. But not all workers, and not all voters, politicians presumed, had made up their minds firmly. Like all issues of race in American history, Chinese immigration struck at people's emotions before it struck at their minds; this was, in fact, a key reason why the issue could generate momentary excitement. If politicians could present the issue quickly, bombard voters with it suddenly, and engulf the nation with it overwhelmingly—before people had a chance to assess the matter rationally—it might just swing a few votes. And a few votes were all politicians needed. Hayes, after all, had beaten Tilden by a single electoral vote in 1876, and seven key states had been decided by razor-thin margins, Democrats winning Indiana (by 1.2 percent), Connecticut (2.4 percent), and New York (2.9 percent), and Republicans winning Ohio (1.1 percent), Pennsylvania (2.3 percent), Wisconsin (2.4 percent), and Illinois (3.5 percent). Aware that a handful of votes could tip any of these states—and possibly the election—politicians flailed desperately to capture them. And politicians, of course, also had their eye on the volatile West Coast. The last congressional race in Oregon had been decided by barely one thousand votes, the gubernatorial contest by a mere seventy-nine votes. Recent races in Nevada were equally tight. And with Greenbacker Kearney threatening to siphon off the anti-Chinese vote in California, every western state was open territory. The early results in Indiana and Ohio dismayed Democrats; with the election hanging precariously, party leaders unleashed a political blitzkrieg, shrewdly banking that enough voters' momentary passions and inner racial fears could shape the outcome. Republicans responded instantly, and in a last-ditch attempt to lure the electorate, politicians of both parties pressed the Chinese race button as it had never been pressed before.[36]

The scheme was hatched in New York City in the office of the *Truth*, an obscure Democratic newspaper controlled by Tammany boss John Kelly. On

October 18, two weeks before election day, *Truth* publisher Joseph Hart found an unsealed envelope on his desk. Inside was a short letter dated January 23, 1880, purportedly written by Garfield to an H. L. Morey, member of the "Employers Union" of Lynn, Massachusetts. The letter, marked "Personal and Confidential," was written on House of Representatives stationery.

Dear Sir,

Yours in relation to the Chinese problem came duly to hand.

I take it that the question of employees is only a question of private and corporate economy, and individuals or companys [*sic*] have the right to buy labor where they can get it cheapest.

We have a treaty with the Chinese Government, which should be religiously kept until its provisions are abrogated by the action of the general Government, and I am not prepared to say that it should be abrogated, until our great manufacturing and corporate interests are conserved in the matter of labor.

Very truly yours,

J. A. Garfield.

In these three sentences, it appeared, Garfield had praised the Burlingame Treaty and placed the needs of capital before labor; more to the point, he seemed poised to welcome Chinese immigrants in unlimited numbers. If true, this private communication belied Garfield's letter of acceptance and exposed the Republican Party as the willing tool of capital with a secret agenda of unrestricted Chinese immigration.[37]

But was the letter genuine? Hart wasn't sure. He took the letter to former representative Abram Hewitt (now running again for the House). Hewitt, a Democrat but friend of Garfield, examined the handwriting and pronounced the letter authentic. So did Speaker of the House Samuel J. Randall (D-Pa.) and Democratic National Committee chairman William Barnum. On October 20, Hart published the letter on the *Truth*'s front page, thereby introducing the most controversial document of the 1880 campaign. After months of disinterest, politicians in the East turned Chinese immigration into the campaign's dominant issue.[38]

The "Morey letter," as it was called, instantly became the talk of the town. "This epistle is the leading topic of conversation and of public discussion here," a Brooklyn lawyer wrote, and the "*Truth*'s office was thronged all day" with people eager to see the original. The newspaper, in fact, had to run off extra editions to keep up with demand. "The *whole city* was virtually flooded with copies," an observer remarked, and "news stands every where . . . were loaded down with . . . the infamous sheet. Republicans, Democrats, Greenbackers *all* looked amazed." Barnum urged every Democratic paper in the country to publish the Morey letter. He also ordered it printed in bulk, "and by noon, thousands of copies were being scattered through the mails to all points of the compass." In less than a week, the *Chicago Times* estimated, half a million had been distributed nationwide.[39]

The Democrats pulled out all the stops to get the message across. They affixed posters of "Garfield's death warrant," as they nicknamed it, to blank walls and hawked "Morey letter" handbills on street corners. "Men are standing to-day at the doors of the public schools," the *Chicago Tribune* reported, "and as the children come out distribute copies" to them to take home to their parents. They translated the document for the benefit of foreign-born voters and stood by factory gates in town after town handing out versions to mill hands as they left work. And for voters whom the translations couldn't fully reach, Democrats printed badges, "headed by a cut of a grinning Mongolian, who smiles at the encouragement the Republican party gives him through its leader." One could not have wandered far in the last week of October 1880 without encountering the Morey letter festooned on posters, walls, and in public squares. And in private homes: one newspaper reported that copies "were distributed directly to servants" and "even posted in the kitchens." With just days to go before the election, Democrats had adroitly and insidiously pushed Chinese immigration to the forefront. "Impromptu meetings" assembled nationwide to denounce both Garfield and the letter. In large cities such as Washington, it "completely superseded all the other issues of the canvass," one newspaper noted, and in small cities such as Toledo, Ohio, the letter was "the sole topic of conversation." The Morey letter "has suddenly forced the Chinese problem forward as the foremost argument in the campaign, overtopping, in interest, business, the tariff, and the solid South," the *Chicago Times* observed. "Aside from the Chinese letter incident, there is not much that is exciting the campaign anywhere in the country." As politicians had hoped, the issue of race electrified voters everywhere.[40]

Garfield, meanwhile, secluded comfortably in his home in Mentor, Ohio, remained aloof, above the mushrooming controversy. "I hoped to answer all my accusers by silence," he wrote Marshall Jewell, the Republican National Committee chairman, to which Jewell responded: "It is a harmless affair if genuine and no denials have been made. I rather imagine that it is a letter you wrote and kept no copy." Garfield disagreed, wiring Jewell that the Morey letter was "a base forgery." Privately he wasn't sure, but the candidate did not expect to lose any sleep over the matter. That night, however, a messenger sent by *New York Herald* editor James Gordon Bennett awakened Garfield at one in the morning with a telegram describing the "great excitement in New York" and beseeching him to disown the "bogus document." The candidate consented and authorized Jewell to declare it a forgery. But still, Garfield was not positive. Making no public comment, he dispatched his private secretary to Washington "to search our files which had been carefully indexed to see if they contained any such letter."[41]

While awaiting word from his secretary, Garfield received a telegram from Jewell imploring him to immediately issue a public denial with his signature attached. Other Republican leaders also pushed him to act quickly. *New York Tribune* editor Whitelaw Reid begged Garfield for "contradiction of your alleged letter on Chinese cheap labor," while *Chicago Tribune* editor Joseph Medill warned, "The Democrats are using it with effect against us, and our 'workers' are feeling considerable uneasiness—indeed alarm." Still, Garfield hesitated. A trace of doubt lingered; he could not absolutely rule out having written the letter. Nonetheless, he authorized Jewell to release his earlier denial to the press. The next day, October 24, his secretary wired him that he could find no record of such a letter in Washington, and on October 25, Garfield received a copy of the *Truth*, which included a lithographic reproduction of the Morey letter. This removed his last doubt: Garfield felt certain it was neither in his handwriting nor in that of any of his staff. Relieved, Garfield finally issued to the press a full denial of the letter with his signature clearly written. On October 26, a facsimile of this denial appeared in the *New York Herald* and in newspapers nationwide. Readers could compare the handwriting and judge for themselves.[42]

Garfield's delay in publicly denouncing the letter almost proved his undoing. The weeklong interval gave Democrats time to mount an offensive and use his silence as evidence of complicity. "We had this election, dead, two weeks ago," one Republican strategist remarked. "Now it is in great doubt, and all through the stupidity of our leaders." Republicans moved frantically to contain the spreading damage. As quickly as Democrats posted handbills of the letter on blank walls, Republicans covered them over with posters charging "forgery." Placard covered placard in towns across the country. Republicans too stood on street corners circulating handbills denying the letter's authenticity, while party leaders highlighted anti-Chinese statements Garfield had made in the past. Representative Jay A. Hubbell (R-Mich.), chairman of the Republican Congressional Committee, cited recent conversations and interviews in which the candidate had called the Chinese "grasshoppers" and expressed fears of "being overrun by alien hordes from Asia." Such comments ensured that the "partisan fury" over the Morey letter would continue right down to election day.[43]

While Republican leaders anxiously awaited Garfield's denial in late October, lesser activists took matters into their own hands. One supporter on Wall

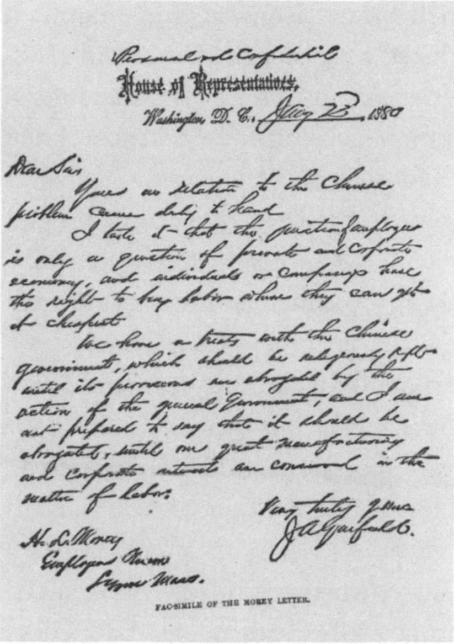

Personal and Confidential
House of Representatives,
Washington, D. C., Jany 23, 1880

Dear Sir
Yours in relation to the Chinese problem came duly to hand
I take it that the question of employes is only a question of private and corporate economy, and individuals or companys have the right to buy labor where they can get it cheapest
We have a treaty with the Chinese government, which should be religiously kept until its provisions are abrogated by the action of the general Government, and I am not prepared to say that it should be abrogated, until our great manufacturing and corporate interests are conserved in the matter of labor.

Very truly yours
J A Garfield.

H. L. Morey
Employers Union
Lynn Mass.

FAC-SIMILE OF THE MOREY LETTER.

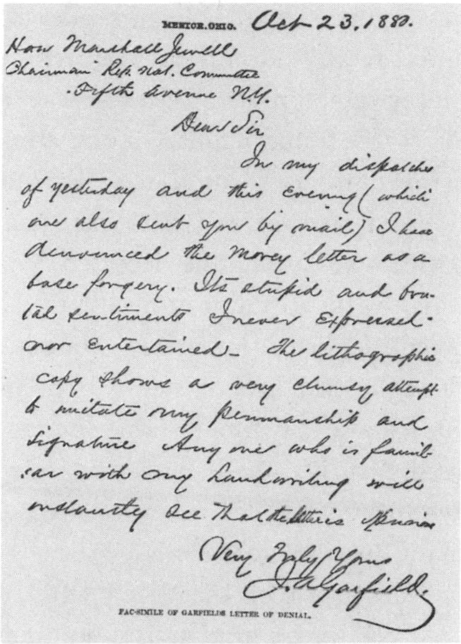

MENTOR, OHIO. Oct 23, 1880.

Hon Marshall Jewell
Chairman Rep. Nat. Committee
Fifth Avenue N.Y.

Dear Sir
In my dispatches of yesterday and this evening (which are also sent you by mail) I have denounced the Morey letter as a base forgery. Its stupid and brutal sentiments I never expressed nor entertained. The lithographic copy shows a very clumsy attempt to imitate my penmanship and signature. Any one who is familiar with my handwriting will instantly see that the letter is spurious

Very Truly Yours
J. A. Garfield.

FAC-SIMILE OF GARFIELDS LETTER OF DENIAL.

Figure 10.4. In the closing days of the 1880 presidential campaign, the Morey letter (left), purportedly written by James Garfield, and the candidate's belated denial (right) appeared side by side in newspapers across the country. The forged letter quickly became the most scrutinized document of the nineteenth century, enabling politicians to turn Chinese immigration into a major campaign issue two weeks before election day. (John Clark Ridpath, *The Life and Work of James A. Garfield, Twentieth President of the United States: Embracing an Account of the Scenes and Incidents of His Boyhood; the Struggles of His Youth; the Might of His Early Manhood; His Valor as a Soldier; His Career as a Statesman; His Election to the Presidency; and the Tragic Story of His Death* [Cincinnati, 1881])

Street spent a day showing the Morey letter to fifty "experts in writing irrespective of political opinion," all of whom pronounced it a fake. The supporter took his "evidence" to campaign chairman Jewell, who "immediately ordered it sent out to all the City papers—and also ordered it telegraphed by special and Associated press dispatches to all parts of the United States." But not all handwriting experts agreed, and Garfield's penmanship became the subject of lengthy editorials. How the candidate dotted his i's, crossed his t's, and inserted periods after the initials in his signature took on tremendous importance. "The democrats," one newspaper remarked, "put a great deal of credit in the 'dot' matter." Experts scrutinized the stationery, and high-level postal workers examined the envelope's postmark. Mystery enhanced the controversy. Who was H. L. Morey, and where was he? Efforts to locate the elusive recipient proved unsuccessful as reporters found that he had either died or disappeared. One reporter turned up a Lynn woman surnamed Morey who claimed to be his mother, but other Lynn residents named Morey denied it, precipitating a family feud. A local hotel proprietor produced a register containing an H. L. Morey signature dated February 1880, but critics dismissed it as fraudulent. Reporters found similarly conflicting claims regarding the existence of the Lynn "Employers Union" to which Morey had allegedly belonged. Controversy reverted to the letter itself. Where had it come from? The *Truth* claimed it had been found among the deceased Morey's papers and forwarded to the publisher by the executor of his estate. The *Tribune* counterclaimed that no such executor existed. Every day brought a new charge, a new lead, a new story. Enough "evidence" existed to prove almost anything, and readers could pick and choose. But evidence no longer mattered. Like the entire Chinese issue itself, facts became lost in a web of specious allegations, underlying motives, and hidden agendas. Assertion accounted for truth as truth became irrelevant in the quest for votes.[44]

Every article on the Morey letter, of course, whether pro or con, kept the issue of Chinese immigration in the forefront while the campaign entered its final week. Even the arrest on October 27 of a *Truth* editor named Kenward Philp, accused of forging the letter, failed to stop the frenzy, for Democrats simply called the arrest a last-ditch effort by Republicans to steal the election. The politics of race hit full gear. "Every democratic stump speaker in the state has been instructed to ring the charges on the sentiments expressed in the letter," one Pennsylvanian remarked, while Abram Hewitt, one of the Morey letter's original boosters and chairman of the congressional committee that had heard workers carefully distinguish between immigration and importation, told an election-eve crowd in New York City, "Chinese emigration would be fatal to this country." Republicans fought back with vigor, attacking the Morey letter as "a malignant lie" and "the vilest, of the Democratic misrepresentations." The *New York Tribune*, once a staunch defender of Chinese immigration, now portrayed the Democrats as the pro-Chinese immigration party and Republicans as the champions of restriction. Party leaders everywhere emphasized Garfield's anti-Chinese stance, and at marches and rallies in the campaign's final weekend, Republicans prominently featured banners warning all Chinese immigrants to leave the country. The Morey letter gave Republicans one last opportunity to wave the "bloody shirt" against the Democrats. "They appealed to the sword in 1860," the influential Robert Ingersoll declared, "now they appeal to the pen."[45]

On November 2, 1880, Americans went to the polls. More than 78 percent of the electorate voted, one of the highest turnouts ever in a presidential contest.

Garfield won the electoral count, 214 to 155, and the popular vote proved the closest in American history: out of nine million ballots cast, Garfield surpassed Hancock by less than 2,000 votes, a mere .02 percent. The narrowest races were in the West, where Hancock won California by a scant 144 votes (out of 164,000 cast) and Nevada by 879 (out of 18,000 cast), while Garfield won Oregon by 664 (out of 41,000 cast). Assessing the impact of the Morey letter on the election is tricky. The chairman of the California Republican Committee told a reporter that he "attributes the disaster [in the state] to the Garfield-Morey letter," a view echoed by Garfield himself, and the returns seem to back this up. Garfield ran behind the ticket in California: although Republican congressional candidates outpolled Democrats by over 600 votes, Hancock won the state. Garfield also ran behind the Republican ticket in Oregon. These split ballots in Hancock's favor suggest that the Morey letter cost Garfield a few crucial votes in the West. Garfield also believed it cost him New Jersey, the only state in the North he failed to carry, but the data are inconclusive. Though New Jersey proved the closest battleground east of the Rockies—Garfield lost the Garden State by just 2,000 votes (out of 264,000 cast)—he actually ran ahead of the Republican ticket by 440 votes and far exceeded Hayes's total in 1876. The Morey letter does not seem to have harmed Garfield seriously in other states east of the Rockies, for he carried all seven states that had been closely fought four years earlier (Indiana, Connecticut, New York, Ohio, Pennsylvania, Wisconsin, and Illinois), several by comfortable margins. The data thus suggest that the Morey letter had a greater impact in the West than it did in the East. The initial excitement the incident sparked did not carry into the voting booth. Again, the issue demonstrated little staying power. Despite all the best efforts of politicians, "the Chinese question," the *Chicago Times* stated, was "not a live issue this side of the Rockies."[46]

In trying to assess the impact of the Morey letter on the outcome of the election, however, one mustn't overlook the essential meaning of the episode: that the entire affair was engineered by politicians, manipulated by politicians, and propelled by politicians. And newspapers—many of them paid party sheets—eagerly exploited the affair by keeping the issue on page one. By both controlling the flow of information and disclosing rumor in the guise of fact, the press shaped, perpetuated, and helped legitimize the importance of the Morey letter. As devised by politicians, the contest came down to a test of which party could present itself as more opposed to Chinese immigration. Chinese immigrants had become the pawns of a nearly perfectly balanced two-party system, and politicians, abetted by the press, used exclusion as a handy lever to try to tip the scales in their favor. Few voices outside the press or the West spurred them on. Virtually no one in the East had mentioned the Chinese since the early summer; for months the issue had lain dormant. Then, in late October, the Democrats, fearing defeat, suddenly catapulted the issue to the front lines, and Republicans raced them head to head with it down to the wire.

For their part, working people remained largely indifferent. "Read it, ye workingmen," counseled the *Cincinnati Enquirer*. The Morey letter "is un-American to the last degree, and it is an expression of hostility to the interests of every laboring man in the United States who is not a Chinaman." Such efforts may have swayed a few workers, but the evidence is slim. The labor press devoted little space to the matter, and labor leaders made scant effort to capitalize on the incident or mobilize around the issue. Despite the herculean efforts of politicians, Chinese exclusion still remained virtually absent from organized labor's agenda. As one Brooklyn reader of the *Irish World and American Industrial Liberator* declared just after the election, a new platform for a new labor party must "emphatically . . . favor . . . a free voluntary immigration to the United States of the citizens of the world."[47]

The Morey letter remains one of the smaller but intriguing mysteries of the nineteenth century. To this day no one knows who wrote it. The accused Kenward Philp was later acquitted, and no other forger was definitively identified.[48] The significance of the letter, however, lies not in its origin but in its use. No letter in American history ever received such immediate and intense scrutiny as the three sentences James Garfield purportedly wrote on January 23, 1880. The letter provided good copy, and politicians and editors—not workers —trumpeted it across the nation. Lost in all the mainstream publicity was the vital distinction workers had long made between immigration and importation, which labor leader Fehrenbatch had carefully, if futilely, explained to candidate Garfield in June. The Morey letter affair demonstrates how easily politicians could overlook workers' demands and, at the same time, generate headlines simply by treating an issue superficially and spouting racism.

Garfield called the Morey letter a "wicked device" designed to catch votes. He was right, but whether the letter was any more wicked a device than Tucker's secret mission on behalf of Evarts the year before or Garfield's own letter of acceptance in July remains open to debate. Ever the politician, Garfield predicted the scandal would boomerang on those who conceived it. "I may be in error," the future president recorded in his diary, "but I confidently believe this forgery will injure the party in whose interest it has been concocted and circulated. Moreover, it is a confession that the Democrats cannot hope to win on the merits of their doctrines and practices." The Republicans, on the other hand, could point proudly to their doctrines and practices. The "doctrines" set forth by James Blaine, the "practices" set in motion by William Evarts, and the promises set in print by James Garfield did, indeed, in the eyes of the Republican candidate, merit votes. Yet was there, ultimately, really much difference? No: in means perhaps, but not in ends. As the *New York Herald* observed, "In this canvass General Garfield stooped to bid for the anti-Chinese vote and win the Kearney crowd, which Hancock, to his credit, did not do." Garfield was justifiably miffed at the Democrats' "unusually desperate" schemes, but ultimately they were nothing more than an extension of Republican tactics.[49]

The Morey letter episode represented the culmination of years of anti-Chinese politics. Capping the 1880 campaign, it showed that bigotry remained the sharpest arrow in the politician's quiver. Democrats and Republicans could shoot their poisonous arrows at will, and in the waning days of Reconstruction, it was open season on a new race. What had once been the party of emancipation had now become the agent of a new racism. As far as Chinese immigration was concerned, political labels no longer mattered. Electioneering suddenly became a contest to see which party could "out-Chinese" the other, whether by legitimate or illegitimate means. While Garfield squeaked by with a razor-thin margin of victory, the politics of race and exclusion won a resounding triumph. Rhetoric, bigotry, and national policy would at last converge as the Chinese temporarily displaced blacks to become the most officially despised people in America. After a brief hiatus inspired by Civil War idealism, racism was back in fashion. Only the target had shifted. The election of 1880 reintroduced racism as a popular political weapon that politicians would wield for years to come.

As the flood of congratulatory telegrams poured in to Mentor, Ohio, in the chilly days of November, the president-elect received word that American diplomats in Peking had signed a new treaty giving the United States the power to restrict Chinese immigration. The path was now clear. No one doubted how Congress and the new president would proceed.

> Sometimes expediency
> is statesmanship of the
> highest order.
> —*New York Tribune*,
> March 10, 1882

CHAPTER ELEVEN

The Gate Must Be Closed

The Angell Treaty and the Race
to Exclude, 1881–1882

James Burrill Angell, president of the University of Michigan, did not favor Chinese exclusion. "The absolute and formal prohibition of the laborers would be diametrically opposed to all our national traditions," he wrote Secretary of State William M. Evarts on March 11, 1880, just as the presidential campaign was gearing up, "and would call down the censure of a very large portion, if not a majority of our most intelligent and high-minded citizens." On the recommendation of Senator George F. Edmunds (R-Vt.), Evarts had tapped Angell in February to head the commission to China to renegotiate the Burlingame Treaty. The secretary of state emphasized that the main purpose for a new treaty was to curb "in some degree the emigration which was threatening to flood the Pacific States." Evarts invited Angell to Washington to confer with Republican senators and President Hayes. "He seemed deeply impressed with the importance of restraining the immigration of the Chinese," Angell later wrote of the president. "I asked if the government supposed the country east of the Rocky Mountains was ready to adopt measures restrictive of Chinese immigration. In reply I was given to understand that the action of such a Commission as they were trying to appoint would of itself have much weight in securing acquiescence in reasonable measures." Angell's mission to China would thus have two goals: diplomatic, to negotiate a new treaty; and political, to further convince easterners of the wisdom of restricting Chinese immigration.[1]

Plainly troubled by abetting exclusion, Angell wavered in accepting the appointment. "There are some indirect methods for sustaining the emigration," he wrote. The United States could forbid entry of Chinese men without families, a restriction that "would almost cut off emigration." But such a solution, Angell admitted, might not be very practical. Chinese men might induce any woman to accompany them "and so immorality could be fostered." A better approach, "indeed the best which has suggested itself to me, would be to ask the Chinese government to agree that no emigrants should come on the present contract system." Angell expounded to Evarts on the evils of imported contract laborers. "It is notorious that contractors pay . . . for them as they would for horses, having no pecuniary dealings at all with the individual Chinaman. The contract is radically different in spirit from our ordinary business contracts." To abolish such contracts—the decade-old demand of American workers—by negotiating a new treaty, Angell agreed to serve as diplomat "from a sense of public duty."[2]

Evarts accepted Angell's stipulations and nominated him to lead the commission. On April 9, 1880, the Senate confirmed Angell and two other commissioners: former assistant secretary of state William H. Trescot, a Democrat from South Carolina, and John Swift, a lawyer and former Republican legislator who had helped draft the California constitution. In May, a week before Evarts raced off to the Republican Convention, he, Angell, and Trescot met in Washington for four days of discussions.[3] They focused on "the difference between European and Asiatic immigration" as well as commercial questions. Few notes remain of their meetings, but Evarts must have persuaded Angell to change his mind on importation; at no time in the course of subsequent communications or negotiations, nor in the treaty itself, was there any mention of contract labor. Evarts had little interest in the distinction between immigration and importation; hence, he did not instruct the commission to negotiate on this subject. The only distinction he made was between immigration restriction and total exclusion. Evarts preferred restriction, he explained to Angell and Trescot (in his typically verbose manner), because of "the widely diffused and so to speak, natural sentiment of our people in favor of the most liberal admission of foreign immigrants who desire to incorporate themselves and their families with our

Figure 11.1. President of the University of Michigan, James B. Angell (1829–1916) led the commission to China in 1880 to revise the Burlingame Treaty. Although he opposed exclusion, the Angell Treaty he negotiated led directly to the Chinese Exclusion Act less than two years later. (Courtesy Bentley Historical Library, University of Michigan)

society, and mingle the stream of their posterity in the swelling tide of native population." Simply stated, the commission's immediate goals were immigration restriction and commercial relations; its ultimate goal was American dominance of China. As Trescot wrote Evarts shortly after arriving in Asia, "I cannot tell you how often since I came here I have felt the force of your declaration that the U.S. was a Pacific power or at least ought to be."[4]

The commissioners set sail in June, a week after the Republican Convention, arriving in China in late July. Negotiations began in Peking with Chinese ministers Pao Chun and Li Hungtsao on October 1, during the height of the presidential campaign. Swift urged that the new treaty empower the United States to exclude Chinese immigrants totally, but Angell and Trescot, following Evarts's advice, suggested simply the power to regulate and restrict. Swift prevailed initially, and the first proposal required China to recognize America's right to prohibit the immigration of Chinese laborers. Objecting immediately, Pao and Li argued that it was only "the rabble"—particularly "the Irish" in California— who advocated exclusion "and that the better class of Americans thought mostly the other way." The U.S. government, they held, was swayed by "the influence of violent men." The American commissioners rebuked them for this insult to the nation's honor and, in Swift's words, "for making any distinction between American citizens." The Chinese apologized and said they had been led to believe these points by former minister George F. Seward. Trescot then explained the unanimity of sentiment among Americans against Chinese immigration, presenting as proof the Republican and Democratic platforms (but not the Greenback platform), copies of which Evarts had passed along.[5]

Angell seized the initiative, convincing Pao and Li to negotiate on immigration. The Chinese commissioners then offered a counterproposal with seven main provisions:

1. The United States could "regulate" rather than "prohibit" the immigration of Chinese laborers, but only if the Chinese government approved.
2. Artisans would not be included as laborers.
3. Regulation would apply only to immigrants landing in California.
4. The length of regulation should be specified.
5. Regulation would apply only to Chinese laborers working for American citizens (thus permitting them to work in the United States for Chinese employers).
6. Chinese merchants and students should be allowed to bring their servants.
7. Chinese immigrants should be fully protected by the law.[6]

The Americans accepted the last two provisions, but rejected numbers 2 through 5. Congress needed the power and flexibility to respond to local situations, Trescot explained: "For example, there might be a demand for Chinese labor in the South and a surplus of such labor in California." To legislate accordingly, the United States needed "a certain elasticity of action" and could not be bound by regional or temporal restrictions. The Americans compromised only on the first provision, accepting, as Angell and Trescot had initially favored, the term "regulate" in place of "prohibit." They refused, however, to give the Chinese government any veto power over such regulation. "We thought that the simplest, the directest, and the only efficient plan," the commissioners wrote, "was to give the control of the subject to the Government of the United States." They assured Pao and Li that the United States would act only with "wise discretion" and "entire justice."[7]

After forty-eight days of talks—during which the Morey letter affair stole headlines back home—the American and Chinese commissioners signed a treaty on November 17, 1880. The key clause on immigration appeared in article 1: "Whenever in the opinion of the Government of the United States, the coming of Chinese laborers to the United States, or their residence therein, affects or threatens to affect the interests of that country, or to endanger the good order of the said country or of any locality within the territory thereof, the Government of China agrees that the Government of the United States may regulate, limit, or suspend such coming or residence, but may not absolutely prohibit it. The limitation or suspension shall be reasonable and shall apply only to Chinese who may go to the United States as laborers, other classes not being included in the limitations." Article 2 defined such "other classes" as teachers, students, merchants, and "their household servants." Article 3 entitled all Chinese in the United States to legal protection (essentially reinforcing the provision of the Civil Rights Act of 1870). The final article required the United States to notify China of any legislation passed in accordance with the treaty and to permit the Chinese Foreign Office to discuss the subject with the secretary of state. As Swift remarked, this last article merely gave China the "right to grumble."[8]

The Chinese had conceded virtually everything the United States demanded, mainly because of their overriding desire for American friendship. Throughout the year China had feared an attack from Russia, and during negotiations, Swift noted, "The Chinese waters were filled with Russian war ships [and] Muscovite troops were massed on the borders." China also dreaded war with Japan and wanted American intervention to force its Asian neighbor out of the Ryukyu Islands. Unprepared for armed conflict and unable to rely on protection from England, the Chinese hoped to curry American favor. Their need for support outweighed their distaste for the insulting terms of the treaty. "The readiness with which the best blood of your people to assist us, in case we should be engaged in war, is the highest proof of sincerest friendship," wrote Chinese leader Li Hung-chang a few months later. "I truly thank your people for this noble offer." In addition to the immigration pact, the two nations signed a second treaty, which lowered trade duties, outlawed the opium trade, and resolved jurisdictional disputes.[9]

The commission had succeeded. Little now stood in the way of a limited restriction of Chinese immigration. In the months to come, however, the U.S. government would abandon the commissioners' promises of both "wise discretion" and "entire justice" in dealing with the issue. It would also stretch "a certain elasticity of action" to the breaking point as Congress would soon terminate Chinese immigration almost completely in a law that would be renewed for decades and enforced with a single-minded resoluteness.

Trescot left Peking on November 20 to carry the two treaties to Washington. Their contents remained a mystery until the *New York Herald* intercepted a copy and published a summary on January 6, 1881. Their disclosure created a furor in the Senate, and George Edmunds demanded an investigation into how they were leaked. This action sparked indignant editorials on freedom of the press, but little came of the senatorial uproar, perhaps because of the almost uniformly positive response the treaties themselves received.[10] Scattered opponents in California complained that the anti-immigration clauses were too mild, but this resistance soon melted away. In Manhattan, some businessmen protested because the ban on the opium trade threatened to give Great Britain a monopoly. "A preposterous petition," the New York Herald remarked on this protest, drafted by "nincompoop New York merchants." These comments fairly set the tone for eastern opinion: opposition remained all but dormant. Such silence surprised the Chicago Times, which expected an outcry from the "sentimental people"—those "adhering to the old notion that America should be an asylum, or a common sewer . . . for all sorts of people from all parts of the world." But there was scant outcry; the "old notion" of America as an "asylum" for people the world over had passed from vogue.[11]

To many, the treaties represented the final achievement of the outgoing administration. Hayes and Evarts, the Herald proclaimed, "have won the blue ribbon of diplomacy." The New York Times voiced no complaints, and the Tribune called the treaties "all that could be desired. . . . It is difficult to see any point in either of them to which any Senator can reasonably raise objection, and their ratification will probably not be delayed."[12]

On this last point, the Tribune jumped the gun. In February, the Senate deferred action until the spring. The chief casualty of this delay was a disappointed William Evarts, who was prevented from officially affixing his signature to the treaties. This task was left to a successor. On March 4, 1881, James A. Garfield was inaugurated president, and he promptly nominated James G. Blaine to be secretary of state. The Senate quickly approved Blaine and the entire cabinet.[13]

The new president ran into problems, however, when the Senate refused to confirm his lesser appointments. Senator Roscoe Conkling (R-N.Y.) and the so-called Stalwart wing of the Republican Party obstructed regular business by opposing Garfield's choices, and a Democratic filibuster over appointments in Virginia further deadlocked the Senate for two months. To resolve the squabbling, President Garfield persuaded the Senate to meet in executive session. Such sessions are technically closed to the public, and the Congressional Record, which normally reports all legislative debate, does not cover them. It was amid this period of executive session and intense Republican infighting between March and May 1881 that the Chinese treaties came up for consideration. As a consequence, no official account of the debate exists. Only the vote was officially recorded.[14]

Despite this news blackout, nothing very essential was concealed. The Senate debated the treaties for two days, on May 4 and May 5. California senators John F. Miller (R-Calif.) and James T. Farley (D-Calif.), who had replaced the retired Aaron Sargent, urged speedy ratification and presented numerous western petitions in support. Only Senator George Frisbie Hoar (R-Mass.) denounced the anti-immigration treaty for being "contrary to the genius of our institutions and to the general doctrine of 'the brotherhood of man.'" Hoar's position won few backers. After just five hours of debate, the Senate ratified the Angell Treaty, as the anti-immigration pact became known, 48 to 4 (with 24 not voting). The sole purpose of this treaty was to give the United States the right to restrict Chinese immigration. *It had no other function.* As the *New York Times* later noted, anyone favoring the Angell Treaty could no longer oppose restriction "on the ground of principle." That defense was now gone. The anemic opposition during the debate demonstrates the broad support that immigration restriction had amassed in Congress. Of seventy-six members in the U.S. Senate, just four dared to swim against the current.[15]

The press appeared to be in an executive session of its own. With ratification taken for granted, newspapers wasted little space on the Senate proceedings. "There will not be any appreciable opposition to the confirmation of the Chinese treaties," the *New York Times* predicted on the eve of debate. And without a fight, the press lost interest. The only objection raised was to the Senate's executive session—"in direct contradiction to the Constitution"—but not to its near unanimous vote of ratification. The *Times*, one of the last holdouts in favor of Chinese immigration, no longer raised its voice in protest, seemingly relieved, as its headline stated, of "A VEXED QUESTION SETTLED." The propriety of exclusion—the ethics of this vexing question—no longer mattered. On the losing end of a long battle, the *Times* took just one parting swipe: "If California were not a doubtful state in national politics, and if the people there were not almost uniformly bitten by the anti-Chinese mania, the 'national' character of this momentous matter would hardly be so apparent." That said, it was now up to Congress to actually restrict Chinese immigration. "And when this is done," the *Times* concluded, "let us hope the Chinese question will disappear forever from American politics."[16]

Ratification of the Angell Treaty marked a legal turning point in the movement to restrict Chinese immigration. The sole obstacle that had blocked the Fifteen Passenger Bill had now been eliminated. There was no doubt that when the 47th Congress convened for its official opening session in December 1881, immigration restriction would top the agenda.[17] Enactment of such a law was a foregone conclusion, and debate began to focus not on *if* Chinese immigration would be restricted but on *how* and to what extent. As politicians commenced formulating bills, organized labor nationwide finally began to lend support. Workers, to be sure, had expressed little interest in the Angell Treaty. Negotiation and ratification passed virtually unnoticed in the labor press and at workers' meetings. Scattered anti-Chinese sentiment erupted in the spring when a Cincinnati cigar manufacturer hired forty Chinese laborers, and eastern cigar makers began pushing the union label—an innovation devised by western cigar makers for the sole purpose of informing customers that no Chinese laborers had worked on the product. Despite these actions, the Cigar Makers' International Union said little about Chinese labor or immigration restriction that fall at its annual four-day meeting in Cleveland. The Angell Treaty never came up. Nor did the treaty receive any mention the entire year in the *Journal of United Labor*, the recently founded newspaper of the Knights of Labor, or at the organization's annual five-day assembly in Detroit in September.[18]

Two months later, however, eastern workers broke their silence. On November 15, 1881, labor leaders gathered in Pittsburgh to form a new association, the Federation of Organized Trades and Labor Unions, which in 1886 would rename itself the American Federation of Labor. Almost two-thirds of the 107 delegates came from Pennsylvania; one, who would be of great significance, came from California.[19] The convention elected John Jarrett, president of the Amalgamated Association of Iron and Steel Workers, as president, and cigar maker Samuel Gompers as one of two vice presidents. For the first three days, delegates wrangled over political issues and membership in the new organization. Some differences were settled amicably, others bred acrimony. In one dispute, Gompers squared off against Sherman Cummin of the Boston Typographical Union. Gompers argued for a strict hierarchical system of organization in which national and international unions chose delegates to the federation. Cummin urged selection by the rank and file so that actual workers and local labor organizations could also be represented. After intense debate, delegates reached a compromise partial to Gompers. The dispute, however, presaged a fight involving Cummin on the convention's last day.[20]

On November 18, Charles F. Burgman, a California tailor representing the Pacific Coast Trades and Labor Unions, delivered a stinging address, describing all the familiar "evils" of Chinese labor. Sent specifically by his organization to pitch Chinese exclusion, Burgman introduced a resolution urging Congress to pass laws "entirely prohibiting the immigration of the Chinese into the United States." Cummin objected at once. American workers, the Boston printer said, had nothing to fear from the Chinese: "The Constitution of the United States guaranteed them the hospitality of our shores, and they should have the same rights as other foreigners." A discussion ensued, for which no transcript exists. The official proceedings recount little more, and newspaper accounts provide minimal detail. The press, however, emphasized the fury of the exchange. The *Chicago Tribune* noted "the sharp fight on the Chinese question," while both the *New York Times* and *Herald* described it as "a heated debate." The *Tribune* added that the dispute marked one of the few divisive moments of the entire convention.[21]

Cummin was clearly in the minority. He tempered his strong objections by moving to replace "entirely prohibiting" with the word "regulating." The amendment lost. Burgman's speech had swayed the convention. Had he not attended, it is likely delegates would have ignored the issue. As Gompers later noted, Burgman had crossed the country "to rouse the East to the dangers of Chinese immigration." But unlike Roach and unlike Kearney, Burgman succeeded, at least at this one convention. With a single dissenting vote—no doubt Cummin's—delegates adopted the following resolution:

> WHEREAS, The experience of the last thirty years in California and on the Pacific Coast having proved conclusively that the presence of Chinese, and their competition with free white labor, is one of the greatest evils with which any country can be afflicted; therefore be it
> RESOLVED, That we use our best efforts to get rid of this monstrous evil (which threatens, unless checked, to extend to other parts of the Union) by the dissemination of information respecting its true character, and by urging upon our representatives in the United States Congress the absolute necessity of passing laws entirely prohibiting the immigration of Chinese into the United States.[22]

California labor had scored a major victory. It had at last convinced an organized group of workers in the East to endorse Chinese exclusion. As Gompers recounted with pride in his autobiography forty years later, the Federation of Organized Trades and Labor Unions (FOTLU) "was the first national organization which demanded the exclusion of coolies from the United States."[23] Gompers was right. The FOTLU resolution of November 18, 1881, officially marked the start nationally of organized labor's endorsement of Chinese exclusion. After resisting for more than a dozen years, union leaders in the East finally acquiesced to the demands of California. Several reasons account for this. The FOTLU had grand hopes for the future as a national body representing workers throughout the country. California, with its vibrant labor movement, could be an important force in strengthening the new organization. Though many workers decried race baiting and remained opposed to exclusion, some seemed indifferent to the issue and even sympathetic. During the Morey letter incident, no one, least of all organized labor, had risen to the defense of the Chinese, and with the momentum of "anti-coolieism" building nationwide as a result of the Angell Treaty and careful political nurturing, workers appeared to be riding the tide of anti-Chinese emotion. Perhaps most important, ratification of the treaty in May had made exclusion all but inevitable, and national labor leaders, as politically savvy as national politicians, saw a way to gain support in the West that might no longer hurt them in the East. As a consequence, the FOTLU jumped on the bandwagon at the last minute and narrowly beat Congress to the finish line.

The FOTLU convention received generally positive reviews from workers, but the Chinese plank excited minimal attention. Several labor papers printed appeals from Burgman and other Californians urging eastern workers to join their anti-Chinese crusade.[24] Publication suggests endorsement, but editorials remained subdued. Meanwhile, the Boston Central Trades and Labor Union held a meeting in December and discussed the appeal of its Pacific brethren. They expressed "sympathy with their experience" and empowered the union's executive committee to call a mass meeting on the subject "if it considered it necessary." The committee never did. Most other labor gatherings failed to mention the Chinese plank or immigration restriction, and the few times the issue surfaced, subtle changes in wording suggest a certain distancing from the FOTLU's hard-line position. In reporting the convention's proceedings in the *Cigar Makers' Official Journal*, Gompers himself transcribed the resolution as favoring "laws entirely prohibiting their importation." While this could reflect the increasingly synonymous nature of the terms "importation" and "immigration," it is noteworthy that Gompers chose the phrase less controversial in labor circles. The terminology used at a meeting of the Amalgamated Trades and Labor Union in New York to ratify the FOTLU platform is more illuminating. Speakers themselves never mentioned Chinese immigration, and in resolutions endorsing the platform, they rewrote the anti-Chinese plank. Instead of "entirely prohibiting the immigration of Chinese into the United States," the New Yorkers substituted, "We . . . condemn the importation of Chinese single men, with their inferior standard of wants." Anti-Chinese sentiment was evident, but the solution remained fuzzy.[25]

While overwhelming consensus among working people toward Chinese exclusion had not yet emerged, staunch opposition no longer existed. And still, to many workers, Chinese immigration remained a side issue at most. The *Fall River Labor Standard*, which presciently called the FOTLU convention "the most important gathering that has met in America for a long time," nonetheless criticized the proceedings: "By a glance over the topics discussed and the resolutions adopted one would almost be tempted to ask if some shrewd capitalist hadn't chosen their subjects for them; carefully selecting the harmless topics for discussion and keeping the important questions in the back ground." The Massachusetts weekly rebuked the delegates for uttering "hardly a passing word" on such vital matters as poverty, the eight-hour day, and workers' disfranchisement. Items such as Chinese immigration and convict labor were nothing but "the skim-milk issues of the day."[26]

In regard to the national political debate on Chinese immigration, 1881 was the most quiescent year in half a decade. The year's single outstanding accomplishment—ratification of the Angell Treaty—passed with little more than a yawn. The lack of any voluble opposition indicates the growing acceptance of Chinese exclusion nationally as well as the understanding that immigration restriction was imminent. Hoar's lonely defense of the Chinese in the Senate sparked ridicule rather than respect and few people anywhere lent him support. With Democrats eager to exclude the Chinese and Republicans eager to take the credit, the Angell Treaty sailed through the Senate practically unchallenged. As the outgoing administration had hoped, the success of the treaty commission apparently helped cement public opinion in favor of immigration restriction. At the very least, it had stifled opposition. Chinese exclusion had become an article of faith, no longer provoking much controversy. And organized labor, despite internal dissension, had at last come around on this "skim-milk issue." But by 1881 it didn't much matter. While politicians frequently invoked the "American workingman" as the nation's glory, he generally remained a mythic entity—white, hard-working, unorganized. The demands of a FOTLU, an Adolph Strasser, or a *Fall River Labor Standard* seldom surfaced in political rhetoric. Organized labor reached people below far more than those above. Its audience was in the factories and workshops, not in the halls of Congress. Had politicians been listening, the Republican and Democratic platforms, as well as the Angell Treaty, would have dealt with importation and contract labor, not with immigration restriction. But politicians had an agenda different from that of organized labor or workers in the East. Consequently, working people had little direct impact on national legislation in this period and almost none at all on the Chinese exclusion debate. The final chapter of this debate was just around the corner. Although a few brave antiexclusionists would revive for one last gasp in 1882, the upcoming debate in Congress would ultimately seal the fate of Chinese immigrants for generations to come. It would also reveal the direction of national immigration policy for the next century and the new course of the Republican Party.

When the 47th Congress officially opened on December 5, 1881, Americans were still reeling from the assassination of President Garfield the past summer.

On July 2, Garfield had left the White House for a trip to New England. While walking arm in arm with Secretary of State Blaine in the Washington railroad depot, a gunman approached and fired two shots. One bullet struck Garfield in the abdomen, and he fell at once. Barely conscious, the president was carried back to the White House, where he lingered for two months. In early September, doctors moved him to the healthier, coastal climate of Elberon, New Jersey. His condition worsened, however, and on September 19, having served just six and a half months as president, Garfield died. The next day, Chester A. Arthur took the oath of office as president of the United States. One of Arthur's first actions as president on October 5 was to proclaim the recently ratified treaties between the United States and China in effect.[27]

Immigration restriction was now up to Congress, where Republicans held a slight advantage: three seats in the Senate and twelve in the House. They thus led the final effort toward exclusion and banked on taking the credit. On the session's first day, Senator John F. Miller (R-Calif.) introduced a bill to exclude Chinese immigrants, and eight days later, Representative Horace F. Page (R-Calif.) offered a similar measure in the House. Modifying its language to conform with the Angell Treaty, Miller's bill (effective sixty days after enactment) "suspended . . . the coming of Chinese laborers" for twenty years. Any Chinese immigrant presently in the United States seeking to leave and return would have to register at customs and secure a passport. The few Chinese exempted from the law, such as those in the diplomatic corps and their servants, would require passports, listing rank and occupation as well as "age, height, and all physical peculiarities." Such passports would need approval by an American diplomat before the individual left China. Any Chinese entering the United States illegally would be subject to a fine of one hundred dollars and a one-year prison term. Ships landing Chinese laborers would be subject to forfeiture, their captains punishable by a fine of five hundred dollars for each illegal immigrant and one year in prison. Forging a passport would be punishable by a fine of one thousand dollars and a five-year prison term. To this bill, Congress later added two vital amendments: the first prohibited Chinese immigrants from obtaining American citizenship (and therefore suffrage); the second defined "Chinese laborers" as both skilled and unskilled workers, as well as miners.[28]

Debate commenced on February 28, 1882. Senators Miller and Hoar, who had clashed a year earlier over the Angell Treaty, were the initial combatants, setting the early tone as well as the terms of the debate. Miller, who had chaired the anti-Chinese committee at the California constitutional convention, began by stressing the measure's legality, the chief stumbling block that had doomed the Fifteen Passenger Bill. The new Angell Treaty not only sanctioned such a law, Miller said, it demanded one. Having gone to such trouble to secure the treaty, failure to follow through would expose the United States to humiliation and dishonor: "A great nation cannot afford inconsistency in action, nor betray a vacillating, staggering, inconstant policy." Without this bill, the United States would be open to charges of "irresolute, fickle, feeble, or petulant" behavior. "Can we afford to make such a confession of American imbecility to any oriental power?" For further authority Miller invoked the Constitution: Chinese exclusion would "promote the general welfare" of the nation.[29]

Having disposed of the legal, diplomatic, and constitutional aspects, Miller emphasized the bill's popularity. Formerly limited to the Pacific Coast, "public sentiment [against the Chinese] . . . seems to have permeated the whole country." Like the treaty commissioners in Peking, he quoted as proof the platforms of the Democratic and Republican Parties, adding that each presidential candidate had favored restriction. On no issue in American history, he said, had the nation ever been so united. Echoing Blaine and countless western members of Congress, Miller stressed how exclusion would help the American laborer, "for wherever there is a white man or woman at work for wages, whether at the shoe bench, in the factory, or on the farm, there is an opening for a Chinaman." Competition with low-paid Chinese immigrants threatened the "public good," he charged, and had created a "new element in American society called the 'hoodlum.'" Immigration restriction could thus strike a dual blow at poverty and "Kearneyism."[30]

These economic arguments, however, paled beside those based on race. Likening the Chinese to "inhabitants of another planet," Miller called them "machine-like . . . of obtuse nerve, but little affected by heat or cold, wiry, sinewy, with muscles of iron; they are automatic engines of flesh and blood; they are patient, stolid, unemotional . . . [and] herd together like beasts." America had no need for the "insignificant, dwarfed, leathery little man of the Orient." Racial distinctions remained paramount. "Why not discriminate?" he asked. "Why aid in the increase and distribution over . . . our domain of a degraded and inferior race, and the progenitors of an inferior sort of men?" Miller welcomed immigrants from Germany, Ireland, Scandinavia, and Italy, but not "these stubborn invaders. . . . Of Chinese we have enough, and [I] would be glad to exchange those we have for any white people under the sun." Concluding his almost two-hour address, the California Republican implored fellow senators to act for the good of the nation. "We ask you to secure to us American Anglo-Saxon civilization without contamination or adulteration with any other. . . . Let us keep pure the blood which circulates through our political system . . . [and] preserve our life from the gangrene of oriental civilization." With the Chinese excluded, America could at last fulfill its destiny, a land dotted with "the homes of a free, happy people, resonant with the sweet voices of flaxen-haired children."[31]

The next day, George Frisbie Hoar spoke against the bill. A lifelong opponent of slavery and a protégé of Charles Sumner, Hoar had represented Massachusetts since 1869, first in the House and then in the Senate. Now fifty-five, Hoar had always considered himself a friend of labor. He had long supported eight-hours legislation and a national bureau of labor statistics. He defended the right of workers to organize and strike, and as a House member in 1871, he had praised both the International Workingmen's Association and the Paris Communards. Yet Hoar was very much the patrician. Born in Concord and descended from Puritans, he had impeccable family credentials: His grandfather Roger Sherman had helped draft the Constitution; his father had helped found the Free-Soil Party in Massachusetts; and his brother, coiner of the phrase "Conscience Whig," had served as attorney general under Grant. His first cousin was William Evarts. Hoar was less a party functionary than a genuine statesman. More than any other senator of his generation, Hoar remained devoted to the ideals of civil rights and racial equality, and his unswerving opposition to the Chinese Exclusion Act reflected his deepest convictions.[32]

Hoar began his speech by invoking the American Revolution, the nation's heritage of "natural rights," and "the great doctrine of human equality affirmed in our Declaration of Independence." Such rights and doctrines, he said, should be secure, "beyond the reach of any government." Hoar compared the Chinese Exclusion Act to the iniquitous Alien laws of 1798. He likened the persecution of the Chinese to the persecution of blacks, American Indians, Jews, and the Irish. The current arguments, he said, recalled those of the discredited Know-Nothings of the 1850s. "[We] must take a race at its best," he said, not its worst. Praising different groups and races, Hoar lauded the Chinese for their various accomplishments, such as inventing gun powder, the compass, and the printing press. On one point only did he agree with Miller: *the real issue was indeed race*. The underlying motive for the bill was "old race prejudice"—"the last of human delusions to be overcome." Such prejudice, he said, "has left its hideous and ineradicable stains in our history in crimes committed by every generation." The Chinese Exclusion Act would be but another crime committed against a race and against the Declaration of Independence. "We go boasting of our democracy, and our superiority, and our strength," he said. "The flag bears the stars of hope to all nations. A hundred thousand Chinese land in California and everything is changed. . . . The self-evident truth becomes a self-evident lie."[33]

Dissecting the bill clause by clause, Hoar found fault with every section. He opposed its harsh penalties and the intrusive powers it granted the govern-

Figure 11.2. As a representative and a senator from 1869 to 1904, George Frisbie Hoar (1826–1904) of Massachusetts carried on the abolitionist legacy, remaining more committed to the Civil War ideals of equal rights and racial justice than anyone else in Congress. Racial prejudice, he observed while leading the fight against the Chinese Exclusion Act, "has left its hideous and ineradicable stains in our history in crimes committed by every generation." (Courtesy Massachusetts Historical Society)

ment, such as allowing customs agents to seize virtually any Chinese visitor. Furthermore, the bill blatantly violated the Angell Treaty, which permitted *restriction* of immigration but not total prohibition. And the treaty by no means, he said directly to Miller, *demanded* restriction. Hoar also criticized the class dimension of the bill. Restriction was to be based "not on conduct, not on character, but upon race and upon occupation. . . . With paupers, lazzaroni, harlots, [and] persons afflicted with pestilential diseases, laborers are henceforth to be classed." Because of the bill's wording, he told his colleagues, "you may deny to the laborer what you may not deny to the scholar or to the idler." Such distinctions he found invidious. "There may be much that is wrong connected with the coming of these people from China," he said, "especially the importation of coolies." By all means, "the trade in human labor under all disguises [should] be suppressed." But this was hardly the bill's aim. "It is not importation, but immigration; it is not importation, but the free coming . . . at whom this legislation strikes its blow." Hoar's rhetoric echoed that of countless eastern workers and labor leaders of the past decade and a half. "As surely as the path on which our fathers entered a hundred years ago led to safety, to strength, to glory," he concluded, "so surely will the path which we now propose to enter bring us to shame, to weakness, and to peril."[34]

In these two speeches, Miller and Hoar presented the extremes of the issue, and according to most observers, the Californian had won the debate. Even former advocates of Chinese immigration conceded the point. The *New York Times* praised Miller for his "masterly statement" that was "admirable in temper and judicial in fairness." His presentation reflected "patient study, perfect candor, and great breadth of view." The *Tribune* concurred, calling Miller's speech "calm and dispassionate." Both journals castigated Hoar. "The state of facts has wholly changed since the new treaty has been concluded with the Chinese," the *Times* observed. Hoar's arguments were either out of date or irrelevant. Attacking the "glittering generalities" of his rhetoric, the *Times* assailed his "doubtful claims" lauding the Chinese for their inventions: "It is idle to reason with stupidity like this." Chinese immigration, the *Tribune* explained, posed "one of the most difficult problems that republican government has yet grappled with." It was too important an issue to "be rightly or safely administered upon the notions of humanitarian half thinkers." A generation had clearly passed. To the *New York Tribune*, once the greatest reform journal of the nineteenth century, the cause of equality and racial justice had become nothing more than a cry of sentimental "half thinkers."[35]

Miller and Hoar, let alone the *Times* and the *Tribune*, had by no means the last word on the subject, as more than twenty senators joined the debate. Backing the bill irrespective of party, westerners attacked Hoar's arguments mercilessly. First they disposed of the Declaration of Independence. Many of the signers owned slaves, Senator John P. Jones (R-Nev.) noted, and Benjamin Franklin himself had discoursed on the right to exclude other races from America. Federal policy toward American Indians offered further justification. The government had established Indian reservations on which "the white men of this country have no right to set foot." Now, if all people have the right to emigrate to the United States, Jones asked with masterful logic, how can we "prevent our own people from entering upon an Indian reservation?" In other words, if the United States could control mobility *within* the nation, surely it could restrict mobility *into* the nation. As early as the seventeenth century, La Fayette Grover (D-Ore.) added, William Penn had set a precedent by decrying "commingling with the Delawares." Settlers "proceeded forthwith to drive out the aborigines from the land with fire and sword," and since the nation's founding, "not a single serious effort has been made to incorporate the natives of America into the body of our people as a part of the nation." By treating the "natives" as nothing but "aliens and outcasts," the founders had set the United States on an exclusionary path. The treatment of Native Americans as well as blacks in American history showed the limitations of Jefferson's dictum, which James Slater (D-Ore.) simply recast: "No one will deny the axiomatic and self-evident truths of the Declaration of Independence, but that they apply in this case may well be denied." Original intent evidently favored exclusion.[36]

Confident that white-supremacist southerners would back them, westerners pushed the race button at every opportunity, likening the Chinese to "rats," "beasts," and "swine." "The Caucasian race has a right," said Henry Teller (R-Colo.), "considering its superiority of intellectual force and mental vigor, to look down upon every other branch of the human family." The United States, Senator Jones added, should admit only "favored races," not those "molded in the spirit of despotism." Race and civilization became one; whether skin color or culture, it was "impossible for a Chinaman to change." Jones stated the issue baldly: "Does anybody suppose for an instant that if the African were not in this country to-day we should be anxious to welcome him? Does any reflecting man believe that he is an advantage to this country? Is it not true if his place were occupied by smaller numbers of intelligent men of our own creative race that the country would be stronger than it is?" As with blacks—whose "presence here is a great misfortune to us to-day"—so with Chinese. "In dealing with foreign immigration," Jones concluded, "the only question we have to consider is what is best for our own race."[37]

Such arguments touched a receptive chord among southern senators, who needed little encouragement to justify exclusion. The Constitution, James Z. George (D-Miss.) said, "was made by the American people for themselves and their posterity, not for the human race," and Samuel B. Maxey (D-Tex.) explained, to the Founding Fathers "posterity" meant the "pure, unmixed Caucasian race." In a brief, racist diatribe, Maxey observed that at least blacks were Americans, receptive to white influence and capable of being uplifted. Not so the Chinese. Maxey feared the impact they would have on the South, where the "naturally superstitious . . . colored man . . . might be carried away from Christian civilization after the Joss god of the Chinaman." Thomas F. Bayard (D-Del.), still with his eye on the White House, called the bill "full of beneficence and kindness" because it would protect the Chinese—a "very ignorant and helpless people"—from unscrupulous importers. Exclusion, Senator George added, was simply a matter of "Anglo-Saxon common sense." Speaking for the white South, the Mississippi Democrat concluded that America did not need "another inferior race."[38]

The decline of Reconstruction had transformed southern senators into ardent exclusionists. Although six of the region's Democrats had opposed the Fifteen Passenger Bill because they looked forward to Chinese laborers underselling or replacing blacks as farmworkers, the present collapse of Reconstruction state governments was undermining Republican power throughout the South and enabling Democrats to return to power. With conservative Democrats slowly regaining control of government machinery in the former Confederacy, whites would soon possess ample weapons to subjugate the region's black population. The dawn of the Jim Crow era of discrimination, disfranchisement, and segregation meant that the Chinese would no longer be "needed." Senator Isham Green Harris (D-Tenn.)—the former Tennessee governor who had chaired the Memphis Chinese Labor Convention in 1869—symbolized this transition of southern sentiment by casting his ballot in favor of Chinese exclusion. Fellow southern senators deftly converted the anti-Chinese argument into a stinging attack on Reconstruction. Whites on the Pacific Coast were unanimously opposed to the Chinese, said Wilkinson Call (D-Fla.), and the federal government was about to grant them relief. Why not grant similar relief to the South where whites thoroughly opposed blacks? For Washington to cave in to the demands of one region and ignore those of another was unfair. Senator Henry L. Dawes (R-Mass.) countered both arguments. No locality should stamp its demands on another, he said. "We are not here to legislate for New England nor for California." At which point, Senator James Farley (D-Calif.) retorted, didn't legislators from New England continually ask for tariff protection? Dawes dodged the question, but the exchange reveals how Chinese immigration could bring to the surface deep-seated animosities between regions over race, economics, and federal intervention.[39]

No doubt the most unusual southerner was Joseph E. Brown (D-Ga.). Former war governor and states' rights Democrat, Brown became a Republican after the war and, enthusiastically endorsing abolition and Radical Reconstruction, served as booster for the "New South." Switching back to the Democratic Party, he made a fortune as a railroad promoter and mine owner, blatantly exploiting convict labor. A "political chameleon," as one historian has called him, he revealed yet a new color when he bucked the Southern tide on Chinese exclusion. Treat all immigrants fairly, Brown said, and they will adapt to American institutions. Blacks proved a perfect example: "Relations between the two races had become very cordial before the emancipation, and the result was their Christianization." Similar results could be achieved with the Chinese. "Take the Chinaman by the hand, treat him as you now treat the African, and you will find him assimilate much more readily than he does with your hand turned against him." The Chinese posed no threat, Brown insisted. In fact, the situation was precisely the opposite: "The tide of emigration has been westward . . . since the days of the Goths and Vandals. . . . The Chinese Empire is in a great deal more danger to-day of being overrun and subverted by Yankee energy and Yankee enterprise on the one side, and the empire of Russia on the other, and England on the ocean, than this country is of being overrun by Chinamen."[40]

Brown made no effort to conceal his motives. China represented a vast market, "a wide field open for us. No people on earth are more interested in that country than the people of the United States." Sounding the tocsin of American imperialism, he added: "We ought to build up a boundless trade there, and it ought to be a great field for white men's energy and thrift and gain." As a southerner, Brown was especially concerned with the cotton trade, for which China seemed the ultimate market. "The 400,000,000 of people in the Chinese empire, use cotton almost exclusively for clothing," he said, and American cotton was the best in the world. Exclusion would only insult China and threaten this potential economic bonanza. Except for his accent, Brown sounded identical to the Yankee capitalists he so evidently admired and modeled himself after. Representing a powerful but small segment of the New South, he would be the only Democrat and the only southerner in the Senate to vote against the first version of the Chinese Exclusion Act.[41]

Brown was an interesting anomaly, but his influence remained minimal. From the outset it was clear that westerners of both parties and Democrats of all regions strongly backed the bill. The crucial test would be among Republicans east of the Rockies. For years the Republican Party, like the Democrats, had used the issue of Chinese immigration restriction for electoral purposes. Now their true colors would be shown. While just a handful joined Hoar in principled opposition to the bill, only a similarly small handful expressed unqualified support. Angus Cameron (R-Wisc.), for example, recoiled from "this overflowing Asiatic hive" and, echoing Blaine, stated, "I am one of those who believe that either the Anglo-Saxon will possess the Pacific slope or the Mongolian will possess it."[42] Most Republican senators from the Northeast and Midwest, however, found themselves in a quandary, trying to reconcile the glowing ideals of the Civil War with the grimy problems of the Gilded Age. They debated the bill furiously, and their infighting illustrates the fundamental changes the party had undergone. It also reveals the new direction in which the Republican Party was heading.

George F. Edmunds helped lead Republicans along this new path. The distinguished senator, often spoken of for the presidency, had represented Vermont for sixteen years. On his second day in office in 1866, he had voted for the Civil Rights Act over President Johnson's veto, and he won plaudits a few weeks later for his principled stance against Colorado statehood because of a "white" suffrage qualification in its constitution. Long an opponent of slavery and discrimination, Edmunds cosponsored the Civil Rights Act of 1870 that guaranteed legal protections for Chinese immigrants, and he helped draft both the Ku Klux Klan Act of 1871 and the Civil Rights Act of 1875. In 1879, he voted against the Fifteen Passenger Bill because it violated the Burlingame Treaty and interna-

Figure 11.3. A fervent Republican who had supported the Civil Rights Acts of 1866, 1870, and 1875, George F. Edmunds (1828–1919) of Vermont was one of the Senate's most respected members. Although he voted against the Chinese Exclusion Act, his speech defending it provided a moral basis for immigration restriction that Republicans quickly latched onto. Chinese exclusion was not wrong, he said, but "a mere question of expediency." (Courtesy Vermont Historical Society)

tional law. A year later, however, he recommended his old friend James Angell to Secretary of State Evarts to negotiate the new treaty. Though currently preoccupied with drafting an antipolygamy bill to outlaw "Mormon abuses" in Utah Territory, Edmunds played a prominent role in the Chinese exclusion debate. Challenging Hoar as the voice of New England, he was the rare senator to command respect across party lines. When he rose to speak on March 7, the mood of the chamber changed abruptly. "A score of senators who had been chatting and smoking in the cloak-rooms hastened to their seats," the *Chicago Times* reported. "Others who were writing letters at their desks promptly laid aside their papers. Crowds of correspondents trooped into the reporters' gallery, and every utterance of the famous Vermont Senator received undivided and interested attention."[43]

Edmunds surprised his listeners. Despite his Radical credentials, he emphasized the futility of trying to overcome differences of race. Integration, amalgamation, and the notion that "all mankind are of one kin . . . one nature . . . [and] one destiny" sounded nice, he said, but "common sense . . . and the common observation of everybody has demonstrated that that is not true." God had wisely separated the races into different parts of the globe, and it would be folly to tamper with this natural order. Sounding more like a westerner, Edmunds stressed how different the Chinese were in culture, religion, and modes of thought. "There is no common ground of assimilation," he said. He cited the South as proof that two essentially different races could not live peacefully side by side, for "no republic can succeed that has not a homogeneous population." Heterogeneity had destroyed ancient Greece, it presently cursed the South, and in the West "it has promoted political discord and discontent among our fellow-citizens." Just as the first duty of a nation is self-preservation, he said, the first duty of a government is creating borders and deciding who may enter and who may not. The great forces motivating the Declaration of Independence were separation, self-government, and the determination to choose who could be part of the polity. In summation, Edmunds said, "every people and every church, every little community . . . must decide what persons other than itself are to be received into it and become a part of it."[44]

Edmunds's approach was a cautious one, combining prudence and expediency. He did not condemn the Chinese or call them inferior; he simply stressed their differentness. The role of government was to acknowledge this differentness and adjust social policy accordingly. Americans had every right to exclude anyone they chose, he argued, and he justified this right in the name of morality. Exclusion was *moral* not because it was *right* but because it was *popular*. After all, Edmunds said in an exchange with Hoar, "who is to decide . . . what the moral law is? Is it he [Hoar]? Is it I? Not at all. It is all; it is the body of the people organized into a government; they and they alone can decide."[45] Here was the key: Edmunds linked morality to majority rule. What "the body of the people" deemed moral was ipso facto moral. Right and wrong could be settled by a popularity contest. This emphasis on "morality"—in place of justice, equality, or right—is crucial to understanding the transformation of Republican ideology. The free-soil, antislavery impulse that had helped launch the party in the 1850s and the abolitionist ideals that had helped sustain it in the 1860s now only constricted it. Without the mandate of the Civil War or an equally strong imperative, Republicans had to restructure their principles to suit the times, and what better principle than morality, especially one based on popular approval? In legitimating exclusion, Edmunds turned pandering for votes into a noble cause. Idealism only induced ridicule; morality—diffuse, open-ended, and malleable—carried far greater clout.

Republicans, of course, had always invoked morality to defend their policies. In his debates with Stephen Douglas in 1858, Lincoln had voiced prevailing Republican sentiment in attacking slavery as "a moral wrong." Such moral judgments had appealed to a higher source, above the Constitution and above the government. Morality transcended laws made by men. But passage of a generation forced Republicans to discard this outmoded basis of morality, which Edmunds shrewdly recast. "The ground upon which we legislate against free love, and polygamy, and all other kinds of moral wickedness, over which we have control by legislative power, is that it belongs to the will of the people . . . to decide upon the conduct of persons who are in it or who are to come to it."[46] Not least of the advantages of this new basis for morality was its flexibility. With a few twists of logic one could justify anything in the name of morality, even racism if that was "the will of the people." Such reasoning would have repercussions well beyond the Chinese Exclusion Act: it would facilitate northern acceptance of Jim Crow policies in the South, ease the Supreme Court's retreat from civil rights in the course of the decade, and foreshadow the "separate but equal" doctrine established nationally fourteen years later in *Plessy v. Ferguson*. Edmunds's argument conceded that the role of government—and the Republican Party—was no longer to lead the people but to follow them (at least as politicians interpreted them). The double irony here is that politicians had led the populace to favor exclusion, which they now claimed to champion because of popular support. Like patriotism for scoundrels, morality became the last refuge for Republicans.

"The effect . . . [of Edmunds] announcing his hearty adhesion [to] the principle underlying this bill," the *Chicago Times* remarked, "and of the brief but unanswerable argument with which he justified it, was even more than commonly noticeable." Edmunds had deftly argued against Chinese immigration and given honorable reasons to "suspend it for a little while." "How should that shock humanity?" he asked. Then came the clincher: though supporting exclusion, Edmunds opposed the bill! Twenty years, he said, was simply too long, a violation of the treaty provision stipulating "reasonable" suspension. He urged colleagues to endorse a ten-year ban. After ten years of excluding Chinese immigrants, he said, the United States could review the law and either renew it or repeal it.[47]

Edmunds's speech opened the floodgates. Republicans latched onto his moral argument and spent more time debating the *length* of exclusion than exclusion itself. Indeed, remarked Senator John Sherman (R-Ohio), length "is the most important feature of the whole bill." He suggested suspending Chinese immigration for five years. "They are not a desirable population," the former treasury secretary noted, "they are not the kind of immigrants which have been useful to our country." James McDill (R-Iowa) also favored a shorter period of suspension, as did John I. Mitchell (R-Pa.), who said he would vote for "reasonable regulation of Chinese immigration."[48]

After Edmunds's speech, the length of exclusion—rather than exclusion itself—became the focal point, as Republicans lined up to endorse the ends of the bill rather than the means. This distinction was best exemplified by Orville

Figure 11.4. In trying to straddle two chairs—the "anti-Chinese" stool of the West and the "pro-Chinese" stool of the East—Senator Edmunds finds he hasn't a leg to stand on. Although the caption suggests the Vermonter's imminent collapse, Edmunds's "greatest effort"—his speech on the morality of Chinese exclusion—helped lay the foundation for the new direction of the Republican Party. (*Puck*, March 22, 1882)

Platt (R-Conn.), then at the beginning of a long and distinguished Senate career. "This is race legislation," he declared, and "all the old arguments that we heard about the danger of social equality between the negro and the white man are resurrected and rehabilitated for the occasion." He denounced the bill as unprincipled and unjust. "Harsh in its provisions, severe . . . in its penalties, the bill reads more like an enactment of the seventeenth century than like a wise, humane, and beneficial statute of the present age and time." But idealism had its limits. "Do not misunderstand me," Platt explained. "I do not say the Chinaman is the equal of the Anglo-Saxon socially or intellectually." Then, indicating Edmunds's influence, he urged an alternative: limit China to one thousand immigrants per year. Such a compromise, he said, would not "improperly" restrict Chinese immigration. Although Platt clothed his sentiments in more elevated rhetoric, his position ultimately differed little from that of Edmunds.[49]

The Vermont senator had masterfully steered his party between the Scylla and Charybdis of equality and exclusion, and fellow Republicans scurried to climb aboard. With the morality of the bill accepted, they spent the bulk of their time mouthing pieties and debating minutiae. The terms of the debate had plainly shifted; no longer focusing on the justice of exclusion, Republicans quibbled over details. Samuel J. R. McMillan (R-Minn.), the only midwestern senator who had opposed the Angell Treaty, successfully pushed for an amendment delaying implementation of the act from sixty days after passage to ninety.[50] Would such a delay really make any difference? And was there really much difference in excluding Chinese immigrants for five years versus ten years or for ten years versus twenty? Or in setting up a quota at a thousand per year? Such details were not trivial, but in comparison with the exclusion versus no exclusion debate, they scarcely mattered. Thanks to the groundwork laid by Blaine, the decision to restrict Chinese immigration had been accepted. Thanks to the nurturing efforts of Evarts and Garfield, Republicans had embraced restriction and campaigned on it. And thanks now to Edmunds, leading senators endorsed it freely. Morality had triumphed. Republican policy was crystal clear: the Chinese must go.

Only a handful dissented, few as eloquently as Joseph R. Hawley (R-Conn.). The former Connecticut governor, who in 1870 had defended Chinese immigration (and importation) in the wake of North Adams, had grown bolder in the intervening years. "A few words in the proposed law may be quoted for a century," he said on March 9, "not as the opening lines of the Declaration of Independence are quoted, as a comfort, a prophecy, a battle-cry, but on the same page as the edict of Nantes, the innumerable decrees tormenting the Jews, . . . [and] the barbarisms that were once heaped upon the . . . negro." Hawley enumerated all the arguments in favor of exclusion and found them wanting. He did not doubt the authority of the United States to ban the Chinese, but with his eye on Edmunds, remarked, "Perhaps we are confounding right and power." Like Hoar, Hawley considered the act a milestone and a precedent: whatever defenses his colleagues employed and whichever way they deigned to vote, the debate over Chinese exclusion revealed the passing of a generation. In an understatement few may have noticed, Hawley remarked, "Our zealous and radical republicanism is fading."[51]

Minutes later the Senate voted. Senate Bill Number 71, inoffensively titled "An act to execute certain treaty stipulations relating to Chinese," passed 29 to 15 (with 32 not voting). Twenty Democrats and nine Republicans voted in favor. All five western Republicans supported the bill; so did four Republicans east of the Rockies: Angus Cameron (Wisc.), Eugene Hale (Maine), Warner Miller (N.Y.), and Philetus Sawyer (Wisc.). Fourteen of the fifteen negative votes came from Republicans. Senator Brown of Georgia was the lone Democrat in opposition.[52]

The House considered the bill five days later, and some seventy representatives took part in the deliberations. Like their colleagues in the Senate, Republicans fell into three groups: those opposed to the bill on principle, those opposed to the bill but not immigration restriction, and those in favor of the bill. The breakdown of the first two groups mirrored the Hoar-Edmunds split, with the former group by far the smallest. No more than six House Republicans who opposed the bill cited principle as a major reason. Godlove S. Orth (R-Ind.), a Republican since the party's earliest days, labeled the bill "a backward step" in the nation's history. So what if the Chinese were "pagans," he asked. Religious freedom remained the "crowning glory" of America, a nation open to all faiths on the globe. The bill set a dangerous precedent. "By its passage," he warned, "you strike a blow at the right of migration which might hereafter affect the emigrant from other lands than China." But Orth was in a distinct minority. Most Republicans opposing the bill attacked details—the length of exclusion, the passport requirement, the penalties for violation—but supported the bill's intent. James Tyler (R-Vt.) thought exclusion for ten years "long enough." So did George Robinson (R-Mass.) (who three years earlier had denounced the Fifteen Passenger Bill as "cheap nostrums"), Robert Hawk (R-Ill.), and Mark Dunnell (R-Minn.), all of whom said they would support exclusion for one decade but not two. Henry Lord (R-Mich.) called the bill "a departure from [the] great and cardinal principles . . . of human rights," but endorsed a ten-year ban nonetheless. As Nathaniel Deering (R-Iowa) remarked, the bill is "extreme . . . sweeping and oppressive," but, he added, "I am willing and anxious" to support "reasonable restrictions."[53]

Typical of these Republicans was Ezra Taylor (R-Ohio). Although little remembered today, Taylor was the focus of considerable attention by virtue of his representing the district of the martyred Garfield. Inheritor of this Republican mantle, Representative Taylor articulated Civil War ideals as poignantly as Senators Hoar and Hawley. The Chinese Exclusion Act, he said, "changes and revolutionizes the traditions and principles of this country." In excluding the Chinese, "we know not when the next wall will be erected. . . . I would deem the new country we will have after this bill becomes law as changed from the old country we have to-day as our country would have been changed if the rebellion of 1861 had succeeded." The bill was based "on passion and prejudice," he claimed. "We talk in regard to the differences between races; and I am astonished at the way we talk. I know our books speak of it learnedly. There are heaps of nonsense in some books." Reciting the antislavery legacy of his party, Taylor proclaimed, "Others may say 'throw sentiment aside,' but the Republican party is founded on sentiment, and it cannot 'throw sentiment aside.'" But then Taylor switched gears: "I hope my remarks have not been understood as favoring a further immigration of the Chinese. . . . I want no more of them. But I talk only of this bill, and I do not mean to be in the least understood as favoring that immigration. . . . I deplore their presence here as much as any man."[54]

Congressmen strongly opposed to the bill nevertheless went on record stating their hostility to Chinese immigrants. Racism and the new morality went hand in hand. "There is not one gentleman who spoke on the other side of this question that has not acknowledged that Chinese immigration is an evil; not one of them," noted Charles Brumm, a pro-exclusion Greenback-Republican from Pennsylvania, with only slight exaggeration; "they only pick flaws in the bill." Observing this broad bipartisan consensus, George Wise (D-Va.) commented, "No gentleman in this discussion has dared . . . to put himself on record as entertaining the opinion that Chinese immigration is desirable, and that it ought not to be restrained and limited." As Aylett Buckner (D-Mo.) acidly observed, the Chinese Exclusion Act "performs the last funeral rite over the dead body of the false and nonsensical dogma of government policy that 'all men are created equal.' "[55]

Few members of Congress troubled themselves with such outdated "dogma." While a handful echoed Hoar and many more echoed Edmunds, by far the greatest number echoed Blaine, as Republicans battled Democrats in claiming to speak—and legislate—on behalf of working people. "I insist that it [the Chinese Exclusion Act] is in the interest of the free and independent laborers of this country everywhere," Benjamin Butterworth (R-Ohio) said, a sentiment endorsed by William Calkins (R-Ind.). "I plant myself upon the broad ground of protection to American labor," Calkins argued, trying to shame his opponents into supporting the bill. "When you go to your people, you who have looms and spindles and forges, you who are going to vote against this bill, I ask you to explain to your laborers how it is possible that you have left the doors all open to a competition by which their labor may entirely be rooted up and destroyed, and by which their children and themselves may become paupers; for that is the inevitable result unless you restrict this immigration." To many congressmen backing the bill, Chinese immigration posed a national emergency; its exclusion would promote and uplift the American worker. "Wise statesmanship demands that we . . . save American labor," said Edwin Willits (R-Mich.), while Stanton Peelle (R-Ind.) declared, "Whatever support to restrictive legislation I may give will be upon the ground of protection to our American laborers." Should Congress fail to exclude Chinese immigrants, noted Tyler of Vermont, "it is starvation and ruin to American laborers." Democrats also invoked working people as the key beneficiaries and advocates of Chinese exclusion. "The question more closely interests the American laboring classes than any other that has lately arisen," stated Morgan Wise (D-Pa.), to which Roswell Flower (D-N.Y.), future governor of New York, added, "I am in favor of any measure that will ameliorate and elevate labor, and I shall vote for this bill on that principle." Chinese exclusion became a litmus test for showing loyalty— both personal and partisan—to the working classes. With sectional differences disappearing, Richard Townshend (D-Ill.) said, the major question dividing the country was class, and the present conflict revealed who are "the friends and foes of labor." The Republican Party, he added, has "ever [been] . . . subservient to monopoly, while the Democratic party has ever been the true friend of labor." Republicans fired back at every opportunity. "As a protectionist, as a Republican," said Addison McClure (R-Ohio), "I stand by . . . white labor." So said virtually every member of Congress who favored the Chinese Exclusion Act. The legislation—which just twenty years earlier, said Senator Sherman, would have been unthinkable, "the death warrant of the man who offered it"—was now in the best traditions of both the nation and each political party. As William Washburn (R-Minn.) observed: "In all its grand history it [the Republican Party] has never failed to respond to the appeals of the oppressed; neither has it ever failed to recognize the great truth that dignity of labor . . . is the bed-rock upon which all governments of the people can alone securely rest. . . . I feel that it is not only a proper exercise of power but the imperative duty of this government to restrict in every reasonable way the class of immigration that this bill is intended to reach."[56]

In just three years, Blaine's battle cry had become the cry of Republicans and Democrats everywhere and accepted as common wisdom. Politicians of both parties had reached consensus not just on Chinese exclusion but on the rationale for Chinese exclusion, and they scrambled to outdo each other in paying homage to the American worker. The congressional debate of 1882 provided a vehicle for politicians to position themselves and their parties for the post-Reconstruction era. "Eloquent allusions to our national traditions may captivate those who look to the past for their inspiration," said Representative Thomas Bayne (R-Pa.), "but they will have but little influence on those who are compelled to deal with the stern realities of the present." And in dealing with these "stern realities," no one doubted the action Congress would soon take. As Cyrus Carpenter (R-Iowa), one of the bill's few opponents who argued on principle, conceded, "I know that I speak for a lost cause." His colleague Edward K. Valentine (R-Nebr.) put it most succinctly. "To protect our laboring classes," he said, "the gate . . . must be closed."[57]

On March 23, the House of Representatives approved the Chinese Exclusion Act, 167 to 66 (with 59 not voting). Republicans contributed almost all the negative votes, but as a party split evenly, 60 to 62 (with 25 not voting). Only four Democrats joined the opposition. Notable affirmative votes included Abram Hewitt (D-N.Y.), Joseph G. Cannon (R-Ill.), and future president William McKinley (R-Ohio). The regional breakdown was pronounced. All seven western representatives voted in favor. The South also supported the bill overwhelmingly, 60 to 2 (with 20 not voting). New England presented the opposite picture, 1 in favor, 19 opposed, and 2 not voting. New England Republicans, with Maine included, opposed the bill unanimously, 0 to 20 (with 4 not voting). Far west and far east Republican representatives thus presented completely reverse images. Republicans from the mid-Atlantic and midwestern states divided more evenly. Mid-Atlantic Republicans favored the bill, 17 to 14 (with 11 not voting), while midwestern Republicans favored the bill, 34 to 26 (with 8 not voting). The data thus suggest an image among Republicans of increasing support for exclusion as one moves from east to west across the country, but individual states belie this. Republicans in Illinois and Michigan favored the bill, 15 to 5 (with 2 not voting), whereas Republicans in Iowa and Kansas, farther west, voted the opposite, 0 to 11 (with 1 not voting). The chief factor among Republicans in the Midwest was the local economy: those from industrialized states tended to favor exclusion more than did those from agricultural states. Taken altogether, three factors—in varying degrees—influenced the vote: region, party, and local economy.[58]

The Republican press generally applauded the bill, but enthusiasm varied. The *Chicago Tribune* lavished praise on it, whereas the *New York Times* simply considered it a fait accompli. Washington had long since settled the issue, claimed the *Times*, by its votes on the Fifteen Passenger Bill and the Angell Treaty. Consequently, all the recent speeches and editorials "are absurdly out of order. . . . Time and again, both political parties have promised to do what has now been done, and nobody has raised a voice of protest or disavowal of responsibility for such promises." Denying that the United States need serve as a home for the oppressed of all nations, the *Times*, paraphrasing Edmunds, scoffed, "As for the assertion that we have no moral right to say who shall and who shall not come into the country, no true American will for one moment admit a doctrine so dangerous, or make a confession so weak." The *New York Tribune* was more circumspect, noting—in what could serve as the new slogan for the Republican Party in the Gilded Age—"sometimes expediency is statesmanship of the highest order." Like many Republican journals, the *Tribune* poked holes in the bill but defended exclusion: "Let it be granted, for the sake of argument, that everything ought to be done that we have a right to do to exclude or restrict Chinese immigration." And yet the *Tribune*, neither pleased with nor proud of the bill's intent, shifted the blame from individuals to a broad consensus: "However repugnant the bill may be to our national sense of justice, it cannot be denied that public sentiment generally upholds the measure as being necessary and expedient, and not to be rejected for merely sentimental reasons." The *Tribune* buttressed this claim with a quote from an anonymous Democratic representative. "I am opposed to the whole theory of the bill," the congressman remarked, "and would like to vote against it, but I must 'keep solid' with my constituents." The *Tribune* concluded, "This was the feeling, doubtless, of many others—both Democratic and Republican—who voted for the bill virtually under duress."[59]

With this comment we have returned full circle: Who was behind the Chinese Exclusion Act? Was it simply the work of politicians, or were the nation's elected leaders responding to the will of the American people? After so many years of agitation on the subject, it was no longer easy to tell. Politicians angling for office had no doubt swung many people to their side, and the momentum in turn, as the unnamed congressman's comment indicates, had forced other politicians to fall into line. "Public opinion" and politicians fed on each other, and by 1882 it had become difficult to separate the two forces. "Among the remarkable social phenomena of the time," the *Chicago Times* noted, "is the change of public opinion on the 'Chinese question' which has taken place within the last three or four years."[60]

Perhaps the nation had indeed come around to Chinese exclusion. If so, the Angell Treaty Commission had fulfilled one of its tasks: converting the American people in favor of Chinese immigration restriction. One of the converts was Angell himself. Speaking in Saratoga, New York, before the American Social Science Association in September 1882, the chief negotiator of the new treaty emphasized the dangers of blind idealism: "The problem of harmonizing so alien a civilization as that of China with ours is probably more difficult than we in the East have supposed. . . . That it is possible that Chinese laborers may, if unrestricted, come to us more rapidly than is well, either for them or for us, is certainly true. Reason about it as we may, I believe the fact will be found constant, that if they are brought rapidly, in large numbers, into any Western country, there will be unpleasant friction between them and the Western people." A suspension of Chinese immigration for five years, Angell concluded, might eliminate this "unpleasant friction." If the treaty commissioner himself, once an adamant opponent of Chinese exclusion, could reverse his own position in less than three years, there is little reason to doubt that Americans nationwide could also. "It has been approved by the press and the people, outside of New England," the *Chicago Tribune* observed, "almost without distinction of party."[61]

But power still remained the core of the issue. Politicians, not "public opinion," fueled the engine of exclusion. "The country may as well understand," a reporter remarked from the capital in March, "that here in Washington . . . the anti-Chinese question attracts interest mainly because it is supposed to be a means of carrying California, Oregon and Nevada next fall." And looking ahead two years, Representative Leopold Morse (D-Mass.) commented that those three western states "are supposed to hold the balance of political power in the next Presidential contest." Politics, politics, politics. Perhaps the *Chicago Tribune* put it best. With Republicans, who held a majority in Congress, able to take credit for exclusion, they could reap the benefits in the West and let the issue disappear in the East. Thus, said the *Tribune*, "there will be no chance for another Morey letter in 1884."[62] Concern over the political impact of the bill dominated the press as the nation waited anxiously for the president's response. Would Chester Arthur sign the bill or veto it? No one knew for sure.

CHAPTER TWELVE

A Mere Question of Expediency

The Chinese Exclusion Act of 1882

Chester Alan Arthur was the most unlikely person ever to occupy the office of president. Prior to his nomination for vice president in 1880, he had never held a single elected position, and allegations of corruption had forced him to resign in 1878 from the only important job he had ever held, collector of customs for the Port of New York. Arthur was not without scruples, however. As a young abolitionist lawyer, he had gained fame by winning the freedom of two slaves whose owner had taken them to New York. During the Civil War he rose to the rank of quartermaster general, and in 1868 he astutely aligned with pro-Grant forces. A savvy politician with high-placed connections, Arthur became a chief lieutenant in Roscoe Conkling's "Stalwart" machine in the Empire State. To placate Conkling and the pro-Grant wing of the party, which were vital to winning New York, Garfield offered Arthur the second spot on the ticket in 1880. Inexperienced, widowed, and always impeccably dressed, the dapper New Yorker accepted the nomination and uttered scarcely a word throughout the campaign. In a rare, unscripted speech before his inauguration, Arthur—the perfect embodiment of the machine politician—seemingly joked about Republicans having bribed voters to win the election.[1]

Arthur's few months as vice president lacked distinction, and when Garfield's assassination elevated him to the presidency in 1881, few people knew where he stood on anything. The "acting president," as critics derisively called Arthur, had expressed no opinion on Chinese immigration, and his first public comment on the subject proved vague. "The prompt and friendly spirit with which the Chinese government, at the request of the United States, conceded the modification of existing treaties should secure careful regard for the interests and susceptibilities of that Government in the enactment of any laws relating to Chinese immigration," he explained in his first annual message in December 1881. "Legislation is necessary to carry their provisions into effect." President Arthur thus opened the door to immigration restriction but allowed himself wide latitude for judging prospective legislation. He made no public statement on the subject in the intervening months, and when the bill to limit Chinese immigration appeared on his desk in March 1882, Arthur—like Hayes three years earlier—had not yet decided whether to sign or veto it.[2]

So uncertain was the president that he held three cabinet meetings on the matter. One lasted four hours, after which the press reported that the president's advisers were evenly split. Three cabinet members urged approval of the bill: Secretary of War Robert T. Lincoln (son of the former president), Interior Secretary Samuel Kirkwood, and Postmaster General Timothy O. Howe (who as senator had opposed the Fifteen Passenger Bill). Three others urged a veto: Secretary of State Frederick Frelinghuysen (who had replaced Blaine), Treasury Secretary Charles Folger, and Attorney General Benjamin Brewster. And the seventh cabinet member, Navy Secretary William Hunt, was, the *Chicago Times* said, "on the fence without definite opinions." Perhaps more significant was that Folger and Brewster opposed only the length of exclusion, not exclusion itself. "There is," the *New York Herald* observed, "a general agreement [in the cabinet] that it would be well to suspend immigration of Chinese for a time." Arthur also heard from Cheng Tsao-ju, the new Chinese minister, who denounced the bill as unjust and "discriminatory." Letters and telegrams, meanwhile, flooded the White House, and several influential Republicans urged a veto. Former president Grant remarked that he "was not in favor of the Chinese coming to this country" but found the legislation "objectionable in its present shape." The aged Thurlow Weed, who had opposed the Fifteen Passenger Bill on principle, now urged suspension of immigration for five years—but not twenty. Staying true to his ideals, the eminent Wendell Phillips, former abolitionist and labor-reform candidate, reiterated his long-held "detestation of all restrictions on Chinese immigration as inconsistent, absurd, unjust and wicked." But Arthur kept everyone guessing. The only hint came from a friend who noted that the president had been much impressed by Edmunds's speech.[3]

Arthur announced his decision on April 4. At 1:20 that afternoon his secretary carried the president's message to the Capitol and placed it on the desk of Senate pro tem David Davis, who suspended ordinary business so that the message could be read. "After careful consideration of Senate bill No. 71," the Senate secretary recited aloud, "I herewith return it to the Senate . . . with my objections to its passage." Arthur's veto message was clear and direct. Seven times he quoted the phrase from the Angell Treaty that permitted the United States to "regulate, limit, or suspend" Chinese immigration but not to "absolutely prohibit it." The twenty-year suspension, Arthur said, violated this clause of the treaty and thereby presented "a breach of our national faith." Arthur feared that the Chinese might retaliate by closing their ports to American ships. "Experience has shown that the trade of the East is the key to national wealth and influence," he said. "It needs no argument to show that the policy which we now propose to adopt must have a direct tendency to repel oriental nations from us and to drive their trade and commerce into more friendly lands." Opposing exclusion for its potential economic consequences, Arthur then poked holes in the bill itself. He criticized the clauses requiring Chinese immigrants to carry passports and register with the government and those preventing Chinese laborers from simply passing through the United States en route to another country. The president then praised the Chinese for their contributions to the nation. He highlighted their "instrumental" role in building the transcontinental railroad and developing the land and industries of the Pacific Coast. "There may . . . be other sections of the country where this species of labor may be advantageously employed," he said, "without interfering with the laborers of our own race." These comments notwithstanding, Arthur fully endorsed the need to restrict Chinese immigration. "Deeply convinced of the necessity of some legislation on this subject," he wrote, "the coming of such laborers . . . endangers good order throughout the country." He urged Congress to reconsider the bill and attempt "a shorter experiment" with Chinese exclusion. In its main points—treaty violation, threats to trade, and willingness to restrict Chinese immigration—Arthur's veto message proved remarkably similar to that of Hayes three years earlier. A day later, the Senate voted 29 to 21 to override the veto, five short of a two-thirds majority.[4]

In rejecting the bill, Arthur stressed that his main criticism was length of exclusion, not exclusion itself. This concern over length—ten years versus twenty—remained the major point of contention among Republicans. The dispute was purely semantic, focusing on the interpretation of a word rather than the intent of the act. "At some shadowy indefinit[e] point between the ten and twenty years," the *Chicago Tribune* noted, "lay the boundary line between 'reasonable' and 'unreasonable' suspension." The effort to define this "indefinite point" monopolized debate and deflected attention from the bill's aim. As Senator John Sherman (R-Ohio) remarked, "Some wise limitation upon the immigration of Chinese to this country would be voted for heartily by members of all political parties, of both houses, with scarcely any distinction." With the principle conceded, politicians' response to Arthur's veto focused not on Chinese immigration but on the political repercussions. "The dignified Senate was thrown into positive disorder immediately after the reading [of the president's message]," the *New York Times* noted. When queried, the first thing congressmen mentioned was the veto's political impact. It "has seriously impaired the future of the republican party," Senator John F. Miller (R-Calif.) said, "and makes it certain that it cannot carry the Pacific coast for some time to come." The hapless Civil War general William Rosecrans, now a Democratic representative from California, predicted that the Republican Party would not even contest the upcoming congressional elections in the West, while Senator James T. Farley (D-Calif.) labeled the veto "the political ruin of Mr. Arthur." Democrats wondered if it would be better to override the veto or simply let the bill die, with the Republicans shouldering the blame. The press also emphasized the political effects. The *Chicago Tribune* called it the "death-knell of the Republican party on the Pacific Coast," and the *New York Tribune*, after interviewing western congressmen, recounted that "some of them went so far as to say that the Republican party had elected its last President." Emphasis on such matters effectively squelched any lingering interest in discussing the future of Chinese immigration or the ethics of exclusion.[5]

The veto caused the predicted uproar in the West. "Expression of indignation, disgust, and discouragement were [*sic*] universal," one paper noted, as Arthur was hanged in effigy and burned at the stake. Easterners were less violent but similarly outraged. At public meetings, Mayor Carter Harrison of Chicago and Tammany boss John Kelly of New York protested the veto, as did many eastern ministers. Rev. George Gallagher, a fiercely antilabor Unitarian, called Chinese immigration "fatal to the principles of our government," a sentiment backed by Presbyterian Rev. Arthur Swazey. While politicians and clergy led the protest, much of the denunciation came from organized labor. A working-class meeting in St. Louis featuring Richard Trevellick and Albert Parsons adopted resolutions opposing Arthur's veto, and the New York Central Labor Union, the Chicago Carpenters Union, and the Washington Federation of Labor took similar stances. In Philadelphia, John Kirchener, a leader of the Knights of Labor and editor of *Labor World*, organized a mass meeting of ten thousand workers to denounce the veto, and in Milwaukee, striking cigar makers carried a banner that portrayed a Chinese immigrant "hurrying to leave the country with umbrellas, old brooms, old shoes and other trash flying after him. The banner bore the inscription: 'Coolie labor the curse of civilization.'"[6]

In the spring of 1882, organized labor rallied behind the bill to ban Chinese immigrants. Recent converts to exclusion, workers endorsed it wholeheartedly when passage in Congress became a foregone conclusion. Yet the nuances in their comments and in editorials in the labor press suggest a slightly but vitally different picture. Whenever possible, workers still stressed the dangers of importation rather than immigration. As John Jarrett, president of both the Amalgamated Association of Iron and Steel Workers and the Federation of Organized Trades and Labor Unions, noted: "The veto has aroused the working people everywhere, and there seems to be a universal sentiment against it. It isn't the Chinese labor that they object to, but coolie cheap labor; just as they object to hordes of cheap Italian or Scandinavian laborers being brought over here." Jarrett's complaint, like those of countless others who had come before him, focused on the *nature* of the immigration, not its origins. So did lengthy resolutions passed by the carpenters and joiners of Kansas City, Missouri, who a half-dozen times used the word "importation" and completely avoided the word "immigration."[7]

The labor press expressed little delight when the bill passed, nor did it express great indignation when Arthur rejected it. "Let us not be misunderstood here," the *Irish World and American Industrial Liberator* explained. "We do not oppose the Chinaman on account of any race prejudice. If our industrial system were what it ought to be, a system under which every worker received the full value of his labor, we should have no reason to fear Chinese immigration." A duplicitous excuse? Perhaps, but the *Carpenter* said much the same thing. While calling the Chinese "dangerous to public health and human decency," the year-old labor paper edited by Peter McGuire stated, "We have no objection against their immigration—when they come here voluntarily— but we do object to their importation in hordes, under slavish contracts made in their native country, and held sacred by their religious fears." The language was virtually identical to that used twelve years earlier at North Adams. The enemy was not immigration but importation or, to be more precise, the importers. "The real fight," explained the *Carpenter*, "should be against the human hyenas who rummage the world over, and induce cheap labor to enter the field of industry and drag down our fellow workmen." The *Cigar Makers' Official Journal* also stressed this distinction between immigration and importation: "We do not object to the Chinese because of their race or their language or their religion, but we do object to an organized effort to introduce cheap laborers into the Republic." The *Journal* also dismissed the popular argument articulated by Senator George Edmunds that a "homogeneous race" was necessary for national survival, claiming instead that a unity of peoples could be best promoted through trade union activity. The editorial laid ultimate blame for Chinese exclusion on national politicians: "The failure of statesmanship in this country to solve the economic problem has necessitated this legislation."[8]

In saying this, the *Journal* laid blame on the nation's leaders for failing to deal with poverty, unemployment, and depression, problems caused by the massive industrial upheavals of the past decade. The United States had no comprehensive economic policy, no blueprint for a sustained recovery, no plan for providing for even the minimal welfare of its people. Neither innovation nor vision emanated from Washington; leaders had failed to lead. They had also failed to listen. Virtually every postwar working-class demand—eight-hours enforcement, public works, a federal bureau of labor—had fallen on deaf ears in the nation's capital. A ban on imported contract labor had been foremost among these long-stated demands. But workers and working-class organizations exerted little pressure on Washington, and Congress made no serious effort to legislate on this subject. The handful of bills introduced on importation during the past twelve years had died in committee. The regulation of imported contract labor involved complex and intricate matters that would require massive bureaucratic machinery to oversee. Mere investigation of charges, congressmen knew, would be a logistical nightmare. Agents would have to be stationed abroad and the entire diplomatic corps mobilized for enforcement. The sensitive matter of imposing American law on foreign soil further complicated the issue. Any statute on importation was bound to face major obstacles in operation.

Exclusion, on the other hand, appeared simple and direct. It involved minimal overhead or outlay of funds. Except for hiring a few extra customs agents to identify and turn back the excluded, no new expenses were anticipated and no expansion of government necessary. Compared with the herculean task required to implement a ban on imported contract labor, blanket exclusion seemed an easy alternative. For politicians, Chinese exclusion was a cheap panacea. And for workers in 1882, it was plainly the best they were going to get. National politicians had come through on little else in the past decade, and legislation on importation was nowhere in sight. Half a loaf—even not of their own choosing—was better than none. Workers in the East maintained a conscious distance from exclusion; although many supported it, they did not embrace it fully. Nor did they react with glee to its passage. It was not what they had asked for, and their words expressed a certain discomfort with exclusion. It was the wrong solution, the wrong approach, but no other remedy from Washington was forthcoming. Congress offered them no alternatives.[9]

Though in the end organized labor backed the bill, opposition persisted. Deeming it wrongheaded and misdirected, the *Paterson Labor Standard* asked, "Why make so much noise about Chinese cheap labor when we see our own children being used in their tender years to bring down our wages?" Recent efforts to import Italian workers led the editor to conclude, "Cheap labor is evidently cheap labor, whether it be Chinese, American or European." The most eloquent statement came not from any editorial but out of a strike in Paterson, New Jersey. Three days after Arthur's veto, seventy-five white and Chinese shirt ironers walked off the job together, demanding a raise of a penny per shirt. The Chinese, a *New York Herald* reporter wrote, "are always ready to join any movement for an increase in pay. The white men say that the Chinamen are more to be depended upon than the Caucasians, for they never knew a China-man to break his word when he resolved to strike. They are always the last to give in, and are considered first class strikers in every sense of the word."[10]

Amid the antiveto atmosphere, several Republicans defended Chinese immigration, none more vigorously than Rev. Henry Ward Beecher. The United States, he explained in a sermon to his Brooklyn congregation, needed some group to offset the Irish: "Now, immigration is good; I want it; but the vote is our big trouble. That is to say, the Irish vote. . . . The Irish people . . . are a vexation to municipal government." By uplifting the Irish to respectability and reforming their "corrupt" voting habits, the Chinese could perform a valuable public service, Beecher said, and because of their alleged docility and disinterest in citizenship, they posed no threat to the body politic. Again the issue came down to politics. In reasoning reminiscent of James Henry Hammond's famous "mudsill" speech of 1859, Beecher declared:

> If there is one thing that is clearer than another it is that all the dominant races—the Irish, English, German, Scotch—. . . have . . . an aspiration that is continually tending to drive them up from humble offices of life to higher duties, and in a score of years we shall have no race that will be willing to do what we call the menial work. It is for a people that will do this that this continent and age are hungering. More and more the other races are going up from the bottom and leaving the underwork of society to the poor of other and less ambitious peoples; and here is a race offered to us that by reason of their training, by the habits of a thousand years, are adapted to do that work.

The Chinese, willing to do the "underwork of society" and demand little in exchange—not citizenship, not suffrage—were, in Beecher's eyes, the ideal immigrants. Who else would do the "menial work"? No one but the "less ambitious" Chinese. Their virtue lay in being at the bottom of the hierarchy of races.[11]

As Beecher preached, a reporter observed, "nearly every one in the church stamped his or her feet" in approval, his "fiery sermon" provoking the most "emphatic demonstration" from his congregation since the Civil War. Beecher's audience extended far beyond the confines of his church. As the most prominent pastor of the Gilded Age, he served as a mouthpiece for the nation's middle and upper classes. Perhaps no sermon of his better captured the fears of the nation's well-to-do citizens or the suppressed hostility toward the Irish embedded in the nation's Protestant majority. Racial superiority, Social Darwinism, and national progress converged neatly in Beecher's colloquy. He compared immigrants to "mud," which, he explained, can be both fertilizing and "miasmatic." National policy, he said, should promote the former and check the latter, and here the Chinese provided the perfect solution: by occupying a perpetual lowly position as the nation's servile labor force (fertilizer for the nation's industry), the Chinese would act as a brake on "miasmatic" political corruption, saving the nation from class war and social decay. Beecher's congregants no doubt worried that his solution might backfire. Suppose the Chinese did demand political rights? Suppose the Irish did not rise in society? Despite his influence, Beecher could not dictate national policy. Yet his words may be taken to reflect the unspoken views of many old-line Protestants and "best men" who opposed Chinese exclusion but maintained little faith or interest in a democratic, egalitarian society.[12]

One other influential group opposed the Chinese Exclusion Act: the merchant community of the Northeast connected with the China trade. Fearing the bill would endanger business, several commercial firms in Boston petitioned Congress to reject the legislation. So did merchants connected with the New York City Board of Trade as well as leading bankers, iron manufacturers, and insurance executives. The Union League Club of New York also drafted a petition signed by its president, former secretary of state William Evarts. The petition claimed that the bill's twenty-year clause and passport requirement violated the Angell Treaty and if enacted would harm trade and "impair the friendly relations" between the two nations. Approving the president's veto, the petitioners urged further "study [of] the subject." What is significant about the Union League petition is that it said nothing against exclusion itself. The same was true for the Boston merchants' petition. Only one petition, that of the New York City Board of Trade, opposed exclusion, but it remained mum on immigration restriction. Eastern merchants' fears that if the bill became law China might retaliate by obstructing commerce were surely sincere, but by equivocating on immigration restriction, they revealed that such restriction would be acceptable if kept within "reasonable" bounds.[13]

Thus at the climax of the Chinese exclusion debate in 1882, class lines separated two of the sides. Organized labor favored the bill, whereas the merchant community opposed it. But the two groups were not really very far apart. Room for compromise existed. Congress knew it. The president knew it. The press knew it. If twenty years seemed "unreasonable" and thereby threatened to violate the treaty, why not compromise on a shorter period of time? As the *New York Tribune* noted, a seven-year suspension would "certainly [be] long enough to give the experiment a fair trial." Ten years would also suffice. "If the bill works satisfactorily there would be no trouble in extending the period as often as necessary." The *Tribune* was both prophetic and judicious: "By using a little prudence and moderation we can undoubtedly accomplish all we need for our own welfare at home, and at the same time avoid the mistake of needlessly damaging our commercial relations abroad."[14]

Congress reconsidered the legislation on April 17. Veteran anti-Chinese crusader Horace F. Page (R-Calif.) introduced a revised version, which reduced the length of exclusion from twenty years to ten. The new bill also substituted the word "certificate" for passport, a mere change in terminology to placate Arthur. Otherwise, the bill was virtually identical to the one the president had vetoed two weeks earlier. Debate was brief but "gave rise," the *New York Tribune* noted, "to one of the most extraordinary scenes ever witnessed" in Congress. "For nearly an hour disorder ruled supreme, and Speaker [J. Warren] Keifer [R-Ohio] lost control of the House. Twenty members at a time were on the floor, shouting for recognition and plying the Speaker with 'parliamentary inquiries,' 'points of order' and 'questions of privilege.'" The Democrats had two strategies: either to delay the vote and blame defeat on the Republicans, or strengthen the bill and thereby insure a second veto. Either way the Democrats hoped to "gain some partisan advantage for themselves." So did the Republicans, who favored a speedy vote. To the very end, politics and political advantage remained the chief motivating force behind every stage of the Chinese Exclusion Act. As a high-placed Republican functionary in California wrote, if the new bill failed, "the Pacific Coast will give a solid Democratic electoral vote. . . . We are now pretty thoroughly discouraged politically; but give us the House bill promptly passing the Senate, & promptly signed, & we can rally. Another *veto*,—a failure in any way to give us such a bill, & our party is swamped forever here." The letter's recipient, Republican national party leader William Chandler, made sure the message got through to his colleagues.[15]

When the Speaker at last restored order, Representative John Kasson (R-Iowa) was the only principal orator. He had opposed the first version of the bill and deplored the partisan spirit presently raging. Eager to unite Republicans and satisfy the West but reluctant to reverse traditional national policy, Kasson declared: "I do not believe it to be just or the duty of the Congress of the United States to make itself a pack of hounds to hunt down any race born and permitted to live on God's earth . . . to exclude them from American soil. . . . We, on this [the Republican] side of the House, have been and will remain the party of liberty, of justice, and of hospitality to all the oppressed nationalities of the earth; and may the day be far distant when we shall abandon that crowning glory of our history." Such a day was not far distant at all, just three weeks away. Moments after Kasson's speech, the House approved the new version of the Chinese Exclusion Act, 201 to 37 (with 53 not voting). Half of the 62 Republicans who had voted against the first bill changed their votes, 22 voting in favor and 10 not casting ballots. Republicans switching sides came from all regions. Six New Englanders did an about-face and supported the new version. So did all three Kansans, three New Yorkers, and ten others, including Kasson. All told, the Republican Party approved the bill, 90 to 34 (with 24 not voting); the Democrats, 101 to 3 (with 29 not voting); and the Greenbackers, 5 to 0. No representative who had supported the first version opposed the second. The final tally indicates the overwhelming bipartisan support for Chinese exclusion in the lower house of Congress—73 percent among voting Republicans, 97 percent among voting Democrats—from every region of the country except New England.[16]

Debate in the Senate lasted slightly longer. In a racist speech, John Tyler Morgan (D-Ala.) said that without exclusion, Chinese immigrants would descend on the South and together with blacks cause "the utter destruction of the last vestige of civilization we have there." During his two-hour tirade, Morgan repeated what had now become a truism: "Is there any doubt about the majority of the people of the United States of both parties concurring . . . that there must be a prohibition . . . of Chinese immigration? Who will dare to rise up and confront the majesty of the people . . . [and] deny its authority in this matter?" As Morgan himself answered, "Only a few."[17]

One of the few was George Frisbie Hoar (R-Mass.). In his final speech on the bill, he denounced Chinese exclusion as both "a violation of the ancient policy of the American Republic" and "a violation of the rights of human nature itself." Joseph R. Hawley (R-Conn.) also made one last attack on the legislation. "It reads as if it came from the dark ages," he declared. "It reads like the old fugitive-slave law." So exacting was Hawley in his humanitarian ideals that the New York Times chided him for "his persistent appeals to the palladium of our liberties." Hawley was indeed persistent. The bill, he said, was a repudiation of the nation's heritage and a subversion of a person's right to work wherever, whenever, and however one chose: "Let this proposed statute be read a hundred years hence, dug out of the dust of ages and forgotten as it will be except for a line of sneer by some historians, and ask the young man not well read in the history of the country what was the reason for excluding these men, and he would not be able to find it in the law. He would find the Chinese laborer excluded for no cause except that he is a laborer." And, Hawley could have added, for the political cause of gaining western votes and inveigling working people nationwide. Like the recently retired Hannibal Hamlin of Maine, Hawley wanted nothing to do with Chinese exclusion: "I leave the bill to posterity for its condemnation. I plant myself here now, this moment, on the ground of unconditional hostility and denunciation. I will make no terms with it now or elsewhere here or hereafter, at any time." But even the eloquent Hawley, founder of Connecticut's Free-Soil and Republican Parties and proud scion of the abolitionist legacy, could not escape the winds of change. "I am willing," he said at last, "to regulate the immigration [from China]. . . . I am willing to limit it; to restrict it." The man who twelve years earlier had said, "Let them come. . . . I don't know how . . . to lock the doors of the United States," had at last modified his position. Humanitarianism evidently had its boundaries, and Hawley's dictum applied no less to himself: "Our zealous and radical republicanism is fading."[18]

A few others spoke. Henry L. Dawes (R-Mass.), like Hoar and Hawley, denounced the bill. Recounting the incident at North Adams in 1870 that had ignited the first national debate on Chinese immigration, Dawes praised the actions of his old friend, shoe manufacturer Calvin T. Sampson—"no man was ever fairer than he"—and defended both contract labor and Chinese immigration. George Edmunds (R-Vt.) also spoke. Ironically, the Vermont Republican apologized for his inability to support the bill, explaining that while he favored exclusion, he felt the ban on citizenship violated the Angell Treaty. Combining Blaine's argument three years earlier that Chinese exclusion could buy labor peace and the *Tribune*'s argument one month earlier that "sometimes expediency is statesmanship of the highest order," Edmunds envisioned immigration restriction as a peacekeeping device that would appease "the sand-lot people" of the Far West: "It does not make any difference which class of the community it is that disturbs the public peace," said this voice of the new Republican morality; "the public peace is disturbed and if you can save it by giving time for reason to restore itself and passion to cool, is it not wise? . . . Then let us protect the Chinamen by having them hold up a little while until they [the sandlotters] get over their trouble. . . . It comes to a mere question of expediency."[19]

Figure 12.1. A former abolitionist, Senator Joseph R. Hawley (1826–1905) of Connecticut had always defended Chinese immigration, and in 1882 he expressed his "unconditional hostility" to the Chinese Exclusion Act. "I leave the bill to posterity for its condemnation," he said. But he then added he was "willing to limit" and "restrict" Chinese immigration. Providing the epitaph to an era, Hawley remarked, "Our zealous and radical republicanism is fading." (Courtesy Connecticut Historical Society, Hartford)

A mere question of expediency. As Blaine had indicated, the goal of government, of statesmanship, of national leaders was to preserve order rather than to serve justice. With slight alterations, the Senate passed the Chinese Exclusion Act, 32 to 15 (with 29 not voting), on April 28. All fifteen negative votes were Republican. Eleven Republicans supported the bill, and thirteen did not vote, eight of whom were paired in opposition. Just 38 percent of Republicans in the Senate officially opposed the Chinese Exclusion Act. The Senate demonstrated considerably more antiexclusion sentiment than did the House, but hardly enough to make a difference and not enough to override a second potential veto. Without debate and without a vote, the House approved the Senate version on May 3. The next day, pro tem David Davis of Illinois, an independent Republican and the only senator who had switched his vote from no to yes, signed the bill and sent it to the White House.[20]

Would President Arthur sign or veto it? In contrast to a month earlier, there was little drama and no excitement. Arthur held no cabinet sessions and received little mail. Although most of his objections remained unmet, few doubted that he would approve the bill. The western vote was too important to his party. With neither fanfare nor ceremony, President Chester Alan Arthur signed the Chinese Exclusion Act on May 6, 1882.[21]

An eerie silence greeted its passage. Newspapers reported the matter perfunctorily with scant comment or criticism. "It is to be hoped," the *New York Times* said succinctly, "that this will settle the much-vexed Chinese question for a time at least."[22] Few others said even this much, and the labor press added practically nothing. No meetings of workers, at least in the East, gathered to celebrate. Nor did any other groups or organizations meet to lavish praise or offer criticism. It appears that initially, most Americans simply wanted to ignore or forget what the nation had just done.

The Chinese Exclusion Act of 1882 was the first law ever passed by the United States barring any group of people from American shores purely because of race or nationality. As many had foreseen, it provided a precedent for future restrictive legislation. "Hereafter," the *Chicago Times* noted, "we are to keep our hand on the door-knob, and admit only those whose presence we desire."[23] For the next hundred years Americans would indeed keep a "hand on the door-knob," barring the Chinese again in 1892, 1902, and 1904, and most Japanese and Koreans a few years afterward. The knob turned tighter in 1917 when the United States barred virtually all Asians and again in 1921 and 1924 when the United States all but closed the door to Europe and Japan. Not until World War II was the Chinese Exclusion Act repealed, but even then the United States restricted immigration to a quota of 105 Chinese per year.[24] The door at last reopened in the 1960s, but shouts to close it again have grown shriller in recent years.

In tracing the origin of the Chinese Exclusion Act, both the California thesis and the national racist consensus thesis offer instructive points: the former illustrates how anti-Chinese sentiment developed in the West, and the latter suggests how Americans nationwide could readily accept anti-Chinese legislation. Both theses, however, essentially leave the politics out. And politics are at the core of the Chinese Exclusion Act. Anti-Chinese hostility, after all, had been rife in California for twenty-five years before the rest of the country took notice and began responding in the mid-1870s, and anti-Chinese imagery had long pervaded the nation during the nineteenth century without precipitating any adverse federal legislation. However racist the beliefs of politicians, workers, and other Americans in the post–Civil War years, Congress made no substantial effort to enact anti-Chinese laws in 1865 or 1870 or 1875. There was little demand for and little to gain from such legislation. But when the national railroad strike jolted the nation in 1877, just as Reconstruction was collapsing, a new era emerged that would make anti-Chinese politics possible nationwide. Suddenly the landscape had changed. Class conflict had forged this change and

(DIS.) "HONORS ARE EASY."
NOW BOTH PARTIES HAVE SOMETHING TO HANG ON.

Figure 12.2. With the Republican elephant leading the way, the Democratic tiger clutches the Chinese immigrant, uprooting the tree of liberty and plunging freedom to the depths below. Placing politics at the center of the Chinese Exclusion Act, cartoonist Thomas Nast caustically puns, "Now both parties have something to hang on." Nast's drawing, when contrasted with his earlier one after the Civil War (see Figure 2.1), illustrates the transformation of the politics of immigration and race from the late 1860s to 1882. In banning Chinese immigrants from the United States, politicians are about to overturn and submerge American ideals forever. Original caption: "(Dis-) 'Honors Are Easy.' Now Both Parties Have Something to Hang On." (*Harper's Weekly*, May 20, 1882)

would keep generating and regenerating a changing political landscape for the duration of the Gilded Age. The fundamental question underlying the era's preeminent economic treatise—Henry George's *Progress and Poverty*, published in 1879—was, How in a nation of such wealth and abundance could there be so much poverty? It was this problem that politicians confronted throughout the Gilded Age and beyond, and in seeking answers, one of the first solutions they grasped was Chinese exclusion. This solution, politicians argued, would protect, uplift, and enrich the working person. As James Blaine said, "I feel and know that I am pleading the cause of the free American laborer and of his children and of his children's children." He was, he insisted, speaking "in defense and advocacy of the interests of the laboring classes." The Chinese Exclusion Act represented class politics on the cheap, a painless way for politicians to ensnare working people's support without providing any genuine solution to their problems.[25]

In the decade and a half following the Civil War, workers east of the Rocky Mountains carefully and repeatedly voiced their opposition to imported contract labor and their support for Chinese immigration. Only at the very end of this period, when exclusion became all but inevitable, did workers finally adopt the cause for their own. But at that point it really didn't matter, except that it enabled politicians to invoke the support of the working classes in whose name they convinced themselves, the nation, and ultimately workers that they were legislating. Their appeals to race and to class eventually struck a chord. As David Roediger, Alexander Saxton, and Gwendolyn Mink have argued, white working-class racism may indeed have been deep and pervasive in the middle and latter decades of the nineteenth century.[26] The important question to ask, however, is not how racist workers were, but how did workers *act* on this racism? When issues of race arose at key historical moments, how did workers respond, and how did their entrenched racism influence their demands, their actions, and their political aims? The answer in this case is, surprisingly, not much. In the 1870s, a decade marked by depression, class conflict, and industrial upheaval, workers east of the Rockies—who composed the vast bulk of the working classes and the national labor movement—remained remarkably consistent in their tolerance toward Chinese immigration. From speeches made at rallies to resolutions passed at meetings, from letters sent to newspapers to slogans scrawled on banners, from offhand comments heard by reporters to prepared testimony delivered before Congress, from all the myriad working-class voices that can be rescued from the past, the great majority of workers who spoke out on the issue, contrary to the claims of countless historians, welcomed Chinese immigrants to America. After more than a dozen years of articulating their political demands for a ban on imported contract labor, legislation was at last passed—not the legislation most workers had wanted but the legislation politicians had fashioned. It was immigration—not importation, not contract labor—that politicians banned. Despite the avalanche of arguments by national politicians appealing to workers' self-interest, few workers in the East revealed much concern over Chinese immigration or Chinese exclusion. It was seldom an issue with which they chose to be associated. Immigration restriction rarely appeared on the working-class agenda in the 1860s and 1870s, and only when politicians placed it on the national agenda and trumpeted the issue in their name did workers finally accept it.

Politics, as Alexander Saxton has demonstrated, was the main channel for explicating and disseminating racial discourse. By spewing, amplifying, and propagating racist stereotypes of the Chinese and linking the well-being of workers to the exclusion of Chinese immigrants, politicians manipulated the two most volatile issues in American society—race and class—and combined them to produce the first race-based immigration act in American history. This manipulation is the essence of the Chinese Exclusion Act. Perhaps no better example of top-down politics exists than this 1882 statute. Both West Coast agitation and general racist tendencies nationwide were essential elements contributing to the climate conducive to Chinese exclusion, but the engine fueling and steering exclusion was politics. Politicians and national party leaders were the glue welding the active anti-Chinese racism of westerners with the nascent anti-Chinese racism of other Americans. In all senses of the term, Chinese exclusion was a *political* act.

Its impact, however, far transcended politics. By sanctioning racism, it perpetuated racism, and by sanctioning racist policy at the highest levels of government, it helped legitimize racist action at every level of society. The Chinese Exclusion Act was the foremost racist law passed after the Civil War. It both symbolized and facilitated the transition from Reconstruction to the Gilded Age, making discrimination more acceptable, more apparent, and more prevalent throughout the nation. All sections of the country, East and West, North and South, united in Congress to promote discrimination and legitimize segregation openly. Though westerners taunted a dwindling handful of eastern idealists for their "mawkish sentimentality" (as one California representative put it), the "equality gush" did not disappear entirely. It was simply redefined to suit the times. No one better captured this emerging ethos than Civil War veteran John Sherwin, an obscure two-term Republican congressman from Aurora, Illinois, who sought to reconcile the ideals of an earlier age with the "stern realities" of the dawning era. "We do not deny the equality of man," Sherwin said, minutes before voting for the Chinese Exclusion Act. "We still assert that all men are born free and equal, but we claim the right to control our own workshops and choose our own associates." One could thus endorse equality in principle and discrimination in practice. Ideals were as malleable as words. But Sherwin did not go unchallenged. Cyrus Carpenter, an equally obscure Republican congressman from Iowa (as well as a Civil War veteran), predicted that a political backlash to the Chinese Exclusion Act would precipitate the law's repeal by 1890. "Common sense and not prejudice," he said, "will then prevail." Carpenter's vision was not borne out. After the Chinese Exclusion Act, prejudice prevailed and predominated, and Sherwin's words more perceptively codified the emerging philosophy of an increasingly segregated society. Equality could be proclaimed from the Capitol to the village square, but it would not be backed up by legislation or public policy. As the Jim Crow era of state-sponsored segregation dawned, more and more Americans, both nationally and locally, would "claim the right to control our own workshops and choose our own associates." From Sherwin's defense of Chinese exclusion in 1882 it was an effortless segue to *Plessy v. Ferguson* in 1896 and the institutionalization of racism in the twentieth century.[27]

The Chinese Exclusion Act neither caused nor made inevitable later restrictions on immigration, but it certainly lent them legitimacy. It made future bans and quota systems easier to justify and easier to accept. By the early twentieth century, when many of the act's original sponsors had long since passed away, Chinese exclusion remained firmly embedded in the nation's laws. "Common sense" did not prevail, and renewals of the act passed with little opposition. The Exclusion Act legitimized racism, and racism legitimized further exclusion. As Senator William M. Stewart, the Nevada Republican who had boldly endorsed Chinese immigration and secured legal protections for all immigrants in 1870, remarked just days before the law's renewal in 1892: "There was a time when there was great diversity of opinion on the question of Chinese immigration to this country, but I think there is practically none now. The American people are now convinced that the Chinese can not be incorporated among our citizens, can not be amalgamated, can not be absorbed, but that they will remain a distinct element." Exclusion, this former defender of immigrant rights concluded, "seems to me a necessity."[28] After permanent renewal in the early 1900s, exclusion no longer appeared an aberration of traditional American policy; it became American policy, it became American tradition, and thus had repercussions for generations to come. The law's legacy, in the form of future restrictions and anti-Asian racism, lingers to this day. Like the Fugitive Slave Act of 1850, the Chinese Exclusion Act of 1882 remains one of the most infamous and tragic statutes in American history. It must also remain one of the most ironic. No national sentiment arose to demand it, no broad effort emerged to prevent it. The Chinese Exclusion Act was a tool shaped and wielded by politicians who, in an era of burgeoning class conflict and razor-sharp electoral margins, championed an issue of paltry national importance in the false name of the working classes in the hopes of gaining a decisive handful of votes. In the name of morality, Gilded Age politicians used amoral tactics to enact an immoral law.

This point was not lost on contemporary observers. Kwong Ki Chiu, a

Chinese scholar residing in Connecticut, identified the underlying motivation behind the Chinese Exclusion Act. "I fear," he wrote on April 29, 1882, just days before 400 million of his fellow countrymen and countrywomen would for generations be excluded from the United States, "that some of the supporters of the anti-Chinese bills do not act from principle, but are seeking, under cover of this bill, to promote some ulterior and selfish end, such as their own re-election or their possible nomination for the Presidency."[29]

In enacting the "anti-Chinese bill" in 1882, politicians not only closed the gate on an entire group of people but also set the standard for how Americans would both frame the immigration debate in the years that followed and come to accept greater and greater restrictions on foreigners seeking refuge and freedom in the United States. More than a century after its passage, the Chinese Exclusion Act still haunts the nation's treatment of immigrants and immigration.

Appendix.
The Chinese
Exclusion Act

An act to execute certain treaty stipulations relating to Chinese.

Whereas, in the opinion of the Government of the United States the coming of Chinese laborers to this country endangers the good order of certain localities within the territory thereof: Therefore,

Be it enacted by the Senate and House of Representatives of the United States of America in Congress assembled, That from and after the expiration of ninety days next after the passage of this act, and until the expiration of ten years next after the passage of this act, the coming of Chinese laborers to the United States be, and the same is hereby, suspended; and during such suspension it shall not be lawful for any Chinese laborer to come, or, having so come after the expiration of said ninety days, to remain within the United States.

SEC. 2. That the master of any vessel who shall knowingly bring within the United States on such vessel, and land or permit to be landed, any Chinese laborer, from any foreign port or place, shall be deemed guilty of a misdemeanor, and on conviction thereof shall be punished by a fine of not more than five hundred dollars for each and every such Chinese laborer so brought, and may be also imprisoned for a term not exceeding one year.

SEC. 3. That the two foregoing sections shall not apply to Chinese laborers who were in the United States on the seventeenth day of November, eighteen hundred and eighty, or who shall have come into the same before the expiration of ninety days next after the passage of this act, and who shall produce to such master before going on board such vessel, and shall produce to the collector of the port in the United States at which such vessel shall arrive, the evidence hereinafter in this act required of his being one of the laborers in this section mentioned; nor shall the two foregoing sections apply to the case of any master whose vessel, being bound to a port not within the United States, shall come within the jurisdiction of the United States by reason of being in distress or in stress of weather, or touching at any port of the United States on its voyage to any foreign port or place: *Provided*, That all Chinese laborers brought on such vessel shall depart with the vessel on leaving port.

SEC. 4. That for the purpose of properly identifying Chinese laborers who were in the United States on the seventeenth day of November, eighteen hundred and eighty, or who shall have come into the same before the expiration of ninety days next after the passage of this act, and in order to furnish them with the proper evidence of their right to go from and come to the United States of their free will and accord, as provided by the treaty between the

The Statutes at Large of the United States of America, from December, 1881, to March, 1883, and Recent Treaties, Postal Conventions, and Executive Proclamations (Washington, D.C., 1883), 22:58–61.

United States and China dated November seventeenth, eighteen hundred and eighty, the collector of customs of the district from which any such Chinese laborer shall depart from the United States shall, in person or by deputy, go on board each vessel having on board any such Chinese laborer and cleared or about to sail from his district for a foreign port, and on such vessel make a list of all such Chinese laborers, which shall be entered in registry-books to be kept for that purpose, in which shall be stated the name, age, occupation, last place of residence, physical marks or peculiarities, and all facts necessary for the identification of each of such Chinese laborers, which books shall be safely kept in the custom-house; and every such Chinese laborer so departing from the United States shall be entitled to, and shall receive, free of any charge or cost upon application therefor, from the collector or his deputy, at the time such list is taken, a certificate, signed by the collector or his deputy and attested by his seal of office, in such form as the Secretary of the Treasury shall prescribe, which certificate shall contain a statement of the name, age, occupation, last place of residence, personal description, and facts of identification of the Chinese laborer to whom the certificate is issued, corresponding with the said list and registry in all particulars. In case any Chinese laborer after having received such certificate shall leave such vessel before her departure he shall deliver his certificate to the master of the vessel, and if such Chinese laborer shall fail to return to such vessel before her departure from port the certificate shall be delivered by the master to the collector of customs for cancellation. The certificate herein provided for shall entitle the Chinese laborer to whom the same is issued to return to and re-enter the United States upon producing and delivering the same to the collector of customs of the district at which such Chinese laborer shall seek to re-enter; and upon delivery of such certificate by such Chinese laborer to the collector of customs at the time of re-entry in the United States, said collector shall cause the same to be filed in the custom-house and duly canceled.

sec. 5. That any Chinese laborer mentioned in section four of this act being in the United States, and desiring to depart from the United States by land, shall have the right to demand and receive, free of charge or cost, a certificate of identification similar to that provided for in section four of this act to be issued to such Chinese laborers as may desire to leave the United States by water; and it is hereby made the duty of the collector of customs of the district next adjoining the foreign country to which said Chinese laborer desires to go to issue such certificate, free of charge or cost, upon application by such Chinese laborer, and to enter the same upon registry-books to be kept by him for the purpose, as provided for in section four of this act.

sec. 6. That in order to the faithful execution of articles one and two of the treaty in this act before mentioned, every Chinese person other than a laborer who may be entitled by said treaty and this act to come within the United States, and who shall be about to come to the United States, shall be identified as so entitled by the Chinese Government in each case, such identity to be evidenced by a certificate issued under the authority of said government, which certificate shall be in the English language or (if not in the English language) accompanied by a translation into English, stating such right to come, and which certificate shall state the name, title, or official rank, if any, the age, height, and all physical peculiarities, former and present occupation or profession, and place of residence in China of the person to whom the certificate is issued and that such person is entitled conformably to the treaty in this act mentioned to come within the United States. Such certificate shall be prima-facie evidence of the fact set forth therein, and shall be produced to the collector of customs, or his deputy, of the port in the district in the United States at which the person named therein shall arrive.

SEC. 7. That any person who shall knowingly and falsely alter or substitute any name for the name written in such certificate or forge any such certificate, or knowingly utter any forged or fraudulent certificate, or falsely personate any person named in any such certificate, shall be deemed guilty of a misdemeanor; and upon conviction thereof shall be fined in a sum not exceeding one thousand dollars, and imprisoned in a penitentiary for a term of not more than five years.

SEC. 8. That the master of any vessel arriving in the United States from any foreign port or place shall, at the same time he delivers a manifest of the cargo, and if there be no cargo, then at the time of making a report of the entry of the vessel pursuant to law, in addition to the other matter required to be reported, and before landing, or permitting to land, any Chinese passengers, deliver and report to the collector of customs of the district in which such vessels shall have arrived a separate list of all Chinese passengers taken on board his vessel at any foreign port or place, and all such passengers on board the vessel at that time. Such list shall show the names of such passengers (and if accredited officers of the Chinese Government traveling on the business of that government, or their servants, with a note of such facts), and the names and other particulars, as shown by their respective certificates; and such list shall be sworn to by the master in the manner required by law in relation to the manifest of the cargo. Any willful refusal or neglect of any such master to comply with the provisions of this section shall incur the same penalties and forfeiture as are provided for a refusal or neglect to report and deliver a manifest of the cargo.

SEC. 9. That before any Chinese passengers are landed from any such vessel, the collector, or his deputy, shall proceed to examine such passengers, comparing the certificates with the list and with the passengers; and no passenger shall be allowed to land in the United States from such vessel in violation of law.

SEC. 10. That every vessel whose master shall knowingly violate any of the provisions of this act shall be deemed forfeited to the United States, and shall be liable to seizure and condemnation in any district of the United States into which such vessel may enter or in which she may be found.

SEC. 11. That any person who shall knowingly bring into or cause to be brought into the United States by land, or who shall knowingly aid or abet the same, or aid or abet the landing in the United States from any vessel of any Chinese person not lawfully entitled to enter the United States, shall be deemed guilty of a misdemeanor, and shall, on conviction thereof, be fined in a sum not exceeding one thousand dollars, and imprisoned for a term not exceeding one year.

SEC. 12. That no Chinese person shall be permitted to enter the United States by land without producing to the proper officer of customs the certificate in this act required of Chinese persons seeking to land from a vessel. And any Chinese person found unlawfully within the United States shall be caused to be removed therefrom to the country from whence he came, by direction of the President of the United States, and at the cost of the United States, after being brought before some justice, judge, or commissioner of a court of the United States and found to be one not lawfully entitled to be or remain in the United States.

SEC. 13. That this act shall not apply to diplomatic and other officers of the Chinese Government traveling upon the business of that government, whose credentials shall be taken as equivalent to the certificate in this act mentioned, and shall exempt them and their body and household servants from the provisions of this act as to other Chinese persons.

SEC. 14. That hereafter no State court or court of the United States shall admit Chinese to citizenship; and all laws in conflict with this act are hereby repealed.

SEC. 15. That the words "Chinese laborers," wherever used in this act, shall be construed to mean both skilled and unskilled laborers and Chinese employed in mining.

Approved, May 6, 1882.

Notes

ABBREVIATIONS

BG *Boston Globe*
CE *Cincinnati Enquirer*
CG *Congressional Globe*
CGa *Cincinnati Gazette*
CMOJ *Cigar Makers' Official Journal*
CR *Congressional Record*
CT *Chicago Times*
CTr *Chicago Tribune*
IW *Irish World* (New York)
IWAIL *Irish World and American Industrial Liberator* (New York)
LC Library of Congress
NYH *New York Herald*
NYLS *New York Labor Standard*
NYS *New York Sun*
NYT *New York Times*
NYTr *New York Tribune*
NYW *New York World*
PI *Philadelphia Inquirer*
SFAC *San Francisco Alta California*
SFC *San Francisco Chronicle*
SR *Springfield (Mass.) Republican*
WA *Workingman's Advocate* (Chicago)

CHAPTER ONE

1. *CR*, 45th Cong., 3d sess., 1301, 1303 (Feb. 14, 1879).

2. Ibid.; James G. Blaine (letter) in *NYTr*, Feb. 24, 1879. Blaine's letter was technically in response to one written by William Lloyd Garrison. See *NYTr*, Feb. 17, 1879.

3. James G. Blaine (letter) in *NYTr*, Feb. 24, 1879; *CR*, 45th Cong., 3d sess., 1302 (Feb. 14, 1879); U.S. Bureau of the Census, *Statistics of the Population of the United States at the Tenth Census (June 1, 1880), Embracing Extended Tables of the Population of States, Counties, and Minor Civil Divisions, with Distinctions of Race, Sex, Age, Nativity, and Occupations; Together with Summary Tables, Derived from Other Census Reports, Relating to Newspapers and Periodicals; Public Schools and Illiteracy; The Dependent, Defective, and Delinquent Classes, Etc.* (Washington, D.C., 1883), 3. The Chinese population in the West in 1880 included those

in the states of California (75,132), Oregon (9,510), Nevada (5,416), and Colorado (612) and in the territories of Idaho (3,379), Washington (3,186), Montana (1,765), Arizona (1,630), Wyoming (914), Utah (501), and New Mexico (57).

4. *CR*, 45th Cong., 3d sess., 800–801 (Jan. 28, 1879), 1400 (Feb. 15, 1879), 2275–76 (Mar. 1, 1879).

5. *CR*, 47th Cong., 1st sess., 1674 (Mar. 7, 1882), 1904 (Mar. 14, 1882), 2126, 2132 (Mar. 21, 1882), 2210 (Mar. 23, 1882), 2608 (Apr. 5, 1882).

6. Ibid., 1645 (Mar. 6, 1882), 2208 (Mar. 23, 1882), app., 41, 44–45, 89 (Mar. 16, 1882). For similar views, see also in ibid. the remarks of Representatives Calkins, 1903–4 (Mar. 14, 1882), James Tyler (R-Vt.), 1938 (Mar. 15, 1882), McClure, 2127 (Mar. 21, 1882), Thomas Bayne (R-Pa.), 2129 (Mar. 21, 1882), Joseph Scranton (R-Pa.), 2131 (Mar. 21, 1882), Butterworth, 2132 (Mar. 21, 1882), William Washburn (R-Minn.), 2162 (Mar. 22, 1882), Robert Hawk (R-Ill.), 2175 (Mar. 22, 1882), Hazelton, 2210 (Mar. 23, 1882), Senator Sherman, 2609 (Apr. 5, 1882), and Representative A. Herr Smith (R-Pa.), app., 49 (Mar. 16, 1882).

7. *CR*, 47th Cong., 1st sess., 2608 (Apr. 5, 1882).

8. Mary Roberts Coolidge, *Chinese Immigration* (New York, 1909), 21–32, 55–56, 69–82, 498. The quotes are from 22 and 23. On Gam Saan, see Ronald Takaki, *Strangers from a Different Shore: A History of Asian Americans* (New York, 1990), 31.

Californians adopted anti-Chinese measures both locally and statewide. Towns in Mariposa and El Dorado Counties passed resolutions barring and expelling Chinese immigrants from their jurisdictions in the 1850s. In 1850, the state legislature enacted the Foreign Miners' License Law, requiring noncitizens and foreign-born citizens to pay twenty dollars a month for mining licenses. Although initially directed against Mexican American and Latin American miners, the law was soon enforced against the Chinese and reenacted in various versions in 1852, 1853, 1855, and 1856. In 1854, the California Supreme Court outlawed Chinese testimony against whites in state court, depriving Chinese immigrants of legal protection. In 1855, California imposed an entry fee of fifty dollars on Chinese immigrants arriving by boat, and in 1860, a monthly tax of four dollars on Chinese fishermen. Also in 1860, California excluded all Chinese (along with blacks and American Indians) from the public schools. In addition to Coolidge, see Lucile Eaves, *A History of California Labor Legislation, with an Introductory Sketch of the San Francisco Labor Movement*, University of California Publications in Economics, vol. 2 (Berkeley, 1910), chap. 3; Ira B. Cross, *A History of the Labor Movement in California* (Berkeley, 1935), 17, 76–77; and Charles J. McClain, *In Search of Equality: The Chinese Struggle against Discrimination in Nineteenth-Century America* (Berkeley, 1994), chap. 1.

On legal obstacles faced by Chinese immigrants in California, Oregon, and elsewhere in the nineteenth century, see Sucheng Chan, ed., *Entry Denied: Exclusion and the Chinese Community in America, 1882–1943* (Philadelphia, 1991); J. A. C. Grant, "Testimonial Exclusion because of Race: A Chapter in the History of Intolerance in California," *UCLA Law Review* 17 (Nov. 1969): 192–201; Hyung-chan Kim, *A Legal History of Asian Americans, 1790–1990* (Westport, Conn., 1994); Hyung-chan Kim, ed., *Asian Americans and the Supreme Court: A Documentary History* (Westport, Conn., 1992); Milton R. Konvitz, *The Alien and the Asiatic in American Law* (Ithaca, N.Y., 1946); McClain, *In Search of Equality*; Ralph James Mooney, "Matthew Deady and the Federal Judicial Response to Racism in the Early West," *Oregon Law Review* 63 (1984): 561–637; Lucy E. Salyer, *"Laws Harsh as Tigers": Chinese Immigrants and the Shaping of Modern Immigration Law* (Chapel Hill, N.C., 1995); John R. Wunder, "The Chinese and the Courts in the Pacific Northwest: Justice Denied?" *Pacific*

Historical Review 52 (May 1983): 191–211; and John R. Wunder, "Chinese in Trouble: Criminal Law and Race on the Trans-Mississippi Frontier," *Western Historical Quarterly* 17 (Jan. 1986): 25–41. Several of these articles are collected in Charles J. McClain, ed., *Chinese Immigrants and American Law* (New York, 1994).

Although Coolidge provided the first comprehensive treatment of the California thesis, she was not the first to articulate it. See Richmond Mayo-Smith, *Emigration and Immigration: A Study in Social Science* (New York, 1890), chap. 11; Chester Holcombe, "The Restriction of Chinese Immigration," *Outlook* 76, Apr. 23, 1904, 971–77; and Prescott F. Hall, *Immigration and Its Effects upon the United States* (New York, 1906), 327–31.

9. Coolidge, *Chinese Immigration*, chaps. 4–6, 18–20; Crocker quoted in U.S. Senate, *Senate Report no. 689, Joint Special Committee on Chinese*, 44th Cong., 2d sess. (Washington, D.C., 1877), 667; U.S. Bureau of the Census, *The Statistics of the Population of the United States, Embracing the Tables of Race, Nationality, Sex, and Selected Occupations. To Which Are Added the Statistics of School Attendance and Illiteracy, of Schools, Libraries, Newspapers and Periodicals, Churches, Paupers and Crime, and of Areas, Families, and Dwellings. Compiled from the Original Returns of the Ninth Census, (June 1, 1870,) under the Direction of the Secretary of the Interior, by Francis A. Walker, Superintendent of Census* (Washington, D.C., 1872), 1:xvii. On the legal history of state and federal jurisdiction over immigration, see Benjamin Klebaner, "State and Local Immigration Regulation in the United States before 1882," *International Review of Social History* 3 (1958): 269–95. On the first congressional efforts to restrict Chinese immigration, see *CG*, 40th Cong., 2d sess., 163 (Dec. 12, 1867), 837–38 (Jan. 29, 1868).

For general historical accounts of Chinese immigrants and Chinese Americans in California and the United States, see Gunther Barth, *Bitter Strength: A History of the Chinese in the United States, 1850–1870* (Cambridge, Mass., 1964); Sucheng Chan, *This Bittersweet Soil: The Chinese in California Agriculture, 1860–1910* (Berkeley, 1986); Jack Chen, *The Chinese of America* (New York, 1980); Ping Chiu, *Chinese Labor in California, 1850–1880* (Madison, Wisc., 1963); Lucy M. Cohen, *Chinese in the Post–Civil War South: A People without a History* (Baton Rouge, 1984); Roger Daniels, *Asian America: Chinese and Japanese in the United States since 1850* (Seattle, 1988); Loren W. Fessler, ed., *Chinese in America: Stereotyped Past, Changing Present* (New York, 1983); Corinne K. Hoexter, *From Canton to California: The Epic of Chinese Immigration* (New York, 1976); S. W. Kung, *Chinese in American Life: Some Aspects of Their History, Status, Problems, and Contributions* (Westport, Conn., 1962); Rose Hum Lee, *The Chinese in the United States of America* (Hong Kong, 1960); James W. Loewen, *The Mississippi Chinese: Between Black and White* (Cambridge, Mass., 1971); Stanford M. Lyman, *Chinese Americans* (New York, 1974); Ruthanne Lum McCunn, *Chinese American Portraits: Personal Histories, 1828–1988* (San Francisco, 1988); Victor G. Nee and Brett de Bary Nee, *A Documentary Study of an American Chinatown* (New York, 1973); Stan Steiner, *Fusang: The Chinese Who Built America* (New York, 1979); Betty Lee Sung, *Mountain of Gold: The Story of the Chinese in America* (New York, 1967); Takaki, *Strangers from a Different Shore*; Shih-shan Henry Tsai, *The Chinese Experience in America* (Bloomington, Ind., 1986); Judy Yung, *Chinese Women of America: A Pictorial History* (Seattle, 1986); and Kil Young Zo, *Chinese Emigration into the United States, 1850–1880* (New York, 1978). See also two outstanding fictional treatments: Maxine Hong Kingston, *Chinamen* (New York, 1976); and Ruthanne Lum McCunn, *Wooden Fish Songs* (New York, 1995).

10. Coolidge, *Chinese Immigration*, chaps. 7–9, 11, 24; the quotes are from 179 and 182. For comparative studies of Chinese exclusion in other countries, see Charles A. Price, *The Great*

White Walls Are Built: Restrictive Immigration to North America and Australia, 1836–1888 (Canberra, 1974); Andrew Markus, *Fear and Hatred: Purifying Australia and California, 1850–1901* (Sydney, 1979); and Robert E. Wynne, *Reaction to the Chinese in the Pacific Northwest and British Columbia, 1850–1910* (New York, 1978).

11. Elmer Clarence Sandmeyer, *The Anti-Chinese Movement in California* (Urbana, Ill., 1939); the quote is from 110–11. For fuller treatment of the early origins of anti-Chinese sentiment in California during the gold rush era, see Rodman W. Paul, "The Origin of the Chinese Issue in California," *Mississippi Valley Historical Review* 25 (June 1938): 181–96, and Ralph Mann, "Community Change and Caucasian Attitudes toward the Chinese: The Case of Two California Mining Towns, 1850–1870," in *American Workingclass Culture: Explorations in American Labor and Social History*, ed. Milton Cantor (Westport, Conn., 1979), 397–422. For an excellent analysis of the middle-class roots of this early anti-Chinese sentiment and how this sentiment followed and developed from hostility toward other foreigners, including Mexicans, South Americans, Australians, Pacific Islanders, and the French, from 1849 to 1852, see Leonard Pitt, "The Beginnings of Nativism in California," *Pacific Historical Review* 30 (Feb. 1961): 23–38. Paul, Mann, and Pitt cover a neglected period of anti-Chinese hostility in California, but none of them deals directly with the California thesis. Nor does Gunther Barth, who in 1964 offered an alternative explanation for why this hostility emerged. White Americans, Barth argued, resented Chinese immigrants because they perceived them as "sojourners" with no intention of settling permanently in the United States. Barth's theory has generated a lively controversy. See Barth, *Bitter Strength*; Anthony B. Chan, "The Myth of the Chinese Sojourner in Canada," in *Visible Minorities and Multiculturalism: Asians in Canada*, ed. K. V. Ujimoto and G. Hirabayashi (Toronto, 1980); Clarence E. Glick, *Sojourners and Settlers: Chinese Migrants in Hawaii* (Honolulu, 1980); Franklin Ng, "The Sojourner, Return Migration, and Immigration History," in *Chinese America: History and Perspectives, 1987* (San Francisco, 1987); Peter Ward, *White Canada Forever* (Montreal, 1978); Edgar Wickberg et al., *From China to Canada: A History of Chinese Communities in Canada* (Toronto, 1982); and Yuen-fong Woon, "The Voluntary Sojourner among the Overseas Chinese: Myth or Reality?" *Pacific Affairs* 56 (Winter 1983/84): 673–90. For a sociological approach to the subject that focuses on the lack of assimilation of Chinese "sojourners" in the twentieth century, see Paul C. P. Siu, "The Sojourner," *American Journal of Sociology* 58 (July 1952): 34–44.

12. Alexander Saxton, *The Indispensable Enemy: Labor and the Anti-Chinese Movement in California* (Berkeley, 1971), esp. chap. 2; the quotes are from 27 and 36. Wilmot quoted in *CG*, 29th Cong., 2d sess., app., 317 (Feb. 8, 1847), with slight variation in Saxton, *Indispensable Enemy*, 34. Although Saxton provides the most comprehensive analysis of the centrality of anti-Chinese politics to the California labor movement, he was not the first to advance this theory. See two fine earlier works: Eaves, *A History of California Labor Legislation*, and Cross, *A History of the Labor Movement in California*.

13. Saxton, *Indispensable Enemy*, esp. chaps. 4–5, but also chaps. 6–8, 12. The quotes are from 108 and 109.

14. Stuart Creighton Miller, *The Unwelcome Immigrant: The American Image of the Chinese, 1785–1882* (Berkeley, 1969). The quotes are from 112, 157, 191, and 201. Although arguing against it, Miller coined the phrase "California thesis." See ibid., chap. 1. In its posing of a broad-based racism that pervaded nineteenth-century America without regard to class or ideology, Miller's work on the Chinese image largely parallels that of George M. Fredrickson on the black image. See Fredrickson, *The Black Image in the White Mind: The Debate on*

Afro-American Character and Destiny, 1817–1914 (New York, 1971). On the emergence of scientific racial theory and the development of racism in America, see also Thomas F. Gossett, *Race: The History of an Idea in America* (Dallas, 1963); Reginald Horsman, *Race and Manifest Destiny: The Origins of American Racial Anglo-Saxonism* (Cambridge, Mass., 1981); William Stanton, *The Leopard's Spots: Scientific Attitudes toward Race in America, 1815–59* (Chicago, 1960); and Ronald Takaki, *Iron Cages: Race and Culture in Nineteenth-Century America* (New York, 1979).

15. Miller, *Unwelcome Immigrant*, 195–96.

16. John R. Commons et al., *History of Labour in the United States* (New York, 1918), 2:150–51; Selig Perlman, *A History of Trade Unionism in the United States* (New York, 1950; first published 1922), 62; Philip Taft, *Economics and Problems of Labor* (Harrisburg, Pa., 1942), 34; Philip Taft, *Organized Labor in American History* (New York, 1964), 302–4; Joseph G. Rayback, *A History of American Labor* (New York, 1959), 140, 142; Gerald N. Grob, *Workers and Utopia: A Study of Ideological Conflict in the American Labor Movement, 1865–1900* (Evanston, Ill., 1961), 26, 57; Herbert Hill, "Anti-Oriental Agitation and the Rise of Working-Class Racism," *Transaction* 10 (Jan./Feb. 1973): 44–46; Herbert Hill, "Race and Ethnicity in Organized Labor: The Historical Sources of Resistance to Affirmative Action," *Journal of Intergroup Relations* 12 (Winter 1984): 12–16 (see also Herbert Hill, "Race, Ethnicity, and Organized Labor: The Opposition to Affirmative Action," *New Politics* 1 [Winter 1987]: 37–43); Robert D. Parmet, *Labor and Immigration in Industrial America* (Boston, 1981), 28–32, 36; A. T. Lane, *Solidarity or Survival? American Labor and European Immigrants, 1830–1924* (Westport, Conn., 1987), 44; Daniels, *Asian America*, chap. 2, esp. 41–43; Takaki, *Iron Cages*, chap. 10, esp. 232–40, 246; David R. Roediger, *Towards the Abolition of Whiteness: Essays on Race, Politics, and Working Class History* (London, 1994), 23. For similar comments, see also Barth, *Bitter Strength*, chap. 8, esp. 202; Dale Baum, "Woman Suffrage and the 'Chinese Question' in Massachusetts, 1865–1876," *New England Quarterly* 56 (Mar. 1983): 72; Mary Ritter Beard, *The American Labor Movement: A Short History* (New York, 1939), 77, 78; Isabella Black, "American Labour and Chinese Immigration," *Past and Present* 25 (July 1963): 67; John Philip Hall, "The Knights of St. Crispin in Massachusetts, 1869–1878," *Journal of Economic History* 18 (June 1958): 165, 168; and Frederick Rudolph, "Chinamen in Yankeedom: Anti-Unionism in Massachusetts in 1870," *American Historical Review* 53 (Oct. 1947): 25, 29.

17. Gwendolyn Mink, *Old Labor and New Immigrants in American Political Development: Union, Party, and State, 1875–1920* (Ithaca, N.Y., 1986), chaps. 1–3. The quotes are from 43, 67, 71, and 73. See also 64.

18. Ibid., 51, 73, 77, 79, 88–89, 106, 108, 115. The quotes are from 51, 106, 108, and 115.

19. Alexander Saxton, *The Rise and Fall of the White Republic: Class Politics and Mass Culture in Nineteenth-Century America* (London, 1990).

20. Ibid., esp. the introduction and chap. 13. The quote is from 301.

21. David R. Roediger, *The Wages of Whiteness: Race and the Making of the American Working Class* (London, 1991). The quotes are from 7, 168, 169, and 179.

CHAPTER TWO

1. Ralph Waldo Emerson, *The Journals and Miscellaneous Notebooks of Ralph Waldo Emerson*, ed. William H. Gilman, Alfred R. Ferguson, and Merrell R. Davis (Cambridge, Mass., 1961), 2:224, 228–29, 378–79; *NYTr*, Sept. 29, 1854; Bayard Taylor, *A Visit to India,*

China, and Japan, in the Year 1853 (New York, 1855), 354; Samuel Goodrich, *The Tales of Peter Parley about Asia for Children* (Philadelphia, 1859), quoted in Stuart Creighton Miller, *The Unwelcome Immigrant: The American Image of the Chinese, 1785–1882* (Berkeley, 1969), 83; Claude M. Fuess, *The Life of Caleb Cushing* (New York, 1923), 2:230–31. By 1862, Taylor's book had gone through sixteen editions.

2. *New York Star*, Aug. 29, Sept. 24, 1870; *SR*, July 6, 1870; *CGa*, July 11, 1870; Helper quoted in *WA*, Sept. 10 and 17, 1870; *NYT*, Sept. 3, 1865; *NYH*, Oct. 30, 1870.

3. Charles Francis Adams Jr., "The Protection of the Ballot in National Elections: A Paper Read at the General Meeting of the Association, at Albany, New York, February 19th, 1869," *Journal of Social Science* 1 (June 1869): 107, 108, 110 n; Wendell Phillips, "The Chinese," *National Standard*, July 30, 1870; John Stuart Mill (letter) in *NYTr*, July 5, 1870.

4. David Montgomery, *Beyond Equality: Labor and the Radical Republicans, 1862–1872* (New York, 1967), 140–41, chaps. 6, 8.

5. Abbott Emerson Smith, *Colonists in Bondage: White Servitude and Convict Labor in America, 1607–1776* (New York, 1975; first published 1947), 3–4; Charlotte Erickson, *American Industry and the European Immigrant, 1860–1885* (Cambridge, Mass., 1957), 3–5 and accompanying notes; Robert J. Steinfeld, *The Invention of Free Labor: The Employment Relation in English and American Law and Culture, 1350–1870* (Chapel Hill, N.C., 1991), chap. 6.

6. *Seventh Annual Report of the Chamber of Commerce of the State of New York, 1864–5*, quoted in *A Documentary History of American Industrial Society*, ed. John R. Commons et al. (Cleveland, 1910), 9:74–75; James D. Richardson, ed., *A Compilation of the Messages and Papers of the Presidents, 1789–1897* (Washington, D.C., 1897), 7:3383; Erickson, *American Industry*, 6–13; Jonathan Philip Grossman, *William Sylvis, Pioneer of American Labor: A Study of the Labor Movement during the Era of the Civil War*, Columbia University Studies in History, Economics, and Public Law, no. 516 (New York, 1945), 146. The Senate and House passed early versions of the bill in June and the final version on July 2. Lincoln signed it the same day (*CG*, 38th Cong., 1st sess., 896 [Mar. 2, 1864], 1793 [Apr. 21, 1864], 3292 [June 27, 1864], 3495, 3530, 3536 [July 2, 1864]). For a text of the bill, see George P. Sanger, ed., *The Statutes at Large, Treaties, and Proclamations of the United States of America from December 1863, to December 1865* (Boston, 1866), 13:385–87. The law exempted contract laborers from the wartime draft and provided for a commissioner of immigration.

7. Erickson, *American Industry*, 6–7, 17, 24, 27–28, 30, 33–35, 38–44; Souper quoted in *Missouri Democrat*, May 15, 1865, May 15 to May 23, 1865, reprinted in Commons et al., *A Documentary History*, 9:78–80.

8. *Iron Molders' Journal*, May 10, 1864, 15–16; *WA*, Nov. 2, 1867; Grossman, *William Sylvis*, 147; Erickson, *American Industry*, 51–52.

9. Erickson, *American Industry*, 13, 50, 52, 53; Iver Bernstein, *The New York City Draft Riots: Their Significance for American Society and Politics in the Age of the Civil War* (New York, 1990), 211. See also Grossman, *William Sylvis*, 145–49; and Montgomery, *Beyond Equality*, 391.

10. *Detroit Union*, quoted in *National Trades' Review*, May 19, 1866; *Fincher's Trades' Review*, Jan. 6, 1866. Edited by Machinists' and Blacksmiths' International Union president Jonathan Fincher, the Philadelphia-based *Fincher's Trades' Review* became the *National Trades' Review* on March 17, 1866. It folded five months later. For articles attacking importation, see, for example, June 17, 1865.

11. *Fincher's Trades' Review*, Mar. 26, 1864, quoted in Erickson, *American Industry*, 54; Erickson, *American Industry*, 54–58, 61; *International Journal of the Iron Molders' Interna-*

tional Union, Jan. 1867, 310 (see also Oct. 1866, 210); *WA*, Nov. 2, 1867; James C. Sylvis, *The Life, Speeches, Labors and Essays of William H. Sylvis, Late President of the Iron-Moulders' International Union; and Also of the National Labor Union* (Philadelphia, 1872), 186; Grossman, *William Sylvis*, 148. Sylvis's sudden death in 1869 dealt a serious blow to the labor movement. For biographical treatment, see Montgomery, *Beyond Equality*, 223–29, and Grossman, *William Sylvis*.

12. *WA*, Sept. 8, 1866.

13. Erickson, *American Industry*.

14. *WA*, Sept. 1, 1866. On the NLU convention, see Montgomery, *Beyond Equality*, chap. 4, esp. 170–80.

15. *WA*, Aug. 24 (also dated Aug. 31), Nov. 2, 1867.

16. Erickson, *American Industry*, 28–30; *CG*, 39th Cong., 1st. sess., 4040, 4041, 4043 (July 23, 1866). The senator was John Conness (R-Calif.).

17. On "the meaning of freedom," see Eric Foner, *Reconstruction: America's Unfinished Revolution, 1863–1877* (New York, 1988), chap. 3. See also ibid., chaps. 4, 10, 11; and Montgomery, *Beyond Equality*, 230–49.

18. *CG*, 39th Cong., 1st sess., 4040–43 (July 23, 1866).

19. *CG*, 40th Cong., 2d sess., app., 505 (Mar. 30, 1868).

20. Proceedings of the National Labor Congress can be found in *WA*, Oct. 10, 1868.

21. Elmer Clarence Sandmeyer, *The Anti-Chinese Movement in California* (Urbana, Ill., 1939), chap. 3; Alexander Saxton, *The Indispensable Enemy: Labor and the Anti-Chinese Movement in California* (Berkeley, 1971), chap. 4. On the decline of nativism, see John Higham, *Strangers in the Land: Patterns of American Nativism, 1860–1925* (New York, 1975; first published 1955), 14–23; John Higham, "Origins of Immigration Restriction, 1882–1897: A Social Analysis," *Mississippi Valley Historical Review* 39 (June 1952): 77; and Maldwyn Allen Jones, *American Immigration* (Chicago, 1960), 248. For an overview of Burlingame's mission to the United States, see Frederick Wells Williams, *Anson Burlingame and the First Chinese Mission to Foreign Powers* (New York, 1912), esp. chap. 3; Knight Biggerstaff, "The Official Chinese Attitude toward the Burlingame Mission," *American Historical Review* 41 (July 1936): 682–701; and Shih-shan Henry Tsai, *China and the Overseas Chinese in the United States, 1868–1911* (Fayetteville, Ark., 1983), 24–39. For background on Burlingame, see David L. Anderson, *Imperialism and Idealism: American Diplomats in China, 1861–1898* (Bloomington, Ind., 1985), chap. 2. For a day-to-day account of the Chinese legation's travels, see the excellent coverage provided by the *New York Herald*. The quotes from Burlingame can be found in *NYH*, Aug. 23, 1868; and "Speech of Mr. Burlingame at a Municipal Banquet in Boston," in Chinese Legation, *Official Papers of the Chinese Legation* (Berlin, Germany, n.d.), 33, 38–39. Other guests besides Emerson included the mayor of Boston, the governor of Massachusetts, Senator Charles Sumner, and Oliver Wendell Holmes.

22. Williams, *Anson Burlingame*, 128–29, 156–57; *NYH*, June 6, June 10, June 18, July 26, 1868; "Speech of Mr. Burlingame at a Municipal Banquet in Boston," 37–39. For a text of the treaty, see Charles I. Bevans, comp., *Treaties and Other International Agreements of the United States of America, 1776–1949* (Washington, D.C., 1971), 6:680–84. The final version of the treaty was signed on July 28, 1868. On the Senate's last-minute changes, see U.S. Senate, *Journal of the Executive Proceedings of the Senate of the United States of America from December 2, 1867, to March 3, 1869, Inclusive* (Washington, D.C., 1887), 16:355–56. I am

indebted to Rodney A. Ross of the National Archives for bringing this document to my attention.

23. U.S. Senate, *Journal of the Executive Proceedings of the Senate*, 16:356; *NYW*, June 11, 1868; *NYH*, July 15, 1868; Tsai, *China and the Overseas Chinese*, 8–12, 24–29; Kil Young Zo, *Chinese Emigration into the United States, 1850–1880* (New York, 1978), chap. 1; Robert L. Irick, *Ch'ing Policy toward the Coolie Trade, 1847–1878* (Republic of China, 1982), 11–13. See also *NYS*, July 28, 1868; and *CG*, 40th Cong., 2d sess., 163 (Dec. 12, 1867), 837–38 (Jan. 29, 1868). Although the official Senate journal and various newspapers recorded the vote on the Burlingame Treaty as unanimous, Senator Garrett Davis (D-Ky.) claimed two years later that he had voted against it. See *NYH*, July 25, July 26, 1868; *NYS*, July 27, 1868; and *CG*, 41st Cong., 2d sess., 5385 (July 8, 1870). For the proceedings of the National Labor Congress, see *WA*, Oct. 10, 1868; and *NYW*, Sept. 22–26, 1868. Blaine quoted in James G. Blaine, "Mr. Burlingame as an Orator," *Atlantic Monthly*, Nov. 1870, reprinted in James G. Blaine, *Political Discussions Legislative, Diplomatic, and Popular, 1856–1886* (Norwich, Conn., 1887), 107. "Mr. Burlingame's success at Pekin [*sic*]," Blaine wrote, "will always remain the distinguishing feature of his remarkable career" (ibid., 106).

24. *WA*, Feb. 6, 1869.

25. *Hide and Leather Interest and Industrial Review*, quoted in *American Workman*, June 5, 1869. On Chinese being removed from the camera's view, see David Montgomery, *The Fall of the House of Labor: The Workplace, the State, and American Labor Activism, 1865–1925* (New York, 1987), 68.

26. Cummings quoted in *American Workman*, June 5, 1869; *Cincinnati Commercial*, quoted in *WA*, Aug. 14, 1869; *WA*, June 12, 1869; *SFC*, June 27, 1869, reprinted in *NYT*, July 8, 1869; Raphael Pumpelly, "Our Impending Chinese Problem," *Galaxy* 8 (July 1869): 31. After conducting a geologic survey in China, Pumpelly became Harvard's first professor of mining in 1866.

27. *NYTr*, July 6, 1869; *NYS*, July 21, 1869; Lucy M. Cohen, *Chinese in the Post–Civil War South: A People without a History* (Baton Rouge, 1984), 65–66; Lennie Austin Cribbs, "The Memphis Chinese Labor Convention, 1869," *West Tennessee Historical Society Papers* 37 (1983): 74–81; *Memphis Appeal*, June 26, 1869, quoted in ibid., 75; *Montgomery Mail*, June 23, 1869, quoted in Sylvia H. Krebs, "John Chinaman in Reconstruction Alabama: The Debate and the Experience," *Southern Studies* 21 (Winter 1982): 376. On the importation of Chinese from Cuba to Louisiana after the Civil War, see Lucy M. Cohen, *Chinese in the Post–Civil War South*, chap. 3.

28. All the major dailies gave prominent coverage to the Memphis Chinese Labor Convention. See especially the *Memphis Appeal*. The best secondhand accounts are Lucy M. Cohen, *Chinese in the Post–Civil War South*, 66–72; Cribbs, "Memphis Chinese Labor Convention"; and Gunther Barth, *Bitter Strength: A History of the Chinese in the United States, 1850–1870* (Cambridge, Mass., 1964), 189–93. The quote by Tye Kim Orr is from *NYTr*, July 15, 1869.

29. The quotes are from *NYT*, July 21, 1869; and *NYS*, July 21, 1869. For further biographical and descriptive information on Koopmanschap, see *St. Louis Republican*, July 15, 1869, reprinted in *NYT*, July 18, 1869; Barth, *Bitter Strength*, 191–93; and Lucy M. Cohen, *Chinese in the Post–Civil War South*, 69 n. 45.

30. *NYTr*, July 16, July 21, 1869; report quoted in *Memphis Avalanche*, July 16, 1869, reprinted in Commons et al., *A Documentary History*, 9:83. The very language of the report

treated the Chinese as if they were products. It talked of "procuring supplies that may be ordered" and money to be "paid on delivery of the laborer at Memphis" (ibid., 82, 83).

31. *NYT*, July 20, 1869; *NYS*, July 21, July 22, 1869; *NYTr*, July 30, 1869. The quote is from *NYT*, July 14, 1869.

32. George S. Boutwell to James F. Casey, July 23, 1869, reprinted in *New Orleans Picayune*, July 27, 1869, cited in Lucy M. Cohen, *Chinese in the Post–Civil War South*, 73; "An Act to Prohibit the 'Coolie Trade' by American Citizens in American Vessels," in *The Statutes at Large, Treaties, and Proclamations of the United States of America, from December 5, 1859, to March 3, 1863*, ed. George P. Sanger (Boston, 1863), 12:340–41.

33. Eliot noted a chain of shipboard horrors including mutinies, massacres, and murders. Of 50,123 "coolies" shipped from China to Cuba from 1847 to 1859, Eliot said, 7,622 died en route from disease or violence. After passing without opposition, the bill was signed by President Lincoln on February 19, 1862. For Eliot's speech, see *CG*, 37th Cong., 2d sess., 350–52 (Jan. 15, 1862). See also ibid., 16 (Dec. 4, 1861), 375, 377 (Jan. 17, 1862), 555–56 (Jan. 30, 1862), 581–82 (Jan. 31, 1862), 593 (Feb. 4, 1862), 838 (Feb. 14, 1862), 849, 855 (Feb. 17, 1862), and 911 (Feb. 22, 1862).

34. Persia Crawford Campbell, *Chinese Coolie Emigration to Countries within the British Empire* (London, 1923), chap. 3; Irick, *Ch'ing Policy*, 11–13; Parker quoted in Lucy M. Cohen, *Chinese in the Post–Civil War South*, 27; *Random House College Dictionary*, rev. ed. (New York, 1980), 295; Noah Webster, *An American Dictionary of the English Language*, rev. ed. (New York, 1846), 953. In the 1846 edition, the term (spelled "cooly") appeared in the appendix. By 1852, it appeared in the main body of the dictionary. The definition of "coolie" has changed little over the years, with one more recent dictionary defining the term as "an unskilled laborer or porter usu[ally] in or from the Far East hired for low or subsistence wages." The ancient word "kūlī" is accented in numerous ways and likely has Tamil origins as well. See Webster, *An American Dictionary of the English Language* (Springfield, Mass., 1852), 264; Webster and Chauncey A. Goodrich, eds., *An American Dictionary of the English Language* (Philadelphia, 1857), 227; Webster, *An American Dictionary of the English Language* (n.p., 1859), 264; Webster, *An American Dictionary of the English Language* (n.p., 1861), 264; and *Merriam-Webster's Collegiate Dictionary*, 10th ed. (Springfield, Mass., 1993), 255.

Twenty years later, Senator James Z. George (D-Miss.) stated that because the law was so vague and weak no one had ever been prosecuted under it (*CR*, 47th Cong., 1st sess., 3404 [Apr. 28, 1882]. See also the speech of Representative A. Herr Smith (R-Pa.), ibid., app., 50 [Mar. 16, 1882]).

On the "coolie" trade, see Irick, *Ch'ing Policy*, 2–6, 46–60; Elliot Campbell Arensmeyer, "British Merchant Enterprise and the Chinese Coolie Trade: 1850–1874" (Ph.D. diss., University of Hawaii, 1979); Tin-yuke Char and Wai Jane Char, "The First Chinese Contract Laborers in Hawaii, 1852," *Hawaiian Journal of History* 9 (1975): 128–34; M. Foster Farley, "The Chinese Coolie Trade, 1845–1875," *Journal of Asian and African Studies* 3 (July and Oct. 1968): 257–70; and Arnold Joseph Meagher, *The Introduction of Chinese Laborers to Latin America: The "Coolie Trade," 1847–1874* (San Francisco, 1978).

35. Lucy M. Cohen, *Chinese in the Post–Civil War South*, 73–74; *NYT*, July 24, July 25, July 26, 1869.

36. *Memphis Avalanche*, July 18, 1869, reprinted in *NYH*, July 25, 1869; *St. Louis Republican*, July 15, 1869, reprinted in *NYT*, July 18, 1869; *NYT*, July 18, July 19, July 20, July 26, July 31, 1869; *NYS*, July 21, Aug. 16, 1869; *NYTr*, July 21, July 29, Aug. 9, Aug. 13, 1869; *Omaha Herald*, quoted in *NYTr*, Aug. 14, 1869 (see also *NYS*, Aug. 2, Sept. 15, 1869); Lucy M. Cohen,

Chinese in the Post–Civil War South, 80–81; *St. Louis Republican*, quoted in R. W. Hume (letter) in *WA*, Aug. 21, 1869.

37. R. W. Hume, "John Chinaman," in *WA*, Aug. 21, 1869; *Irish Republic*, quoted in *National Anti-Slavery Standard*, Aug. 7, 1869.

38. R. W. Hume (letters) in *WA*, May 15, June 26, July 17, July 24, Aug. 7, Aug. 21, 1869. Whereas Hume's letters and poems in the *Workingman's Advocate* focused heavily on the alleged evils of Chinese immigration and its effects on American workers, his articles in the *National Anti-Slavery Standard* and its successor, the *National Standard*, seldom mentioned the subject. See, for example, *National Anti-Slavery Standard*, Aug. 28, Sept. 4, Nov. 20, 1869; and *National Standard*, Apr. 16, Sept. 10, Oct. 15, Oct. 22, Dec. 17, 1870.

39. See, for example, "Mountaineer" (letter) in *WA*, July 10, 1869; J. T. C. (letter) in ibid., July 31, 1869; and "H" (letter) in ibid., Aug. 7, 1869. George Prindle (letter) in *WA*, July 17, 1869 (see also George Prindle [letter] in ibid., July 31, 1869); Zerob (letter) in ibid., Aug. 21, 1869.

40. *WA*, Sept. 14, 1869; *NYTr*, Aug. 17, 1869.

41. *NYTr*, Aug. 20, Aug. 23, 1869; *WA*, Sept. 4, Sept. 11, 1869; R. W. Hume (letter) in ibid., Sept. 4, 1869.

42. *NYTr*, Aug. 23, 1869.

43. *CG*, 41st Cong., 2d sess., 3 (Dec. 6, 1869), 86 (Dec. 13, 1869), 300–301 (Dec. 22, 1869).

44. Ibid., 1389 (Feb. 18, 1870), 2895 (Apr. 22, 1870), 2950 (Apr. 25, 1870), 3238 (May 5, 1870), 4126 (June 6, 1870), 5124 (July 2, 1870), 5150–51 (July 4, 1870), 5387 (July 8, 1870).

45. Ibid., 4112 (June 6, 1870), 4275–79, 4284 (June 9, 1870), 4317–18 (June 10, 1870), app., 410 (May 27, 1870), 452–53 (June 9, 1870).

46. Ibid., 4538–39 (June 17, 1870), 4754–55 (June 23, 1870).

CHAPTER THREE

1. "Testimony of C. T. Sampson," in Massachusetts Bureau of the Statistics of Labor, *Report of the Bureau of Statistics of Labor, Embracing the Account of Its Operations and Inquiries from March 1, 1870, to March 1, 1871* (Boston, 1871), 98–107. See also the testimony of Alfred L. Wood, Daniel Luther, Oliver A. Brown, W. E. Haskins, Isaac Tyler, Edward Gregson, L. W. Lemoine, and Lucius A. Ellis, and "Conclusions," in ibid., 108–17. *SR*, June 18, 1870; *Boston Advertiser*, June 15, 1870, reprinted in *NYS*, June 18, 1870. On Sampson, see *Adams Transcript*, Mar. 24, 1870; Frederick Rudolph, "Chinamen in Yankeedom: Anti-Unionism in Massachusetts in 1870," *American Historical Review* 53 (Oct. 1947): 7–9, 12–13. On North Adams, see *Adams Transcript*, Oct. 6, 1870; Timothy Coogan, "The Forging of a New England Mill Town: North and South Adams, Massachusetts, 1780–1880" (Ph.D. diss., New York University, 1992); Willis F. Spear, *History of North Adams, Mass., 1749–1885* (North Adams, 1885); and S. Proctor Thayer, "Adams and North Adams," in *History of Berkshire County, Massachusetts*, vol. 1 (New York, 1885). On the Crispins, see David Montgomery, *Beyond Equality: Labor and the Radical Republicans, 1862–1872* (New York, 1967), 141–42, 369; Alan Dawley, *Class and Community: The Industrial Revolution in Lynn* (Cambridge, Mass., 1976), chaps. 5–8; and Don D. Lescohier, *The Knights of St. Crispin, 1867–1874: A Study in the Industrial Causes of Trade Unionism*, Bulletin of the University of Wisconsin, no. 355, Economics and Political Science Series, vol. 7, no. 1 (Madison, 1910). Lescohier must be used with great caution.

2. "Testimony of C. T. Sampson," 103–7. Although Sampson tried to keep the contract

secret, several newspapers published its contents. See, for example, *Adams Transcript*, Aug. 18, 1870.

3. *WA*, June 11, 1870.

4. *Boston Advertiser*, June 15, 1870, reprinted in *NYS*, June 18, 1870; *NYS*, June 22, 1870; *SR*, June 13, June 15, June 18, 1870; *NYH*, June 26, 1870. The Chinese arrived in North Adams just in time to be counted for the 1870 census, which recorded their names and ages. According to the census, there were 7 Chinese aged fourteen; 16 aged fifteen; 16 aged sixteen; 16 aged seventeen; 11 aged eighteen; 1 aged nineteen; 2 aged twenty-two; 1 aged twenty-six; 2 aged twenty-eight; and 3 in their thirties (U.S. Bureau of the Census, *Population Schedules of the Ninth Census of the United States*, Microfilm roll 601, Massachusetts, 2, Berkshire County [Washington, D.C., 1965], 301–3).

5. *NYTr*, June 18, 1870.

6. *NYH*, June 26, 1870; *SR*, June 25, 1870; *Albany Journal*, June 23, 1870.

7. *NYH*, June 26, 1870; *SR*, June 15, 1870; *Albany Journal*, June 25, 1870; *Boston Advertiser*, reprinted in *NYH*, June 21, 1870; Massachusetts Bureau of the Statistics of Labor, *Report*, 108–15. Crispins may have taken heart from a point noted by the *Report*, which hinted that the Chinese could "learn and practice both combination and strike, as they have done in their own country with fearful result, or as in Calcutta, where, as the London *Spectator* declares, they have built the most powerful trade-union in the world" (ibid., 116–17).

8. *NYS*, July 1, 1870. The New York City meeting received wide coverage. For the most complete accounts, see July 1 editions of the *New York Tribune*, *Sun*, and *Herald*.

9. *NYS*, July 1, 1870; *NYTr*, July 1, 1870; *NYH*, July 1, 1870.

10. *NYS*, July 1, 1870; *NYH*, July 1, 1870; *NYT*, July 1, 1870.

11. Iron Molders' International Union, *Proceedings of the Tenth Session of the Iron Molders' International Union, in Convention Assembled, at Philadelphia, July 6th, 1870* (Philadelphia, 1870), 51–52 (see also 75); *WA*, July 2, July 9, July 30, Aug. 13, Nov. 5 and 12, 1870; *Rochester Democrat*, June 25, 1870. *CGa*, June 27, July 9, 1870; *Missouri Republican*, July 8, July 12, 1870; *Albany Journal*, June 23, 1870; *NYTr*, July 1, 1870. The New York Workingmen's Assembly in Albany had taken the identical stance the previous winter (*WA*, Feb. 5, 1870).

12. *NYTr*, July 22, 1870.

13. Stuart Creighton Miller, *The Unwelcome Immigrant: The American Image of the Chinese, 1785–1882* (Berkeley, 1969), 177.

14. *NYTr*, June 30, 1870. Swinton's manifesto was later reprinted as a sixteen-page pamphlet. See John Swinton, *The New Issue: The Chinese-American Question* (New York, 1870). On Swinton, see Richard O. Boyer and Herbert M. Morais, *Labor's Untold Story* (New York, 1980; first published 1955), 80–81; and *National Cyclopedia of American Biography* (New York, 1924), 8:251.

15. John R. Commons et al., eds., *A Documentary History of American Industrial Society* (Cleveland, 1910), 9:257–59, 262; *CE*, Aug. 18, 1870; *WA*, Aug. 27, 1870; *CGa*, Aug. 20, 1870.

16. *CGa*, Aug. 22, 1870; *NYTr*, Aug. 22, Aug. 25, 1870; *WA*, Aug. 27, 1870; Montgomery, *Beyond Equality*, 124.

17. Commons, *A Documentary History*, 9:266–67; *CGa*, Sept. 13, 1870. For historians who have misread this resolution, see, for example, John R. Commons et al., *History of Labour in the United States* (New York, 1918), 2:150–51; Selig Perlman, *A History of Trade Unionism in the United States* (New York, 1950; first published 1922), 62 and note; Rudolph, "Chinamen in Yankeedom," 25; John Philip Hall, "The Knights of St. Crispin in Massachusetts, 1869–1878," *Journal of Economic History* 18 (June 1958): 165, 168; Gerald N. Grob, *Workers and Utopia: A*

Study of Ideological Conflict in the American Labor Movement, 1865–1900 (Evanston, Ill., 1961), 57; Isabella Black, "American Labour and Chinese Immigration," *Past and Present* 25 (July 1963): 67; Dale Baum, "Woman Suffrage and the 'Chinese Question' in Massachusetts, 1865–1876," *New England Quarterly* 56 (Mar. 1983): 72; and A. T. Lane, *Solidarity or Survival? American Labor and European Immigrants, 1830–1924* (Westport, Conn., 1987), 44. See also Miller, *Unwelcome Immigrant*, 196–97; and Alexander Saxton, *The Indispensable Enemy: Labor and the Anti-Chinese Movement in California* (Berkeley, 1971), 105.

18. *New York Star*, Apr. 26, 1871; *WA*, Sept. 10 and 17, 1870, Sept. 23, 1871, Mar. 21, 1874; *NYH*, June 26, 1871; Montgomery, *Beyond Equality*, 191, 192, 198, 373, 401; platform quoted in *Boston Transcript*, Sept. 8, 1870; *NYTr*, Sept. 9, 1870. The *Workingman's Advocate* also noted Cummings's "amiable disposition." The Crispin leader became impoverished and died of consumption in 1874, leaving a wife and four children. He was forty-two years old.

19. *Boston Transcript*, Sept. 8, 1870; Wendell Phillips, "The Chinese," *National Standard*, July 30, 1870; *WA*, Aug. 13, Oct. 1, 1870. Phillips praised the platform and accepted the nomination. Two other parties also nominated Phillips for governor: the Woman Suffrage Party and the Prohibitory Party. Phillips had long supported woman suffrage but was not a prohibitionist. In the general election, Phillips received 21,900 votes (14.5 percent) (Montgomery, *Beyond Equality*, 369–70).

20. *NYS*, June 22, 1870; *Boston Advertiser*, reprinted in ibid.; *NYS*, Dec. 14, 1870; *Hampshire Gazette and Northampton Courier*, June 28, 1870; Lucy M. Cohen, *Chinese in the Post–Civil War South: A People without a History* (Baton Rouge, 1984), 76–78, 89–91, 95; *SR*, June 24, Sept. 9, 1870; *WA*, Sept. 24, 1870; *Boston Commonwealth*, Aug. 20, 1870.
Palmer found that many clients wanted Chinese as domestics, so he revised his plans to import workers singly rather than "in colonies" (*SR*, Sept. 9, 1870).

21. A leading member of Sisson, Wallace was a brother of Central Pacific Railroad president Charles Crocker. On the firm providing Chinese laborers for the railroad, see U.S. Senate, *Senate Report no. 689, Joint Special Committee on Chinese*, 44th Cong., 2d sess. (Washington, D.C., 1877), 674. The *Trans-Continental* was a novelty newspaper published from a printing press taken aboard the first railroad car to cross the country and return, from May to July 1870. The advertisement appeared in eight issues: May 24 (Niagara Falls); May 26 (Omaha); May 27 (Cheyenne, Wyo.); June 25 (San Francisco); June 27 (Promontory Point, Utah); June 28 (Laramie, Wyo.); June 30 (Burlington, Iowa); and July 4, 1870 (Boston).

22. *NYS*, June 18, July 9, July 11, 1870; *NYTr*, June 30, 1870; *Boston Transcript*, July 5, July 12, Aug. 1, 1870; *SR*, July 29, 1870; *WA*, Sept. 24, 1870; *St. Louis Republican*, July 30, 1870; *New York Star*, Aug. 10, 1870.

23. *Utica Observer*, reprinted in *Albany Journal*, June 20, 1870; *NYTr*, July 2, Aug. 31, 1870; *NYH*, June 26, 1870; *Punchinello*, July 23, 1870, 265; *Boston Advertiser*, reprinted in *NYS*, June 22, 1870; *NYS*, Aug. 31, Sept. 2, 1870; R. W. Hume, "Chow-Chow and His Friends," in *WA*, Jan. 1, 1870; Massachusetts Bureau of the Statistics of Labor, *Report*, 461–63.

24. *SR*, July 9, 1870; *Nation*, July 7, 1870; *CGa*, June 27, 1870. The two historians quoted are, respectively, Rudolph, "Chinamen in Yankeedom," 28, and Miller, *Unwelcome Immigrant*, 75. In his antiquarian account of the incident at North Adams, Rudolph downplayed the significance of the event and made numerous factual errors. He based his article on just a handful of sources, and as a consequence, he misstated the ages of the Chinese immigrants, misunderstood the position of eastern workers, and failed to place the event in appropriate historical context.

25. *NYTr*, July 5, 1870; *Boston Commonwealth*, July 9, 1870. President Ulysses S. Grant and Rev. Henry Ward Beecher also delivered speeches but said nothing on the Chinese.

26. *NYTr*, July 5, 1870; *Boston Commonwealth*, July 9, 1870; Charlotte Erickson, *American Industry and the European Immigrant, 1860–1885* (Cambridge, Mass., 1957), 163; *Dictionary of American Biography* (New York, 1931), 4:421. Hawley edited the *Hartford Evening Press* during its association with the American Emigrant Company in the 1860s. When the *Press* merged with the *Hartford Courant* in 1867, Hawley became editor of the *Courant*.

27. *CG*, 41st Cong., 2d sess., 5121 (July 2, 1870); Act of March 26, 1790, chap. 3, 1 Stat. 103, quoted in Charles J. McClain, *In Search of Equality: The Chinese Struggle against Discrimination in Nineteenth-Century America* (Berkeley, 1994), 70.

28. *CG*, 41st Cong., 2d sess., 5122 (July 2, 1870), 5152, 5159–61, 5168–69, 5175–77 (July 4, 1870); 5386, 5389 (July 8, 1870).

29. Ibid., 5123 (July 2, 1870), 5156, 5173 (July 4, 1870). On the origin of Sumner's amendment, see ibid., 40th Cong., 1st sess., 728–29 (July 19, 1867); ibid., 3d sess., 1159 (Feb. 13, 1869); and ibid., 41st Cong., 2d sess., 5123 (July 2, 1870), 5154–55 (July 4, 1870).

30. Ibid., 41st Cong., 2d sess., 5123, 5124 (July 2, 1870), 5173, 5176, 5177 (July 4, 1870). The racist wording of the nation's naturalization laws remained in effect until 1952. See Roger Daniels, *Asian America: Chinese and Japanese in the United States since 1850* (Seattle, 1988), 43–44, chaps. 6–7.

31. Ibid., 5124 (July 2, 1870), 5149, 5161–62, 5171, 5175 (July 4, 1870).

32. Ibid., 5125 (July 2, 1870), 5151 (July 4, 1870).

33. *Dictionary of American Biography* (New York, 1936), 9:14; William M. Stewart, *Reminiscence of Senator William M. Stewart of Nevada*, ed. George Rothwell Brown (New York, 1908), esp. 21, 26, 77–78, 151, 167, 199–201, 205, 219–24, 231–38. See also Russell R. Elliott, *Servant of Power: A Political Biography of Senator William M. Stewart* (Reno, 1983); William Gillette, *The Right to Vote: Politics and the Passage of the Fifteenth Amendment* (Baltimore, 1965), 55–61, 67, 71, 78, 79, 157–58, 159; and McClain, *In Search of Equality*, 37–40. There is some confusion over Stewart's date of birth, some placing it in 1827. See *Dictionary of American Biography*, 9:13, 15.

On May 25 along strict party lines, the Senate passed the Civil Rights Act of 1870, 48 to 11 (with 13 not voting). The House passed it 133 to 58 (with 39 not voting) on May 27, and it became law on May 31, 1870 (*CG*, 41st Cong., 2d sess., 3809 [May 25, 1870], 3884 [May 27, 1870]). The Civil Rights Act of 1866 had guaranteed legal rights to "all citizens." In drafting the clause of the Civil Rights Act of 1870, Senator Stewart extended these rights to "all persons," whether citizens or not, thus including Chinese immigrants. The 1870 law ultimately invalidated the many discriminatory taxes levied against the Chinese in California and overturned the state's ban on Chinese giving testimony in court against whites. Stewart's close connection to the Central Pacific Railroad no doubt contributed to his attitude toward Chinese immigration, but the Nevada senator may have had deeper, personal motives for sponsoring the Civil Rights Act in 1870. Seventeen years earlier, a Nevada County, California, jury had convicted a white man of murdering a Chinese immigrant, largely on the testimony of three Chinese witnesses. In 1854, California chief justice Hugh C. Murray overturned the verdict, ruling that Chinese, like blacks and American Indians, could not give evidence in court against whites. Thus, the murderer went free. Setting a precedent, which California enacted into law in 1863, Murray's ruling barred Chinese from testifying against whites in state courts—a fateful decision that left Chinese immigrants defenseless before the law. The district attorney who had prosecuted the murder case in 1853 was twenty-eight-year-old William Stewart. For an excellent overview, see McClain, *In Search of Equality*, 20–23, 29–42.

In his largely negative biography, Elliott condenses Stewart's contributions to the 1870 Senate debate on the Chinese to one paragraph and completely ignores the senator's careful distinctions between immigration and importation. He also ignores Stewart's contribution to the Civil Rights Act of 1870.

Stewart had met and befriended Twain in California and the senator considered him "a member of my family." The two men later had a falling out, and in his book *Roughing It*, Twain accused Stewart of cheating him in a business deal.

In 1871, President Grant offered Stewart a seat on the Supreme Court, which Stewart declined. He retired from the Senate in 1875 and was reelected twelve years later. After flirting with the Populists in the 1890s, he returned to the Republicans and served until 1905, capping a remarkable Senate career of twenty-nine years. In a curious sidenote, the mansion he built on Dupont Circle in Washington later served as the residence of the Chinese minister to the United States (Elliott, *Servant of Power*, 65, 66; Mark Twain, *Roughing It* [New York, 1962; first published 1871], 232–33; Stewart, *Reminiscence*, 17, 219–24, 261, 278, 318; *Letters of Mrs. James G. Blaine*, ed. Harriet S. Blaine Beale [New York, 1908], 1:204 and 204 n).

34. *CG*, 41st Cong., 2d sess., 5155–58 (July 4, 1870).

35. Ibid., 5150–51 (July 4, 1870), 5379, 5382–86, 5388 (July 8, 1870).

36. Indicative of the Republican split on the issue, Radical Republican Ben Wade, former Senate pro tem, squarely endorsed the right to import workers, whereas Charles Sumner (although he backed the American Emigrant Company) opposed it. On Wade, see Baum, "Woman Suffrage," 73; on Sumner, see Jonathan Philip Grossman, *William Sylvis, Pioneer of American Labor: A Study of the Labor Movement during the Era of the Civil War*, Columbia University Studies in History, Economics, and Public Law, no. 516 (New York, 1945), 146, and *CG*, 41st Cong., 2d sess., 4539 (June 17, 1870). For Senator Cameron's comment, see *CG*, 41st Cong., 2d sess., 5390 (July 8, 1870).

37. *Boston Commonwealth*, June 25, 1870; *SR*, Sept. 24, 1870; *CGa*, July 9, 1870; *NYTr*, June 18, June 24, June 30, July 7, July 28, 1870.

38. *National Anti-Slavery Standard*, Aug. 21, 1869, Apr. 16, 1870; Frederick Douglass to Charles Sumner, July 6, 1870, reprinted in Frederick Douglass, *The Life and Writings of Frederick Douglass: Reconstruction and After*, ed. Philip S. Foner (New York, 1955), 4:222; George W. Julian, "The Coolie Traffic and the Land Question," *National Standard*, Aug. 6, 1870; William Lloyd Garrison, "Hostility to the Chinese," *New York Independent*, Aug. 18, 1870. See also Frederick Douglass, "Composite Nation" (lecture in the Parker Fraternity Course, Boston, 1867), Frederick Douglass Papers, Douglass Memorial Home, Anacostia, Washington, D.C., and David J. Hellwig, "Black Reactions to Chinese Immigration and the Anti-Chinese Movement, 1850–1910," *Amerasia* 6 (1979): 28–29.

39. Howe quoted in *Woman's Journal*, July 16, 1870, 217; L. Maria Child (letter) in *National Standard*, Sept. 17, 1870; Blackwell quoted in *Woman's Journal*, July 16, 1870, 221; James M. Ashley (letter) in *National Standard*, Oct. 1, 1870. Phillips called Ashley's letter "simply atrocious" (ibid.). On Ashley, see *Dictionary of American Biography* (New York, 1943), 1:389–90.

40. Child (letter) in *National Standard*, Sept. 17, 1870. On Irish American attitudes toward slavery and abolition, see Iver Bernstein, *The New York City Draft Riots: Their Significance for American Society and Politics in the Age of the Civil War* (New York, 1990), and David R. Roediger, *The Wages of Whiteness: Race and the Making of the American Working Class* (London, 1991), chap. 7. On the abolitionists' split over women's rights, see Ellen Carol

DuBois, *Feminism and Suffrage: The Emergence of an Independent Women's Movement in America, 1848–1869* (Ithaca, N.Y., 1978).

41. Eric Foner, *Politics and Ideology in the Age of the Civil War* (New York, 1980), 126; Troup quoted in *SR*, July 1, 1870; Saxton, *Indispensable Enemy*, 36. On working-class contributions to and participation in the abolitionist movement, see Debra Gold Hansen, *Strained Sisterhood: Class and Gender in the Boston Female Anti-Slavery Society* (Amherst, Mass., 1993); John Jentz, "The Antislavery Constituency in Jacksonian New York City," *Civil War History* 27 (June 1981): 101–22; Bruce Laurie, "The 'Fair Field' of the 'Middle Ground': Abolitionism, Labor Reform, and the Making of an Antislavery Bloc in Antebellum Massachusetts" (unpublished paper in the possession of the author, 1995); Edward Magdol, *The Antislavery Rank and File: A Social Profile of the Abolitionists' Constituency* (Westport, Conn., 1986); and Leonard L. Richards, *"Gentlemen of Property and Standing": Anti-Abolition Mobs in Jacksonian America* (New York, 1970).

CHAPTER FOUR

1. *SR*, Sept. 24, 1870. The journals that sent reporters to North Adams included the *Albany Times, Boston Advertiser, Boston Herald, Frank Leslie's Illustrated Newspaper, Harper's Weekly, New York Globe, New York Tribune, New York World, Springfield Republican*, and *Troy Times*.

2. The worker quoted was the indefatigable labor activist and feminist Jennie Collins (*NYH*, June 30, 1870). On the depth of the depression, the literature is tremendous. For a fine overview, see Eric Foner, *Reconstruction: America's Unfinished Revolution, 1863–1877* (New York, 1988), chap. 11. In September 1870, James B. Hervey imported about seventy Chinese laborers to wash and iron shirts at his laundry establishment in Belleville, New Jersey. Workers' response to this action echoed that of workers in North Adams. For an overview, see Daniel Leistman, "Chinese Labor at the Passaic Steam Laundry in Belleville," *New Jersey History* 112 (Spring/Summer 1994): 20–33.

3. On the introduction of bills relating to importation or contract labor, see *CG*, 41st Cong., 3d sess., 58 (Dec. 12, 1870); ibid., 42d Cong., 1st sess., 78 (Mar. 13, 1871); ibid., 2d sess., 1581 (Mar. 11, 1872), 2909 (Apr. 30, 1872); ibid., 3d sess., 450 (Jan. 9, 1873), 1295 (Feb. 12, 1873); *CR*, 43d Cong., 1st sess., 925 (Jan. 26, 1874); ibid., 2d sess., 2 (Dec. 7, 1874), 32 (Dec. 9, 1874); and ibid., 44th Cong., 1st sess., 194 (Dec. 13, 1875). The only bill remotely connected to contract labor that passed in this period was an 1874 law stating that "whoever shall . . . bring into the United States . . . any person inveigled or kidnaped in any other country, with intent to hold such person in involuntary confinement or to any involuntary service . . . shall be deemed guilty of felony." This act aimed to outlaw the Italian padrone system and was never directed against the Chinese (*CR*, 43d Cong., 2d sess., 4443 [June 1, 1874]. See also Gunther Peck, "Reinventing Free Labor: Immigrant Padrones and Contract Laborers in North America, 1885–1925," *Journal of American History* 83 [Dec. 1996]: 848–71).

4. For Mungen's speech, see *CG*, 41st Cong., 3d sess., 351–60 (Jan. 7, 1871).

5. The "anti-coolie" act stated that "a permit or certificate shall be prepared and signed by the consul or consular agent of the United States . . . containing the name of such person, and setting forth the fact of his voluntary emigration . . . but the same shall not be given until such consul or consular agent shall be first personally satisfied by evidence produced of the truth of the facts stated therein" (George P. Sanger, ed., *The Statutes at Large, Treaties,*

and Proclamations of the United States of America, from December 5, 1859, to March 3, 1863 [Boston, 1863], 12:340–41).

6. Doc. 43 in U.S. Congress, *Papers Relating to the Foreign Relations of the United States Transmitted to Congress with the Annual Message of the President, December 4, 1871, Preceded by a Synoptical List of Papers and Followed by an Alphabetical Index of Persons and Subjects* (Washington, D.C., 1871), 207–10. The document is dated April 25, 1871. As noted in Chap. 2, "coolie" was also spelled "cooly."

7. Ibid., Doc. 47 (enclosures 63 [Sept. 12, 1871], 74 [Aug. 14, 1871], 392 [Aug. 15, 1871], 430 [Sept. 11, 1871]), 219–21; Mary Roberts Coolidge, *Chinese Immigration* (New York, 1909), 49 n. 13; George Anthony Peffer, "Forbidden Families: Emigration Experiences of Chinese Women under the Page Law, 1875–1882," *Journal of American Ethnic History* 6 (Fall 1986): 28–46 (see esp. 31–35). See also Lucie Cheng Hirata, "Free, Indentured, Enslaved: Chinese Prostitutes in Nineteenth-Century America," *Signs* 5 (Autumn 1979): 3–29. It should be noted as well that the charges against Bailey, which had nothing to do with his 1871 investigation, were not leveled until 1879, long after he issued his report.

8. Winn quoted in *WA*, May 13, 1871; *WA*, June 3, Sept. 30, 1871, Feb. 15, June 21, 1873, Mar. 28, 1874. Cameron also ran a lengthy anti-Chinese series (ibid., Aug. 24, Aug. 31, Sept. 7, Sept. 14, Oct. 5, Oct. 12, Nov. 16, 1872) and a hysterically anti-Chinese poem (Sam Booth, "They Are Coming," ibid., Aug. 2, 1873). For Mungen's speech, see ibid., Feb. 4, Feb. 11, Feb. 18, Feb. 25, Mar. 4, Mar. 11, and Mar. 18, 1871. A carpenter by trade, the Virginia-born Winn was a prominent leader of the anti-Chinese and eight-hour-day movements in California. See Lucile Eaves, *A History of California Labor Legislation, with an Introductory Sketch of the San Francisco Labor Movement*, University of California Publications in Economics, vol. 2 (Berkeley, 1910), 21–22, and Ira B. Cross, *A History of the Labor Movement in California* (Berkeley, 1935), chap. 4.

9. *WA*, Oct. 4, 1873; U.S. House of Representatives, *Petition of the Citizens of Beaver County, Pennsylvania, relative to Chinese Laborers, Feb. 3, 1873*, 42d Cong., 3d sess., Misc. Doc. 81 (Washington, D.C., 1873); W. J. N. (letter) in *NYTr*, Aug. 27, 1872; Mason quoted in *WA*, Feb. 8, 1873. On threats to import Chinese laborers, see *NYS*, Dec. 3, Dec. 6, Dec. 14, 1870; *WA*, Feb. 4, Apr. 29, 1871; *NYT*, Apr. 25, 1871; and Leistman, "Chinese Labor," 29.

10. *Proceedings of the Eleventh Session of the Iron Molders' International Union in Convention Assembled, at Troy, N.Y., July 10, 1872* (Cincinnati, 1872), 16–18, 60. See also *Iron Molders' International Journal*, Sept. 30, 1872, 7–8, Oct. 31, 1872, 3, 5, Mar. 31, 1873, 3, and Apr. 30, 1873, 8.

11. *Iron Molders' International Journal*, June 30, 1873, 9; *Iron Molders' Journal*, Oct. 10, 1874, 65. See also *Iron Molders' International Journal*, Oct. 31, 1872, 5; *CGa*, quoted in ibid., June 30, 1873, 5; and *Iron Molders' Journal*, Nov. 10, 1874, 98. (Both the Iron Molders' International Union and the *Iron Molders' International Journal* dropped the word "international" from their names in 1874. Ironworkers were lobbying Congress to incorporate the union, and lawmakers frowned on the word "international.")

12. *Allegheny Mail*, reprinted in *NYH*, Sept. 27, 1874; Herbert G. Gutman, "The Workers' Search for Power in the Gilded Age," in Gutman, *Power and Culture: Essays on the American Working Class*, ed. Ira Berlin (New York, 1987), 90–91; *Pittsburgh Leader*, reprinted in *WA*, Oct. 3 and 10, 1874; *NYTr*, Sept. 28, 1874; John Higham, *Strangers in the Land: Patterns of American Nativism, 1860–1925* (New York, 1975; first published 1955), 48; *Iron Molders' Journal*, Nov. 10, 1874, 104–5.

13. *Allegheny Mail*, reprinted in *NYH*, Sept. 27, 1874; *WA*, Oct. 24, 1874; Herbert G. Gutman, "Labor in the Land of Lincoln: Coal Miners on the Prairie," in Gutman, *Power and*

Culture, 150–56, 175–85; Higham, *Strangers in the Land*, 47–48; James C. Sylvis, *The Life, Speeches, Labors and Essays of William H. Sylvis, Late President of the Iron-Moulders' International Union; and Also of the National Labor Union* (Philadelphia, 1872), 186.

14. *WA*, Aug. 19, 1871, Mar. 2, Mar. 16, 1872; *Hartford Labor Journal*, reprinted in ibid., Apr. 27, 1872. See also *WA*, Sept. 21, 1872.

15. *WA*, July 19, July 26, 1873, Apr. 25, 1874, Apr. 24, 1875. On the National Labor Union, its foray into presidential politics, and the organization's subsequent collapse, see David Montgomery, *Beyond Equality: Labor and the Radical Republicans, 1862–1872* (New York, 1967), chaps. 4, 10. Justice Davis had hoped the National Labor Reform Party nomination would boost his chances for a spot on the Democratic or Liberal Republican tickets. When this failed to materialize, Davis withdrew, leaving the party stillborn. In the crazy election year of 1872, one can only speculate what may have happened had the Labor Reformers selected a different candidate, such as Wendell Phillips, whose name had been placed in nomination at the convention by delegate Samuel P. Cummings (*WA*, Mar. 2, 1872).

16. U.S. Bureau of the Census, *The Statistics of the Population of the United States, Embracing the Tables of Race, Nationality, Sex, and Selected Occupations. To Which Are Added the Statistics of School Attendance and Illiteracy, of Schools, Libraries, Newspapers and Periodicals, Churches, Paupers and Crime, and of Areas, Families, and Dwellings. Compiled from the Original Returns of the Ninth Census, (June 1, 1870,) under the Direction of the Secretary of the Interior, by Francis A. Walker, Superintendent of Census* (Washington, D.C., 1872), 1:xvii (hereafter referred to as *Ninth Census*); U.S. Bureau of the Census, *Statistics of the Population of the United States at the Tenth Census (June 1, 1880), Embracing Extended Tables of the Population of States, Counties, and Minor Civil Divisions, with Distinctions of Race, Sex, Age, Nativity, and Occupations; together with Summary Tables, Derived from Other Census Reports, Relating to Newspapers and Periodicals; Public Schools and Illiteracy; the Dependent, Defective, and Delinquent Classes, Etc.* (Washington, D.C., 1883), 3. Sampson imported fifty more Chinese to North Adams in the early 1870s, bringing the total in his factory to more than a hundred. On prejudice and racist legislation in the North, see Leon F. Litwack, *North of Slavery: The Negro in the Free States, 1790–1860* (Chicago, 1961), esp. chap. 3, and William Gillette, *The Right to Vote: Politics and the Passage of the Fifteenth Amendment* (Baltimore, 1965). The total population of the United States in 1870 was 38,925,598, and in 1880, 50,155,783.

The census likely undercounted the total number of Chinese in the United States. In 1880, for example, it counted 909 Chinese in New York State, but the *New York Herald* estimated in March 1879 that there were 1,800 in New York City alone and raised the number to almost 3,000 by year's end. (The *Herald* also estimated the city's Chinese businesses: 300 laundries, 50 grocery stores, 20 tobacco stores, 10 drugstores, and 6 restaurants.) The *New York Times* estimated the Chinese population in New York and vicinity at 4,500 in 1880. There were thus probably more Chinese than the census officially stated (*NYH*, Mar. 18, Sept. 15, 1879; *NYT*, Mar. 6, 1880).

17. Higham, *Strangers in the Land*, 49–50.

18. Ibid.; Robert E. Weir, *Beyond Labor's Veil: The Culture of the Knights of Labor* (University Park, Pa., 1996), chap. 1; David R. Roediger, *The Wages of Whiteness: Race and the Making of the American Working Class* (London, 1991), 8, 55, 87, 179; "An Irish Workman" (letter) in *Boston Pilot*, Aug. 24, 1878. The literature on white working-class racism is extensive. See, for example, Roediger, *Wages of Whiteness*; David R. Roediger, *Towards the Abolition of Whiteness: Essays on Race, Politics, and Working Class History* (London, 1994);

Alexander Saxton, *The Rise and Fall of the White Republic: Class Politics and Mass Culture in Nineteenth-Century America* (London, 1990); and Gwendolyn Mink, *Old Labor and New Immigrants in American Political Development: Union, Party, and State, 1875–1920* (Ithaca, N.Y., 1986).

19. *CR*, 43d Cong., 1st sess., 716 (Jan. 16, 1874), 1463–64 (Feb. 13, 1874). See also the speech of Representative John Coghlan (R-Calif.) in *CG*, 42d Cong., 2d sess., 1737–41 (Mar. 16, 1872).

20. *San Francisco Examiner*, Apr. 29, 1873, reprinted in *WA*, June 7, 1873; *San Francisco Shop Senate*, July 5, 1873, reprinted in *WA*, Aug. 2, 1873; Cross, *A History of the Labor Movement in California*, chap. 4, esp. 84–85; Alexander Saxton, *The Indispensable Enemy: Labor and the Anti-Chinese Movement in California* (Berkeley, 1971), 104–9. See also Henry George, "The Kearney Agitation in California," *Popular Science Monthly* 17 (Aug. 1880): 440–41; Rodman W. Paul, "The Origin of the Chinese Issue in California," *Mississippi Valley Historical Review* 25 (June 1938): 181–96; Leonard Pitt, "The Beginnings of Nativism in California," *Pacific Historical Review* 30 (Feb. 1961): 23–38; and Elmer Clarence Sandmeyer, *The Anti-Chinese Movement in California* (Urbana, Ill., 1939). Clergy in California soon followed merchants and manufacturers into the anti-Chinese camp, their numbers growing as the decade wore on. See Robert Seager II, "Some Denominational Reactions to Chinese Immigration to California, 1856–1892," *Pacific Historical Review* 28 (Feb. 1959): 49–66.

21. James D. Richardson, ed., *A Compilation of the Messages and Papers of the Presidents, 1789–1897* (Washington, D.C., 1897), 9:4242; *CR*, 43d Cong., 2d sess., 19 (Dec. 8, 1874), 1599 (Feb. 22, 1875), 2161 (Mar. 3, 1875). On reports of Chinese prostitution, see Stuart Creighton Miller, *The Unwelcome Immigrant: The American Image of the Chinese, 1785–1882* (Berkeley, 1969), 163, 164, 171, 181, 182–83. See also Sucheng Chan, "The Exclusion of Chinese Women, 1870–1943," in *Entry Denied: Exclusion and the Chinese Community in America, 1882–1943*, ed. Chan (Philadelphia, 1991), 94–146; Hirata, "Free, Indentured, Enslaved"; and Peffer, "Forbidden Families." For excellent fictional treatment of a Chinese woman smuggled into America as a prostitute in the 1870s, see Ruthanne Lum McCunn, *Thousand Pieces of Gold* (Boston, 1981). The Page Act also banned the immigration of criminals, except those guilty of political crimes.

22. *Ninth Census*, 1:xvii.

23. The literature on "critical elections," political realignments, and the various party systems is enormous. See V. O. Key Jr., "A Theory of Critical Elections," *Journal of Politics* 17 (Feb. 1955): 3–18; Richard P. McCormick, *The Second American Party System* (Chapel Hill, N.C., 1966); William Nisbet Chambers and Walter Dean Burnham, eds., *The American Party Systems: Stages of Political Development* (New York, 1967); Walter Dean Burnham, *Critical Elections and the Mainsprings of American Politics* (New York, 1970); Paul Kleppner, *The Third Electoral System, 1853–1892: Parties, Voters, and Political Cultures* (Chapel Hill, N.C., 1979); and Richard L. McCormick, *The Party Period and Public Policy: American Politics from the Age of Jackson to the Progressive Era* (New York, 1986). See also John A. Garraty, *The New Commonwealth, 1877–1890* (New York, 1968), chap. 6.

24. Eric Foner, *Reconstruction*, 488–511, Schurz quoted on 500; Montgomery, *Beyond Equality*, 368–86, Godkin quoted on 380. See also Sidney Fine, *Laissez Faire and the General-Welfare State: A Study of Conflict in American Thought, 1865–1901* (Ann Arbor, Mich., 1956), esp. chaps. 3–5; John G. Sproat, *"The Best Men": Liberal Reformers in the Gilded Age* (New York, 1968); Michael McGerr, *The Decline of Popular Politics: The American North, 1865–1928* (New York, 1986); and Michael Perman, *The Road to Redemption: Southern Politics, 1869–*

1879 (Chapel Hill, N.C., 1984). For differing views on the Liberal Republicans, see Richard Allan Gerber, "The Liberal Republicans of 1872 in Historiographical Perspective," *Journal of American History* 62 (June 1975): 40–73.

25. Eric Foner, *Reconstruction*, 505–9, Greeley quoted on 508.

26. Kirk H. Porter and Donald Bruce Johnson, comps., *National Party Platforms, 1840–1968* (Urbana, Ill., 1970), 41–48. The Democratic and Liberal Republican platforms differed only in punctuation and grammar. Other parties—the anti-Greeley Straight-Out Democrats, the Labor Reformers, and the Prohibitionists—also issued platforms and nominated candidates, and feminist Victoria Woodhull became the first woman to run for president. These minor parties further helped make 1872 an unusual election year but had little impact on the outcome.

27. Sproat, *"Best Men,"* 82–88; Eric Foner, *Reconstruction*, 505–11.

28. Sproat, *"Best Men,"* 87.

29. Eric Foner, *Reconstruction*, 512–13; Burnham, *Critical Elections*, 32.

CHAPTER FIVE

1. Philip A. Roach to Manton Marble, June 7, 1880, Manton Marble Papers, LC.

2. Ibid.

3. *NYH*, Feb. 23, 1876; *NYTr*, Feb. 23, 1876. For a sampling of labor meetings during the winter of 1875–76, see *National Labor Tribune* (Pittsburgh), Jan. 8, 1876; *NYH*, Jan. 11, Mar. 15, Mar. 25, 1876; *IW*, Jan. 22, 1876; *NYS*, Mar. 24, Mar. 25, 1876. For background on the Order of United American Mechanics, see Bruce Laurie, *Working People of Philadelphia, 1800–1850* (Philadelphia, 1980), 174–76. John Higham called the Order "a mere fragment" after the Civil War and described a major regrowth in the late 1880s. The intervening years remain a mystery (John Higham, *Strangers in the Land: Patterns of American Nativism, 1860–1925* [New York, 1975; first published 1955], 13, 23, 57, 64). The Order's meeting in 1876 supports historians' claims that the years following the Civil War were, with the exception of California, marked by a decline in nativism nationwide (ibid., 14–23; John Higham, "Origins of Immigration Restriction, 1882–1897: A Social Analysis," *Mississippi Valley Historical Review* 39 [June 1952]: 77; and Maldwyn Allen Jones, *American Immigration* [Chicago, 1960], 248).

4. Mary Roberts Coolidge, *Chinese Immigration* (New York, 1909), 112; *SFAC*, Mar. 21, Mar. 23, Mar. 26, Mar. 29, 1876; Elmer Clarence Sandmeyer, *The Anti-Chinese Movement in California* (Urbana, Ill., 1939), 57–59. Bryant's address was also prompted by a recent Supreme Court ruling declaring a state law restricting entry of Chinese women into the country unconstitutional.

5. *SFAC*, Apr. 6, 1876.

6. Ibid., Apr. 4, Apr. 12, Apr. 15, 1876; Sandmeyer, *The Anti-Chinese Movement in California*, 60–62; California Senate, *Chinese Immigration; Its Social, Moral, and Political Effect. Report to the California State Senate of Its Special Committee on Chinese Immigration* (Sacramento, 1878; reprint, 1971), 60, 63, 64; California Senate, *Chinese Immigration. The Social, Moral, and Political Effect of Chinese Immigration. Testimony Taken before a Committee of the Senate of the State of California, Appointed April 3d, 1876* (Sacramento, 1876; reprint, 1970).

7. *Facts upon the Other Side of the Chinese Question: with a Memorial to the President of the U.S. from Representative Chinamen in America* (n.p., 1876), 18, 19.

8. The queue ordinance was declared unconstitutional three years later. See *The Invalidity of the "Queue Ordinance" of the City and County of San Francisco. Opinion of the Circuit Court*

of the United States, for the District of California, in Ho Ah Kow vs. Matthew Nunan, Delivered July 7th, 1879 (San Francisco, 1879). Because this decision applied the Fourteenth Amendment's equal protection clause to noncitizens as well as citizens, Charles J. McClain hails it as a landmark case in both American jurisprudence and the Chinese quest for civil and legal rights. The San Francisco Board of Supervisors, it might be added, had passed a queue ordinance in 1873, but Mayor William Alvord had vetoed it. McClain argues persuasively that from the 1850s onward, Chinese immigrants consistently fought discriminatory legislation passed against them and profoundly influenced the development of American jurisprudence (McClain, *In Search of Equality: The Chinese Struggle against Discrimination in Nineteenth-Century America* [Berkeley, 1994], esp. 48–50, 73–76). For an early example of such efforts, see *Remarks of the Chinese Merchants of San Francisco, upon Governor Bigler's Message, and Some Common Objections; with Some Explanations of the Character of the Chinese Companies, and the Laboring Class in California* (San Francisco, 1855).

9. *SFAC*, Mar. 23, May 9, 1876; *SFC*, May 10, 1876; *San Francisco Bulletin*, Mar. 23, 1876, quoted in Sandmeyer, *The Anti-Chinese Movement in California*, 58.

It appears that McDonald, though appointed, never went. On other anti-Chinese meetings in the West, see *SFAC*, Apr. 1, Apr. 5, May 10, May 13, May 27, June 8, 1876. On Pixley, see Gerald Stanley, "Frank Pixley and the Heathen Chinee *(A Phylon Document),*" *Phylon* 40 (Sept. 1979): 224–28.

10. Peter Thomas Conmy, *Philip Augustine Roach, 1820–1889, California Pioneer* (San Francisco, 1958), 5; *NYT*, Apr. 28, 1889. For other biographical information on Roach, see *McGee's Illustrated Weekly*, July 28, 1877, 149, and *IW*, Oct. 31, 1874.

11. *WA*, May 20, 1876.

12. Ibid.; Philip A. Roach to Manton Marble, June 7, 1880, Marble Papers; Frank M. Pixley to John Strathman (letter), reprinted in *SFC*, June 15, 1876; *Nation*, Apr. 13, May 18, 1876.

13. *SFC*, June 21, July 19, 1876; *IW*, July 1, 1876.

14. *SFC*, June 16, July 19, 1876; Frank M. Pixley to John Strathman (letter), reprinted in ibid., June 15, 1876; Frank M. Pixley to Mayor A. J. Bryant (letter), reprinted in ibid., June 4, 1876; Philip A. Roach to Thomas F. Bayard, Jan. 16, 1879, Thomas F. Bayard Papers, LC.

15. *CR*, 44th Cong., 1st sess., 477 (Jan. 18, 1876), 901 (Feb. 7, 1876), 2793 (Apr. 20, 1876).

16. Ibid., 2850–57 (May 1, 1876).

17. Ibid. As the Senate's leading suffragist, Sargent introduced the first constitutional amendment to enfranchise women in 1878 and invited Elizabeth Cady Stanton and Susan B. Anthony to testify before the Senate. His wife, Ellen Clark Sargent, was president of the California Woman Suffrage Association, and his daughter, Dr. Elizabeth C. Sargent, was a prominent suffragist. See Elizabeth Cady Stanton, Susan B. Anthony, Matilda Joslyn Gage, [and Ida Husted Harper], eds., *History of Woman Suffrage* (New York, 1882), 2:483–84; (Rochester, 1886), 3:70–75, 108–11, 121, 245–47; 4:135, 287, 366, 481, 487; (New York, 1922), 5:150, 328, 623.

18. *SFAC*, May 8, 1876; U.S. Senate, *Senate Report no. 689, Joint Special Committee on Chinese*, 44th Cong., 2d sess. (Washington, D.C., 1877), 679; *CR*, 44th Cong., 1st sess., 3099–3101 (May 16, 1876), 3183–86 (May 18, 1876).

19. Republican Party, *Proceedings of the Republican National Convention, Held at Cincinnati, Ohio, Wednesday, Thursday, and Friday, June 14, 15, and 16, 1876, Resulting in the Nomination for President and Vice-President Rutherford B. Hayes and William A. Wheeler*, comp. M. A. Clancy and William Nelson (Concord, N.H., 1876), 58; Donald Bruce Johnson,

comp., *1840–1956*, vol. 1 of *National Party Platforms*, rev. ed. (Urbana, Ill., 1978), 58. On Hawley's comments, see above, Chap. 3.

20. Republican Party, *Proceedings of the Republican National Convention*, 58–63; *CR*, 44th Cong., 1st sess., 4418 (July 6, 1876); *SFAC*, June 16, 1876; *NYTr*, June 16, 1876; *New York Witness*, quoted in *SFC*, July 4, 1876.

21. Philip A. Roach to Manton Marble, June 7, 1880, A. J. Bryant to Manton Marble, June 17, 1876, Marble Papers; California delegates quoted in *St. Louis Globe-Democrat*, June 25, 1876; *NYS*, June 27, 1876; Johnson, *1840–1956*, 50; Democratic Party, *Official Proceedings of the National Democratic Convention, Held in St. Louis, Mo., June 27th, 28th and 29th, 1876. With an Appendix Containing the Letters of Acceptance of Gov. Tilden and Gov. Hendricks* (St. Louis, 1876), 97–99. Appointed collector of the port of San Francisco in 1884, Hager was, in the words of Senator William M. Stewart, among the most "zealous opponent[s] of Chinese immigration" he had ever known (*CR*, 50th Cong., 1st sess., 7304 [Aug. 7, 1888]; Christian G. Fritz, "A Nineteenth Century 'Habeas Corpus Mill': The Chinese before the Federal Courts in California," *American Journal of Legal History* 32 [1988]: 366).

22. *CR*, 44th Cong., 1st sess., 4418–21 (July 6, 1876), 4491, 4507 (July 10, 1876), 4671–72 (July 17, 1876), 4678, 4705 (July 18, 1876), 5060 (Aug. 2, 1876), 5676 (Aug. 15, 1876).

23. *SFC*, May 8, June 14, June 17, July 19, 1876; Frank M. Pixley to A. J. Bryant (letter), reprinted in *SFC*, June 4, 1876; *NYH*, May 4, June 5, June 8, 1876; *St. Louis Globe-Democrat*, Apr. 7, May 5, June 12, 1876.

24. *NYW*, Aug. 1, 1876.

25. Ibid., June 5, June 14, June 19, June 29, July 1, July 2, 1876; Philip A. Roach to Manton Marble, June 7, 1880, Marble Papers. See also *NYW* editorial (June 14, 1876) supporting the California Supreme Court's ruling of Chinese immigration restriction laws as unconstitutional.

26. Thomas J. Vivian, "John Chinaman in San Francisco," *Scribner's Monthly* 12 (Oct. 1876): 862; *NYH*, Aug. 15, 1876. The campaign can be followed in any of the major dailies. For a sample of speeches and rallies, see *NYW*, Oct. 5, Oct. 14, Nov. 13, 1876; *NYS*, Oct. 13, Nov. 3, Nov. 5, 1876; and *NYH*, Nov. 2, 1876.

27. *National Labor Tribune* (Pittsburgh), Apr. 22, Apr. 29, May 27, 1876; *Workingman's Map* (Indianapolis), Apr. 15, Apr. 22, June 17, June 24, July 1, 1876; *IW*, May 6, 1876; *WA*, May 20, 1876; *NYLS*, Dec. 9, 1876.

28. *Socialist* (New York), June 10, June 17, 1876; *WA*, June 10, 1876.

29. *Socialist* (New York), June 3, 1876. See also *NYLS* (successor to the *Socialist*), Sept. 30, Dec. 23, 1876. In response to the June 3 editorial, the *San Francisco Chronicle* denounced the *Socialist*, "professedly an organ of the working classes," for its "stupidity and ignorance" on the Chinese issue: "The laboring men of San Francisco understand this question far better than the senseless agitators at the East" (*SFC*, June 14, 1876).

30. For detailed accounts of labor meetings, see *National Labor Tribune* (Pittsburgh), Apr. 22, 1876; *Workingman's Map* (Indianapolis), May 6, July 1, 1876; *Chicago Inter-Ocean*, Sept. 20, 1876; *NYS*, June 22, Aug. 8, Aug. 13, Oct. 25, Oct. 31, Nov. 1, Nov. 3, 1876; *NYW*, Aug. 10, Aug. 11, 1876; and *NYH*, Apr. 10, June 14, July 11, July 12, July 22, July 31, Aug. 1, Aug. 2, Aug. 10, Aug. 11, Sept. 15, Oct. 14, Nov. 4, 1876.

For early Greenback-Labor conventions and meetings, see *IW*, Mar. 25, May 27, June 10, Sept. 23, Oct. 7, Oct. 28, 1876; *NYH*, Feb. 17, Feb. 23, Mar. 10, Mar. 16, May 27, June 18, Aug. 31, Sept. 27, 1876; and *St. Paul Anti-Monopolist*, May 25, 1876. Literature on the Greenbackers remains woefully slim. See Fred Emory Haynes, *Third Party Movements since the Civil War with Special Reference to Iowa: A Study in Social Politics* (Iowa City, 1916), chaps. 8–14; Paul Kleppner, *The Cross of Culture: A Social Analysis of Midwestern Politics, 1850–1900* (New York, 1970), 15, 120–24; R. C. McGrane, "Ohio and the Greenback Movement," *Mississippi Valley Historical Review* 11 (Mar. 1925): 526–42; Ralph R. Ricker, *The Greenback-Labor Movement in Pennsylvania* (Bellefonte, Pa., 1966); Clyde O. Ruggles, "The Economic Basis of the Greenback Movement in Iowa and Wisconsin," *Proceedings of the Mississippi Valley Historical Association* 6 (1912/13): 142–62; and Irwin Unger, *The Greenback Era: A Social and Political History of American Finance, 1865–1879* (Princeton, 1964).

31. *NYLS*, Sept. 23, 1876; *NYH*, Aug. 10, 1876. For an overview of the collapse of the International Workingmen's Association, see Bruce Laurie, *Artisans into Workers: Labor in Nineteenth-Century America* (New York, 1989), 178–81.

32. *NYH*, June 23, Oct. 14, Oct. 15, Oct. 27, 1876; *NYS*, June 5, 1876; *Socialist* (New York), July 1, 1876.

33. *Congressional Quarterly's Guide to U.S. Elections*, 2d ed. (Washington, D.C., 1985), 339; *CT*, Dec. 14, 1877; *Socialist* (New York), July 22, 1876.

CHAPTER SIX

1. *IW*, Apr. 7, 1877. For another example of Irish-Chinese cooperation, see ibid., June 10, 1876. Created to introduce Chinese youths to Western ideas, the Chinese Educational Mission lasted from 1872 to 1881. The significance, role, and day-to-day functioning of this school deserve greater study. For an introduction, see Charles A. Desnoyers, " 'The Thin Edge of the Wedge': The Chinese Educational Mission and Diplomatic Representation in the Americas," *Pacific Historical Review* 61 (May 1992): 241–63; Timothy T. Kao, "An American Sojourn: Young Chinese Students in the United States," *Connecticut Historical Society Bulletin* 46 (July 1981): 65–77; Thomas E. LaFargue, *China's First Hundred: Educational Mission Students in the United States, 1872–1881* (Pullman, Wash., 1942), esp. chap. 3; and Ruthanne Lum McCunn, *Chinese American Portraits: Personal Histories, 1828–1988* (San Francisco, 1988), 16–25. On Yung Wing, the first Chinese graduate of an American college (Yale, 1854) and later China's associate minister to the United States, see Yung Wing, *My Life in China and America* (New York, 1909), and Edmund H. Worthy Jr., "Yung Wing in America," *Pacific Historical Review* 34 (Aug. 1965): 265–87.

2. Because March 4 fell on a Sunday, Hayes's inauguration was delayed until March 5. On the 1876 election, see C. Vann Woodward, *Reunion and Reaction: The Compromise of 1877 and the End of Reconstruction* (Boston, 1951), and Keith Ian Polakoff, *The Politics of Inertia: The Election of 1876 and the End of Reconstruction* (Baton Rouge, 1973). The term "Rutherfraud" was coined by *New York Sun* editor Charles A. Dana. See Herbert J. Clancy, *The Presidential Election of 1880* (Chicago, 1958), 31 n. 28.

3. U.S. Senate, *Senate Report no. 689, Joint Special Committee on Chinese*, 44th Cong., 2d sess. (Washington, D.C., 1877), with quotes from iv–viii, 672, 677, 685 (for the list of questions and groups represented, see 2–3; for the list of witnesses, see 1255–57); *CR*, 44th Cong., 2d sess., 1961 (Feb. 27, 1877), 2004–5 (Feb. 28, 1877), app., 117–19 (Feb. 28, 1877); U.S. Senate, *Views of the Late Oliver P. Morton on the Character, Extent, and Effect of Chinese Immigration to the United States*, 45th Cong., 2d sess., Misc. Doc. 20 (Washington, D.C., 1878). Every prominent politician in California belonged to the Anti-Chinese Union, whose stated goal was to ban Chinese immigration and "compel the Chinese living in the United States to withdraw from the country." Honorary vice presidents included Senators Aaron

Sargent and Newton Booth, Representatives Horace Page, John Luttrell, and William Piper, Governor William Irwin, former senator Eugene Casserly, former representatives James Johnson and John Coghlan, future senator James Farley, Mayor Andrew Bryant, State Senator Philip Roach, and Frank Pixley (U.S. Senate, *Senate Report no. 689*, 1169–70).

4. Loren W. Fessler, ed., *Chinese in America: Stereotyped Past, Changing Present* (New York, 1983), 138–39. On the widespread coverage of the "Chico Massacre," see, for example, *NYT*, Mar. 16, Mar. 17, Mar. 18, Mar. 24, 1877.

The most horrendous incidents of white violence directed against Chinese immigrants include an 1871 riot in Los Angeles that left nineteen Chinese dead, an 1880 riot in Denver that left one Chinese dead, the 1885 massacre in Rock Springs, Wyoming, that left twenty-eight Chinese dead, and an 1887 attack near the Snake River in Oregon that left ten Chinese dead. Shih-shan Henry Tsai counts fifty-five anti-Chinese riots in the late nineteenth century, most in California, but ranging from South Dakota to Alaska. The most brutal year was 1885, when the Rock Springs massacre sparked violence in Seattle, Tacoma, and other towns in Washington Territory. President Grover Cleveland ordered federal troops to suppress the outbreaks, the first time American soldiers protected Chinese settlers. See *The Chinese Massacre at Rock Springs, Wyoming Territory, September 2, 1885* (Boston, 1886); Patrick Joseph Healy and Ng Poon Chew, *A Statement for Non-Exclusion* (San Francisco, 1905), 211–44; Jules Alexander Karlin, "The Anti-Chinese Outbreak in Tacoma, 1885," *Pacific Historical Review* 23 (Aug. 1954): 271–83; Jules Alexander Karlin, "The Anti-Chinese Outbreaks in Seattle, 1885–1886," *Pacific Northwest Quarterly* 39 (Apr. 1948): 103–30; Charles J. McClain, *In Search of Equality: The Chinese Struggle against Discrimination in Nineteenth-Century America* (Berkeley, 1994), chap. 7; *NYT*, Aug. 20, 1995; Craig Storti, *Incident at Bitter Creek: The Story of the Rock Springs Chinese Massacre* (Ames, Iowa, 1991); Shih-shan Henry Tsai, *The Chinese Experience in America* (Bloomington, Ind., 1986), 67–72; and Roy T. Wortman, "Denver's Anti-Chinese Riot, 1880," *Colorado Magazine* 42 (Fall 1965): 275–91. Several of these articles are collected in Roger Daniels, ed., *Anti-Chinese Violence in North America* (New York, 1978). Violence against Chinese Americans continued throughout the twentieth century. For recent incidents, see *NYT*, Dec. 13, 1995.

5. *NYH*, Mar. 11, Mar. 15, Mar. 16, Mar. 17, May 25, 1877; *NYLS*, Aug. 11, 1877, May 5, 1878; Henry George, *Progress and Poverty: An Inquiry into the Cause of Industrial Depressions and of Increase of Want with Increase of Wealth. The Remedy* (San Francisco, 1879). The railroad strike can be followed in any of the major dailies. See, for example, the *New York Herald* and *Chicago Times*. For secondary accounts, see Robert V. Bruce, *1877: Year of Violence* (New York, 1959); Philip S. Foner, *The Great Labor Uprising of 1877* (New York, 1977); and David R. Roediger, "America's First General Strike: The St. Louis Commune of 1877," *Midwest Quarterly* 21 (Winter 1980): 196–206.

6. Bruce, *1877*; *NYT*, July 25, 1877; *New York Times, World, Herald*, and *Sun* quoted in Richard O. Boyer and Herbert M. Morais, *Labor's Untold Story* (New York, 1980; first published 1953), 59, 62. On Beecher's comments, see Bruce Laurie, *Artisans into Workers: Labor in Nineteenth-Century America* (New York, 1989), 133, 154–55.

7. Ira B. Cross, *A History of the Labor Movement in California* (Berkeley, 1935), 89–92; Elmer Clarence Sandmeyer, *The Anti-Chinese Movement in California* (Urbana, Ill., 1939), 64–65; Alexander Saxton, *The Indispensable Enemy: Labor and the Anti-Chinese Movement in California* (Berkeley, 1971), 114; Neil Larry Shumsky, *The Evolution of Political Protest and the Workingmen's Party of California* (Columbus, Ohio, 1991), parts 1, 3.

8. James Bryce, *The American Commonwealth*, 3d ed. (New York, 1905; first published

1894), 2:431–32; Cross, *A History of the Labor Movement in California*, chap. 7; Lucile Eaves, *A History of California Labor Legislation, with an Introductory Sketch of the San Francisco Labor Movement*, University of California Publications in Economics, vol. 2 (Berkeley, 1910), 27–36; Ralph Kauer, "The Workingmen's Party of California," *Pacific Historical Review* 13 (Sept. 1944): 278–91; Sandmeyer, *The Anti-Chinese Movement in California*, 64–65; Saxton, *Indispensable Enemy*, 118–19; Shumsky, *Evolution of Political Protest*, parts 1, 3; Henry George, "The Kearney Agitation in California," *Popular Science Monthly* 17 (Aug. 1880): 440–41; J. C. Stedman and R. A. Leonard, *The Workingmen's Party of California: An Epitome of Its Rise and Progress* (San Francisco, 1878).

9. *NYTr*, Nov. 7, 1877; Samuel Gompers, *Seventy Years of Life and Labor: An Autobiography* (New York, 1925), 2:147. The strike was well covered by the major New York newspapers. For the best accounts, see *CMOJ*, Oct. 1877 through Jan. 1878, and the almost daily reports in the *New York Herald*. See also Gompers, *Seventy Years*, 1:110, 134–63.

10. Gompers, *Seventy Years*, 1:148–51; *CMOJ*, Nov. 10, 1877; *NYH*, Oct. 19, Oct. 21, Oct. 23, Oct. 28, Oct. 30, Nov. 18, 1877, Jan. 6, 1878; *NYTr*, Oct. 24, 1877.

11. *NYH*, Oct. 17, Oct. 19, 1877, Jan. 6, 1878; *NYTr*, Oct. 31, 1877; *NYLS*, Oct. 21, Nov. 11, 1877; potter quoted in *CMOJ*, Nov. 10, 1877.

12. *NYTr*, Oct. 19, Nov. 10, 1877; *NYH*, Nov. 6, Nov. 7, Nov. 18, 1877; *CMOJ*, Nov. 10, 1877. See also *NYLS*, Nov. 18, 1877, and *NYTr*, Nov. 11, 1877.

13. *CMOJ*, Nov. 10, Dec. 24, 1877; *NYH*, Nov. 13, 1877, Jan. 6, 1878.

14. Gompers, *Seventy Years*, 1:134, 154; *CMOJ*, Dec. 10, 1877, Feb. 10, May 10, 1878.

15. *CMOJ*, May 10, June 10, 1878; *NYLS*, Jan. 27, 1878.

16. *NYLS*, Dec. 16, 1877, Feb. 10, Feb. 17, Feb. 24, Mar. 3, Mar. 17, June 30, July 14, 1878; "A Factory Slave" (letter) in ibid., Dec. 9, 1877. "Chineize" was also spelled "Chinaize." See *NYLS*, Aug. 11, 1877, Feb. 17, June 2, 1878.

17. *Socialist* (Detroit), Feb. 9, Mar. 23, Mar. 30, Apr. 20, 1878; Helverson (letter) in ibid., Mar. 16, 1878; B. E. G. Jewett (letter) in ibid., May 4, 1878; J. B. Rumford (letter) in *National Socialist* (Cincinnati), June 29, 1878.

18. Knights of Labor, *Record of the Proceedings of the General Assembly of the ********* [Knights of Labor] held at Reading, Pennsylvania, January 1–4, 1878* (n.p., 1878), 28–32; *CT*, July 1, 1878; *CTr*, quoted in *NYLS*, July 14, 1878. The Six Companies were six separate Chinese American benevolent associations based in San Francisco that derived from six geographic districts in Kwangtung Province in southeastern China, the source of most Chinese immigration. Dominated by merchants, the *huiguan*, or "meeting hall," as the Chinese called the companies, served as mutual-aid and support organizations, providing medical care, lodging, financial assistance, and guidance to Chinese immigrants. The Six Companies—whose numbers actually varied from four to eight in the nineteenth century—were often portrayed as secretive, nefarious societies, and many Americans accused them of importing immigrants from China. Although the huiguan supplied credit to assist immigration, recent historians have found little evidence to support the charge of importation. The companies also fought discriminatory legislation and became one of the leading voices of the Chinese American community. Some of the companies survive to this day. See Him Mark Lai, "Historical Development of the Chinese Consolidated Benevolent Association/ Huiguan System," in *Chinese America: History and Perspectives, 1987* (San Francisco, 1987), 13–51; William Hoy, *The Chinese Six Companies* (San Francisco, 1942); Shih-shan Henry Tsai, *China and the Overseas Chinese in the United States, 1868–1911* (Fayetteville, Ark., 1983), 31–38; and McClain, *In Search of Equality*, 13–16.

19. Edwin R. Meade, *The Chinese Question: A Paper Read at the Annual Meeting of the Social Science Association of America, held at Saratoga, N.Y., Sept. 7th, 1877* (New York, 1877). The first two quotes are from *NYH*, Sept. 8, 1877; Wells quoted in speech of Meade in *CR*, 44th Cong., 2d sess., app., 118 (Feb. 28, 1877), and *Chicago Inter-Ocean*, Sept. 8, 1877. See also *SFC*, May 8, 1876. For background on the American Social Science Association, see Thomas L. Haskell, *The Emergence of Professional Social Science: The American Social Science Association and the Nineteenth Century Crisis of Authority* (Urbana, Ill., 1977).

20. White and Hodge quoted in *CR*, 45th Cong., 3d sess., 1267 (Feb. 13, 1879); William C. Bryant to Miss J. Dewey, Jan. 21, 1875, quoted in Stuart Creighton Miller, *The Unwelcome Immigrant: The American Image of the Chinese, 1785–1882* (Berkeley, 1969), 178; M. J. Dee, "Chinese Immigration," *North American Review* 127 (Jan.–Feb. 1878): 506–26. See also James A. Whitney, *The Chinese and the Chinese Question* (New York, 1880). Dee was not the first to apply Darwinian theory to Chinese immigration. Nine years earlier, Harvard professor Raphael Pumpelly wrote, "The teeming population of our hemisphere two or three centuries hence may have more Chings and Changs in their geneological [*sic*] trees than Smiths and Browns; for, other things being equal, the predominant blood will be that of the race best able to maintain an undiminished rate of increase; and the vitality of the Chinese nation during a constant struggle for life seems to bespeak for it at least equally favorable prospects in less crowded homes" (Pumpelly, "Our Impending Chinese Problem," *Galaxy* 8 [July 1869]: 24).

21. *SFC*, Oct. 16, Nov. 4, Nov. 30, 1877; *BG*, July 28, 1878.

22. *NYTr*, Nov. 30, Dec. 7, 1877; *CT*, Dec. 7, Dec. 21, 1877.

23. *NYTr*, Dec. 18, 1877. On Mills, see *Dictionary of American Biography* (New York, 1934), 7:6–7.

24. *NYLS*, Oct. 7, 1877; *CR*, 45th Cong, 1st sess., 195 (Oct. 29, 1877); ibid., 2d sess., 68 (Dec. 7, 1877), 81, 98 (Dec. 10, 1877), 251, 271 (Jan. 10, 1878), 310, 318, 320 (Jan. 14, 1878), 383 (Jan. 17, 1878); *CT*, Jan. 19, 1878.

25. *BG*, Feb. 27, 1878; *CR*, 45th Cong., 2d sess., 3226 (May 7, 1878), 3772–73 (May 25, 1878), 4782 (June 17, 1878). For Sargent's speech, see ibid., 1544–53 (Mar. 7, 1878).

26. *CTr* and *Chicago Inter-Ocean*, quoted in Bruce C. Nelson, *Beyond the Martyrs: A Social History of Chicago's Anarchists, 1870–1900* (New Brunswick, N.J., 1988), 58–59; *CT*, Apr. 30, May 6, May 7, May 11, June 14, June 15, 1878; *CE*, quoted in *CT*, May 3, 1878; *NYTr*, quoted in *CT*, May 13, 1878; *NYH*, May 4, May 7, May 18, May 28, June 10, June 13, June 14, June 15, 1878; *BG*, May 18, May 26, 1878; *NYW*, quoted in *BG*, Apr. 8, 1878.

27. Nelson, *Beyond the Martyrs*, 58–59; *CT*, June 5, June 14, July 9, 1878; *BG*, May 26, 1878; *NYH*, May 23, June 20, June 21, 1878; Sandmeyer, *The Anti-Chinese Movement in California*, 66; Kauer, "The Workingmen's Party of California," 283.

28. *NYH*, Nov. 23, 1877, Feb. 24, 1878. By 1881 there were more than three hundred Greenback newspapers. See list in *Wisconsin Standard*, June 23, June 30, 1881.

29. *Cleveland Labor Advance*, Mar. 2, 1878; *St. Paul Anti-Monopolist*, Feb. 28, May 23, 1878; *Oshkosh Greenback Standard*, Mar. 22, Apr. 5, May 24, 1878; Cary quoted in ibid., June 21, 1878. The *Oshkosh Greenback Standard* changed its name to the *Oshkosh Standard* in October 1878 and to the *Wisconsin Standard* in August 1880. *BG*, May 23, June 6, 1878; *CT*, July 24, 1878; *NYH*, Mar. 28, May 10, June 19, June 30, 1878; *IW*, May 18, June 15, Aug. 3, 1878; Edward McPherson, *A Hand-Book of Politics for 1878: Being a Record of Important Political Action, National and State, from July 15, 1876, to July 15, 1878* (New York, 1878), 161–62, 167–68; Terence V. Powderly, *The Path I Trod* (New York, 1940), 76; Gompers, *Seventy Years*, 1:136;

Congressional Quarterly's Guide to U.S. Elections, 2d ed. (Washington, D.C., 1985), 794–97; Fred Emory Haynes, *Third Party Movements since the Civil War with Special Reference to Iowa: A Study in Social Politics* (Iowa City, 1916), 114.

30. *SFAC*, July 2, 1878.

CHAPTER SEVEN

1. Kearney's itinerary during the first six weeks of his tour included twenty-one speeches in ten states: Boston (Aug. 5, Aug. 8), Marblehead (Aug. 10), Lynn (Aug. 12), Lowell (Aug. 13), Brighton (Aug. 14), Indianapolis (Aug. 18), Chicago (Aug. 20), Bloomington, Ill. (Aug. 21), St. Louis (Aug. 22), Cincinnati (Aug. 23), Newport, Ky. (Aug. 24), Columbus (Aug. 26), Washington, D.C. (Aug. 29), Philadelphia (Aug. 30), Newark, N.J. (Sept. 2), Jersey City, N.J. (Sept. 3), New York City (Sept. 6), Brooklyn (Sept. 7), Troy (Sept. 11), and Baltimore (Sept. 12). Local papers carried his speeches everywhere he went. For the best overall coverage, see the *Boston Globe* and the *New York Herald*. On the size of the crowd in New York City, see *Irish World*, Sept. 14, 1878.

2. *SFAC*, Dec. 24, 1878.

3. *Nation*, Aug. 1, 1878.

4. Biographical information on Kearney, although sketchy, is gleaned from *BG*, July 28, Aug. 9, 1878; *NYH*, July 28, 1878; Henry George, "The Kearney Agitation in California," *Popular Science Monthly* 17 (Aug. 1880): 433–53; Hubert Howe Bancroft, *1860–1890*, vol. 7 of *History of California*, vol. 24 of *The Works of Hubert Howe Bancroft* (San Francisco, 1890), 357 n. 22; Doyce B. Nunis Jr., ed., "The Demagogue and the Demographer: Correspondence of Denis Kearney and Lord Bryce," *Pacific Historical Review* 36 (Aug. 1967): 269–88; Russell M. Posner, "The Lord and the Drayman: James Bryce vs. Denis Kearney," *California Historical Quarterly* 50 (Sept. 1971): 277–84; and *Dictionary of American Biography* (New York, 1961), 5:268–69. The quote is from Denis Kearney to Lord Bryce, Nov. 14, 1889, reprinted in Nunis, "The Demagogue and the Demographer," 280.

The pronunciation of Kearney's name remains something of a mystery. Doggerel writers frequently rhymed it with "blarney," but in the only specific extant description, railroad baron and former California governor Leland Stanford said it was pronounced "cur-nee." This, of course, coming from a fiercely anti-Kearney Republican, may simply have been a crude pun. Journalists, it might be added, frequently misspelled his first name "Dennis." See "A New Ballad of Secession," *NYS*, Feb. 24, 1879, and the interview with Stanford, *NYH*, May 15, 1880.

5. *BG*, July 28, 1878; James Bryce, *The American Commonwealth*, 3d ed. (New York, 1905; first published 1894), 2:431; Bancroft, *1860–1890*, 357 n. 22; Denis Kearney to Lord James Bryce, Nov. 14, 1889, in Nunis, "The Demagogue and the Demographer," 280, 281; George, "The Kearney Agitation in California," 439. On the Workingmen's Party, see Ralph Kauer, "The Workingmen's Party of California," *Pacific Historical Review* 13 (Sept. 1944): 278–91, and Neil Larry Shumsky, *The Evolution of Political Protest and the Workingmen's Party of California* (Columbus, Ohio, 1991), chaps. 1, 7. Shumsky argues persuasively that Kearney and the Workingmen's Party were in the tradition of the preindustrial crowd.

6. *Boston Journal*, July 25, 1878; *NYT*, Aug. 6, 1878; *BG*, Aug. 6, Aug. 9, Aug. 11, 1878; *NYS*, Aug. 9, Aug. 13, 1878.

7. *NYTr*, Aug. 7, Sept. 7, 1878; *NYH*, Aug. 21, 1878; *BG*, Aug. 6, Aug. 9, 1878; *NYS*, Aug. 6, 1878; Tony Hart interviewed in *St. Louis Globe-Democrat*, reprinted in *CGa*, Aug. 15, 1878.

8. This is a composite drawn from slightly different versions in *NYS*, Aug. 6, 1878, and *IW*, Aug. 17, 1878. See also *BG*, Aug. 6, 1878.

9. *NYS*, Aug. 6, Aug. 11, Aug. 13, 1878; *NYTr*, Sept. 7, 1878; *CGa*, Aug. 24, 1878.

10. *NYH*, Aug. 24, 1878; *BG*, Aug. 9, Aug. 11, 1878; *NYTr*, Sept. 3, Sept. 7, 1878.

11. *BG*, Aug. 11, 1878; *NYTr*, Sept. 7, 1878; *CGa*, Aug. 24, 1878.

12. *CGa*, Aug. 24, 1878; *SFC*, Oct. 28, 1878; *NYTr*, Sept. 7, 1878.

13. *BG*, Aug. 11, 1878; *IW*, Aug. 17, 1878; *Washington Post*, Aug. 30, 1878; *SFC*, Aug. 26, 1878; *Boston Pilot*, Aug. 17, 1878; "An Irish Workman" (letter) in ibid., Aug. 24, 1878; *NYS*, Aug. 6, 1878.

14. For more on Butler, see Hans L. Trefousse, *Ben Butler: The South Called Him BEAST!* (New York, 1957). See also David Montgomery, *Beyond Equality: Labor and the Radical Republicans, 1862–1872* (New York, 1967), 360–68.

15. *IW*, Aug. 17, 1878; *BG*, Aug. 15, Dec. 10, 1878. For other examples of crowds cheering Butler, see *BG*, Aug. 6, 1878; *NYS*, Aug. 9, Aug. 13, 1878; and *NYTr*, Sept. 7, 1878.

16. Kearney interviewed in *Boston Herald*, July 29, 1878, reprinted in *NYH*, July 30, 1878; *Boston Pilot*, Aug. 17, 1878; *BG*, Aug. 9, Aug. 31, 1878; *NYTr*, Sept. 7, 1878.

17. *SFC*, Aug. 24, 1878; *BG*, Aug. 9, Aug. 14, 1878; *NYS*, Aug. 11, Sept. 4, 1878; *NYTr*, Sept. 7, 1878.

18. *Boston Transcript*, Aug. 6, Aug. 9, 1878; *PI*, Aug. 29, 1878; *NYT*, Aug. 30, 1878; *CT*, Aug. 21, 1878; *Pomeroy's Illustrated Democrat*, Sept. 7, 1878; *Indianapolis Sun*, Aug. 19, 1878; *Nation*, Aug. 1, 1878; *Harper's Weekly*, Sept. 28, 1878, 766; *Pottsville Miner's Journal*, Aug. 9, 1878; *NYTr*, Sept. 5, 1878; *Boston Pilot*, Aug. 17, 1878; *New York Irish-American*, Sept. 14, 1878. The extent of anti-Kearney editorials is near endless. See also *Boston Journal*, Aug. 3, 1878; *NYS*, Aug. 6, 1878; *NYH*, Aug. 9, Aug. 17, 1878; *New York Express*, Sept. 7, 1878; *NYW*, Sept. 8, 1878; and *SR*, Sept. 28, 1878.

19. *NYLS*, Aug. 11, 1878; *IW*, Sept. 14, 1878.

20. Blaine quoted in *CT*, reprinted in *Hartford Courant*, Sept. 5, 1878; Ch'en Lan-pin, *Shih-mei chi-lueh* (A brief account of my ministry in America), quoted in Charles A. Desnoyers, "Self-Strengthening in the New World: A Chinese Envoy's Travels in America," *Pacific Historical Review* 60 (May 1991): 213; *NYH*, Sept. 11, 1878. After ordering subordinates to translate press accounts of Kearney's speeches into Chinese, Ch'en—then en route to Washington to open the office of the Chinese legation—found that the newspapers made him "so full of anger that, having collected basketfuls of them, I can't bear to [record] them further." For examples of anti-Kearney sermons, see Rev. A. Vincent Group, "America's Fatal King: Kearney's Communism," in *PI*, Sept. 2, 1878, and Rev. W. C. Steele in *NYH*, Sept. 11, 1878.

21. *BG*, July 28, Aug. 18, 1878; *IW*, Sept. 14, 1878; Uriah Stephens to Terence V. Powderly, Aug. 3, 1878, Terence V. Powderly Papers, Catholic University, Washington, D.C.; *CTr*, Aug. 19, 1878; *CGa*, Aug. 19, 1878; *NYS*, Sept. 3, 1878; *NYTr*, Sept. 7, 1878.

22. *NYS*, Aug. 13, Sept. 3, 1878; *NYTr*, Sept. 3, Sept. 4, 1878; *BG*, Aug. 11, 1878.

23. *BG*, Aug. 9, 1878; *Boston Transcript*, Aug. 9, 1878; *NYS*, Aug. 9, 1878.

24. *NYTr*, Aug. 7, 1878; *NYS*, Aug. 6, 1878; *BG*, Aug. 6, 1878; *IW*, Aug. 17, 1878.

25. *Boston Transcript*, Nov. 4, 1878; *NYT*, Sept. 7, 1878; *SFC*, Sept. 7, 1878; *IW*, Sept. 14, 1878; *NYS*, Aug. 30, Sept. 7, 1878; *NYTr*, Sept. 7, 1878; *SFAC*, Aug. 30, 1878; *Indianapolis Sun*, Aug. 19, 1878; *NYH*, Aug. 21, Aug. 30, 1878; *Brooklyn Eagle*, Sept. 8, 1878.

26. *Portland Eastern Argus*, Aug. 12, Aug. 14, 1878; *NYTr*, Aug. 7, 1878; *NYS*, Aug. 13, Sept. 3,

1878; *CT*, Aug. 20, 1878; *SFC*, Aug. 30, 1878; George, "The Kearney Agitation in California," 448, 452; *NYH*, Aug. 21, 1878; *PI*, Aug. 31, 1878.

27. *Portland Eastern Argus*, Aug. 14, 1878; *Boston Transcript*, Aug. 9, 1878; *SFC*, Aug. 19, 1878; *CT*, Aug. 21, 1878; *NYS*, Aug. 13, 1878.

28. *NYS*, Aug. 13, 1878; *BG*, Aug. 9, 1878; *NYH*, Aug. 31, 1878; *NYTr*, Aug. 7, 1878; *Boston Transcript*, Aug. 9, 1878; *NYW*, Sept. 8, 1878; *CE*, Aug. 24, 1878. For examples of hecklers, see *SFC*, Aug. 18, Sept. 3, 1878, and *NYTr*, Sept. 7, 1878.

29. *NYTr*, Sept. 7, 1878; *Boston Journal*, Aug. 13, 1878; *Washington Post*, Aug. 30, 1878; *SFC*, Aug. 31, 1878. For slightly different wording of the Philadelphia resolution, see *Philadelphia Public Ledger*, Aug. 31, 1878.

30. *BG*, Aug. 1, 1878; *NYTr*, Aug. 30, Sept. 5, 1878; *PI*, Aug. 30, 1878; *NYT*, Sept. 4, 1878; Powderly to Charles Litchman, Aug. 24, 1878, Powderly Papers; *Washington Star*, Aug. 30, 1878; *Boston Transcript*, Oct. 1, 1878; *Indianapolis Sun*, Aug. 30, 1878.

31. *Washington Post*, Aug. 13, Aug. 29, Sept. 3, 1878. For accounts of the meetings of the National Workingmen's Assembly, see ibid., and *Washington Star*, Aug. 13, Aug. 15, Aug. 21, Aug. 28, Sept. 3, Sept. 10, 1878. *Indianapolis Sentinel*, Aug. 19, 1878; *SFAC*, Aug. 20, 1878; *NYH*, Aug. 11, Aug. 21, 1878; *NYS*, Aug. 13, 1878; *CT*, Aug. 13, Aug. 23, 1878; *CTr*, Aug. 25, 1878.

32. *St. Louis Post*, Aug. 23, Aug. 24, 1878; *CT*, Aug. 23, 1878; *Voice of Labor*, cited in *St. Louis Globe-Democrat*, Aug. 21, 1878; *Volkszeitung* (Cincinnati), quoted in *SFAC*, Aug. 20, 1878; *Boston Labor Standard*, Oct. 26, 1878; *Washington Post*, Aug. 13, 1878; *NYH*, July 29, Aug. 8, 1878; *NYTr*, Aug. 2, 1878. Other Socialist organs also denounced Kearney and his anti-Chinese message. See, for example, *NYLS*, Aug. 11, 1878; *National Socialist* (Cincinnati), Aug. 17, 1878; *Communist* (St. Louis) and *Volksstimme des Westens*, quoted in *St. Louis Globe-Democrat*, Aug. 21, 1878. For similar comments from individual Socialists in Missouri, Ohio, and New Jersey, see *St. Louis Globe-Democrat*, Aug. 21, 1878; *Indianapolis Sun*, Aug. 1, 1878; and *NYH*, July 29, 1878. For background on Goldwater, see Bruce C. Nelson, *Beyond the Martyrs: A Social History of Chicago's Anarchists, 1870–1900* (New Brunswick, N.J., 1988), 38, 40, 42, 57, 66, 202–3.

33. "Mechanic" (letter) in *NYTr*, Aug. 17, 1878; "Dad" (letter) in *NYS*, Aug. 17, 1878; "By a Mechanic" (letter) in *New York Witness*, Aug. 15, 1878; *St. Louis Post*, Aug. 23, 1878. See also "Toil" (letter) in *PI*, Aug. 17, 1878; "An Irishman" (letter) in *NYH*, Sept. 7, 1878; and John Colton (letter) in *SR*, Aug. 20, 1878.

34. *PI*, Sept. 13, 1878; *Boston Pilot*, Aug. 17, 1878; John Dorthy (letter) and "An Irish Workman" (letter) in ibid., Aug. 24, 1878; "O'Brien" (letter) in ibid., Aug. 31, 1878. See also "A Workingman" (letter) in ibid., Sept. 7, 1878. For anti-Chinese articles, see ibid., Dec. 15, 1877, Apr. 13, and July 6, 1878.

35. *NYT*, July 29, Sept. 8, 1878; *Brooklyn Eagle*, Sept. 8, 1878; *SFC*, Aug. 19, Nov. 12, 1878; *Volksstimme des Westens*, quoted in *St. Louis Globe-Democrat*, Aug. 21, 1878. See also *IW*, Aug. 10, 1878; *Boston Journal*, July 29, 1878; *National Socialist* (Cincinnati), Aug. 24, 1878; and *CTr*, Aug. 19, 1878. I am indebted to Richard Gyory for the German translation. Perhaps the most elaborate banner featuring a "fine painted sketch" appeared at the Indianapolis rally: "[It] represented a landscape, with mountains in the back-ground, from which the sun of labor is rising shedding glorious beams marked 'Equality,' 'Justice,' 'Fraternity,' 'Progress,' etc. At one side the Goddess of Liberty is striking the chains from the limbs of a wage-slave— a stout mechanic, who falls on his knees and worships the rising sun. At the other side of the picture is a scaffold, under which is a row of tombstones bearing the epitaphs of Tom Scott,

Vanderbilt, U. S. Grant, Jay Gould, and the principal capitalistic newspapers of the country" (*National Socialist*, Aug. 24, 1878).

36. *SR*, Sept. 12, 1878; Denis Kearney, "To the Workingmen of Massachusetts," Sept. 21, 1878, in *BG*, Oct. 1, 1878.

37. *SFC*, Sept. 18, 1878; *Boston Journal*, Sept. 26, Oct. 2, Oct. 3, Oct. 4, 1878; *Boston Transcript*, Oct. 2, Oct. 3, 1878; *Pittsfield Sun*, Oct. 16, 1878; *BG*, Oct. 2, Oct. 3, 1878; *Chicago News*, Aug. 21, 1878.

38. *NYW*, Nov. 5, 1878; *Boston Journal*, July 25, 1878. For accounts of Kearney's speeches in the fall, see *BG*, Oct. 8, Oct. 11, Oct. 16, Oct. 17, Oct. 19, Oct. 21, Oct. 28, Nov. 3, Nov. 4, 1878, and *Pittsfield Sun*, Oct. 30, 1878.

39. *Boston Transcript*, Sept. 30, Nov. 1, 1878; *Pittsfield Sun*, Sept. 25, 1878; *SR*, Nov. 1, 1878; *NYW*, quoted in *SFC*, Sept. 24, 1878; *BG*, July 8, Sept. 8, Oct. 27, 1878; *Indianapolis Sun*, Oct. 21, 1878; *SFC*, Nov. 3, 1878; Richard S. West Jr., *Lincoln's Scapegoat General: A Life of Benjamin F. Butler, 1810–1893* (Boston, 1965), 369. Reports of Butler's speeches appeared in the *Boston Globe* almost every day from September 5 to September 12 and from September 27 to November 5. For a brief summary of the campaign, see Trefousse, *Ben Butler*, 240–41. A complete account of this lively campaign remains to be written.

40. *SFC*, Oct. 11, 1878; *SR*, Nov. 13, 1878; *BG*, Nov. 13, 1878; *NYW*, Nov. 13, 1878.

41. *NYH*, Nov. 14, 1878. The *Boston Globe* failed to cover this meeting.

42. *BG*, Nov. 18, 1878; *NYW*, Nov. 20, 1878.

43. *BG*, July 28, 1878; *Pittsfield Sun*, Aug. 28, 1878; *Philadelphia Times*, quoted in *SR*, Sept. 24, 1878; *NYW*, Aug. 10, 1878.

44. *BG*, Aug. 6, 1878.

45. U.S. House of Representatives, *Investigation by a Select Committee of the House of Representatives relative to the Causes of the General Depression in Labor and Business, Etc.*, 45th Cong., 2d sess., Misc. Doc. 29 (Washington, D.C., 1879). A list of witnesses appears on 673–75.

46. Ibid., 41.

47. Ibid., 103.

48. Ibid., 103–4.

49. *CMOJ*, Aug. 10, Sept. 10, 1878; *New York Dispatch*, Aug. 11, 1878.

50. *CT*, Aug. 3, Aug. 23, 1878; *NYT*, Aug. 6, 1878; *NYTr*, Aug. 3, Sept. 7, 1878; *New York Dispatch*, Aug. 11, 1878. For examples of misquoted or incomplete excerpts, see *NYTr*, Aug. 6, 1878; *NYH*, Aug. 3, 1878; *SR*, Aug. 3, 1878; and *PI*, Aug. 3, Aug. 6, 1878. Strasser's testimony refutes Herbert Hill's contention that Strasser was one of "two men, above all others . . . responsible for organized labor's crusade against Asian workers," and Gwendolyn Mink's contention that Strasser "defended the anti-Chinese posture of [his] California colleagues and actively involved [himself] in the exclusion movement." See Herbert Hill, "Race and Ethnicity in Organized Labor: The Historical Sources of Resistance to Affirmative Action," *Journal of Intergroup Relations* 12 (Winter 1984): 14, and Gwendolyn Mink, *Old Labor and New Immigrants in American Political Development: Union, Party, and State, 1875–1920* (Ithaca, N.Y., 1986), 79. For a humorous account of the Hewitt Committee, see Heinz Ickstadt and Hartmut Keil, eds., "A Forgotten Piece of Working-Class Literature: Gustav Lyser's Satire of the Hewitt Hearing of 1878," *Labor History* 20 (Winter 1979): 127–40.

51. *SFC*, Nov. 12, 1878; *SFAC*, Dec. 24, 1878; *CT*, Aug. 19, 1878; Sargent interviewed in *Washington Star*, Nov. 26, 1878. On Walsh, see Robert Ernst, "The One and Only Mike Walsh," *New-York Historical Society Quarterly* 26 (1952): 43–65; Sean Wilentz, *Chants Demo-*

cratic: New York and the Rise of the American Working Class, 1788–1850 (New York, 1984); and Edward Pessen, "Pre-Industrial New York City Labour Revisited: A Critique of a Recent Thompsonian Analysis," *Labour/Le Travail* 16 (Fall 1985): 233–37. Wilentz focuses on Walsh's class-based populism and basically ignores his racist appeal. On Watson, see C. Vann Woodward, *Tom Watson: Agrarian Rebel* (New York, 1938).

52. *SFC*, Aug. 29, 1878; *IW*, Sept. 7, 1878.

53. *SFC*, Dec. 27, 1878.

CHAPTER EIGHT

1. Theron Clark Crawford, *James G. Blaine: A Study of His Life and Career from the Standpoint of a Personal Witness of the Principal Events in His History* (Philadelphia, 1893), 23; Chauncey M. Depew, *My Memories of Eighty Years* (New York, 1922), 141–46; Stevens quoted in Donald Barr Chidsey, *The Gentleman from New York: A Life of Roscoe Conkling* (New Haven, 1935), 40–41; George Frisbie Hoar, *Autobiography of Seventy Years* (New York, 1903), 1:200; *NYH*, Feb. 15, 1879.

2. Eric Foner, *Reconstruction: America's Unfinished Revolution, 1863–1877* (New York, 1988), 467, 468; Chandler quoted in David Saville Muzzey, *James G. Blaine: A Political Idol of Other Days* (New York, 1934), 155; Blaine quoted in Richard Hofstadter, *The American Political Tradition and the Men Who Made It* (New York, 1948), 176; James A. Garfield, Diary, Apr. 14, 1880, James A. Garfield Papers, LC; *NYT*, Apr. 15, 1884, quoted in John G. Sproat, *"The Best Men": Liberal Reformers in the Gilded Age* (New York, 1968), 119; Mark Wahlgren Summers, *The Press Gang: Newspapers and Politics, 1865–1878* (Chapel Hill, N.C., 1994), 150; Charles Edward Russell, *Blaine of Maine: His Life and Times* (New York, 1931), 3; Crawford, *James G. Blaine*, 36–37.

No politician of the Gilded Age deserves a modern biography more than Blaine. The paucity of his private papers has no doubt deterred many scholars. Along with a slew of campaign biographies written in 1884, sympathetic accounts of the Plumed Knight include Crawford, *James G. Blaine*; Gail Hamilton [Mary Abigail Dodge], *Biography of James G. Blaine* (Norwich, Conn., 1895); Edward Stanwood, *James Gillespie Blaine* (Boston, 1906); and Muzzey, *Blaine*. For a more critical account, see Russell, *Blaine of Maine*. See also Norman E. Tutorow, *James Gillespie Blaine and the Presidency: A Documentary Source Book* (New York, 1989).

3. *CR*, 45th Cong., 2d sess., 318 (Jan. 14, 1878); ibid., 3d sess., 447 (Jan. 14, 1879), 791–92 (Jan. 28, 1879). The first version of the bill had limited the number of Chinese passengers to ten, and the effective date was September 1, 1878.

4. The report appears in *CR*, 45th Cong., 3d sess., 793 (Jan. 28, 1879). For Page's and Willis's speeches, see ibid., 795–99 (Jan. 28, 1879).

5. *NYH*, Feb. 5, 1879; for Townsend's speech, see *CR*, 45th Cong., 3d sess., 794–95 (Jan. 28, 1879); for Hardenbergh's speech, see ibid., app., 200 (Jan. 28, 1879); ibid., 800 (Jan. 28, 1879). In the only other speech on the House floor, Representative John Luttrell (D-Calif.) endorsed the bill but mainly delivered a partisan attack on the Republicans (ibid., 798 [Jan. 28, 1879], app., 59–61 [Jan. 28, 1879]). Four other members of the House favoring the bill inserted speeches in the *Congressional Record*: Carter Harrison (D-Ill.); Horace Davis (R-Calif.); Dudley Haskell (R-Kans.); and Hernando Money (D-Miss.). Two nonvoting delegates also inserted speeches: Orange Jacobs (R-Washington Territory); and William Corlett

(R-Wyoming Territory). Conger's provision was later incorporated into the bill by the Senate (ibid., app., 26–27, 28–33, 36–38, 51–57 [Jan. 28, 1879]).

6. *CR*, 45th Cong., 3d sess., 794, 800–801 (Jan. 28, 1879), app., 31–33 (Jan. 28, 1879); *NYT*, Jan. 31, 1879.

7. For Sargent's speech, see *CR*, 45th Cong., 3d sess., 1264–67 (Feb. 13, 1879).

8. Ibid.

9. Ibid., 1270 (Feb. 13, 1879), app., 91, 92, 94 (Feb. 14, 1879).

10. Ibid., 1268, 1269, 1271 (Feb. 13, 1879), 1303 (Feb. 14, 1879), app., 89–99 (Feb. 14, 1879).

11. For Blaine's speech, see *CR*, 45th Cong., 3d sess., 1299–1303 (Feb. 14, 1879).

12. James G. Blaine (letter) in *NYTr*, Feb. 24, 1879.

13. Ibid.; *CR*, 45th Cong., 3d sess., 1302 (Feb. 14, 1879).

14. *Congressional Quarterly's Guide to U.S. Elections*, 2d ed. (Washington, D.C., 1985), 339; *Portland Eastern Argus*, Mar. 7, 1879; *Utica Herald*, quoted in *SR*, Feb. 21, 1879.

15. Fred Emory Haynes, *Social Politics in the United States* (Boston, 1924), 161; George C. Gorham to Blaine, Sept. 13, 1878 (microfilm reel no. 8), James G. Blaine Papers, LC. See also John Tyler Jr. to John Sherman, Feb. 19, Feb. 25, 1879, John Sherman Papers, LC. As James Garfield observed, "A curious phenomenon is presented in the fact that the Greenback Party shows more signs of activity since the election than before and seems to be bent on proselyting the people and increasing its strength" (Garfield, Diary, Dec. 4, 1878, Garfield Papers).

On Gorham's familiarity and past experiences with the Chinese issue, see Alexander Saxton, *The Indispensable Enemy: Labor and the Anti-Chinese Movement in California* (Berkeley, 1971), 81–89.

16. *NYW*, Feb. 23, 1879.

17. The song, "President McMullen," was sung "with great success at the London Theatre" in New York City. See John E. Murphy, *Murphy and Mack's Rafferty Blues Songster* (New York, [1880?]), 20, and Murphy, *Murphy and Mack's McMullen Family Songster* (New York, 1879).

18. *NYS*, Feb. 25, 1879.

19. The scrapbook filled with clippings can be found on microfilm reel no. 16 of the Blaine Papers. Correspondence can be found on earlier reels. *NYW*, Feb. 26, Feb. 27, 1879; *NYS*, Feb. 20, 1879; Crawford, *James G. Blaine*, 23.

20. Philip A. Roach to Bayard, Jan. 16, Jan. 18, 1879, and Eugene Casserly to Bayard, Feb. 14, 1879, Thomas F. Bayard Papers, LC.

21. *CR*, 45th Cong., 3d sess., 1310–11 (Feb. 14, 1879); *San Francisco Call*, Feb. 16, 1879, reprinted in *NYW*, Feb. 25, 1879; A. W. Dickson to Bayard, Feb. 21, 1879, Bayard Papers. As secretary of state from 1885 to 1889, Bayard engaged in lengthy treaty negotiations with China, at one point urging extension of the period of Chinese exclusion to thirty years, and for another thirty years thereafter. See Charles Callan Tansill, *The Foreign Policy of Thomas F. Bayard, 1885–1897* (New York, 1940), chap. 5. On Bayard's deep-seated racism, see Jean Baker, *Affairs of Party: The Political Culture of Northern Democrats in the Mid–Nineteenth Century* (Ithaca, N.Y., 1983), chap. 5.

22. *CGa*, Sept. 12, 1870; *CR*, 45th Cong., 3d sess., 1306, 1310 (Feb. 14, 1879).

23. *NYT*, Feb. 17, 1879; *CGa*, Feb. 18, Feb. 19, 1879. For similar editorials emphasizing the purely political nature of the bill, see *Washington Star*, Jan. 29, 1879; *NYS*, Jan. 30, Feb. 18, 1879; *CT*, Feb. 3, 1879; *Boston Journal*, Feb. 3, 1879; *Hartford Courant*, Feb. 15, 1879; *NYTr*, Feb. 19, 1879; and *PI*, Feb. 24, Mar. 3, 1879.

24. On Hamlin, see H. Draper Hunt, *Hannibal Hamlin of Maine: Lincoln's First Vice-President* (Syracuse, N.Y., 1969); *Dictionary of American Biography* (New York, 1932), 8:196–98. For Hamlin's speech, see *CR*, 45th Cong., 3d sess., 1383–87 (Feb. 15, 1879). For Hamlin's other comments during the debate, see ibid., 1274, 1275, 1276 (Feb. 13, 1879), 1301–2, 1305, 1314–15 (Feb. 14, 1879). The quotes are from 1302, 1314, 1315, and 1383.

25. *CR*, 45th Cong., 3d sess., 1276 (Feb. 13, 1879), 1315 (Feb. 14, 1879), 1385, 1387 (Feb. 15, 1879). The description of Hamlin is from *SFC*, Feb. 16, 1879.

26. *CR*, 45th Cong., 3d sess., 1275 (Feb. 13, 1879), 1312 (Feb. 14, 1879), 1389, 1390 (Feb. 15, 1879).

27. *NYH*, Feb. 15, 1879; *Albany Journal*, Feb. 17, 1879; *CR*, 45th Cong., 3d sess., 1312 (Feb. 14, 1879).

28. *CR*, 45th Cong., 3d sess., 1300–1301 (Feb. 14, 1879), 1385, 1386 (Feb. 15, 1879).

29. Ibid., 1301, 1315 (Feb. 14, 1879), 1386 (Feb. 15, 1879).

30. Ibid., 1384 (Feb. 15, 1879).

31. Ibid., 1383, 1386 (Feb. 15, 1879). Hamlin's most recent biographer writes that "Hamlin enjoyed one of his finest hours as a statesman when he championed American national honor by opposing the Chinese Exclusion Bill" (Hunt, *Hannibal Hamlin*, 212).

32. *CR*, 45th Cong., 3d sess., 1315 (Feb. 14, 1879), 1391–92, 1393, 1394, 1398 (Feb. 15, 1879).

33. Ibid., 1274, 1275 (Feb. 13, 1879), 1312 (Feb. 14, 1879), 1390, 1392 (Feb. 15, 1879); Lincoln quoted in Hofstadter, *American Political Tradition*, 102.

34. *CR*, 45th Cong., 3d sess., 1305, 1307 (Feb. 14, 1879).

35. Ibid., 1309, 1311 (Feb. 14, 1879), 1386, 1390, 1393, 1394, 1400 (Feb. 15, 1879). On Senator Davis's party affiliation, see below, Chap. 12, n. 20.

36. Ibid., 1390–91, 1399, 1400 (Feb. 15, 1879). The Senate rejected a similar amendment minutes before the final vote.

37. Ibid., 1400 (Feb. 15, 1879); *Puck*, Feb. 26, 1879; *CTr*, Feb. 17, 1879. The amended version of the Fifteen Passenger Bill passed by the Senate excepted four groups: sea captains "in stress of harbor"; Chinese rescued from shipwrecked vessels; Chinese government ministers; and Chinese students with certificates from their government.

It is noteworthy that six of the Democrats voting *against* the bill came from the South. They still looked forward to importing scores of Chinese to their region. Coincidentally, Isham Green Harris, who had chaired the Memphis Chinese Labor Convention in 1869, was presently a senator from Tennessee. He was absent from Washington, however, during the entire debate. One senator, Isaac Christiancy (R-Mich.), had just resigned from the Senate and was succeeded by fellow Republican Zachariah Chandler. Chandler, however, had not yet taken his seat, and his name does not appear in the official tally.

38. *CR*, 45th Cong., 3d sess., 1796 (Feb. 22, 1879).

39. *Washington Star*, Feb. 25, 1879; *SFC*, Feb. 25, Feb. 28, 1879; *NYH*, Feb. 18, Feb. 28, 1879; *Virginia City (Nevada) Enterprise*, quoted in ibid., Feb. 17, 1879; Governor Jno. H. Kinkead to Blaine, March 6, 1879 (microfilm reel no. 16), Blaine Papers; *NYTr*, Feb. 25, Feb. 26, 1879; *CT*, Feb. 27, 1879. The Nevada Senate, San Francisco Board of Supervisors, Sacramento Board of City Trustees, and California Republican State Committee also endorsed the bill unanimously and urged Hayes to sign the bill. On the growing anti-Chinese sentiment among California clergy, see Robert Seager II, "Some Denominational Reactions to Chinese Immigration to California, 1856–1892," *Pacific Historical Review* 28 (Feb. 1959): 49–66.

40. *NYH*, Feb. 22, Feb. 28, 1879; *CT*, Feb. 17, Feb. 22, Feb. 25, Feb. 26, Feb. 27, 1879; *Daily Stock Report* (San Francisco), reprinted in ibid., Feb. 22, 1879; *SFC*, Jan. 30, 1879; *Paterson*

Labor Standard, Feb. 22, 1879; *Puck*, Mar. 5, 1879; "A New Ballad of Secession," in *NYS*, Feb. 24, 1879; Rev. Howard Henderson (letter) in *CE*, Apr. 27, 1880.

41. *PI*, Feb. 17, 1879; *Hartford Courant*, Feb. 15, 1879; *Brooklyn Eagle*, Feb. 17, Feb. 24, 1879. See also ibid., Feb. 22, 1879. *NYW*, Feb. 17, Feb. 23, 1879; *Louisville Courier-Journal*, reprinted in *CT*, Feb. 22, 1879; *Poughkeepsie Eagle*, Feb. 24, 1879, reprinted in *NYW*, Feb. 25, 1879; *New York Irish-American*, Mar. 8, 1879; *SR*, Feb. 20, 1879; *Cincinnati Commercial*, quoted in *Boston Times*, Feb. 24, 1879, reprinted in *NYW*, Feb. 25, 1879.

42. *CT*, Feb. 17, 1879; *CE*, Feb. 15, 1879; *CTr*, Feb. 25, 1879; *Nation*, Feb. 20, 1879. See also *Albany Journal*, Feb. 15, Feb. 18, Feb. 24, 1879.

43. *CGa*, Feb. 18, Feb. 25, Mar. 3, 1879. On the *Gazette*'s pro-exclusion stance in 1870, see above, Chap. 3.

44. *NYTr*, Feb. 8, Feb. 19, Feb. 21, Feb. 24, 1879; see also Jan. 21, 1879.

45. *NYT*, Jan. 29, Jan. 31, Feb. 17, Feb. 19, Feb. 24, Mar. 4, 1879. See also Feb. 15 and Feb. 18, 1879. Other journals that had spoken for a generation of Republicans expressed identical themes. See, for example, *Hartford Courant*, Feb. 15, Feb. 17, Feb. 24, 1879; *Boston Journal*, Feb. 3, Feb. 18, 1879; and *PI*, Feb. 15, Feb. 17, 1879.

46. *Boston Post*, quoted in *St. Louis Post-Dispatch*, Feb. 24, 1879.

47. *NYT*, Feb. 21, Feb. 28, 1879; *NYH*, Jan. 29, Feb. 28, 1879; *PI*, Mar. 3, 1879. See also *NYT*, Feb. 19, 1879; *NYH*, Mar. 1, 1879; and *New York Commercial*, reprinted in *SFC*, Feb. 21, 1879.

48. *NYH*, Feb. 10, 1879; *Methodist* (Baltimore), cited in ibid., Feb. 23, 1879; Gary Pennanen, "Public Opinion and the Chinese Question, 1876–1879," *Ohio History* 77 (Winter/Spring/Summer 1968): 144; *NYT*, Feb. 19, 1879. For antibill sentiment, see *New York Independent*, *Baptist Weekly*, *National Baptist*, *Christian Intelligencer*, and *Christian Union*, summarized in *NYH*, Feb. 23, 1879. See also *NYT*, Feb. 18, 1879; *PI*, Feb. 25, 1879; and *CGa*, Feb. 24, 1879. For pro-bill sentiment, see Rev. Charles Taylor (Methodist Episcopal) in *CE*, Jan. 22, 1879; Rev. C. W. Wendte (Unitarian) in *CGa*, Feb. 24, 1879; and *Alliance* (Chicago), Feb. 22, 1879, and *Christian Cynosure* (Chicago), Mar. 6, 1879, both clippings in microfilm reel no. 16, Blaine Papers.

49. *NYTr*, Feb. 17, Feb. 25, Feb. 27, 1879; *NYT*, Feb. 27, 1879; *IWAIL*, July 12, 1879; *NYH*, Feb. 19, 1879; *New Haven Register*, reprinted in *CT*, Feb. 28, 1879; George William Curtis to Rutherford B. Hayes, quoted in Pennanen, "Public Opinion," 148; Frederick Wells Williams, *The Life and Letters of Samuel Wells Williams, LL.D., Missionary, Diplomatist, Sinologue* (New York, 1889), 429. One of Barnum's chief circus attractions was "Chang the Giant" of China, a fact that may or may not have influenced the great showman's attitude toward Chinese immigration.

Along with Frederick Douglass, Henry Highland Garnet was one of the most respected black leaders in the nation. Both men had been militant abolitionists and, like many blacks, they firmly opposed Chinese exclusion. When it came to anti-Chinese stereotypes and prejudices, however, views of the black community tended to mirror those of whites. See David J. Hellwig, "Black Reactions to Chinese Immigration and the Anti-Chinese Movement, 1850–1910," *Amerasia* 6 (1979): 25–44; Leigh Dana Johnsen, "Equal Rights and the 'Heathen Chinee': Black Activism in San Francisco, 1865–1875," *Western Historical Quarterly* 11 (Jan. 1980): 57–68; and Arnold Shankman, "Black on Yellow: Afro-Americans View Chinese-Americans, 1850–1935," *Phylon* 39 (Spring 1978): 1–17.

50. *Paterson Labor Standard*, Feb. 22, 1879; *National Labor Tribune* (Pittsburgh), Mar. 8, 1879. It should be noted that the *Labor Tribune* of Feb. 15, 1879, is missing. *Socialist* (Chicago), Nov. 30, 1878, Feb. 15, Mar. 8, Mar. 15, 1879; *IWAIL*, Mar. 1, Mar. 8, 1879. See also

IWAIL, Apr. 19, 1879. For a variety of working-class and Socialist opinions on Chinese immigration and discomfort with exclusion, see the lively correspondence of "Rusticus," "Leo," "Justus," and W. G. H. Smart, in *Socialist* (Chicago), Jan. 11–Apr. 26, 1879.

51. *CMOJ*, Mar. 10, May 10, 1879; *BG*, Jan. 20, Jan. 31, Feb. 17, Feb. 18, Feb. 22, 1879; George B. Perry to Ben Butler, Feb. 18, 1879, Benjamin F. Butler Papers, LC; *Paterson Labor Standard*, Nov. 23, 1878; *NYH*, Feb. 12, Feb. 16, Feb. 21, 1879; *CT*, Feb. 23, 1879; Knights of Labor, *Record of the Proceedings of the Second Regular Session of the General Assembly, Held at St. Louis, Mo., January 14–17, 1879* (n.p., 1879). For other labor meetings during the winter of 1879, see, for example, *Socialist* (Chicago), Mar. 1, 1879; *CT*, Jan. 13, Jan. 27, Feb. 3, Feb. 24, 1879; *BG*, Jan. 27, Jan. 28, Jan. 29, Jan. 31, Feb. 1, Feb. 3, Feb. 6, Feb. 19, Feb. 27, Mar. 3, 1879; *Brooklyn Eagle*, Feb. 15, 1879; *NYH*, Mar. 3, 1879; and *CE*, Mar. 2, 1879. These myriad meetings, which covered the entire gamut of working people's concerns, said nothing on Chinese immigration.

On February 18, three days after approving the Fifteen Passenger Bill, the Senate rejected the anti–tenement house measure, and the House failed to consider it. Cigar makers then turned to state legislatures for relief, and four years of persistent lobbying led to a New York law abolishing tenement house labor in 1883. The courts, however, declared the law unconstitutional. The attorney for the manufacturers was former secretary of state William M. Evarts. See *CMOJ*, Mar. 10, May 10, 1879, and Samuel Gompers, *Seventy Years of Life and Labor: An Autobiography* (New York, 1925), 1:183–98.

52. *CE*, Feb. 24, 1879; *Washington Star*, Feb. 25, 1879; *IWAIL*, Sept. 27, 1879. On earlier meetings of the National Workingmen's Assembly, see *Washington Star*, Jan. 7, Jan. 14, Jan. 21, Jan. 28, Feb. 4, Feb. 11, and Feb. 19, 1879. Interestingly, on March 3, the association gave special praise to Senator Sargent, but only on behalf of his efforts in the Government Printing Office. Nothing was said about his efforts on behalf of the Fifteen Passenger Bill (ibid., Mar. 4, 1879).

53. *CE*, Dec. 28, 1878, reprinted in *SFC*, Jan. 3, 1879; *CE*, Jan. 23, 1879; *SFC*, Dec. 28, 1878, reprinted in *National Labor Tribune* (Pittsburgh), Jan. 11, 1879; *Socialist* (Chicago), May 3, 1879; *CTr*, Mar. 2, 1879; *CT*, Mar. 2, 1879. For more commentary on eastern workers' apathy regarding Chinese immigration, see *Boston Pilot*, Jan. 4, 1879, and *San Francisco Call*, Feb. 25, 1879, clipping in microfilm reel no. 16, Blaine Papers. On the anti-Chinese movement in Australia, see Charles A. Price, *The Great White Walls Are Built: Restrictive Immigration to North America and Australia, 1836–1888* (Canberra, 1974), and Andrew Markus, *Fear and Hatred: Purifying Australia and California, 1850–1901* (Sydney, 1979). The official report of the Illinois legislature, it might be added, failed to mention Morgan's testimony on the Chinese. See Illinois House of Representatives, *Illinois House. Report of Special Committee on Labor* (Springfield, 1879).

54. *CE*, Feb. 20, Feb. 24, 1879; *CT*, Mar. 2, 1879. For a more detailed account of working-class activity in early 1879, see Andrew Gyory, "Rolling in the Dirt: The Origins of the Chinese Exclusion Act and the Politics of Racism, 1870–1882" (Ph.D. diss., University of Massachusetts at Amherst, 1991), 651–53.

55. *NYTr*, Feb. 19, 1879; *Cleveland Herald*, Feb. 25, 1879, clipping in microfilm reel no. 16, Blaine Papers; *SFC*, Feb. 21, 1879. See also *BG*, Mar. 10, 1879, and Joaquin Miller (letter) in *NYTr*, Feb. 25, 1879. Some historians have echoed this argument and blamed Chinese exclusion on Irish immigrants. See, for example, Mary Roberts Coolidge, *Chinese Immigration* (New York, 1909).

56. Accounts of the cabinet meeting appeared in many newspapers. See, for example,

Washington Star, Jan. 3, 1879; *BG*, Jan. 4, 1879; and *Portland Eastern Argus*, Jan. 6, 1879. The quotes are from *CT*, Jan. 4, 1879, and *NYH*, Jan. 4, 1879.

57. *NYH*, Feb. 14, Feb. 19, 1879; *SR*, Feb. 24, 1879; *CGa*, Feb. 18, Feb. 24, 1879; *SFC*, Jan. 21, 1879; *NYT*, Feb. 18, 1879; Edmund H. Worthy Jr., "Yung Wing in America," *Pacific Historical Review* 34 (Aug. 1965): 278–79. See also U.S. House of Representatives, *Message from the President of the United States, Transmitting, in Response to a Resolution of the House of Representatives, a Report from the Secretary of State in Relation to the Negotiations concerning the Immigration of Chinese to the United States, April 12, 1880*, 45th Cong., 2d sess., Executive Doc. 70 (Washington, D.C., 1880); Ch'en Lan-pin and Yung Wing were the same two men who directed the Chinese Educational Mission in Connecticut (see above, Chap. 6, n. 1). Although Ch'en was the official Chinese minister and Yung his associate, Yung, who was completely bilingual, often spoke for the legation, particularly during Ch'en's numerous absences abroad. See Earl Swisher, "Chinese Representation in the United States, 1861–1912," *University of Colorado Studies* 5 (1967), reprinted in Swisher, *Early Sino-American Relations: The Collected Articles of Earl Swisher*, ed. Kenneth W. Rea (Boulder, Colo., 1977), 184–85. On the establishment of the Chinese legation, see Shih-shan Henry Tsai, *China and the Overseas Chinese in the United States, 1868–1911* (Fayetteville, Ark., 1983), 38–42.

58. Rutherford B. Hayes, *The Diary of a President, 1875–1881, concerning the Disputed Election, the End of Reconstruction, and the Beginning of Civil Service*, ed. T. Harry Williams (New York, 1964), 187–88 (Feb. 20, 1879), 192 (Feb. 28, 1879).

59. *New York Graphic*, Feb. 24, 1879, quoted in *SFC*, Feb. 25, 1879; Garfield, Diary, Feb. 23, Feb. 24, 1879, Garfield Papers. Garfield had also met privately with Evarts in January to discuss the Fifteen Passenger Bill and Chinese immigration. See ibid., Jan. 26, 1879.

60. *CR*, 45th Cong., 3d sess., 2275–76 (Mar. 1, 1879). Moments after receiving Hayes's message, the House failed to muster a two-thirds majority to override the president's veto, 110 in favor, 96 opposed, and 84 not voting (ibid., 2276–77 [Mar. 1, 1879]).

61. *CE*, Mar. 6, 1879; *BG*, Feb. 26, 1879.

62. Garfield, Diary, Feb. 24, 1879, Garfield Papers.

63. Elmer Clarence Sandmeyer, *The Anti-Chinese Movement in California* (Urbana, Ill., 1939), 91; Saxton, *Indispensable Enemy*, 137.

64. *Cleveland Daily Advance*, Jan. 11, 1879.

CHAPTER NINE

1. The California constitution of 1879 is readily available. See, for example, Edward F. Treadwell, ed., *The Constitution of the State of California* (San Francisco, 1923). For background on the charter, see Carl Brent Swisher, *Motivation and Political Technique in the California Constitutional Convention, 1878–79* (Claremont, Calif., 1930); James Bryce, *The American Commonwealth*, 3d ed. (New York, 1905; first published 1894), 1:711–24, 2:437–42; and Ira B. Cross, *A History of the Labor Movement in California* (Berkeley, 1935), 118. On the vote, see Swisher, *Motivation and Political Technique*, 109. In urging ratification, Kearney wrote, "I made a thorough canvass of the state, speaking in some cases three times in one day." See Denis Kearney to Lord Bryce, Nov. 14, 1889, quoted in Doyce B. Nunis Jr., ed., "The Demagogue and the Demographer: Correspondence of Denis Kearney and Lord Bryce," *Pacific Historical Review* 36 (Aug. 1967), 285.

2. Alexander Saxton, *The Indispensable Enemy: Labor and the Anti-Chinese Movement in California* (Berkeley, 1971), 127–32, 138; Henry George, "The Kearney Agitation in Califor-

nia," *Popular Science Monthly* 17 (Aug. 1880): 445–49. Other historians have also stressed the moderateness of the California constitution. See, for example, Ralph Kauer, "The Working-men's Party of California," *Pacific Historical Review* 13 (Sept. 1944): 283–85.

3. *NYTr*, May 16, May 23, 1879; *NYW*, May 16, 1879; *NYH*, May 16, May 22, 1879; *IWAIL*, May 31, 1879; *BG*, May 24, Aug. 28, 1879. See also *CT*, May 10, 1879.

4. *Socialist* (Chicago), May 24, 1879; *CT*, May 19, 1879. The *Times's* version of the resolution substituted the term "working people" for "workingmen." For a sampling of workers' meetings during this period, see *CT*, May 19, July 5, 1879; *BG*, July 5, 1879; *NYH*, July 5, 1879; *Washington Star*, July 5, 1879; *Trades* (Philadelphia), July 12, 1879; *Socialist* (Chicago), July 12, 1879; and *IWAIL*, July 19, 1879. For an overview of labor sentiment in the East in 1879, see Andrew Gyory, "Rolling in the Dirt: The Origins of the Chinese Exclusion Act and the Politics of Racism, 1870–1882" (Ph.D. diss., University of Massachusetts at Amherst, 1991), 695–97, 711–16.

5. U.S. House of Representatives, *Investigation by a Select Committee of the House of Representatives relative to the Causes of the General Depression in Labor and Business; and as to Chinese Immigration* [hereafter *Investigation*], 46th Cong., 2d sess., Misc. Doc. 5 (Washington, D.C., 1879), 251, 257–58, 263, 277, 314, 318, 361, 467–68; *Boston Pilot*, Aug. 9, 1879. The congressional committee had met in Chicago three weeks earlier, from July 28 to August 1. Of the thirty-six Chicagoans who testified (one-third of them workers), only one, a rolling-mill manufacturer, urged Chinese exclusion (*Investigation*, 5–237, esp. 230–36). After meeting in San Francisco from August 15 to August 19, the committee met in Des Moines, September 2; New York, October 28; and Boston, November 4, 1879.

6. *Investigation*, 320–24, 338–50, 467–68. Healy gave some of the most hilarious testimony ever heard before a congressional committee. See *Investigation*, 320–24. He later became one of the West Coast's chief defenders of Chinese immigration. See Patrick Joseph Healy, "A Shoemaker's Contribution to the Chinese Discussion," *Overland Monthly* 7 (Apr. 1886): 414–21; Patrick Joseph Healy, *Some Reasons Why an Exclusion Law Should Not Be Passed* (San Francisco, 1902); and Patrick Joseph Healy and Ng Poon Chew, *A Statement for Non-Exclusion* (San Francisco, 1905).

Gibson, who had spent many years in China, wrote one of the earliest works on Chinese immigration. See Otis Gibson, *The Chinese in America* (Cincinnati, 1877).

7. Neil Larry Shumsky, *The Evolution of Political Protest and the Workingmen's Party of California* (Columbus, Ohio, 1991), 203–4; Neil Larry Shumsky, "San Francisco's Crowd: The Workingmen's Party of California, 1877–1879" (unpublished paper in possession of the author), 19–20; M. M. Marberry, *The Golden Voice: A Biography of Isaac Kalloch* (New York, 1947), 229, 250, 253–55, 259–60; George, "The Kearney Agitation in California," 447; *CE*, Apr. 27, 1880; *IWAIL*, Sept. 13, 1879; *Boston Pilot*, Aug. 30, 1879.

8. *IWAIL*, Sept. 13, 1879; Marberry, *Golden Voice*, 260–63.

9. In a fitting climax to this macabre episode, Kalloch's son shot De Young to death in 1880. A friendly jury acquitted the son of murder (Marberry, *Golden Voice*, 294–300).

10. Shumsky, "San Francisco's Crowd," 15; Kauer, "The Workingmen's Party of California," 287.

The Republican majority by state in the House of Representatives was very tenuous. After winning California, Republicans held a nineteen to eighteen advantage, with Indiana still divided among six Republicans, six Democrats, and one Greenbacker.

The historian Mary Roberts Coolidge questioned the validity of the California referendum because of the bias of the wording. The ballot itself was marked "Against Chinese

Immigration" in very small letters. Thus to vote in favor of Chinese immigration, a voter had to read the ballot carefully, then physically cross out the word "Against" and write in "For." Coolidge's point is well taken but hardly convincing. Mere laziness on the part of the voters cannot account for the dismal showing of pro-Chinese forces. One could double, quadruple, even multiply by ten the pro-Chinese vote and the outcome would not be appreciably different. A referendum in Nevada one year later produced comparable results: opposed to Chinese immigration, 17,209 (98.9 percent); in favor, 183 (1.1 percent). As the historian Lucile Eaves has written, "Even when one makes allowance for the influence of any peculiarities in the printing of the ballots, the results of these elections indicate a remarkable uniformity of public opinion. . . . There can be no question that the great majority of the citizens of these states [California and Nevada] were thoroughly convinced that men of this race [the Chinese] were unfitted for membership in an American commonwealth." See Mary Roberts Coolidge, *Chinese Immigration* (New York, 1909), 123–24, and Lucile Eaves, *A History of California Labor Legislation, with an Introductory Sketch of the San Francisco Labor Movement*, University of California Publications in Economics, vol. 2 (Berkeley, 1910), 159.

11. *NYH*, Aug. 30, 1879; *NYTr*, Aug. 28, 1879; *National View* (Washington), Aug. 30, Sept. 20, Nov. 1, Dec. 13, 1879; *CT*, Aug. 19, 1878. Numerous mainstream newspapers applauded Kearney for his peacekeeping efforts. See, for example, *SFAC*, Aug. 24, 1879; *NYH*, quoted in ibid., Aug. 25, 1879; and *Indianapolis Journal*, quoted in *SFC*, Aug. 28, 1879. For more Greenback praise of Kearney, see *National View*, Sept. 13, Sept. 27, Oct. 25, 1879, and *NYH*, Sept. 25, 1879. For opposition within the Workingmen's Party of California to Kearney's collusion with the Greenbackers, see *National View*, Oct. 25, 1879.

12. *NYH*, Dec. 19, 1879; *CE*, Dec. 20, 1879; *CT*, Dec. 20, 1879, Jan. 9, Jan. 10, Jan. 13, 1880; *Chicago Express*, Jan. 14, 1880. Few newspapers covered this conference.

13. *NYS*, Jan. 17, 1880; *NYTr*, Jan. 17, 1880; *New York Star*, Jan. 17, 1880; *NYH*, Jan. 17, 1880; *IWAIL*, Jan. 31, 1880; *CT*, Jan. 26, 1880; *CTr*, Jan. 26, Jan. 28, 1880; *Washington Star*, Dec. 23, Dec. 30, 1879, Jan. 6, Jan. 13, Jan. 20, Jan. 27, 1880. The Kearney quote is from the *New York Sun*. For weeks after his visit to Chicago, Greenbackers and members of the Trade and Labor Council bickered over who should pay for the hall rented for his speech. See *CT*, Feb. 16, Feb. 27, 1880, and *CTr*, Mar. 1, 1880. The *Paterson Labor Standard* (Jan. 24, 1880) printed one sentence on Kearney's tour. On Parnell's visit, see Eric Foner, "Class, Ethnicity, and Radicalism in the Gilded Age: The Land League and Irish America," in *Politics and Ideology in the Age of the Civil War* (New York, 1980), 150–200.

14. *Chinatown Declared a Nuisance!* (n.p., 1880); Charles J. McClain, "In *Re Lee Sing*: The First Residential-Segregation Case," *Western Legal History* 3 (1985): 182; Rev. Howard Henderson (letter) in *CE*, Apr. 27, 1880; *St. Louis Post-Dispatch*, Mar. 9, 1880; *Boston Pilot*, Mar. 20, 1880; *NYH*, Mar. 2, Mar. 11, 1880. For a summary of these events, see Saxton, *Indispensable Enemy*, chap. 7; Cross, *A History of the Labor Movement in California*, 123–24; and Marberry, *Golden Voice*, chap. 11. The events can also be followed in the San Francisco press and in eastern journals such as the *Chicago Times* and the *New York Herald*. Other towns in California, such as Nevada City, passed ordinances to evict Chinese residents from their jurisdictions. See McClain, "In *Re Lee Sing*," 185.

15. Yung and Evarts quoted in Shih-shan Henry Tsai, *China and the Overseas Chinese in the United States, 1868–1911* (Fayetteville, Ark.), 1983), 51–52; *CT*, Mar. 1, Mar. 5, 1880; *NYS*, Mar. 7, 1880; *New York Star*, Mar. 5, 1880; *BG*, Mar. 20, 1880; *NYH*, Mar. 5, Mar. 6, Mar. 7, 1880; *NYT*, Mar. 6, Mar. 20, 1880; *St. Louis Globe-Democrat*, quoted in *CT*, Mar. 5, 1880. A

low transcontinental fare of thirty-five dollars, the *Globe-Democrat* noted, helped induce the exodus.

16. *NYH*, Mar. 11, Mar. 14, Mar. 20, Apr. 18, 1880; *Puck*, Mar. 17, 1880, 24–25. See also *NYT*, Mar. 6, 1880. I have been unable to determine whether Mrs. Timothy Sargent was any relation to Senator Aaron Sargent.

17. *NYH*, Mar. 9, Mar. 19, Mar. 20, 1880; *NYTr*, Mar. 21, 1880; *NYT*, Mar. 20, 1880; Beverley Tucker to William M. Evarts, Aug. 11, 1879, William M. Evarts Papers, LC.

18. *Puck*, Mar. 17, 1880, 24–25.

19. *CT*, Mar. 16, Mar. 20, 1880; *CTr*, Mar. 16, 1880. On the meeting's planning, see *CT*, Mar. 12, 1880.

20. *CT*, Mar. 20, 1880.

21. *Chicago News*, Mar. 6, 1880. On the national nature of the strike wave, see *NYH*, Feb. 23, Feb. 26, Mar. 1, Mar. 15, Mar. 16, Mar. 19, Mar. 21, Mar. 22, Mar. 23, Mar. 25, Mar. 26, 1880; *NYT*, Mar. 9, Mar. 22, 1880; *BG*, Feb. 10, Mar. 4, Mar. 5, Mar. 14, Mar. 23, 1880; *NYS*, Mar. 31, 1880; *CT*, Mar. 31, 1880; *St. Louis Post-Dispatch*, Mar. 20, Mar. 22, 1880; and *Chicago News*, Mar. 12, Mar. 19, 1880.

22. *NYS*, Mar. 17, 1880; *NYT*, Mar. 12, Mar. 16, Mar. 17, Mar. 21, 1880; *New York Star*, Mar. 18, 1880; *NYTr*, Mar. 19, 1880; *NYH*, Feb. 26, Mar. 15, Mar. 16, Mar. 20, Mar. 30, 1880; *IWAIL*, Mar. 27, 1880.

23. *NYS*, Mar. 18, 1880; *NYT*, Mar. 18, 1880.

24. *Nation*, Mar. 18, 1880; *Chicago News*, Mar. 16, 1880; Saxton, *Indispensable Enemy*, 145–46; *BG*, Apr. 9, May 4, May 8, 1880 (supplement); *Brooklyn Eagle*, May 15, 1880; *IWAIL*, May 22, May 29, 1880; *Fall River Labor Standard*, May 15, 1880; *Paterson Labor Standard*, May 29, 1880. For denunciation of Kearney's sentence, see, for example, *Chicago News*, Mar. 20, 1880, and *NYS*, Mar. 27, 1880.

Some speakers compared the imprisonment of Kearney with that of *Paterson Labor Standard* editor Joseph P. McDonnell, who was serving time in jail following his libel conviction for exposing rotten working conditions in a local New Jersey brickyard. See *BG*, Apr. 9, 1880, and Herbert G. Gutman, "A Brief Postscript: Class, Status, and the Gilded Age Radical. A Reconsideration," in *Work, Culture, and Society in Industrializing America: Essays in American Working-Class and Social History* (New York, 1977), 260–93.

25. *Fall River Labor Standard*, Feb. 28, 1880. On the strike by cigar makers, see *St. Louis Post-Dispatch*, Aug. 20, Aug. 22, Aug. 23, Aug. 27, Aug. 29, Aug. 30, Sept. 1, Sept. 12, Sept. 18, Oct. 29, 1879; *CT*, Aug. 26, Aug. 30, 1879; and *Trades* (Philadelphia), Sept. 13, 1879.

CHAPTER TEN

1. *CT*, May 30, May 31, 1880. See also *SFC*, May 17, June 1, 1880, and *CTr*, May 31, 1880.

2. The best account of Grant's final run for the presidency is William B. Hesseltine, *Ulysses S. Grant, Politician* (New York, 1967; first published 1935), chap. 26. Grant's world tour is covered well in William S. McFeely, *Grant: A Biography* (New York, 1982), chap. 25. See also John Russell Young, *Around the World with General Grant: A Narrative of the Visit of General U. S. Grant, Ex-President of the United States, to Various Countries in Europe, Asia, and Africa, in 1877, 1878, 1879. To Which Are Added Certain Conversations with General Grant on Questions Connected with American Politics and History*, 2 vols. (New York, 1879). On Grant's arrival in San Francisco, see *SFC*, Sept. 21, 1879. On preparations, see ibid., from Sept. 16 through Sept. 20, 1879.

3. *NYH*, Aug. 16, 1879.

4. This chapter is by no means a definitive history of the 1880 election; it deals only with the impact of Chinese immigration on the campaign. For extended treatments of the election, see Herbert J. Clancy, *The Presidential Election of 1880* (Chicago, 1958); Leonard Dinnerstein, "Election of 1880," in *History of American Presidential Elections, 1789–1968*, ed. Arthur M. Schlesinger Jr. (New York, 1971), 2:1491–1516; Justus Doenecke, *The Presidencies of James A. Garfield and Chester A. Arthur* (Lawrence, Kans., 1981), chap. 2; Alan Peskin, *Garfield* (Kent, Ohio, 1978), chaps. 21–22; John M. Taylor, *Garfield of Ohio: The Available Man* (New York, 1970), chaps. 1, 13–15; Margaret Leech and Harry J. Brown, *The Garfield Orbit* (New York, 1978), chap. 10; and Robert Granville Caldwell, *James Garfield: Party Chieftain* (New York, 1931), chap. 14. The quote is from Dinnerstein, "Election of 1880," 1491.

5. E. B. Kennedy et al., *Our Presidential Candidates and Political Compendium. Also Containing Lives of the Candidates for Vice-President—the Proceedings of the Three National Conventions—the Three Platforms and the Three Letters of Acceptance* (Newark, N.J., 1880), 7–8. For descriptions of the convention, see Taylor, *Garfield of Ohio*; Peskin, *Garfield*; and Thomas C. Reeves, *Gentleman Boss: The Life of Chester Alan Arthur* (New York, 1975).

6. *CT*, June 2, June 3, 1880; *CTr*, June 3, 1880; *NYT*, June 3, 1880.

7. Republican Party, *Proceedings of the Republican National Convention, Held at Chicago, Illinois, Wednesday, Thursday, Friday, Saturday, Monday and Tuesday, June 2d, 3d, 4th, 5th, 7th and 8th, 1880. Resulting in the Following Nominations: For President, James A. Garfield, of Ohio. For Vice-President, Chester A. Arthur, of New York*, comp. Eugene Davis (Chicago, 1881), 160–69.

8. *NYT*, June 6, June 7, 1880; *Philadelphia Press*, June 7, 1880; *NYTr*, June 6, 1880; *Boston Pilot*, June 12, 1880.

9. *NYH*, June 5, 1880; *CT*, May 31, 1880. Exact tallies of the thirty-six ballots can be found in Kennedy et al., *Our Presidential Candidates*; Republican Party, *Proceedings of the Republican National Convention*; and any of the major dailies. See, for example, *CT*, June 9, 1880. The four minor candidates and their support on the first ballot were John Sherman (93), George F. Edmunds (34), Elihu B. Washburne (30), and William Windom (10).

10. James G. Blaine, *Twenty Years of Congress: From Lincoln to Garfield. With a Review of the Events Which Led to the Political Revolution of 1860* (Norwich, Conn., 1886; first published 1884), 2:666.

11. *CE*, June 21, 1880. Hancock narrowly led Bayard on the first ballot, 171 to 153½. Henry B. Payne of Ohio received 81 votes and Thurman 68½. On Hancock, see *Reminiscences of Winfield Scott Hancock, by His Wife* (New York, 1887); David M. Jordan, *Winfield Scott Hancock: A Soldier's Life* (Bloomington, 1988); Kennedy et al., *Our Presidential Candidates*, 166–218; and John M. Taylor, "General Hancock: Soldier of the Gilded Age," *Pennsylvania History* 32 (Apr. 1965): 187–96. On Tilden's withdrawal, which many dismissed as a ploy actually to gain the nomination, see Alexander Clarence Flick, *Samuel Jones Tilden: A Study in Political Sagacity* (New York, 1939), chaps. 34–35.

12. *CT*, June 24, June 26, 1880; Donald Bruce Johnson, comp., *1840–1956*, vol. 1 of *National Party Platforms* (Urbana, Ill., 1978), 57; *CE*, June 25, 1880; *NYH*, July 6, 1880; *SFAC*, June 15, 1880; *Puck*, July 14, 1880; *Oshkosh Standard*, July 22, 1880. On the interchangeability of the planks, see, for example, the comments of former abolitionist George W. Julian and the flamboyant merchant (and racist) George Francis Train (George W. Julian, "The Issues of 1880—Character of the Candidates," in *Later Speeches on Political Questions with Select*

Controversial Papers, ed. George W. Julian and George Julian Clarke [Indianapolis, 1889], 180; Train quoted in *Oshkosh Standard*, July 1, 1880).

13. *NYH*, Mar. 24, 1880; *NYT*, Mar. 25, 1880; *Oshkosh Standard*, Mar. 11, 1880. For other state and local Greenback conventions, see ibid., Apr. 29, May 20, June 3, 1880; *CT*, Apr. 22, Apr. 30, June 2, 1880; and *BG*, May 12, 1880. On Kearney's release from prison, see *SFC*, May 28, May 29, 1880.

14. Kennedy et al., *Our Presidential Candidates*, 74–79; *CT*, June 10, 1880; *CTr*, June 10, 1880; *IWAIL*, June 26, 1880.

15. *CT*, June 10, 1880.

16. Kennedy et al., *Our Presidential Candidates*, 75; *CT*, June 11, 1880; *NYT*, June 11, 1880; *New York Commercial Advertiser*, quoted in *SFC*, June 13, 1880. Accounts of the Kearney-Spencer exchange vary slightly. On Spencer, see Elizabeth Cady Stanton, Susan B. Anthony, Matilda Joslyn Gage, [and Ida Husted Harper], eds., *History of Woman Suffrage* (New York, 1882), 2:539–40, 543, 587, 597; (Rochester, 1886), 3:12–16, 26–27, 28, 30, 35, 66–67, 97, 103, 152–54, 160, 166–67.

17. Kennedy et al., *Our Presidential Candidates*, 80–83, 92. For slight differences in the Greenback platform, compare with Johnson, *1840–1956*, 57–58. Like the resolution on the Chinese, the resolution on woman suffrage was ambiguously worded: "That every citizen of due age, sound mind, and not a felon, be fully enfranchised, and that this resolution be referred to the States, with recommendation for their favorable consideration" (ibid., 58).

18. Garfield interviewed in *Wheeling Intelligencer*, reprinted in *San Francisco Post*, Dec. 7, 1878, reprinted in *CTr*, June 20, 1880. See also James A. Garfield, Diary, Nov. 3, 1878, James A. Garfield Papers, LC. Garfield abstained on the Fifteen Passenger Bill but later voted to sustain the president's veto. See *CR*, 45th Cong., 3d sess., 800–801 (Jan. 28, 1879), 2276–77 (Mar. 1, 1879). On Garfield's opposition to Chinese immigration, see above, Chap. 8.

19. E. M. Gibson to Garfield, June 9, 1880, C. Curtiss to Garfield, June 9, 1880, Sargent cited in Thomas Nichol to Garfield, July 8, 1880, Horace F. Page to Garfield, June 9, 1880, and George C. Gorham to Garfield, June 17, 1880, all in Garfield Papers. See also John Harmon to Garfield, June 8, 1880, and Charles A. Buckbee to Garfield, June 1880, both in Garfield Papers.

20. *NYW*, July 21, 1880. See also *NYT*, July 13, 1880.

21. John Fehrenbatch to Garfield, June 16, 1880, Garfield Papers. For background on Fehrenbatch, see David Montgomery, *Beyond Equality: Labor and the Radical Republicans, 1862–1872* (New York, 1967), 193, 194, 210, 331. H. C. Traphagen, a member of the Cincinnati Trades Assembly and organizer for the Knights of Labor, remarked a month later that "the restriction against the *Chinese* is in contradiction to a Republic, inhuman and tyranical [*sic*]" (H. C. Traphagen to John Samuel, July 4, 1880, John Samuel Papers, State Historical Society of Wisconsin, Madison; I am indebted to James Danky and Harold L. Miller for bringing this letter to my attention). Traphagen was a political enemy of Fehrenbatch. It is noteworthy that in spite of this antagonism, they both opposed Chinese exclusion. See H. C. Traphagen to Terence V. Powderly, Sept. 19, 1880, Terence V. Powderly Papers, Catholic University, Washington, D.C.

22. J. G. Blaine to Garfield, July 4, 1880, Garfield Papers.

23. My interpretation of Evarts closely follows Walter LaFeber, *The New Empire: An Interpretation of American Expansion, 1860–1898* (Ithaca, N.Y., 1963), 39–46. He calls Evarts "one of the more underrated Secretaries of State." The quote from Evarts is on page 40. For general background, see *Dictionary of American Biography* (New York, 1959), 3:215–18.

Curiously, this three-thousand-word article devotes less than a sentence to Evarts's years as secretary of state. On Evarts's early connections with the Republican Party and the New York City Bar Association, see Brainerd Dyer, *Public Career of William M. Evarts* (Berkeley, 1933), 28–34, 152–53. For extended treatment of Evarts, see also Chester Leonard Barrows, *William M. Evarts, Lawyer, Diplomat, Statesman* (Chapel Hill, N.C., 1941). Like many Gilded Age figures, Evarts deserves a modern biography.

24. LaFeber, *New Empire*, 42–46. The colleague was John Russell Young, chronicler of Grant's round-the-world tour and future minister to China (John Russell Young to Evarts, Mar. 4, 1880, William M. Evarts Papers, LC). The French project in Panama—which at the time was ruled by Colombia—failed, as natural forces doomed construction, delaying for a generation American seizure of the Panamanian isthmus and the digging of the canal.

25. On Evarts's earlier actions relating to Chinese immigration, see above, Chaps. 6 and 8. On Seward, see Ari Hoogenboom, *The Presidency of Rutherford B. Hayes* (Lawrence, Kans., 1988), 181–83; and David L. Anderson, "The Diplomacy of Discrimination: Chinese Exclusion, 1876–1882," *California History* 57 (Spring 1978): 34–39. See also *Brooklyn Eagle*, Jan. 19, 1880, and *BG*, Apr. 14, 1880. Shortly after his dismissal, Seward wrote one of the earliest treatises on Chinese immigration. See George F. Seward, *Chinese Immigration, in Its Social and Economical Aspects* (New York, 1881).

26. Beverley Tucker to Evarts, Aug. 11, Aug. 25, Aug. 29, 1879, Evarts Papers; Beverley Tucker to Garfield, June 1, 1881, William H. Hunt to Beverley Tucker, July 3, 1881, Garfield Papers. Evarts's dislike of Grant stemmed from Grant's decision not to appoint him chief justice in 1876. See Garfield, Diary, Mar. 5, 1876, Garfield Papers. On Tucker, see *Dictionary of American Biography* (New York, 1936), 10:37–38.

27. Beverley Tucker to Evarts, Aug. 11, Aug. 25, Aug. 29, 1879, Evarts Papers.

28. Beverley Tucker to Evarts, Aug. 25, Aug. 29, 1879, Evarts Papers. On the treaty commission, see James Burrill Angell, *The Reminiscences of James Burrill Angell* (New York, 1912), chap. 6. Despite treaties with the United States and European powers permitting immigration, the Chinese government disapproved of the practice and had long tried to prevent its people from leaving China. See Kil Young Zo, *Chinese Emigration into the United States, 1850–1880* (New York, 1978), chap. 1, and Shih-shan Henry Tsai, *China and the Overseas Chinese in the United States, 1868–1911* (Fayetteville, Ark., 1983), chap. 1.

29. William M. Evarts to Garfield, July 5, 1880, Garfield Papers. An archivist has misdated this section of the letter "September."

30. Garfield's letter in Kennedy et al., *Our Presidential Candidates*, 17–24. The letter can also be found in virtually any newspaper dated July 13, 1880.

31. Thurlow Weed to Evarts, July 17, 1880, Evarts Papers; *Cleveland Leader*, quoted in *CT*, July 14, 1880; *NYTr*, July 13, 1880; *Cincinnati Commercial*, quoted in *CT*, July 13, 1880; Garfield, Diary, July 26, 1880, Garfield Papers; *NYH*, July 13, 1880. See also *CGa*, July 13, 1880.

32. Hancock's letter in Kennedy et al., *Our Presidential Candidates*, 162–65; *Washington Star*, July 31, 1880; *CT*, July 30, 1880.

33. *SFC*, Aug. 1, Aug. 10, Oct. 20, 1880.

34. Ibid., Aug. 4, Sept. 23, Oct. 7, Oct. 26, Oct. 27, Oct. 31, 1880. See also *CE*, Oct. 25, 1880. *SFAC*, Aug. 3, Sept. 9, 1880; *Truth* (New York), Aug. 16, 1880. On the treaty commission, see, for example, *SFC*, June 15, June 16, June 17, Aug. 4, 1880; *SFAC*, June 14, June 16, 1880; and Chester Holcombe, "The Restriction of Chinese Immigration," *Outlook* 76, Apr. 23, 1904, 974. The *San Francisco Chronicle* believed that Hayes's tour would help the anti-Chinese cause: "It is only through the visits of prominent men that we may hope for any alteration of

the opinion existing at the East on this subject—an opinion shared by all parties and all classes alike" (Sept. 8, 1880). On Scharrett, see above, Chap. 9. On black migration to the Midwest, see Nell Irvin Painter, *Exodusters: Black Migration to Kansas after Reconstruction* (New York, 1976).

35. *CT*, Apr. 12, 1880; *Congressional Quarterly's Guide to U.S. Elections*, 2d ed. (Washington, D.C., 1985), 339; Taylor, *Garfield of Ohio*, 214–16; Garfield to Edwards Pierrepont, Oct. 16, 1880, quoted in ibid., 216.

36. *Congressional Quarterly's Guide*, 339, 340, 513, 522, 794–800.

37. The Morey letter can be found in practically any newspaper dated October 20 or 21, 1880. See, for example, *CT*, Oct. 21, 1880.

38. For lively accounts of the Morey letter affair, see Clancy, *The Presidential Election of 1880*, 233–37; Peskin, *Garfield*, 505–8; Caldwell, *James Garfield*, 306–10; and Ted C. Hinckley, "The Politics of Sinophobia: Garfield, the Morey Letter, and the Presidential Election of 1880," *Ohio History* 89 (Autumn 1980): 381–99.

39. Henderson Benedict to Garfield, Oct. 21, 1880, H. M. Munsell to Garfield, Oct. 22, 1880, Garfield Papers; *CE*, Oct. 22, 1880; *CGa*, Oct. 22, 1880; *CT*, Oct. 21, Oct. 26, 1880.

40. *CTr*, quoted in *SFC*, Oct. 29, 1880; *Cincinnati Tribune*, quoted in *SFC*, Oct. 27, 1880; D. E. Hening to Garfield, Oct. 21, 1880, C. S. Hall to Garfield, Oct. 25, 1880, Garfield Papers; *CE*, Oct. 22, Oct. 25, Oct. 26, Oct. 30, 1880; *CT*, Oct. 26, Oct. 28, 1880; Hinckley, "The Politics of Sinophobia," 397 n. 24.

41. Garfield, Diary, Oct. 21, Oct. 22, Oct. 23, Oct. 24, Oct. 25, 1880, Marshall Jewell to Garfield, Oct. 21, 1880, John K. Valentine to S. W. Dorsey, Oct. 21, 1880, included in John K. Valentine to Garfield, Oct. 21, 1880, all in Garfield Papers; Hinckley, "The Politics of Sinophobia," 394.

42. Garfield, Diary, Oct. 23, Oct. 24, Oct. 25, 1880, Garfield Papers; Whitelaw Reid to Garfield, Oct. 24, 1880, quoted in Hinckley, "The Politics of Sinophobia," 393; Joseph Medill to Garfield, Oct. 21, 1880, Garfield Papers; *NYH*, Oct. 26, 1880.

43. *Rochester Union and Advertiser*, Nov. 1, 1880 (extra); I am indebted to Daniel Clifton for bringing this document to my attention. *Fall River Labor Standard*, Oct. 30, 1880; *CGa*, Oct. 27, 1880; *CTr*, reprinted in *SFC*, Oct. 24, 1880. See also *CGa*, Oct. 23, 1880, and *Cincinnati Times*, Oct. 28, 1880.

44. H. M. Munsell to Garfield, Oct. 22, 1880, Garfield Papers; *NYH*, Oct. 27, 1880; *NYW*, Oct. 27, 1880; *NYTr*, Oct. 25, 1880; John Clark Ridapth, *The Life and Work of James A. Garfield, Twentieth President of the United States: Embracing an Account of the Scenes and Incidents of His Boyhood; the Struggles of His Youth; the Might of His Early Manhood; His Valor as a Soldier; His Career as a Statesman; His Election to the Presidency; and the Tragic Story of His Death* (Cincinnati, 1881), 476. See also *CTr*, Oct. 28, 1880, and *CE*, Oct. 22, Oct. 29, 1880. For all the various allegations regarding Morey, see *CT*, Oct. 23, Oct. 28, 1880; *NYH*, Oct. 22, 1880; *CE*, Oct. 25, Oct. 27, 1880; *NYW*, Oct. 26, Oct. 27, Oct. 29, Oct. 31, Nov. 1, Nov. 2, 1880; *NYTr*, Oct. 31, Nov. 2, 1880; *Brooklyn Eagle*, Oct. 29, Nov. 1, 1880; and *Rochester Union and Advertiser*, Nov. 1, 1880 (extra). One rumor surfaced that Ben Butler had masterminded the forgery. See *CE*, Oct. 25, 1880.

45. *NYTr*, Oct. 28, Oct. 30, 1880; *CGa*, Oct. 28, Oct. 29, 1880; *Rochester Union and Advertiser*, Nov. 1, 1880 (extra); *CT*, Oct. 26, Oct. 30, 1880; *Truth* (New York), Oct. 29, 1880; *Columbus Herald*, quoted in *SFC*, Oct. 27, 1880; *CE*, Oct. 29, 1880; D. E. Hening to Garfield, Oct. 21, 1880, Richard C. McCormick to Garfield, Oct. 26, 1880, Garfield Papers; *NYH*, Oct.

30, 1880; Ingersoll quoted in the *Chicago Inter-Ocean*, reprinted in *SFC*, Oct. 29, 1880. See also *NYTr*, Oct. 22, 1880.

46. *Congressional Quarterly's Guide*, 287, 339–40, 791, 798–800; *NYH*, Nov. 4, 1880; Garfield, Diary, Nov. 3, 1880, Garfield Papers; *CT*, Oct. 27, 1880. The final tally was Garfield, 4,446,158 (48.27 percent); Hancock, 4,444,260 (48.25 percent); Weaver, 305,997 (3.33 percent); and minor candidates, 14,005 (.15 percent). Other sources give slightly different vote counts. The *Encyclopedia of American History* gives Garfield a plurality of 7,000 votes; the Census Bureau gives him a plurality of 39,000. I have relied on the *Congressional Quarterly's* data because they are both the most definitive and the most detailed (Richard B. Morris and Jeffrey B. Morris, eds., *Encyclopedia of American History* [New York, 1996], 287; U.S. Bureau of the Census, *Historical Statistics of the United States, Colonial Times to 1970* [Washington, D.C., 1975], 2:1073). In 1880, California joined the rest of the nation in holding congressional elections in even-numbered years.

Although many newspapers downplayed the Morey letter's impact on the election, several blamed it for contributing to an anti-Chinese riot in Denver on November 1 that destroyed the Chinese quarter and left one Chinese immigrant dead. See Roy T. Wortman, "Denver's Anti-Chinese Riot, 1880," *Colorado Magazine* 42 (Fall 1965): 275–91.

47. *CE*, Oct. 22, 1880; *IWAIL*, Nov. 20, 1880. See also *IWAIL*, Nov. 6, Nov. 13, 1880, and *Fall River Labor Standard*, Nov. 20, 1880. The *Journal of United Labor*, the newly founded monthly newspaper of the Knights of Labor, never mentioned the Morey letter.

48. Clancy, *The Presidential Election of 1880*, 237 n. 102. An 1884 book by John I. Davenport claimed that the forger was a New York lawyer and "Hancock Republican" named Henry Hercules Hadley (*NYT*, Aug. 16, 1884). Ted Hinckley notes that only one person, James O'Brien, alias Robert Lindsay, served time in prison in connection with the Morey letter. O'Brien was convicted of perjury—not forgery—in the investigation that followed and spent five years in Sing Sing ("The Politics of Sinophobia," 395).

49. Garfield, Diary, Oct. 21, Oct. 29, 1880, Garfield Papers; *NYH*, Nov. 8, 1880; Garfield to "My Dear Boys" (Hal and Jimmie, Garfield's sons), Oct. 31, 1880, reprinted in Leech and Brown, *The Garfield Orbit*, 306.

CHAPTER ELEVEN

1. James B. Angell to William M. Evarts, Mar. 11, 1880, William M. Evarts Papers, LC; James Burrill Angell, *The Reminiscences of James Burrill Angell* (New York, 1912), 128–30. Chapter 6 covers Angell's mission to China. See also David L. Anderson, *Imperialism and Idealism: American Diplomats in China, 1861–1898* (Bloomington, Ind., 1985), chap. 6.

2. Angell to Evarts, Mar. 11, 1880, Evarts Papers.

3. Angell, *Reminiscences*, 131–32. While in Washington, Angell also met with Peter Parker, former U.S. commissioner and minister to China, and the historian George Bancroft. "Both of them," Angell discovered, "were opposed to unlimited immigration of the Chinese. Mr. Bancroft said he did not want to see the young men in Massachusetts towns forced to compete with the Chinese who had such low standards of living" (ibid., 131).

4. Chester Holcombe, who served as secretary and interpreter for the commission, later claimed that Evarts, Angell, and Trescot never discussed Chinese immigration in their meetings in Washington. Angell's own account, however, refutes this (Chester Holcombe, "The Restriction of Chinese Immigration," *Outlook* 76, Apr. 23, 1904, 974). William Henry Trescot to William M. Evarts, Aug. 15, 1880, Evarts Papers; Evarts quoted in U.S. Congress,

Papers Relating to the Foreign Relations of the United States, Transmitted to Congress, with Annual Message of the President, December 5, 1881 (Washington, D.C., 1882), 196. These papers, hereafter cited as *Foreign Relations*, include the official correspondence between the U.S. commission and the secretary of state, along with other relevant documents.

5. Angell, *Reminiscences*, 133–36, 142; *NYH*, Dec. 6, 1880; *SFC*, reprinted in ibid., Jan. 28, 1881; *Foreign Relations*, 173–78, 196; David L. Anderson, "The Diplomacy of Discrimination: Chinese Exclusion, 1876–1882," *California History* 57 (Spring 1978): 39–44.

Angell himself noted two years later: "It is a very great and a very common mistake in the East[ern United States], to suppose that the opposition to the continuance of unlimited immigration from China has been cherished or stimulated only by the Dennis Kearneys, and other sand-lot orators of his ilk. A large proportion of the most serious and right-minded citizens of the Pacific States came to believe that the public welfare required that some check should be put upon this coming of Chinese laborers." See James B. Angell, "The Diplomatic Relations between the United States and China," *Journal of Social Science* 17 (May 1883): 27. The remarks were contained in a speech delivered on September 7, 1882.

6. *Foreign Relations*, 178, 183, 188, 195–98.

7. Ibid., 182–83, 195–98; Angell, *Reminiscences*, 142–44. For a summary of the negotiations from a different viewpoint, see Mary Roberts Coolidge, *Chinese Immigration* (New York, 1909), chap. 10.

8. *SFC*, reprinted in *NYH*, Jan. 28, 1881. For a text of the treaty, see *The Statutes at Large of the United States of America, from December, 1881, to March, 1883, and Recent Treaties, Postal Conventions, and Executive Proclamations* (Washington, D.C., 1883), 22:826–27.

9. *SFC*, reprinted in *NYH*, Jan. 28, 1881; Li Hung-chang to John Russell Young, Feb. 14, 1881, John Russell Young Papers, LC. On the threat of war, see the interview with Angell in *NYTr*, Feb. 22, 1882; *NYH*, Dec. 6, 1880, May 3, 1881; E. M. House to James Gordon Bennett, enclosed in John Russell Young to William M. Evarts, Mar. 4, 1880, John Russell Young to William M. Evarts, Mar. 25, 1880, Evarts Papers; and E. M. House to James Gordon Bennett, Mar. 27, 1880, Young Papers. For a brief overview, see Shih-shan Henry Tsai, *China and the Overseas Chinese in the United States, 1868–1911* (Fayetteville, Ark., 1983), 53. For a text of the second treaty, see *Statutes at Large*, 22:828–30. Li Hung-chang, who had met with Grant during the former president's recent world tour, resented the United States for its shabby treatment of Chinese immigrants. John Russell Young, Grant's chronicler, recalled Li's concern for them and how he "used to grow angry and flushed and strike the table with his hand when he spoke of the Chinese in California." Li ultimately swallowed his anger in exchange for diplomatic support (John Russell Young to William M. Evarts, Mar. 26, 1880, Evarts Papers).

10. *Foreign Relations*, 210; *NYH*, Jan. 6, Jan. 14, Jan. 24, 1881. As one editorial stated, "Looking at the question practically nothing is more absurd than the effort to maintain secrets in a body as large as the Senate, and especially in a matter like the Chinese Treaty, about which no one cares a farthing" (*NYH*, Jan. 24, 1881).

11. *NYH*, Jan. 19, 1881; *CT*, Jan. 18, Mar. 21, 1881.

12. *NYH*, Dec. 2, 1880; see also Jan. 15, Mar. 10, 1881. *NYT*, Jan. 11, 1881; *NYTr*, Jan. 15, 1881. "The supremacy of American influence in the Pacific Ocean, and the unlimited development of American commerce with and in China," the *Tribune* stated, "may ultimately be seen to have depended upon the successful negotiation of these treaties."

13. *CT*, Feb. 18, 1881; *NYH*, May 4, 1881. Garfield had actually settled on Blaine as early as

December 1880. See Justus Doenecke, *The Presidencies of James A. Garfield and Chester A. Arthur* (Lawrence, Kans., 1981), 33.

14. Doenecke, *The Presidencies of James A. Garfield and Chester A. Arthur*, chap. 3, esp. 41–45; U.S. Senate, *Executive Journal of the Senate*, 47th Cong., special session, commencing Friday, March 4, 1881 (Washington, D.C., 1881), 66 (May 5, 1881). I am indebted to Rodney A. Ross of the National Archives for bringing this document to my attention.

15. The four dissenters were Henry L. Dawes (R-Mass.), Joseph R. Hawley (R-Conn.), George Frisbie Hoar (R-Mass.), and Samuel J. R. McMillan (R-Minn.). The tally was not revealed at the time and the press gave conflicting accounts. On the vote, see U.S. Senate, *Executive Journal*, 66 (May 5, 1881). On the debate, see *NYH*, May 5, May 6, 1881, and *NYT*, May 5, May 6, 1881. The quote from the *Times* is from Apr. 4, 1882. On California sentiment, see *NYH*, May 2, May 3, 1881.

16. *NYT*, May 4, May 6, 1881. See also *NYTr*, May 5, May 6, 1881, and *NYH*, May 3, 1881.

17. The 47th Congress, elected in 1880, actually held two early special sessions, the deadlocked one noted above, from March 4 to May 20, 1881, and a second one from October 10 to 29 (*CR*, 47th Cong., special sess., 1, 471, 505; ibid., 1st sess., 1).

18. *CT*, Apr. 23, 1881; *CMOJ*, May 10, Oct. 10, 1881. See also *CMOJ*, June 10, July 10, Aug. 10, 1881, and *Carpenter*, June 1881. On the origin of the union label, see Ira B. Cross, *A History of the Labor Movement in California* (Berkeley, 1935), 136–38, and Alexander Saxton, *The Indispensable Enemy: Labor and the Anti-Chinese Movement in California* (Berkeley, 1971), 73–74. The *Journal of United Labor* began publication on May 15, 1880. In its first two years of existence the newspaper printed three articles relating to the Chinese: a vicious letter from the Knights' "Executive Committee in San Francisco"; a piece on Chinese jugglers ("a sight so wonderful"); and a description of Chinese "lepers" departing from California (*Journal of United Labor*, Aug. 15, Nov. 15, Dec. 15, 1880). At the annual gathering of the Knights of Labor in 1880, delegates passed a resolution opposing "Chinese coolie importation." This is the only record of the Chinese issue ever surfacing at a Knights of Labor convention from the first one in 1878 through 1882. See Knights of Labor, *Record of the Proceedings of the General Assembly of the ********* [Knights of Labor] held at Reading, Pennsylvania, January 1–4, 1878* (n.p., 1878); *Record of the Proceedings of the Special Session of the General Assembly, Held at Philadelphia, Penn., June 6, 1878* (n.p., 1878); *Record of the Proceedings of the Second Regular Session of the General Assembly, Held at St. Louis, Mo., January 14–17, 1879* (n.p., 1879); *Record of the Proceedings of the Third Regular Session of the General Assembly, Held at Chicago, Ill., Sept. 2–6, 1879* (n.p., 1879); *Record of the Proceedings of the Fourth Regular Session of the General Assembly, Held at Pittsburgh, Pa., Sept. 7–11, 1880* (n.p., 1880), 223, 249–50; *Record of the Proceedings of the Fifth Regular Session of the General Assembly, Held at Detroit, Mich., Sept. 6–10, 1881* (n.p., 1881); *Record of the Proceedings of the Sixth Regular Session of the General Assembly, Held at New York City, N.Y., Sept. 5–12, 1882* (n.p., 1882).

19. The geographic breakdown was as follows: Pennsylvania, 69; New York, 8; Illinois, 6; Ohio, 6; Massachusetts, 3; Michigan, 3; Missouri, 3; West Virginia, 3; and one each from California, Indiana, Maryland, New Jersey, Rhode Island, and Wisconsin. See *Report of the First Annual Session of the Federation of Organized Trades and Labor Unions of the United States and Canada Held in Pittsburgh, Pennsylvania, December 15, 16, 17 and 18, 1881*, in American Federation of Labor, *Proceedings of the American Federation of Labor 1881, 1882, 1883, 1884, 1885, 1886, 1887, 1888* (Bloomington, Ill., 1906), 7–9 [hereafter *Report of the First*

Annual Session]. Note that the session is misdated. The convention actually took place November 15–18, 1881.

20. Ibid.; Samuel Gompers, *Seventy Years of Life and Labor: An Autobiography* (New York, 1925), 1:219–28. David Montgomery mistakes Sherman Cummin for Samuel P. Cummings, former leader of the Knights of St. Crispin. Cummings had died in 1874 (David Montgomery, *Beyond Equality: Labor and the Radical Republicans, 1862–1872* [New York, 1967], 464; *WA*, Mar. 21, 1874). On Cummings, see above, Chap. 3 n. 18.

21. *Report of the First Annual Session*, 20; Gompers, *Seventy Years*, 1:227–28; *CTr*, Nov. 19, 1881; *NYT*, Nov. 19, 1881; *NYH*, Nov. 19, 1881. On Burgman, see Saxton, *Indispensable Enemy*, chap. 8.

22. *Report of the First Annual Session*, 4; Gompers, *Seventy Years*, 1:220. Gompers's account of the founding convention of the Federation of Organized Trades and Labor Unions and the anti-Chinese movement contains numerous mistakes. In an attempt to exaggerate the importance of the convention (which did not need it), Gompers stated erroneously that the resolution was adopted unanimously. He also placed Denis Kearney's major visit to New York (in 1878) *after* the convention rather than before it and misspelled the names of Kearney, Burgman, and Cummin (*Seventy Years*, 1:224, 2:161).

23. Gompers, *Seventy Years*, 1:228. On Gompers's racism and deep-seated anti-Chinese proclivities, see Arthur Mann, "Gompers and the Irony of Racism," *Antioch Review* 13 (June 1953): 203–14.

24. See, for example, *Paterson Labor Standard*, Oct. 22, 1881; *Iron Molders' Journal*, Oct. 31, 1881; *CMOJ*, Nov. 11, Dec. 15, 1881; *IWAIL*, Nov. 19, 1881; and *Carpenter*, Jan. 1882.

25. *Fall River Labor Standard*, Dec. 17, 1881; *Paterson Labor Standard*, Dec. 24, 1881; *CMOJ*, Dec. 15, 1881, Jan. 15, 1882; *NYH*, Jan. 6, 1882. For other labor gatherings, see, for example, *NYH*, Dec. 3, Dec. 29, Dec. 30, 1881; *CT*, Dec. 29, 1881; and *Chicago Express*, Jan. 7, 1882. See also a list drawn up by a Washington, D.C., labor activist of eleven demands, none of which mentioned Chinese immigration (*Paterson Labor Standard*, Dec. 24, 1881).

26. *Fall River Labor Standard*, Nov. 26, 1881.

27. *Statutes at Large*, 22:826, 828. For a more detailed account of the assassination and Garfield's last days, any of the standard biographies suffice. See, for example, Alan Peskin, *Garfield* (Kent, Ohio, 1978), chap. 25.

28. *CR*, 47th Cong., 1st sess., 5 (Dec. 5, 1881), 89 (Dec. 13, 1881). See also ibid., 217 (Dec. 19, 1881), 561 (Jan. 23, 1882), 630, 645 (Jan. 26, 1882), and 737 (Jan. 30, 1882). For a text of the bill, see ibid., 1480–81 (Feb. 28, 1882), and for amendments, 1749, 1750 (Mar. 9, 1882). For a text of the Chinese Exclusion Act as it ultimately passed, see Appendix.

29. *CR*, 47th Cong., 1st sess., 1481–88 (Feb. 28, 1882).

30. Ibid.

31. Ibid.; *NYH*, Mar. 1, 1882.

32. On Hoar, see George Frisbie Hoar, *Autobiography of Seventy Years*, 2 vols. (New York, 1903), and Richard E. Welch Jr., *George Frisbie Hoar and the Half-Breed Republicans* (Cambridge, Mass., 1971). Hoar remained a chief advocate of federal aid to public and black education. In 1890, he sponsored the Federal Election, or "Force," Bill, the last major effort to protect black voting rights in the South until the 1960s. Hoar was also a leading proponent of woman suffrage and spoke out strongly against the anti-Catholic American Protective Association. As Hoar grew older he became more conservative toward labor. On his earlier attitudes, see Montgomery, *Beyond Equality*, 372–73.

33. *CR*, 47th Cong., 1st sess., 1515–23 (Mar. 1, 1882). Hoar's comments on Chinese inven-

tions sparked opposition from Senator John P. Jones (R-Nev.), who, quoting scientific racist J. A. de Gobineau, argued that the Chinese did not invent these items "but stole them from stray Aryan Caucasian people who had wandered into their midst" (ibid., 1582 [Mar. 3, 1882]).

34. Ibid., 1516, 1517, 1523 (Mar. 1, 1882).

35. *NYT*, Mar. 4, Mar. 9, Mar. 24, 1882; *NYTr*, Mar. 3, 1882.

36. *CR*, 47th Cong., 1st sess., 1546 (Mar. 2, 1882), 1635 (Mar. 6, 1882), 1740 (Mar. 9, 1882).

37. Ibid., 1484, 1485 (Feb. 28, 1882), 1636, 1645 (Mar. 6, 1882), 1713 (Mar. 8, 1882), 1741, 1742, 1744 (Mar. 9, 1882).

38. Ibid., 1583–84 (Mar. 3, 1882), 1637 (Mar. 6, 1882), 1715 (Mar. 8, 1882). Southerners seemed obsessed with the racial differences between blacks and Chinese, which Representative Emory Speer (D-Ga.) summarized succinctly: The "negro" was "deeply emotional," the Chinese "cold"; the "negro" was "sympathetic and kind-hearted," the Chinese "callous and indifferent"; the "negro" was susceptible to poetry and eloquence, the Chinese not; the "negro" was "intensely religious" ("perhaps sometimes he backslides . . . but he can be converted again"), the Chinese had no god, fearing only the devil; the "negro" loved rhythm and music, the Chinese loved discordant sounds and disharmony. All told, Speer concluded, "a typical negro is infinitely superior to a typical Chinaman" (ibid., 2029 [Mar. 18, 1882]).

39. Ibid., 1638 (Mar. 6, 1882), 1670 (Mar. 7, 1882), 1753 (Mar. 9, 1882). Most Southerners who spoke connected the Chinese issue to Reconstruction. See, for example, the speeches of Bayard, George, and Augustus Garland (D-Ark.), in ibid., 1586, 1588 (Mar. 3, 1882), and 1637 (Mar. 6, 1882).

40. Ibid., 1643 (Mar. 6, 1882). For Brown's speech, see ibid., 1639–44. For background on Brown, see Joseph H. Parks, *Joseph E. Brown of Georgia* (Baton Rouge, 1977), and C. Vann Woodward, *Tom Watson: Agrarian Rebel* (New York, 1938), 56–61, 66, 68, 70–71, 84–86, 106, 110–11. The historian quoted is Eric Foner, *Reconstruction: America's Unfinished Revolution, 1863–1877* (New York, 1988), 299.

41. *CR*, 47th Cong., 1st sess., 1643 (Mar. 6, 1882).

42. Ibid., 1636 (Mar. 6, 1882).

43. *Dictionary of American Biography* (New York, 1931), 3:24–27; *CT*, Mar. 8, 1882; *CG*, 41st Cong., 2d sess., 3753 (May 24, 1870). Although an influential senator for twenty-five years and arguably the most distinguished person ever to serve Vermont, no full-length biography of Edmunds exists.

44. *CR*, 47th Cong., 1st sess., 1674 (Mar. 7, 1882), 1710–11 (Mar. 8, 1882).

45. Ibid., 1709 (Mar. 8, 1882).

46. Ibid.

47. *CT*, Mar. 8, 1882; *CR*, 47th Cong., 1st sess., 1674 (Mar. 7, 1882).

48. *CR*, 47th Cong., 1st sess., 1748, 1751, 1752, 1753 (Mar. 9, 1882), 2608 (Apr. 5, 1882). By votes of 23 to 23 (with 30 not voting) and 20 to 21 (with 35 not voting), the Senate twice rejected an amendment reducing the period of exclusion to ten years (ibid., 1707 [Mar. 8, 1882], 1752 [Mar. 9, 1882]).

49. Ibid., 1702–3, 1705, 1706 (Mar. 8, 1882).

50. Ibid., 1715 (Mar. 8, 1882).

51. Ibid., 1738–39 (Mar. 9, 1882). On Hawley's earlier statements, see above, Chap. 3.

52. Ibid., 1753 (Mar. 9, 1882).

53. Ibid., 1937, 1938 (Mar. 15, 1882), 2174, 2175 (Mar. 22, 1882), 2186, 2187–88 (Mar. 23, 1882 [misdated Mar. 22]), 2216 (Mar. 23, 1882), app., 51 (Mar. 16, 1882). In addition to Orth, other

Republicans making arguments based largely on principle included William Moore (Tenn.), Cyrus Carpenter (Iowa), Charles Skinner (N.Y.), Thomas Browne (Ind.), and Rufus Dawes (Ohio). See ibid., 2035–36, 2037–38, 2040–41 (Mar. 18, 1882), 2177–82, 2183 (Mar. 23, 1882 [misdated Mar. 22]). Two Democrats also opposed the measure on principle: Leopold Morse, the only Democrat from Massachusetts, called the bill "un-Democratic, un-Republican, un-American"; and Augustus Hardenbergh (D-N.J.), who had argued eloquently against the Fifteen Passenger Bill, said that the United States could not simply "close its ports. . . . That nation which refuses the common dictates of humanity to another, whatever its condition, must pay the penalty of that disobedience to a diviner law, which is but the law of justice and of right." To Hardenbergh, morality was not, as Edmunds had claimed, subject to majority rule. Echoing Hoar and many a worker, Hardenbergh added, "I would make by laws all such contracts [to import labor] void, but I would not close my country's ports to the inhabitants of whatever clime who may seek acquaintance with the institutions of freedom" (ibid., 2184 [Mar. 23, 1882 (misdated Mar. 22)], app., 92–93 [Mar. 16, 1882]). On Robinson's earlier comment, see above, Chap. 8.

54. Ibid., 1980, 1982, 1983, 1984 (Mar. 16, 1882). Charles Joyce (R-Vt.) took a similar position. "This bill," he said, "is a bold and audacious denial of this great principle of expatriation; it is a declaration limiting and circumscribing human rights; it flies in the face of the spirit and genius of our institutions, and would . . . fix a stigma and a blot upon the history of our country." He then quickly added, "I do not claim that a large influx of Chinese would be either desirable or profitable" (ibid., 2184–85 [Mar. 23, 1882 (misdated Mar. 22)]).

55. Ibid., 2043 (Mar. 18, 1882), 2139 (Mar. 21, 1882), app., 63 (Mar. 22, 1882). Among the more unusual opponents of the bill was Mississippi Democrat Charles Hooker. A former rebel who had lost an arm fighting for the Confederacy, Hooker denounced all the arguments based on racial differences and nonassimilation. Such charges had long been waged against blacks, he said, who had been termed "ignorant, uneducated, uneducable . . . unreligious . . . [and] far more pagan than the Chinese." But events of the past twenty years had proved these charges baseless, for "when the manacles were stricken from their limbs by the proclamation of Mr. Lincoln and the results of the war, they sprung at once into the arena flaming with the intelligence of the nineteenth century. They have occupied your pulpits, your school-houses and your halls of legislation." Such swift advancement, Hooker argued, revealed the "civilizing" influence of American institutions: "It is true that the Chinaman has the misfortune to have a yellow skin and almond-shaped eyes. It was the misfortune of the colored man that he had a black skin. But even with that misfortune our civilization reached him, and he is now a full-fledged American citizen, with the ballot in his hand, and with all the powers, duties, and responsibilities of an intelligent American freeman. Now do you not think that if we could produce these results on the African we might try our influence on the Chinaman, particularly as they are a people always distinguished for their intelligence?" Hooker certainly stood apart from his southern and Democratic colleagues. Considered one of "the most graceful speakers in the House," he had a voice "clear, strong, and musical." His demeanor was "natural and dignified," the *Chicago Times* noted, and "his empty sleeve" only added distinction to his presence. Yet the views of this reconstructed southerner may not have been totally ingenuous. According to the *Chicago Tribune*, the four-term Mississippi congressman wanted to import Chinese laborers to the South (ibid., 2134–38 [Mar. 21, 1882]; *CT*, Mar. 22, 1882; *CTr*, Mar. 22, 1882).

56. *CR*, 47th Cong., 1st sess., 1903–4 (Mar. 14, 1882), 1938 (Mar. 15, 1882), 2030 (Mar. 18,

1882), 2127, 2132 (Mar. 21, 1882), 2162, 2163 (Mar. 22, 1882), 2213, 2215 (Mar. 23, 1882), 2608 (Apr. 5, 1882), app., 42, 45 (Mar. 16, 1882), 70 (Mar. 22, 1882).

For similar views, see also the remarks of Senators James Z. George (D-Miss.), 1637 (Mar. 6, 1882), and Henry Teller (R-Colo.), 1645 (Mar. 6, 1882), and Representatives Horace F. Page (R-Calif.), 1936–37 (Mar. 15, 1882), George Cassidy (D-Nev.), 1978 (Mar. 16, 1882), Campbell Berry (R-Calif.), 2034 (Mar. 18, 1882), Thomas Bayne (R-Pa.), 2129 (Mar. 21, 1882), Joseph Scranton (R-Pa.), 2131 (Mar. 21, 1882), Robert Hawk (R-Ill.), 2175 (Mar. 22, 1882), John Richardson (D-S.C.), 2177 (Mar. 23, 1882 [misdated Mar. 22]), John Sherwin (R-Ill.), 2208 (Mar. 23, 1882), George Hazelton (R-Wisc.), 2210 (Mar. 23, 1882), Andrew Curtin (D-Pa.), 2220 (Mar. 23, 1882), J. Hyatt Smith (R/D-N.Y.), app., 40 (Mar. 16, 1882), A. Herr Smith (R-Pa.), app., 49–50 (Mar. 16, 1882), Henry Harris (D-N.J.), app., 50 (Mar. 16, 1882), John Dezendorf (R-Va.), app., 52 (Mar. 16, 1882), Edward K. Valentine (R-Nebr.), app., 87–89 (Mar. 16, 1882), and Daniel Ermentrout (D-Pa.), app., 89 (Mar. 16, 1882).

57. Ibid., 2038 (Mar. 18, 1882), 2128 (Mar. 21, 1882), app., 89 (Mar. 16, 1882).

58. Ibid., 2227 (Mar. 23, 1882). The four Democrats opposing the bill were Edward Bragg (Wisc.), Augustus Hardenbergh (N.J.), Charles Hooker (Miss.), and Leopold Morse (Mass.). The exact breakdown of the vote was as follows: Yes—97 Democrats, 60 Republicans, 5 Greenbackers, 2 Readjusters; No—4 Democrats, 62 Republicans; Not Voting—33 Democrats, 25 Republicans. Excluded from these data are four representatives with split affiliations. Voting yes were one Greenback-Republican, one Greenback-Democrat, and one Republican-Democrat. One Greenback-Democrat did not vote. In addition to the fifty-nine representatives listed as "not voting," one more—the Speaker of the House, a Republican— did not vote. By tradition, the Speaker votes only to break a tie and is not listed in the official tally.

The regional categories include the following states: West—Calif., Colo., Nev., Ore.; South—Ala., Ark., Fla., Ga., Ky., La., Miss., N.C., S.C., Tenn., Tex., Va.; New England— Conn., Mass., N.H., R.I., Vt. (plus Maine); Mid-Atlantic—Del., Md., N.J., N.Y., Pa.; Midwest—Ill., Ind., Iowa, Kans., Mich., Minn., Mo., Nebr., Ohio, W.Va., Wisc.

59. *CTr*, Mar. 15, Mar. 19, Mar. 24, Mar. 28, 1882; *NYT*, Mar. 24, 1882. See also *NYT*, Mar. 7, 1882. *NYTr*, Mar. 10, Mar. 24, Apr. 6, 1882. As the *Chicago Tribune* summed up, the debate was "characterized by hard facts upon one side and sentiment on the other" (*CTr*, Mar. 18, 1882).

60. *CT*, Mar. 9, 1882.

61. Angell, "Diplomatic Relations between the United States and China," 34, 35; *CTr*, Mar. 28, 1882. Angell delivered the speech on September 7, 1882.

62. *NYH*, Mar. 18, 1882; *CR*, 47th Cong., 1st sess., 2184 (Mar. 23, 1882 [misdated Mar. 22]); *CTr*, Mar. 24, 1882.

CHAPTER TWELVE

1. On Arthur, see George Frederick Howe, *Chester A. Arthur: A Quarter-Century of Machine Politics* (New York, 1935), and Thomas C. Reeves, *Gentleman Boss: The Life of Chester Alan Arthur* (New York, 1975).

2. James D. Richardson, ed., *A Compilation of the Messages and Papers of the Presidents, 1789–1897* (Washington, D.C., 1898), 8:42. On the term "acting president," see, for example, *CTr*, Mar. 28, 1882.

3. *CTr*, Mar. 27, Apr. 1, Apr. 2, Apr. 5, 1882; *CT*, Mar. 30, Mar. 31, Apr. 4, 1882; Shih-shan

Henry Tsai, *China and the Overseas Chinese in the United States, 1868–1911* (Fayetteville, Ark., 1983), 66; *NYH*, Mar. 29, 1882; *NYTr*, Mar. 27, Mar. 29, 1882.

4. *CT*, Apr. 5, 1882; *NYT*, Apr. 5, 1882. For the text of Arthur's message, see *CR*, 47th Cong., 1st sess., 2551–52 (Apr. 4, 1882). On the vote to override, see ibid., 2617 (Apr. 5, 1882).

5. *CTr*, Apr. 5, 1882; *CR*, 47th Cong., 1st sess., 2608 (Apr. 5, 1882); *NYT*, Apr. 5, 1882; *NYTr*, Apr. 5, 1882; *CT*, Apr. 5, 1882. The senator most gratified by Arthur's veto was George Frisbie Hoar, his face "beaming with pleasure which he did not care to suppress" (*CT*, Apr. 5, 1882).

6. *Carpenter*, May 1882; *CT*, Apr. 7, Apr. 16, May 7, 1882; *NYH*, Apr. 3, Apr. 17, 1882; Jno. S. Kirchener to Terence V. Powderly, Apr. 7, 1882, Terence V. Powderly Papers, Catholic University, Washington, D.C.; *NYTr*, Apr. 7, 1882; *Chicago Express*, May 13, 1882; *Chicago News*, Apr. 28, 1882; *IWAIL*, Apr. 29, 1882; *CTr*, Apr. 6, 1882; *Truth* (San Francisco), May 31, 1882; *CMOJ*, May 15, 1882. For a sample of West Coast opinion, see excerpts reprinted in *CT*, Apr. 5, 1882. For pro-bill sentiment among workers while Congress was deliberating, see Robert D. Layton to Terence V. Powderly, Mar. 16, 1882, and enclosed circular, Powderly Papers; resolution of Pennsylvania miners in *NYH*, Mar. 19, 1882; resolutions of the Chicago Trade and Labor Assembly in *CT*, Mar. 13, Mar. 20, 1882; and resolutions of Canton, Ohio, cigar makers addressed to Representative William McKinley (R-Ohio) in *Canton Repository*, reprinted in *CMOJ*, Apr. 15, 1882.

7. *CT*, Apr. 21, 1882; *Carpenter*, Feb. 1882.

8. *IWAIL*, Apr. 15, 1882; *Carpenter*, June 1882; *CMOJ*, Mar. 15, 1882. McGuire began publishing the *Carpenter* in St. Louis in May 1881 and moved the paper to New York City the following December.

9. In 1885, Congress finally acceded to workers' demands and passed the Foran Act, outlawing contract labor. As many had anticipated, the law proved difficult to enforce and largely ineffective. Its failure no doubt steered many workers to the anti-immigration camp. The Chinese Exclusion Act, ironically, also proved difficult to enforce, necessitating revisions in the 1880s and 1890s, all of which passed with little opposition. The Scott Act of 1888, for example, which prevented Chinese who had left the United States from returning and barred issuance of new certificates for readmission, passed the Senate by a vote of 37 to 3. One of the three voting against it was the indomitable George Frisbie Hoar (*CR*, 50th Cong., 1st sess., 8369 [Sept. 7, 1888]; *The Statutes at Large of the United States of America, from December, 1887, to March, 1889, and Recent Treaties, Postal Conventions, and Executive Proclamations* [Washington, D.C., 1889], 25:476–79). On the Foran Act, which merits far greater study, see Charlotte Erickson, *American Industry and the European Immigrant, 1860–1885* (Cambridge, Mass., 1957). On enforcement of the Chinese Exclusion Act, see Lucy E. Salyer, *"Laws Harsh as Tigers": Chinese Immigrants and the Shaping of Modern Immigration Law* (Chapel Hill, N.C., 1995).

10. *Paterson Labor Standard*, May 20, June 17, 1882; *NYH*, Apr. 8, 1882. See also *Chicago News*, Apr. 13, 1882. The *New York Tribune* claimed strikers sought a raise of a half cent per shirt (Apr. 8, 1882).

11. Beecher's sermon reprinted in *NYH*, Mar. 27, 1882. Beecher's rhetoric included one of the earliest references to the "melting pot": "When the cook has gathered from the sea and from the forest and the garden all the substances required for a great banquet he mixes them together in due proportion. Separately they may not be pleasant to the taste; but he throws in a little salt and some pepper and other condiments, and when the banquet is ready these condiments that have been thrown in make the dish provoke the appetite of the world. I tell you one of the most important condiments ever thrown into this national broth that we are

stewing here is the Irish. If they don't give spice and piquancy to it then my palate is sadly at fault."

12. Ibid.

13. Petition of George C. Richardson and Co. in *CR*, 47th Cong., 1st sess., 3076 (Apr. 20, 1882). See also *NYTr*, Apr. 7, 1882, and *NYT*, Apr. 13, 1882. Petition of New York City Board of Trade in *CR*, 47th Cong., 1st sess., 2878 (Apr. 14, 1882). See also *NYTr*, Apr. 14, 1882; and *NYH*, Apr. 14, 1882. Petition of Union League Club of New York City, Apr. 14, 1882, in *CR*, 47th Cong., 1st sess., 3207 (Apr. 24, 1882). See also *NYTr*, Apr. 14, 1882.

14. *NYTr*, Apr. 8, 1882.

15. *NYTr*, Apr. 18, 1882; George A. Nourse to William E. Chandler, Apr. 21, 1882, William E. Chandler Papers, LC. For a complete text of the Chinese Exclusion Act, see *The Statutes at Large of the United States of America, from December, 1881, to March, 1883, and Recent Treaties, Postal Conventions, and Executive Proclamations* (Washington, D.C., 1883), 22:58–61.

16. *CR*, 47th Cong., 1st sess., 2972–74 (Apr. 17, 1882). Of the four Democrats who had opposed the first bill, only Hooker of Mississippi changed his vote and abstained. Kasson, interestingly, was the only politician singled out for praise in T. Fulton Gantt's 1887 working-class novel *Breaking the Chains: A Story of Industrial Struggle*. See Mary C. Grimes, ed., *The Knights in Fiction: Two Labor Novels of the 1880s* (Urbana, Ill., 1986), 55.

The exact breakdown of the vote was as follows: Yes—101 Democrats, 90 Republicans, 5 Greenbackers, 2 Readjusters; No—3 Democrats, 34 Republicans; Not Voting—29 Democrats, 24 Republicans. Excluded from these data are four representatives with split affiliations. Voting yes were two Greenback-Democrats and one Republican-Democrat. One Greenback-Republican did not vote. One representative had died since the first vote on March 23. As in the first vote, the Speaker of the House did not cast a ballot and was not listed in the official tally (see above, Chap. 11, n. 58).

17. *CR*, 47th Cong., 1st sess., 3266–70 (Apr. 25, 1882).

18. Ibid., 3264, 3265 (Apr. 25, 1882), app., 183–86 (Apr. 26, 1882); *NYT*, Apr. 27, 1882. For Hawley's speech in 1870, see above, Chap. 3.

19. *CR*, 47th Cong., 1st sess., 3354–57 (Apr. 27, 1882), 3412 (Apr. 28, 1882); *NYTr*, Mar. 10, 1882.

20. *CR*, 47th Cong., 1st sess., 3412 (Apr. 28, 1882), 3532 (May 3, 1882), 3588 (May 4, 1882). A former Supreme Court justice, Davis had been a close confidant of Lincoln. He long considered himself a Republican, but an independent one, and in 1877, Democrats in the Illinois legislature unanimously elected him senator. Because no Republicans had supported him, Davis voted with the Democrats on organizational matters during the first half of his Senate term. In 1880, he backed Hancock for president. In 1881, however, Republicans in the Senate unanimously elected him pro tem (not a single Democrat voted for him) and claimed him as one of their own. Davis considered himself above party, but for statistical purposes I have counted him as a Democrat during the first half of his term and a Republican during the second half. Davis, as noted earlier, had been nominated for president by the National Labor Reform Party in 1872 but withdrew when he failed to win nomination by the Liberal Republicans. See Willard L. King, *Lincoln's Manager, David Davis* (Chicago, 1960), chaps. 22–24.

21. *Statutes at Large*, 22:61.

22. *NYT*, May 9, 1882.

23. *CT*, Apr. 25, 1882.

24. On May 5, 1892, the United States extended the Chinese Exclusion Act for another

decade. Two years later, on March 17, 1894, the United States and China signed a new treaty stipulating that "for a period of ten years . . . the coming . . . of Chinese laborers to the United States shall be absolutely prohibited." With the 1892 law set to expire after ten years, the United States passed a new version on April 29, 1902. Seeking to ban Chinese immigrants forever, the United States passed the final version of the Chinese Exclusion Act on April 27, 1904, stipulating that "all laws in force on the twenty-ninth day of April, nineteen hundred and two, regulating, suspending, or prohibiting the coming of Chinese persons or persons of Chinese descent into the United States . . . are hereby, reenacted, extended, and continued, without modification, limitation, or condition." Chinese exclusion remained in effect for sixty-one years. Its repeal in 1943 was largely a diplomatic measure stemming from World War II. *The Statutes at Large of the United States of America, from December, 1891, to March, 1893, and Recent Treaties, Conventions, and Executive Proclamations* (Washington, D.C., 1893), 27:25–26; *The Statutes at Large of the United States of America, from December, 1901, to March, 1903, Concurrent Resolutions of the Two Houses of Congress, and Recent Treaties, Conventions, and Executive Proclamations*, vol. 32, pt. 1 (Washington, D.C., 1903), 176–77; Charles I. Bevans, comp., *Treaties and Other International Agreements of the United States of America, 1776–1949* (Washington, D.C., 1971), 6:691–94; *The Statutes at Large of the United States of America, from November, 1903, to March, 1905, Concurrent Resolutions of the Two Houses of Congress, and Recent Treaties, Conventions, and Executive Proclamations*, vol. 33, pt. 1 (Washington, D.C., 1905), 428; Fred W. Riggs, *Pressures on Congress: A Study of the Repeal of Chinese Exclusion* (New York, 1950).

25. Henry George, *Progress and Poverty: An Inquiry into the Cause of Industrial Depressions and of Increase of Want with Increase of Wealth. The Remedy* (San Francisco, 1879); James G. Blaine (letter) in *NYTr*, Feb. 24, 1879; *CR*, 45th Cong., 3d sess., 1302 (Feb. 14, 1879).

26. On Saxton, Mink, Roediger, and others, see above, Chap. 1.

27. *CR*, 47th Cong., 1st sess., 2038 (Mar. 18, 1882), 2206 (Mar. 23, 1882). The two quotes from westerners were, respectively, by Representatives Campbell Berry (R-Calif.) and George Cassidy (D-Nev.) (ibid., 1979 [Mar. 16, 1882], 2035 [Mar. 18, 1882]).

28. Ibid., 52d Cong., 1st sess., 3559 (Apr. 23, 1892).

29. Kwong Ki Chiu (letter) in *NYH*, May 1, 1882. Compiler of *A Dictionary of English Phrases with Illustrative Sentences*, Kwong had served as translator and interpreter for the Chinese Educational Mission in Connecticut from 1875 to 1881. See Ruthanne Lum McCunn, *Chinese American Portraits: Personal Histories, 1828–1988* (San Francisco, 1988), 21.

Bibliography

MANUSCRIPT COLLECTIONS

Madison, Wisconsin
  State Historical Society of Wisconsin
    International Workingmen's Association Papers
    John Samuel Papers
New York, New York
  Cooper Union
    Peter Cooper Papers
    Abram Hewitt Papers
  Tamiment Institute Library, New York University
    United Hatters Collection
Washington, D.C.
  Catholic University
    Terence V. Powderly Papers
  Douglass Memorial Home, Anacostia
    Frederick Douglass Papers
  Library of Congress
    Thomas F. Bayard Papers
    James G. Blaine Papers
    Anson Burlingame Papers
    Benjamin F. Butler Papers
    William E. Chandler Papers
    Henry L. Dawes Papers
    William M. Evarts Papers
    James A. Garfield Papers
    Horace Gray Papers
    Robert G. Ingersoll Papers
    John A. Logan Papers
    Manton Marble Papers
    Eli T. Sheppard Papers
    John Sherman Papers
    Robert Wilson Shufeldt Papers
    John Russell Young Papers

GOVERNMENT DOCUMENTS

Bevans, Charles I., comp. *Treaties and Other International Agreements of the United States of America, 1776–1949*. Vol. 6. Washington, D.C., 1971.

California Senate. *Chinese Immigration. The Social, Moral, and Political Effect of Chinese Immigration. Testimony Taken before a Committee of the Senate of the State of California, Appointed April 3d, 1876*. Sacramento, 1876. Reprint, 1970.

——. *Chinese Immigration; Its Social, Moral, and Political Effect. Report to the California State Senate of Its Special Committee on Chinese Immigration*. Sacramento, 1878. Reprint, 1971.

Chinese Legation. *Official Papers of the Chinese Legation*. Berlin, Germany, n.d.

Congressional Globe.

Congressional Quarterly's Guide to U.S. Elections. 2d ed. Washington, D.C., 1985.

Congressional Record.

Illinois House of Representatives. *Illinois House. Report of Special Committee on Labor*. Springfield, 1879.

The Invalidity of the "Queue Ordinance" of the City and County of San Francisco. Opinion of the Circuit Court of the United States, for the District of California, in Ho Ah Kow vs. Matthew Nunan, Delivered July 7th, 1879. San Francisco, 1879.

Massachusetts Bureau of the Statistics of Labor. *Report of the Bureau of Statistics of Labor, Embracing the Account of Its Operations and Inquiries from March 1, 1870, to March 1, 1871*. Boston, 1871.

——. *Tenth Annual Report of the Bureau of Statistics of Labor, January, 1879*. Boston, 1879.

——. *Eleventh Annual Report of the Bureau of Statistics of Labor, January, 1880*. Boston, 1880.

——. *Twelfth Annual Report of the Bureau of Statistics of Labor, January, 1881*. Boston, 1881.

——. *Thirteenth Annual Report of the Bureau of Statistics of Labor, March, 1882*. Boston, 1882.

Missouri Bureau of the Statistics of Labor. *Fourth Annual Report of the Bureau of Labor Statistics of the State of Missouri, for the Year Ending December 31, 1882*. Jefferson City, 1883.

Richardson, James D., ed. *A Compilation of the Messages and Papers of the Presidents, 1789–1897*. 10 vols. Washington, D.C., 1896–99.

Sanger, George P., ed. *The Statutes at Large, Treaties, and Proclamations of the United States of America, from December 5, 1859, to March 3, 1863*. Vol. 12. Boston, 1863.

——. *The Statutes at Large, Treaties, and Proclamations of the United States of America, from December 1863, to December 1865*. Vol. 13. Boston, 1866.

The Statutes at Large of the United States of America, from December, 1881, to March, 1883, and Recent Treaties, Postal Conventions, and Executive Proclamations. Vol. 22. Washington, D.C., 1883.

The Statutes at Large of the United States of America, from December, 1887, to March, 1889, and Recent Treaties, Postal Conventions, and Executive Proclamations. Vol. 25. Washington, D.C., 1889.

The Statutes at Large of the United States of America, from December, 1891, to March, 1893, and Recent Treaties, Conventions, and Executive Proclamations. Vol. 27. Washington, D.C., 1893.

The Statutes at Large of the United States of America, from December, 1901, to March, 1903,

Concurrent Resolutions of the Two Houses of Congress, and Recent Treaties, Conventions, and Executive Proclamations. Vol. 32, pt. 1. Washington, D.C., 1903.

The Statutes at Large of the United States of America, from November, 1903, to March, 1905, Concurrent Resolutions of the Two Houses of Congress, and Recent Treaties, Conventions, and Executive Proclamations. Vol. 33, pt. 1. Washington, D.C., 1905.

U.S. Bureau of the Census. Historical Statistics of the United States, Colonial Times to 1970. 2 vols. Washington, D.C., 1975.

——. Population Schedules of the Ninth Census of the United States. Microfilm roll 601, Massachusetts, 2, Berkshire County. Washington, D.C., 1965.

——. The Statistics of the Population of the United States, Embracing the Tables of Race, Nationality, Sex, and Selected Occupations. To Which Are Added the Statistics of School Attendance and Illiteracy, of Schools, Libraries, Newspapers and Periodicals, Churches, Paupers and Crime, and of Areas, Families, and Dwellings. Compiled from the Original Returns of the Ninth Census, (June 1, 1870,) under the Direction of the Secretary of the Interior, by Francis A. Walker, Superintendent of Census. Washington, D.C., 1872.

——. Statistics of the Population of the United States at the Tenth Census (June 1, 1880), Embracing Extended Tables of the Population of States, Counties, and Minor Civil Divisions, with Distinctions of Race, Sex, Age, Nativity, and Occupations; Together with Summary Tables, Derived from Other Census Reports, Relating to Newspapers and Periodicals; Public Schools and Illiteracy; The Dependent, Defective, and Delinquent Classes, Etc. Washington, D.C., 1883.

U.S. Congress. Papers Relating to the Foreign Relations of the United States Transmitted to Congress with the Annual Message of the President, December 4, 1871, Preceded by a Synoptical List of Papers and Followed by an Alphabetical Index of Persons and Subjects. Washington, D.C., 1871.

——. Papers Relating to the Foreign Relations of the United States, Transmitted to Congress, with Annual Message of the President, December 5, 1881. Washington, D.C., 1882.

U.S. House of Representatives. Investigation by a Select Committee of the House of Representatives relative to the Causes of the General Depression in Labor and Business; and as to Chinese Immigration. 46th Cong., 2d sess., Misc. Doc. 5. Washington, D.C., 1879.

——. Investigation by a Select Committee of the House of Representatives relative to the Causes of the General Depression in Labor and Business, Etc. 45th Cong., 2d sess., Misc. Doc. 29. Washington, D.C., 1879.

——. Message from the President of the United States, Transmitting, in Response to a Resolution of the House of Representatives, a Report from the Secretary of State in Relation to the Negotiations concerning the Immigration of Chinese to the United States, April 12, 1880. 45th Cong., 2d sess., Executive Doc. 70. Washington, D.C., 1880.

——. Petition of the Citizens of Beaver County, Pennsylvania, relative to Chinese Laborers, Feb. 3, 1873. 42d Cong., 3d sess., Misc. Doc. 81. Washington, D.C., 1873.

U.S. Senate. Executive Journal of the Senate. 47th Cong., special session, commencing Friday, March 4, 1881. Washington, D.C., 1881.

——. Journal of the Executive Proceedings of the Senate of the United States of America from December 2, 1867, to March 3, 1869, Inclusive. Vol. 16. Washington D.C., 1887.

——. Report of the Committee of the Senate upon the Relations between Labor and Capital, and Testimony Taken by the Committee. 5 vols. Washington, D.C., 1885.

——. Resolutions Adopted by a Convention of the Iron-Molders' International Union Held at Philadelphia in July 1870. 41st Cong., 3d sess., Misc. Doc. 13. Washington, D.C., 1870.

———. *Senate Report no. 689, Joint Special Committee on Chinese*. 44th Cong., 2d sess. Washington, D.C., 1877.

———. *Views of the Late Oliver P. Morton on the Character, Extent, and Effect of Chinese Immigration to the United States*. 45th Cong., 2d sess., Misc. Doc. 20. Washington, D.C., 1878.

NEWSPAPERS AND PERIODICALS

Adams Transcript
Albany Journal
American Workman (Boston)
Atlantic Monthly
Baltimore Sun
Boston Commonwealth
Boston Globe
Boston Journal
Boston Labor Standard
Boston Pilot
Boston Transcript
Brooklyn Eagle
Brookville (Pa.) Graphic
Bulletin de l'Union Républicaine de Langue Française (New York)
Carpenter (St. Louis and New York)
Chicago Express
Chicago Inter-Ocean
Chicago News
Chicago Times
Chicago Tribune
Cigar Makers' Official Journal
Cincinnati Enquirer
Cincinnati Gazette
Cincinnati Star
Cincinnati Times
Cleveland Daily Advance
Cleveland Labor Advance
Cleveland Weekly Advance
Communist (St. Louis)
Fall River Labor Standard
Fincher's Trades' Review (Philadelphia)
Frank Leslie's Illustrated Newspaper
Galaxy
Granite Cutters' National Journal
Hampshire Gazette and Northampton Courier
Harper's New Monthly Magazine
Harper's Weekly
Hartford Courant
Indianapolis Sentinel

Indianapolis Sun
Industrial Age
International Journal
International Journal of the Iron Molders' International Union
Irish World (New York)
Irish World and American Industrial Liberator (New York)
Iron Molders' International Journal
Iron Molders' Journal
Jefferson County (Pa.) Graphic
Journal of Social Science
Journal of United Labor
Lippincott's Magazine
Locomotive Firemen's Monthly Magazine
McGee's Illustrated Weekly
Miners' National Record
Missouri Republican (St. Louis)
Nation
National Anti-Slavery Standard
National Labor Tribune (Pittsburgh)
National Socialist (Cincinnati)
National Standard
National Trades' Review (Philadelphia)
National View (Washington, D.C.)
New York Dispatch
New York Express
New York Globe
New York Graphic
New York Herald
New York Independent
New York Irish-American
New York Labor Standard
New York Mail
New York Post
New York Scottish-American Journal
New York Star
New York Sun
New York Telegram
New York Times
New York Toiler
New York Tribune
New York Witness
New York World
North American Review
Northampton Free Press
Oshkosh Greenback Standard
Oshkosh Standard
Overland Monthly

Paterson Labor Standard
Philadelphia Bulletin
Philadelphia Inquirer
Philadelphia Press
Philadelphia Public Ledger
Pittsfield Sun
Pomeroy's Illustrated Democrat
Popular Science Monthly
Portland (Maine) Eastern Argus
Potter's American Monthly
Pottsville (Pa.) Miners' Journal
Puck
Punchinello
Putnam's Monthly
Rochester Democrat
Rochester Union and Advertiser
St. Louis Globe-Democrat
St. Louis Post
St. Louis Post-Dispatch
St. Louis Republican
St. Paul Anti-Monopolist
San Francisco Alta California
San Francisco Chronicle
Scribner's Monthly
Socialist (Chicago)
Socialist (Detroit)
Socialist (New York)
Southern Workman (Hampton, Va.)
Sovereigns of Industry. Bulletin! (Worcester, Mass.)
Springfield (Mass.) Republican
Trades (Philadelphia)
Trans-Continental
Truth (New York)
Truth (San Francisco)
Washington National Republican
Washington Post
Washington Star
Wisconsin Standard (Oshkosh)
Woman's Journal
Woodhull and Claflin's Weekly
Workingman's Advocate (Chicago)
Workingman's Map (Indianapolis)

PROCEEDINGS

American Federation of Labor. *Proceedings of the American Federation of Labor 1881, 1882, 1883, 1884, 1885, 1886, 1887, 1888.* Bloomington, Ill., 1906.

Brotherhood of Locomotive Firemen. *Journal of the Proceedings of the First Twelve Annual Conventions of the Brotherhood of Locomotive Firemen, from 1874 to 1885, Inclusive.* Terre Haute, Ind., 1885.

Democratic Party. *Official Proceedings of the National Democratic Convention, Held in St. Louis, Mo., June 27th, 28th and 29th, 1876. With an Appendix Containing the Letters of Acceptance of Gov. Tilden and Gov. Hendricks.* St. Louis, 1876.

Iron Molders' International Union. *Proceedings of the Tenth Session of the Iron Molders' International Union, in Convention Assembled, at Philadelphia, July 6th, 1870.* Philadelphia, 1870.

———. *Proceedings of the Eleventh Session of the Iron Molders' International Union, in Convention Assembled, at Troy, N.Y., July 10, 1872.* Cincinnati, 1872.

Iron Molders' Union of North America. *Proceedings of the Twelfth Session of the Iron Molders' Union of North America, in Convention Assembled, at Richmond, Va., July 8, 1874.* Cincinnati, 1874.

———. *Proceedings of the Thirteenth Session of the Iron Molders' Union of North America, Convened at Cleveland, Ohio, July 5, 1876.* N.p., 1876.

———. *[Proceedings of the] Fourteenth Session of the Iron Molders' Union of North America, Convened at Louisville, Ky., July 10, 1878.* N.p., 1878.

———. *[Proceedings of the] Sixteenth Session of the Iron Molders' Union of North America, Convened at Brooklyn, N.Y., July 10, 1882.* N.p., 1882.

Kennedy, E. B., S. D. Dillaye, Henry Hill, and F. C. Bliss. *Our Presidential Candidates and Political Compendium. Also Containing Lives of the Candidates for Vice-President—the Proceedings of the Three National Conventions—the Three Platforms and the Three Letters of Acceptance.* Newark, N.J., 1880.

Knights of Labor. *Record of the Proceedings of the General Assembly of the ********* [Knights of Labor] held at Reading, Pennsylvania, January 1–4, 1878.* N.p., 1878.

———. *Record of the Proceedings of the Special Session of the General Assembly, Held at Philadelphia, Penn., June 6, 1878.* N.p., 1878.

———. *Record of the Proceedings of the Second Regular Session of the General Assembly, Held at St. Louis, Mo., January 14–17, 1879.* N.p., 1879.

———. *Record of the Proceedings of the Third Regular Session of the General Assembly, Held at Chicago, Ill., Sept. 2–6, 1879.* N.p., 1879.

———. *Record of the Proceedings of the Fourth Regular Session of the General Assembly, Held at Pittsburgh, Pa., Sept. 7–11, 1880.* N.p., 1880.

———. *Record of the Proceedings of the Fifth Regular Session of the General Assembly, Held at Detroit, Mich., Sept. 6–10, 1881.* N.p., 1881.

———. *Record of the Proceedings of the Sixth Regular Session of the General Assembly, Held at New York City, N.Y., Sept. 5–12, 1882.* N.p., 1882.

———. *Record of the Proceedings of the Seventh Regular Session of the General Assembly, Held at Cincinnati, Ohio, Sept. 4–11, 1883.* N.p., 1883.

———. *Record of the Proceedings of the Eighth Regular Session of the General Assembly, Held at Philadelphia, Pa., Sept. 1–10, 1884.* N.p., 1884.

———. *Record of the Proceedings of the Ninth Regular Session of the General Assembly, Held at Hamilton, Ontario, October 5–13, 1885.* N.p., 1885.

Republican Party. *Proceedings of the Republican National Convention, Held at Cincinnati, Ohio, Wednesday, Thursday, and Friday, June 14, 15, and 16, 1876, Resulting in the Nomina-*

tion for President and Vice-President Rutherford B. Hayes and William A. Wheeler. Compiled by M. A. Clancy and William Nelson. Concord, N.H., 1876.

——. *Proceedings of the Republican National Convention, Held at Chicago, Illinois, Wednesday, Thursday, Friday, Saturday, Monday and Tuesday, June 2d, 3d, 4th, 5th, 7th and 8th, 1880. Resulting in the Following Nominations: For President, James A. Garfield, of Ohio. For Vice-President, Chester A. Arthur, of New York*. Compiled by Eugene Davis. Chicago, 1881.

Socialistic Labor Party. *Socialistic Labor Party. Platform, Constitution, and Resolutions, Adopted at the National Congress of the Workingmen's Party of the United States, Held at Newark, N.J., December 26, 27, 28, 29, 30, 31, 1877, together with a Condensed Report of the Congress Proceedings*. Cincinnati, 1878.

——. *Socialistic Labor Party. Platform, Constitution, and Resolutions, together with a Condensed Report of the Proceedings of the National Convention, Held at Allegheny, Pa., December 26, 27, 28, 29, 30 and 31, 1879, and January 1, 1880*. Detroit, 1880.

CONTEMPORARY PUBLICATIONS AND PUBLISHED DOCUMENTS

Adams, Charles Francis, Jr. "The Protection of the Ballot in National Elections: A Paper Read at the General Meeting of the Association, at Albany, New York, February 19th, 1869." *Journal of Social Science* 1 (June 1869): 91–111.

Angell, James B. "The Diplomatic Relations between the United States and China." *Journal of Social Science* 17 (May 1883): 24–36.

Bancroft, Hubert Howe. *1860–1890*. Vol. 7 of *History of California*. Vol. 24 of *The Works of Hubert Howe Bancroft*. San Francisco, 1890.

Blaine, James G. *Political Discussions Legislative, Diplomatic, and Popular, 1856–1886*. Norwich, Conn., 1887.

Bowles, Samuel. *Our New West*. Hartford, Conn., 1869.

Bryce, James. *The American Commonwealth*. 3d ed. 2 vols. New York, 1905; first published 1894.

Chinatown Declared a Nuisance! N.p., 1880.

The Chinese Massacre at Rock Springs, Wyoming Territory, September 2, 1885. Boston, 1886.

Commons, John R., Ulrich B. Phillips, Eugene A. Gilmore, Helen L. Sumner, and John B. Andrews, eds. *A Documentary History of American Industrial Society*. 11 vols. Cleveland, 1910–11.

The Commune in 1880. Downfall of the Republic! New York, 1877.

Conwell, Russell H. *Why and How the Chinese Emigrate*. Boston, 1871.

Crawford, Theron Clark. *James G. Blaine: A Study of His Life and Career from the Standpoint of a Personal Witness of the Principal Events in His History*. Philadelphia, 1893.

Dee, M. J. "Chinese Immigration." *North American Review* 127 (Jan.–Feb. 1878): 506–26.

Facts upon the Other Side of the Chinese Question: with a Memorial to the President of the U.S. from Representative Chinamen in America. N.p., 1876.

Gantt, T. Fulton. *Breaking the Chains: A Story of Industrial Struggle*. In *The Knights in Fiction: Two Labor Novels of the 1880s*, edited by Mary C. Grimes, 27–133. Urbana, Ill., 1986.

George, Henry. "The Kearney Agitation in California." *Popular Science Monthly* 17 (Aug. 1880): 433–53.

——. *Progress and Poverty: An Inquiry into the Cause of Industrial Depressions and of Increase of Want with Increase of Wealth. The Remedy*. San Francisco, 1879.

Gibson, Otis. *The Chinese in America*. Cincinnati, 1877.

Goodrich, Samuel G. *The Child's Second Book of History, Including the Modern History of Europe, Africa, and Asia. Illustrated by Engravings and Sixteen Maps, and Designed as a Sequel to the "First Book of History,["] by the Author of Peter Parley's Tales*. Boston, 1840.

Hamilton, Gail [Mary Abigail Dodge]. *Biography of James G. Blaine*. Norwich, Conn., 1895.

Healy, Patrick Joseph. "A Shoemaker's Contribution to the Chinese Discussion." *Overland Monthly* 7 (Apr. 1886): 414–21.

———. *Some Reasons Why an Exclusion Law Should Not Be Passed*. San Francisco, 1902.

Healy, Patrick Joseph, and Ng Poon Chew. *A Statement for Non-Exclusion*. San Francisco, 1905.

Julian, George W., and George Julian Clarke, eds. *Later Speeches on Political Questions with Select Controversial Papers*. Indianapolis, 1889.

McCabe, James D. *The Life and Public Services of Gen. James A. Garfield, Twentieth President of the United States. Embracing a Full Account of His Early Life; His Struggles with Poverty and Efforts to Obtain an Education; His Brilliant Services as a Soldier and Statesman; His Election to the Presidency; His Able and Patriotic Administration; His Manful Battle with Rings and Corruption in High Places. Together with the History of His Assassination, Giving All the Incidents of His Long and Painful Illness, the Surgical Treatment, the Consultations of the Eminent Physicians, Daily Scenes at the Sufferer's Bedside, Last Hours and Death, the Funeral Cortege, Burial, Etc*. Cincinnati, 1880.

McNeill, George, ed. *The Labor Movement: The Problem of To-day*. New York, 1891.

McPherson, Edward. *A Hand-Book of Politics for 1872: Being a Record of Important Political Action, National and State, from July 15, 1870, to July 15, 1872*. New York, 1872.

———. *A Hand-Book of Politics for 1878: Being a Record of Important Political Action, National and State, from July 15, 1876, to July 15, 1878*. New York, 1878.

Meade, Edwin R. *The Chinese Question: A Paper Read at the Annual Meeting of the Social Science Association of America, Held at Saratoga, N.Y., Sept. 7th, 1877*. New York, 1877.

Murphy, John E. *Murphy and Mack's McMullen Family Songster*. New York, 1879.

———. *Murphy and Mack's Rafferty Blues Songster*. New York, [1880?].

National Democratic Committee. *The Campaign Text Book. Why the People Want a Change. The Republican Party Reviewed: Its Sins of Commission and Omission. A Summary of Leading Events in Our History under Republican Administration. Issued by the National Democratic Committee*. New York, 1880.

Pumpelly, Raphael. "Our Impending Chinese Problem." *Galaxy* 8 (July 1869): 22–33.

Quigley, Hugh. *The Irish Race in California, and on the Pacific Coast, with an Introductory Historical Dissertation on the Principal Races of Mankind, and a Vocabulary of Ancient and Modern Irish Family Names*. San Francisco, 1878.

Remarks of the Chinese Merchants of San Francisco, upon Governor Bigler's Message, and Some Common Objections; with Some Explanations of the Character of the Chinese Companies, and the Laboring Class in California. San Francisco, 1855.

Ridpath, John Clark. *The Life and Work of James A. Garfield, Twentieth President of the United States: Embracing an Account of the Scenes and Incidents of His Boyhood; the Struggles of His Youth; the Might of His Early Manhood; His Valor as a Soldier; His Career as a Statesman; His Election to the Presidency; and the Tragic Story of His Death*. Cincinnati, 1881.

Ridpath, John Clark, and Selen Connor. *Life and Work of James G. Blaine*. Philadelphia, 1893.

Seward, George F. *Chinese Immigration, in Its Social and Economical Aspects*. New York, 1881.

Sloan, George M. *The Telephone of Labor*. Chicago, 1880.

Spear, Willis F. *History of North Adams, Mass., 1749–1885*. North Adams, 1885.

"Speech of Mr. Burlingame at a Municipal Banquet in Boston." In Chinese Legation, *Official Papers of the Chinese Legation*, 33–40. Berlin, Germany, n.d.

Stanton, Elizabeth Cady, Susan B. Anthony, Matilda Joslyn Gage, [and Ida Husted Harper], eds. *History of Woman Suffrage*. 6 vols. New York and Rochester, 1881–1922.

Stedman, J. C., and R. A. Leonard. *The Workingmen's Party of California: An Epitome of Its Rise and Progress*. San Francisco, 1878.

Swinton, John. *The New Issue: The Chinese-American Question*. New York, 1870.

Sylvis, James C. *The Life, Speeches, Labors and Essays of William H. Sylvis, Late President of the Iron-Moulders' International Union; and Also of the National Labor Union*. Philadelphia, 1872.

Taylor, Bayard. *A Visit to India, China, and Japan, in the Year 1853*. New York, 1855.

Thayer, S. Proctor. "Adams and North Adams." In *History of Berkshire County, Massachusetts*. Vol. 1. New York, 1885.

Vivian, Thomas J. "John Chinaman in San Francisco." *Scribner's Monthly* 12 (Oct. 1876): 862–72.

Webster, Noah. *An American Dictionary of the English Language*. Rev. ed. New York, 1846.

———. *An American Dictionary of the English Language*. Springfield, Mass., 1852.

———. *An American Dictionary of the English Language*. N.p., 1859.

———. *An American Dictionary of the English Language*. N.p., 1861.

Webster, Noah, and Chauncey A. Goodrich, eds. *An American Dictionary of the English Language*. Philadelphia, 1857.

Whitney, James A. *The Chinese and the Chinese Question*. New York, 1880.

Young, John Russell. *Around the World with General Grant: A Narrative of the Visit of General U. S. Grant, Ex-President of the United States, to Various Countries in Europe, Asia, and Africa, in 1877, 1878, 1879. To Which Are Added Certain Conversations with General Grant on Questions Connected with American Politics and History*. 2 vols. New York, 1879.

MEMOIRS, REMINISCENCES, LETTERS, AND AUTOBIOGRAPHIES

Angell, James Burrill. *The Reminiscences of James Burrill Angell*. New York, 1912.

Blaine, James G. *Twenty Years of Congress: From Lincoln to Garfield. With a Review of the Events Which Led to the Political Revolution of 1860*. 2 vols. Norwich, Conn., 1886; first published 1884.

Blaine, Mrs. James G. *Letters of Mrs. James G. Blaine*. Edited by Harriet S. Blaine Beale. 2 vols. New York, 1908.

Depew, Chauncey M. *My Memories of Eighty Years*. New York, 1922.

Douglass, Frederick. *The Life and Writings of Frederick Douglass: Reconstruction and After*. Vol. 4. Edited by Philip S. Foner. New York, 1955.

Emerson, Ralph Waldo. *The Journals and Miscellaneous Notebooks of Ralph Waldo Emerson*. 16 vols. Edited by William H. Gilman, Alfred R. Ferguson, and Merrell R. Davis. Cambridge, Mass., 1960–1982.

———. *The Letters of Ralph Waldo Emerson*. 6 vols. Edited by Ralph L. Rusk. New York, 1939.

Garrison, William Lloyd. *To Rouse the Slumbering Land, 1868–1879: The Letters of William*

Lloyd Garrison. 6 vols. Edited by Walter M. Merrill and Louis Ruchames. Cambridge, Mass., 1971–1981.

Gompers, Samuel. *Seventy Years of Life and Labor: An Autobiography*. 2 vols. New York, 1925.

Hancock, Winfield Scott. *Reminiscences of Winfield Scott Hancock, by His Wife*. New York, 1887.

Hayes, Rutherford B. *The Diary of a President, 1875–1881, concerning the Disputed Election, the End of Reconstruction, and the Beginning of Civil Service*. Edited by T. Harry Williams. New York, 1964.

Hoar, George Frisbie. *Autobiography of Seventy Years*. 2 vols. New York, 1903.

Powderly, Terence V. *The Path I Trod*. New York, 1940.

Stewart, William M. *Reminiscence of Senator William M. Stewart of Nevada*. Edited by George Rothwell Brown. New York, 1908.

Twain, Mark. *Roughing It*. New York, 1962; first published 1871.

Williams, Samuel Wells. *The Life and Letters of Samuel Wells Williams, LL.D., Missionary, Diplomatist, Sinologue*. Edited by Frederick Wells Williams. New York, 1889.

Young, John Russell. *Men and Memories: Personal Reminiscences*. New York, 1901.

Yung Wing. *My Life in China and America*. New York, 1909.

BOOKS

Anderson, David L. *Imperialism and Idealism: American Diplomats in China, 1861–1898*. Bloomington, Ind., 1985.

Baker, Jean. *Affairs of Party: The Political Culture of Northern Democrats in the Mid–Nineteenth Century*. Ithaca, N.Y., 1983.

Barrows, Chester Leonard. *William M. Evarts, Lawyer, Diplomat, Statesman*. Chapel Hill, N.C., 1941.

Barth, Gunther. *Bitter Strength: A History of the Chinese in the United States, 1850–1870*. Cambridge, Mass., 1964.

Beard, Mary Ritter. *The American Labor Movement: A Short History*. New York, 1939.

Bernstein, Iver. *The New York City Draft Riots: Their Significance for American Society and Politics in the Age of the Civil War*. New York, 1990.

Boyer, Richard O., and Herbert M. Morais. *Labor's Untold Story*. New York, 1980; first published 1955.

Bruce, Robert V. *1877: Year of Violence*. New York, 1959.

Burnham, Walter Dean. *Critical Elections and the Mainsprings of American Politics*. New York, 1970.

Caldwell, Robert Granville. *James Garfield: Party Chieftain*. New York, 1931.

Campbell, Persia Crawford. *Chinese Coolie Emigration to Countries within the British Empire*. London, 1923.

Chambers, Walter Nisbet, and Walter Dean Burnham, eds. *The American Party Systems: Stages of Political Development*. New York, 1967.

Chan, Sucheng. *This Bittersweet Soil: The Chinese in California Agriculture, 1860–1910*. Berkeley, 1986.

——, ed. *Entry Denied: Exclusion and the Chinese Community in America, 1882–1943*. Philadelphia, 1991.

Chen, Jack. *The Chinese of America*. New York, 1980.

Chidsey, Donald Barr. *The Gentleman from New York: A Life of Roscoe Conkling*. New Haven, 1935.

Chiu, Ping. *Chinese Labor in California, 1850–1880*. Madison, Wisc., 1963.

Choy, Philip P., Lorraine Dong, and Marlon K. Hom. *The Coming Man: Nineteenth Century American Perceptions of the Chinese*. Seattle, 1994.

Chu, Limin. *The Images of China and the Chinese in the "Overland Monthly," 1868–1875, 1883–1935*. San Francisco, 1974.

Clancy, Herbert J. *The Presidential Election of 1880*. Chicago, 1958.

Cohen, Lucy M. *Chinese in the Post–Civil War South: A People without a History*. Baton Rouge, 1984.

Cohen, Warren I. *America's Response to China: An Interpretive History of Sino-American Relations*. New York, 1971.

Commons, John R., David J. Saposs, Helen L. Sumner, E. B. Mittelman, H. E. Hoagland, John B. Andrews, Selig Perlman, Don D. Lescohier, Elizabeth Brandeis, and Philip Taft. *History of Labour in the United States*. 4 vols. New York, 1918–35.

Conmy, Peter Thomas. *Philip Augustine Roach, 1820–1889, California Pioneer*. San Francisco, 1958.

Coolidge, Mary Roberts. *Chinese Immigration*. New York, 1909.

Cross, Ira B. *A History of the Labor Movement in California*. Berkeley, 1935.

Daniels, Roger. *Asian America: Chinese and Japanese in the United States since 1850*. Seattle, 1988.

——, ed. *Anti-Chinese Violence in North America*. New York, 1978.

Dawley, Alan. *Class and Community: The Industrial Revolution in Lynn*. Cambridge, Mass., 1976.

Doenecke, Justus. *The Presidencies of James A. Garfield and Chester A. Arthur*. Lawrence, Kans., 1981.

DuBois, Ellen Carol. *Feminism and Suffrage: The Emergence of an Independent Women's Movement in America, 1848–1869*. Ithaca, N.Y., 1978.

Dyer, Brainerd. *Public Career of William M. Evarts*. Berkeley, 1933.

Eaves, Lucile. *A History of California Labor Legislation, with an Introductory Sketch of the San Francisco Labor Movement*. University of California Publications in Economics, vol. 2. Berkeley, 1910.

Elliott, Russell R. *Servant of Power: A Political Biography of Senator William M. Stewart*. Reno, 1983.

Erickson, Charlotte. *American Industry and the European Immigrant, 1860–1885*. Cambridge, Mass., 1957.

Fairchild, Henry Pratt. *Immigration: A World Movement and Its American Significance*. New York, 1913.

Fessler, Loren W., ed. *Chinese in America: Stereotyped Past, Changing Present*. New York, 1983.

Fine, Sidney. *Laissez Faire and the General-Welfare State: A Study of Conflict in American Thought, 1865–1901*. Ann Arbor, Mich., 1956.

Flick, Alexander Clarence. *Samuel Jones Tilden: A Study in Political Sagacity*. New York, 1939.

Foner, Eric. *Free Soil, Free Labor, Free Men: The Ideology of the Republican Party before the Civil War*. New York, 1970.

——. *Politics and Ideology in the Age of the Civil War*. New York, 1980.

——. *Reconstruction: America's Unfinished Revolution, 1863–1877*. New York, 1988.

Foner, Philip S. *The Great Labor Uprising of 1877*. New York, 1977.

——. *History of the Labor Movement in the United States*. 7 vols. New York, 1947–87.

Formisano, Ronald P. *The Transformation of Political Culture: Massachusetts Parties, 1790s–1840s*. New York, 1983.

Fredrickson, George M. *The Black Image in the White Mind: The Debate on Afro-American Character and Destiny, 1817–1914*. New York, 1971.

Friday, Chris. *Organizing Asian American Labor: The Pacific Coast Canned-Salmon Industry, 1870–1942*. Philadelphia, 1994.

Fuess, Claude M. *The Life of Caleb Cushing*. 2 vols. New York, 1923.

Garraty, John A. *The New Commonwealth, 1877–1890*. New York, 1968.

Gillette, William. *The Right to Vote: Politics and the Passage of the Fifteenth Amendment*. Baltimore, 1965.

Glick, Clarence E. *Sojourners and Settlers: Chinese Migrants in Hawaii*. Honolulu, 1980.

Gossett, Thomas F. *Race: The History of an Idea in America*. Dallas, 1963.

Grob, Gerald N. *Workers and Utopia: A Study of Ideological Conflict in the American Labor Movement, 1865–1900*. Evanston, Ill., 1961.

Grossman, Jonathan Philip. *William Sylvis, Pioneer of American Labor: A Study of the Labor Movement during the Era of the Civil War*. Columbia University Studies in History, Economics, and Public Law, no. 516. New York, 1945.

Gutman, Herbert G. *Power and Culture: Essays on the American Working Class*. Edited by Ira Berlin. New York, 1987.

——. *Work, Culture, and Society in Industrializing America: Essays in American Working-Class and Social History*. New York, 1977.

Hall, Prescott F. *Immigration and Its Effects upon the United States*. New York, 1906.

Hansen, Debra Gold. *Strained Sisterhood: Class and Gender in the Boston Female Anti-Slavery Society*. Amherst, Mass., 1993.

Haskell, Thomas L. *The Emergence of Professional Social Science: The American Social Science Association and the Nineteenth Century Crisis of Authority*. Urbana, Ill., 1977.

Haynes, Fred Emory. *James Baird Weaver*. Iowa City, 1919.

——. *Social Politics in the United States*. Boston, 1924.

——. *Third Party Movements since the Civil War with Special Reference to Iowa: A Study in Social Politics*. Iowa City, 1916.

Hesseltine, William B. *Ulysses S. Grant, Politician*. New York, 1967; first published 1935.

Higham, John. *Strangers in the Land: Patterns of American Nativism, 1860–1925*. New York, 1975; first published 1955.

Hoexter, Corinne K. *From Canton to California: The Epic of Chinese Immigration*. New York, 1976.

Hofstadter, Richard. *The American Political Tradition and the Men Who Made It*. New York, 1948.

Hoogenboom, Ari. *The Presidency of Rutherford B. Hayes*. Lawrence, Kans., 1988.

——. *Rutherford B. Hayes: Warrior and President*. Lawrence, Kans., 1995.

Horsman, Reginald. *Race and Manifest Destiny: The Origins of American Racial Anglo-Saxonsim*. Cambridge, Mass., 1981.

Howe, George Frederick. *Chester A. Arthur: A Quarter-Century of Machine Politics*. New York, 1935.

Hoy, William. *The Chinese Six Companies*. San Francisco, 1942.

Hunt, H. Draper. *Hannibal Hamlin of Maine: Lincoln's First Vice-President*. Syracuse, 1969.

Hunt, Michael H. *The Making of a Special Relationship: The United States and China to 1914*. New York, 1983.

Hunt, Rockwell D. *California in the Making: Essays and Papers in California History*. Westport, Conn., 1974; first published Caldwell, Idaho, 1953.

Hutchinson, E. P. *Legislative History of American Immigration Policy, 1798–1965*. Philadelphia, 1981.

Irick, Robert L. *Ch'ing Policy toward the Coolie Trade, 1847–1878*. Republic of China, 1982.

Isaacs, Harold M. *Scratches on Our Minds: American Images of China and India*. New York, 1958.

Johnson, Donald Bruce, comp. *1840–1956*. Vol. 1 of *National Party Platforms*. Rev. ed. Urbana, Ill., 1978.

Jones, Maldwyn Allen. *American Immigration*. Chicago, 1960.

Jordan, David M. *Winfield Scott Hancock: A Soldier's Life*. Bloomington, 1988.

Keller, Morton. *Affairs of State: Public Life in Late Nineteenth Century America*. Cambridge, Mass., 1977.

Kim, Hyung-chan. *A Legal History of Asian Americans, 1790–1990*. Westport, Conn., 1994.

———, ed. *Asian Americans and the Supreme Court: A Documentary History*. Westport, Conn., 1992.

King, Willard L. *Lincoln's Manager, David Davis*. Chicago, 1960.

Kingston, Maxine Hong. *Chinamen*. New York, 1976.

Kleppner, Paul. *The Cross of Culture: A Social Analysis of Midwestern Politics, 1850–1900*. New York, 1970.

———. *The Third Electoral System, 1853–1892: Parties, Voters, and Political Cultures*. Chapel Hill, N.C., 1979.

Konvitz, Milton R. *The Alien and the Asiatic in American Law*. Ithaca, N.Y., 1946.

Kung, S. W. *Chinese in American Life: Some Aspects of Their History, Status, Problems, and Contributions*. Westport, Conn., 1962.

LaFargue, Thomas E. *China's First Hundred: Educational Mission Students in the United States, 1872–1881*. Pullman, Wash., 1942.

LaFeber, Walter. *The New Empire: An Interpretation of American Expansion, 1860–1898*. Ithaca, N.Y., 1963.

Lane, A. T. *Solidarity or Survival? American Labor and European Immigrants, 1830–1924*. Westport, Conn., 1987.

Laurie, Bruce. *Artisans into Workers: Labor in Nineteenth-Century America*. New York, 1989.

———. *Working People of Philadelphia, 1800–1850*. Philadelphia, 1980.

Lee, Rose Hum. *The Chinese in the United States of America*. Hong Kong, 1960.

Leech, Margaret, and Harry J. Brown. *The Garfield Orbit*. New York, 1978.

Lescohier, Don D. *The Knights of St. Crispin, 1867–1874: A Study in the Industrial Causes of Trade Unionism*. Bulletin of the University of Wisconsin, no. 355. Economics and Political Science Series, vol. 7, no. 1. Madison, 1910.

Litwack, Leon F. *North of Slavery: The Negro in the Free States, 1790–1860*. Chicago, 1961.

Loewen, James W. *The Mississippi Chinese: Between Black and White*. Cambridge, Mass., 1971.

Lyman, Stanford M. *Chinese Americans*. New York, 1974.

McClain, Charles J. *In Search of Equality: The Chinese Struggle against Discrimination in Nineteenth-Century America*. Berkeley, 1994.

——, ed. *Chinese Immigrants and American Law*. New York, 1994.

McClellan, Robert. *The Heathen Chinee: A Study of American Attitudes toward China, 1890–1905*. Columbus, Ohio, 1971.

McCormick, Richard L. *The Party Period and Public Policy: American Politics from the Age of Jackson to the Progressive Era*. New York, 1986.

McCormick, Richard P. *The Second American Party System*. Chapel Hill, N.C., 1966.

McCunn, Ruthanne Lum. *Chinese American Portraits: Personal Histories, 1828–1988*. San Francisco, 1988.

——. *Thousand Pieces of Gold*. Boston, 1981.

——. *Wooden Fish Songs*. New York, 1995.

McFeely, William S. *Grant: A Biography*. New York, 1982.

McGerr, Michael. *The Decline of Popular Politics: The American North, 1865–1928*. New York, 1986.

McKenzie, R. D. *Oriental Exclusion*. Chicago, 1928.

Magdol, Edward. *The Antislavery Rank and File: A Social Profile of the Abolitionists' Constituency*. Westport, Conn., 1986.

Marberry, M. M. *The Golden Voice: A Biography of Isaac Kalloch*. New York, 1947.

Marcus, Robert D. *Grand Old Party: Political Structure in the Gilded Age, 1880–1896*. New York, 1971.

Mark, Diane Mei Lin, and Ginger Chih. *A Place Called America*. N.p., 1993; first published 1982.

Markus, Andrew. *Fear and Hatred: Purifying Australia and California, 1850–1901*. Sydney, 1979.

Mayo-Smith, Richmond. *Emigration and Immigration: A Study in Social Science*. New York, 1890.

Meagher, Arnold Joseph. *The Introduction of Chinese Laborers to Latin America: The "Coolie Trade," 1847–1874*. San Francisco, 1978.

Merriam-Webster's Collegiate Dictionary. 10th ed. Springfield, Mass., 1993.

Miller, Stuart Creighton. *The Unwelcome Immigrant: The American Image of the Chinese, 1785–1882*. Berkeley, 1969.

Mink, Gwendolyn. *Old Labor and New Immigrants in American Political Development: Union, Party, and State, 1875–1920*. Ithaca, N.Y., 1986.

Montgomery, David. *Beyond Equality: Labor and the Radical Republicans, 1862–1872*. New York, 1967.

——. *The Fall of the House of Labor: The Workplace, the State, and American Labor Activism, 1865–1925*. New York, 1987.

Morgan, H. Wayne. *From Hayes to McKinley: National Party Politics, 1877–1896*. Syracuse, 1969.

Morris, Richard B., and Jeffrey B. Morris, eds. *Encyclopedia of American History*. New York, 1996.

Muzzey, David Saville. *James G. Blaine: A Political Idol of Other Days*. New York, 1934.

Nee, Victor G., and Brett de Bary Nee. *A Documentary Study of an American Chinatown*. New York, 1973.

Nelson, Bruce C. *Beyond the Martyrs: A Social History of Chicago's Anarchists, 1870–1900*. New Brunswick, N.J., 1988.

Nevins, Allan. *Abram S. Hewitt, with Some Account of Peter Cooper*. New York, 1935.

Painter, Nell Irvin. *Exodusters: Black Migration to Kansas after Reconstruction*. New York, 1976.

Parks, Joseph H. *Joseph E. Brown of Georgia*. Baton Rouge, 1977.

Parmet, Robert D. *Labor and Immigration in Industrial America*. Boston, 1981.

Perlman, Selig. *A History of Trade Unionism in the United States*. New York, 1950; first published 1922.

Perman, Michael. *The Road to Redemption: Southern Politics, 1869–1879*. Chapel Hill, N.C., 1984.

Peskin, Alan. *Garfield*. Kent, Ohio, 1978.

Plesur, Milton. *America's Outward Thrust: Approaches to Foreign Affairs, 1865–1890*. DeKalb, Ill., 1971.

Polakoff, Keith Ian. *The Politics of Inertia: The Election of 1876 and the End of Reconstruction*. Baton Rouge, 1973.

Porter, Kirk H., and Donald Bruce Johnson, comps. *National Party Platforms, 1840–1968*. Urbana, Ill., 1970.

Prendergast, Thomas F. *Forgotten Pioneers: Irish Leaders in Early California*. San Francisco, 1942.

Price, Charles A. *The Great White Walls Are Built: Restrictive Immigration to North America and Australia, 1836–1888*. Canberra, 1974.

Random House Collegiate Dictionary. Rev. ed. New York, 1980.

Rayback, Joseph G. *A History of American Labor*. New York, 1959.

Reeves, Thomas C. *Gentleman Boss: The Life of Chester Alan Arthur*. New York, 1975.

Richards, Leonard L. *"Gentlemen of Property and Standing": Anti-Abolition Mobs in Jacksonian America*. New York, 1970.

Ricker, Ralph R. *The Greenback-Labor Movement in Pennsylvania*. Bellefonte, Pa., 1966.

Riggs, Fred W. *Pressures on Congress: A Study of the Repeal of Chinese Exclusion*. New York, 1950.

Rodgers, Daniel P. *The Work Ethic in Industrial America, 1850–1920*. Chicago, 1978.

Roediger, David R. *Towards the Abolition of Whiteness: Essays on Race, Politics, and Working Class History*. London, 1994.

——. *The Wages of Whiteness: Race and the Making of the American Working Class*. London, 1991.

Russell, Charles Edward. *Blaine of Maine: His Life and Times*. New York, 1931.

Salyer, Lucy E. *"Laws Harsh as Tigers": Chinese Immigrants and the Shaping of Modern Immigration Law*. Chapel Hill, N.C., 1995.

Sandmeyer, Elmer Clarence. *The Anti-Chinese Movement in California*. Urbana, Ill., 1939.

Saxton, Alexander. *The Indispensable Enemy: Labor and the Anti-Chinese Movement in California*. Berkeley, 1971.

——. *The Rise and Fall of the White Republic: Class Politics and Mass Culture in Nineteenth-Century America*. London, 1990.

Schwartz, Bernard, ed. *Statutory History of the United States, Civil Rights, Part 1*. New York, 1970.

Shumsky, Neil Larry. *The Evolution of Political Protest and the Workingmen's Party of California*. Columbus, Ohio, 1991.

Smith, Abbott Emerson. *Colonists in Bondage: White Servitude and Convict Labor in America, 1607–1776*. New York, 1975; first published 1947.

Smith, Shirley W. *James Burrill Angell: An American Influence*. Ann Arbor, Mich., 1954.

Sproat, John G. *"The Best Men": Liberal Reformers in the Gilded Age*. New York, 1968.

Stanton, William. *The Leopard's Spots: Scientific Attitudes toward Race in America, 1815–59*. Chicago, 1960.

Stanwood, Edward. *James Gillespie Blaine*. Boston, 1906.

Steiner, Stan. *Fusang: The Chinese Who Built America*. New York, 1979.

Steinfield, Robert J. *The Invention of Free Labor: The Employment Relation in English and American Law and Culture, 1350–1870*. Chapel Hill, N.C., 1991.

Storti, Craig. *Incident at Bitter Creek: The Story of the Rock Springs Chinese Massacre*. Ames, Iowa, 1991.

Summers, Mark Wahlgren. *The Press Gang: Newspapers and Politics, 1865–1878*. Chapel Hill, N.C., 1994.

Sung, Betty Lee. *Mountain of Gold: The Story of the Chinese in America*. New York, 1967.

Swisher, Carl Brent. *Motivation and Political Technique in the California Constitutional Convention, 1878–79*. Claremont, Calif., 1930.

Swisher, Earl. *Early Sino-American Relations: The Collected Articles of Earl Swisher*. Edited by Kenneth W. Rea. Boulder, Colo., 1977.

Taft, Philip. *Economics and Problems of Labor*. Harrisburg, Pa., 1942.

——. *Organized Labor in American History*. New York, 1964.

Takaki, Ronald. *Iron Cages: Race and Culture in Nineteenth-Century America*. New York, 1979.

——. *Strangers from a Different Shore: A History of Asian Americans*. New York, 1990.

Tansill, Charles Callan. *The Foreign Policy of Thomas F. Bayard, 1885–1897*. New York, 1940.

Taylor, John M. *Garfield of Ohio: The Available Man*. New York, 1970.

Treadwell, Edward F., ed. *The Constitution of the State of California*. San Francisco, 1923.

Tretousse, Hans L. *Ben Butler: The South Called Him BEAST!* New York, 1957.

Tsai, Shih-shan Henry. *China and the Overseas Chinese in the United States, 1868–1911*. Fayetteville, Ark., 1983.

——. *The Chinese Experience in America*. Bloomington, Ind., 1986.

Tutorow, Norman E. *James Gillespie Blaine and the Presidency: A Documentary Source Book*. New York, 1989.

Tweedy, John. *A History of the Republican National Conventions from 1856 to 1908*. Danbury, Conn., 1910.

Unger, Irwin. *The Greenback Era: A Social and Political History of American Finance, 1865–1879*. Princeton, 1964.

Wallace, Anthony F. C. *St. Clair: A Nineteenth-Century Coal Town's Experience with a Disaster-Prone Industry*. Ithaca, N.Y., 1987.

Ward, Peter. *White Canada Forever*. Montreal, 1978.

Ware, Norman J. *The Labor Movement in the United States, 1860–1895: A Study in Democracy*. Gloucester, Mass., 1959; first published 1929.

Weir, Robert C. *Beyond Labor's Veil: The Culture of the Knights of Labor*. University Park, Pa., 1996.

Welch, Richard E., Jr. *George Frisbie Hoar and the Half-Breed Republicans*. Cambridge, Mass., 1971.

West, Richard S., Jr. *Lincoln's Scapegoat General: A Life of Benjamin F. Butler, 1818–1893*. Boston, 1965.

Wickberg, Edgar, et al. *From China to Canada: A History of Chinese Communities in Canada*. Toronto, 1982.

Williams, Frederick Wells. *Anson Burlingame and the First Chinese Mission to Foreign Powers*. New York, 1912.

———. *A Sketch of the Relations between the United States and China*. N.p., 1910.

Woodward, C. Vann. *Reunion and Reaction: The Compromise of 1877 and the End of Reconstruction*. Boston, 1951.

———. *Tom Watson: Agrarian Rebel*. New York, 1938.

Wu, William. *The Yellow Peril: Chinese Americans in American Fiction, 1850–1940*. Hamden, Conn., 1982.

Wynne, Robert E. *Reaction to the Chinese in the Pacific Northwest and British Columbia, 1850–1910*. New York, 1978.

Yung, Judy. *Chinese Women of America: A Pictorial History*. Seattle, 1986.

Zo, Kil Young. *Chinese Emigration into the United States, 1850–1880*. New York, 1978.

ARTICLES

Anderson, David L. "The Diplomacy of Discrimination: Chinese Exclusion, 1876–1882." *California History* 57 (Spring 1978): 32–45.

Armstrong, William A. "Godkin and Chinese Labor." *American Journal of Economics and Sociology* 21 (Jan. 1962): 91–102.

Baum, Dale. "Woman Suffrage and the 'Chinese Question' in Massachusetts, 1865–1876." *New England Quarterly* 56 (Mar. 1983): 60–77.

Biggerstaff, Knight. "The Official Chinese Attitude toward the Burlingame Mission." *American Historical Review* 14 (July 1936): 682–701.

Black, Isabella. "American Labour and Chinese Immigration." *Past and Present* 25 (July 1963): 59–76.

Chan, Anthony B. "The Myth of the Chinese Sojourner in Canada." In *Visible Minorities and Multiculturalism: Asians in Canada*, edited by K. V. Ujimoto and G. Hirabayashi. Toronto, 1980.

Char, Tin-yuke, and Wai Jane Char. "The First Chinese Contract Laborers in Hawaii, 1852." *Hawaiian Journal of History* 9 (1975): 128–34.

Choy, Philip P. "Golden Mountain of Lead: The Chinese Experience in California." *California Historical Quarterly* 50 (Sept. 1971): 267–76.

Collomp, Catherine. "Unions, Civics, and National Identity: Organized Labor's Reaction to Immigration, 1881–1897." *Labor History* 29 (Fall 1988): 450–74.

Cribbs, Lennie Austin. "The Memphis Chinese Labor Convention, 1869." *West Tennessee Historical Society Papers* 37 (1983): 74–81.

Daniels, Roger. "American Historians and East Asian Immigrants." *Pacific Historical Review* 43 (Aug. 1974): 449–72.

Desnoyers, Charles A. "Self-Strengthening in the New World: A Chinese Envoy's Travels in America." *Pacific Historical Review* 60 (May 1991): 195–219.

———. " 'The Thin Edge of the Wedge': The Chinese Educational Mission and Diplomatic Representation in the Americas." *Pacific Historical Review* 61 (May 1992): 241–63.

Dinnerstein, Leonard. "Election of 1880." In *History of American Presidential Elections, 1789–1968*, edited by Arthur M. Schlesinger Jr., 2:1491–1516. New York, 1971.

Farley, M. Foster. "The Chinese Coolie Trade, 1845–1875." *Journal of Asian and African Studies* 3 (July and Oct. 1968): 257–70.

Fritz, Christian G. "A Nineteenth Century 'Habeas Corpus Mill': The Chinese before the Federal Courts in California." *American Journal of Legal History* 32 (1988): 347–72.

Gerber, Richard Allan. "The Liberal Republicans of 1872 in Historiographical Perspective." *Journal of American History* 62 (June 1975): 40–73.

Gillette, William. "Election of 1872." In *History of American Presidential Elections, 1789–1968*, edited by Arthur M. Schlesinger Jr., 2:1303–30. New York, 1971.

Grant, J. A. C. "Testimonial Exclusion because of Race: A Chapter in the History of Intolerance in California." *UCLA Law Review* 17 (Nov. 1969): 192–201.

Gutman, Herbert G. "The Tompkins Square 'Riot' in New York City on January 13, 1874: A Reexamination of Its Causes and Its Aftermath." *Labor History* 6 (Winter 1965): 44–83.

Hall, John Philip. "The Knights of St. Crispin in Massachusetts, 1869–1878." *Journal of Economic History* 18 (June 1958): 161–75.

Hellwig, David J. "Black Reactions to Chinese Immigration and the Anti-Chinese Movement, 1850–1910." *Amerasia* 6 (1979): 25–44.

Higham, John. "Origins of Immigration Restriction, 1882–1897: A Social Analysis." *Mississippi Valley Historical Review* 39 (June 1952): 77–88.

Hill, Herbert. "Anti-Oriental Agitation and the Rise of Working-Class Racism." *Transaction* 10 (Jan./Feb. 1973): 43–54.

——. "Race and Ethnicity in Organized Labor: The Historical Sources of Resistance to Affirmative Action." *Journal of Intergroup Relations* 12 (Winter 1984): 5–49.

——. "Race, Ethnicity, and Organized Labor: The Opposition to Affirmative Action." *New Politics* 1 (Winter 1987): 31–82.

Hinckley, Ted C. "The Politics of Sinophobia: Garfield, the Morey Letter, and the Presidential Election of 1880." *Ohio History* 89 (Autumn 1980): 381–99.

Hirata, Lucie Cheng. "Free, Indentured, Enslaved: Chinese Prostitutes in Nineteenth-Century America." *Signs* 5 (Autumn 1979): 3–29.

Holcombe, Chester. "The Restriction of Chinese Immigration." *Outlook* 76, Apr. 23, 1904, 971–77.

Hubbard, Lester A. "John Chinaman in the West." *Western Humanities Review* 4 (Autumn 1950): 311–21.

Ickstadt, Heinz, and Hartmut Keil, eds. "A Forgotten Piece of Working-Class Literature: Gustav Lyser's Satire of the Hewitt Hearing of 1878." *Labor History* 20 (Winter 1979): 127–40.

Jentz, John. "The Anti-Slavery Constituency in Jacksonian New York City." *Civil War History* 27 (June 1981): 101–22.

Johnsen, Leigh Dana. "Equal Rights and the 'Heathen Chinee': Black Activism in San Francisco, 1865–1875." *Western Historical Quarterly* 11 (Jan. 1980): 57–68.

Kao, Timothy T. "An American Sojourn: Young Chinese Students in the United States." *Connecticut Historical Society Bulletin* 46 (July 1981): 65–77.

Karlin, Jules Alexander. "The Anti-Chinese Outbreak in Tacoma, 1885." *Pacific Historical Review* 23 (Aug. 1954): 271–83.

——. "The Anti-Chinese Outbreaks in Seattle, 1885–1886." *Pacific Northwest Quarterly* 39 (Apr. 1948): 103–30.

Kauer, Ralph. "The Workingmen's Party of California." *Pacific Historical Review* 13 (Sept. 1944): 278–91.

Key, V. O., Jr. "A Theory of Critical Elections." *Journal of Politics* 17 (Feb. 1955): 3–18.

Klebaner, Benjamin. "State and Local Immigration Regulation in the United States before 1882." *International Review of Social History* 3 (1958): 269–95.

Krebs, Sylvia H. "John Chinaman and Reconstruction Alabama: The Debate and the Experience." *Southern Studies* 21 (Winter 1982): 369–83.

Lai, Him Mark. "Historical Development of the Chinese Consolidated Benevolent Association/*Huiguan* System." In *Chinese America: History and Perspectives, 1987*, 13–51. San Francisco, 1987.

Leistman, Daniel. "Chinese Labor at the Passaic Steam Laundry in Belleville." *New Jersey History* 112 (Spring/Summer 1994): 20–33.

McClain, Charles J. "In *Re Lee Sing*: The First Residential-Segregation Case." *Western Legal History* 3 (1985): 179–96.

McGrane, R. C. "Ohio and the Greenback Movement." *Mississippi Valley Historical Review* 11 (March 1925): 526–42.

Mann, Arthur. "Gompers and the Irony of Racism." *Antioch Review* 13 (June 1953): 203–14.

Mann, Ralph. "Community Change and Caucasian Attitudes toward the Chinese: The Case of Two California Mining Towns, 1850–1870." In *American Workingclass Culture: Explorations in American Labor and Social History*, edited by Milton Cantor, 397–422. Westport, Conn., 1979.

Matthews, Fred H. "White Community and 'Yellow Peril.'" *Mississippi Valley Historical Review* 50 (1964): 612–33.

Miller, Stuart Creighton. "An East Coast Perspective to Chinese Exclusion, 1852–1882." *Historian* 33 (Feb. 1971): 183–201.

Mooney, Ralph James. "Matthew Deady and the Federal Judicial Response to Racism in the Early West." *Oregon Law Review* 63 (1984): 561–637.

Ng, Franklin. "The Sojourner, Return Migration, and Immigration History." In *Chinese America: History and Perspectives, 1987*. San Francisco, 1987.

Nunis, Doyce B., Jr., ed. "The Demagogue and the Demographer: Correspondence of Denis Kearney and Lord Bryce." *Pacific Historical Review* 36 (Aug. 1967): 269–88.

Olmsted, Roger. "'The Chinese Must Go!'" *California Historical Quarterly* 50 (Sept. 1971): 285–94.

Ong, Paul M. "The Central Pacific Railroad and Exploitation of Chinese Labor." *Journal of Ethnic Studies* 13 (Summer 1985): 119–24.

Paul, Rodman W. "The Origin of the Chinese Issue in California." *Mississippi Valley Historical Review* 25 (June 1938): 181–96.

Peck, Gunther. "Reinventing Free Labor: Immigrant Padrones and Contract Laborers in North America, 1885–1925." *Journal of American History* 83 (Dec. 1996): 848–71.

Peffer, George Anthony. "Forbidden Families: Emigration Experiences of Chinese Women under the Page Law, 1875–1882." *Journal of American Ethnic History* 6 (Fall 1986): 28–46.

Pennanen, Gary. "Public Opinion and the Chinese Question, 1876–1879." *Ohio History* 77 (Winter/Spring/Summer 1968): 139–48.

Pitt, Leonard. "The Beginnings of Nativism in California." *Pacific Historical Review* 30 (Feb. 1961): 23–38.

Posner, Russell M. "The Lord and the Drayman: James Bryce vs. Denis Kearney." *California Historical Quarterly* 50 (Sept. 1971): 277–84.

Roediger, David R. "America's First General Strike: The St. Louis Commune of 1877." *Midwest Quarterly* 21 (Winter 1980): 196–206.

Rudolph, Frederick. "Chinamen in Yankeedom: Anti-Unionism in Massachusetts in 1870." *American Historical Review* 53 (Oct. 1947): 1–29.

Ruggles, Clyde O. "The Economic Basis of the Greenback Movement in Iowa and Wisconsin." *Proceedings of the Mississippi Valley Historical Association* 6 (1912/13): 142–62.

Saxton, Alexander. "Historical Explanations of Racial Inequality." *Marxist Perspectives* 2 (Summer 1979): 146–68.

Seager, Robert, II. "Some Denominational Reactions to Chinese Immigration to California, 1856–1892." *Pacific Historical Review* 28 (Feb. 1959): 49–66.

Shankman, Arnold. "Black on Yellow: Afro-Americans View Chinese-Americans, 1850–1935." *Phylon* 39 (Spring 1978): 1–17.

Shumsky, Neil L. "San Francisco's Workingmen Respond to the Modern City." *California Historical Quarterly* 55 (Spring 1976): 46–73.

Siu, Paul C. P. "The Sojourner." *American Journal of Sociology* 58 (July 1952): 34–44.

Spoehr, Luther W. "Sambo and the Heathen Chinee: Californians' Racial Stereotypes in the Late 1870s." *Pacific Historical Review* 40 (May 1973): 185–204.

Stanley, Gerald. "Frank Pixley and the Heathen Chinee *(A Phylon Document)*." *Phylon* 40 (Sept. 1979): 224–28.

Taylor, John M. "General Hancock: Soldier of the Gilded Age." *Pennsylvania History* 32 (Apr. 1965): 187–96.

Weinstein, Robert A. "North from Panama, West to the Orient: The Pacific Mail Steamship Company." *California History* 57 (Spring 1978): 46–57.

Woon, Yuen-fong. "The Voluntary Sojourner among the Overseas Chinese: Myth or Reality?" *Pacific Affairs* 56 (Winter 1983/84): 673–90.

Worthy, Edmund H., Jr. "Yung Wing in America." *Pacific Historical Review* 34 (Aug. 1965): 265–87.

Wortman, Roy T. "Denver's Anti-Chinese Riot, 1880." *Colorado Magazine* 42 (Fall 1965): 275–91.

Wunder, John R. "The Chinese and the Courts in the Pacific Northwest: Justice Denied?" *Pacific Historical Review* 52 (May 1983): 191–211.

———. "Chinese in Trouble: Criminal Law and Race on the Trans-Mississippi Frontier." *Western Historical Quarterly* 17 (Jan. 1986): 25–41.

UNPUBLISHED PAPERS AND DISSERTATIONS

Arensmeyer, Elliot Campbell. "British Merchant Enterprise and the Chinese Coolie Trade: 1850–1874." Ph.D. diss., University of Hawaii, 1979.

Coogan, Timothy. "The Forging of a New England Mill Town: North and South Adams, Massachusetts, 1780–1880." Ph.D. diss., New York University, 1992.

Gardner, John B. "The Image of the Chinese in the United States, 1885–1915." Ph.D. diss., University of Pennsylvania, 1961.

Gyory, Andrew. "Rolling in the Dirt: The Origins of the Chinese Exclusion Act and the Politics of Racism, 1870–1882." Ph.D. diss., University of Massachusetts at Amherst, 1991.

Laurie, Bruce. "The 'Fair Field' of the 'Middle Ground': Abolitionism, Labor Reform, and the Making of an Antislavery Bloc in Antebellum Massachusetts." Unpublished paper in possession of the author, 1995.

Miller, Stuart Creighton. "The Chinese Image in the Eastern United States, 1785–1882." Ph.D. diss., Columbia University, 1966.

Ring, Martin R. "Anson Burlingame, S. Wells Williams, and China, 1861–1870: A Great Era in Chinese-American Relations." Ph.D. diss., Tulane University, 1972.

Shumsky, Neil Larry. "San Francisco's Crowd: The Workingmen's Party of California, 1877–1879." Unpublished paper in possession of the author, n.d.

Somma, Nicholas A. "The Knights of Labor and Chinese Immigration." M.A. thesis, Catholic University of America, 1952.

Index

Abolition, 9, 13–14, 15, 59, 232

Abolitionists, 14, 44, 47, 56–58, 74, 102, 151–52, 155, 162, 242

"An Act to Encourage Immigration" (contract labor law), 12, 20–21, 23–25, 54, 270 (n. 6); repealed by Congress, 12, 25; passed by Congress, 20

"An Act to Prohibit the 'Coolie Trade' by American Citizens in American Vessels." *See* "Anti-Coolie" Act

Adair, A. B., 180

Africa, 33, 35, 51, 54, 101

African Americans. *See* Blacks

Africans, 18, 35, 51, 83, 84, 228, 229

Albany Journal, 42

Allegheny Mail, 66

Alvord, William, 284 (n. 8)

Amalgamated Association of Iron and Steel Workers, 219, 246

American and Foreign Anti-Slavery Society, 162

American Emigrant Company (AEC), 19–23, 50, 277 (n. 26), 278 (n. 36)

American Federation of Labor, 219

American Indians, 13, 54, 58, 68, 166, 225, 227, 266 (n. 8), 277 (n. 33)

American Miners' Association, 23

American Protective Association, 310 (n. 32)

American Revolution, 19, 225

American Social Science Association, 18, 101–2, 240

Angell, James B., 212–15, 307 (nn. 3, 4); on Chinese immigration, 212–13, 240, 308 (n. 5); meets with Hayes, 212; recommended by Edmunds, 212, 231

Angell Commission, 211, 240; appointed, 197, 199, 202, 212; planning of, 212–14, 307 (nn. 3, 4); negotiates treaty, 214–16

Angell Treaty, 223, 226, 231, 234, 239, 243, 249, 252, 308 (nn. 10, 12); text of, 215–16; Senate debate on, 217–18; ratification of, 218, 222, 309 (n. 15); working-class response to, 219, 221; cited by Arthur, 244. *See also* Angell Commission; Burlingame Treaty

Anthony, Susan B., 192, 284 (n. 17)

Anti-Chinese laws. *See* "Anti-Coolie" Act; Chinese Exclusion Act; Chinese immigrants: laws against; Fifteen Passenger Bill; Page Act; Queue ordinance

Anti-Chinese movement. *See* California: anti-Chinese movement in; Chinese immigrants; San Francisco: anti-Chinese protests in; West Coast: anti-Chinese movement on

Anti-Chinese Union, 93, 286 (n. 3)

Anti-Chinese violence. *See* Chinese immigrants: violence against

"Anti-Coolie" Act, 32, 33, 62–63, 71, 273 (n. 33), 279 (nn. 3, 5). *See also* "Coolie" trade

Arbeiter-Union (New York), 43, 131

Arthur, Chester A., 241, 245; nominated vice president, 190, 242; becomes president, 223; background of, 242–43; on Chinese, 243; ponders Chinese Exclusion Act, 243–44; veto compared to Hayes's, 243, 244; vetoes Exclusion Act, 244–45, 314 (n. 5); signs Exclusion Act, 253

Ashley, James M., 58

Asia, 1, 33, 35, 36, 53, 68, 100, 173, 197, 214, 216

Asian immigrants, 1, 6, 33, 35, 36, 53, 173, 254. *See also* Chinese immigrants; Japanese immigrants; Korean immigrants

Associated Press, 113, 207

Atlantic Monthly, 162

Auburn (New York) Advertiser, 147

Australia, 164

Axtell, Samuel B., 38

Bailey, David H., 62–63, 71, 280 (n. 7)

Bancroft, George, 307 (n. 3)

Barnum, P. T., 162, 297 (n. 49)

Barnum, William, 204, 205

Bayard, Thomas F., 148–49, 150, 228, 295 (n. 21), 303 (n. 11)

Bayne, Thomas, 238, 266 (n. 6), 313 (n. 56)

Beaver Falls, Pa., 64, 70

Beecher, Henry Ward, 277 (n. 25); on railroad strike, 95; criticized by Kearney, 114; on Fifteen Passenger Bill, 162; and adultery charge, 173, 196; on Chinese, 246–47; on Chinese Exclusion Act, 246–47; on melting pot, 314 (n. 11)

Belgian immigrants, 21, 66

Belgium, 20

Belleville, N.J., 279 (n. 2)

Bennett, James Gordon, 205–6

Berry, Campbell, 313 (n. 56), 316 (n. 27)

Bigler, John, 7

Blacks, 51–52; racism against, 10, 13, 30, 68, 73, 149, 225, 228–29, 266 (n. 8), 277 (n. 33); stereotypes of, 18; compared to Chinese, 30, 51–52, 101, 277 (n. 33), 311 (n. 38); and civil rights, 51–52, 53–54, 73; in Congress, 137, 152; on Chinese, 297 (n. 49)

Blackwell, Henry, 58

Blaine, James G., 3–6, 16, 62, 84, 138, 181, 193, 210, 223, 224, 230, 235, 237, 238, 243, 252, 253, 256; and Fifteen Passenger Bill, 3–4, 142–45, 150, 153, 161, 164, 165, 167, 168; on Chinese, 3–6, 135, 142–45, 164, 196; and election of 1880, 4, 6, 145–48, 174, 184, 185–87, 189–90, 196; background of, 4, 135, 136–37; on Burlingame Mission, 27–28, 272 (n. 23); and election of 1876, 84, 87; criticizes Kearney, 118; campaigns against Butler, 128; appointed secretary of state, 136, 190, 217, 308 (n. 13); called Plumed Knight, 137; on Burlingame Treaty, 142; political motives of, 145–48, 167, 185–86; and California election, 146–48, 174; and Garfield, 168, 196, 223; linked to Kearney, 187; advises Garfield on Chinese, 196; and Tucker, 198; on Burlingame, 272 (n. 23)

Blair, George, 107

Blissert, Robert, 43–44, 107, 183, 186

Bohemian immigrants, 98–100

Booth, Newton, 141, 287 (n. 3)

Boston Advertiser, 40, 48

Boston Central Trades and Labor Union, 221

Boston Commonwealth, 56

Boston Eight-Hour League, 88

Boston Globe, 119, 120, 127, 129; on red scare, 105; on Kearney, 112, 119, 130; on Chinese issue, 170

Boston Herald, 113

Boston Journal, 111–12, 122

Boston Labor Standard, 124

Boston Navy Yard, 163

Boston Pilot, 69, 174; on Kearney, 118, 125; on Chinese, 125–26; on Republican platform (1880), 189

Boston Post, 136, 161

Boston Transcript, 119, 120, 121–22, 127; on Kearney, 117, 128

Boston Typographical Union, 219

Boutwell, George S., 32

Bragg, Edward, 313 (n. 58)

Breaking the Chains, 315 (n. 16)

British Guiana, 31

Brooklyn Eagle, 159

Brown, Joseph E., 229–30, 235

Browne, Thomas, 312 (n. 53)

Bruce, Blanche K., 152

Brumm, Charles, 237

Bryant, Andrew J., 76, 78, 79, 85, 93, 158, 283 (n. 4), 287 (n. 3)

Bryant, William Cullen, 102

Bryce, James, Lord, 97, 111

Buckner, Aylett, 237

Burgman, Charles F., 219–20, 221, 310 (n. 22)

Burlingame, Anson, 26–27; mission to United States, 26–28; Blaine on, 272 (n. 23)

Burlingame Treaty: negotiation of, 26–27, 271 (n. 22); ratification of, 27, 271 (n. 22), 272 (n. 23); response to, 27–28; protests against, 78–79, 82, 86; resolution to renegotiate, 82, 104, 181; and Democratic platform (1876), 85; and Hayes, 104, 165–67, 212–13; and Evarts, 107–8, 165–67, 197, 199, 200, 212–15; and Fifteen Passenger Bill, 139, 142, 147, 153–56, 160, 161–62, 165–68, 197, 230; and Garfield, 139, 200, 204; and Blaine, 142, 147; and Hamlin, 153–55; and merchants, 161–62; and Democratic platform (1880), 190–91; and Greenback-Labor platform (1880), 193–94; and Morey letter, 204; renegotiation of, 212–16, 243. *See also* Angell Treaty

Burnham, Walter Dean, 75

Butler, Benjamin F., 84; on Chinese, 50; background of, 50, 115–16; and Kearney, 109, 115–16, 126–28; and election of 1878, 109, 115–16, 126–28, 130; and Morey letter, 306 (n. 44)

Butterworth, Benjamin, 5, 237, 266 (n. 6)

California, 1, 8, 16, 76, 98, 109, 266 (n. 3); arrival of Chinese immigrants in, 6–7, 8, 67; anti-Chinese movement in, 7–8, 9–10, 11–12, 14, 67–68, 69, 70–71, 78–79, 83–84, 85–86, 96–97, 102–4, 111, 149, 157–59, 169–70, 172–74, 176–77, 197–99, 252, 254, 282 (n. 21), 286 (n. 3), 300–301 (n. 10), 305 (n. 34); politics in, 7–8, 9–10, 97, 172, 173–75, 198; political power and importance of, 71, 75, 90, 145–48, 167, 196, 203, 218, 240–41, 245, 250; State Senate, 78–79, 80, 84; constitutional convention, 106, 158, 169, 223; and Fifteen Passenger Bill, 145–49, 157–59, 296 (n. 39); and election of 1879, 147, 172, 173–74, 185, 198, 300 (nn. 9, 10); and secession, 158–59; constitution, 169–70, 197, 300 (n. 2); and eastern response to constitution, 170–71; referendum on Chinese immigration, 172, 173, 174, 300–301 (n. 10); state supreme court, 174, 266 (n. 8), 277 (n. 33), 285 (n. 25); Chinese exodus from, 177, 184, 301 (n. 14); and election of 1880, 185–87, 188, 193, 194–95, 197–200, 201–2, 203, 209, 307 (n. 46); Hayes's visit to, 202, 305 (n. 34); and Angell Treaty, 215, 217, 218; and Chinese Exclusion Act, 223–25, 227, 245, 250; anti-Chinese laws in, 266 (n. 8), 277 (n. 33), 283–84 (nn. 4, 8). *See also* California thesis; San Francisco; West Coast; Workingmen's Party of California

California thesis, 6, 8, 10, 15, 254, 267 (n. 8), 268 (nn. 11, 14)

Calkins, William, 5, 237, 266 (n. 6)

Call, Wilkinson, 229

Cambria Iron Works, 30

Cameron, Andrew C., 29, 36, 40, 44, 46, 63–64, 87; on Chinese, 29, 36, 40, 63–64, 87

Cameron, Angus, 230, 235

Cameron, Simon, 56

Campbell, Dugald, 41

Campbell, Persia Crawford, 33

Canada, 21, 32, 36, 65, 138

Canadian immigrants, 21, 29, 36, 39

Cannon, Joseph G., 139, 238

Carey, Henry C., 19

Carnegie, Andrew, 20

Carpenter, Cyrus, 238, 257–58, 312 (n. 53)

Carpenter, 246, 314 (n. 8)

Carpenters Union (Chicago), 245

Cary, Samuel F., 107

Cashman, William, 42–43

Casserly, Eugene, 38, 55, 149, 287 (n. 3)

Cassidy, George, 313 (n. 56), 316 (n. 27)

Central Pacific Railroad Company, 7, 31, 276 (n. 21), 277 (n. 33)

Chamber of Commerce: San Francisco, 157, 158; New York, 161; Philadelphia, 161

Chandler, William, 250

Chandler, Zachariah, 137, 296 (n. 37)

Chang the Giant, 297 (n. 49)

Chase, Salmon P., 20

Chase, Solon, 164

Cheng Tsao-ju, 243

Ch'en Lan-pin, 118, 299 (n. 57); on Kearney, 118, 291 (n. 20); on Fifteen Passenger Bill, 166

Chicago Amalgamated Trades and Labor Unions, 101

Chicago Carpenters Union, 245

Chicago City Council, 105

Chicago Inter-Ocean, 105

Chicago News, 169, 182

Chicago Times, 101, 243; on Republican platform (1876), 90; on Chinese issue, 90, 190, 202, 209, 240; on Kearney, 117, 121; on Fifteen Passenger Bill, 159; on party platforms (1880), 190, 191; on Hancock's letter of acceptance, 201; on Morey letter, 205; on immigration, 217, 242, 254; on Edmunds, 231, 233; on Hooker, 312 (n. 55)

Chicago Trade and Labor Council, 124, 164, 170–71, 180–81, 301 (n. 13)

Chicago Tribune, 188, 194, 205, 206, 220; on red scare, 105; on Fifteen Passenger Bill, 160; on Chinese Exclusion Act, 239, 240, 241, 245, 313 (n. 59); on Arthur's veto, 245

Chico Massacre, 94

Child, Lydia Maria, 57–58

China, 7, 17, 18, 30, 31, 34, 51, 61, 68, 71, 82, 103, 154–55, 162, 179, 229–30, 249, 308 (n. 9); called Celestial Empire, 10; emperor of, 18, 26, 156; and Burlingame, 26–28; and emigration, 28, 199, 305 (n. 28); and "coolie" trade, 32–33, 36, 53, 58, 61–63, 66, 273 (n. 33), 279 (n. 5); and Bailey, 62–63; protests treatment of immigrants, 118, 177, 308 (n. 9); and Grant, 186–87; and Evarts, 197; and Evarts doctrine, 197; and Angell Commission, 197, 199, 200, 211, 212–16, 223; and threat of war, 216; and Six Companies, 288 (n. 18); and Bayard, 295 (n. 21). *See also* Angell Commission; Angell Treaty; Burlingame Treaty; Chinese diplomats; Chinese Educational Mission; Chinese Exclusion Act; Chinese immigration; Chinese legation; "Coolie" trade; Six Companies; U.S.-Chinese relations

Chinese Aid and Emigration Society, 178

Chinese diplomats, 26–28, 107, 118, 166, 177, 186–87, 197, 198–99, 214–16, 243, 278 (n. 33), 286 (n. 1), 299 (n. 57), 308 (n. 9). *See also* Angell Commission; Angell Treaty; Burlingame Treaty; China; Chinese Educational Mission; Chinese immigration; Chinese legation; U.S.-Chinese relations

Chinese Educational Mission, 92, 286 (n. 1), 299 (n. 57), 316 (n. 29)

Chinese Exclusion Act (1882), 1–2, 5, 6, 11, 14, 15, 16, 44, 61, 70, 95, 314 (n. 9); significance of, 1–2, 6, 15–16, 254–60; politicians invoking working-class support for, 3–6, 237–38; bars Chinese from citizenship, 223; includes miners, 223; synopsis of, 223; Miller's speech on, 223–25; debate in Senate on, 223–35, 251–53; Hoar's speech on, 225–26; comments by westerners on, 227–28; comments by southerners on, 228–30, 311 (n. 39), 312 (n. 55); vote on, 230, 235, 238–39, 251, 253, 313 (n. 58), 315

(n. 16); Edmunds's speech on, 231–33; effect of Edmunds's speech on, 233–35; debate in House on, 235–38, 250–51, 257–58, 311 (n. 39), 312 (nn. 53–55); Taylor's speech on, 236; press response to, 239–41; pondered by Arthur, 243–44; vetoed by Arthur, 244; veto message on, 244, Senate fails to override, 244; response to veto of, 244–47, 248–50; working-class response to, 245–47; Beecher's sermon on, 248–49; response of merchants to, 249–50; signed by Arthur, 253; renewed, 254, 258; repealed, 254, 316 (n. 24); response by Kwong to, 258–59; text of, 261–64; amendments to, 311 (n. 48)

Chinese Exclusion Act (1892), 1, 254, 258, 315 (n. 24)

Chinese Exclusion Act (1902), 1, 254, 316 (n. 24)

Chinese Exclusion Act (1904), 1, 254, 316 (n. 24)

Chinese immigrants: numbers of, 4, 6, 7, 29, 30, 67–68, 72, 225, 265 (n. 3), 275 (n. 4), 281 (n. 16); and citizenship, 6, 51, 90, 223; come to America, 6–7, 67; in gold rush era, 6–8; middle- and upper-class response to in West, 6–8, 9, 70, 78–79, 83, 97, 103, 149, 157–59, 172–73, 188, 194–95, 198, 268 (n. 11), 282 (n. 20), 308 (n. 5); importation of, 7, 12, 30–32, 33–35, 47–48, 60–61, 62–63, 123, 131–33, 168, 196, 279 (n. 2), 296 (n. 37); laws against, 7, 71, 79, 84, 266 (n. 8), 277 (n. 33), 283 (n. 4), 284 (n. 8), 285 (n. 25), 288 (n. 18), 301 (n. 14), 314 (n. 9); working-class response to in West, 7–8, 9, 12, 69, 70, 96–97, 102–3, 158, 173, 176–77, 214; working-class response to in East, 10, 11–12, 14–15, 29–30, 34–37, 38, 40–47, 50, 63–64, 66–67, 69, 80, 87–90, 91, 98–101, 110, 116–17, 119–20, 124–26, 128, 131–34, 162–65, 168, 170–71, 180–84, 186, 195–96, 219–22, 245–48, 256–57, 293 (n. 50), 300 (n. 5), 314 (n. 6); middle- and upper-class response to in East, 10, 17–18, 27–28, 33–34, 48–50, 56–58, 60, 80–81, 84, 86, 101–2, 103, 110, 119–20, 159–62, 167, 177–79, 182–83, 240, 248–50, 300 (n. 5), 307 (n. 3); and term "John Chinaman," 18; and right to emigrate, 26–28; and Senate debate on importation, naturalization, and immigration, 37–38, 50–56, 153; and suffrage, 47, 54, 56, 90, 153, 223, 248; laws defending, 53–54, 277 (n. 33); defend rights, 79, 177, 259, 284 (n. 8), 288 (n. 18), 308 (n. 9); violence against, 90, 94, 96–97, 173–74, 176–77, 287 (n. 4), 307 (n. 46); and naturalization, 90, 153; and Six Companies, 101, 288 (n. 18); leave California, 177–80, 184, 301 (n. 14). See also California; China; Chinese diplomats; Chinese Exclusion Act; Chinese legation; "Coolie" trade; Fifteen Passenger Bill; Morey letter; North Adams, Mass.; Page Act; Queue ordinance; West Coast

Chinese legation, 107, 278 (n. 33), 286 (n. 1), 299 (n. 57); and Burlingame Mission, 26–28, 162; on Kearney, 118, 291 (n. 20); on Fifteen Passenger Bill, 166; on treatment of Chinese, 177; on Chinese Exclusion Act, 243. See also China; Chinese diplomats; U.S.-Chinese relations

Chinese-U.S. relations. See U.S.-Chinese relations

Choy Chew, 34

Christiancy, Isaac, 296 (n. 37)

Cigar makers, 43, 131–34, 219, 245–46, 298 (n. 51); on Chinese, 43, 98–100, 131–34, 184, 245–46, 314 (n. 6); strike by (1877–78), 97–100, 101, 103, 131, 163, 288 (n. 9); on Fifteen Passenger Bill, 163; strike by (1879), 184; strike by (1882), 245

Cigar Makers' International Union, 43, 131, 132–33, 219; and strike (1877–78), 97–100

Cigar Makers' Official Journal, 99–100, 221, 246–47; and Fifteen Passenger Bill, 162; on Chinese, 246

Cincinnati Commercial, 30; on Fifteen Passenger Bill, 159; on Garfield's letter of acceptance, 201

Cincinnati Enquirer, 122, 164–65, 176; on Fifteen Passenger Bill, 159, 164–65, 167; on Morey letter, 210

Cincinnati Gazette: on Chinese, 18, 56; on working-class sentiment, 43, 46; on Republicans, 150; on Fifteen Passenger Bill, 150, 160

Cincinnati Trades and Labor Assembly, 163, 195, 304 (n. 21)

Civil Rights Act (1866), 51, 53, 230, 277 (n. 33)

Civil Rights Act (1870), 53–54, 216, 230, 277 (n. 33)

Civil Rights Act (1875), 230

Civil service reform, 73

Civil War, 9, 89, 95, 96; ideals and legacy of, 9, 14, 24, 52, 59, 68–69, 74, 75, 85, 151, 232, 236; and imported labor, 19–20, 21; and slavery, 24, 59

Clarkson, J. F., 123

Class conflict, 15, 77, 91, 94–96, 97, 104, 254–56; mentioned by Blaine, 143. See also Communism; Railroad strike of 1877; Red scare; Socialists

Clergy, 83, 95, 114, 118, 158, 162, 173, 245, 282 (n. 20)

Cleveland, Grover, 287 (n. 4)

Cleveland Herald, 165

Cleveland Leader, 201

Coghlan, John, 282 (n. 19), 287 (n. 3)

Collins, Jennie, 279 (n. 2)

Colonial era, 19

Commons, John R., 11

Communism, 95, 96, 105–6, 111–12, 117, 128

Conger, Omar, 139, 295 (n. 5)

Congress, 1, 56, 61, 71–72, 74, 78, 79, 94, 103–4, 106, 107, 138, 163, 171, 181, 184, 218, 221, 222, 241, 247, 250, 254, 309 (n. 17); and power to restrict immigration, 7; and first effort to restrict Chinese immigration, 7, 28; and Foran Act, 12, 314 (n. 9); and eight-hour legislation, 19; and "An Act to Encourage Immigration," 20, 23–25; and Page Act, 71; and election of 1872, 74; and investigation of Chinese immigration (1876–77), 84, 85, 87, 93–94; and election of 1876, 92–93; and resolution to renegotiate Burlingame Treaty, 104; and election of 1878, 106–7, 146; and investigation of depression and Chinese immigration, 172–73. See also Elections—1879; House of Representatives; Senate; specific laws

Congressional Record, 217

Conkling, Roscoe: mocks Sumner, 52; on Fifteen Passenger Bill, 156, 161; obstructs Senate, 217; and Arthur, 242

Conness, John, 25, 271 (n. 16)

Constitution, 24, 58, 73, 146, 151, 219, 224, 228, 232. See also specific amendments

Cooke, Jay, 137

Coolidge, Mary Roberts, 6–8, 10, 63, 267 (n. 8), 298 (n. 55), 300–301 (n. 10)

"Coolie" trade, 32, 36, 53, 58, 61–63, 66, 273 (n. 33), 280 (n. 7); defined, 32–33, 273 (n. 34). See also "Anti-Coolie" Act

Cooper, Peter, 89, 123, 128

Corbett, Henry, 55

Cornell University, 102

Crédit Mobilier, 137

Crispins. See Knights of St. Crispin

Critical elections, 72

Crocker, Charles, 7, 31, 93–94, 276 (n. 21)

Cross, Ira B., 70

Cuba, 32, 33, 202, 273 (n. 33)

Cuban immigrants, 98, 99

Cummin, Sherman, 219–20, 310 (nn. 20, 22)

Cummings, Samuel P., 29–30, 36, 41–42, 45–47, 281 (n. 15); on Chinese, 29–30, 36, 41–42, 45–47; background of, 46, 276 (n. 18), 310 (n. 20)

Curtin, Andrew, 313 (n. 56)

Cushing, Caleb, 18

Daily Advance (Cleveland), 168

Daily Stock Report (San Francisco), 158

Dana, Charles A., 286 (n. 2)

Daniels, Roger, 11

Davenport, John I., 307 (n. 48)

Davis, David, 67, 156, 244, 253, 281 (n. 15), 296 (n. 35), 315 (n. 20)

Davis, Garrett, 54, 272 (n. 23)

Davis, Horace, 294 (n. 5)

Davis, Jefferson, 61

Dawes, Henry L., 151, 229, 252, 309 (n. 15)

Dawes, Rufus, 312 (n. 53)

Declaration of Independence, 52, 54, 84, 225, 227, 228, 232, 235

Dee, M. J., 102

Deering, Nathaniel, 236

Delaney, W. W., 45

Democratic Party, 12, 96; before Civil War, 8–9, 13, 72; and election of 1868, 27, 72; and election of 1872, 72–74, 281 (n. 15), 283 (n. 26); and election of 1874, 74; and convention (1876), 76, 85; and election of 1876, 76–77, 78–79, 85–87, 89; and platform (1876), 76–77, 85, 86, 87, 90, 168; on Fifteen Passenger Bill, 140, 148–50; and convention (1880), 190–91; and election of 1880, 190–92, 201–11, 303 (nn. 11, 12); and platform (1880), 190–92, 215, 220, 303 (n. 12); and Hancock's letter of acceptance, 201–2; and Morey letter, 203–8, 209–11; and Senate filibuster, 217; and Chinese Exclusion Act, 235, 237–38, 250–51, 253, 312 (nn. 53–55), 313 (n. 58), 315 (n. 16); invokes working-class support for Exclusion Act, 237–38

Depew, Chauncey, 136

Depression of 1870s, 9, 15, 19, 59, 61, 65, 74–75, 89, 94, 97, 104, 107, 131, 143, 172, 176, 247, 256

Detroit Union, 21

Devens, George, 165

De Young, Charles, 173, 300 (n. 9)

Dezendorf, John, 313 (n. 56)

Dickens, Charles, 82

Douai, Adolph, 43, 131, 134

Douglas, Stephen, 232

Douglass, Frederick, 56, 297 (n. 49)

Draymen and Teamsters' Union, 111

Dunnell, Mark, 236

Eagle Iron Works, 21

Eaves, Lucile, 301 (n. 10)

Edmunds, George F., 52, 216, 239, 247, 303 (n. 9), 311 (n. 43); on Chinese, 5, 231–32; on Fifteen Passenger Bill, 155, 156, 230; recommends Angell, 212; background of, 230–31; speech on Chinese Exclusion Act by, 231–33, 252; and effect of speech by, 233–35, 237, 239, 244

Eight-hour day, 19, 73, 88, 106, 163, 193, 247, 280 (n. 8)

Elections:

—1856, 72

—1860, 72, 196

—1864, 72

—1868, 27, 72

—1870 (Mass.), 46–47, 276 (n. 19)

—1872, 66–67, 71, 72–74, 281 (n. 15), 283 (n. 26), 315 (n. 20); platforms, 73–74

—1874, 74

—1876, 7–8, 12, 75, 76–77, 84–87, 90–91; platforms, 12, 76–77, 84–85, 86, 90, 168, 184; Republican convention, 84–85, 87; Democratic convention, 85, 87; and Greenback-Labor Party, 89, 106, 107; and Workingmen's Party of the United States, 89–90; disputed returns of, 92–93, 146, 196; vote of, 145–46, 202, 203, 209

—1877, 94, 106

—1878, 106–7, 109, 115–16, 126–29, 146

—1879 (Calif.), 146–47, 169–70, 172, 173–75, 176, 183–84

—1880, 4, 12, 135, 145–47, 148, 184, 300 (n. 10); platforms, 12, 187–89, 190–92, 193–94, 215, 220; and Greenback-Labor Party, 175; Republican convention, 185–86, 187–90, 213, 303 (n. 9); Garfield nominated, 189; Hancock nominated, 190; Arthur nominated, 190, 242; Democratic convention, 190–91, 303 (n. 11); Greenback-Labor convention, 192–94; Weaver nominated, 193; Garfield's letter of acceptance, 195–96, 200–202; and working-class activity, 195–96, 210; Blaine advises Garfield during, 196; Evarts's role in, 196–201, 213; Hancock's letter of acceptance, 201–2; gubernatorial races, 202; strategy in, 203; and Morey letter, 203–8, 209–11; vote of, 208–9, 307 (n. 46); Garfield wins, 209

—1884, 241

Electoral college, 71; and election of 1876, 90, 92–93, 145, 196; and election of 1880, 167, 209

Eliot, Thomas Dawes, 32, 273 (n. 33)

Emancipation, 9, 14, 15, 24, 58, 59, 72, 73, 83, 106, 150, 152, 168, 211. See also Abolition; Slavery

Emerson, Ralph Waldo, 17, 26, 271 (n. 21)

Emigrant companies, 19–20, 21–22, 23, 26, 30, 40, 48, 50, 65, 276 (n. 21)

Enforcement Act. See Civil Rights Act (1870)

England, 20, 21, 44, 65

English, J. L., 85

English immigrants, 19, 21, 65; compared to Chinese, 44, 88; praise for, 248

Ennis, John, 43, 107

Erickson, Charlotte, 22

Ermentrout, Daniel, 313 (n. 56)

Europe, 20, 22, 23, 35, 36, 53, 68, 100, 101, 173, 254. See also specific countries and regions

European immigrants, 1, 6, 19–23, 29, 53, 54, 173, 254; compared to Chinese, 35, 101, 143, 248. See also specific countries and regions

Evarts, William M., 235, 298 (n. 51), 304 (n. 21); on Chinese, 107–8; on Fifteen Passenger Bill, 165–66, 168, 197, 299 (n. 59); drafts veto of Fifteen Passenger Bill, 166, 197; and Yung, 177; background of, 196–97; and Angell Commission, 197, 199, 202, 212–14, 217, 231, 307 (n. 4); and Tucker mission, 197–200, 210; advises Garfield, 200–201; and Hoar, 225; on Chinese Exclusion Act, 249; and Grant, 305 (n. 26)

Evarts doctrine, 197

Fall River Labor Standard, 221–22

Farley, James T., 218, 229, 245, 287 (n. 3)

Federal Election Bill, 310 (n. 32)

Federalist Party, 8

Federation of Organized Trades and Labor Unions (FOTLU), 219–22, 246, 309 (n. 19), 310 (n. 22)

Fehrenbatch, John, 195–96, 210, 304 (n. 21)

Fifteen Passenger Bill, 3–6, 169, 184, 185, 190, 194, 218, 223, 236, 239, 243, 294 (n. 3), 294–95 (n. 5), 298 (nn. 51, 52); Blaine's speech on, 3–4, 5–6, 142–45, 147–48; debate in Senate on, 3–4, 140–45, 148–57; debate in House on, 5, 138–40, 312 (n. 53); political aspects of, 5–6, 146–48, 150, 167–68; and Burlingame Treaty, 139, 142, 147, 153–56, 160, 161–62, 165–68, 230; Sargent's speech on, 140–41; western senators on, 141–42; Hamlin's speech on, 150–55; amendments to, 155–56, 296 (nn. 36, 37); response of merchants to, 157, 158, 161–62; response in West to, 157–59, 296 (n. 37); response of clergy to, 158, 162; response in East to, 159–63; response of workers to, 162–65, 298 (n. 52); response of Hayes to, 165–67; response of Evarts to, 165–67, 299 (n. 59); response of Chinese legation to, 166; vetoed by Hayes, 166, 197, 299 (n. 60), 304 (n. 17); veto message on, 166–67, 197; response of Garfield to, 166–67, 299 (n. 59), 304 (n. 17); and South, 228, 296 (n. 37); House fails to override, 299 (n. 60)

Fifteenth Amendment, 53, 54, 58, 73

Filley, Giles, 20–21

Fincher, Jonathan, 23, 270 (n. 10)

Fincher's Trades' Review, 21, 270 (n. 10)

First Amendment, 51, 183, 217

Fitch, Thomas, 38
Flower, Roswell, 237
Folger, Charles, 243
Foner, Eric, 58–59, 72
Foran Act, 12, 314 (n. 9). *See also* "An Act to Encourage Immigration"; Imported labor
Foreign Emigrant Aid Society, 19, 30
Foreign Miners' License Law, 266 (n. 8)
Forrest, Nathan Bedford, 33
Fourteenth Amendment, 27, 73, 284 (n. 8)
France, 20, 197
Franklin, Benjamin, 227
Freedmen's Bureau Act, 51
Free-Soilers, 9, 13, 14, 50, 74, 150, 225, 232, 252
Frelinghuysen, Frederick, 243
French immigrants, 29, 77, 88, 101
Frew, William, 105–6
Fugitive Slave Act, 1, 251, 258

Gallagher, George, 245
Gam Saan, 6, 7, 16
Gantt, T. Fulton, 315 (n. 16)
Garfield, James A., 235, 236; nominated president, 5, 189–90; campaigns against Butler, 128; on Blaine, 137, 168; and Fifteen Passenger Bill, 139, 166, 168, 194, 299 (n. 59), 304 (n. 18); on Chinese, 168, 194, 206; and election of 1880, 189–90, 191–92, 194–96, 200–202, 203–11, 242, 307 (n. 26); appoints Blaine secretary of state, 190, 217, 308 (n. 13); and Republican platform (1880), 191–92; criticized by Kearney, 192; lobbied by California, 194–95; letter of acceptance by, 195–96, 200–202, 210; and Tucker, 198; and Morey letter, 204–8; elected president, 209, 307 (n. 46); inaugurated, 217; assassinated, 222–23, 243; on Greenback-Labor Party, 295 (n. 15)
Garnet, Henry Highland, 162, 297 (n. 49)
Garrison, William Lloyd, 57–58, 162, 265 (n. 2)
Genghis Khan, 27
George, Henry, 94, 121, 170, 255
George, James Z., 228, 273 (n. 34), 313 (n. 56)
German immigrants, 19, 29, 68, 90, 97–100, 119, 126; compared to Chinese, 35, 43, 88, 101, 177, 201, 224; praise for, 77, 224, 248. *See also* Prussian immigrants
Germany, 19, 68, 224. *See also* Prussia
Gibson, E. M., 194–95
Gibson, Otis, 173, 300 (n. 6)
Giddings, Joshua, 53
Gift, George W., 33
Gobineau, J. A. de, 311 (n. 33)
Godkin, E. L., 48, 73, 80
Gold rush, 6, 9, 53
Goldwater, Sam, 124, 134

Gompers, Samuel: and strike by cigar makers, 97, 98, 99; and Greenbackers, 107; and FOTLU convention, 219–20, 221, 310 (n. 22)
Goodrich, Samuel, 17
Gorham, George C., 146, 148, 195
Gould, Jay, 176, 293 (n. 35)
Grant, Ulysses S., 54, 79, 93, 277 (n. 25), 293 (n. 35); and Page Act, 71; on Chinese, 71, 82, 186–87, 243; and election of 1872, 73, 74; meets with Roach, 81; meets with Pixley, 82; and election of 1880, 186–87, 189, 198–99, 242; and world tour, 186–87, 198, 305 (n. 24), 308 (n. 9); meets with Chinese officials, 186–87, 198, 308 (n. 9); and Tucker, 198; on Chinese Exclusion Act, 243; and Stewart, 278 (n. 33); and Evarts, 305 (n. 26)
Great Britain. *See* England; Scotland; Wales
Greeley, Horace, 17, 73, 74
Greenback-Labor Party, 89, 106, 138, 146, 164, 237, 289 (n. 28); called "rag baby," 106; and Toledo platform, 106–7; and Kearney, 111, 117, 119, 122–23, 125, 174–75, 192–94, 301 (nn. 11, 12); and election of 1878 (Mass.), 116, 127–28; and planning convention (1880), 175; and election of 1880, 175, 192–94, 198, 204, 300 (n. 10); and convention (1880), 192–94; nominates Weaver, 193; and platform (1880), 193–94, 215, 304 (n. 17); and Chinese Exclusion Act, 237, 251, 313 (n. 58), 315 (n. 16); Garfield on, 295 (n. 15)
Greenbacks, 73, 89, 96, 106
Greenback Standard (Oshkosh, Wisc.), 107
Grob, Gerald N., 11
Grover, La Fayette, 141, 227
Gunton, George, 88

Hadley, Henry Hercules, 307 (n. 48)
Hager, John S., 85, 285 (n. 21)
Hale, Eugene, 235
Hamlin, Hannibal: and naturalization, 52, 153; on Burlingame Treaty, 104, 153–55, 156; background of, 150; and Fifteen Passenger Bill, 150–51, 153–55, 156, 161, 165, 168, 296 (n. 31); on Chinese, 153; on Irish, 153, 165; retirement of, 252
Hammond, James Henry, 248
Hancock, Winfield Scott, 315 (n. 20); background of, 190; and election of 1880, 190–92, 201–2, 209, 211, 303 (n. 11), 307 (n. 46); nominated president, 190, 303 (n. 11); and Democratic platform (1880), 191–92; letter of acceptance by, 201–2, 211; loses election, 209, 307 (n. 46)
Hardenbergh, Augustus, 139, 312 (n. 53), 313 (n. 58)

Harper's Weekly, 117–18, 162
Harris, Henry, 313 (n. 56)
Harris, Isham Green, 31, 229, 296 (n. 37)
Harrison, Carter, 245, 294 (n. 5)
Hart, Joseph, 204
Hart, Tony, 112
Hartford Labor Journal, 66
Harvard Law School, 196
Harvard University, 30, 272 (n. 26), 289 (n. 20)
Hawaii, 198
Hawk, Robert, 236, 266 (n. 6), 313 (n. 56)
Hawley, Joseph R.: on Chinese, 50; on importation, 50; background of, 50, 235, 252, 277 (n. 26); at Republican convention (1876), 84; on Chinese Exclusion Act, 235, 236, 251–52; on Angell Treaty, 309 (n. 15)
Hayes, Rutherford B., 103, 104, 107, 217, 286 (n. 2); vetoes Fifteen Passenger Bill, 5, 166–67, 169, 197, 299 (n. 60); and election of 1876, 87, 90, 92–93, 196, 202, 203, 209, 286 (n. 2); nominated president, 87; elected president, 90, 92–93; votes for, 90, 92–93, 111, 202, 203, 209; and disputed returns, 92–93, 196; as lame-duck president, 93, 145; and railroad strike, 95; Kearney votes for, 111; meets with Kearney, 135; on Chinese, 135, 166; on Fifteen Passenger Bill, 158, 165–67, 168, 296 (n. 39); veto message of, 166–67; visits California, 202, 305 (n. 34); meets with Angell, 212; veto compared to Arthur's, 243, 244
Hazelton, George, 5, 266 (n. 6), 313 (n. 56)
Healy, Patrick J., 173, 300 (n. 5)
Helper, Hinton Rowan, 18
Hervey, James B., 279 (n. 2)
Hewitt, Abram, 131–32, 204, 208, 238
Hewitt Committee, 107, 131–34, 172
Hide and Leather Interest and Industrial Review, 29, 37, 39
Higham, John, 68
Hill, Herbert, 11, 12, 293 (n. 50)
Hinchcliffe, John, 23, 89
Historiography, 6–15, 44, 46, 49, 69–70, 72–73, 168, 170, 187, 254, 256, 257, 267 (n. 8), 268 (nn. 11, 12), 275 (n. 17), 276 (n. 24), 293 (n. 50), 298 (n. 55), 300 (n. 2), 301 (n. 10)
Hoar, George Frisbie, 231, 232, 235, 236, 237, 252, 312 (n. 53), 314 (nn. 5, 9); on Blaine, 136; on Fifteen Passenger Bill, 151, 155; background of, 152, 225, 310 (n. 32); on Angell Treaty, 218, 222, 223, 309 (n. 15); speech on Chinese Exclusion Act by, 223, 225–26, 227, 251
Hodge, Charles, 102
Holcombe, Chester, 307 (n. 4)
Holmes, Oliver Wendell, 271 (n. 21)
Homrighausen, Fred, 43

Hong Kong, 62
Hooker, Charles, 312 (n. 55), 313 (n. 58), 315 (n. 16)
House of Representatives: and Fifteen Passenger Bill, 5, 138–40, 157, 294 (n. 5), 299 (n. 59); debates importation, 38; and Civil Rights Act (1870), 53, 277 (n. 33); and election of 1872, 74; and election of 1874, 74; and Roach delegation, 82; and Burlingame Treaty, 82, 104; and resolution to investigate Chinese immigration, 85; and resolution to renegotiate Burlingame Treaty, 104; and Hewitt Committee, 107, 131–34; and Constitution, 146; and election of 1879, 146–47, 172, 174, 300 (n. 10); and election of 1880, 146–47, 174, 300 (n. 10); and investigation of depression and Chinese immigration, 172–73; and Morey letter, 204; debates Chinese Exclusion Act, 223, 235–38, 250–51, 312 (nn. 53–55); and vote on Exclusion Act, 238–39, 251, 313 (n. 58), 315 (n. 16); fails to override Hayes's veto, 299 (n. 60); and election of 1880, 300 (n. 10). *See also* Congress; Hewitt Committee; Senate; *specific laws*
Howard, Jacob, 37
Howe, Julia Ward, 57
Howe, Timothy O., 51, 104, 155, 156, 243
Howells, William Dean, 162
Hubbell, Jay A., 206
Hume, Robert W., 34–35, 36, 48, 274 (n. 38)
Hungarian immigrants, 66
Hunt, Samuel, 163
Hunt, William, 243

Illinois legislature, 164, 298 (n. 53)
Imperialism, 197, 198, 214, 230, 308 (n. 12)
Imported labor, 12, 19–25, 30–32, 33–35, 39–41, 47–48, 50, 60–61, 64–66, 70, 96, 100–101, 123, 131–32, 168, 247, 279 (nn. 2, 3, 5), 296 (n. 37), 314 (n. 9). *See also* "An Act to Encourage Immigration"; "Anti-Coolie" Act; Chinese immigrants; "Coolie" trade; Foran Act
Indentured servitude, 19
Indiana, 146–47, 202, 203, 209, 300 (n. 10)
Indianapolis Sun, 120, 123
Industrial Congress, 67, 195
Ingersoll, Robert, 208
International Workingmen's Association, 90, 225
Ireland, 19, 35, 65, 68, 92, 176
Irish American press, 118, 125–26, 159. See also *Boston Pilot*; *Irish World*; *Irish World and American Industrial Liberator*
Irish immigrants, 14, 19, 35, 39, 44, 48, 51, 58, 80, 112, 119; blamed for anti-Chinese movement,

8, 153, 165, 214, 298 (n. 55); stereotypes of, 18, 112, 172, 178, 248–49, 314–15 (n. 11); compared to Chinese, 43, 44, 48, 88, 92, 101, 177, 178, 201, 224; opposition to, 68, 69; pro-Chinese sentiments of, 69, 92, 125–26, 134, 159, 173; praise for, 77, 224, 248; Beecher on, 248–49, 314–15 (n. 11)

Irish World (New York), 92, 120; on Burlingame Treaty, 87; on Kearney, 118, 119

Irish World and American Industrial Liberator (New York), 174; on Fifteen Passenger Bill, 162–63, 183, 210; on Chinese, 246; on Chinese Exclusion Act, 246

Iron Molders' International Journal, 280 (n. 11)

Iron Molders' International Union, 21–22, 43, 65, 280 (n. 11)

Iron Molders' Journal, 66, 280 (n. 11)

Iron Molders' Union, 20–21, 280 (n. 11)

Irwin, William, 78, 103, 158, 287 (n. 3)

Italian immigrants, 65–66, 70, 279 (n. 3); compared to Chinese, 66, 246, 248; praise for, 77, 224

Italy, 66, 224

Japan, 197, 216, 254

Japanese immigrants, 1, 141, 254; compared to Chinese, 88

Jarrett, John, 219, 246

Jefferson, Thomas, 227

Jewell, Marshall, 205–6, 207

Jewett, B. E. G., 100–101

Jim Crow, 1–2, 16, 229, 233, 258

"John Chinaman," 18

Johnson, Andrew, 23, 26, 27, 53, 196, 230

Johnson, James, 287 (n. 3)

Johnson, Reverdy, 25

Jones, John P., 84, 141, 227, 228, 311 (n. 33)

Journal of United Labor, 219, 307 (n. 47), 309 (n. 18)

Joyce, Charles, 312 (n. 54)

Julian, George W., 56, 303 (n. 12)

Kalloch, Isaac, 173–74, 176, 198, 300 (n. 9)

Kasson, John, 251, 315 (n. 16)

Kearney, Denis, 140, 143, 148, 153, 157, 173, 178, 182, 220, 308 (n. 5); on Chinese, 97, 102–3, 111, 116–17, 127, 192–93; and Workingmen's Party of California, 97, 107, 148, 290 (n. 5); speech and style of, 97, 112–17, 175–76, 193; and California constitution, 106, 169, 299 (n. 1); eastern tour of (1878), 108, 109–31, 133, 134–35, 138, 164, 183, 203, 290 (n. 1); and Workingmen's Party of Boston, 109, 110, 129; and Butler, 109, 115–16, 126–27, 128; background of, 110–11; on strikes, 111; and Greenback-Labor

Party, 111, 116, 117, 119, 122–23, 125–27, 128, 174–75, 192–94, 203, 301 (nn. 11, 12); description of, 112; on Beecher, 114; press on, 117–18, 183, 301 (n. 11); Blaine on, 118; Ch'en Lan-pin on, 118, 291 (n. 20); response to in East, 118–31, 134–35, 170, 180, 183–84; meets with Hayes, 135; on Fifteen Passenger Bill, 158; calms San Francisco, 174, 301 (n. 11); and election of 1880, 175, 192–94, 203, 211; eastern tour of (1880), 175–76, 184; arrested, 111, 177; jailed, 183, 302 (n. 24); linked to Blaine, 185, 187; on Garfield, 192; released from jail, 192; at Greenback-Labor convention (1880), 192–94; pronunciation and spelling of name of, 290 (n. 4); and Gompers, 310 (n. 22)

Kearneyism, 128, 141, 224

Keifer, J. Warren, 250

Kelly, John, 203, 245

Kinkead, Jonathan, 185

Kirchener, John, 245

Kirkwood, Samuel, 243

Knights of Labor, 69, 101, 107, 119, 163, 219, 245, 304 (n. 21), 307 (n. 47), 309 (n. 18), 315 (n. 16)

Knights of St. Crispin, 29–30, 39–42, 45–46, 48, 63, 64, 275 (n. 7), 310 (n. 20); background of, 29, 39; in North Adams, 39–42; on Chinese, 40–42, 45–46, 64

Know-Nothings, 68, 77, 100, 126, 139, 159, 225

Koopmanschap, Cornelius, 30–32, 33–34, 35, 47, 61, 179; background of, 31

Korean immigrants, 1, 254

Kuhn, Conrad, 43

Ku Klux Klan, 33, 54, 72

Ku Klux Klan Act, 230

Kwong Ki Chiu, 258–59, 316 (n. 29)

Kwong, Chong, Wing and Company, 40

Labor World, 245

Lane, A. T., 11

Latin America, 31, 33, 197. *See also* South America; *specific countries*

Latin Americans, 266 (n. 8)

Laws. *See* "An Act to Encourage Immigration"; "Anti-Coolie" Act; Chinese Exclusion Act; Chinese immigrants: laws against; Chinese immigrants: laws defending; Civil Rights Act; Fifteen Passenger Bill; Foran Act; Naturalization Act; Page Act; Queue ordinance; Scott Act

Leopold, Prince of England, 187

Letter of acceptance, 195. *See also* Garfield: letter of acceptance by; Hancock: letter of acceptance by

Liberal Republicans, 72–74, 96, 102, 281 (n. 15), 283 (n. 26), 315 (n. 20)

Li Hung-chang, 186, 216, 308 (n. 9)
Li Hungtsao, 214–15
Lincoln, Abraham, 20, 72, 84, 150, 155, 198, 232, 243, 273 (n. 33), 315 (n. 20)
Lincoln, Robert T., 243
Lindsay, Robert, 307 (n. 48)
Lord, Henry, 236
Louisville Courier-Journal, 159
Low, Abiel Abbot, 161
Low, Seth, 161
Lucker, Henry, 36
Luttrell, John, 287 (n. 3), 294 (n. 5)

McClure, Addison, 5, 238, 266 (n. 6)
McDill, James, 233
McDonald, Mark, 79, 284 (n. 9)
McDonnell, Joseph P., 302 (n. 24)
McGregor, Hugh, 124–25
McGuire, Peter J., 119, 124, 246, 314 (n. 8)
Machinists' and Blacksmiths' International Union, 195, 270 (n. 10)
McKinley, William, 238
McLean, Charles, 45–46, 47
McLogan, P. H., 180
McMillan, Samuel J. R., 155, 234, 309 (n. 15)
McNeill, George, 88, 101
Marble, Manton, 76, 85, 86
Marx, Karl, 14
Mason, Samuel, 60, 64
Massachusetts Association of Working Women, 47
Massachusetts Bureau of the Statistics of Labor, 42
Massachusetts Labor Reform Party, 46–47
Matthews, Richard, 43
Matthews, Stanley, 151, 155
Maxey, Samuel B., 228
Meade, Edwin R., 93, 101
Medill, Joseph, 206
Melting pot, 314 (n. 11)
Memphis Appeal, 30
Memphis Chinese Labor Convention, 17, 30–32, 33, 47, 229, 272 (n. 30), 296 (n. 37)
Merchants, 10, 19, 31, 34, 70, 83, 106, 120, 132, 155, 158, 161–62, 167, 172–73, 179, 197, 215, 216, 217, 230, 249–50, 282 (n. 20), 288 (n. 18)
Methodist (Baltimore), 162
Mexicans and Mexican Americans, 7, 177, 266 (n. 8)
Mexico, 9, 32, 138, 198
Michigan State Labor Union, 64
Mill, John Stuart, 18
Miller, John F., 226, 227; on Angell Treaty, 218, 223; speech on Chinese Exclusion Act by, 223–25; on Arthur's veto, 245

Miller, Stuart Creighton, 10–11, 18, 44
Miller, Warner, 235
Mills, Darius Ogden, 103
Miners, 7, 20, 21, 23, 65–66, 70, 223
Mining camps, 6, 7, 266 (n. 8)
Mink, Gwendolyn, 11–12, 14, 256, 293 (n. 50)
Missionaries, 10, 30, 31, 162, 167, 173
Mississippi Valley Immigration Labor Company, 31
Mitchell, John H., 83, 141
Mitchell, John I., 233
Montgomery, David, 19, 72, 310 (n. 20)
Montgomery Mail, 30
Moore, William, 312 (n. 53)
Morey, H. L., 204, 207–8
Morey letter, 203–8, 209–11, 215, 220, 241, 307 (nn. 46–48); text of, 204
Morgan, Edwin, 25
Morgan, J. P., 161
Morgan, John Tyler, 251
Morgan, Thomas J., 164, 298 (n. 53)
Mormons, 231
Morrell, Daniel J., 30
Morrill, Lot, 24–25
Morse, Leopold, 240, 312 (n. 53), 313 (n. 58)
Morton, Levi P., 161
Morton, Oliver P., 51, 52, 93
Mungen, William, 61–62, 63
Murray, Hugh C., 277 (n. 33)

Nation, 73, 80; on Chinese issue, 48–49; on Fifteen Passenger Bill, 160
National Anti-Slavery Standard, 35, 58, 274 (n. 38)
National Labor Bureau of Colored Men, 43
National Labor Congress, 25–26, 36–37, 45–47. *See also* Industrial Congress; National Labor Union
National Labor Reform Party, 66–67, 71, 281 (n. 15), 283 (n. 26), 315 (n. 20). *See also* Massachusetts Labor Reform Party
National Labor Tribune (Pittsburgh), 87; and Fifteen Passenger Bill, 162
National Labor Union (NLU), 23, 25–26, 41, 45–47, 66–67, 89, 193, 195. *See also* National Labor Congress
National racist consensus thesis, 10, 15, 254
National railroad strike. *See* Railroad strike of 1877
National Socialist (Cincinnati), 100
National Standard, 58, 274 (n. 38)
National Typographical Union, 41
National View (Washington, D.C.), 175
Native Americans. *See* American Indians
Nativism, 9, 11–12, 26, 76–77, 283 (n. 3)

Naturalization, 90; Senate debate on, 50–53, 54, 153; laws, 51, 53, 277 (n. 30). *See also* Chinese immigrants: and citizenship; Naturalization Act; Suffrage

Naturalization Act (1790), 51

Naturalization Act (1870): Senate debate on, 50–53, 54, 153; passes, 52. *See also* Naturalization; Naturalization Act (1790)

Navy, 96, 174

Nevada, 53, 72, 145–46, 167, 185, 203, 209, 240, 266 (n. 3), 296 (n. 39), 301 (n. 10). *See also* West Coast

New Jersey, 209

New York Amalgamated Trades and Labor Union, 221

New York Central Labor Union, 245

New York City Bar Association, 196

New York City Board of Trade, 249

New York Dispatch, 133

New York Herald, 41, 94, 98, 105, 158, 179, 186, 205, 206, 220, 248; on Chinese, 18; on Burlingame Mission, 27; on Crispins, 48; on Burlingame Treaty, 86; on Chinese issue, 87; on railroad strike, 95; on Kearney's tour, 124; on domestics, 177; on party platforms (1880), 191; on Garfield's letter of acceptance, 201; on election of 1880, 211; publishes Angell Treaty, 216; on merchants' protest, 217; on Angell Treaty, 217, 308 (n. 10); on Arthur's cabinet, 243

New York Irish-American, 118, 159

New York Italian Labor Company, 65

New York Labor Standard, 94, 98, 100, 118

New York Star, 18, 177

New York Sun, 48, 119, 120, 125, 158–59, 183, 286 (n. 2); on Chinese, 32; on railroad strike, 95; on Blaine, 147

New York Times, 30, 34, 44, 120, 177, 179, 182, 183, 220; on Chinese, 18, 32, 33, 161; on Roach, 80; on railroad strike, 95; on Kearney, 117; on Kearney banners, 126; on Blaine, 137; on Fifteen Passenger Bill, 140, 150, 160–61; on Republican platform (1880), 189; on Angell Treaty, 217, 218; on Hoar, 227; on Miller, 227; on Chinese Exclusion Act, 239, 254; on Arthur's veto, 245; on Hawley, 251–52

New York Tribune, 3, 17, 44, 73, 97, 98, 119, 120, 121, 125, 143, 148, 206, 208, 250, 252; on Chinese, 17, 48, 160; on Chinese issue, 56, 103, 160; on Republican platform (1876), 84; on Kearney, 112, 118, 175; Kearney on, 113; on Fifteen Passenger Bill, 159, 160, 165; on Irish and anti-Chinese sentiment, 165; on Republican platform (1880), 189; on Garfield's letter of acceptance, 201; on Chinese Exclusion Act,

212, 239–40; on Angell Treaty, 217; on Hoar, 227; on Miller, 227; on Arthur's veto, 245

New York Witness, 84, 109, 125

New York Workingmen's Association, 44

New York World, 76, 86; on Burlingame Treaty, 27; on Chinese, 86; on Chinese issue, 86, 148; on railroad strike, 95; on red scare, 105; on Kearney meetings, 122; on Kearney, 127, 129; on Blaine, 147, 148; on Fifteen Passenger Bill, 147, 159

North Adams, Mass., 38, 39–43, 47, 48–50, 55, 59, 60, 64, 65–66, 70, 99, 100, 157, 181, 235, 246, 252; background of, 38, 39; Chinese in, 39–41, 60, 67, 275 (n. 4), 281 (n. 16); working-class protests in, 40–42, 43, 49; press coverage of, 60, 279 (n. 1)

North American Review, 102

Norway, 20

Nye, James W., 55

Oakland Merchants' Exchange, 158

O'Brien, James, 307 (n. 48)

Ohio, 202, 203, 209

Open-door policy, 6, 26, 56, 68–69, 155, 167, 217

Opium War, 10

Order of United American Mechanics, 77–78, 283 (n. 3)

Oregon, 145–46, 158, 167, 185, 203, 209, 240, 266 (n. 3). *See also* West Coast

Organized labor. *See* Chinese immigrants: working-class response to in East; Chinese immigrants: working-class response to in West; Working classes; *specific working-class organizations and unions*

Orth, Godlove S., 236

Oshkosh Standard, 185, 192, 289 (n. 29)

Pacific Coast Trades and Labor Unions, 219

Pacific Mail Steamship Company, 96

Page, Horace F., 70, 82, 103, 287 (n. 3); and Page Act, 71; on Chinese, 138; on Fifteen Passenger Bill, 138, 141; advises Garfield, 195; and Chinese Exclusion Act, 223, 250, 313 (n. 56)

Page Act, 71, 138, 282 (n. 21)

Palmer, Julius, 47, 276 (n. 20)

Panama Canal, 197, 305 (n. 24)

Panic of 1873. *See* Depression of 1870s

Pao Chun, 214–15

Paris Communards, 225

Parker, Gifford, 179

Parker, Peter, 33, 307 (n. 3)

Parmet, Robert D., 11

Parnell, Charles Stewart, 176

Parsons, Albert, 95, 105, 119, 245

Paterson Labor Standard, 162, 248, 302 (n. 24)

Payne, D. O., 188
Peelle, Stanton, 5, 237
Peffer, George Anthony, 63
Penn, William, 227
Perkins, George C., 158
Perlman, Selig, 11
Philadelphia Centennial Exposition, 90
Philadelphia Inquirer, 117, 121
Philadelphia Press, 189
Philadelphia Public Ledger, 86
Philadelphia Times, 130
Phillips, Wendell, 56, 281 (n. 15); on Chinese, 18, 47, 243–44; runs for governor, 47, 276 (n. 19); endorses Butler, 128
Philp, Kenward, 208, 210
Phrenology, 118
Piano makers, 182–83, 184
Piano manufacturers, 182–83
Pickering, Loring, 172
Pierce, Edward L., 84
Pierrepont, Edwards, 188
Pillow, Gideon J., 31
Pinkertons, 202
Pioneers of the Territorial Days of California, 81
Piper, William, 83, 287 (n. 3)
Pittsfield Sun, 128, 130
Pixley, Frank, 93, 287 (n. 3); and eastern tour, 79, 80, 82, 85, 86; background of, 80; meets with Grant, 82; seconds Blaine's nomination, 189
Platt, Orville, 233–34
Plessy v. Ferguson, 2, 233, 258
Polish immigrants, 66, 101, 124
Polk, James K., 79
Pomeroy, Samuel, 37
Pomeroy's Illustrated Democrat, 117
Portland Board of Trade, 158
Portland (Maine) Eastern Argus, 121
Pottsville Miners' Journal, 118
Poughkeepsie Eagle, 159
Powderly, Terence V., 107, 119, 123
Princeton University, 102
Prindle, George, 35
Progress and Poverty, 94, 255
Prostitution, 71, 80, 86, 138
Prussia, 20, 23. *See also* Germany
Prussian immigrants, 20–21, 23. *See also* German immigrants
Puck, 178, 191–92
Pumpelly, Raphael, 272 (n. 26), 289 (n. 20)
Purdy (iron molder), 43

Queue ordinance, 79, 84, 283–84 (n. 8)
Quong, Sam, 179

Racist consensus thesis. *See* National racist consensus thesis
Railroad strike of 1877, 94–95, 96, 97, 104, 105, 111, 141, 143, 254, 287 (n. 5); mentioned by Blaine, 4, 143
Rainey, Joseph H., 137
Randall, Samuel J., 204
Rayback, Joseph G., 11
Reconstruction, 13, 52, 59, 72–73, 74, 190, 311 (n. 39); ideals and legacy of, 9, 68–69, 83, 85, 151; end of, 16, 73, 74, 77, 93, 95, 228–29, 254, 257
Red scare, 104–6, 108, 138, 143, 176
Reid, Whitelaw, 206
Republican Party, 15–16, 25, 27, 32, 96, 116; invokes working-class support for Chinese Exclusion Act, 3–6, 15, 237–38; and Fifteen Passenger Bill, 4–5, 140, 146–47, 155, 161, 166; origins of, 9, 13, 72, 77, 106; and election of 1876, 12, 77, 78–79, 84–85, 89; and platform (1876), 12, 84–85, 86, 87, 90, 168; and election of 1880, 12, 185–90, 194–96, 197–211, 303 (nn. 9, 12); and platform (1880), 12, 187–89, 191–92, 215, 222, 303 (n. 12); and Radicals, 30, 37–38, 50–56, 72, 82–83, 115, 135, 150, 229, 231, 235, 252; and immigration-importation debate, 37–38, 50–56; and moderates, 51; and election of 1872, 72–74; and platform (1872), 73–74; and election of 1874, 74; and election of 1878 (Mass.), 128; and convention (1880), 185–86, 187–90, 303 (n. 9); and lobbying by California, 194–95; and Garfield's letter of acceptance, 195, 200–201; and Morey letter, 204–8, 209–11; obstructs Senate, 217; and Chinese Exclusion Act, 223, 233–35, 235–40, 241, 244–45, 250–51, 253, 313 (n. 58), 315 (n. 16); and morality, 232–33, 234–35, 252
Richardson, John, 313 (n. 56)
Roach, Philip A., 93, 109, 193, 220, 287 (n. 3); on Chinese, 7, 78, 80–81; meets with Tilden, 76–77; and eastern tour, 76–77, 79–82, 84, 85, 86, 183, 186, 189, 203; background of, 79–80; meets with Grant, 81; on Fifteen Passenger Bill, 148–49, 158
Robinson, George, 139, 236
Rockford (Illinois) Free Press, 147
Rock Springs Massacre, 287 (n. 4)
Roediger, David R., 11, 12, 14, 69, 256
Rome, Ga., 65, 70
Rosecrans, William, 245
Roughing It, 278 (n. 33)
Rudolph, Frederick, 276 (n. 24)
Russia, 216
Russian immigrants, 101

Saffin, William, 65
St. Louis Globe-Democrat, 86
St. Louis Post-Dispatch, 176–77
St. Louis Republican, 34, 86
Sampson, Calvin T., 39–42, 48, 61, 67, 100;
    imports Chinese, 39–41, 67, 274 (n. 2), 281
    (n. 16); criticized by workers, 41–42; defended
    by Garrison, 57; defended by Dawes, 252
Sanborn, Franklin B., 102
Sandlots. *See* San Francisco: sandlots
Sandmeyer, Elmer Clarence, 8, 10, 26, 168
San Francisco, 4, 8, 12, 82, 98, 99, 110, 129; arrival
    of Chinese immigrants in, 7; anti-Chinese
    protests in, 7–8, 9, 70, 78–79, 96–97, 102–3,
    172–73; Board of Supervisors, 78–79, 176, 284
    (n. 8), 296 (n. 39); congressional committee
    meets in (1876), 93; sandlots, 96–97, 102–3,
    111, 159, 173–74, 176–77, 252; violence in,
    96–97, 173–74, 176–77; anti-Chinese violence
    in, 96–97, 176–77; Chamber of Commerce,
    157, 158; congressional committee meets in
    (1879), 172–73; Board of Health, 176; Chinese
    exodus from, 177; Grant's arrival in, 186–87,
    198. *See also* California; West Coast; Working-
    men's Party of California
San Francisco Alta California, 84, 108; on
    Chinese, 7; on party platforms (1880),
    191
San Francisco Chronicle, 30, 103, 135, 173; on
    Roach's tour, 85; on Chinese issue, 86, 135,
    164; on letters of acceptance (1880), 201–2;
    on *Socialist*, 285 (n. 29); on Hayes's visit, 305
    (n. 34)
San Francisco Examiner, 70, 80
Sargent, Aaron A., 70, 104, 109, 143, 286–87
    (n. 3), 302 (n. 16); on Chinese, 38, 82–83, 93,
    104; on Chinese issue, 70; speech on Chinese
    by (1876), 82–83, 88, 104, 181; background of,
    82–83, 284 (n. 17); praised by workers, 88, 298
    (n. 52); and congressional investigation, 93,
    104; speech on Chinese by (1878), 104; criti-
    cizes Kearney, 134; on Fifteen Passenger Bill,
    140–41, 160; advises Garfield, 195; retirement
    of, 218
Sargent, Elizabeth C., 284 (n. 17)
Sargent, Ellen Clark, 284 (n. 17)
Sargent, Mrs. Timothy, 177–79, 302 (n. 16)
Sawyer, Philetus, 235
Saxton, Alexander, 8–10, 12–14, 26, 59, 70, 168,
    170, 256, 257
Scandinavia, 20, 224. *See also* Norway; Sweden
Scandinavian immigrants, 20, 66, 224, 246. *See
    also* Swedish immigrants
Schaefer, John, 172, 173
Scharrett, Henry, 179, 202

Schilling, Robert, 89
Schurz, Carl, 51, 72–73, 128
Schwab, Justus, 124
Scientific racism, 10, 102, 311 (n. 33). *See also*
    Social Darwinism
Scotland, 20, 21, 44, 65
Scott, Alexander, 23
Scott, Tom, 292 (n. 35)
Scott Act, 314 (n. 9)
Scottish immigrants, 21, 44, 65, 70, 248
Scranton, Joseph, 266 (n. 6), 313 (n. 56)
Scribner's Monthly, 87
Secession, 158–59
Senate: and Fifteen Passenger Bill, 3–4, 140–45,
    148–57, 296 (nn. 36, 37), 298 (n. 51); and Bur-
    lingame Treaty, 27, 82, 104; debates importa-
    tion, 37–38; debates naturalization, 50–53, 54;
    debates Chinese immigration and importa-
    tion, 50–56; and election of 1872, 74; and
    Roach delegation, 81–82; Sargent's speech in
    (1876), 82–83, 181; and resolution to investi-
    gate Chinese immigration, 85; and resolution
    to renegotiate Burlingame Treaty, 104, 168;
    and tenement house labor, 163, 298 (n. 51);
    confirms Angell Commission, 213; and execu-
    tive session, 217; debates Angell Treaty, 217–18;
    ratifies Angell Treaty, 218, 309 (n. 15); debates
    Chinese Exclusion Act, 223–35, 251–53, 311
    (n. 48); and vote on Exclusion Act, 235, 253;
    fails to override Arthur's veto, 244; and Scott
    Act, 314 (n. 9); and Davis, 315 (n. 20). *See also*
    Congress; House of Representatives; *specific
    laws*
Seward, George F., 197, 215, 305 (n. 25)
Seward, William H., 20, 26, 196
Shannon, T. B., 173
Sherman, John, 5, 6, 51, 233, 238, 245, 266 (n. 6),
    303 (n. 9)
Sherman, Roger, 196, 225
Sherman, William T., 81, 106
Sherwin, John R., 5, 257, 258, 313 (n. 56)
Sing Man, 34
Sisson, Wallace, 48, 276 (n. 21)
Six Companies, 101, 288 (n. 18)
Skinner, Charles, 312 (n. 53)
Slater, James, 227
Slavery, 8–9, 13, 24, 32, 55, 58, 59, 63, 72, 151, 152,
    202, 232. *See also* Abolition; Abolitionists;
    "An Act to Encourage Immigration"; Blacks;
    "Coolie" trade; Emancipation; Imported
    labor; South; Thirteenth Amendment; Work-
    ing classes: connection of importation to
    slavery by
Smart, William G. H., 183
Smith, A. Herr, 266 (n. 6), 313 (n. 56)

Smith, J. Hyatt, 313 (n. 56)
Social Darwinism, 102, 289 (n. 20)
Socialist (Chicago), 162–63
Socialist (Detroit), 100
Socialist (New York), 88–89, 285 (n. 29)
Socialistic Labor Party, 124. *See also* Working-
 men's Party of the United States
Socialists, 105, 107, 111; form party, 89–90; on
 Chinese, 90, 124–25, 298 (n. 50); on red scare,
 105; and Kearney, 119, 124–25, 292 (n. 32)
Souper, Thomas, 20
South, 8, 18, 94, 95, 143, 190, 215, 232, 233, 310
 (n. 32); and Reconstruction, 16, 54, 73, 74; on
 plans to import Chinese, 30–32, 33, 179; and
 importation of Chinese, 47, 202; and "solid
 South," 187, 205; and Chinese Exclusion Act,
 228–30, 238–39, 251, 257, 311 (nn. 38, 39), 312
 (n. 55); and Fifteen Passenger Bill, 228, 296
 (n. 37)
South American immigrants, 7
Spanish immigrants, 98
Speer, Emory, 311 (n. 38)
Spencer, Sara Andrews, 193
Springfield Republican, 40, 42; on Chinese issue,
 48, 60; on imported labor, 56
Sproat, John, 74
Stanford, Leland, 31, 290 (n. 4)
Stanton, Elizabeth Cady, 284 (n. 17)
Stauber, Frank, 105
Stephens, Uriah, 119
Stevens, Thaddeus, 53, 136
Steward, Ira, 88
Stewart, William M., 41, 52–55, 285 (n. 21); on
 Chinese, 37–38, 53–54, 258, 277 (n. 33); back-
 ground of, 53–54, 277 (n. 33)
Storrs, Emory, 188
Strasser, Adolph, 163, 186, 222; and strike by
 cigar makers, 97, 99; on Chinese, 131–33, 293
 (n. 50); testifies before Hewitt Committee,
 131–34
Strikes, 21, 29–30, 34, 39, 48, 59, 60, 66, 97, 104,
 111, 141, 165, 178, 182, 248; by railroad workers,
 4, 94–95, 96, 97, 104, 105, 111, 143, 254, 287
 (n. 5); by ironworkers, 20–21, 65; by bricklayers, 21; by miners, 21, 65–66; in Europe, 22;
 by shoemakers, 29–30, 37, 39, 123; by factory
 workers, 64; by cigar makers, 97–100, 101, 103,
 131, 163, 184, 288 (n. 9); Chinese in, 97–100,
 184, 248, 275 (n. 7); by piano makers, 182–83,
 184; by shirt ironers, 248, 314 (n. 10)
Suez Canal, 34
Suffrage: and Chinese, 47, 54, 56, 90, 153, 223,
 248; and blacks, 52, 53, 73, 137, 153, 230; and
 women, 82, 192–93, 276 (n. 19), 284 (n. 17),
 304 (n. 17), 310 (n. 32)

Sumner, Charles, 20, 38, 50–52, 54, 225, 271
 (n. 21), 278 (n. 36)
Supreme Court, 67, 233, 278 (n. 33), 283 (n. 4),
 305 (n. 26), 315 (n. 20)
Swazey, Arthur, 245
Sweden, 20
Swedish immigrants, 29, 66
Swift, John, 213, 214–15
Swinton, John, 44–45, 46, 47
Swiss immigrants, 101
Sylvis, William H., 21–23, 66, 271 (n. 11)

Taft, Philip, 11
Tailors' Union (New York), 42
Takaki, Ronald, 11
Tamerlane, 27
Tammany Hall, 203, 245
Tariff, 23, 72, 187, 205, 229
Taylor, Bayard, 17
Taylor, Ezra, 236
Taylor, Zachary, 6
Teller, Henry M., 5, 228, 313 (n. 56)
Tenement house labor, 97–99, 163, 298 (n. 51)
Third party system, 72
Thirteenth Amendment, 24, 58, 73
Thurman, Allan G., 148, 149–50, 156, 190, 303
 (n. 11)
Tilden, Samuel J.: meets with Roach, 76–77, 85;
 and election of 1876, 76–77, 87, 92, 196, 202,
 203; nominated president, 87; and disputed
 returns, 92–93, 196; and election of 1880, 190,
 303 (n. 11)
Townsend, Martin, 139, 140
Townshend, Richard, 237
Train, George Francis, 303 (n. 12)
Trans-Continental, 48, 276 (n. 21)
Transcontinental railroad, 7, 29, 31, 93, 244, 276
 (n. 21)
Traphagen, H. C., 304 (n. 21)
Trescot, William H., 213, 214, 215, 216, 307
 (n. 4)
Trevellick, Richard, 23, 45, 89, 193, 245
Troup, Alexander, 41, 45, 59, 89
Trumbull, Lyman, 51
Truth (New York), 203–4, 206, 208
Tsai, Shih-shan Henry, 287 (n. 4)
Tucker, Beverley, 197–200, 210
Turkish immigrants, 101
Twain, Mark, 53, 81, 278 (n. 33)
Tye Kim Orr, 30, 31
Tyler, James, 236, 237, 266 (n. 6)

Union League Club, 249
Unions. *See* Working classes; *specific working-
 class organizations and unions*

U.S.-Chinese relations, 18, 104, 107, 162, 181, 186, 197–99, 200, 286 (n. 1), 299 (n. 57), 305 (n. 28), 307 (nn. 3, 4); and emperor, 18, 26, 156; and Burlingame Mission, 26–28, 162; and "coolie" trade, 32–33, 36, 53, 58, 61–63, 66, 280 (n. 7); and "Anti-Coolie" Act, 32–33, 71, 279 (n. 5); and Bailey report, 62–63; and Grant, 71, 186–87, 198–99, 308 (n. 9); and commerce, 154–55, 160, 161–62, 167, 197–99, 216, 217, 230, 308 (n. 12); and Fifteen Passenger Bill, 154–56, 166–67; and Evarts, 165–66, 197–200; and Li Hung-chang, 186, 308 (n. 9); and George Seward, 197; and Angell Commission, 197, 199, 200, 211, 212–16; and Tucker, 197–99; and Chinese Exclusion Act, 243, 258–59, 314 (n. 9), 315–16 (n. 24); and Bayard, 295 (n. 21); and Chinese legation, 299 (n. 57). See also Angell Treaty; Burlingame Treaty; China; Chinese diplomats; Chinese Educational Mission; Chinese legation; "Coolie" trade; Six Companies
University of Michigan, 212
Utica Herald, 146

Valentine, Edward K., 5, 238, 313 (n. 56)
Violence. See Chico Massacre; Chinese immigrants: violence against; Railroad strike of 1877; Rock Springs Massacre; San Francisco: anti-Chinese violence in; San Francisco: violence in
Virginia City (Nevada) Enterprise, 158
Voice of Labor (Missouri), 124
Volkszeitung (Ohio), 124

Wade, Ben, 278 (n. 36)
Wadleigh, Bainbridge, 155
Walbridge, Hiram, 34
Wales, 20, 65
Walsh, Mike, 134, 294 (n. 51)
Washburn, William, 238, 266 (n. 6)
Washburne, Elihu B., 303 (n. 9)
Washington, George, 51, 190
Washington Federation of Labor, 245
Washington Star: on Kearney and Greenbackers, 123; on Fifteen Passenger Bill, 157; on Hancock's letter of acceptance, 201
Watson, Tom, 134
Weaver, James B., 193–94, 307 (n. 46)
Webster, Daniel, 151
Weed, Thurlow: on Fifteen Passenger Bill, 162; on Garfield's letter of acceptance, 201; on Chinese Exclusion Act, 243
Wells, David A., 102
West Coast, 16, 68, 254, 257; anti-Chinese movement on, 4, 7–8, 14, 15, 29, 69–71, 78–79,

96–97, 219–20, 257; political importance of, 4, 15, 90, 145–47, 150, 187, 198–99, 203, 240–41, 253; Chinese population on, 4, 67, 265 (n. 3); and anti-Chinese members of Congress, 37–38, 55, 70, 82–84, 107, 140–42, 223–25; and Fifteen Passenger Bill, 140–42, 157–59; and election of 1880, 185–87, 188, 189, 190–91, 194–95, 201–2, 209; and Angell Treaty, 218; and Chinese Exclusion Act, 223–25, 227–28, 232, 238, 240–41, 245, 252. See also California; Nevada; Oregon; San Francisco
Whaley, J. C. C., 25–26
Whig Party, 8–9, 225
White, Andrew, 102
Whiteness, 14, 69
Wilentz, Sean, 294 (n. 51)
Williams, George H., 25, 37, 54, 55
Williams, John, 33
Williams, S. Wells, 162
Willis, Albert, 138, 141
Willits, Edwin, 5, 237
Wilmot, David, 9
Wilmot Proviso, 9
Wilson, Henry, 37, 52
Windom, William, 303 (n. 9)
Winn, Albert, 36, 63, 280 (n. 8)
Wise, George, 237
Wise, Morgan, 237
Women's rights, 58, 74, 82, 192–93, 284 (n. 17). See also Suffrage: and women
Woodhull, Victoria, 283 (n. 26)
Woolsey, Theodore, 162
Working classes: racism of, 7–8, 11–12, 13–15, 44, 256; ideology of, 8–10, 11–12, 13–15, 58–59, 68–70, 99–100, 256–57; terminology of, 14; connection of importation to slavery by, 20–21, 41–44, 59, 66, 88–89, 183; distinction between immigration and importation by, 22–23, 25–26, 36–37, 41–44, 45–47, 59, 64, 66, 67, 68–70, 88–89, 101, 131–34, 183–84, 195–96, 221–22, 246–47, 256–57; anti-Chinese sentiment of, 116–17, 119, 162–65, 170–71, 180–82, 219–21, 245–47; response to Chinese Exclusion Act by, 245–47. See also Chinese immigrants: working-class response to in East; Chinese immigrants: working-class response to in West; specific working-class organizations and unions
Workingman's Advocate (Chicago), 29, 35, 45, 46, 47, 80, 274 (n. 38); urges Chinese exclusion, 29, 40, 44, 63–64, 87; on Chinese, 29, 40, 63–64
Workingman's Map (Indianapolis), 87, 89
Workingmen's Party of Boston, 110, 129
Workingmen's Party of California, 97, 106, 107,

111, 169, 170, 172, 173, 174, 175, 176, 198, 290 (n. 5), 301 (n. 11)

Workingmen's Party of the United States, 89–90, 107. *See also* Socialistic Labor Party

World War II, 141, 254, 316 (n. 24)

Wren, Thomas, 138

Yale University, 101, 162, 196

Young, John Russell, 186, 305 (n. 24), 308 (n. 9)

Yung Wing, 92, 299 (n. 57); on Fifteen Passenger Bill, 166; on treatment of Chinese immigrants, 177